THE FLAME OF FREEDOM
The German Struggle against Hitler

Claus Schenk Graf von Stauffenberg

EBERHARD ZELLER

THE FLAME
OF FREEDOM

The German Struggle against Hitler

UNIVERSITY OF MIAMI PRESS
CORAL GABLES, FLORIDA

Translated from the German by R. P. Heller and D. R. Masters

TRANSLATORS' NOTE

In preparing this English translation of Eberhard Zeller's *Geist der Freiheit*, we have thought it necessary to make a few cuts. But nearly all are short and none of them, we believe, involves any matter of substance. We have also retained the bulk of the author's copious notes. This we have done, first, because many of them seem to us to have an intrinsic interest and to cast much additional light on the text; and, secondly, because they will enable the student, if he so wishes, to go to the original German sources. Indeed, in the preface to the German edition the author expressed the hope that his work might serve as an historical survey, or even a textbook, of the events described.

R. P. H.
D. R. M.

CONTENTS

THE ANTECEDENTS

THE TWENTIETH OF JULY

THE ANTECEDENTS

I. LUDWIG BECK
THE CHIEF OF THE GERMAN GENERAL STAFF
IN THE STRUGGLE AGAINST THE WAR

"It is now a question of final decisions affecting the fate of the nation. History will hold these leaders guilty if they do not act in accordance with their professional and political conscience. Their military obedience ends where their knowledge, their conscience and their sense of responsibility forbid the carrying out of an order. If their advice and warnings in such a situation are not heeded, they have the right and the duty before their people and history to resign from their posts. If they all act with a united will, then it will be impossible to make war. In this way, they will have saved their Fatherland from the worst, from catastrophe. It shows a lack of stature and a failure to recognize one's obligations when a soldier of the highest rank at such times sees his duties only in the limited framework of his military tasks and is not conscious of the highest responsibility to the whole nation. Extraordinary times demand extraordinary actions."[1]

With these words Ludwig *Beck*, the German Chief of the General Staff from 1933 to 1938, went beyond the traditions which had been normally binding on a senior German officer. He sought to evoke in the man, to whom the words were addressed, General Brauchitsch, the Commander-in-Chief of the Army, a higher sense of responsibility than faithfulness to duty. He was ready to accept all the consequences for himself. Six years later he paid for it with his life.

His forebears had been Hessian officers. His father, an expert in iron and iron-smelting, scholar and businessman, had settled in Biebrich in the Rhineland as manager of a foundry. Here Beck, who was born in 1880, grew up with his two brothers in a pleasant property close to the Rhine. Later, he went to the *Gymnasium* in Wiesbaden. In the First World War he had posts in the General Staff and from the winter of 1916–17 he was in the High Command of the Army Group "Deutscher Kronprinz". Here he established a close and lasting friendship with the Chief of the General Staff, Count von der Schulenburg, a man whom he greatly admired.

In the Army of the Weimar Republic he rose to the rank of Lieutenant-General. On October 1, 1933 he achieved the position for which his gifts destined him. He was responsible for the training of the future General Staff and, as such, was less in the public eye than the C.-in-C. of the Army. But his formative influence was stronger than that of any other senior officer in those years. The "thoughtful and heart-warming speech", which he made in October 1935 in connection with the 125th anniversary of the Military Academy was long remembered by many of his listeners who came to recognize in his portrait of Moltke the features of their own Chief of Staff.[2]

"Refined and gracious in disposition, modest in outward appearance and behaviour"—so an officer who was close to him describes him—"the perfect gentleman in his dealings with everyone. He had certainly the wisest and best-trained head in the Army; his industry was prodigious; he was exact in detail, imaginative in large matters and careful in weighing issues. Unprejudiced in regard to men or things, he valued honest advisers, recognized different and contrary opinions and possessed to perfection the wisdom to listen. Great self-control and constant self-discipline preserved him from over-hasty judgements and decisions."[3]

In a memorandum on the duties of the most senior of all General Staff officers, Beck wrote these words which also apply to himself : "He is responsible for the theoretical and practical training of the General Staff and also for its education and conduct in terms of character and personality. He must practise what he preaches. Any discrepancy between his words and actions would be fatal for him and disastrous for the General Staff. If, therefore, he finds himself in a situation which, after conscientious appraisal, leaves him no alternative, he must vacate his place to another, in the interests of the General Staff—even if his opinion may be objectively wrong. There must be no doubt about his consistency."[4]

Beck was a German nationalist but without the narrow understanding and aims with which many in the bourgeois parties, the universities and the national para-military organizations pursued an inflexible ideal. The twenty-five years he lived from Versailles to his death showed that he could move with the times and that for him the destiny of Germany was something more than a fond national faith. Beck regarded the strategy of the mighty Ludendorff as indefensible, and sided with his Chief, Schulenburg, who had for some time, even at the cost of disgrace, advocated a negotiated peace. But the collapse in November 1918 seemed to a man like Beck, who had taken part in the severest struggles for the Army's survival, the work of subversion—a long-prepared stab in the back, as his letter of November 28, 1918, put it.[5] The German Republic was for the majority of officers only a necessary consequence of the war with which they had to come to terms, if they could not throw

4

it off, as Kapp had tried to do. In spite of the Republic's historical roots in German history and its future prospects, those officers, who were loyal to the traditions of the Empire, felt they could not actively support it and infuse the spirit of the new national state into the Reichswehr, so long as they saw themselves and their function merely tolerated as a necessary evil by the spokesmen of the new Republic. The reservations of the Reichswehr might perhaps have been overcome, or lessened, if the new state had enjoyed many years of peaceful and successful existence. But this was not granted to the improvised democracy, which was burdened with Versailles and constantly shaken by internal crises. Seeckt, the "marble statue" at the Ministerial tables of the Republic, was certainly not ill-advised to keep his Reichswehr out of politics in the chaotic post-war years; and in this way he enabled the Army to help the new state to establish itself. But his controversial thesis that the important thing was that the soldier should be firmly in the hands of the leadership, and all else was of no account, showed later to what extent this army, which was, as it were, on call, was placed in a vacuum where there was nothing to appeal to its enthusiasms. Three young officers of his old Ulm Regiment, who had sought to escape from this situation and disobeyed regulations, were supported by Beck, when he appeared as witness for the defence in the Reich court, at risk to his career. They had formed National Socialist cells in the Reichswehr. "Two-thirds of the young officers in the Reichswehr think as I do," one of them had said, "and what else are we to think? For have we any other ideas, an ideal or outlet for our patriotism?" (October 1930.)[6]

The loyalty, with which the officers of the Reichswehr served the unloved and prosaic Weimar state, was insufficient. For this loyalty was really only acceptable to them because they hoped, as a body of genuine soldiers, to survive the wretched period and then to serve a future Germany, which would free itself from the limitations of Versailles and, as a sovereign state, revive the traditions of its national life.

The final crisis of the Weimar Republic which began 1929–30 made friendlier relations between Army and State impossible. The picture of increasing confusion, even disintegration, which domestic politics provided, only increased the reservations of soldiers, who expected from a government authority and stability, above all else. At this time Reich Chancellor Brüning, following the improvement in Germany's position due to Stresemann's achievements, had so far succeeded on the laborious path of negotiations as to get a promise to cancel German war debts. This was largely the result of Brüning's emphasis on the increasing radical trends in Germany,

5

which could not be a matter of indifference to the former Allies. However, a large part of the war debts had been transformed into no less onerous economic obligations. By the decision of the Disarmament Conference of December 11, 1932, Germany was in principle conceded equality in arms questions; but, owing to the ties of Versailles, she was not yet in a position to defend herself effectively. She could conclude economic agreements, but not alliances. The customs union with Austria, which both countries desired, was forbidden.

The successes in foreign affairs during these years either came too late or were not clear, or impressive, enough for the harassed Germans. For, meanwhile, since the end of 1929, and beginning with bank failures in the USA, a world economic crisis had affected Germany with particular force. And by the end of 1932 this had reduced about a third of the German population to poverty. Out of this poverty came anarchy. At the Reichstag election of November 6, 1932, the NSDAP (National Socialist German Workers' Party), with about 12 million votes, emerged as the strongest party. The Communist Party, with about 6 million, was third and had also grown. The Social Democratic Party, with a good 7 million, was barely stronger than the Communists and was clearly no longer in a position to keep in its own ranks those who wanted action. The bourgeois parties fell back. The red of the "right- and left-wing Bolshevists" dominated the streets and the masses; and it paralysed the activity of the Reichstag, to the point where it was incapable of functioning. This, in turn, made it impossible to see the end of the crisis and made people doubt whether it could be overcome by normal means. Attempts by the Chancellors, von Papen and von Schleicher, to take the wind out of the sails of the National Socialists, by resorting to national slogans and measures, failed. Bankruptcies and the auctioning of farms increased daily. An army of nearly 7 million unemployed imposed additional burdens on those still at work and gave dangerous nourishment to the unrest which was expediting the revolution.

In this situation it seemed that, to block the progress of Communism, there was now only a choice between military dictatorship and Hitler's Chancellorship. The Reichswehr would only have reluctantly supported a dictatorship to save the Republic from Hitler. It is true that the majority of officers had followed the growth of the NSDAP uneasily : the radical opinions cultivated in that party and its appeals to the masses were too alien to them. On the other hand, because Hitler was a nationalist politician with a movement which knew how to appeal to unusual forces, he inevitably seemed to them an ally. He, like themselves, was fighting against Versailles,

6

against arms limitations and for a strong, independent and united Germany.[7] In October 1931 the German National Party leader, Hugenberg, together with Hjalmar Schacht, led his party into an alliance with Hitler. This "Harzburger Front" was originally intended as a tactical move against Brüning but it was later to have far-reaching consequences. It was then that sympathy with Hitler, which had certainly never been unreserved, came to be expressed more clearly in the Officer Corps as well, and he was regarded as a coming force in the state. Had he dared to make an unconstitutional attempt to take over the state, the Reichswehr would still have been ready at the end of 1932 to use force against him on Hindenburg's orders. But it was different when he succeeded with Hindenburg's help in coming to power legally.

The eighty-six-year-old Reich President had adopted an attitude of sober reserve towards Hitler—he had called him "the Bohemian corporal". But, faced with the difficult decision of January 1933, he decided to ask him to form a new government as Chancellor (January 30). The Chief of the Army Command, Freiherr von Hammerstein, had in a personal audience, three days earlier, spoken against appointing Hitler and had found Hindenburg to be of a similar opinion. But later the former Chancellor von Papen and the President's son, Oskar von Hindenburg, succeeded in changing his mind. General von Schleicher, the Chancellor who had just been relieved of office, tried, after the decision had been taken, to get a military state of emergency declared with the help of the trade unions.[8] The majority of officers were on Hindenburg's side. Beck, too, saw no other solution than that of summoning Hitler from opposition to responsibility and of testing him in the task he had promised to solve. This was to master the anarchy at home and to secure equality for Germany abroad.

Beck spent the first five years of the new régime as the second most senior officer, after Colonel-General Freiherr von Fritsch, the C.-in-C. of the Army. These were years of hopes fulfilled, but also of deep and increasing concern. Hitler's determined and peremptory policies did not scruple to exploit his opponents' weaknesses; but they succeeded, not without some moments of very dangerous exposure, in untying, one by one, the remaining bonds of the Versailles Treaty which the Germans had never regarded as morally binding, and in winning back for Germany equality abroad and freedom of movement.

In his speech to the Reichstag on May 17, 1933, Hitler was able, simultaneously, to reassure the outside world about his intentions and to demand equal status for Germany. On October 14, 1933 he announced Germany's withdrawal from the League of Nations and the Disarmament Conference, when a period of a further eight years had been set for actual equality of status. Hitler pointed out that the other signatories of the Versailles Treaty had not kept their obligations to disarm, although fifteen years had passed and Germany had, in fact, disarmed. With Germany's withdrawal he created, without departing from legally defensible positions, the conditions both for his policy of bilateral pacts and agreements and for the, initially, secret process of German rearmament. A start was made with this in the course of 1934.

In January 1935 the Saar returned to Germany as the result of an overwhelming plebiscite vote; and Hitler solemnly declared—and this certainly gave the Germans satisfaction—that he had no further territorial claims to make against France. But when France increased her period of military service, he replied with an announcement of conscription in Germany and with the fixing of the German Army strength at 500 000 men, composed of thirty-six divisions (Versailles had allowed 100 000 men). Shortly after, on June 18, 1935, Hitler concluded a naval agreement with the British government, which permitted Germany a third of the strength of the British fleet. It was not so much on account of this particular success that Hitler called June 18 his happiest day. It was because with this treaty, his foreign policy to date was tacitly recognized. Germany was once again an equal negotiating partner; and the world had shown itself ready to meet just German demands for the revision of Versailles.[9] But, in this case, Britain had not acted in harmony with France and Italy. When France now tried to cover herself with an agreement with Russia, Hitler used the ratification of the Franco-Russian Pact to occupy the Rhineland (March 7, 1936) which had been demilitarized by Versailles, and to denounce the Locarno Pact, which he had until then accepted. In a note he simultaneously offered France and Belgium a twenty-five-year Pact of Mutual Assistance.

In all these steps the German Head of State certainly acted aggressively and ruthlessly, and he did not hesitate to reinterpret his own promises in a new situation, or to break them. But he always took great care to provide excuses for his action and exploited the former Allies' horror of war and their growing feeling that the old provisions of Versailles were an obstacle to understanding. In addition, his future course was still not sufficiently obvious to them to provoke military counter-action. Hitler followed up his revisionist measures at their expense with words and gestures, such as offers of pacts, which were repeatedly to create the impression that, while he acted very imprudently in destroying Versailles, he was basically a man of peace and reason. An example was the impact of his

Reichstag speech of May 21, 1935. And had he not, on January 26, 1934, concluded a non-aggression pact with Poland, that is to say, with the one state with which the Weimar Republic had had particularly bad and strained relations? By seemingly restraining Germany's not unjustified claims against Poland, he created an impression of statesmanlike moderation and wisdom—even if, in doing so, he intended, chiefly, to strike a blow against the French system of alliances and the policy of collective security. In addition, he skilfully exploited Mussolini's Abyssinian adventure, and Italy's consequent isolation in Europe, to bring about a rapprochement between Germany and Italy. This led, during October 1936, to a secret agreement to found the "Berlin–Rome Axis" and so improved Germany's external position that henceforth mere police actions against the Reich were no longer possible.

On the fourth anniversary (1937) of his accession to power Hitler declared in a lengthy account of his stewardship that the period of surprises was over. The plans, which on June 24, 1937, he asked the General Staff to work out, could be regarded as coming within the framework of what every state entrusts to expert consideration in peace time to meet defence requirements in hypothetical situations. On the other hand, Beck knew from participants that Hitler had put forward an over-all plan for future operations at a conference in the Reich Chancellery on November 5, 1937, in which only seven men took part (in addition to Hitler and his military Adjutant, the Commanders-in-Chief of the three arms of the Wehrmacht, the Reich Minister of War, and the Reich Minister of Foreign Affairs). He had expressed his intention of attacking Czechoslovakia and Austria in the period 1943–45 at the latest and, indeed, earlier, if the foreign situation provided an opportunity. Hitler had unmistakably sought to justify his intentions, not with the need to ensure Germany's defence against an attack, but with Germany's increasing population, which compelled her to acquire greater living space by conquest.[10]

When Hitler ordered German troops into Austria (March 12–14, 1938)—General Beck had not known of the project until two days before—this action could still be explained as a revision of Versailles and defended as the fulfilment of just German demands. For the "Anschluss" had only achieved what had long been desired by the German national movement in both countries, but been refused in 1918–19 on the orders of the victorious powers. The Republic of Austria had in face of this refusal put the concept of the Anschluss at the head of its new Constitution with the words: "Austria is an integral part of the German Reich." Counter-currents, which appeared in Austria after 1933, were directed more against an

9

Anschluss with a National Socialist Germany than against an Anschluss as such. But now, with the march into Austria, Beck, like many Germans, anxiously wondered what were Hitler's next aims and how much longer the world would accept his unscrupulous methods. When, shortly afterwards, the secret order to prepare an attack on Czechoslovakia reached the Army leaders, opinions were divided in the Officer Corps. One could point to the fact that the very nature of Czechoslovakia, as a Czech national state founded at Versailles, put great strains on relations between the Czechs and the various nationalities, especially the very strong German minority; and that this was intolerable for the new Germany—quite apart from the strategic threat. But for Beck and those who knew of the November talks it was clear that, in this case, it could not be just a question of revisionism, however much the situation of the Sudeten Germans might demand help, but a deliberate step towards the goals which Hitler had outlined and which must have far-reaching consequences. Hitler's policy of week-end surprises during France's internal crises or, as in the case of Austria, his dishonest treaties and deceptive manoeuvres, were bound to make his behaviour look like that of a highwayman who, while protesting his poverty, took any booty he wanted in an unguarded moment. "Not what we do, but the way we do it, is so bad : it is a policy of force and perfidy"[11] was how Beck put it. How much longer could others believe the constant promises, that this was the last surprise, that no further claims would be made, that war in Europe was senseless and not intended, once Hitler's blackmailing dishonesty was seen through? The moment, when all trust in him and Germany would disappear, and France's and Britain's loss of political reputation with their Allies would force them into an overwhelming alliance, could no longer be far off.

Internally, Germany had been transformed to an even greater extent in the five years since that crisis winter of 1932–33. Hitler had succeeded in a short time in widening the limited powers accorded to him as Chancellor, to the unlimited ones he exercised as Führer, particularly after Hindenburg's death on August 2, 1934. The material side of life was restored in a quick upsurge which even foreigners admired although, thanks to her measures against the Jews, Germany was hardly able to profit from the improvement in the international economy. Comprehensive building programmes got the economy moving again; industry was expanded, largely for the purposes of rearmament; and agriculture which, as everywhere, had suffered from debt and migration from the land, acquired a new status and was protected by law from commercial speculation and increased its output. The system of social assistance and medical care was expanded; the development of natural resources, including foodstuffs, was promoted; healthy living for young people became the order of the day and their involvement in crime was reduced. New city districts, even whole towns, for the workers, were established round old and new industries. The Volkswagen was on the way. The old idea of the Autobahnen came to fruition, and they were conceived not only for their utility, but also as an integral part of the German landscape.

Imports and exports had declined. The new Germany remained divorced from the liberal international economy by stringent currency restrictions. Relying on an extensive system of autarchy, it had to accept some limitations in the supply of normal consumer goods and in foreign travel. From 1937–38 this was to serve the publicly declared priority for armaments, which consumed vast quantities of foreign exchange.

No account was given of where the public authorities found the thousands of millions of marks for the manifestly vast projects for roads, state buildings and, above all, the increasing armaments. But as long as Schacht was seen to be at work, there was confidence in the "miracle".

There was nothing more to be seen of the discord which had been unleashed, almost to the point of civil war, during the winter 1932–33. The outward improvement; the talk of the national community; the slogan "The common interest before the interest of the individual"; the duty of everyone to show that he was playing his part somewhere in this state and participating in the ritual, such as the Nazi salute, had all given its citizens a common identity. This, however, remained on the surface and did not preclude growing distrust between individuals. People grumbled about the amount of compulsion coming from the party, about the compulsion to volunteer, about the compulsion only to hear and speak one opinion. And people were annoyed by the abuses of officials, great and small. But one had to recognize, in general, that the great majority of these people had trust in Hitler, had work and were happy. Revolution was no longer—or not yet again—to be feared or hoped for.

But there were other alarming and recurring developments in 1937–38, which prosperity and Führer-worship could not obliterate —developments which, in Beck's words, made this state look like the "first stage towards Bolshevism".

During the five years the churches held their ground by constant struggle and sacrifice. Attempts to integrate them more closely by force were abandoned or postponed. But the year 1937 brought significant inroads, such as the persecution of priests after the Encyclical *"Mit brennender Sorge"* (March 14) and the arrest of the well-known Dahlem pastor, Niemöller, as head of a "Confessional Church" (July 1). The new "Weltanschauung" which, Freisler later said, resembled Christianity in only one respect—in that it claimed the whole man—was intolerant. Whatever it might have contained, it suppressed spiritual freedom and the spiritual life. And what was much worse : the more its ideals were accepted, the more they confused conceptions of ethics and honour by judging all actions solely from the viewpoint of the state and the "people", who were now accorded a highly mythical status. This appeared in its most injurious and obvious form in the field of justice with the fateful thesis : "Law is what serves the people."

As dangerous as the spirit, or lack of spirit, in the new régime were its tools : the state propaganda of a Joseph Goebbels which, in the service of politics, created and produced by force, popular opinion and excitement, according to the needs of the moment; the inclusion of all in one of the many organizations, which made it possible to carry out every "inspired" move; and finally the great network of Gestapo, SD (Security Service) and concentration camps, seldom visible but everywhere effective.

In the case of some unpleasant, even horrible, happenings in the early days, it could be assumed that they were the work of wild revolutionaries. But for the way the old order was forcibly overturned, one had to look for a comparison in Russia rather than in the West. The destruction, indeed the extermination, of political opponents and of persons who had other views, especially the Jew, who was stamped as the supreme enemy, became a principle and revealed the fanatical and vulgar crudeness of the system.

Hindenburg had laid down that the Army and its leaders were to play the role of independent guardians in the state and to hold the balance against radical developments. At first, this role of the Army was respected by Hitler. Indeed, it was strengthened by his intervention on June 30, 1934, when the Chief of Staff of his SA (the Storm Battalions) had tried to infiltrate into the Army or, rather, to take it over. Before Röhm could act he was liquidated with a great part of the higher SA leaders in a coup led by Hitler himself. However necessary was the defeat of the enemy and his plans in the eyes of the Reichswehr, there was a terrible warning in the illegality of the proceedings, in which political opponents of earlier years, like the Reichswehr Generals von Bredow and von Schleicher, were shot down. Then, at a ceremony four weeks later, Hitler was able, with the help of his submissive Reich Minister of War, von Blomberg, to deprive the Army of its independence, without the use of force and almost without being noticed. On the occasion of the funeral parade for Hindenburg and Hitler's assump-

12

tion of the highest office, the German soldier was called on to renew his oath in these terms :

"I swear by God this holy oath that I will give unconditional obedience to the Führer of the German Reich and people, Adolf Hitler, the Supreme Commander of the Wehrmacht and that, as a brave soldier, I will be ready at all times to give my life for this oath."

Until then the oath had run :

"I swear by God this holy oath that I will at all times, truly and sincerely, serve my people and Fatherland and that, as a brave soldier, I will be ready at all times to give my life for this oath."

Ludwig Beck, who like the other Generals on that August 2, had been unexpectedly called on to swear the oath in its new form, called the day the blackest of his life. From then on, the leadership of the Army, which could and did feel responsible for the fate of Germany, was made directly answerable on oath to Hitler.

With rearmament and the target of a three- to five-fold increase in the Army's strength—an aim which was pursued with excessive speed despite the objections of Fritsch and Beck—the Army was bound to lose more of its independence and cohesion as many reactivated soldiers and young officers and NCOs of the Hitler state joined the forces. This process was accelerated by the fact that Göring's own Air Force, in rivalry to the Army, received special promotion from the new state, and that the SS under Himmler began to build up military-type units which, unlike the Army, did not give a military salute.

Although Hitler always responded with soothing assurances to Fritsch's remonstrations, there was other evidence to show that the SS troops were meant to form the cadres for the real National Socialist People's Army and, so, later, take the place of the old Army which was regarded as outmoded and still a prisoner of caste feeling. Nothing was said by Hitler himself about these plans : in fact, disputes between Fritsch and Himmler were settled by him without laying down any principle. The conference of November 5, 1937, had shortly followed this. It showed that Hitler needed the Army and was not yet ready to subordinate it to the SS. Indeed, thanks to events in the last three years, the Army had received a powerful impetus both externally and in its standing with the public. But its unity and its ability to act within the state had declined without Fritsch and Beck being able to prevent this process.

In Beck's view, it was not clear, up to the beginning of 1938, how much of the hostility and humiliations which had been encountered, was due to the exuberance of independent authorities exercising their power and how much was official policy. Like most Germans, he was still not ready at this stage to equate the man, whose words had moved so many, who had set to work great and unselfish forces in Germany and who had achieved much with them, with those elements of National Bolshevism (Hitler's charge against Röhm) who were spreading terror and popular neo-paganism.

The unexpected "Fritsch crisis"[12] in the first months of 1938 helped Beck to recognize clearly the outline and depth of the landscape, as if it had been illuminated by a rare streak of lightning. He learnt of the conference in the Reich Chancellery on November 5, 1937, from Fritsch and Neurath.[13] Blomberg, Fritsch and Neurath opposed Hitler's ideas. After a discussion with Beck, Neurath again warned Hitler on January 14, 1938, and offered to resign. Shortly before the Reich Economics Minister, Schacht, had insisted on resigning because his objections to monetary and economic policies had been ignored. On February 4 it was announced that the Reich War Minister von Blomberg, who was Hitler's first Field-Marshal, as well as the C.-in-C. of the Army, Freiherr von Fritsch, and the Reich Foreign Minister, Freiherr von Neurath, had resigned for reasons of health. In addition, sixteen senior officers were retired. The War Ministry was abolished and a High Command of the Wehrmacht (OKW) was created under the compliant General Wilhelm Keitel; this organization was placed directly under Hitler and over the three arms of the Wehrmacht. In this way Hitler became Commander-in-Chief of the entire Wehrmacht without any intermediary.

The public announcement celebrated this day as a "milestone in the National Socialist leadership of the state" and praised it as "a deliberate strengthening of all national energies by their most powerful concentration".[14] Before the later assembled senior officers Hitler's remarks, which were a combination of what was true and false, seemed to humiliate the "old" Army for the purpose of enthroning a new one which had complete faith in his leadership.

Blomberg was dismissed because of a recent marriage which, judged even by National Socialist standards, was unacceptable to the Officer Corps. The pretext needed to take action against Fritsch was found in an old, forgotten "court record" in which his name appeared in a homosexual charge. The Army was allowed to have a military court which, with difficulty, was able to unravel a web of dark intrigues and malicious plots and to prove that the person of the Colonel-General had nothing to do with the charge. It also emerged from the case that the Gestapo, although it knew of the confusion in the names, had compelled the witness for the prosecution, a homosexual and blackmailer with several previous convictions, to stand by his false evidence in court. An inspector was called to account; but nothing was said about those responsible—Göring,

14

Himmler and Heydrich; and the false witness was shot without trial. Outwardly Hitler appeared to have been misled; but even when the intrigue was revealed, he did only his minimum duty to clear the honour of the Colonel-General and did not revoke his dismissal. The German public only read of congratulations and an honour which Fritsch received when his health was restored.

"The Führer always knew how to exploit an opportunity. It was, as some said, 'a bloodless 30th June'. The Army was subdued without any fuss. It had triumphed in 1934. The Party took its revenge in 1938."[15]

For Hitler the scandal of the War Minister—he had been a witness at the wedding—was certainly unexpected and embarrassing. But he seized on it to achieve what he had long desired: Army leaders who were more compliant than independent and from whom he could expect co-operation with himself and his plans.

For about a week before the new C.-in-C. was appointed, Beck represented Fritsch in the top post. He did not feel justified in taking counter-action before a court inquiry; he would have regarded that as mutiny. But before it came to that—Brauchitsch in the meantime having taken over the office of C.-in-C.—the new Army was called on to undertake its first, still flower-strewn, task by marching into Austria. And the reincorporation of the German sister country was for Hitler's leadership such a triumph that all the deep concern connected with the case against Fritsch (March 10–18) was submerged in it. The General went, suffered, and was silent. Beck felt it was disastrous that the Army had suffered a defeat which it should never have had to accept—disastrous, above all, because it could no longer confront the war plans with the necessary independence and self-respect.

In August Winnig's book there is an account of a meeting with Beck in the spring of 1938: "We talked during the whole evening. He judged Ludendorff uncommonly harshly—the Ludendorff of the First World War; he did not take the Protector of the Tannenberg League seriously. In this way, we soon came to the present, which Beck frankly called the first stage towards Bolshevism. It was diverting to observe how he changed the subject and spoke of Trakehnen horses and animal breeding, of the elk reserve Ibenhorst or other East Prussian attractions, as soon as a third person came near us. It was getting very late. We promised to keep in touch —I now knew that here was a man of spirit and will in one of the most important posts, watchful and ready. For that reason, I went my way contentedly through Potsdam that night."[16]

Sooner than it perhaps seemed likely that evening of the meeting, Beck had to act and had to stake himself, his life and his position on the outcome. Once he was convinced that Hitler's war plans were threatening disaster, he deliberately exceeded his military role and, with his great powers of intellect and exposition, tried to influence decisions in the political field, where Hitler had expressly denied his right to take part. He conducted this struggle on his own, not as the holder of the senior responsible post but standing in the background, as adviser to General von Brauchitsch who, in spite of apparent agreement with him, was still basically undecided.

On May 28, 1938, at a conference in the Reich Chancellery in which Beck took part, Hitler spoke about Germany's position in terms similar to those of November. He announced an early attack on Czechoslovakia and referred to the possibility of a war later becoming necessary in the West. On May 30 the three arms of the Wehrmacht received this order, which began : "It is my unalterable decision to crush Czechoslovakia in the near future by military action." They were instructed to make preparations "as quickly as possible".[17]

Beck thought the hour had come to take decisive action. He had no troops under his command and was only adviser and one of five assistants to his Commander-in-Chief. On May 29 he approached the new C.-in-C. of the Army, in writing and in a personal interview, to argue against Hitler's ideas of the day before. He put forward the same ideas which he had set down in his memorandum at the beginning of May. He repeated his arguments in still more urgent form on June 3. He spoke of the "complete inadequacy of the senior military hierarchy until now" and continued : "Constant professional advice for the Commander-in-Chief of the Wehrmacht (that is to say, Hitler) in matters of war strategy and operations must be demanded, as well as a clear demarcation and observance of responsibilities. If something is not quickly done to change the intolerable situation and if the present anarchy becomes permanent, then one can only see the fate of the Wehrmacht in peace and war and, therefore, the fate of Germany in a future war, in the blackest colours."[18]

His oral and written pronouncements, as the published record shows, always had something compelling about them, thanks to the measured and sober way in which he first marshalled the details, then went on to the over-all picture, from which the directives for action seemed to flow automatically. These views, it seemed, had either to be totally accepted or totally rejected. Hitler rejected them as the presumptuous objections of a feckless man who was the prisoner of outmoded ideas. Göring used to say that such wise heads lacked heart. In the meantime, Beck felt an almost unique responsibility as a custodian who had to keep watch over the destructive powers of a modern war and continued to believe that in the twentieth century, too, only "a just war" was worthy of a people.

On June 13 Hitler once again assembled the Generals on the Barth airfield near Stralsund in Pomerania. He announced an honour for Colonel-General Fritsch, on whom the command of an artillery regiment was bestowed; he had the details of the judgment and the reasons for the acquittal read out, and he described his own attitude. He spoke apparently in complete sincerity, expressed his deep regret over the "tragic happening" in which he himself had been misled. But he explained why the Colonel-General who, for the rest, had received every possible satisfaction, could not be reinstated; and he stressed the unique position of the Wehrmacht, against which other elements must not conduct a deliberate campaign. According to the report of one of the participants, he ended by imploring the Commanders "not to desert the flag in this serious crisis". Hitler's words obviously did not fail to have their effect. Brauchitsch himself told the Generals that he had decided to take his departure because of the treatment meted out to Fritsch. Now Hitler had told him there would inevitably be war in the coming weeks. In these circumstances, he felt he could not leave his post and urged others, who had had similar views, to stay.[19]

Beck made a new move. In the draft of his memorandum he had proposed resignation, if Hitler did not change his mind. The fair copy which he handed over on July 16 contained nothing of that. Instead, it contained an appeal to the C.-in-C. and Commanding Generals to try to compel Hitler to give up his preparations for war. The speech, of which a record has been kept, contained clearly and sharply formulated details about the planned move on the part of the Generals, gave a warning of an ignominious end to Germany and found its climax in the sentences reproduced at the beginning of this book. They appealed to the conscience of the C.-in-C. to remember his responsibility to the whole nation, to recognize the limits of his obedience as a soldier and to meet extraordinary times with extraordinary actions. Beck was, as one who heard his conversations at this time reported, "inflexibly determined to bring matters to a head".[20]

Three days later he was again with Brauchitsch and pressed him to use the move planned by the Generals to bring about at the same time the necessary show-down with the SS. Otherwise, he thought it would be impossible to re-establish the proper rule of law. In a further conversation on July 29 he suggested to him this formulation for his action : "The C.-in-C. of the Army, with his senior Generals, regrets that he cannot assume responsibility for the conduct of such a war, without making himself guilty before the nation

17

and history. They will, therefore, resign if the Führer insists on war." Beck added that the form of this declaration could "not be phrased to sound sufficiently compelling, hard and brutal". Apart from the possibility of war, one must, he said, prepare "for an internal conflict, which need only take place in Berlin", in co-operation with the General Commanding Berlin, von Witzleben, and the Police President, Count Helldorf. The second half of September would probably be the appropriate time. Thus the plan for a coup d'état was mentioned for the first time by Beck.[21]

Beck persuaded Brauchitsch to assemble the Army Group Commanders and the Commanding Generals in the first week of August, before Hitler could speak to them. This had been scheduled for the 15th on the troop training field at Jüterbog. Beck literally prepared the speech which the C.-in-C. was to make. It was later called Beck's military testament as Chief of the General Staff of the German Army.[22] Following a review of the international situation on the lines of the former memoranda, it showed that the conflict with Czechoslovakia could not be a limited one and that Germany, because of her present situation (arms, alliances, financial state and morale), was not equal to a world war which could be expected with certainty. Brauchitsch was meant to end : "I intend to explain to the Führer my attitude to a military solution of the Czech question and the resulting problems for the political leadership in the next few days. I must ask from you, gentlemen, that you will stand behind me through thick and thin, and follow me unconditionally on the path that I must take in the interests of our German nation."

Beck's efforts came to nothing. At the meeting Brauchitsch, who did not stick to the plan, got him to deliver his July memorandum and called on General Adam, the Commander proposed for the West, to speak. Adam supported Beck and concluded : "I am very pessimistic : that is the truth." To which Brauchitsch replied : "I share your view entirely. When you have next to speak to the Führer, you must say the very same." Adam answered : "I have the courage to do so." Beck rushed to him and shook both his hands saying : "Adam, I congratulate you." According to the report, there were then heard "only slightly dissenting opinions" (such as those of Reichenau and Busch), to which Beck replied "in a sharp tone" unusual with him. But a joint resolution was not called for. Brauchitsch dismissed the gathering with the simple observation that the senior officers were united in rejecting a war.[23]

Beck was present at the inspection in Jüterbog. Hitler announced that he had definitely decided to solve the Czech question that autumn. Beck tried to get Brauchitsch to define his attitude on the spot, but the latter avoided doing so. Having returned to Berlin,

Beck on August 18 addressed a request to the C.-in-C. to arrange for him to be relieved of his post as Chief of the General Staff. Brauchitsch, plainly not unhappy with this solution, supported the request.

Hitler's consent arrived on August 21. But it was requested that, for reasons of foreign policy, the resignation should be kept secret for the time being.

A highly-gifted man of Moltke's and Schlieffen's school, Beck resigned at a time when the greatest prospects were opening up before him; and he deliberately chose to have no part in a war in which, in other circumstances, his life and career could have found fulfilment.

On August 27 Beck handed over to General Halder and once again assembled his closest associates on the *Tirpitzufer*. "When we entered the room," one who was present says, "Beck stood erect by his writing desk at the window, unmoved by anyone's greeting, with his hands folded, his fine, spiritual face looking weary, almost other-worldly, the gaze of his great, handsome eyes fixed on the distance. He made a speech to us for about a quarter of an hour, classical in form and construction and wise in content. Its gist was once again to make clear to the assembled officers his efforts to secure an independent, free and creative role for the Chief of the General Staff. This he had sought but had only imperfectly achieved in the prevailing circumstances. The exhortation to independence of judgement and firmness of character in action made a great impression. ...I believe that even those few listeners who regarded Beck's departure as actually necessary could not ignore the dignity, seriousness and the proud sense of responsibility of the man who, for character and ability, was to be the last real Chief of the General Staff of Germany."[24]

Beck withdrew from office, but did not feel relieved of his duty. He could now expect to be watched at every step and with every letter he wrote and received. But he knew how to conduct his private life in such a way that he was not interfered with. In fact, he kept up with all events, spoke with many people, whom he received almost exclusively as individual callers, visited himself or met on a neutral ground,[25] and he operated by proxy where he could not be present in person. He became the brain-centre of responsible planning for all the efforts which, up to the 20th July, 1944, were directed towards a coup. "The great figure behind the scenes," as a perhaps controversial source calls him, never hesitated to expose himself to risks. After the dismissal of Freiherr von Fritsch, Hitler is said to have remarked of him: "The only man whom I fear is Beck. That man could do something against me."[26]

II. BECK'S ALLIES

Of those who worked with Beck, Hans *Oster* must be mentioned first. It was he who spent a great deal of time in the room of the Chief of the General Staff and who kept Beck precisely informed about military and political events after his resignation. The Colonel, who later became a Major-General, was seven years younger than Beck and came from a pastor's home on the banks of the Elbe. His whole bearing was that of the slim horse-rider; and he was plainly influenced by the years he had served as a young officer in the Imperial Army. Towards the Kaiser, who had fled to Holland, he always felt a personal sense of loyalty. The later years he spent in the Reichswehr, which were interrupted by periods of civilian life, did not stamp him to the same degree. Before 1933 he was in close touch with the Generals von Schleicher, von Bredow and von Hammerstein, the most determined opponents of Hitler in the Wehrmacht. In 1933 he worked under General von Bredow, who was murdered in the Röhm putsch, and from 1935 under (later) Admiral Canaris in the Abwehr (Military Intelligence) department of the German High Command. From the beginning he was opposed to the new rulers of Germany and proceeded to investigate and record all the horrors which he either saw or anticipated, in order to collect incriminating material for the day when Hitler could be overthrown. Secretly he organized a highly complex nerve centre of intelligence which kept him informed about events in the Reich Chancellery and in the *Berghof,* as well as about the plans of the SS. And he made available to the Opposition the knowledge and the opportunities provided by his office. He was able, ostensibly in the course of his duties, to find like-minded persons and to bring them together : he became the busy middle-man between them all. The offices of the Abwehr were also open to civilians. One was used to seeing the most extraordinary figures in a great variety of dress picking their way through this beehive of activity. Whoever wanted to work in this humming atmosphere had to have many faces or an impenetrable one; his right hand never dared to know what his left hand was doing; his element was a game of life and death and his more than entertaining day's work was to catch without being caught. Oster, although often near to disaster, worked for many years in this element, until he was betrayed by a movement of his hand when trying to push aside a note in order to save another.

Those who saw Oster in his office, speaking to four different persons from the four secret telephone lines on his table, were alarmed by this sort of simultaneous game, especially when they knew that he was working for two sides and often in spheres where high treason and betrayal of one's country could hardly be disentangled.* But Oster, as we are assured by men who saw through his considerable reserve, never acted frivolously, even if he liked to affect a military arrogance which went with his Saxon accent. Those who worked with him knew his driving patriotism and his deep devotion to the religion and ethical code of his youth. We know the kind of decisions such a man had to take. Thus, after a severe conflict between his judgement and conscience, he took it on himself, because he hoped a storm might clear the atmosphere, to warn both Holland and Norway of the imminent German attack hanging over them. He thought that an attack, if beaten off at the outset, or rendered impossible in the eyes of the world, would come as a severe rebuff to Hitler and lead to an early end to the war and to a change of régime and deliverance at home. From the military point of view he was profoundly convinced that the possible sacrifices which this step might cost his own people bore no comparison with the sufferings of the hundreds of thousands of victims and the incalculable destruction that the war would bring to the other peoples of Europe—a war which, because of the rival strengths, could never be won by Germany.

Admiral Canaris was often disturbed by the activities of Oster, which he did not properly comprehend; but he fully recognized his devotion and, at his own peril, constantly covered up and saved Oster in critical situations. For Oster was frequently imprudent in his daring impetuosity and boundless aversion to the régime. Early in 1943 Canaris could protect him no longer and Oster had to retire to private life where he was closely watched. He was arrested after the 20th July, 1944, endlessly questioned and taken away. He was executed in the last month of the war.

His love of horses, his capacity for sharing pleasures with his friends, his constant encouragement of, and sympathy with, others, were the mark of a self-possessed, believing nature, which one of his friends described in the phrase "a man after God's heart". It is reported how Oster answered SS officers, who plied him in prison with questions : "Gentlemen, the issues are clear : the die is cast."[1]

The note he wrote to his son shows, what fellow-prisoners confirm, that he retained his composure and faith in God to the end. "We shall all remain to our last breath the decent fellows we were

*The Germans make a distinction between "Hochverrat" which is high treason against the state and "Landesverrat" which is the betrayal of one's country abroad.

21

brought up to be as children and as soldiers. Let come what will! The only fear we have is that of the anger of God, when we are not upright and decent and fail to do our duty."

It is clear that many of the human contacts and agreements brought about by Oster remained effective up to the 20th July, 1944; but after his retirement his name is no longer encountered in the actual preparations. He lived in a suburb of Leipzig like an exile whose steps were constantly watched. On the day after the 20th July a telegram arrived in Dresden which the Deputy Commanding General of the IV Army Corps von Sch. sent on : it appointed Oster liaison officer for Saxony.[2] But, even without this, Oster would not have escaped his fate. Papers found at Zossen, which put into the hands of the Gestapo some of the documents collected by him, including the diary notes of Canaris, shortly afterwards laid bare his long and bitter opposition.

A friend of Oster and one who worked closely with him, particularly after the Fritsch crisis, was Reichsgerichtsrat Hans von *Dohnanyi*. Despite his youth, he quickly worked his way up to become the personal assistant of the Reich Minister of Justice, Gürtner, and during the war he was given special responsibilities in the Abwehr. He had an unusually lucid mind and a determined but rather reserved and strict character. Like Oster, he came from a Protestant family. His role was to act as the judicial conscience, as well as the moral instigator of the decisions taken in this group. During his arrest he vainly tried to put off his fate by infecting himself with diphtheria bacilli : he was carried to his death paralysed. Others who belonged to this circle, whose activities were uncovered early but who were not eliminated until much later, were Justus *Delbrück*, son of the historian and relative and colleague of Dohnanyi; and pastor Dietrich *Bonhoeffer*, Dohnanyi's brother-in-law. Another, who worked closely in Berlin with Oster and was able to elude all suspicion in a foreign post of the Abwehr in Zagreb until the 20th July, 1944, but who was then seized and executed shortly before the fall of Berlin, was Carl Ludwig Freiherr von *Guttenberg*. He was a much loved, chivalrous figure from the Catholic landed aristocracy of other days who, right up to and including the war, published the "Weisse Blätter" in Neustadt on the Saale. Amid the prevailing monotony of the general press he stood out as the dedicated guardian of his local area.[3]

Admiral Wilhelm *Canaris*, after his flight from Chile in the First World War, worked for a year for the German Secret Service in Spain. In 1918 he was a U-boat Commander in the Mediterranean. At the end of the war he fought for the Government against the revolutionaries; and in 1920 he fought with Ehrhardt and Kapp

22

against the government for "the reconstruction of the Fatherland". In the following decade he rose rapidly, sometimes doing administrative work in the Admiralty, sometimes in command of a ship, an enthusiastic officer and a German nationalist opposed to Versailles. In spite of some reservations, he approved of Hitler's Chancellorship; and in 1934 he became chief of the German military Abwehr, in succession to Captain Patzig, who had fallen out with the War Minister and the SS. When he took up the post, he was forty-seven years old with a fresh complexion and already snow-white hair. Even more than Oster, who was almost the same age, he was the epitome of the Secret Service officer : urbane and astute, observant even in matters that seemed vague and remote, imaginative in investigation, cautious in his own judgements, difficult to catch, always on the trail of things, a lover of adventure and contrived confusion. In addition, this man, who was born on the Lower Rhine, had an intuitive and restless nature, one which, however kind and solicitous towards others, never completely opened up and made friendships. It was only with his dogs that he seemed really at home. Shadows from that world of moods and fantasies which were so real to him, often inhibited him more than the weight of knowledge of one who knows the essence of a matter from too many sides. Aversions could make him physically sick. He was small; he darted about; and his movements were short and precise. It was noticed that even in summer he easily took cold and put on a coat. He always carried medicines in his pockets which he took frequently and offered freely. The countries of the south, Spain, Italy, and Greece attracted him—one of his ancestors had come from Lake Como to Bernkastel on the Moselle. He spoke Spanish fluently. He had had his adventures in the First World War and he particularly loved the Spanish "posada" with its medley of people, the smoke of the hearth, and the smell of wine. At such times, he liked to put on an apron and to stand at the fire to do the roasting. In the south, especially in Cervantes' part of the world, it seemed to his companions that his natural complexion assumed an even livelier hue. This was perhaps a legacy from his forebears. He combined a lively imagination with a sense of reality that bordered on the improbable, and behind it all there was an often almost scurrilous sense of humour.[4]

It was Canaris's particular fate—and one which he deliberately did not evade, even when it was still possible—to be the Secret Service Chief to a man and a party, with whom, after bitter experience, he no longer had anything in common and whose policies he thought disastrous. This was in spite of the fact that he had once devoted his services to Hitler because he regarded him as the restorer

23

of national sovereignty and German hopes for the future. This fate cast a shadow over Canaris, even when he acted from the purest of motives. As one can see from his own statements, he himself felt that an office like his should not be carried by one man. But to hand it over, without defending himself to the last, to those dangerous and unscrupulous rivals, who fought and intrigued for it so long, and who would clearly have used it for their purposes, would have struck him as an intolerable capitulation. He preferred to accept a twilight reputation for himself and the often very difficult decisions about what he owed his country and the fighting forces and what his conscience demanded of him in order to limit the disgrace, to prevent or right a wrong, to ward off an evil. The Nuremberg trials revealed the efforts he made to prevent the human exterminations in the East and the killing of French Generals, such as Giraud and others, in captivity. He expressly protested to his chief Keitel against the military Abwehr service being used for such acts of murder.[5]

His main task was to obtain intelligence and to pass this on to the Army, the Air Force and the Navy for evaluation. His biographer, Abshagen, shows how, in this respect, he strove to provide exact and complete information. It was different with his oral and written statements to people like his chief, Keitel, or to Hitler himself : here, while complete material was at the disposal of the competent authorities, he deliberately coloured reports to put obstacles in the way of certain moves which he feared; for example, when an attempt was being made to get Spain to enter the war. These efforts, however honest and sensible in particular cases—and who dared to judge them at the time?—could do great harm if they interfered with some great but not easily discernible over-all plan. This bore heavily on Canaris's activities from 1938 onwards and he genuinely wanted to get away from the dilemma and find a solution in liberation.[6]

Freiherr von Weizsäcker, who spoke of very few as openly as he did of Canaris, wrote about him : "One cannot overlook him as a phenomenon. He is one of the most interesting phenomena of the time, of a type brought to light and perfected under dictatorship, a combination of disinterested idealism and shrewdness, such as is particularly rare in Germany. As wise as serpents, as pure as doves. This combination is rare with us. As a young naval officer, Canaris had been very enterprising and adventurous. That was shown in the First World War. He commanded his U-boat with distinction. He was versed in foreign languages and had friends everywhere. Whether he had Greek blood I do not know; but, at all events, he passed for a cunning Odysseus. This much even Hitler must have recognized; otherwise, he would have hardly entrusted his whole military intelligence to a sailor. But he had not seen into his heart. Even the Gestapo for many years did not know what kind of man he was. Canaris had the gift of getting people to talk, without revealing himself. His pale blue eyes did not uncover the depth of his being. Very seldom, and only through a narrow crack, did one see his crystal-clear character, the deeply moral and tragic side of his personality."[7]

Canaris dissociated himself from all the direct planning for a coup with the remark : "Just get on with it." We may conclude this was because he realized that he, who was so cautious, so convinced of disaster, who only saw difficulties and could not believe in success, was not the man for this. But for years he provided help, created contacts, and passed on information. He courageously protected those in danger, and for a long time cultivated, in a spirit of professional co-operation but, in fact, at the cost of wearing down his strength, contacts with the SS especially with Heydrich, then Kaltenbrunner, Müller and Schellenberg, in order to save what was possible. The crisis which led to Oster's dismissal left him in office, but a year later he was out-manoeuvred and had to step down (Spring 1944). One of his department chiefs, Colonel Hansen, became Chief of the Service and was later put under the RSH (The Central Reich Security Office). He, too, like many others who worked in the Abwehr, was one of the men of the 20th July and was executed.

Three days after the 20th July Canaris was arrested in his Berlin home by Schellenberg, his former partner in talks and later successor from the ranks of the SS. He was subjected to the same humiliating custody as many others. Parts of his diary were found with a collection of Oster's documents in a security safe. This evidence, which led to more cross-examinations, lengthened the wretched lives of both men almost to the point where they hoped to be saved. Participation in the conspiracy of the 20th July could not be proved against them. But it was decided that, because they knew so much, they must not survive. In the first light of April 9, 1945, Canaris was ignominiously executed with Oster, Bonhoeffer and five or six others in Flossenbürg, the notorious place of execution in the Upper Palatinate Forest.[8]

In looking round for a senior officer who commanded troops, Oster approached the Commander of the Berlin Military District, General, as he then was, Erwin von *Witzleben*. Oster had known him earlier as his superior officer and in him he had soon found a man of the same mind, who regarded June 30, 1934 (the action against Röhm and others) and February 4, 1938 (Fritsch's dismissal and Hitler's assumption of the command of the Wehrmacht) as an insult to the German Officer Corps and looked forward to the day

25

when this insult could be avenged. He had been born in Breslau in 1881 in a Prussian family with an old officer tradition. The rise of Hitler never affected him very deeply : he left politics to others. He loved, above all things, the country, the woods, hunting and clear-cut decisions. In bearing and manner, he had the authority of a soldier who commands and whose strictness harmonized with his own undeniable self-discipline. He carried himself erect, with his head up and his eyelids half-closed. He spoke rather quietly and could have been taken for a General from the entourage of Kaiser Wilhelm I. In 1942 he was relieved of his command and was not employed again. Through his Adjutant, Ulrich Wilhelm Count Schwerin-Schwanenfeld, to whom reference will be made later, he remained connected with the plans for resistance and a coup. "A straight, honest officer," so Schacht judges Witzleben, "born and brought up an aristocrat, more a Corps Commander than an officer of the General Staff".[9] Towards Beck, he, the Field-Marshal, adopted an attitude of respectful loyalty right to the end. He was amongst the first of those to be sentenced and to die for the 20th July.

General of the Armoured Troops, Erich *Hoepner*, Commander of the 1st Light Division in Wuppertal, also declared himself ready in December 1938 to take part in a coup. Later he made a great name for himself as Commander of the 6th Armoured Division in the German advance in France and Russia; but, in the first months of 1942, he was dishonourably discharged from the Wehrmacht by Hitler, because in the previous serious winter crisis before Moscow he had withdrawn troops on his own initiative. He was executed along with Witzleben.[10]

With General Karl Heinrich von *Stülpnagel*, who was one of his Quartermasters, Beck had a close understanding during his period of office. He is the same person whom we find again in an important position in Paris on 20th July. He was a few years younger than Beck and, because of his unwavering chivalry, moderation, and dependability, was regarded as the embodiment of the best Prussian type, especially by South Germans. He combined an academic nature and great knowledge with the unmistakable appearance of a soldier of the old school. In contact with the most diverse types, even the vulgar, he often showed his great adaptability and was capable of fine nuances in his speech.

In 1940 he became Chairman of the German Armistice Commission after the Treaty of Compiègne.[11] Later, we see him in Southern Russia as Commander of the Seventeenth Army, where at the end of 1941 he was relieved of his post after the loss of Rostov.[12] On March 1, 1942, he became Military Commander in

France and from 1943 onwards he built up his position in Paris in such a way that he was later able to work from it for the revolution he wanted. As for the criticism levelled against him in his certainly difficult office—that he was either too hesitant, or too hard —one might agree with the remark of one of his staff "that his deeds and omissions were dominated by his wish to be able to play the part assigned to him in the final struggle against Hitler".[13]

Another of Beck's Quartermasters, who knew at first hand of his move in the summer of 1938 and who took part in the preparations for the coup in September 1938 and always continued to stand by Beck, was General Eduard *Wagner*, later Quartermaster-General. He was particularly active in the preparation of the 20th July and committed suicide after its failure.

General Franz *Halder*, also Quartermaster under Beck, had succeeded Beck as Chief of the General Staff with the latter's encouragement. June 30, 1934, had deeply angered him without actually bringing a break between him and Hitler. But soon Hitler became for him merely the destroyer of the Fatherland and the personification of evil. In the autumn of 1937 he had, a report says, talked of the use of force against Hitler to the Army C.-in-C., Freiherr von Fritsch, and after the latter's "infamous dismissal", spoke to Beck of "practical opposition".[14] In his first talks with Colonel Oster, to whom he had been particularly recommended by Beck, he confessed himself in passionate terms to be an enemy of Hitler and offered to take part in a coup, if Hitler really went to war. He had an important part in the plan for a coup d'état in September 1938. In the autumn of 1939, when the Polish campaign was over, he tried a new approach, while, as Chief of the General Staff, he was busy with the preparations for the attack in the West. During the years of German successes in the war, he held his office without receiving particular commendation from Hitler. After several serious clashes, including one in which Halder says that Hitler went for him "foaming at the mouth and with clenched fists",[15] he was dismissed on September 4, 1942, with the remark that, for the tasks which still faced the Army, it was not a question of professional ability, but of the ardour of National Socialist belief : the secret of Moltke's successes, it was said, had been the ardour of his monarchist conviction. Halder was of Bavarian origin. At first sight a little schoolmasterish with pince-nez and well-brushed hair, he was regarded as extraordinarily knowledgeable and painstaking in his field, precise and instructive in argument, honourable in his aims. His capacity for work was almost limitless, thanks to a tough constitution and severe self-discipline. But his capacity for action was limited by a weak and very impressionable nature. After the 20th

27

July he was arrested and was only released at the end of the war.[16]

Of Beck's entourage there remains to be mentioned a man, whom he himself honoured and whose similar attitude he found fortifying : Colonel-General Kurt Freiherr von *Hammerstein-Equord*. Hammerstein had been previously known as the "Red General", because he got on with the trade unions and was opposed to certain "German Nationalist" views of the old Officer Corps. In 1933 he was ready to use the Reichswehr against Hitler as he was forcing his way to power, but then had to accept Hindenburg's veto.[17] In January 1934 he requested, and received, his discharge as Chief of the Army Command. June 30, 1934, which involved Generals who thought like himself, left him untouched. The longer he lived in retirement, the more Hammerstein, who took an active interest in affairs and had an independent outlook, felt himself divided from the leading soldiers. Brüning, with whom he had much in common, described him early in 1939 as the only General who could remove Hitler.[18] He was, according to him, a man without nerves, who when the time came would light a Brazil cigar, place himself in a chair and give the order to fire. But Hammerstein had no command. Only in September 1939 when the Polish War had begun, did he get an Army Command in the West. It is reported[19] that the General, who could be secretive even with his own friends, decided to use his new command of troops for a coup and to seize Hitler while on an inspection tour in the West. But, after a few days, Hitler declined the proffered invitation, and retired the Colonel-General again. He died in April 1943.[20]

In accordance with his ideas of his office and duty, Ludwig Beck, as Chief of the General Staff, sought talks with responsible men outside his own military field. He had confidential contacts with Freiherr von Weizsäcker who in April 1938 became State Secretary in the Foreign Office under Ribbentrop. Later he prepared the way for a rapprochement between Weizsäcker and Halder who often exchanged messages through Canaris. A number of younger members of Weizsäcker's staff were also involved.

There were other contacts with Carl Goerdeler, the former Mayor of Leipzig, with Hjalmar Schacht, President of the Reichsbank and still Reich Economics Minister. Important information, not otherwise available, about internal measures and secret SS and Party matters were provided by Regierungsrat Hans-Bernd Gisevius, who was close to Oster. He had good contacts with the Police President of Berlin, Count Helldorf, and with the Director of the Reich Criminal Police, SS Standartenführer Nebe. In addition, the Vice-President of the Berlin Police, Count Fritz von der Schulenburg, was known to be sympathetic.

III. FIRST ATTEMPTS AT A COUP 1938–39

On September 1, 1938, Halder took Beck's place. It was clear to the initiated that war was to be reckoned with before the end of the month. Before this, the Party Rally in Nuremberg was to take place, which, if it were not suddenly cancelled, was expected to produce a heightening of tension.

Halder met Schacht, whose views greatly impressed him. He believed that, if there were a German attack on Czechoslovakia, military intervention by the Western powers was absolutely certain. Erich Kordt expressed the same opinion during a visit to von Brauchitsch arranged by Oster. As he says in his account, he ended : "In your hands, Colonel-General, now lies the fate of the German Army and with it that of the German people. You now carry the entire responsibility."[1] In the meantime Witzleben worked out a plan[2] on General Staff lines to occupy Berlin and to seize power in the Reich in co-operation with Major-General Count Brockdorff-Ahlefeldt, his subordinate as the Commander of the Potsdam (23rd) Division who was later to become known as the defender of Demyansk. He also took into his confidence other troop commanders in the area. To help him, H. B. Gisevius worked in Witzleben's offices, ostensibly doing some research on family matters : his special task was the difficult one of determining the position and strength of party offices and SS troops in and around Berlin and taking account of this in the plans. In accordance with a suggestion, which clearly owed its origin to him and Oster, that an initial, legal move should be made against "the criminal Gestapo", they proposed to inform Hitler in the Reich Chancellery of the intolerable conditions and force him to dismiss Himmler and Heydrich at once. If he refused, Hitler was to be removed from the Reich Chancellery in a sudden swoop and held at an unknown place. Further, with Witzleben's forces, it was proposed to occupy the Government quarters, the SS strong-points and all communications in Berlin, to arrest the most important party leaders and members of the Government, and to issue appropriate orders for simultaneous action at once to the Military District Commanders. Detailed preparations, especially information about the opposition to be expected, about the signals centres, repeater stations and transmitters, as well as about the routine in, and physical layout of, the Reich Chancellery, were necessary : here, in particular, Erich Kordt, as Chief of the

Ministerial Bureau in the Foreign Office, offered his help. Witzleben was confident and thought, when the precise plan was drawn up, that he could successfully carry out the coup. The public was to be fed with contradictory rumours in the first few hours and independent action from any "liberators" was to be made difficult. Then it was proposed to come forward as soon as possible with statements showing Hitler was deliberately provoking a world war and setting forth the crimes of his régime. Possibly there would also be an announcement that Hitler would shortly be put on public trial or—this, too, was also considered—that he had become insane. The first ten hours would be decisive; in this period the Commanding Generals in the Reich would have to succeed in ensuring their exclusive control. The SS *Leibstandarte* in Munich were regarded as an important body of troops on Hitler's side. General Hoepner, who was with his Wuppertal Armoured Division in the Thuringian Forest in preparation for the Sudeten affair, was ready to attack them, should they be ordered to Berlin to rescue Hitler. The period from September 14–16 was accepted as the approximate date of the operation, since the Party Rally in Nuremberg was expected to end on September 11. But there was need for great vigilance so as not to miss the moment for action. Hitler would give the order to attack Czechoslovakia; but the advance would not begin forthwith because, once that had happened, it would no longer be possible to call a halt. According to Halder's assurance, the "calendar", in spite of all intentions to take lightning action, envisaged forty-eight hours between the first order and the actual attack. This meant that the domestic military operation, which had been organized to begin in a matter of hours, could take place in this interim period.

The plan for the coup rested on a few men. It was uncertain until the last moment whether the C.-in-C. of the Army, von Brauchitsch, would co-operate. If he refused, Witzleben was determined to take action against him as well. The Germans, as a whole, encouraged by the Anschluss with Austria, heard only of daily and often bloody attacks by the Czechs and of the Sudeten German minority helplessly trying to defend itself. That incidents were created, that cause and effect were conveniently confused, and that the temperature of the daily news reports could be regulated without reference to the facts and according to a prepared plan, was known only to a few initiated persons at the time. To judge by the official picture, action by Germany seemed justified; indeed, failure to act would be discreditable. And it was readily accepted as certain that Britain and France, who were known to have obligations to assist Czechoslovakia, would not in these circumstances resort to arms.

For the purpose of a coup in Germany it was, therefore, very important that there should be a forthright declaration, particularly from Britain, exposing the irresponsible attitude to war of Germany's leaders.[3]

In the middle of August the conservative politician, Ewald Heinrich von Kleist-Schmenzin, had gone to London with the knowledge of the Abwehr Chief, Canaris, and had spoken to Vansittart, Lord Lloyd and Churchill. At the beginning of September, without knowing about him, Major Böhm-Tettelbach had followed, sent by Halder, Oster and Beck.[4] A few days later, Sir Horace Wilson and, in a secret night audience (on September 5) the British Foreign Secretary, Halifax, were approached by the German chargé d'affaires in London, Theo Kordt, with the same end in view. They urged firmness towards Hitler and his policy of force. Only in this way, they argued, might it be possible to avoid a war; and the National Socialist régime would not survive such a diplomatic defeat. "Should Hitler still insist on his policy of war," Kordt said, "then I am in a position to assure you that the political and military circles for whom I speak, will 'take arms against a sea of troubles and, by opposing, end them'." Kordt ended his message, as he himself has said, with the words : "The German patriots see no other way out of the dilemma than close co-operation with the British government in order to prevent the great crime of war."[5] The British Embassy Secretary was spoken to in similar terms in the diplomats' train in Nuremberg where he was a guest.[6]

It became known later that just as the German diplomat was received in the London Foreign Office and was frankly describing, at risk to his life, the situation in Germany, a decision was taken to send the Prime Minister to negotiate with Hitler. The British were not in a position to reciprocate the German frankness.[7] What filtered through to them from this other Germany carried too little weight as far as they were concerned. It seemed like a party feud of injured and impotent men at a foreign court.[8] Chamberlain, by whatever other motives he was prompted, turned to peace at any price—at the price, as he later learned, of a world war.

The older generation will remember what tension hung over that September of 1938. Hitler thought the hour had come for which he had long wished : to take the first major step, in the confidence of his arms, towards winning territory for his over-populated country. Others prayed to heaven that it would permit them to strike down the great destroyer of the country, the demolisher of justice and morality. The memorable weeks were very sunny—it was expected they would produce a good wine : they brought out all the charms of our country in the rural areas but were full of explosive

31

tension in the cities. Countless special trains ran to Nuremberg; small towns seemed for a while quite emptied of men; then, when the wave returned, there were call-ups and new departures to the garrisons and to the frontiers. They were weeks of continuous newspaper attacks, and it was apparent that Hitler was becoming increasingly vehement in his unyielding attitude.

The Party Rally brought no startling declaration. The mass display of power seen then had never been witnessed before—except perhaps in Soviet demonstrations. The relationship between Hitler and his hundreds of thousands of supporters was shown in the mighty pomp of a spectacle which outdid itself and seemed on the point of explosion. Was anyone troubled in all this deafening tumult by the knowledge that in the eyes of Hitler, who had taken it on himself to decide the fate of the masses, the death of thousands weighed as lightly as the happiness of thousands? He no longer spoke the language of persuasion : he thundered, jeered, scolded and threatened his own people, as well as foreigners. No calmer tone relieved his voice of tension. He seemed like one driven to action, whom resistance inhibited, like a person who struck with words in order to create the heavy atmosphere, which made it easier for him to set things alight. Of his true intentions the keenly awaited final speech gave little indication. But the appeal to Benes, the President of the Czechoslovak Republic, was of striking urgency—an appeal to respect the right of self-determination. A power like the newly-risen Reich, Hitler claimed, could not much longer look on at the oppression of people of its own blood. Almost more threatening, and certainly understood by men like Beck, seemed the attack on the enemy at home, on the intelligentsia and the upper classes who, it was said, did not understand the national revolution and were full of cowardice. With the evening of the "cathedral of light", the great arc made by searchlights around "the Führer and his people", the last Party Rally ended. Hasty military movements followed.[9]

On September 13, Hitler came to Berlin. In Beck's and Witzleben's circle every step he took was followed with the greatest excitement. Then it became known on September 14 that the British Ambassador had announced that the visit of the British Prime Minister, which he had suggested, would take place on the following day. Hitler left Berlin on September 14 to receive his guests the next day in Berchtesgaden. This was the first unexpected rebuff for the conspirators.

A talk with Witzleben took place in Oster's home on how to seize Hitler's person as soon as possible. The former *Stahlhelm* leader and member of the Ehrhardt Free Corps Brigade, Lieutenant-Colonel Friedrich Wilhelm Heinz, as well as naval Lieutenant

Liedig, took part. Heinz undertook to form an assault party from the former *Young-Stahlhelm* and the *Stahlhelm* Student Ring Langenmarck, which was to force its way into the Reich Chancellery. After about a week the assault party was available and was held in readiness, dispersed among a number of houses in Berlin. Halder, like Witzleben and Beck, was opposed to assassination; but the young assault group were clearly determined on a radical solution, because they were convinced that, as long as he lived, Hitler would represent a force which was stronger than the conspirators, stronger even than Witzleben's Army Corps.[10]

The negotiations with Chamberlain dragged on. From September 22 to 24 he was in Godesberg for a second, and again fruitless, conversation with Hitler. This time it was no longer a question of the form the plebiscite would take in the Sudeten territories, as Chamberlain had expected, but, as became increasingly clear, according to the report of Erich Kordt, a question of the complete dismantling of the Czechoslovak state with the participation of Poland and Hungary.[11] On September 26 a British special envoy brought a last compromise proposal. Hitler gave Prague an ultimatum which, according to the interpreter present, expired on September 28 at 2 o'clock in the afternoon. On the evening of September 26 Hitler addressed a big meeting in Berlin. He said his demand for the separation of the Sudeten territory was "his last territorial demand".[12] On the evening of the next day, although annoyed by a troop display which had not been applauded and which was to heighten tension, he rejected the British proposal and decided to issue orders to march on September 30. Oster had the note rejecting the proposal in his hands during the night September 27–28; and early next day he was with Beck, Witzleben and Halder. The moment had come. The C.-in-C. of the Army, who was particularly enraged by the note rejecting the proposal, now also decided to co-operate. He drove to the Reich Chancellery to get a final assurance and Witzleben went to the Military District to await the call there and to give the order to move.

In the Reich Chancellery they reckoned with war. Just as Brauchitsch arrived, a message from Mussolini came through Attolico, the Italian Ambassador. Asked by Britain to mediate, Mussolini, who was worried about his own treaty obligations, proposed a meeting in Munich on September 29 of the four Heads of government of Germany, Britain, France, and Italy. He believed there would be speedy agreement on the point at issue. Hitler, still affected by the impression of the previous day, declared his agreement after some hesitation—against Ribbentrop's advice, but at the insistence of Neurath and Brauchitsch. The danger of war was banished. Witzleben waited in vain. Twenty-four hours later the four statesmen began their talks in Munich. In an agreement a formula was found which satisfied fully Hitler's claims. Another twenty-four hours later German troops occupied those border areas of Czechoslovakia with a German population—"the Sudetenland"—as far as the agreed boundary line. The German Führer now enjoyed such a reputation for success with his people that even his most determined opponents had serious reservations whether the proposed scheme would have succeeded, even if it had been carried out by people who were divinely inspired.

In these days after Munich Goerdeler wrote in a letter to America : "The Munich agreement was nothing but a complete capitulation by France and Britain to inflated charlatans. . . . The end to the German people's sufferings under a brutal tyranny and methods of the Middle Ages has been deferred for a long time. By shrinking from a risk, Chamberlain has made a war inevitable. The British and French peoples will now have to defend their freedom with arms." In a later epilogue of his we read : "Influential Britons and Americans were told before this war that Hitler would unleash it and bring terrible misfortune to the world. They thought we Germans who gave this warning were men without national feeling. They did not realize that we love our Fatherland with all our heart and desire its greatness and honour, but that we knew from our suffering what course the satanic and demonic Hitler would take. In spite of our warning, Chamberlain ran after Hitler in 1938. At that time British firmness could have avoided war and exposed Hitler. We do not wish to lessen the responsibility which we Germans have to carry. But the tragedy before us was not caused only by us Germans; nor have we Germans in this tragedy made the least sacrifices for our conviction. When we free ourselves, the world will learn what decent Germans have endured and suffered, and how many of them have died a death of torment for German honour and for the freedom of the world."[13]

Beck's views were similar to Goerdeler's when he learned the result of Munich. He regarded Britain's and France's agreement as disastrous weakness and saw the world conflict, which he had expected at once, as not avoided, but only deferred, to become something much more extensive. Churchill spoke in the same terms.[14]

With the victory which the other powers handed Hitler by their yielding, they "decimated" the opposition which had been raised in Germany against him. And they cut the ground from under the feet of his principal opponents; since, if the European powers surrendered inexplicably to the demands of this man and paid him "homage", how should his subject people, who lived on the words he hammered into them daily, be persuaded by a few men to revolt? If there had for a while been a feeling that there might be a new world war, Munich had been the great test of this man. He had been proved right in a dangerous situation and could now claim unconditional support for the future. His plans and aims were not announced; and acts of inhumanity were denied, or excused as popular anger.

During the Sudeten crisis Beck had been appointed C.-in-C. of the First Army in the West with headquarters in Wiesbaden. After the crisis had ended successfully for Germany with the conclusion of the Munich Agreement, Hitler let Beck know that he now expected him to draw the consequences of his action in July. Beck handed in his resignation and on October 31 he was promoted to the rank of Colonel-General and retired from the Army. The German public was then briefly informed for the first time of the change in the post of Chief of the General Staff.

Outwardly, the year which followed Munich was filled with a series of new successes for Hitler—successes which, it seemed, were the almost natural consequences of the events of the summer of 1938.[15] Let us briefly recall the order of events. On October 3 Chamberlain, who had just come home proclaiming "peace in our time", announced in the House of Commons a programme of British rearmament.[16] On October 9, in his speech in Saarbrücken, Hitler openly departed from the Munich Agreement and made new demands. The next day he spoke to the State Secretary of his Foreign Office about the need to "liquidate" the Czech problem within a few months. There followed, on October 29, the Vienna Arbitration Award, in which the German and Italian Foreign Ministers allocated parts of Czechoslovakia to Hungary; Poland, by means of an ultimatum at the beginning of the month, had extorted another part of Czechoslovakia, the Olsa territory. On November 7 the attaché in the German Embassy in Paris, Ernst von Rath, was shot by a young Jew of Polish origin. Goebbels used the occasion to proceed against everything Jewish in Germany—persons and property—in a fierce, but coldly calculated frenzy, which caused widespread horror not only abroad, but also amongst Germans, who had until then gone along with the régime. At the end of January 1939 an offer by the Prague Government to ally and subordinate itself to the Reich was rejected; at the same time the movement for secession and independence in Slovakia and Ruthenia was pressed on. When Prague removed the two autonomous governments and proclaimed a state of emergency, Hitler intervened. He demanded that Slovakia should declare her independence and he forced Hacha, Benes's successor as President, to surrender Czechoslovakia's freedom in Berlin on the night March 14–15. On the afternoon of the next day Hitler drove, on the advice of his escorting officer, Rommel, in an open car, past the advancing troops to Prague. And that night, as he looked down from the Hradschin, he drafted the new statute for Bohemia and Moravia, which were declared a "Reich Protectorate". On March 18 in Vienna he affirmed his protection for Slovakia, which had now become independent. Then the Lithuanian Foreign Minister was summoned to Berlin; on March 23 the Memel Land, which had been taken away from Germany sixteen years earlier, returned to the Reich. Simultaneous attempts to win Danzig and a route through the Corridor encountered strong opposition from the Polish Foreign Minister, Beck, on March 26. Five days later in London Beck reached a very important preliminary agreement for a British-Polish alliance. Relying on this, he resisted all Hitler's demands during the coming months. On April 3 Hitler ordered the German High Command to prepare an attack on Poland and one that could begin on September 1.[17] On April 14 Roosevelt sent a warning message to Hitler and Mussolini. On April 27 it was decided in Britain to call up reservists. The day after, Hitler in his Reichstag speech,[18] which was also his only answer to the American President, abrogated the Anglo-German Naval Agreement of 1935 and the German-Polish Non-Aggression Pact of 1934. From now on he concentrated on the details of patching up the neglected relations with Russia.[19] In August, thanks to the open arming of the Germans, there was a customs dispute in Danzig and a serious worsening of relations with Poland, whilst in Moscow the envoys of the Western Powers and Germany, who were living in the same street, competed with each other for a Russian alliance. For a time the outcome was uncertain; then on the evening of August 24, certainly his most brilliant day, Ribbentrop, coming via Königsberg, landed in Tempelhof with the Russo-German alliance in his pocket. This had been achieved by abandoning the Baltic states and Bessarabia to Russia and by agreeing beforehand to divide Poland. On the afternoon of August 25 Hitler, having three days before delivered a several hours' tirade to the Commanders-in-Chief, gave the order to advance on the next day. But he countermanded this three hours later when news came from London of the definite conclusion of an assistance pact with Poland. An hour later a letter arrived from Mussolini in which he said he was not sufficiently armed to take part in a war. After six eventful days of negotiations, which are a story of their own and saw serious crises in which Hitler wavered, his determination to attack finally prevailed, despite strong and persistent opposition. In this opposition the men of the "Beck group", as they may be called,

36

above all Hassell, Weizsäcker, Goerdeler, Popitz, Canaris, Oster, Schacht, Planck, Jessen and their associate, General Georg Thomas, the Head of the Military Economics Office, were particularly active.[20]

Early on September 1, the war against Poland began without prior announcement. On September 3 Britain and France declared war against Germany. Similar declarations followed from Canada, Australia, New Zealand and the Union of South Africa. On the eighteenth day of fighting the Russians marched into Eastern Poland, ostensibly to protect the threatened minorities. On September 29 Warsaw surrendered, the last bulwark of quickly conquered Poland. Danzig and the territories, which formerly belonged to Germany, together with a part of what subsequently became Polish territory, were incorporated in the Reich as Gau Danzig and Wartheland. Poland west of the Bug, in accordance with the earlier German-Russian agreements, was declared a Government-General, under German suzerainty. Eastern Poland, including the White Ruthenian and Galician territories, went to Russia. At the end of September a start was made to move the majority of the German fighting units to the western frontiers of the Reich. Britain and France waited; they had not intervened whilst the Germans fought in Poland.

At the beginning of October Ludwig Beck received definite information that Hitler was now preparing to attack the West and would adopt the plan of advancing against France through Holland and Belgium, thus violating their neutrality. Like the majority of the senior officers in the Army, he was convinced that such an attack must fail for purely technical reasons and could not be justified. But he was also convinced that Hitler's plans, which, according to his orders (Directive No. 6 for the conduct of the war) aimed at the "final military defeat of the West", must lead to a European catastrophe, especially since Russia was appearing on the scene as a new European power, thanks to her advance to the Baltic. In addition to all this, there came in the first half of October the first reliable, although very secret, information, about an SS terror régime in Poland and the disclosure of Hitler's plan to liquidate the Polish people and hold them in subjection. Von Brauchitsch agreed with Halder that Hitler's Western offensive must be opposed with every professional argument. The three Army Group Commanders in the West—von Leeb, von Rundstedt, and von Bock also protested in memoranda against the plan to attack. Colonel-General Ritter von Leeb, who was particularly opposed to this project, told Brauchitsch that he was ready to accept "any consequence that seemed necessary".[21] Halder, after the events of September 1938,

37

had ordered Lieutenant-Colonel i. G. Grosscurth to work out a General Staff plan for a coup to meet the circumstances and he kept back at the Elbe two armoured divisions which were moving from the East to the West. At the end of October he sent K. H. von Stülpnagel to visit the front in the West to find out on which Commanders reliance could be placed in the case of action. Oster and von Stülpnagel communicated with Beck, who could not come out into the open, but who followed events with enthusiasm and vigour and co-ordinated the military undertaking with an over-all plan of political action. Goerdeler, von Weizsäcker and von Hassell co-operated with him in the political field.

A memorandum of the Foreign Office, which was drawn up at the end of October by Hasso von Etzdorf and Erich Kordt, and which has been substantially preserved,[22] sought to outline "the threatening catastrophe", which would materialize with an attack on Belgium. It argued that it would bring together an increasing alliance, reinforced by the USA, such as Germany could not cope with. Of the USA, it said : "They will send not only material but also men filled with a crusading spirit." Since, it claimed, Hitler could no longer achieve a compromise peace, it was only left to him to burn his boats, to blow his bridges and force his way forward. His "infallibility" was a blasphemous legend. "His successes were apparent successes, or the result of a natural development, in which the disadvantages caused by his methods outweighed the advantages." After giving examples, there followed the sentence : "Never was Germany nearer to chaos and Bolshevism than now after six years of the Hitler régime, which in recent weeks has succeeded in handing over twenty million people to Bolshevism." To the objection that a coup d'état would find no support now "after a brilliant military campaign", the answer was : "The débacle will only be recognized once it is there. The coup d'état would then, of course, be popular; but it would come too late and would no longer ward off the catastrophe into which we would all be plunged, with or without Hitler, and even with our fine Polish laurels. For once the fury of war is let loose, it cannot be coaxed back by reason. War follows its own inexorable laws and every Army Command wants, above all, to be victorious—i.e. to destroy now. The relative unpopularity of the undertaking must, therefore, be accepted with the necessary degree of civic courage." On the question of the oath, the memorandum, which was drafted to win over the military, claimed that this had lost its validity "because Hitler, forgetting his own obligations, is preparing to sacrifice Germany to his diabolic aims. In consequence, the German soldier is relieved of his military oath; but it remains his highest national duty to remain loyal to

38

the German Fatherland against its destroyer." A section on "honourable peace" concluded that political intervention could only be successful, if a military defeat, or a 9th November 1918, was avoided. With that, the memorandum returned to the theme of the urgency of the task. For the recipients, who read it and apparently approved it—by not reporting it, they made themselves accomplices —knew that there were only about two weeks to go before the date for the attack.

On November 1 one of the authors of the memorandum was with Oster and, in answer to his request, declared himself ready to use his freedom to move about within the Reich Chancellery to make a bomb attack. It was only through successful assassination, Oster said, that the Generals would feel freed from their scruples, and from the oath they swore to Hitler when he was alive. Oster undertook to provide the explosive by November 11.[23]

In the meantime, it already looked on November 4 as if the hour was approaching. Beck and Goerdeler were informed. On November 5 Hitler had finally to confirm the order for the attack on November 12 so as to allow sufficient time for troops to move into position. Brauchitsch drove with Halder to the Reich Chancellery. Beginning with notes and then speaking impromptu, he once again gave his reasons for opposing the offensive in the West, which Hitler had decided should begin on November 12. He was overwhelmed by a hurricane outburst of Hitler's and brusquely dismissed from the audience. Hitler hurled out the threat that he knew the "spirit of Zossen" (Zossen was the Headquarters of the Army High Command) and would destroy it.

From other indications, too, there was reason to believe that the plan for the coup had been betrayed and that the Army leadership could expect a fate like that of 30th June 1934.[24] On his return, Halder gave orders for all documents to be quickly destroyed. When after twenty-four hours nothing happened, they began to think again. Halder was pressed to act. He was opposed to assassination and found no support even from Canaris. Brauchitsch retreated into a sort of inner no-man's land. He was heard to say : "I won't do anything; but I won't oppose it, if someone else does it."

On November 7 Beck informed Brauchitsch that, if he declined to lead the coup d'état, he, Beck was ready to take over the responsible command to ensure that the action was coherently directed from above, on condition that the three Army Group Commanders would not oppose it.

That mid-day the Army movements in the West were halted for the first time. In the evening the Belgian and Dutch monarchs offered to act as peace mediators.

The events of November 8 were confusing and unexpected for the planners of the coup d'état. As he did every year, Hitler went at 8 o'clock in the evening to meet his old circle of comrades in the *Bürgerbräu* beer-cellar in Munich. He began what promised to be a long speech, but ended it surprisingly quickly and then left the hall. Shortly afterwards, a powder charge exploded which tore the speaker's rostrum and the adjacent pillar into pieces and strewed the hall with wreckage. There were six dead and sixty-three injured. Canaris and Oster themselves made inquiries and were confronted with a riddle, just as were Heydrich, the Gestapo, and the Security Service—a fact which has never been disproved to this day, despite some suspicions. Hitler later told his faithful companions how he had suddenly felt unwell after starting the speech and a secret intuition had prompted him to leave. Despite all suppositions of a conspiracy on the part of one side or the other, even with the knowledge of Hitler, and short of fresh light being cast on the subject, the most improbable explanation today must be regarded as the true one; that the would-be assassin, Elser, had planted the explosive on his own, while the Generals were conspiring, and had only missed his target by a mysterious hair's breadth.[25]

Elser's action, it would seem, from the only source available, prevented the execution of the proposed coup. With the more stringent control over munitions stores which immediately followed, Oster had to give up his efforts to get hold of explosives.[26]

Bad weather; also apparently arguments, accepted with reluctance, that training was incomplete and preparations inadequate; and, perhaps, too, the proposal to alter the plan of attack, so that the main emphasis was not on the right flank but on a tank thrust against Sedan, all brought about a new postponement of the day of attack. On November 23 Hitler spoke, in a speech lasting several hours, to the Commanders-in-Chief and General Staff officers about the coming war of conquest. He mocked the anxious "prophets" who saw only catastrophe in all the decisions he took, and he stormed against the reactionary Generals and the "antiquated upper class" which had failed in 1914 and, once more, against the "spirit of Zossen", although he did not mention names. He said : "I will shrink from nothing and will destroy everyone who is against me. But if, as in 1914, Commanders-in-Chief have nervous breakdowns, what must we ask of an ordinary rifleman?... I will stand or die in this struggle. I will not survive the defeat of my people. Abroad no capitulation : at home no revolution."[27]

With this speech of Hitler's, unexcelled in brutality, cynicism, and lack of restraint, we must regard the attempts at a coup d'état, which were made during these weeks, as ended. Insults and threats from Hitler did not act as a stimulus; they had, on the contrary, a paralysing effect. "The charge of cowardice has made the brave cowards again" was the way Oster put it.[28]

So far as is known, only one of the Generals, not belonging to the group privy to the plan for the coup, protested to Hitler against the insults to the senior officers who had, after all, fought for him in the Polish war; and that was Guderian. Von Brauchitsch, against whom Hitler's mistrust, bordering on contempt, was particularly directed, did not feel able to do the same. The resignation, which he offered, was declined. Goerdeler said in his report to von Hassell that it looked as if Hitler with this speech "has made an impression on the harmless soldiers, whereas more intelligent men had the impression of a raving Genghis Khan".[29]

About the end of December there seemed to be another crisis looming.[30] Information about SS murders in Poland deeply shook those who learned about them; and the Russian attack on Finland implicated the German Government, particularly in the eyes of its Italian ally. The date for the attack in the West was still put off. Another attempt was to be made to bring about a revolt. Witzleben was to lead the coup in Berlin, and Beck was to take over the military command and make appeals to the German people. Oster and Goerdeler went to see Witzleben. Popitz and Hassell prepared a new basic law for the state and the ordinances for the transition period. At the beginning of January Beck sought a personal interview with Halder to persuade him to agree to joint action. But Halder thought it was now impossible to act against Hitler, the man of unbroken success, who had the younger generation, including the officers, completely on his side. He believed that only defeats could provide new possibilities of action. In addition, it appeared difficult now to get hold of troops. Beck wanted to force through a peace and Germany's political liberation, even in opposition to the majority. Momentarily impotent on the military side, he tried to use political arguments. Attempts were made in various ways, chiefly private, to re-establish the broken contacts with British political leaders (Theo Kordt in Berne, Ulrich von Hassell in Arosa, and the former Chancellor Wirth in Lausanne-Ouchy). Dr Josef Müller, who was attached to the German Abwehr, and who had the credentials of the Beck-Goerdeler-Oster group, was able, with the help of the Pope, to have an exchange in Rome with the British Minister to the Vatican, Osborne. A year after Munich the British Government of Chamberlain and Halifax had at last come to a different view of the prospects and value of a Resistance movement in Germany and had expressly allowed its representative at the Vatican to exchange views. This took place between October 1939 and February 1940.

41

In this exchange, as far as can be judged from the still unpublished documents, remarkable concessions were made to a non-National Socialist government in Germany : certainly the frontiers of 1937, probably the inclusion also of Austria and the Sudetenland and, in addition, a promise not to exploit the domestic crisis during a transition with any external military attack. A year earlier such an assurance from Britain might have encouraged the uprising, which was ready to be launched; but now Beck, Halder, Goerdeler, and Thomas, had this offer set down (perhaps in edited form) in the so-called "Document X"; and, in the quite altered circumstances, it proved to be ineffectual. Brauchitsch, who saw the document at the beginning of April, was disposed to have the person who brought it arrested as a traitor. About the same time Halder sent a written refusal in response to Goerdeler's pressing demands, observing once again that action would only be possible after a defeat. It would not be possible to overthrow Hitler and establish another government before world-wide military involvements created a new situation.[31]

On April 9 there began the surprising move of the German Navy against Norway which, thanks to its extraordinary success, banished still further thoughts of a German coup. At Beck's request the negotiator at the Vatican was told at the beginning of May : "The Generals cannot decide to act. Hitler will attack. The attack is imminent."[32] Beck felt that after what had happened such information was necessary with an eye to the whole future. Shortly afterwards, on the evening of May 9, Oster, acting on his responsibility, informed the threatened Dutch of the time of the attack. But after so many delays they hardly took the report seriously. On May 10 the "phoney war" ended and gave way to the real war : the German attack on Belgium, Holland and France.

All that Ludwig Beck and his colleagues had tried to do for almost two years to curb and overthrow Hitler disappeared without Hitler, who had remained the victor, and his contemporaries, hearing about it. Only when the documents were found at Zossen on September 22, 1944—Beck was then dead—did the Gestapo and, through it, Hitler get knowledge of it. But it was kept from the public. When, after the war, the German people were apprised of the secret history of these years, in addition to what was already public knowledge, they learned with tremendous horror of what had happened in their name and also of the actions of those who had sought a way out. Most of the conspirators were then no longer alive.

At first Beck had other plans; but then he decided not to leave Berlin after his retirement. We must assume that he wished to remain near to events and did not yet consider himself relieved of his task. In the many changes and divisions of the ensuing years, it is now clear that he was always accepted, whether his views were completely endorsed or not, as the central figure, who co-ordinated the groups of the Resistance. This thoughtful soldier possessed not only character and the ability to influence others; he also had the gentlemanly bearing of a man who knew how to respect those who were simple and differently constituted from himself. In his presence there was no room for rival egotisms. His sincerity brought unity amongst conflicting personalities. He was sometimes referred to as "The dear God" in the conversations of his friends and all troubles were brought to him. He did not like loose talk about the Fatherland; but there was something about him which imposed, and demanded, values that looked beyond the lot of the individual.

Whoever went to the Goethestrasse and asked for his home discovered that even ordinary people knew General Beck and spoke of him with respect. His daughter, who became a widow in the Second World War, kept house for him. He cultivated his garden and, under the influence of contemporary events and with them in mind, devoted himself to the science, and especially the history, of war. The fate of Germany on the fronts and at home occupied him keenly; and not a day passed without visitors bringing him news and impressions of what was happening and voicing their anxieties to him. We often find it said that at, every phase of the war, he had an overall picture, that he was able to present it in clear outlines and that his predictions were often astonishingly accurate. He took a lively part in, and several times spoke himself at, the meetings and lectures of the "Wednesday Club",[33] where people with specialist knowledge met in a wider milieu and exchanged views. One of the members has described Beck's impressive but somewhat taciturn personality in these terms : "The slim man of medium height with the narrow head was the perfect type of senior Prussian officer. Everything about him was so formed and disciplined that it had become second nature, a law unto itself. His slender, finely modelled and altogether sculptured face was, in its every movement, made to harmonize with his personality. Mind and will formed a unity which gave Beck something of the features of a wonderfully spiritual-looking piece of statuary. The eyes were the finest thing about the face : they were wise, very spiritual eyes which would occasionally light up with the charm of human warmth, something not very common in his profession. It is difficult to give a picture of the power which emanated from this clear mind and, even more, from his humanity. Twice I had the fortune to see him at my home. . . . When he was in the garden in Lichtenrade—Ulrich Wilcken[34] was

43

sitting next to him, listening to the song of the blackbirds and enjoying the perfume of the elder blossom—it was fascinating to see with what courtesy Beck carefully left the old man at his side undisturbed, until he drew him into one of those conversations which, for all their lightness, were much more than mere conversations. He avoided talking about his former life—I hardly ever heard from him any condemnation or criticism of the Generals. Rather he would in a few lines give character sketches of individuals, would sketch Dietl or Rommel and bring out something of the real personality and abilities of the man he was describing. Occasionally one clearly noticed the deliberate rule of silence he had imposed on himself and how, in spite of all his open friendliness, he reserved what was important for special times and special company. . . . But when this man allowed his wonderful smile to light up for a moment, and this smile gave a hint of an inner life, which no one would have suspected in him, there was not a person to resist him. And it was understandable that the ageing man found honour and real enthusiasm among the young. The mere fact that a man like Ludwig Beck was still possible in the world of 1940 was, of itself, a cause for rejoicing."[35]

In another place in his memoirs Paul Fechter relates how once, during the war, he came away with Beck from an autumn commemoration ceremony at Berlin University. "We strolled along the grey Unter den Linden. We said little, then Beck suddenly stopped and asked : 'Did you know the last piece of music that was played?' I said : 'Yes' and told him : it was the Chorale from Bach's The Art of the Fugue. He looked at me thoughtfully for a while : 'That was the most other-worldly thing that I have ever heard,' he said half to himself. 'Very remarkable.' We went on. I felt that he was somewhat preoccupied and said nothing. And suddenly he continued, half to himself and half to me : 'One should take note of that —for all eventualities. Don't you think?' "[36]

In the bitter years, when illness also took toll of Beck, the shadow of disappointment rested more heavily on the normally firm and bold eyes, which were hidden behind dark glasses when he went his dangerous ways. His fine, nervous hands began to tremble with impatience and excitement. The disheartening effect of failure impaired his strength to act. But the fact that Beck stood resolutely with the conspirators on that day in July, the last of his life, shows that, in spite of all the grief for what had been denied, his devotion never slackened and that this sixty-four-year-old man felt to the last that he had obligations towards the younger members, just as they had always measured their actions against his judgement.

IV. CARL FRIEDRICH GOERDELER
MEN OF THE RIGHT

In the memorandum, in which the two authors from the Foreign Office tried in October 1939 to explain to the senior officers their right and duty to intervene with force, they had, adapting Schiller, recalled the law : "The fury of war, once let loose, cannot be coaxed back by reason. . . ." The authors could hardly realize the double significance of these remarks concerning the fate of their people. For, not only was Hitler unable to turn back from the course of his victories and grandiose schemes and, as reason demanded, to call off what had become a limitless war, before catastrophe overwhelmed everything. But, in addition, no reasonable argument on the part of the Resistance movement could oppose him while the series of victories remained unbroken, or overthrow him, in the ebbing fortunes of the war. For the Resistance the critical moment had passed with the attack in the West; it had resulted not, as expected, in a quick military collapse, but in an unanticipated success for Germany.

Hassell noted on June 24, 1940, after the victory in France : "No one can deny the magnitude of Hitler's victory. But that does not alter the real nature of his deeds and the terrible dangers to which all higher values are now exposed. A demonic Spartacus can wreak nothing but destruction if the opposition does not act in time. One could despair under the weight of the tragedy of not being able to take pleasure in the successes."[1] Another described the tragic conflict of those who, in war-time, had become alive to the dangers and wanted to act, in the phrase : "Hitler must be destroyed and at the same time the German people must be saved from disaster. How can we few, with an eye to reality, bring this about?"[2]

Actually, apart from the obvious fact of the powerlessness of the few facing a highly armed state, these people were confronted with something quite different. Hatred for Hitler in the course of such a terrible war did not absolve one from devotion and service to the Fatherland. In all the many countries occupied by Germany the Resistance movement called for action against the foreign conqueror and enemy, and found outlets for the greatest enthusiasm. But here were people resisting a conqueror from their own ranks on whom the country depended in war-time in thousands of ways. How could he, the individual, be struck, without striking the whole community?

45

And in another way, too, they were affected by the war. If it brought victory and elation, it would also raise Hitler in the estimation of his people and condemn every plan directed against him, which came at an unpropitious time, as "psychological nonsense". If it brought suffering and defeat, an attempt at a coup would only increase the danger, and brand those who dared to undertake it, now and always, as traitors, who had not stabbed Hitler in the back, but their own people.

The attempted coups of 1938 and 1939 had been planned by a small circle and with comparatively little political preparation. But it had to be recognized that, with the continuation of the war, any assassination of Hitler would be meaningless, if at that moment, there were not the able and necessary men at the top ready to cope with all the tasks, who had to hand properly thought-out plans to bring about an orderly transition.

These reasons generally explain why even resolute opponents of Hitler rejected all attempts to intervene by force; and it is not sufficient to say that they finally succumbed to Hitler's great successes and "God's judgement", as evinced by his achievements. Those, however, who were not content to accept the apparently inevitable and who wanted to act, had to find people with similar ideas and had to go from group to group, ignoring differences of class, religious beliefs and political allegiance. Action could only spring from a united will. Thus it was that the military, in contrast to previous attempts, went outside its own sphere and sought co-operation with genuine political forces. Allies were found among the former Right and former Left, among men of the church, the administration and industry, the Foreign Office, the technical colleges, the workers' movement and the aristocracy. They could only serve their cause in secrecy. Whatever part of Germany they came from, their class or profession, they were part of the Hitler state and, somewhere or other, merged their lives with the great events of the war. To describe them individually in a history of the 20th July, 1944 would be most appropriate to their position and the time. If we treat them in groups, as is required by a review, we must remember that this rather formal pattern was often interrupted and broken up by real divisions. We cannot attempt here to go into these divisions, to follow the variety of groups and circles, their special services and tasks, the stages of their conversations and programmes, their quarrels and reconciliations. But we can try to summarize the forces which tried during the war to intervene in German history and which were associated with Claus Stauffenberg and his plan for a revolt.

* * *

46

If the word "National Socialism" broadly represented a programme which sought to combine the nationalism of the Right and the socialism of the Left in a new unity, it was obvious from the beginning that, whereas the representatives of the Right were drawn into the movement, those of the Left were excluded by persecution. So if we find the men of the former Left generally from the outset on the side of the Opposition, those of the Right are to be found there only after a period of years. In the interim they held responsible posts; then they resigned or started oppositional activities while still in office. They served the new state with roughly similar reservations, but with loyalty, because they hoped that the good would prevail over all that was bad. But sooner or later events made them ask whether, and how, co-operation was still justifiable, or what was demanded from the individual in the way of counter-action. The answers were as various as the men who asked the questions; and it is impossible, as has been attempted, to judge character according to when a person's eyes were opened and to insist on courage and self-sacrifice as the norm. Some, like Beck, gave up their office, when they could achieve nothing. Others avoided this step and tried privately to steer between duty and conscience. Others, again, withdrew and sought a new life abroad. Some names, soon forgotten in the Germany of those days, have only through the history of the 20th of July become known again as those of the main participants of the attempted uprising.

Of these the most frequently named is Dr Carl Friedrich *Goerdeler*. With him Prussia's revolt of conscience against the usurper found its strongest voice and perhaps its most passionate instigator. The name Goerdeler could later stand as the title of a history of the German Resistance movement.[3]

The son of a judge, he was brought up in the small West Prussian towns of Schneidemühl and Marienwerder in the spirit of the old Prussian conservative civil service with its regard for the monarchy. The problems of the German frontier population, in particular, developed his political awareness; and, after a short period of studying law and history, he was very soon doing the work that suited him : local government and economics, preferably as head of a large city community. After apprentice years spent in the very different Rhineland industrial area of Solingen, he returned to the East in the First World War. Early in 1918 he was given the task of building up again the financial administration of White Russia and Ruthenia. Put in authority over Russians, he did his duty carefully, justly and ably, and helped the country, which had been neglected in war, back to prosperity. In doing so, he set a great example. When he went,

47

he wrote: "What the future will bring to this country I do not know. The Germans, who did not come with hostile intentions and who lived here peacefully in spite of all the hard necessities of war which they also experienced at first hand, wish the land of Minsk blessing upon its work."[4]

Shortly afterwards, in June 1919, Goerdeler planned, with the national Free Corps movement in West Prussia, a "crushing" of Poland during the weeks before the peace of Versailles. The idea was to create in advance of the treaty a fait accompli, which would prevent the surrender of German territory in the East. There were a few days of feverish confusion and unsuccessful attempts to act against his own government and the veto of the Army Command. . . . Goerdeler failed with his revolt; and the peace, which brought about the fateful Polish Corridor, was concluded. There followed ten years in the mayor's office in Königsberg. Then in May 1930 Goerdeler was unanimously elected by the city council and senate Mayor (Oberbürgermeister) of Leipzig. This was due to his reputation and personality, not to his party allegiance; otherwise, he would have had to belong to the Social Democratic Party. He was able to master the financial difficulties of Leipzig and to make it, after a few years, one of the best administered German cities. His reputation spread beyond the frontiers of the Reich. At the end of 1931 he was appointed by Hindenburg, with the full powers he demanded, Reich Commissioner for Price Control in the Brüning government. During the winter 1931–32 he succeeded in getting the rising prices reduced by a tenth. Hindenburg continued to seek his advice without always following it. Brüning's suggestion, at his audience on the memorable May 30, 1932, that Goerdeler should be appointed Chancellor in succession to him, was rejected by Hindenburg, on Schleicher's insistence, in favour of the Presidential cabinet of Papen. Goerdeler declined to become Economics and Labour Minister in the "cabinet of barons"—he later regarded this as a mistake—although he felt himself equal to the task and feared the great economic crisis would bring a revolution at home. Goerdeler felt increasingly alienated from Hugenberg and the men of the extreme Right, who held the power in the circle around the aged Hindenburg. He had no part in their intrigues, which produced the different Chancellorships up to Hitler's time.

He put his hopes in the new national Government and its Chancellor, Hitler, although he disliked its crudeness and libellous propaganda. He had expressly refused to join the Party. In November 1934 he was appointed, a second time, Reich Commissioner for Savings, this time by Hitler. In January 1935 he was asked to co-operate on the new plans for local government, on which he had earlier

48

worked for several years with the mayor of Königsberg, Lohmeyer, in the executive committee of the German Local Government Association. His memorandum of autumn 1934 addressed "To the Reich Chancellor, Adolf Hitler", dealt primarily with economic questions. But it was also an open and courageous move against the rule of the Party in the Third Reich, an attempt to press on the Führer a reform programme in the old Prussian style. In August 1936 Goerdeler presented a memorandum, which Göring had requested, on foreign exchange, with emphatic warnings against further deficit financing and the extension of credit. It also criticized plans for economic autarchy and precipitate rearmament. Some weeks later Göring's Four Year Economic Plan was proclaimed and launched by Hitler at the Nuremberg Party Rally. It was a very harsh rebuff for Goerdeler, who also had to face some personal criticism, when he was re-elected Mayor of Leipzig for another twelve years. But the Party increased its attacks; and it tried to circumscribe Goerdeler's independence and to denigrate him. There was a demand that the statue of Mendelssohn in front of the *Gewandhaus* in Leipzig, the statue of a Jew, should be removed. Goerdeler refused to consider the matter. But, on returning from a lecture trip to Finland, he learned in Stockholm that Haake, one of his deputy mayors, behind whom the Party district leader stood, had had the statue removed, in order, it was said: "to spare him a painful decision". Back in Leipzig, Goerdeler at once demanded that the statue should be put back; and, when this was refused, he handed in his resignation. On the last day of March 1937 at the age of fifty-two, he took leave of his colleagues in the city administration. In his motives there is a foretaste of what prompted Ludwig Beck to take a similar step a year later.

After leaving office in Leipzig, Goerdeler looked for a job in industry, where he had earlier acquired many contacts. A post as financial adviser, offered some time earlier by Gustav Krupp, was vetoed by Hitler when his name was put forward; but no objections were raised to a more discreet form of co-operation with Robert Bosch in Stuttgart. Goerdeler refused Krupp's offer of private compensation to the value of 100 000 marks; but he agreed later, when this sum was put at his disposal for travel abroad. This he was able to undertake in accordance with his own plans, although it was also of use to Krupp. A diplomat without a brief, Goerdeler visited Britain, France, the USA, Canada, and many smaller countries. He made many contacts, some of them close and friendly, with politicians and economists in these countries, such as could hardly be established with the official emissaries of the Third Reich. In his talks with British, French, and American statesmen, he constantly

49

urged them not to allow themselves to be forced gradually by Hitler to abandon the Versailles Treaty system, but to take the initiative openly themselves with a view to clearing up all outstanding problems. His reports of his journeys were originally intended also for Hitler and Göring, and they make his intentions clear. They were meant to convince and persuade Hitler to adopt a policy of understanding, instead of one of isolation and threats of force. His arguments, in consequence, were often presented from Hitler's point of view. In this way, Goerdeler did not appear as an opponent of Nazism, but rather as a well-meaning, if very firm, admonisher. However, in a memorandum of December 1937, which he left behind in New York, he spoke without reservation and in quite different terms. In this he looked forward to an uprising on the part of the Germans, which would free them from lawlessness and moral disintegration and create a liberal state, based on the rule of law. Shortly afterwards, in January 1938, he met Beck and Fritsch in Berlin. There is no doubt that he spoke to them in the sense of his New York memorandum, rendered perhaps more vivid by his impassioned eloquence. At the time of Beck's resignation, and during the September crisis, Goerdeler was again abroad, as he was in the months before the outbreak of war.

In a memorandum of July 1, 1940, which is clearly addressed to an officer, he gave full praise to the Wehrmacht for the unexpectedly speedy victory it had just achieved over France. But he went on to speak at length about human responsibility. He saw what had been achieved coming to naught : "This war," he said "does not serve a positive, constructive purpose, but fantastic schemes such as have not been entertained since Napoleon's time." Hitler, he argued, like many conquerors, would never be able to rule such an area in a way which safeguarded the honour and freedom of the peoples living in it—an indispensable condition of their achieving the highest ends. Impoverishment of the masses, the destruction of cultural values, the extermination of the intelligentsia, especially in the East, the eclipse of all national freedom and independence, would follow, and, what he called, "the upsurge of brutality, of philistinism, of inexperience and ignorance". The memorandum ended with the appeal to resist Napoleon, which Freiherr vom Stein addressed to Frederick William III on October 12, 1808 : "For the honest man there is no salvation but in the conviction that the wicked is capable of all evil.... To have faith in the man, of whom it was said with so much truth that he had hell in his heart and chaos in his head, is more than blindness.... If, in any case, nothing but misfortune and suffering can be expected, then it is better to take a decision which is honourable and

50

noble and offers compensation and grounds for solace, should things turn out badly."[5]

In addition to his activities in industry, which allowed Goerdeler considerable freedom in war-time to travel about Germany and sometimes even to Sweden or Switzerland, he worked with unbelievable physical energy for the coup he so much desired. To judge by the number of people he won over to the cause, his influence was perhaps the greatest of all those who were active against Hitler. Not for nothing were a million marks later put on his head as a fugitive. He never spared himself. Just as he knew how to stir others, so he threw himself into any action which seemed necessary; and we can believe that he was ready to appear before Hitler himself with his demands. He was four years younger than Beck and six years older than Hitler. Dressed in his wide-brimmed hat, or as an inconspicuous civilian ("itinerant preacher" or "country pastor" were code-names for him), he travelled in his tireless way, through Germany and to the Eastern front. He got the reputation with the military—the higher, the better—of being troublesome. He dared to make appearances where he repeatedly feared he would be taken away, and he prepared wherever he could, the ground for the revolt. In his sanguine manner, he wanted to speak, to convince and to mould the future with the new plans for the State he was always drawing up and with the speeches he would make as Chancellor. Often he was so absorbed in his own ideas of what should be that he over-simplified the real state of affairs and produced too facile solutions; but even those, who did not agree with his views and predictions, were moved by the directness and sincerity of this complete patriot. For somehow he still believed in a sound world, or one that could be made sound; and he never, as long as he was free, succumbed to the poison of despair and self-torment, which overwhelms even the noblest of characters. Friends and former subordinates have described his warm-hearted and chivalrous manner. It was precise but, at the same time, considerate of others' views. When the old Prussian came to the surface, his rather muffled voice acquired an impressive tone, even in his speeches. The story is told how in 1943, or 1944, he asked an intermediary to tell his friends that, should he be arrested, as seemed likely, then they should act. But should the overriding interests of the Fatherland make action impossible, he expected them to put something into his hands (here he indicated an exploding bomb) during his trial before the People's Court : "For I do not intend to leave this iniquitous world quietly and unceremoniously."[6]

Goerdeler, as Price and Savings Commissioner, had had to impose austerity on the nation and was, in general, against any irresponsible method of creating financial credit, even Schacht's. He once said : "The ending of unemployment is not a miracle but, with 40 000 million marks' debts, a schoolboy's trick and an unscrupulous act."[7] But he also regarded self-denial as a virtue for a politician, even in his private life. As Mayor of Leipzig, he preferred in 1933 to pay out of his own pocket for a reception for lawyers, who were meeting there, rather than charge it up to the city treasury and so set an example of the extravagant use of public money. While in prison, he wrote of the "simplicity" of Hitler, "who wallows in millions (the Eher publishing house and Reich Treasury), eats and drinks simply, but panders to all other luxuries and corrupts everyone. 50 000 marks a year extra for every Minister and every Marshal! And he gives each of the Marshals in this lost war 250 000 marks or estates. . . ."[8]

To persuade the hesitant, and to clarify his own ideas, Goerdeler liked to summarize his arguments in the form of a memorandum. Even more than Beck, he composed memoranda, drafts and appeals, which, as Ritter says, "are written in a strangely old-fashioned style, sometimes diffuse, but always most enlightening and at times very reminiscent of morality sermons".[9] Even in political life, Goerdeler believed in the power of reason against all the forces of evil. Hence his solutions often proved too simple and his "democracy of the ten commandments" did not take account of the demonic forces which had been unleashed on the world. He thought always of what was immediate and possible, and of what resulted from insight; that which a determined statesman ought to accomplish. As such, he wanted to arouse people, evoke their responsibility to God and the Fatherland, inspire courage and set free the hesitant. Thus, he presented all his causes in bold outlines; he saw approaching collapses which did not occur or only happened much later, and hopes of action which were no longer attainable. For this reason he often received negative responses from the Generals who distrusted his optimism; and, even in the conversation of the men of the Resistance movement, he evoked contradiction and, indeed, dissension with his wishful thinking and artless proposals. But hardly anyone could resist the charm of his direct appeal and his imperturbability which survived the most serious crises.

Many times Goerdeler traced the course of recent German history, the Empire of Wilhelm II, the First World War, the Republic, the Third Reich, and the Second World War, and thought about the outlines of a new Germany and a new Europe. The essence of his thinking about Germany survived substantially from the days when he wanted to march against the Poles; but his views about the course that was necessary changed over the years. He spoke of the in-

52

capacity and guilt of the German Nationalists and of the even more extreme all-German Right, and he toyed with Socialist ideas. In the spring of 1941 his publication Das Ziel ("The Goal") revealed his ideas for a German constitution. When in September 1944 he was sentenced to death, but was still alive to write treatises, he once again wrote down his plans in detail.

As with all the Opposition's plans for a new order, so with Goerdeler's,[10] we must not forget that they were especially intended for the emergency period following the coup. They were not thought of as a final solution, even if Goerdeler's detailed plans emphasized the factor of stability. Goerdeler did not think of restoring the party system of the Weimar constitution, or of setting up a Western-type state, for which the conditions were lacking in Germany. One could not, he felt, ignore Hitler, who had conceived the "People's Community" (Volksgemeinschaft), and one must "make the workers share in the responsibility for the state". But where could one begin in Germany and where find the leaders for a new government? Goerdeler thought the only hope lay in the emergence of capable men from the distinctive "cell on which the state is built", the town or village community (Gemeinde). From here the way led in his plan through the local council, the district council and the provincial council to the Reichstag and his Second Chamber, the Reichsstaendehaus. Admittedly, this was not absolutely direct; and only half of these chambers were to be filled with men from this background. For the other half the professions, the corporations, and the parties, could send their members. In addition, free appointments could be made. The principle of selecting the political leadership was emphatically vested in the Gemeinde, city or district. Organically, one could only proceed from the small to the larger, with equal rights for all elements of the nation.

Goerdeler did not exclude the emergence of a new political movement and thought that three parties, elected by simple majorities, were appropriate to a new liberal state. But, initially, the system should be built on proven ability and administrative experience. Thus Goerdeler based his ideas about the state on his belief in his own abilities. It was part of his strength that he felt he was capable of leading Germany out of the crisis and of winning the support of his people in his role of conscientious and just father of his country. But his plans—and this is why they gradually lost their validity with the continuation of the war—presupposed freedom of action and no protracted occupation of Germany by the victorious powers.

Goerdeler wanted to create a strong political authority but to guard against arbitrary and one-party rule. He wanted also to allow room for freedom and competition in the economy without permitting the community to be endangered by the selfishness of large organizations. As Head of State he thought there should be a monarch, an hereditary or elected Emperor (negotiations went on with a scion of the House of Hohenzollern) or a Reich Commissioner, such as Beck, as guardian of the constitution. Under the new régime self-government at Gemeinde level was to be given priority; the powers of the provinces (*Gaue*) were to be deliberately restricted; but the Reich administration was to be provided with strong powers. Accordingly only the Gemeinden and the Reich were to raise taxes.

On the road to self-government, a new trade union movement was regarded as urgent. It might be called the "German Trade Union"; and membership would be compulsory for workers and clerical employees. It was to take over the business of wage negotiations and labour exchanges, as well as of social insurance and education. In addition, it would have its own enterprises which would be run and worked commercially, without state subsidies. The management of mineral resources and of the great transport and supply concerns would be conducted as a state monopoly for the common good, without prejudicing free competition.

The churches, too, would once again enjoy unfettered independence. The state would only retain the right to confirm senior appointments and would give the church no subsidies. The church was, perhaps after the American pattern, to rely much more on the free initiative of its members and to take over practical tasks in the field of education and welfare. In Goerdeler's view, the Protestant churches, by confining their activities to services and Sunday sermons, had developed too much into "pastors' churches".

After a successful coup, German courts were to pass judgments on violations of the law, on cases of corruption, and on all acts of inhumanity which had been committed in the past. But Party membership and lack of courage and political insight were not to be grounds for punishment or loss of promotion. It seemed particularly important that the purge should come from within, uninfluenced by the victorious powers. Only in this way could there be a "renewal".

When Goerdeler thought about the future shape of Europe, Germany was assigned the role of Europe's frontier territory against Bolshevism. Once the war-time laws had been rescinded, Goerdeler hoped that Britain, France, Germany, and the smaller states would freely join an economic union with common European reconstruction projects, police troops, and arbitration courts. As the war went on, the withdrawal of the German front line modified the original territorial claims which Goerdeler thought Germany would have

to make. After the Casablanca Declaration on unconditional surrender, Goerdeler saw an increasing danger of a one-sided domination of the Continent by the Russians and their totalitarian system;
this, he thought, would eventually deprive the West of all the fruits
of its sacrifices in the war. At the same time, he saw the scarcely
lesser danger that the victorious powers would impose on the Germans another senseless "*Diktat*" of revenge and thus prevent that
genuine "renewal" which alone could provide a defence against
Bolshevist Russia.

At the close of a memorandum intended for Churchill and the
British Government, which he was able to send at the end of May
1943 through his friends, the brothers Jakob and Markus Wallenberg, who were directors of a Swedish bank, Goerdeler wrote char-
acteristically : "This is the plan. Germany has enough capable men
to carry it out. But it is precisely they who, while respecting and
desiring the independence of all other nations, passionately reject
the interference of other nations in German affairs. So, when one
hears that Poland demands East Prussia and parts of Silesia, that
it is intended to influence German education and do in Germany
what Germans themselves must do, and what only they can do
with success, the outlook for the future of Europe and the white
peoples is bleak. For that future can only be based on their free
alliance, on independence and respect, not on new degradation. We
ourselves will bring Hitler and his fellow-criminals to justice because
they have stained our good name. But we will also defend our independence."[11]

Goerdeler retained his faith in a new Germany and a future
Europe right up to the months of his imprisonment; and he always
tried to understand what rational motives prompted the actions
of the statesmen of the West. So long as he was free, there hardly
passed a day when he did not think about his own political actions,
about the coup and reconstruction, and speak to people about it—
so strongly did he feel that he had the vocation and calling to work
with his whole being for the "overriding interests of the Fatherland".
His name remains bound up with the history of these years as an
impassioned warning voice, an advocate of justice against injustice,
a man who urged on and encouraged others, even in the darkest
moments of a journey which led him from disappointment to disappointment and, finally, to death.

Hjalmar *Schacht* occupies a unique, and often controversial, position. For the outsider it will always be difficult to decide how far
desire for personal advancement and prestige, or a strong will,
supported by a most gifted intellect, determined the actions and
words of this much praised and much criticized man. His ministerial

55

colleague and, at times, strong opponent, Reich Finance Minister, Count Schwerin-Krosigk, who wrote one of the best and most readable chapters of his book about Schacht, says : "With Schacht one was always torn between admiration and instinctive repugnance. His life was full of contradictions." Schwerin-Krosigk praised Schacht's skill in conversation, his quickness, his inexhaustible wealth of original ideas, his combative spirit and his boundless courage; but he also thought that his egotism was excessive and prevented him from admitting mistakes. "He stretched the truth, until he seemed to be the only one who had acted entirely correctly, and eventually he himself believed that events had occurred, as he had represented them."[12] Schacht himself in his *Abrechnung mit Hitler* (English title : *Account Settled*) gives the following outline of events. After he had, as a banking expert, achieved financial independence, which he insisted on as a pre-condition of taking public service, he became Reich Currency Commissioner in 1923–24 and, later, President of the Reichsbank. In 1930 he criticized the weakness of the government and then resigned and travelled abroad a good deal. In speeches which he made, particularly in countries which were creditors of Germany, he tried to convince his listeners that German reparations were an intolerable burden and had disadvantages for all. He regarded the deferment of payments as a result of the Hoover Moratorium of 1931 and the Lausanne Agreement of 1932, which virtually cancelled Germany's debt obligations, as the product of his efforts. Disgusted by the parliamentary quarrels, during which time the unemployment figure rose to nearly 7 million, and impressed by the growing danger of radicalism on the Right and on the Left, he advocated calling on Hitler, the leader of the strongest party, to assume responsibility for the government of the country. He signed the famous petition of bankers, economists, and industrialists addressed to Reich President Hindenburg in November 1932.[13] To Hitler himself he once wrote at this time : "I have no doubt that things can end only in one way, and that is in your Chancellorship. . . . Your movement is intrinsically so right and necessary that its victory, in one form or another, is inevitable."[14] He hoped, in particular, that the proven ability of this national leader to act would create work and restore Germany's national sovereignty. At Hitler's request, he took over the Reichsbank again in 1933. On August 2, 1934, the day of Hindenburg's funeral parade, he became Reich Economics Minister. After the announcement of conscription, Hitler appointed him, by a secret law in May 1935, General Plenipotentiary for the military economy. With these personal plenary powers he accomplished extraordinary things for German rearmament. The way he created money and credit amongst a poor people with his

MEFO bills and put them to work aroused widespread astonishment, like the magic of a great expert who brings order out of confusion. Foreign economists are reported to have said at the time that he was able to work simultaneously with 237 different mark currencies.[15] Severer critics regarded him as a juggler, whose conscience should not be called to account. Goerdeler called his achievement "a schoolboy's trick with 40 000 million marks' debt". In any case Schacht very soon saw that to go further would lead to bankruptcy, and he implored Hitler to curb public expenditure. But, now the vehicle was going at full speed, he was powerless against the man who, since September 1936, had been responsible for the Four Year Plan and who chiefly personified the new lack of restraint in money matters : Göring.[16] Awkward as he could be and uncompromising as he increasingly became, Schacht was more and more opposed to the new methods of creating credit, which, he thought, would drive the Government into a war. Nor did he refrain from criticizing the way the new Party bosses were exceeding all limits. When Goerdeler left Leipzig, he was still engaged in his struggle. But a few months later he, too, withdrew by taking a long holiday; and he was eventually dismissed in December 1937 as Reich Economics Minister. But he agreed, for public purposes, to continue as Minister without Portfolio and as President of the Reichsbank. Schacht seldom wore the Golden Party Badge which he received; but he used to make sarcastic comments about it. The events of 1938 profoundly modified his predictions and views of the system for which he was still working. The story is told of a dinner with a colleague in the summer of this year : "When Dr Schacht appeared, it was obvious that he was fuming about something. During the meal it suddenly came out when, in a state of great excitement, he shouted point-blank to my wife : 'Madam, we have fallen into the hands of criminals : how could I have guessed that?' "[17]

At that year's Christmas speech to the staff of his Bank, Schacht, as he himself says, openly condemned the recent measures against the Jews as a disgrace. When asked by Hitler to explain, he answered : "My Führer, had I known that you approve these happenings, I should have been silent." In January 1939 he was also relieved of his post as President of the Reichsbank, after Hitler had had several clashes with him and had had to listen to his often mordant and unorthodox views.

A letter, which Schacht sent to Göring in November 1942, when the call-up of fifteen and sixteen year-olds was being considered, left little to be desired for the outspokenness of its criticisms. It led to Schacht, from then on, joining the opponents of the régime who were closely watched.[18]

After that, he never took a prominent part. As he once said, he was his own resistance circle. And the others were not encouraged to bring him over to their ranks, partly because his name abroad was too closely associated with Hitler and the trade unions deeply distrusted him. Through General Lindemann, he remained informed about the preparations for a rising in 1944. After the 20th July he was arrested and put through the same mill of interrogations as the others. Because Lindemann did not incriminate him as an accomplice of the planned uprising, he avoided the worst. He was freed at the end of the war and the case against him at the Nuremberg trials ended with his acquittal.

In 1938 Schacht, who was still at that time a member of the Government, toyed with the idea of a coup in co-operation with Beck, Goerdeler, Oster, and Halder; and, as far as his nature allowed, he gave it his support. This happened, for instance, in the Fritsch crisis, when he and Goerdeler tried to persuade the Generals to go over to active resistance, and then in the September plan, which he enthusiastically promoted. Clearly, for Beck, Oster, and for Canaris, the acuteness and range of his political judgement were particularly important. So they always chose him to enlighten the Generals about the great events at home and abroad, with which they were less conversant, and to give them the necessary political support for any action that was required. For this purpose, Schacht met Halder, Witzleben, Brauchitsch, Raeder, Rundstedt, and others and, according to his own testimony, put himself at the disposal of a new government. The calm, superior and sometimes caustic arguments he brought to the conversations were, as we can see from the reports, difficult for his listeners to refute. But it is not known to what extent these talks were successful in preparing the way for action. Brauchitsch, who, admittedly, was committed in another direction in the meantime, declined a visit from Schacht in August 1939.

However different were the characters of Schacht and Goerdeler, their paths during these years were similar. It is true that Schacht had supported Hitler's rise to power with greater expectations; but both performed their duties under the new régime with all their strength. However, they reached a point where they saw the corruption of what had been begun with so much hope, and the disaster of faulty policies, so outweigh everything else that they left and went over to the Opposition. Schacht supported the Opposition for a limited period when there were still hopes for a change; Goerdeler did the same for years, and even without hope, until his last day of freedom. It is moving to read what each wrote about the other, although it does not give the whole picture of their mutual impressions. Schacht, looking back in 1948, wrote of Goerdeler : "Goerdeler was a man of irreproachable character, great courage and untiring urge to act. But he was, in Dr Josef Müller's words, an engine which ran too noisily. His plans and moods were always changing. He was not very realistic, although he larded all his predictions and expositions with figures and tables—predictions which were never realized on time and expositions which disregarded many possibilities. This is the reason why Goerdeler never succeeded in getting one of the Field-Marshals to act, although he repeatedly tried to do so with several, at risk to himself."[19]

Goerdeler, for his part, wrote of Schacht in his last notes in prison : "He bears responsibility for the National Socialist debt policy up to the beginning of 1939. But that does not alter the fact that he has the virtuosity of an artist in his complete mastery of the problems of money, currency and banking, that he knows the laws of economics, that he is a brave man of character, one of the ablest heads and best patriots Germany has had since Bismarck. God grant that he will remain alive! Therefore do not judge him for his ambition or for the false choice he made when he attacked Brüning in Harzburg in 1931 and came out in favour of Hitler...."[20]

The name of another man must now be mentioned who, as a high official of the Reich, knew of Beck's plans in the summer of 1938, supported them as far as he could, and was one of the confederates in the next four years : Ernst von *Weizsäcker*, State Secretary in the Foreign Office. At eighteen he joined the Navy and spent the First World War on warships and, later, as naval liaison officer in Hindenburg's and Ludendorff's General Headquarters. From 1920 onwards he was an official of the Foreign Office in various countries, such as Switzerland, Denmark and Sweden. In 1938 he was offered, and accepted, the office of State Secretary to the newly appointed Reich Foreign Minister, Ribbentrop. He took this decision from a sense of responsibility which, he felt, forbade him to withdraw, for personal reasons, at a time of increasing danger for the Reich and to retreat before the new masters in the Office. He disliked the diplomatic war forced on him in the summer of 1938, which made him an active tool of covert aggression. And it helped him, like Beck and the others, to foresee that war was inevitable—a war which he thought Germany could not face politically. Consequently, he approved Beck's attempt to organize resistance and he permitted his subordinates to undertake activities, particularly in the hope of influencing the British Government. In August 1939 he made strenuous efforts to prevent the outbreak of war.[21] The loyalty which he felt he owed both to his Office and his Fatherland presented him with an almost insuperable dilemma.

Those who had broken with Hitler and who were "outside", inevitably felt as disappointed by the apparently unswerving loyalty and constant prudence of the State Secretary, as Ribbentrop and his foreign affairs staff were annoyed by the way Weizsäcker ran the Foreign Office on the "old lines" and always pursued watered-down policies. If one thought one could still do good in such an office— and Nuremberg made this clear[22]—then one had to play the part of Penelope. Often by a tip to his friends, Weizsäcker succeeded in unravelling what he had earlier had to weave; and, in this, he was understood by the younger people, who followed him and were ready for a revolt. What he achieved over the years, as a moderating and restraining influence, was recognized, when in 1943, he left Berlin to go as Ambassador to the Vatican.[23] It was there that he saw the end of the war. Several years later, he was brought before the International Court in Nuremberg and tried and sentenced as the main defendant in the trial of the Foreign Office. Shortly after his release, he died.

His role was inseparably connected with the circle of young diplomats, whom he brought to the fore and allowed, in close co-ordination with himself, to work for a counter-movement. They were united in their admiration of Weizsäcker and in their rejection of the evil and perfidy of the system and its policy of force which, they thought, would lead to Bolshevism. Many of them also supported the revolt in 1944, after Weizsäcker was replaced by Wilhelm Keppler, Hitler's close and proven agent. Among the members of this circle were the brothers Theo and Erich Kordt, Hasso von Etzdorf, Eduard Brücklmeier, Albrecht von Kessel, Hans-Bernd von Haeften, and Adam von Trott zu Solz. Three of them were executed.[24]

In the winter of 1938–39, Ludwig Beck came into contact with other Reich officials, either still in office or retired, who had ideas similar to his own and who had become aware of him largely through the "Wednesday Club". These men, such as Hassell, Popitz and Jessen, advised him and participated in the planning right up to the 20th July.

Ulrich von *Hassell*, who was born in 1881, belonged to an old Hanoverian family and had entered the Diplomatic Service in 1911 under the Monarchy. He had survived a bullet which entered his heart during the battle of the Marne. The years after the First World War took him from Italy to Spain, Denmark and Yugoslavia, and then, in 1932, back to Italy, of which he was particularly fond. As Ambassador at the Quirinal, he opposed a military alliance with Italy and was, for this reason, dismissed from the post in December 1937. An attempt to get reinstated with Göring's help in the spring of 1938 was unsuccessful. Once marked by Hitler's disfavour, he could only, like Goerdeler, obtain positions with the help of industry : this allowed him to travel abroad and to observe the European scene which was so much after his heart. His published diaries, which begin in September 1938, reveal his serious doubts, indeed his critical rejection of the prevailing system, and his search in the many talks he had with responsible persons for ways of bringing about a change. From them emerges, in particular, his horror at the decline in human standards, which he notes and describes in detail, and the feeling on every page of his responsibility as a German. For him, the talk of ·a European family of nations, as his attitude to Dante shows, had a real meaning, based on civilized traditions; and on that he founded his plans to bring Europe together in a new form, by means of economic and cultural rapprochement, while, at the same time, respecting national characteristics. For Germany, he preferred the monarchist conception. Thanks to his opportunities to talk with Göring and his friendship with the British Ambassador, Henderson, he was able to follow at first hand, and actually participate in, the events of the last days before the outbreak of war. His knowledge of those events appears to have been chiefly responsible for his death sentence after the 20th July. It seems that his active participation in the preparatory talks about a new government,[25] in which he was particularly successful in mediating between the younger and older generations, incriminated him less.

It did, however, transpire that the men of the 20th July had thought of him as a possible Foreign Minister. A courtier of refined and exacting standards, an inexhaustible raconteur, an eloquent master of conversation : that is how Hassell is remembered by many at home and abroad, who spent any time with him. We must also recall his impetuosity, his cool daring, his aristocratic disregard of danger from the time the Fronde began; his superior, defiant composure before the foaming judge, when he said : "Herr Präsident, I have not lived sixty-two years to be told by you that I am a liar"; his last letters scribbled before the executioner seized him in which he thanked his dear wife, a daughter of the famous Tirpitz, for the fortune of a happy life and urged her to remain kind and not to become embittered. In all this, we see features of a life which remind us of the aristocratic world of old.

Professor Johannes *Popitz*, who was four years younger than Beck, had made a name in the time of the Weimar Republic as an expert and official in administration, especially in finance, and he had taught at Berlin University. In 1933 he became Prussian Finance Minister. Although an official of the old school, he welcomed the Hitler régime and was convinced that the good elements

61

among the Germans would prevail over the defects and wrongs of the new movement, of which he himself was a victim, and that they would help to make something lasting out of it. But he saw this goal constantly recede; and Hans Oster, with whom he was for many years in contact, reported his observations to him. The events connected with the dismissal of Colonel-General Fritsch and the Sudeten crisis, presented Popitz, who supported Beck, with an insuperable dilemma; and, after the persecution of the Jews in November 1938, which he openly condemned, he asked to be relieved of his office. When that was refused, he felt from then onwards a greater responsibility to work for a change from within. He believed that it must be possible to force a split in the system itself. Göring, to whom he had access, as party member and ministerial colleague, was, for a time, under his influence. When nothing could be done with him—Göring's vanity and weakness were too obvious—Popitz tried in August 1943 to talk with Himmler himself and, with cautious feelers, to win him over to the idea of a revolt. This venture encountered much criticism in the circle of the Opposition and, after a few weeks, thanks to the arrest of the go-between, it ended without a second talk with Himmler. Even after the failure of this attempt, Popitz tried some independent approaches himself, because he was clearly opposed not only to Goerdeler's views, but also to those of the Socialists. Until 1943 Popitz was earmarked for the future post of Minister of Culture, and later Minister of Finance. But from 1944 onwards his name no longer appears in the surviving lists.

A "provisional basic law for the state", which Popitz drew up after many talks with Jessen, Hassell, Planck, and Beck, and "Guiding principles for the administration of the law on the state of siege", whose author is said to be Langbehn, have survived.[26] Drafted for the chaotic transition period, they establish an absolute, centralized rule on the part of the Reich Commissioner (*Reichsverweser*), or Head of State. He governs through his representatives (*Statthalter*) in the newly-constituted provinces (*Länder*), which are merely administrative regions. Popitz thought that genuine representative government would only be possible at a later date. This, as his daughter has said, he conceived somewhat in the form of Rhenish liberalism. According to her, he had always been opposed to the German Nationalists and his views on the restoration of the Monarchy were only prompted by tactical considerations.[27]

Popitz was arrested the day after the 20th July. His friends in Himmler's entourage deferred his end, by giving him assignments after he was condemned to death, perhaps in the hope of saving him from the rope. On thirty-nine wide-ranging questions they demanded from him, as they did from Goerdeler, memoranda about Germany's post-war reconstruction, about his ideas on Reich and administrative reform, about reorganization of Reich territory and much else. This was to prove to posterity how greatly their opponents valued the political knowledge of these men. His execution on February 2, 1945, together with Goerdeler, came on orders from higher authority; it left his answers to these questions unfinished.

Those close to Popitz knew his kindness. More apparent in conversation was his extraordinarily clear and critical mind "whose superior calibre, often to Popitz's own sorrow, some found a little too hard or bitter".[28] His sarcasm was as sure of its aim, although not so spiteful, as that of his ministerial colleague from the Reichsbank. The profound and serious look of a thoughtful Roman head lent an emphasis to his learned expositions and searching questions, which even a man like Göring, it seemed, found attractive. The extraordinary intellectual and practical expertise of the Minister was only part of his richly endowed nature. Those who went to his home found an atmosphere of good taste and educated humanism. He himself seemed to be at one with the things, the books, and pictures, which he loved to have about him, a man of intellectual freedom and sincerity, who still drew inspiration from the classics.

The clearly defined personality of Popitz had its influence on a circle of important men, not concerned with the history of the Resistance and including the surgeon, Sauerbruch, and the constitutional lawyer, Carl Schmitt. One of them, who also collected round himself a lively group of largely younger people, interested in political matters, owed his contacts with the Opposition movement principally to Popitz. This was Albrecht *Haushofer*. He was born in 1903 and worked as Professor of Geo-Politics at the Berlin Technical College for Politics. At first he directed his activities clearly to working with, and serving, the new régime, as was shown in his personal relations with Rudolf Hess. Later, he went more and more his own way and in 1941 he ended his work with the Foreign Office. Thanks to his capacity for world-wide perspectives, his stimulating mind and gift for languages, Haushofer had a special attraction for young people and knew how to arouse in them a patriotic and European conscience, which carried some through the fortunes of war, after faith in Hitler had been destroyed. Haushofer disappeared after the 20th July, but was later arrested and shot, without trial and without ceremony, during the last days of the war, as the enemy was approaching. There are sonnets of his, which he composed in prison, as one purified, who looks back after having taken many winding paths.

Among other men in Popitz's circle, who should be named in

connection with the Opposition, was Haushofer's friend, the adventurous Dr Carl *Langbehn*. Born in 1901, he was a lawyer and notary, who courageously used his contacts with the highest SS authorities for a coup d'état. It is indicative of how dangerous the situation had become that even Goerdeler regarded him as suspect and unsuitable for this task.[29] There was also Erwin *Planck*, Brüning's personal secretary, who later had a prominent position in the wholesale iron trade. The son of the famous physicist, and a friend of General von Schleicher, he was very much affected by the events of June 30, 1934. Finally, there was Jens *Jessen* who was particularly active in connection with the 20th July. All the persons named were executed.

Professor Jens Jessen was a friend of Popitz from earlier years. Thanks to him he had come to Berlin University as a lecturer in economics. He was born in 1895 of Friesian peasant stock, the fifth of ten children, in the most northern district of Germany. Jessen belonged to a different generation from that of Beck and Popitz, not so much in point of age as of experience. He belonged to the generation of front-line soldiers who had gone to war as volunteers from school. Those who survived studied at the universities after the war under conditions of great privation. They felt that they had sealed with their blood a common destiny with thousands of their compatriots, without any reference to class; and, at first, they had little desire to resume the threads of bourgeois life, as Jessen put it. After several years abroad, which made him conversant with public affairs, as a specialist in banking and trade in Denmark and the Argentine, he opted in 1927 for an academic career in Germany. And, without becoming a member of the Party, he soon supported Hitler's movement and his friends with his own northern fighting spirit and independence, at a time when "educated" people still abominated it. It is characteristic of him that he would, however, add when speaking to his friends : "Once they are in power, I shall be in opposition. That I know." He thought this movement was the only one adequate and strong enough to act as a counter-weight to the Communism which was threatening Europe. But if it were to succeed, he thought one must "avoid encumbering it with elements, which did not really belong to the movement, and ensure that rigidity, imposed by the Party bosses, did not divert the movement from its path or cripple it".[30] His years after 1933 reflect a recurring fate. His position as Director of the Institute for World Trade and Ocean Traffic in Kiel which the new régime had given him, he soon had to leave when he began a campaign against irregularities which were covered up by the Party. He refused to depart from the principles of decency and patriotic socialism, as he understood them. He passionately tried

64

to save "the idea" of the movement and did not object to sending his pupils to the SS, where he felt, the important decisions would be taken. Ohlendorf, "once an ideal character", is an example; his alienation and fanaticism later produced a profound crisis in Jessen.[31] When in 1937–38 the new unrestrained credit policy began in the Reich, and the universities, particularly the economic science faculties, were held on a tighter doctrinal rein, Jessen, who was still content to call himself a "war volunteer" felt increasingly constrained to go into opposition and to invent a bold form of double-talk. In the sort of language which was still allowed, he advocated a turning away from the public course of state socialism and, as he saw it, of irretrievable Bolshevization. Together with Beck, Popitz, and von Hassell, Jessen formed the real conspiratorial group in the "Wednesday Club". Jessen, it seems, was the one most eager to act amongst them, the first to regard assassination as inevitable, and to work out methods of bringing it about, in his own purposefully brave and silent manner. Fechter describes him as tall and slim "with Danish features and with that un-bourgeois matter-of-factness towards life which was the mark of those who remembered and who had directly experienced the years of inflation. He was both cool and temperamental, acute, wise, and a good hater."[32] Jessen kept in close contact with Oster and Goerdeler and was a friend of von Tresckow. In 1941, in spite of two serious wounds from the First World War, he was called up and, as Captain, got the section at the Quartermaster-General's which was in charge of traffic between Germany and the front. In this position he performed valuable services for the Opposition. At his home in Berlin he was a very generous host and important meetings took place there right to the end. Jessen was executed, not for treason, but for a serious case of withholding information from the authorities.

V. MEN OF THE LEFT

A DISTINCTIVE group of men, who took part in and influenced the 20th July, had earlier been members of the Socialist movement. They were not a homogeneous group; several were of marked individuality and greatly intent on bringing about a "renewal" in German life. Their common ground was that they regarded the First World War, in which most of them had served throughout as young volunteers, as a decisive personal and political watershed. They had looked forward with lively hopes to the new order which, they thought, would clear away so much that was out of date. When these hopes were not fulfilled and other forces, which they thought belonged to the past, rose again to power in the new Republic, these men were driven to take part in the political scene.

It was inevitable that these people, who in the years before 1933 had bitterly opposed the advance of National Socialism, were the first to feel the counter-measures of the new régime. Branded as the "Marxist" intelligentsia and the creatures of the "November criminals", they were abused and outlawed and spent years in the first merciless concentration camps. It is easy to understand how they, as victims of oppression, saw in their daily lives the darker side of the régime—more fully than, and differently from, all other Germans. But we know that some were able to lift themselves above their own personal fate and refused to become the victims of bitterness and despair. When they were again released—although not always completely free—and found a living in trade or industry, their opposition was unbroken. They knew about each other and about those who stood with them. Their hopes were directed towards casting off again the yoke of the "huge prison", as Leuschner described it in a letter of August 20, 1939,[1] and towards founding a more genuine people's state.

But when they looked at Hitler's Germany, they were not spared some bitter reflections. For they had to admit that this man, unlike any other German popular leader before him, had founded a "people's community", in which the remnants of class differences had disappeared; that much was being done for social welfare; and that the worker was provided with work, good wages and leisure. Three-quarters of all Germans, and perhaps a still higher proportion of workers, had to be regarded as followers of Hitler. How was one to get them to revolt? How was one to persuade them that all

this was only oppression, a bait, a way of rendering them powerless, so that they would have no other thoughts, and work for rearmament, while Hitler pursued political aims which could only
be realized by war? How could one talk to them of human freedom
and of the rights of the individual? Had the Weimar Republic
and the Social Democratic movement, then, achieved so little that
all this was possible, indeed inevitable? If what they saw happening
in Germany seemed a mockery of their conception of Socialism and
a totalitarian Bolshevist system, they—or, at any rate, some of them
—also judged severely the failure of the party, for which they themselves had worked.[2] They were heard to complain that parliamentary bureaucracy, desire for office, quarrels about doctrine and a
mistaken lack of patriotism had been rampant in the party. They
thought a different kind of revolutionary spirit was necessary to
provide a new European conception of the state in the world of
capitalism and communism which were so opposed but inwardly
so akin. This state would get away from the rule of the masses and
enable spiritual freedom and the right of the individual to prosper
again and develop.

It is clear from the evidence that this group of men realized that
the horrifying disintegration of human society, which had originally
raised the social problem, could not be explained or remedied in a
purely political context. They themselves had learnt this from far-
seeing men. They were more likely to feel tempted to regard any
intervention in the highly complex and closely co-ordinated world
of their day as hopeless. But, in spite of this, they were urged on
by their instinctive desire for action to do what was possible, and
to find a way out of the present crisis.

Wilhelm *Leuschner*[3] was a person with a gift for rallying and
organizing men. He was astute and skilled in negotiation, and was
looked upon by all as the indisputable leader of their cause in the
Diaspora, which had been forced upon them. He was the same age
as Hitler, and a wood-worker by calling. For years he had been a
Darmstadt city councillor and a member of the Hesse provincial
parliament; and in 1928–33 he was Hesse Minister of the Interior.
He had been born in Bayreuth, and was the son of a stove-fitter. By
a deliberate course of training he had schooled himself for his wide-
ranging tasks without, however, ever suffering from either an inferiority complex or pretentiousness. He is described as "quiet and composed, dependable, accurate and extraordinarily manly" but there
was also some magic quality about his presence, "something scintil-
lating, not easily grasped and unfathomable".[4] His great physical
powers of resistance were further hardened by his years of imprisonment : he scorned a soft bed and liked a simple chair. When, in

67

camp, he went to have his head shaven, he dared to resist, as not one in hundreds did; and, disclaiming heroic gestures, explained, when he later saw his shame-faced colleagues, that it had not been worth the barber shaving his few hairs. . . . He liked to do things in his own way, such as fitting out his home, and adopting unconventional ideas : as a young man he once, with the help of a ladder, painted a picture on the ceiling over the bed of his invalid mother.

At the centre of his trade union work, which he started early, was the desire to provide the worker with education and a dignified life. He took part, as a pupil and a teacher, at the adult education institutes, and wrote, when calling for a ninth school year at the *Volksschule* : "One does not send a child of fourteen into the world : one trains him." During his first weeks of arrest in 1933 he was occupied with Goethe's *Wilhelm Meister*. He was an active member of the Hesse provincial parliament and its Vice-President and Minister of the Interior in the years when fanaticism was gathering force. He was the originator of one of the first plans for Reich administrative reform which was to start with the creation of a Reich province of Greater Hesse by combining Hessian and Prussian areas. He was a member of the executive and, after Leipart's departure, was nominated chairman, of the German General Trade Union Federation, which numbered nearly 4½ million members. He was the workers' representative at the preliminary conference of the ILO in Geneva in January 1933. In these positions and duties Leuschner certainly proved himself to be one of the resolute politicians of the later years of the Weimar Republic. And, through Geneva, he acquired a reputation abroad : he himself spoke French and English. By his significant silence at the Geneva meeting of the International Labour Conference in June 1933, Leuschner made clear to all his refusal to put his reputation at the disposal of the new régime and its prominent Labour Front leader, Ley. When he returned to Germany he was arrested and remained in custody for two years. After that he had an opportunity to go abroad. But he decided to stay at home. He took over a small factory in Berlin, in which virtually only trade union people worked. He thus provided himself with a new cachet but also with the entirely respectable opportunity of cultivating his contacts throughout Germany and neighbouring countries. His factory was engaged on the production of beer taps and developed a new hardening process for aluminium. In war-time he worked for the Navy, and remained in Berlin busy preparing a revolt. The defeats and disasters which had become inevitable made him hope for the day, when it would be possible to drive a wedge between Hitler and the German workers. Leuschner, who was often called "Uncle" in the circle of conspirators, was experienced in the formation of cells and in the tactics of the underground; and he made the network of his political friends a system of strong-points throughout the Reich. In this way, he was able to reach out to factory floors without the authorities of the Labour Front suspecting anything. He deliberately aimed at large associations; in 1932–33 these had been short-sightedly neglected. He had an understanding with the men of the former Christian unions who belonged to the political centre and who were associated with the Franconian, Jakob *Kaiser*; he established contact with Ernst *Lemmer*, the former Secretary-General of the Hirsch-Duncker trade union; and he reached agreement with the men of the once largest employees' union of the Right, the German Nationalist Shop Clerks' Union, whose spokesman was Max *Habermann*.[5] It was widely felt in these groups that it had been wrong to fight each other over trivialities, when only strong and united action could have blocked the way to dictatorship. How difficult was it now to make any progress! Speeches on the shop-floor and membership lists, revolutionary meetings and open challenges could no longer help to launch the popular movement that was wanted; no written or broadcast word could be openly expressed. All that remained possible were oral agreements and exchanges in accordance with agreed signs. Friends who had somewhere come to agreement and taken on tasks could find themselves dispersed the next day to the ends of the earth, thanks to the exigencies of the war, without any possibility of contact. That Leuschner and his friends were nevertheless able to create a considerable secret network—although it never came to political fruition after the failure of the 20th July—is shown by the names of the many dead, which the trade unionists and Socialists mourned. It can also be proved that many ramifications escaped the attention of the Gestapo.[6]

On August 20, 1939, shortly before the Russo-German alliance opened the gates of war, Leuschner wrote to a friend abroad : "I am afraid there will be war this autumn and that it will last for years.... We are quite unable to prevent the catastrophe. We are caught in a huge prison. To rebel would be as suicidal as if prisoners were to rise up against their heavily armed guards." Yet from the start of the war, Leuschner was determined not to give in to the all-pervading atmosphere of force, to remain vigilant, to construct new bridges and to seek contacts with the military, from whom alone a change could still be hoped for. Leuschner had once known General von Hammerstein well. In the first year of the war Canaris and Oster established contact with him; he himself communicated with

Olbricht through intermediaries; and Beck came to the factory as an ordinary visitor. At the hostel in the Askanischer Platz there took place the first meeting with Goerdeler who, in the years of their co-operation, always had a great admiration for Leuschner, in spite of some real differences. Leuschner, in close contact with Goerdeler and the circle round Stauffenberg and Leber, took an important part in the plans for a revolt on the 20th July and was proposed as Vice-Chancellor in the new régime.

On his return from Geneva, Leuschner had voluntarily surrendered to the police, when he saw someone else mistakenly arrested for himself at the platform-barrier. Similarly, he found it intolerable after the 20th July that his wife, who had covered his escape in Berlin by some secret back-stairs, should be in the hands of the Gestapo. He remained and, with a warrant out for his arrest, lived a hazardous life moving between those who knew his secret and those who suspected nothing, until an ordinary woman betrayed him. He refused to be handcuffed and promised not to escape. Shouted down by the President of the Court, who accused him of "boundless ambition", and declared, along with Goerdeler, Hassell and the others in court, to be "lepers amongst our people", Leuschner declined to make a final statement. There followed three weeks of torment after the death sentence. His fellow-prisoners at the time found him always "upright and unbowed" and pastors of both confessions said he would only discuss personal affairs. His last brief words to his friends were : "Tomorrow I shall hang. Unite !" And on his way to the gallows he made the same, silent exhortation with a gesture of his hands.

Leuschner, who in the war years had himself become an independent factory owner, saw modern socialism somewhat in the following terms. After the revolutionary generation of the workers' movement, which had started with the class war of the Communist Manifesto, the present generation had a quite different task. This was to achieve the full integration into the state of the workers who, in the meantime, had become a social force and had achieved equality, and to give them the rights and responsibilities which were their due "not only in a social but also in a political, spiritual and cultural sense". "With the revolution of 1918 Germany ceased to be an authoritarian state. . . . Today the working classes are fighting for a state which previously they regarded as something hostile."[7] Every talented child, he thought, should have an equal chance of advancement at school. Leuschner wanted the same nine-year basic schooling for all to be followed by instruction in a trade or further education. And, above all, he demanded good instruction in German. For him the worker was no longer a sort of servant; "The question of the

70

economic foundations of our state," he said, "concerns the workers. . . . We are not only assuming a function here for ourselves, but a national and European function." "First we saw how the individualist destroyed the state; now we see how the state destroys the individual. But there is a third possibility which is not a compromise, but something higher and different : the human personality." In accordance with these high aims, he thought the new trade union ought to develop a work ethos that was no longer based on feelings of oppression and lack of privilege, but one that would give the worker a feeling of responsibility, appropriate to his professional and personal qualifications. Leuschner had many arguments with Goerdeler about the organizational form of this trade union, which the former Mayor of Leipzig emphatically wanted. Only in the winter of 1942–43 was agreement reached about the shape of a "German Trade Union". It was to be centrally controlled and divided into thirteen different industrial categories with individual works' secretariats. By law all workers and employees over eighteen years of age were to belong to it as a self-governing organization of the workers. Its functions included : "Social insurance, wage agreements, arbitration, and the sending of elected representatives to the boards of management, the supervisory boards and the shop stewards' councils of all major economic undertakings."

At the same time Leuschner was greatly concerned with ideas for reconstructing the German state and with interim solutions in the period of chaos that was anticipated. For him, too, the basic ideas of Freiherr vom Stein on self-government were the starting-point. But he deliberately catered for an interim period of post-war confusion, where there would be no elections and the first elements of government to reappear would be the result of local initiative. There was to be a Reichstag and Upper House (Senate). The Upper House was to act as a delaying element in countering the changing moods of an unthinking electorate. Leuschner, in spite of strong resistance from Goerdeler, insisted on getting rid of proportional representation. Only *one* representative was to be elected, if necessary after a second ballot, in each constituency. In this way, in addition to stressing the importance of personality, it would constantly be brought home to the voter that compromise was inevitable in politics. "The voter in this situation," wrote Ludwig Bergsträsser in the memorandum secretly drafted at the time for Leuschner, "would then be made directly aware that politics cannot be conducted in a vacuum in accordance with pure principles, that moderation is necessary, that the better is often the enemy of the good and that, in politics as in human life, one is often in the awkward position

71

of having to choose between two evils. It showed lack of political understanding if one dismissed such compromises as horse-trading (as Goerdeler did), when they are, in fact, vital to politics. We have had, in the meantime, enough unfortunate experience of policies which lack compromise." Reichstag and Senate together were to elect the Head of State, the President. Leuschner would only consider a restoration of constitutional monarchy, which was discussed and enthusiastically canvassed by some sections of the Opposition circles, if all other agreement failed. Finally, the memorandum once again referred to Leuschner's dictum that forms of organization were not so important as the responsible co-operation of the citizen. What would help to arouse this in future was not glorified discipline, but the development of personality and civic education.[8]

Hermann *Maass* helped Leuschner in his work and was in his factory. He had been in the youth movement and was, until 1933, secretary of the German Youth Associations. He is described as a "man of firm and clear conviction and resolute character".[9] "He spoke earnestly and gravely, and only after he had resolved some difficult inner conflict. As the guardian of legality and of the immutability of an accepted law, he compelled his friends to justify themselves, to scrutinize their actions and to observe the written law. Certainly, a man with his feelings of responsibility and his spiritual incorruptibility was of incalculable value in a time of turmoil."[10]

Leuschner had strong local ties with two men who had been friends since youth : Theodor *Haubach* and Carlo *Mierendorff*. Both were born just before the turn of the century (1896 and 1897); both left the Ludwig-Georg Gymnasium in Darmstadt in 1914; both were war volunteers who were wounded several times and received high decorations.[11] They studied in the restless post-war years in Heidelberg under Alfred Weber, Gothein and Gundolf and received their doctorates in 1922.

Haubach had a busy life in Hamburg, first in the *Weltwirtschaftliches Archiv*, and then as foreign editor of the "Hamburger Echo".[12] The promptings of his conscience and his sense of responsibility made him stand in the front line of democracy. As an "officer of socialism" he spoke at many meetings, won over young people and was a co-founder of the *Reichsbanner Schwarz-Rot-Gold*, the league of Republican war-veterans. He took part, as the spokesman of the younger people, in the Hofgeismar circle. This group sought to get beyond antiquated ideas of the class struggle and the conflicts of economic interests, and felt called upon to work for a spiritual revival of socialism, and an acceptance of the idea of a Greater

German state. In 1928 Carl Severing, the former Prussian, and then Reich, Minister of the Interior, brought Haubach to Berlin to be Head of the Press Department. He remained in this office until 1930, when the Social Democratic Party left the government. At the time of the revolution of 1933 he was Head of the Press Department at the Berlin Police Headquarters. In September 1933 he ended a funeral speech for an old party friend with the words : "Today our lips are sealed and our flags are rolled up; but even in our silence our thoughts salute you, Nikolaus Osterroth, with the immortal hope and noble greetings of freedom." In 1934 he was arrested and, without being charged or brought to court, had to work for two hard years in the desolate swamps of the Emsland. After his release, he struggled along with difficulty, until he found a responsible post in an industrial undertaking whose owner became his friend. He continued in this work during the war and could have made a living from it. But he was irked by what was happening to Germany and he instinctively refused to acquiesce in what seemed to him to be shameless indifference, and was driven on to run greater risks.

When war broke out, Haubach said : "The task that falls to us is like the tragic conflict of the classical drama. Hitler must be destroyed and, at the same time, the German people must be saved from disaster. How can we few, with an eye to reality, bring this about?" His published letters, because they might be seen by strangers, say hardly anything about, or make only indirect references to, the times; but they reveal a profound and friendly nature and, by certain undertones, help us guess the reasons which led such a patriot to become an accomplice of the revolt in the middle of the war.

In the days of July 1938 when Beck was engaged in his struggle, Haubach wrote from Berlin : "I am gaily involved in the history of philosophy. I am just reading Spinoza and Descartes and have only today come across in the latter the truly royal observation, which makes this philosopher a prince amongst his kind, that the greatest human virtue is, not truth or goodness or a sense of duty, but *admiratio*, the capacity to admire."

When Haubach once heard of the scandal which city children from Hamburg had caused in a Bavarian town, he wrote : "What was complained about was serious enough : lack of respect for an alien way of life and, above all, for an alien faith. The children, corrupted by free-thinking, make fun of the Catholic faith, laugh at church-goers and pictures of the saints, and generally behave, not like guests, but like billeted soldiers. How right old Goethe was when he said that the three forms of respect—respect for what is over us, about us, and beneath us, were the basis of all moral and spiritual life."[13]

Haubach had been able to devote the year 1941 entirely to recovering his strength after an illness and to achieving that fruitful calm, without which he thought he could do nothing for other people. In 1942 he was busy thinking about a coup and was ready to accept for himself the serious consequences and responsibilities that such an attempt must involve. Mierendorff, who was impetuously launched on the same course, and who, as a revolutionary, was the centre of the whole circle, was often in Berlin. Haubach pinned his hopes on the strength of his friend, if the longed-for day should really come. The news that Mierendorff had been killed in an air-raid affected him deeply in December 1943. Moved by the after-glow cast by this "princely life", as he described it, Haubach referred in a letter[14] to the "light from the light of eternity, without which we cannot live—live in the real and original sense of the word"; and he sought the strength to transform this evil into his own salvation. Later he gave the moving memorial speech for his friend—the kind that a man hardly ever made in these times for a friend and which reflected honour on them both.

The loss of Mierendorff was a very painful blow to Haubach. But he devoted himself more closely to the project of a coup and this provided him with new tasks each day. His letters of the spring and summer of 1944, which contain nothing of this, strike a particularly personal note : he contrasts what is victorious and lasting in nature and in outstanding individuals with the terrible things that were happening. We see a calm acceptance of fate, such as can only proceed from a triumph over daily dangers and from an absolute inner preparedness. In a profound and moving letter of July 6, 1944, he exchanged views with Pastor May in Neu-Kaliss about two passages in the Bible which refer to men as "gods". He believed they should be interpreted in terms of Genesis's "Man made in the image of God" and recalled that the early Greek Homeric period used several words for divine and godlike. "The more I try to fathom the dark wisdom of the two Testaments, the more I feel that in recent centuries the essential idea of the divine message has been obscured. It seems to me a great fault in the practice of the Church that it always reminds him who prays of his miserable, depraved and inferior nature, and does not, at the same time, speak of his capacity to be the creature and image of God." Haubach added in his own writing : "I ask you for your priestly blessing, dear Pastor. And will you include in your prayers a man like myself, who trembles at the troubles of the time but who also hopes?"

Two weeks after the 20th July Haubach was still free. Then his

74

participation was discovered. There was the evidence that in Leuschner's plan he was to have had the office for popular education and propaganda. Shortly before his arrest, Haubach wrote : "Wherever Germany was in trouble, there was I, too. Those gentlemen will not find me a fainthearted figure among the accused. They may even be surprised. This time last year I stood on the burning roof-tops of Berlin. And, today, I must show whether I am a patriot !"[15] It is reported that Haubach so annoyed the angry President of the Court with his proud closing words, justifying his action, that the President at once reopened the case and eventually imposed the death sentence, instead of imprisonment which the prosecution had demanded. After five months of imprisonment Haubach was executed in January 1945. The volume of Hölderlin, which he had in prison until the last day, was returned to its owner. Next to the late poem *"Ich bin nichts mehr, ich lebe nicht mehr gerne"* ("I am nothing more, I no longer wish to live") was Haubach's pencil note : "And I still love this world in spite of everything. Still. October 13, 1944."

When Haubach was executed, not a year had passed since he had ended his speech at Mierendorff's grave with the words : "But he who knows that everything in the world is part of a whole, that reality and dreams are interrelated, and that the invisible, spiritual order limits and conditions the visible, knows also that transformation by death does not affect the essential living being. This radiant strength which once imbued our friend and companion and which flourished in the fair, earthly light, does not evaporate in the infinite and does not dissolve, because it is part of the constantly creative strength of love."[16]

Mierendorff was a restless genius of a man, whose many gifts developed early in the highly stimulating and cultural atmosphere of Darmstadt and were given further impetus by the confusion of the war and the post-war period. We hear of reading evenings among school friends, hand-written art reviews, revolutionary societies, and letterblock and hand-presses acquired with difficulty, to publish the "Dachstube" (The Garret). Mierendorff sent his contributions to the "Dachstube" from the field; the most impressive was the "Autumn in Lorraine—dedicated to a royal Prussian hospital administration with humble thanks". This was written by him when he was twenty years old and shows an almost frightening exultation in life and pulsating impatience for action.

When he returned from the war, Mierendorff published in November 1918 an appeal in the last number of the "Dachstube" : "Our times have become the measure of all values and woe be to the art which ignores them. We wait for you, friends, for your warm support. Seek direction, means and ends. Let an irresistible urge towards the future carry us high and be our creed." Zuckmayer, Mierendorff's friend, describes the time they spent together:[17] "The events of this first winter after the collapse were painful and bitter—the Spartacus struggles, the outrageous murder of Liebknecht and Rosa Luxemburg under the eyes of our democratic government, the appearance of the Free Corps, the hopelessly confused rebellion of the Workers' Councils in several cities and their cruel suppression, which trampled down everything that was free and new. Painful and disappointing was the failure of the Wilson Mission, the lack of understanding on the part of the victorious powers, who were already digging the grave of German freedom and helping its most bitter enemies to rise again. . . . Conversation with Mierendorff was always lively, never dull; it revolved round the same vital questions, which still form the main topics of our life today. In those days we were determined to, and convinced we could, solve and clarify every one of them—and certainly by the time we were thirty. Carlo with his great energy would also have had the equipment to do it. I cannot ever remember when he was really tired, except for those famous twenty minutes, when sometimes, in sudden attacks of almost Bismarckian weakness, he would sleep off, during a party, on a sofa in a room next door. But then he would turn up again, as if refreshed from a holiday trip, and resume the very last sentence he had broken off."

Although he favoured more radical change, Mierendorff deliberately joined the Social Democratic Party because he believed that only with its help could "the evil of 1918", the lost revolution, still be saved. His party career certainly gave him much trouble. During his political years he was reduced to nervous despair by what was described as that "cowardly and unimaginative party officialdom clinging like pitch to its offices".[18] He opposed the Reichswehr policy, on which the Government was embarking, and wanted a truly European alliance. Speaking at mass meetings, he showed great and original gifts. "When he mounted the rostrum, hearts went out to him, whether they willed it or not. Even when he stormed, raged and fumed, even when he made his opponent a laughing-stock and put him to shame, there was always a breath of goodness about him, that magic lustre of men of good-will—nothing mean, crafty, ordinary, no demagogy, no propaganda. His strength was untiring : he once spoke at twelve mass meetings all over the Reich in one week; he was always on form; his voice was always sound; and he looked like . . . a complete man."[19]

For ten years Darmstadt remained the field of his activity. Nothing happened there in which his voice was not heard. In 1930 he took over the press office in Leuschner's Hessian Ministry of the Interior. In the spring of 1933 he returned to Germany from Switzerland : "What will our workers think, if we leave them there alone? They cannot get to the Riviera!" he said. He was quickly seized and taken through the streets of Darmstadt "in triumph, like a captured beast".[20] He was kept for four years under arrest, most of that time doing heavy work in stone quarries. During the war he worked in industry. As soon as there was the possibility of a revolt, he was again anxious to take risks; and great hopes were put on his future role as an eloquent and popular leader. In the spring of 1943, when a Darmstadt friend spoke to him, he was drafting his first radio speech, which he hoped he would soon be able to deliver, as well as a plan to hold down, or dig out, the pockets of resistance in Bavaria, especially those round Berchtesgaden. It is said that he remarked at the time : "From now on we can only move forward—to victory or to the gallows."[21] In December, having just left his bomb-wrecked home in Berlin, he was killed in a British bombing attack on Leipzig, "to the very great horror of his friends, who found that his death left a gap which could never be filled".[22]

A person, who worked with him, said about Mierendorff : "Politics were his obsession. . . . In his hands every idea was transformed into an action, to which he devoted himself passionately. He used to hit on the right thing with incredible sureness; and he was a man who had a grasp of all the forces at work in Europe and judged them correctly. He had a magic about him, which can only come from a fullness of life."[23]

Ludwig *Schwamb*, born in 1890, is mentioned as a helper, "a guard who kept a prudent look-out", who arranged for many of his friends to meet in Berlin and provided a safe and congenial atmosphere in which they could develop their ideas. He had once been a Staatsrat in Leuschner's Ministry in Darmstadt. Leuschner, Mierendorff and Leber first met at his home. A "rare friend in good and bad days", Annedore Leber describes him. "He disliked force, foolhardy enterprises and two much passion. His path had to be clear and untroubled like the mirror of his soul. But the friend was stronger in him. As a symbol of loyalty to his friends, he went to his death."[24] He was executed with Haubach.

Adolf *Reichwein* belonged, like Haubach and Mierendorff, to the younger generation of front-line veterans. He was born in 1898 into a family of farmers and teachers in what was then the Prussian province of Hesse-Nassau, and grew up on the Rhine and at the foot of the Taunus Mountains. During the war he was decorated as the leader of an assault party. He recovered from a severe lung wound and a bayonet cut in the arm and was twenty years old at the time of the collapse. He went to the university with an open curiosity stimulated by the youth movement and with a strong community spirit, which alienated him from anything that smacked of aesthetic affectation. He wrote an historical thesis for his doctorate at Marburg under Friedrich Wolters on Chinese influence on eighteenth-century Europe. For Reichwein, Goethe and Hölderlin remained the guiding spirits, even after he became a teacher : he used to say he did not want to see them disembodied in literature. He once wrote, with the insight which is derived from the enjoyment of work : "Thanks to Goethe, we have been made fully aware of the great inborn capacity of man : to grasp divine reality in the visible world."

He followed his bent and, on leaving the university, he turned to popular education. From 1922 onwards, he worked in the Berlin Ministry and in work camps, especially those of the Silesian youth association, such as Löwenberg and Boberhaus, which tried, for the first time, to bring together young workers, farmers and students in practical training for life. In Jena he directed the residential adult education institute of the Zeiss works on the same principles, combining instruction, sport, and physical adventure. The aim was to train the young worker to be conscious of his true value and to understand the basic conditions of the modern world and thus be able to play a useful role. It was said of him that he was not a Socialist in the doctrinaire sense, but a modern man with a strongly developed desire for social education. Whenever the militant political socialism of his young friends became too much for him, he used to tell them that socialism was something which had to be reflected every day in an individual's every action. "Are you not, in your bitterness and understandable hatred, extinguishing the holy flame of real human freedom which you ought to preserve for future generations?" he asked.[25] He was also heard to say, that one could only be horrified by wars such as we have seen. Today men should prove themselves in a different way : they should go together to that frontier where the technical aids of modern life cease to be of any avail and the struggle with man and the elements demands the age-old virtues—where decisions cannot be avoided. A journey to Lapland with his young workers from Jena demanded such a test. At this time Reichwein wrote to his non-political friends from the university : "Politics are not something that we think of in times of trouble, in order to get back to a happier state of affairs and then dismiss from our service as no longer necessary. They are not only a means to happiness but are valuable in themselves as the expression of a creative life." And elsewhere he said : "The conflict is no longer between bourgeoisie and workers but between a pluto-

78

cracy of a few capitalists and the mass of people to which we all belong. . . . Today economics and politics are opposed to culture—for political events are now, in the last analysis, only economics. How can politics be freed from economics and made to serve cultural ends ?"[26]

Following a tragic period in his life in which his little son was accidentally drowned and his first marriage broke up under the strain, Reichwein took a year's leave for research in the late autumn of 1926. Here he was helped by the Minister of Culture, Becker, who took a fatherly interest in him. He went round the world, in a way one would hardly have expected from someone travelling on a scholarship in order to study the economics of the world's raw materials and much else. He drove at his leisure in an old Ford across North America, had an accident in the Rocky Mountains, wrote, drew, and went to the fur-trappers and lumberjacks of Alaska. He served as a sailor, helping out as navigation officer, went to Japan and China, and then back to California. He crossed Mexico on horse and in a boat. The "bueno" he brought back he always subsequently spoke with the invincible joie de vivre of a scholar of a peculiar kind—one who had taken his doctorate in nature's school, and who said of himself that he loved life in all its forms because only this love brought knowledge. When he returned home, the Prussian Minister of Culture chose him as his personal assistant and entrusted him with the care of the proposed teaching academies. They were, in Reichwein's words, "a new and unique synthesis of scientific theory and educational practice", intended as schooling, preparation and initiation for the future career of a teacher and, as such, "only possible outside the universities". Yet they thought of developing the new academies into full-blown colleges.[27] One suggestion is characteristic of Reichwein : that sessions and instruction should only be held in winter; in summer each student should be allowed to go out and do whatever he chose, whether it was learning a trade or art, or travelling. He thought this would enrich the common academic life in winter and produce a new generation of teachers. In 1930 Reichwein himself went to the Teaching Academy in Halle as Professor of Politics and Social Sciences. He wanted personally to try out in the teacher's college what he had theoretically laid down on behalf of the Minister. At this time, when there were already 5 million unemployed, Reichwein wrote : "How few of us today can still find the peace to talk, without concern, about the future of things which are not directly 'economics'? But it will be the mark of statesmen, if they can calmly and deliberately defend the great and important traditions of our cultural life." Reichwein thought that "the spiritual potential of our

79

people, without which we cannot face the moral, psychological and intellectual demands of the coming decades" would decisively "depend on the existence of a formative teaching profession, which can provide intelligent leadership, not only in educating the individual, whether child or adult, but also the social group, the local community and the family".[28]

The three years in Halle—Reichwein was not yet thirty-two when he started—were a high-watermark in his life and influence. Of few teachers at this time could such reports have been written as about him. Even the young National Socialists among his pupils who disagreed with him wanted him on their side. "He knew what grips young men and excites them and he was able to stimulate them positively in favour of his own daring schemes. His affirmation of life, his great joy in action and in the happier sides of life, although he was well aware of the darker ones which had to be surmounted, radiated from every word he spoke."[29] In a notable essay on the Dane, Grundtvig, he gave new life to his phrase "Freedom is the spirit's element". He was often on the move. He was particularly fond of his little *Klemm* aircraft, his "dream of birch wood and raw silk". It offered him, as Saint-Exupéry has described it, the thrill of a bird's eye view and also the chance to prove himself. It often set him down unexpectedly on a meadow, where there were nearby tented camps, friends' meetings and gatherings. Reichwein, with his windswept red hair and gentle eyes, would step out, and introduce a fresh note to the discussion with all the magic of a richly-enjoyed life. Later, he would talk through the night to the campers about his experiences all over the world in his rather harsh voice. "In these years he had an aura about him which came from adventure, the power to help, and a spiritual presence."[30] At the end of 1932 Reichwein, as a deliberate challenge, joined the Social Democratic Party, to which he had previously avoided tying himself. He was relieved of his post in May 1933. He sold his aircraft, remarking that even in the air it was impossible any longer to be a free man and, turning down a professorship in Turkey, asked the new Minister for a one-class village school. He came to Tiefensee in the Niederbarnim district near Berlin and devotedly ran the school on the lines he thought right : a cheerful and matter-of-fact approach, close to nature, which gradually trained the youngster to show consideration for others. A friend saw Pestalozzi's words brought to life here : "The great basis of all education is a trained awareness of one's capabilities."

It was not his professorship in Halle but the years in Tiefensee which resulted in Reichwein's name, long after he was dead, having a special reputation among teachers, and also being given to a

Teacher's Academy. His *"Schaffendes Schulvolk"* (Creative School), which tells of Tiefensee, has been newly recognized as a treasury of information and it is at its most moving in its attempt to solve— more by practical example than theory—the problem of freedom and authority between parents, teachers and children, in a manner which points to the future.

In 1939 Reichwein was appointed to the Folklore Museum in Berlin with the task of harnessing the museum collections to popular education. This was a task after his own heart. He gained information about forgotten techniques of weaving; he dug out formulae for vegetable dyes; took instruction from an old blacksmith in decorative work; and in carefully arranged exhibitions covering every field, and through the medium of attractive displays, aroused interest in the revival of old skills. But he did not mean that fine old things should be copied or imitated; rather "that we should want to learn something about their very nature, and about the honest, simple and painstaking way of using working materials and of making things from them".[31] He held courses in town and country; sought support from governments and local authorities, from women's organizations and the labour service, for the training of handicraft teachers and craft instruction; and he had great success with all this. He thought we must adopt a different attitude to the things we use every day, and establish some sort of affinity with working materials. He regarded as wrong the American tendency to let things end up as junk after a short period of use. Thrift was more than an economic virtue. The pious way our fathers regarded bread, he thought, ought to govern our attitude to all things. . . .

Reichwein's work in Tiefensee and Berlin was in the words of a friend, "certainly like a striking and boldly conceived fabric, densely woven, rich in colours, and durable—a pattern for the future. But at the same time it became an ever thinner cover for his political involvement."

Like Tiefensee before, so in war-time, the Princesses' Palace in Unter den Linden became a meeting place for men who were increasingly worried about Germany's future. Reichwein took up again the contacts which he had from the past—especially from his time in Jena—and which had in the meantime become dangerous. He moved closer to Count Moltke, whom he knew from the days of the Silesian work camps. With him and Gerstenmaier he started the talks and plans of the Kreisau circle, which were to consider what was to be done in the débâcle which would follow Hitler's expected defeat. He introduced Mierendorff and Haubach to Moltke. The death of Mierendorff, whom he valued particularly highly as a born leader of men, affected him deeply. The bombs

81

in Berlin deprived him of his worldly possessions; and his wife and four children, who were at first put up in Kreisau with Count Moltke, he thought would be fated to remain nomads. A letter written at Easter 1944 reveals today—as it could not then for the uninitiated recipient—that Reichwein was devoting all his energies to the revolt. "Sometimes," he wrote, "I envy those who take refuge in their books and leave it to others to fight the daily struggle for the future. But when I am in this mood of renunciation, I am strengthened in the conviction that epochs can only find fulfilment, once the threshold has been won. And the fewer the fighters, the greater the responsibility of the few. I have so often seen in my own life how lack of will to fight produces lost opportunities. A terrible field of fruitless efforts remains behind us. As far as I am concerned, I don't want to share responsibility for these lost opportunities."[32]

In June 1944 it was decided, largely due to Leber, to try to make contact with the Communists of the underground, with a view to clarifying the situation for the day of the uprising. Reichwein used his former contacts to arrange a meeting. He himself went to the meetings; and from the second one on July 4 he did not return. He fell into the Gestapo net. Even torture did not make him disclose what was on foot. Before the People's Judge there was no scope for his frank and courageous nature, which was almost defenceless against common and crude behaviour. At his trial he spoke no word for posterity. We merely have the picture of that moment when the judge pronounced the death sentence : the proud discipline of a spirit which has victoriously emerged from all the agonizing torment of humiliation.[33]

Ernst von *Harnack*[34] combined the intellectual heritage of the Harnack family—his father was the Berlin theologian—and the artistic heritage of his mother's family, Thiersch. After the First World War, he joined the Social Democratic Party when he was thirty-two. He served the Prussian Government, latterly in Merseburg as Regierungspräsident of the province of Saxony, until he was forced to vacate his post by Papen in 1932. In 1933 he was finally dismissed by Hitler and penalized with a reduced pension. Three years later, the book of his experiences "The Practice of Public Administration" was published, but was at once withdrawn. Then, so as not to be inactive, he tried his hand as an ordinary worker. When he was again dismissed, he set up an office in the middle of Berlin and worked in the cloth trade. People who could not otherwise have met came to his office without attracting attention; and here he provided refuge for victims of persecution, for friends from his party, for priests, Jews and half-Jews. They found him a sympathetic and courageous helper, a property administrator and even a lawyer, when they were in conflict with the police or the authorities. We realize what he sometimes took upon himself when we recall his description of himself : "I am not by nature brave. I have to make a mighty effort to overcome fear."

In the years 1938–39 Harnack came into close contact with Goerdeler, Beck, and Julius Leber, whom he greatly admired. In the autumn and winter of 1939 he took part in the plans for a coup. Once the war had started, he was certain that Hitler would never make peace and that the German people would no longer be able to rid themselves of him by legal means. He thought the only hope lay in creating mutual trust between the old trade unions and the leading military figures, and in getting them to act together. He himself, therefore, tried to establish as many bridges as possible and, particularly, to influence the Generals whom Hitler had sacked.[35] It is known that he visited Colonel-General Guderian at a time when the latter was in disgrace and a civilian; but the General received him with reserve. When in 1942 his cousin, Dr Arvid Harnack and his wife,[36] who had been questioned in some detail about him, were executed, Ernst von Harnack moved into the dangerous front line. He played the perilous game with great seriousness, but with little concern for himself. After the 20th July he remained hidden for a while, but was seized at the end of September when he thought the danger had passed.

His unconcern was not light-headedness. An outlaw in his own country, he never lost face or was untrue to himself. Early on he had seen in Egmont a kindred spirit. To devote himself to a higher cause was more important to him than life or death. Thus, he regarded the defence he wrote in prison as an "artistic" duty; he was not concerned with what was prudent or useful to himself, but only wished to say merely what he thought he owed to himself and to the role he had played. "Great issues were at stake," he said, "and I have not come to my present position thoughtlessly. . . . I also had to provide testimony for my father. . . . Then, too, I had before my eyes the fearless conduct of my cousin and his equally brave wife, who had to take the same path. I have no right to be deflected from my decision by regard for surviving members of my family."[37] After his encounter with the President of the People's Court, who sentenced him to death, it was reported by a prison inmate[38] that Harnack returned curiously elated; he derived keen satisfaction from his conduct at this time, because he had succeeded in standing and speaking unshaken, like the man he was, and had to be. To have had to be ashamed of himself would have affected him more than the words which spelt out his death. It was characteristic of him that he did not later fail to praise his opponents for "an excellent knowledge of the documents in his case and proceedings, which, in many ways, were conducted in a gentlemanly way". Sentenced to death, he spent five weeks in chains, day and night, and had to remain in his cell on the third floor of the prison in the Lehrterstrasse, even during air-raid warnings. He was executed on March 5, 1945.

Harnack's opposition to the régime which outlawed him, was characterized by his remark that "a system without humility or goodness is condemned to failure". Force and revolution were alien to him; for he saw too clearly the limitations of mere administrative measures. He was a man of many parts, born into a spiritual tradition. And as a senior official, he saw his office exclusively in terms of service, of providing, preserving, planning, and unceasingly trying to master present-day developments and conditions with the help of the guiding images which played so great a part in his life. The obstacles on such a path, particularly in Communist Merseburg, must have been unending. Harnack, it appeared, found reserves of strength in the enjoyment of the arts. For him figures from literature became alive in conversation. He knew how to organize parties; to transform people tired of the daily round; to put addresses into verse; to give pleasure by presenting his own paintings; and, in a joyful mood of devotion, to cultivate music at home with his family and friends, when he himself played the flute. All this, however, was far from him, as he languished within the walls of his last cell : they restricted him in one respect, only to strengthen him in another.[39]

But one is glad to know that at the end he was able, through the cell wall, to ask his neighbour, who had been allowed to keep his violin, to play his favourite music : the powerful *"Jerusalem, Du hochgebaute Stadt"*, Bach's *"Wenn ich einmal soll scheiden"* and the old Christian heroes' hymn of the seventh century "Vexilla regis prodeunt".

Julius *Leber*, born in 1891, was, like Mierendorff, in his revolutionary energy, a man of toughness and determination, uncompromising in his affirmations and rejections, bold and fervent in his ideas, with an innate gift for winning followers. Among all those in the Socialist camp, it was he who played the leading role in the summer of 1944. The vindictive judge, before whom Leber stood with the other men of the 20th July, described him, in a talk to a small circle, as the most important figure in the political constellation, and designated him "the German Lenin".[40]

Leber was born in humble circumstances in what was then German Alsace. His father worked as a mason and the mother managed a small farm. The boy was soon left to his own devices and had to earn his living. After learning to be a salesman in a wall-paper factory, which he found unsatisfying, he went back to school. He was older than his fellow-pupils and divided from them by his clear and unyielding opposition to the views of the bourgeois world. In 1912 he matriculated and then studied economics and history until the war. On August 3, 1914, he volunteered, and quickly became an officer. He spent the whole war at the front, except for the time when he was gassed and had a leg wound. In 1918 as an Alsatian, Leber opted for Germany, but also emphatically for a Franco-German reconciliation. Even twenty years later this seemed to him more important than the question of whether Germany and Austria should become a single state. He decided to continue to serve in the Army, and with his troops, which were incorporated in the provisional Reichswehr, he was given duties in connection with the protection of the eastern frontier. At the time of the Kapp "putsch" in 1920, he put his troops at the service of the Republic against superior forces on Kapp's side, was overpowered, and only just escaped a summary court martial. At the end of the year he got his doctorate and in the new year he turned to politics. Lübeck became his new home and the city of his activities. He became the editor of the "Lübecker Volksbote", and the Socialist Party leader and member of the *Bürgerschaft*, which was both the city and provincial parliament, of what was then a Free Hansa city. From 1924 he was a member of the Reichstag. It is said that in few of the larger cities of Germany the Communists had as little influence as in Lübeck and that Hitler liked to avoid the city : in both cases, Leber's influence can be seen. With his powerful figure and impressive head Leber came to be associated with the workers of this city, although he did not speak their dialect. In the written and spoken word he liked to be direct, penetrating and sharp. "Lukewarmness and good-naturedness are greater crimes in politics than flagrant injustice. They make one the laughing stock of one's opponents and the object of ridicule amongst the indifferent," he once said. He could also always find the telling phrase when discussing grave issues, as well as in the cut-and-thrust of extempore speaking. "His capacity for mental concentration", writes one who often saw Leber, "the quickness of his mind, and his ability to get to the heart of a question were amazing. This came out in the debates in the Lübeck Bürgerschaft in which his opponents had no easy task. To all interruptions he reacted with great humour and hit the nail on the head, as no one else could. He often had the whole house laughing on his side."[41] He complained about German parliaments, saying : "Today one party speaker after another comes forward with a thick, carefully prepared manuscript which he has put

85

together and sifted some days before by the sweat of his brow, and reads it in a well-modulated voice. He does not care what the previous speaker has said, and what comes after him is of no account. . . . The suggestion has been made that, by way of a radical reform, the rostrum in the Reichstag should simply be removed and the members compelled to stand up from their seats, and to speak more or less spontaneously on the British pattern. But how many members can do that in Germany?. . . Go to the popular assemblies and look at the speakers—they even read their jokes! Even a speaker like Westarp has a pile of papers in front of him! . . . The art of speaking is the art of projecting and defending a conviction spontaneously. May our schools and colleges learn, at last, from the British college clubs! For the man, who can speak spontaneously, can also learn quickly to think spontaneously!"[42]

It was characteristic of Leber, who knew he was hasty and impatient, that he could write of himself : "There are not many people of my profession who take so much trouble about speaking even a few words before others. I have often spent hours and days trying to find a single formula. I take comfort from the fact that I have regarded my most important task very seriously and that here I have been strict, very strict, with myself."

From Leber's leader articles, speeches and notes in his Lübeck years, which have been collected in the book *Ein Mann Geht Seinen Weg* (*A Man Goes On His Way*), we can read twelve years of German history in extracts. We can see how a politician like him, who combined passion and judgement, as Max Weber demanded, saw these times and tried to shape them by his judgements and through his actions. He never failed to devote himself wholeheartedly to the cause and never learned fear—even in the "years of struggle". Once at a meeting, when all his people had been driven out of the hall by superior force and he was left to defend himself alone on the speaker's platform, he broke a chair and fought his way out, almost unharmed, brandishing a chair leg in each hand against the frenzied mob. In a speech of his in 1929 it is reported that he said : "Goebbels, the clown of the Reichstag, said he wanted to argue with everyone except me. He behaves like those boxers at fairs who challenge everyone to fight, but decline the rigours of a fight, when someone looks dangerous."[43]

In the first night after Hitler had been appointed Reich Chancellor Leber was attacked. Some of his people rushed to his assistance and one of the assailants was killed. After a short while Leber was released but he turned down two opportunities to flee. In spite of warnings, he went to the Reichstag on March 23, was handcuffed before the entrance and taken away. The court recognized

86

that in the incident of January 30 Leber had acted in self-defence, but he was sentenced to several years' imprisonment by the judge for being the "spiritual author" of the events which had unleashed this kind of fighting. He wrote on August 31, 1933, the day he was sentenced, a characteristic letter:

"The finality of the heavy sentence, imposed on me this morning, is the lowest point in the crisis curve of my life in recent years. Now it can go no lower. I do not need to tell you that the sentence does not frighten me. From now on, things can only get better and, you will see, they *will* get better. The monstrous catastrophe, which has befallen our ideas and faith, had, in all circumstances, to be a catastrophe of the same personal consequence and inexorability.... As for the attitude of individuals to the catastrophe, there are three courses open to those involved. First, death, or extinction, in order to bridge with this voluntary, or involuntary, sacrifice of life, the abyss which separates the past from what the future holds spiritually, so at least to leave behind the light of the sacrificial flame on the other side. The second course leads, ever deeper and deeper, through the abyss of fate and then reveals the upward path: this demands that one should prove oneself and directly accept what fate brings. The third course would be that of withdrawal, the escape from decision and fate, to avoid and, as it were, to snap one's fingers at it, in the vague hope of some lucky development which would right everything.... Decisions are less free than we believe. They are the result of character and are determined in the human breast by the stars that shine or do not shine within it.... At all events, in spite of thousands of considerations of every kind, I have at last, consciously or unconsciously, taken the path lighted up for me by the star within me. I had to take the way to the end; otherwise nothing would have happened, and nothing would have counted in my sight. And, while I write this, a great inner contentment passes through me, a calm and unshakable firmness. I know that I have now only one great duty: not to lose faith in myself. No fate is quite pointless. Each has its laws and purposes. And only he is quite deserted and lost, who does not understand the language of this fate, because he is too poor to be able to receive it, because nowhere in his soul has he the ear to listen to the distant murmurings of the deep springs which determine his fate. I have told you once in a letter that there is really only one justification for life, and that is that it should be illumined by a profound passion and strength of feeling, which lights up all the avenues and rooms of the inner being, and thus becomes reality. One's attitude to existence is conditioned entirely by such strength. Whoever does not possess it, does not live, or lives no differently from the worm, which has the same life even when it is cut in two. . . . I go to my prison with my head high and without spiritual depression. In these last few days, I have drawn up an account and entered the individual items, without hypocrisy and without self-deception. And the result? There is quite a big task to be fulfilled—for myself, for you, and for an ideal. I do not know whether I shall prove myself in this task. But I hope the experience I now have to endure will prepare me for it."[44]

The peculiar severity of his detention; the obvious malice with which they tried to break him; his being put in a punishment squad, which was under particularly harsh orders, all showed that Leber was regarded as an especially dangerous and hated opponent. According to reports, he was held for a year in a dark cell : "In this year they refused him everything in his bare and airless cell—bed, chair, table, employment, exercise and warm food. Even when the temperature was 18 degrees below freezing point he lay on the bare floor at night without blanket, straw, or coat."[45]

Although so persecuted, he wrote with self-possession : "History passes pitiless judgements. Let not the present rulers, who think their hour has come, be deceived on this point. But let us leave all this to take its course, and should it not be granted to me to reach my harbour again, then I can still recall Nietzsche's proud words : 'Perish in the act. . . . I know no better purpose in life than to squander a great soul and to perish for a great and impossible cause.' Greet my friends and tell them that I am in good heart, that my sense of humour is unimpaired and that it is an honour for me to sit in my cell, so long as I cannot be a free man."[46]

We read in other letters from prison : "Basically life is only beautiful because of its tensions. Among my early 'beautiful memories', I recall only a few rare occasions that give me a joy as tense as that which fills me now in the expectation of your visit. And if that week passes as quickly as the present, then my life will be almost perfect. When the inspector passed through the cell yesterday and asked me how I was, I could only answer him that I was spending a happy time under his authority. He thought I was mad. But this inner calm and concentration, induced by the narrowness of the cell, actually creates conditions which make for more spiritual happiness than the frantic haste of the free life. . . . Here the heart is put into the scale without any make-weight. Here it is quite impossible to delude oneself about anything, for one is always alone within four bare walls which, in the long months, become as bright as the mirror of the soul."[47]

Leber spoke meaningfully, and unmoved by his own suffering, of the world's failure to understand what was really happening : "How little the outside world understands of events is shown by its reaction to the so-called atrocity propaganda. As if the decisive thing were the fact that Jews, Social Democrats and priests are maltreated, or as if it greatly signified that I, or hundreds or thousands, are in prison! That is not very important. Not even for us, the main victims. We put up with four years of war with the same equanimity with which we now let this revolution pass over us. The only important thing is the fate of the people in the context of freedom and humanity. Only that interests us. . . ."

Contrary to expectation, Leber was released, on May 5, 1937. He passed through the Sachsenhausen camp gate spiritually and physically unbroken. A friend visited him on the second day of his freedom. After several hours' talk, he said : "Here I came to inform you about political life in Germany today. But you camp-inmates seem to know more than us. Your contacts are better than ours."[48] Leber spoke of his experience in camp and added : "So long as I was able to keep my self-respect, I did not give up hope. But when they tried to make me do what was unworthy, I knew I would not survive the humiliation. What I had to endure for my refusal, I regarded almost as a relief."[49]

Leber became a coal merchant in Berlin. The minute office building of the firm in Schöneberg, of which he was part owner, became a meeting place for friends and, until the 20th July, a conspirators' hearth with flaming coals! From 1938 onwards, Leber skilfully evaded those who were instructed to keep watch on him, and he regularly met Leuschner and Mierendorff. At the beginning of the war, he travelled to General Falkenhausen in Dresden, who was known to be a determined opponent of Hitler amongst the Generals. While it was Leuschner's aim to create new bridges and build up contacts, Leber took up the challenge and infused an elemental, radiant strength into the rising spirit of revolt against Hitler.

We see evidence of Leber's instinct for politics, his original and passionate political energy, which wanted to grasp and mould the outside world, in those reflections which he wrote secretly during the first months of his arrest in 1933 under the title : "Thoughts on the Banning of German Social Democracy".[50] Some of his party friends—Socialists and sociologists—intoxicated themselves with clever theories of the stages of historical development and thought they could grasp the future in their thinking. Leber relegated all these ideas to the second rank, and put in the forefront the great, creative figures who appear where no clever man suspects them and who aspire to the highest "even at the risk of perishing in some

89

impossible cause". We sketch out here a few features of the memorandum, which reveal Leber's attitude to the state and which, in spite of the outdated theme, still provide today an impressive political testament. He rejected the confused conception of the rule of the masses, beyond which the old social democracy was unable to proceed, and set against all doctrine the individual "fighting personalities", who alone could accomplish constructive work in the state. Above all, he was concerned with the problem of selection and with the establishment of real contact between the leaders and the led. He insisted that the leaders, as representatives of the people, should govern, as long as they were in office, and should use their authority in accordance with their own will and conscience. They must have the opportunity and the power to give real form to their visions and intentions. He thought it should be possible for them, as educators of their people, to pursue policies, in certain circumstances, which were against the wishes of the people. But when the current of popular confidence took another direction, then the leaders must accept the consequences. There was no rule of the people without authority, and no real freedom without a strong régime. The parties Leber saw as "stone weights in the scales of the government's existence" which registered the people's mood. To base the election of the people's representatives on proportional lists, as the Weimar constitution did, was, he thought, a very great evil. Then, instead of some hundreds of persons elected by popular confidence, came the rule of the organizations and the secretariats. The real wielders of power exercised their influence behind closed conference doors, anonymously and without visible responsibility. The people did not know, and did not see enough of, the men, to whom they were asked to accord trust and full powers. Such a rule by party bureaucracies, whatever its complexion, only promoted general mediocrity in the long run. Democracy demanded a sense of responsibility and self-discipline from everyone who wanted his place in the machinery of state. Extremism and lack of responsibility in attitudes and criticism were incompatible with that external order, which guaranteed everyone so large a measure of individual freedom of opinion. A strong state authority must here impose limits to popular thought but in a form which gave every citizen the feeling of the maximum personal freedom.

On another occasion Leber once said "There are all sorts of ways of frightening people. But love grows only from humanity and justice. And, without love, there can be no patriotism. I sometimes wonder whether I shall ever see a Fatherland based on justice."[51]

For his own, and all parties, in 1928, and later, he said; "You have got to govern or be in clear opposition. Not to be ready to assume responsibility for the one or to have the courage for the other, but to prefer a policy of sailing with the wind rather than one of taking a firm line, is the biggest mistake a political party can make."

In 1924 he complained about those who did not wholeheartedly support the new state: "We had the power, we had behind us the power of this endless procession of men, we had behind us the gigantic power of the trade unions! And yet what has become of the German Republic? What is still left of it for us? Why has it all passed away and evaporated? Why must we now make such efforts to save what remains? The talk is now about the forms of the Republic and the colours of the Republic! No one speaks any more of the spirit of the Republic. . . . Let us recall Danton's words to his executioner: 'Show my head to the people and shout: Long Live the Republic!' And let us recall the last words of Danton on the scaffold: 'We went our way, although we knew that we could only look forward to blood and death. For this reason we succeeded. Future ages will speak of Danton although he is now dragged to the scaffold like a criminal. My children will become orphans today, but they will be proud of their father. Long live the Republic!' "

In his speeches on behalf of the Reichswehr, which earned him the reputation of a right-wing Socialist and some enmity in the ranks of his own party, there is a passage, in which he compared the present with the time of the wars of liberation: "Stein, Gneisenau, and Scharnhorst were convinced that the traditions of monarchy had collapsed and that, instead, new impulses for the state had to be found in the young Third Estate, in the citizen's consciousness of freedom. What was the result? They were described as a clique of rebels and were insulted as wretched demagogues. Nevertheless, they went their way. A man like Scharnhorst was abused as a 'pitiful peasant lout'. When Scharnhorst was given the task of reorganizing the state, which had collapsed, of creating a new basis for the old feudal state, he appealed to the new estate, the Third Estate. Is it not time that the Reichswehr remembered that we have a similar situation in the structure of our state today? Why has no Scharnhorst hit on the idea that the new state, the power of the state, the army, must now appeal to the Fourth Estate, to create a new basis for the state and its power?"

In a speech in the Reichstag in March 1931 Leber rejected a moral distinction, with which the French Minister of War had thwarted Franco-German understanding: "Monsieur Maginot has enough classical education to know Tacitus. . . . He says in one place: 'These two great peoples are separated by a great river, by a chain of mountains and by mutual fear of each other.' Is it not time to replace the mutual distrust between these two civilized European nations with a policy of trust, a policy of peace? A greater authority on the history and science of war than M. Maginot dealt with this in some detail in his political testament. That was Napoleon. He wrote : 'It is time that the kings of Europe came to agreement; for in this continent there are no more grounds for sustaining hate between the nations.'

"I believe these words of Napoleon apply also to republican 'kings'. The French parliamentary report carries the brief comment in connection with M. Maginot's speech : 'Applause from the Right'. It is high time that the statesmen of both countries began to conduct policies and to make speeches, so that the parliamentary reports no longer talk of 'applause from the right' but of 'applause from the intelligent and reasonable'."

Reading Leber's speeches we are sometimes struck by his Napoleonic brevity. And we may recall Theodor Heuss's words : "Although he had no love for the barrack square, he had fundamentally a soldierly nature and even laughed, without any attempt to deny it, when I once told him that he, the Alsatian, was made of the stuff out of which Napoleon moulded his Marshals. The heavy, broad-shouldered body with its impressive, bold head could easily lead one to make such a comparison."[52]

Although Leber was just as uncompromising as the other Socialists in his attitude to the forces of capitalism and their liberal, political outlook, he differed from most of the men in his party, as far as we can see, in this : he clearly saw, at a very early stage, the future course and the aggressive nature of Soviet power and, as a German workers' leader, resolutely opposed it from within. As early as 1924 he took the view that the German Communist Party must be banned. But he regarded such a ban as a minor external measure which must be followed by an entirely new internal bid to prevent what would otherwise be inevitable radicalization, that is to say, the enslavement of Germans. He recognized early on—more so than most bourgeois politicians—that the masses were ready for a change. He felt he must contribute all in his power to seeing that the workers' movement emerged from its old-fashioned, obstinate class quarrels and its negative discontent, and become a militant organization, not for its own advantage but to mould the new all-embracing state with a faith that appealed to the heart. There is evidence that Leber went a long way on this path in opposing false ideas in his own party. In small things and great, he built the foundations of a social state with an unswerving sense of judgement. But Hitler overtook him and, by casting him into prison, sought to paralyse his influence, because he was a dangerous opponent to have at large. We can imagine how such a man, regardless of the hate which raged within him, followed the fate of the country and how, behind the barbed wire of his camp, continued to develop his ideas.

The war, with its threatening catastrophe and its decisions in East and West, created a new situation, where Leber's advice was especially sought by the other men of the Resistance. Leber always insisted that the front in the East must be held, and he approved of the attempt to approach the governments of the West with a view to opening their eyes to the danger which a Russian advance into German territory would have for all. He himself took an important part in drafting the messages which were sent to the other side and, as long as he was free, he was at the centre of those who were both planning and taking action.

We have a report which shows the man in the last period of his imprisonment.[53] In the small prison yard the prisoners took their daily silent walk, at a distance from each other and closely guarded, so that conversation was impossible. With Leber were the Socialists, Maass, Haubach and Dahrendorf. The survivor, Dahrendorf, writes : "We breathed the air in deeply. We looked for the glance of a friend. We suspected our fate—it was a competition with death, Theo Haubach once called to me. That thought moved me, and perhaps it showed in my bearing and face. Julius Leber looked at me searchingly, as we passed at a distance. His body straightened, and his face seemed to say in a spirit of friendship and comfort : 'Don't let go : keep your bearing!' " Dahrendorf also writes : "I often saw him, deep in thought, serious and very determined, the epitome of strength and unbroken spirit. Julius Leber knew what was in store for him. For four nights in August 1944 he was questioned. Terrible were the tortures with which they tried to force him to make a statement about the preparations for the 20th July. Julius Leber bore them and was silent. Then they told him that the Gestapo had arrested his wife and two children in order to break his resistance. Only those who knew Leber can realize how profoundly this news affected him. But he did not betray how shaken he was. Then, with great self-control, he made a statement which, in all essentials, related only to himself."

On October 24, 1944, Leber was condemned to death by the People's Court under the presidency of Freisler for betraying his country abroad, for helping the enemy and for high treason to the state.[54] But the sentence was not immediately carried out. In the following months of imprisonment Leber became very thin and acquired an almost youthful agility. The red scars on his wrists he dismissed with a gesture of indifference when someone referred to them. He eagerly listened to news of the war and of the advance of the foreign armies. But he was ready each day to be summoned to death. "The loneliness of the cell is not an oppressive burden," Leber wrote at this time. "I often think of the monks in the Middle Ages, who withdrew from the world in order to devote themselves to their thoughts within four small walls. Many of them found great happiness and deepest fulfilment in it. . . . I have thought a lot in the last weeks and have become convinced that the love, of which the human soul is capable and which is stronger than anything else in man and in the world, proves that this soul must be of divine origin. Divine origin also means immortal."[55]

On January 5, 1945, Julius Leber was executed. That he was wholly devoted to Germany, his Fatherland, is attested also by those who have praised his work for larger international organizations. "For so good and just a cause the sacrifice of one's life is an appropriate price. We have done what lay in our power. It is not our fault that all turned out like this and not otherwise."[56] Those were the words which Leber sent as a last message to his friends.

VI. THE KREISAU CIRCLE

FROM Reichwein and Haubach who had earlier had close contact with the "religious socialists" around Paul Tillich, a bridge led to a more complex circle of men centred on the unmistakably towering figure of the young Count von Moltke. In this loose, rather personal study group, which sprang to life secretly during the war and which was later named the *Kreisau circle* after Moltke's Silesian property, we have the most impressive example of the unifying force of a movement against Hitler. Here young noblemen, originally from the conservative Right, and administrators of old estates, who were also active as lawyers and state officials, met representatives of the two Christian faiths and former workers' leaders for the purpose of open discussions. Together, without cloaking their differences and often to the accompaniment of serious quarrels, they laid the basis for a community to cope with the future emergency. They were not so much concerned with devising an ideal state to take the place of the existing one, as with preparing a sober and responsible body of men and equipping them to cope with the German collapse. This moment they considered would inevitably come; indeed, they welcomed it as providing the best chance for Germany's future. Important voices among them rejected any idea of an assassination right up to 1944 : they felt that Hitler's rule could only disappear in defeat and had to be patiently borne to the end. Only in this way could the necessary purification and conversion be achieved.[1] If Hitler were killed while he was still powerful, they felt it would create amongst the Germans the legend of a great man betrayed and he would return to cast an even more fateful shadow over Germany's future. When the agony turned out to be longer, and even more terrible, than had been expected, when the sacrifices and destruction constantly grew, even members of the Kreisau circle came to believe that it was wrong to wait any longer, and agreements were made with the men of the Stauffenberg circle. The courts were of the opinion that only Count Yorck, Trott zu Solz and Father Delp were directly involved in the conspiracy; and they were sentenced accordingly. The others were sentenced to death or to imprisonment for ideas and talk hostile to the state or for failing to report subversive activities.

Helmuth James von *Moltke*, the great-grand-nephew of the Marshal of Bismarck's time, had an English mother who was the daughter of a Chief Justice of the Court of the Union of South

95

Africa in the Transvaal. Moltke belonged to the generation whose important adolescent years were passed in the decade after the First World War : he was born in 1906. During his training to be a judge, unemployment, the critical alienation of large sections of the nation from the life of the state and the threatening eruption of uncontrollable forces were a decisive experience. This had the effect of suppressing the gayer and more nonchalant side of his nature; it gave the impression of a rather cool, proud and inflexible mind and, in spite of his kindness to others, it imparted a trace of sadness and remoteness, which some of his entourage found deeply moving.[2] Before 1933 Moltke had tried, with some men of the former youth movement, to bring together young people of all classes in the Löwenberg work camps. He hoped that by sharing their work and leisure they would become aware of their duties and their community of interest in the social state. To Moltke, who lived in Eastern Germany after Versailles, the problem of the coexistence of peoples seemed one of particular urgency. Here, between Breslau and Königsberg, Germans and non-Germans were compelled to live together in such a way that emphasis on national sovereignty, in the tradition of the nineteenth century, would always lead to trouble, never to peace. So attempts were made to separate national from political factors and, through cultural autonomy, to make coexistence possible for the minorities. These ideas led automatically—and particularly for someone like the young Moltke—from small things to great. It was proposed to reject the essentially outmoded views of nationality among the European peoples, and to evoke and fashion an entirely different conception of solidarity. This seemed all the more urgent because of the new threats before which frontier disputes between the countries of Europe seemed senseless and self-destructive. Moltke had formed such ideas before Hitler's accession to power in Germany. But what then happened under Hitler on the road to a great European war gave a new and almost consuming passion to these ideas. When Moltke had succeeded in reclaiming the Kreisau property, which had been lost as a result of inflation—it was an inheritance from the Marshal—he divided up a large part of his land into independent peasant lots and was not deterred by the criticism voiced by the large land-owners. As an expert in international law in Berlin, he was able by his defence to help many victims of persecution to get themselves and their property over the German frontiers. During the war Moltke served as an adviser in international law with the OKW in Berlin and had close contacts with the Abwehr. He opposed the maltreatment of prisoners of war and the foreign civilian population, particularly in occupied Russia; he saved Jews in Denmark by giving forewarning of an intended move against them; and, thanks to his legal objections, ensured that a plan was abandoned to shoot as traitors all Frenchmen who were found fighting on the allied side when the Germans occupied Tunisia.[3] Moltke was deprived of his freedom in January 1944 and was executed after a year in gaol. At first, the only charge brought against him was that he had warned a friend, who had later been seized by the Gestapo; then, after the attempted assassination in July, his name was found amongst the papers of the conspirators, and the Kreisau contacts, although misrepresented and incompletely understood, became subjects for the attention of the fanatical Freisler. "Count Helmuth von Moltke was the most outstanding personality that I met in those years," one report says.[4] He was unusually lean, tall and dark. The owner of the Kreisau property near Schweidnitz in Silesia did not answer the usual description of a Silesian Junker. Highly educated, and mentally agile, he possessed the social attributes of an English nobleman. In fact, he had practised as an English barrister in London. He made at first a cool, impersonal impression, as if he wished to subordinate all personal considerations to the facts of the case. That was the Moltke taciturnity, a family inheritance. He was silent, not in the sense of having few words, but about everything which was not strictly relevant. . . . The imperturbability of the Count in his miserable humiliation and his smile—ironic and courteous—which could encourage his fellow-prisoners and drive his non-German guards to anger and despair, are attested by reports. They allow us to guess something of the anguish which Moltke endured at this time and which led him out of his melancholy absorption with death to the open heights of grateful Christian affirmation. The day after the state prosecutor had demanded the death sentence for him, Moltke was brought back to the court with the others and heard the sentence. They were not able to prove his participation in the planned coup d'état; at the most, they could show that he failed to report what he knew. But his thoughts called for the death sentence : "We have only thought. . . . We have had nothing to do with practical operations. We are being executed because we *thought* together," Moltke wrote in his moving farewell letter to his wife.[5] One of those whose life was spared tells of the journey home in the green prisoners' car : he had a "wonderful talk" with him about Peter Yorck, who had been executed months before and was particularly close to Moltke, as well as about the others. He adds : "Moltke was happy and had an infectious warmth and sense of comradeship."

The Moltkes had various ties of friendship and marriage with the family of Count Peter *Yorck von Wartenburg* which likewise came from Silesia. The family of Yorcks, which Marshal Yorck von Wartenburg made famous, later became especially known for its interest in philosophy and literature. Peter Yorck's grandfather had had a learned correspondence with Dilthey and, as a result of his intense love of books, had built up a large library. This included, in particular, treasures of German romantic and classical literature, as well as the first edition of Luther's works which, it is said, was always brought out at reading sessions.[6] Peter Yorck was born in 1904 and grew up as one of a large family in a home stamped by his father's influence. Like the somewhat younger Moltke, he turned to the study of law and political science and worked until the war in state posts : for a long time he was personal assistant to the Price Commissioner and Gauleiter Joseph Wagner. At the same time he administered his property in Kauern in Silesia, to which he was very attached. He served with the troops as a tank officer in the Polish campaign; and from 1942 onwards he served with the Eastern Department of the Military Economics Office and made many important contacts because he spent those years in Berlin and also had opportunities to travel. Both in the country and his official position, in the world of books and of men, Yorck had his own careful and tactful way of going about things. This gave the somewhat softly spoken and reserved heir of a great name a more effective and far-reaching influence than a casual contact might have suspected.[7] Even in his last letter just before his death, he was preoccupied with the planting in his garden at home. He derived much experience from the practical work of agriculture.[8] What Moltke perhaps discussed, in more theoretical terms, Yorck was able to clothe with flesh and blood; for he could contribute his own experiences and took, for his starting-point, life as it is lived in terms of men and opportunities. On such occasions the often almost wistful man thawed and engaged in argument as master and friend in the social life he enjoyed. Moltke, thanks to his Anglo-Saxon blood and knowledge of Anglo-Saxon life, was more concerned with the wider world in which he saw Germany wilfully taking no part. Yorck, however, felt passionately as a German; and the alien domination at home and abroad, which was robbing the Germans of their ideals and their soul, made him, as he once jokingly called himself, with a touch of melancholy, "an unhappy rebel in the cause of freedom, human dignity and right". Thus the two friends complemented each other. Moltke was all attack, intellect and sharpness : Yorck, on the other hand, was tempered warmth, common-sense, ability to inspire confidence and to win over with urbanity.

From January 1944 onwards Stauffenberg had several talks with Yorck, his cousin.[9] He told him about the plan for a coup d'état and secured his agreement to co-operate. Yorck's name appears on one of the surviving lists as State Secretary to the Vice-Chancellor. On 20th July he was at hand in the Bendlerstrasse. One of his duties was to install the officers who were to ensure the continued administration in the highest Reich offices. He later destroyed the written instructions on this subject.[10] When he was questioned, he stressed particularly, among the reasons for his break with the Nazi state, the way the law had been devalued, as was to be seen in the extermination measures against the Jews and in the behaviour of the Germans in the occupied territories. He was one of the first accused to come before the People's Court and he was executed on August 8, 1944, having been sentenced by Freisler before the details of the Kreisau circle and Yorck's many-sided role as intermediary became known.

He said in his last letter that from death he hoped for expiation, expiation also "for what is the responsibility of us all. May the remoteness from God of our days be reduced a mite by it." He continued : "Also, for my part, I die a death for the Fatherland. If it looks very inglorious, even shameful, I go this last way upright and unbowed and I hope that you will not see in it arrogance or blindness, but faithfulness unto death. We wanted to light the torch of life : now a sea of flames surrounds us, what a fire !"[11]

A third individual, a friend of Moltke and Yorck, who often came to the talks in Moltke's home in the Derfflingerstrasse, was Dr Eugen *Gerstenmaier*. Shortly before, he had established himself as a lecturer in systematic theology at Berlin University, but was relieved of his post because of "public criticism of National Socialism". As a close colleague of Bishop Wurm of Württemberg, he then entered the church's Foreign Relations Office, where, from the beginning of the war, he had the task of cultivating relations between the German Evangelical Church and foreign churches. During the war he had the special duty of looking after the interests of the foreign workers in the Reich, some of whom had come to work voluntarily and some under duress. He was to concern himself with individual cases and to alleviate the lot of all in a country engaged in a pitiless war. This job required not so much an introverted theologian, as a militant and active man, who thought it the church's duty to intervene against injustice, insults and oppression. Those who had anything to do with the young *Konsistorialrat* did not have the impression of meeting a pastor. It was understandable that he seemed an "outsider" to some of his theological colleagues— and not only to the Quietists whom he shocked. After his intermediate examination, he had spent eight years in industry. Then he caught up on his examinations and was involved in philosophical and theological studies, especially Kant and Hegel, until quite different experiences during the war and contact with the Kreisau circle and the men of the 20th July led him away from academic niceties to prove his abilities in a more active field. His impetuous manner and his sometimes drastic Swabian nature tended to have, it is said, an animating effect on discussions. In January 1943,[12] there was an important meeting to try to bring about a compromise between the Kreisau circle and Goerdeler, at which Ulrich von Hassell was also present. After Goerdeler had sought to bridge the differences in a rather conciliatory spirit, Gerstenmaier made himself the frank and lucid spokesman of the social programme of the younger members. True to his character, he came out clearly on Stauffenberg's side and used his position to take part in the preparations for the revolt. Although his contact with Goerdeler, his presence in the Bendlerstrasse on the 20th July and his close relations with Moltke were known, he was able to defend himself successfully before the People's Court. The death penalty demanded by the prosecution was transformed into seven years' imprisonment. Gerstenmaier was one of the few from the Moltke circle to survive the critical period. He himself has told of his experiences : he had to shackle madmen at his side and to unload the dead. After the war, he came to prominence as the Head of the Evangelical Relief Organization and, like Bishop Wurm, made a courageous protest against the injustice to which Germany was then subjected.

A year after the end of the war, he wrote : "The greatest and most costly attempt of the Germans to help themselves . . . that was the theme of the organized resistance in all groups and circles of the German Opposition movement, which found its most visible, but not its only, expression in the 20th July 1944. It was never a question of imposing one party programme in preference to another, of ambition, or spoils, but always of saving Germany from the claws of a system and a group of men, who, by the most brutal and cunning use of power, had resorted to criminal acts and megalomania. I say that not to deal an extra kick to the dead lions and panthers, but because I think that no one is inwardly obliged to remain loyal to Hitler and his system for Germany's sake. Whatever may be said against the conditions in which we are at present compelled to live, we must fairly recognize that they are the consequences of Hitler's policy. Dazzled by the idea of National Socialism, disgusted by the quarrels of the parties and incomprehensibly blind to what stood behind the man—all in all, foolishly but fairly, the German people gave Hitler a chance. And, perhaps with misgivings, but without resistance, the majority surrendered to him. That is our fault, our great fault. Thereafter, it was beyond the power of an individual, indeed beyond the power of a group of men determined to do everything possible, to break the bonds into which Hitler's total system of terror had been able to cast us. Only an outsider or dilettante can hold that against us, who has himself never truly risked all. . . . When we, a small group of lost men, were waiting on the evening of the 20th July 1944 in the OKH in the Bendlerstrasse in Berlin for the last assault of the advancing SS units, knowing full well that this last attempt of the Germans to help themselves had failed, I heard neither Stauffenberg nor anyone else complain. We had tried to do what we thought we owed Germany and the world before God and our conscience; we had done it with the means which we were able to get hold of, after careful planning and endless efforts. The rest was in God's hands. 'In the end one can do no more than die for the cause,' said Ulrich Wilhelm Count Schwerin-Schwanenfeld, as we were overpowered, handcuffed to each other, and led away."[13]

Another similar confession of faith is taken from an appeal which Gerstenmaier wrote for the sixth anniversary of the 20th July : "The attempted coup d'état of the 20th July 1944, in all its stages, in each chapter of its preparations, and in the will and mind of all its participants, had always one sole aim. The aim was to save Germany. Doubtless there were, and are, people for whom this aim was not, and is not, particularly sympathetic. It may be connected with the fact that, abroad, the attempted coup d'état found approval only slowly and with great reservations. In so far as this concerns the former enemies of Germany, we can understand this attitude. For the 20th July was neither planned nor risked for the sake of the Allies' war aims. Nor was it undertaken for the sake of this or that political doctrine. It was planned and risked solely to save Germany, to save her blood and territory, to save her freedom and her ultimate dignity before the judgement of world history. The attempt may have failed—the prospects were always 2 : 1 against success—but it had to be risked. For this attempt was the last opportunity to spill Germany's blood in order to free her from wicked tyranny. It was also an attempt to snatch millions of oppressed and insulted people of many European nations from the terrible authority of the murderers and criminals of Buchenwald and Auschwitz, the very murderers who had burdened the name of Germany with shame. This attempt had to be made, whatever the risk. At the same time, it was necessary to save the Reich from the collapse which would cost millions their homes and their lives."[14]

As President of the German Bundestag, Gerstenmaier once wrote later : "It must also be said that the Kreisau circle had left behind not only Hitler's dictatorship, but also the Weimar democracy. In their concepts they had not foreseen that the old forms—curiously enough at the behest of the Russians—would again be bestowed upon us by the occupation powers in the autumn of 1945. . . . I hardly dare suggest what they would have thought of the lively activities in and between our parties today. We cannot, therefore, seriously ask whether the men of the Kreisau circle under Moltke and Mierendorff would be popular today; but we cannot for a moment doubt that they would be urgently needed. They are needed—for the problem that faced them is the still unresolved one of European democracy."

Another Protestant who co-operated was Pastor Harald *Pölchau*. He was the chaplain in the prison at Tegel, through which many political prisoners passed. At great danger to himself, he was constantly able to establish contacts between the prisoners and their families. It was his fate to be with his own friends in the weeks or hours before their violent deaths—friends with whom, when they were still free, he had shared ideas of building a new order. In a similar office and with similar devotion, the Catholic priest, *Buchholz*, worked in Plötzensee, where the majority of those sentenced for the 20th July were executed.

Moltke thought it also necessary to reach agreement with the Catholics. At the beginning of 1942 we know he approached the Jesuits in Munich and asked for a sociologist with whom he could discuss the question of the workers and the planning of a Christian social order. With the approval, and at the wish of the provincial superior, Father *Roesch*, Father Alfred *Delp* reported to him. He was in future to have very active and friendly relations with him and Gerstenmaier, and together with them and Haubach, he gave his stamp to the Kreisau entourage.

Delp, who was born in 1907, was a year younger than Moltke and the same age as Stauffenberg. During his years at the Gymnasium he had gone over to the Catholic Church and at nineteen he had joined the Jesuit Order. Later he was one of the most acute and imaginative members of the staff of "Stimmen der Zeit", the organ of the Jesuits; and, thanks to his persuasive speaking, his social work and his writings,[15] he acquired a large circle of friends in the parish of St. George in Munich. What is remarkable about this young Jesuit priest is that he did not believe, as many of his kind, that the Church was still one of the leading forces and powers of humanity.[16] Rather, he saw it as the task of those few, who were still truly filled with God, to win back the world from quite other paths by the strength of their mission.

He thought the churches themselves had played their part in producing the man of the masses, collectivism and forms of dictatorship. He said: "It remains to be seen whether the churches can once again produce a creative type of man who is imbued with divine strength.

"That a type of man has been produced, before whom, we might say, even the spirit of God stands perplexed and finds no access, because everything is distorted by bourgeois security and safeguards, need not be regarded merely as a phenomenon of the past. This type still exists. This type has laid down the path along which we are moving. Basically, this type has not been superseded, because all counter-movements do not in fact reject it, but only the exclusion of a part of humanity from the possibilities of this type. Most modern movements set out to make it possible for those, who are still excluded, to live as good a bourgeois life as possible. The Church has played its part in promoting and distorting bourgeois man. And the bourgeois man has not failed to spread himself in the Church and to plant the ideals of human weakness inside the Church. . . .

"Contemporary man is in general not merely godless. He has fallen into a way of life in which he is incapable of receiving God. . . . In what does this incapacity lie? It lies in the stunting of certain human organs so that they can no longer perform their normal function. Similarly, in the structure and form of human life which make too great demands on man and do not allow him to be himself. . . . What is to be done? There are three possibilities. Proclaim God's order and await everything from its new recognition; or bring man back to order and await healthy conditions, as a result of his own recovery; or bring the outer world back to order and await the success of man. We must do all three. The revolution of the twentieth century needs at last its theme and the possibility of creating a new and durable background for human beings."

There is an impressive memorandum written by Delp on New Year's Eve 1944–45. In this he looked out at the world with lively interest from the loneliness of his cell. It shows how the talks of the Kreisau circle were conducted on a level which extended beyond Germany itself. Here are some passages :

"It is difficult to summarize in a few words the year which ends tonight. It was many-sided. And what its real splendour and message is, I do not yet know.

"In general, it has not brought a decision. The suffering, the hardship and the weight of destiny and events have become more intense than anyone would ever have imagined. The world lies in ruins. Everyone holds on desperately to the scraps he still has at hand, because they are the last things man can call his own. Hardly anyone has yet an idea of the connections between the scene of ruins and corpses in which we live and the collapse and destruction of the spiritual world. And if so, then they are stated merely as a fact to be registered, not to frighten, or to serve as a lesson for a new start. To such an extent are we already nihilized and bolshevized! It is fortunate that vital interests still justify opposition to the horde from the steppes. For the West would no longer survive this alliance with nihilism.

"Of the old civilized nations of the West, Portugal slumbers like Sleeping Beauty. What happens there will be the result of others' decisions. Spain is being thrown into the crucible again, because she wrongly survived the last test and solved dishonestly the problem set her. Today there are no feudal possibilities, not even in the masquerade of popular tribunes. There are only social possibilities and these Spain has missed. To her bitter cost and to the bitter cost of the Church which shares her guilt.... Russia cannot be fathomed. Visit Russia. Is Bolshevism the prelude to a Russian imperialism of the most measureless kind? When the steppe dreams, it does so on the grand scale and without moderation. Or does Bolshevism need the national characteristics and interests of Russia? The Slavs can destroy, annihilate and carry off so much. But they cannot yet lead and build. France is, as always, perplexed when the Western arch becomes insecure or collapses. She needs a genuine dialogue with Germany, otherwise she is extreme and immoderate, almost like Russia. But she uses reason and, is, therefore, more dangerous. That England's time is drawing to a close I also gradually believe. The British are no longer bold enough and no longer spiritual enough. The philosophy of utility has infected their essence and paralysed the muscles of the heart. They still have great memories, even great traditions and bearing, but the men . . . ? Germany is fighting with all her heart for survival. One thing is certain. There can be no Europe without Germany and without Germany taking a leading part. But a Germany in which the original Western streams of Christianity, the Germanic (not the Teutonic) world and antiquity, no longer flow in their purity, is not Germany and is no blessing for the West. But here, too, apart from the brutal question of the outcome of the war, the question of bread and relief of need takes precedence over all deeper questions. In other words : here, too, we have the social problem.

"The prospect for the West at this turn of the year is a sad one. From two sides alien and uncomprehending forces intervene in our lives—Russia and America! . . . It remains to consider the Vatican and the Church. It will certainly be established one day in the future that the Pope has done his duty and more. . . . This shows the changed situation : amongst the great partners of the bloody conflict there is no one who fundamentally listens to the Church. We have over-estimated the political mechanism of the Church and let

104

it run on at a time when it lacked the spiritual fuel. . . . First, this war which, it seems, no one side can now win, must be brought to its terrible end. The problem facing the countries, as well as the European continent, is, to put it crudely, man in a three-fold sense. How to house and feed him; how to employ him so that he can feed himself—the economic and social revival; and how he can be brought to face himself—the spiritual and religious awakening. Those are the problems of the Continent, they are the problems of the individual states and nations. And they—and not some stylistic reforms —are the problems of the Church. If these three problems are solved without us, or against us, then this part of the world is lost to the Church, even if in all churches the altars are turned round and the Gregorian chant is sung in all parishes."

Delp stood with Moltke and Gerstenmaier and three other confederates before the People's Judge. "Our case turned on the destruction of Moltke and myself. Everything else was of secondary importance," Delp wrote. While the court based the death sentence on Moltke merely on his offence of having failed to report information, it also accepted high treason in the case of Delp. It had been discovered that the young Jesuit father had provided his house in Munich for a secret discussion, although he himself had taken part only at the beginning, and that in June 1944 he had been in Bamberg for a long talk with Count Stauffenberg.[17] It was the impression of others that Delp accepted the sentence of high treason not without satisfaction, since he was not to be allowed to live; just, as at the Bamberg meeting, he had come out unreservedly for action and in support of Stauffenberg. When the tension relaxed after the announcement of the sentence, Delp once again became his agile, eloquent and witty self, and on the melancholy return journey he beguiled the company with his laughter. Moltke was executed on January 23, just two weeks after his sentence, together with Haubach, who had also been sentenced in the meantime. Delp followed on February 2. On his way to execution, Delp called with a smile to the prison chaplain, who greeted him : "In a few minutes I shall know more than you."[18] In his last notes he wrote : "It is a time for sowing, not for harvest. God sows : one day He will also reap the harvest. One thing I want to try to do : at least, to fall as fertile and healthy seed on the soil. One day others ought to be able to live better and more happily. I ask my friends not to mourn, but to pray for me and to help me, as long as I need help. And to be sure afterwards that I was sacrificed, not killed. I did not think this would be my path. My sails wanted to stand tautly before the wind : my ship wanted to set out on a great voyage and the flags and pennants were to fly proudly and high in every storm. But, perhaps, they would have become the wrong flags, perhaps it would have been the wrong course or the wrong freight for the ship and false booty. I do not know. Nor do I want to console myself with a cheap disparagement of life and earthly things. Quite honestly and simply : I should like to live on and, more than ever now, continue to work and proclaim many new words and values which I have only lately discovered. But it has turned out otherwise. It remains for me to thank many men for their loyalty, kindness, and love : the Order and the Brothers in it, who provided me with a beautiful and genuine field of spiritual life; and the many good people I was able to meet. Those whom I have in mind will know. Alas, my friends, to think the hour never struck and the day never dawned that would have permitted us freely and openly to associate ourselves with the Word and the work for which we were being spiritually prepared. Remain true to the silent command which always called us. Continue to love this people, now spiritually so forsaken, betrayed and helpless—and, basically, so lonely and confused, despite all the parades and declamatory self-assurance. If, by reason of one man's existence, there is a little more love and kindness, a little more light and truth in the world, then this life has had a purpose. . . . So farewell. My crime is that I had faith in Germany—a faith that looked beyond a possible interim period of suffering and darkness; that I did not believe in that naïve and arrogant trinity of pride and force (NSDAP = Third Reich = German people); and that I did this as a Catholic Christian and a Jesuit. These are the values for which I stand here on the edge of the abyss and must await for him to cast me down : Germany, beyond today, as something new and real; Christianity and the Church as the secret longing and the invigorating and healing force of this country and people; the Order as the home of a type of men who are hated because they are not understood or known in their free allegiance, or because they are feared as a reproach and a challenge by others in their own arrogant, pathetic lack of freedom."

The agreement of the Jesuit provincial superior, Father Roesch, and his visit to Kreisau were not concealed from the Gestapo. He, too, whose humane moderation and spiritual superiority guided and influenced the younger ones, was brought before the court,[19] as an active opponent of Hitler and held under arrest for a long time. He escaped with his life. At the first Kreisau meeting, after Steltzer had spoken on relations between church and state, Roesch gave an address on the "Catholic world". He was sent to a "conclave" with Steltzer in order to draft that part of the memorandum which deals with church and culture. He was also present at the second meeting. At the third he was represented by Delp.

Lawyers and officials, who took part, also derived their attitude and inspiration from their church. For instance, Paulus *van Husen*, a Westphalian Catholic, a former member of the Mixed Commission in Upper Silesia and later *Oberverwaltungsgerichtsrat*, an expert in international law and a very active helper in Moltke's endeavours. Amongst the Kreisau documents, the surviving draft on the treatment of violators of the law is largely his work. Another was Hans *Lukaschek*, a Silesian, and a former member of the Centre Party, who had been with van Husen in the Mixed Commission and had been until 1933 Oberpräsident of his home province. Yet another was Dr Theodor *Steltzer*, who came from a Prussian judge's family in Holstein. Steltzer had studied political science before the First World War and, what was unusual for a man of his origins, had sought contacts in socialist circles. In the war, after a severe wound, he served as a General Staff officer in the Supreme Army Command on the staff of General Gröner. Later, he returned as *Landrat* to his home in Holstein and, until he was relieved of his post in 1933, devoted himself to educational work in the district and local community. Later he was concerned with the ecumenical movement. In the Second World War he was a transport officer in Norway and became acquainted with Bishop Berggrav, the Head of the Church, and a powerful opponent of Hitler. Steltzer himself tried to alleviate the hard fate of the Norwegians and to do all in his power to prevent what he regarded as breaches of international law by the occupation power. As a participant in the Kreisau meetings, he took a lively part in the discussions and the preparations of the memoranda. The People's Court sentenced him to death; but his execution was deferred, thanks to the intervention of someone close to Himmler, and he thus escaped with his life. Steltzer was, of all the Kreisau participants, the most vigorous opponent of assassination and the use of force.[20]

Other men, who took part in an advisory capacity in the work of the Kreisau circle, should be mentioned here : Hans *Peters*, professor of constitutional law at Breslau University; Dietrich von *Trotha*, the lawyer, a cousin of Moltke; and Horst von *Einsiedel*, the sociologist who, with Moltke, founded the Löwenberg work camps. He died later in Russian captivity.

Particular mention should be made of two young diplomats, who were friends and who had close relations with Yorck and Moltke and supplied the circle with up-to-date information about events abroad. Legationsrat Hans-Bernd von *Haeften* was born in 1905, a member of an old Lower Rhenish family.[21] His mother was a von Brauchitsch who, it is said, was of a more resolute spirit than her brother, the Field-Marshal. A tradition of Protestant piety, which went beyond Sunday church-going and influenced his every action, formed the background to his adolescence and retained its hold on his adult life. More than any of his friends, who all felt themselves much more torn by the spiritual struggle, he seemed to found his life on this solid moral basis. Before 1933 he had been an exchange student at Oxford. Later he worked under Ambassador von Papen in Vienna, and, after that, he spent several years as a cultural adviser in Bucharest. It is significant that, during this work in Rumania, he made close contact with the Roman Church and was not afraid of being called a "clerical". He tried to ally himself with the forces of good wherever he found them. During the war he was in the Foreign Office in Berlin and devoted himself, often to the limit of his physical powers, to his growing two-fold task : to serve his Fatherland honestly in the Foreign Office and, at the same time, to work with the circle of conspirators for a change of régime. In this spirit of revolt, in his occasionally passionate impatience, in his vigilant attitude amid the tumult of external events and in his readiness to help where he was needed, Haeften showed a strength which a stranger would not have suspected, who had only seen the kind and obliging manners of the man. He was a tall, good-looking man, anxious to do what was good and right, almost too conscious of his own failings and of the sins of the world. "His firmness of character, the clear path of his life and his wise head and heart"[22] gave him his standing among his friends. In the months before the 20th July Haeften was in Berlin. His part in the planning of the revolt could not be disguised and quickly led to his arrest.

Legationsrat Adam von *Trott zu Solz*, who was born in 1909, spent an eventful but sheltered youth in a pleasant valley of Hesse-Kassel. Later, with the maturity of manhood, he lived a life of adventure and acquired a wide knowledge of the modern world. As he wrote in one of his last letters, he believed that he inherited from his father, who had been a high official in the Prussian civil service, his deep love of Germany which never failed to call him back from the wider world and the favours and esteem which it offered him.[23] To his mother, who was particularly close to him, he owed his insatiable curiosity, his restlessness, and a strong sense of being born to a high destiny. The days and nights, which he had spent as a boy together with a friend in the "Trott's Wood", left their impact in later years. And although, when among quite different people abroad, he went about as one of them and spoke their language, he still kept his roots in Germany and identified himself with one of Jean Paul's figures in their "still inviolate valleys and woods".[24]

Trott was tall and was a conspicuous figure in the street. His

108

English friends found "a sense of power in his manner", and they jokingly complained that he had no right "to look so imposing" as he did. But, in fact, they recognized that, with all the strength which his appearance lent him, he was completely without arrogance; and they expressed surprise at how easily and naturally he made friends with all classes in England and Germany, and how devoted children were to him from the first contact. Even as a boy, people had been struck by his lively concern for the situation of others, by the way he knew how to develop his own qualities and by that easy, mutual friendliness with people who were otherwise reserved. A later friend writes about this quality : "Love is the only great and disarming standard which all those, who are capable of it and blessed with it, can bring to bear against the theories of hate. Adam Trott possessed this love. His nature radiated it. It was this which enabled him to recognize qualities in others and for others to recognize his own. This mitigated all feelings of weakness and inferiority in the people with whom he came into contact."[25]

Trott studied law and philosophy. At twenty he produced a thesis on "Hegel's philosophy of the state and international law". He wrote in a notebook at this time : "Reject all influences which do not aid or support creative purposes"; "Is not the terrible pressure of life today explained by the fact that its great spiritual forces are not being utilized and that, therefore, they are not consciously part of the whole?"[26]

A friend describes his bohemian bachelor household.[27] When one entered there were the hairbrush and the open volumes of Karl Marx and Hölderlin together on the table; and soon one was talking about revolt and a change of régime in the Fatherland. From 1931 to 1933 Adam Trott was a Rhodes Scholar at Oxford. British reports say that he was able, as few young Germans were, to enter fully into the life of Oxford but, at the same time, to remain, recognizably and completely German—for which he was respected. He made many friendships, some of which were vividly remembered after his death.[28] In the years between, in which Trott did the necessary training in German courts, he constantly felt inhibited, because the new régime implied he was "politically and personally unsuitable".[29] But he had new opportunities to study outside Germany. He embarked on this period, six months in the USA and fourteen months in China, with the intention of returning to Germany, in spite of all the advice he received to the contrary. He wanted to be on the spot with all his accumulation of experience when the great showdown came.[30] In December 1938 he was back again. His friends noticed how the East had matured him, had given him a deep calm and the strength to act. And he now made it his aim to secure an important position in the régime which he so much hated. But, on his return home, his immediate concern was to try, in every possible way, to prevent the outbreak of war. Before the fighting destroyed all hopes, he visited London three times in 1939 and, as we have already indicated, tried in talks with important people like Lord Lothian and Lord Halifax to get a clear statement from Britain which, it was thought, would curb Hitler's desire for war.[31] A member of the British Parliament put forward Trott's views; but those in power went other ways. The report of his impressions of his British talks, which the German Foreign Office asked him to submit, was drafted by Trott with considerable self-control, in Hitler's own idiom. But it was also drafted deliberately as a warning of Britain's determination and as a warning against war. At this time he was already in touch with Beck, Goerdeler, Schacht and Leuschner.

In October 1939, as soon as the war in Poland was over, Trott, with the authorization of the Foreign Office, accepted a repeated telegraphic invitation to attend a conference of the Institute of Pacific Relations in the USA. He got the last ship from Genoa which, thanks to its courageous captain, was able to break the British blockade near Gibraltar. In New York he met a large circle of people, thanks to introductions from his Oxford friends, from Hjalmar Schacht, and from Dr Brüning. With Dr Brüning, who was in America, he had long talks. He spoke twice to the Assistant Secretary of State, Messersmith, and got a memorandum drawn up by the German–American, Paul Scheffer, on which he himself had worked, through to the Secretary of State, Cordell Hull, and, it seems, also to Roosevelt.[32] According to F. Morley, the aim of the memorandum was "to ensure that the idea of a war of annihilation did not drive all those into the arms of National Socialism who had begun to come together to overthrow Hitler". For this purpose a peace programme was demanded, in which Germany, freed of Hitler, would have to make sacrifices and provide guarantees, but in which the Allies would not make excessive demands, e.g. they would not deprive Germany of territory she had in 1933. Trott warned against a premature peace with the existing German Government; for nothing seemed more fatal to him than a second Munich. In the final paragraphs of the memorandum, which he added himself, he advocated an alliance with "the constructive elements in those countries actually disturbing the peace" and the assumption of joint responsibility for the Western world, which would produce a new realistic social order, and end wars among its members. It seems that President Roosevelt was impressed and that Trott was able to dispel distrust in himself and inspire confidence wherever he went. But, thanks not least to the manner of his journey at the outbreak of the war, there was a suspicion that he was a Nazi agent. This was seized on by Judge Felix Frankfurter of the Supreme Court, a close adviser of Roosevelt and behind whom there were influential industrial interests. Frankfurter, incidentally, knew Trott from Oxford days. So Trott's mission failed. Friends tried to persuade him to stay in the USA but his reply was : "It is clear to me that, failing sure signs of probable liquidation, my place in the coming days is at home."³³ At the beginning of 1940, he returned to Germany via Japan, Peking, and Siberia. Before he got back, his mother received a letter from Peking from a friend who took a fatherly interest in Trott. The friend wrote : "It is difficult for me to tell you how wonderful this short time together again was in so grave an hour. ... Adam's character struck me as clear and refined, strong but remote from all violence, kind without weakness, matured to manliness, and purified by two years of profound experiences of the world...."³⁴ Trott attributed a severe case of jaundice, with which he returned home, to his anguish and disappointment about the war which no political consideration could now check.

Only then did he succeed in entering the Foreign Office in Berlin. He remained there the four years until his arrest and was entrusted with various tasks in the Cultural Affairs Department.³⁵ During this period, Trott tried, in as far as the war allowed it and at increasing risk to himself, to maintain the contacts of his Kreisau friends and the growing circle of the German Resistance movement at home with the neutral and occupied countries of the Continent. He also sought to protect people liable to persecution in the occupied countries, and, by providing active proof that there was another spirit than that of narrow hatred in Germany, to promote the feeling of a common European solidarity in this time of crisis. Although he was careful not to violate military security, he often tried himself, or through others, to get his views through to responsible people on the enemy's side. Today we know of some of his writings, which seem to have been drafted with hindsight : for instance, the memorandum which Visser't Hooft, Secretary-General of the Ecumenical Council of the Church, took in April 1942 from Geneva to Sir Stafford Cripps in England;³⁶ the message which was brought to the American, A. W. Dulles, in Berne, in 1943; the "Reply to the Six Peace Points of the American Churches" in November 1943; and a second message to Dulles in April 1944. His memorandum of 1944, which he himself regarded as his testament after the 20th July, "Germany Between East and West", has not yet been found. Presumably, it was available to his judges. Trott said of it to one of his friends after the 20th July : "You will see that everything will turn out as we predicted."[37]

In his office, his close friends were Hans von Haeften, and Alexander Werth. He had a particularly fruitful association with Julius Leber. Trott experienced a powerful new impulse, which even left a physical mark, "a great feeling of human fulfilment", as a report says, when at the beginning of 1944 he got to know Count Stauffenberg on Leber's recommendation. The two quickly became friends in an extraordinary way. Stauffenberg frequently came to Trott's house "Am wilden Eber". The memorandum "Germany Between East and West", which Trott drafted for him, greatly impressed Stauffenberg, who based his own ideas on it. Adam Trott never for a moment hesitated to take, from his own deep conviction, the same path which he saw Stauffenberg's active genius had taken. In Trott's person Stauffenberg found a powerful and passionate helper, to whom nature, in addition to his height, his powerful forehead and his dark, shaggy eyebrows over blue, deep-set eyes, gave not only gravity but also the joy of youthful laughter and the gift of effective "laconic eloquence", as his friends called it. When someone pointed out that he was conspiring in the ante-room of the friend and loyal colleague of the Führer, he remarked that it was safest to nest in the pockets of the scarecrow. To the question what was State Secretary Keppler like, he answered : "He has the scepticism of a cunning peasant crossed with sublime faith in the Führer." And in reply to the question how he felt about the war, he said he was "pale and calm".[38]

In Verona, in May 1944, Trott had again to choose whether he should go over to the other side in Rome which was then about to fall. There was much to be said for it because he expected his arrest each day. A duty trip offered him an easy way of going over without attracting attention. But he wanted to go back to Berlin, where he knew his friends were hard-pressed. He wanted to be at hand when Stauffenberg needed him. "This friendship," a report at this time on Trott concludes "must—in spite of all opposition and prospects—have revived in him positive hopes for the future. It was like a last gift from heaven which wanted to grant this earthly fulfilment to his extraordinary and prematurely ended life."[39] Friends remember him in his last months. Intellect, imagination and will-power, which had earlier pulled him in different directions, seemed now "illumined, purified and concentrated to make him a formidable influence".... All this was reflected in his face which seemed free of the fear of those weeks and almost handsomer, as though no blow could affect it which was not the result of a higher dispensation.

After the 20th July Trott knew he would be arrested in Berlin. Different people competed to help him to escape at risk to themselves. He remained. "I feel like a tree without branches," he said on July 21 to a cousin, who knew everything, on a walk through the Grunewald. He was arrested on July 25 and on August 14 he stood with Haeften before the People's Court. Haeften was executed on the following day, but Trott was held back another twelve days because it was hoped he would make a statement. Shortly before his death, he said farewell to his wife and daughter on a small prison form. Mindful of his daughters, he wrote : "Today there is a clear 'Peking sky' and the trees are rustling. Teach our dear sweet little ones to understand these signs from God—and the profounder ones—not only with thankfulness, but also with an active and valiant spirit."[40]

Other participants in Moltke's and Yorck's discussions have been mentioned already. It will cause no surprise to find them active in this circle and on friendly terms. Adolf Reichwein, whom Moltke knew from the days of the Silesian work camps; Theo Haubach and Carlo Mierendorff, both introduced by Reichwein; and Hermann Maass, associated with the others through the former youth movement. Mierendorff, in particular, it seems, gave their circle its strongest stamp as a political force. He had gone to the greatest pains to find, and engage, suitable men all over the Reich and to undertake the practical planning. His death and Moltke's arrest, a few weeks later, put an end to the joint work of the Kreisau circle. Even if some differences of opinion were never bridged, it is remarkable how far the men of the Church were able to accept the views of the Socialists, and how far, again, the Socialists found thesmelves impelled to underwrite a Christian basis for the state. As far as can be seen, Julius Leber only came into close contact with Moltke towards the end of 1943. Apparently, Mierendorff and the others kept him informed of what was going on. He generally approved; but he did not want to bind himself to the political principles which had been worked out and which he occasionally said were too theoretical.

To complete the picture of the Kreisau discussion circle, we should remember the wives. As hostesses, they created a congenial atmosphere; but they also met the men on their own level, and contributed their own ideas and experiences, as did Countess Freya Moltke, and Countess Marion Yorck.

Moltke's plan was to ask specialists to consider particular fields of the future state administration, to discuss the results of their deliberation in a small circle, and then to put them before a plenary meeting. From this would emerge the principles, which were to be laid before the groups round Beck, Goerdeler, and other responsible conspirators to form the basis of a coherent policy. As a further step, it was thought necessary to find the men for the individual provinces (Länder) and to provide them with political instructions. The boundaries of these provinces were newly fixed in accordance with the plans of Haushofer and Schulenburg.[41] These men were to take over important posts in the transition period, such as those of provincial commissioner and trade union or church representative.

Security required work to be done in small groups and contact to be maintained with the centre through a spokesman. Only the name Moltke was the common watchword for all participants; and Berlin and Munich were the most frequent meeting places. When the plans were elaborated and it became necessary to get a common view of the matters which had been explored separately, Moltke invited the participants to three memorable week-end meetings on his estate near Schweidnitz (Whitsun 1942, October 1942 and Whitsun 1943). Half of the participants of these meetings lost their lives. The atmosphere of the meetings can still be recaptured from the accounts of the survivors. Special approaches and exits were devised and those not invited were kept away. Some, who met in the castle, saw each other for the first time. But, thanks to the sponsorship of the host, there was complete mutual trust. And everyone, whether from the East or West, South German, landowner, priest, lawyer or workers' leader, teacher or diplomat, came prepared to consider the opinion of others and to banish that old German evil, unbending egotism, in order to serve the common good, and to decide on measures to deal with the coming collapse. They were little concerned with victory or defeat : at these meetings they sought to find out the reasons for the collapse of man and society, which had made the rise of Hitler possible, and to discover what could help people to stand firm in such a period of confusion. The talks were conducted at this level. Pressed on all sides as they were by terrible new experiences each day, they lost no time in complaint and accusation. They always tried to look at the spread of calculating violence and cold-blooded destruction, which appeared to seize men, in their hundreds of thousands, not merely as the consequence of Hitler and his devotees, but as a deeper Mene Tekel, or writing on the wall : evidence of a sickness which, originating in age-old roots, had now broken out in the German body and confounded its neighbours. Moltke and his friends felt acutely the disgrace and responsibility with which the German name was now burdened. They bore it without any benevolent indulgence towards themselves, and did not look abroad and say "The others are no better". But it was clear to them that similar symptoms were to be seen in other peoples; and in their contacts abroad they sought by their admissions, their entreaties and their readiness to help, to build for the emergency a community of "enlightened" people who, rising above national hatred and ordinary resentments, would be moved in their own hearts by the same call in adversity. If others thought about the goal of destroying Hitler's rule, the Kreisau circle saw the real task beginning after that, in the spiritual struggle which faced the victors and the defeated. The later warning phrase about the "Hitler in ourselves"[42] might have been uttered in the Kreisau circle.

They discussed political questions as part of the great spiritual problem of their generation. The Socialists saw practical tasks to be solved : new roots for the industrial working masses alienated from the land; the need to master a tyrannical technology; the nationalization of the basic industries; wresting power from those international economic and capitalist forces interested in war; a new integration of the individual in the social state; and a new responsibility for the individual between the extremes of compulsion and freedom. These sort of questions were placed in the Kreisau circle, particularly under the influence of Moltke and Delp, in a larger spiritual context and were discussed in great depth, irrespective of what had to be done immediately.

The political questions formed part of the great spiritual problem of their generation. Counsel was sought in Nietzsche and Burckhardt, as well as in contemporary thinkers like Ortega y Gasset and Bernanos. The question was asked : how could man, who went through the nineteenth century and who realized undreamed-of possibilities, at the cost of his inner life becoming cold, arid and vulgar, find his way back to a state where he could achieve a sense of moderation. How could man free himself from the lie of existence, which enjoined him not to care about uniting the most incompatible things but avidly to increase the poison which killed him? How could man re-establish contact with the vital forces in the nation, state and nature; how could he re-establish the contact with God as it existed, for instance, in the Christian age and made possible a happy, all-embracing community? When they looked at the present, they saw a common fate : hardly anywhere was a spiritual, integrated life possible. In public affairs from East to West, openly or covertly, there was a power struggle in the name of the independent state, or of an independent economy in league with independent research. They felt that this unrestrained world was increasingly heading for collapse and would soon, with the lately discovered secrets, be in a position to destroy all physical life or to damage it to the marrow and to depopulate the earth.

As a result of these reflections, Europe and the West acquired for those gathered in Kreisau a new and important meaning and imposed obligations, before which national destinies paled into insignificance. They saw that anarchy in natural science and technology, as well as in social affairs, originated in Europe. And they saw Europe, because of its heritage, faced with the great task of promoting a conversion. Yorck spoke of the dividing line before the People's Judge : "The totalitarian claim of the state on the citizen with its elimination of his religious and moral responsibility to God." In the principles worked out by the Kreisau circle "the divine order" was emphatically made the basis of standards between men and nations. Only a state constructed in this way could, they thought, ensure the necessary freedom of conscience, the human dignity, the protection of the family, and the proper development of the community. Moltke attached importance to his affirmation that pure moral principles did not suffice, as he had once believed. Only belief in God provided the strength to dare and to sacrifice everything.

The rebuilding of Germany, as part of a new European democracy, it was thought, should rest both on the Christian churches, which were also expected to contribute to a "renewal", and on workers who attached importance to their freedom. But it was necessary to begin modestly : it seemed to Moltke and his friends that the key to the whole question lay in the faith of those who had been "enlightened" by the crisis, who had consciously gone through the fire and were ready to make sacrifices for the common cause. And Moltke proved that he lived according to this principle.

Moltke particularly cultivated contacts with England and sought to establish with his friends there the kind of community of thought and action he aimed at (see the important letter to Lionel Curtis of 1942).[43] Other members of the circle were in touch with like-minded people in other countries. And there were hopes that it would be possible to raise a common "Resistance movement" to the level where it could ignore meaningless frontiers and become a sort of order of enlightened persons who could be identified by their actions.

Of course, it was anticipated that there might be difficulties because it was precisely Germans who were calling for such an association. But Moltke and, with him, some others of his circle, did not shy away from the full consequences of such an attitude. And for this they have been severely criticized by their own people and outsiders. He confessed even to foreign friends that he wanted victory for the other side and accepted suffering and defeat for his own country for the sake of a necessary transformation. From the beginning Moltke rejected Hitler. He was convinced that the new régime worked for the Devil, even if it always seemed to deny this in its pronouncements, and sometimes by its measures made one think that it really wanted to achieve a desirable break-through. Right from the start of the war, he regarded a victory for Hitler as unthinkable and a "New Europe" created and controlled by him just as alien and repugnant as, for instance, a Europe over-run by America or Russia.

In their discussion about the future form of the state the men of Kreisau agreed in rejecting every form of monopoly or state capitalism, whether in authoritarian or liberal guise. Likewise, they seemed to agree that Germany could not take over a form of democracy which had been developed elsewhere. They thought they ought not to tie themselves politically to anything more than the easily recognizable "natural organizations" of the local community (*Gemeinde*) and district (*Kreis*). Proceeding cautiously from here on the principle of self-government, in what was really an unpolitical country, they hoped to create a new sense of participation in community life and a new civic feeling—a "grass-roots democracy", as it is called in the English-speaking world.

Apparently only two examples of the Kreisau memoranda have survived. The more complete of the two, parts of which survived under a rainwater butt in Kreisau castle, has now been published.[44] Dated August 9, 1943, it contains drafts, which were elaborated in the following year: "First Instructions to the Provincial Commissioners (*Landesverweser*); "Principles of the New Order" dealing with the reconstruction of the Reich as well as questions affecting the church, education and the economy; directives on the "Punishment of Violators of the Law" with special "Advice for Cases involving the Punishment of Violators of the Law by the International Community"; and a memorandum signed by Moltke on the results of the first talks in May 1942, which dealt mainly with the church, schools, and technical colleges. The "Instructions to the Provincial Commissioners" assumed "that parts of the province are militarily occupied or separated, or that there is even no government of the German Reich or at least that it is not in a position to give binding orders". It went on : "It is vitally necessary that, in such circumstances, responsible leaders in the provinces and parts of provinces should act in unison and in harmony on basic questions, without being able to secure formal agreement with each other or to establish contact. In this way the inner unity of the German provinces as a national cultural entity would be maintained and strengthened."

Contrary to other interpretations, Gerstenmaier thinks the documents, to be completely understood, assumed a successful coup d'état, which really the Kreisau circle always had in mind. But he adds : "Nevertheless, this consideration shows that the Kreisau circle itself was concerned almost exclusively with the political, cultural, economic and legal problems with which a new German government would be faced after Hitler's disappearance. Military matters were not their speciality. They were neither army leaders nor did they have any organized power. Their field was that of ideas; their task was to draw up a new state order based on the rule of law; their intention was to overcome the ideology of the totalitarian state; and their aim was to build up Germany in the spirit of Christianity and social justice and to incorporate it into a united Europe."[45]

Here is a brief summary of the recommendations of the Kreisau circle, as they are known, from documents or oral communication :

Man stood above the state. Respect for man as an individual with responsibility towards himself and God must influence and limit all demands of the state. Through Christian piety this respect for conscience and the dignity of fellow-men could still be founded in the hearts of men, lies and hatred overcome and an impulse given to purpose and order, without which every society must seem barren, coercive and extortionate. If the churches were to succeed in their work of transformation, they must return to their old, common faith and abandon rigidity. They had the comprehensive task of leading and persuading men spontaneously to respect and love each other. But in order not to debase the word "Christian", it was not to appear in any government plan.

The rigid system of a highly centralized, all-powerful authority was at this time as great an evil as a Germany divided into small, independent units with all the physical and spiritual limitations that led to. The provinces should have about three to five million inhabitants. Their boundaries, could, with minor alterations, coincide with the Military Districts of the Reich. Prussia would disappear among the new provinces. The weight of political life would be in the provinces which already formed, or could become, an agricultural, economic and cultural unity. At their head there would be a Provincial Commissioner; the Governor (*Landeshauptmann*) would head the government with ministers for special fields; and a provincial parliament and upper house (*Landesrat*) would be at their side in an advisory capacity.

Together the provinces would form the Reich, the Federal State. This would consist of a Reich Commissioner (Reichsverweser), a Reich Lower House (Reichstag), and a Reich Upper House (*Reichs-*

rat). Special principles were laid down for election procedure from local government to the Reich Commissioner. The Reich would be responsible for foreign affairs, would supervise customs and the economy, would organize communications and ensure the defence of the country. The schools would be "Christian" schools with religious instruction in both confessions as a compulsory subject and, when possible, undertaken by clergymen. *Hochschulen* (technical colleges) were to be distinct from the Reich universities. The latter were seats of universal research and learning which required evidence of study at a classical Gymnasium or a completed course at a Hochschule. They themselves would award the master's degree and, like a college, would have their members, teaching staff and students, on the same premises. The old school books were to be withdrawn at once and, until new ones were available, instruction was to be undertaken temporarily without books. The danger of trying to give instruction which was too "modern" or too "practical" must be recognized, because, in this way, too much stress was put on the training of man for the technical world of today. Internally, there must be courage to advance towards a form of socialism which was genuine and not merely a superficial show. It was appreciated that success would depend on the extent to which the example of voluntary limitation amongst the rich was effective ("Great possessions mean more responsibility rather than more privilege.") The outward forms accorded with the suggestions of the Socialists with which the men of the church agreed almost without amendment; nationalization of the basic industries, that is to say, mining, the iron and steel industry, the chemical and power industries and, if possible, also insurance. There would be effective co-responsibility for the individual in the factory; the trade unions would be restored as distinct factory unions, and ties with the factory and the land would be promoted by the provision of housing estates, etc.

The judicial system would be given back its independent status. There were to be independent judges not subject to dismissal who, as a result of their special selection and salaries, would enjoy a respected position, as in England. All police actions were to be subject to the jurisdiction of the proper administrative court. Men who supported Hitler were to vacate senior posts. But no one was to be persecuted because he was a member of the Nazi Party. But whoever had committed crimes or violated the law, at home or abroad, was to be judged in German courts or, if this were not possible, in an international court in which there should be three judges of the victorious powers, two from neutral countries and one German judge.

Just as the province was subordinated to the Reich, so the Reich, faced as it would be with great tasks and dangers, would, in future, need an international community transcending individual states. This was not to remain a mere slogan. As soon as the free consent of all the participating nations was assured "the spokesmen of this order must have the right to demand from every individual obedience and respect, even, if necessary, willingness to sacrifice life and property for the highest political authority of the international community."

In their common search for ways to prevent disaster, the men of the Kreisau circle did not stand still, however one-sided they were thought. They looked everywhere, particularly in the church and in the workers' movement, to find men who thought like themselves and to form larger associations. This was the case especially with Moltke, Mierendorff and Delp.

Delp, it is known, worked unremittingly from autumn 1942 onwards to creat contacts with the movement of Catholic clubs, particularly the workers' associations (through the editor Nikolaus *Gross*, President *Müller*, and Bernhard *Letterhaus*, all of whom died as the result of the 20th July.[46] And Moltke and Mierendorff prepared the way for talks with the Catholic bishops. In Bavaria Delp succeeded in getting entry into a circle of men who, ever since the first catastrophic winter of the Russian campaign, were looking for a way out of the crisis[47] and whom he now brought into contact with the aims of the Kreisau circle. At the centre of this group were the former Bavarian Minister to the Reich Government, Colonel Franz *Sperr* and Dr Eduard *Hamm*, once Reich Economics Minister and then until 1933 President of the German Industrial and Trade Association—names which, in earlier years, were to be met in Ulrich von Hassell's confidential entourage. Other members were the lawyer Dr Franz *Reisert*, who belonged to a very active group in Augsburg, Prince *Fugger-Glött*, Lieutenant-Colonel Rudolf *Giehrl* and Otto *Gessler*, Reich Defence Minister 1920–28. Colonel-General Franz *Halder* was also one of those in the know. At the end of 1942 Moltke put forward his views and won support, once an assurance was given that in a future settlement Bavaria would not be divided up and would have the same degree of independence as in Bismarck's Reich. Crown Prince Ruprecht, Prince Fugger, or even Halder were named as possible choices for the post of Bavarian Provincial Commissioner. The orders issued for the 20th July appointed Gessler Political Representative. Sperr was executed after the 20th July because his and Delp's direct connections with Stauffenberg had become known. Hamm anticipated the fate which threatened him; he committed suicide in prison by leaping to his death.[48]

Moltke was not able to form any closer ties with Goerdeler and his circle than those which resulted from their common opposition to Hitler. Moltke did not like Goerdeler's political activities (he once referred to "chancy, conspiratorial methods"). He thought his ideas too workaday and parliamentary and, particularly in the social field, they seemed to him to be more the result of concessions than of a revolutionary impulse towards "renewal".[49] He had frequent exchanges with Popitz, who was sympathetic to Moltke's conception of socialism. With the military centre of the Resistance in Berlin there was a good deal of close contact, for example, through Counts Yorck and Schulenburg and through Trott and Schwerin.

As Steltzer shows, the political work of the Moltke circle ceased with Moltke's arrest in January 1944. We cannot say today what actual progress was made with the formation of the "leadership circles" in the provinces. All that can be said is that information about all the people prepared to co-operate was passed on to Stauffenberg; that the majority were known to him and put their services at his disposal.

Whether, judged by the post-war situation, we are disposed to see some false conclusions in the ideas of the Kreisau circle, or we regret that so little of their plans has been achieved, there is no doubt that in them the danger of the "stab in the back" has been hardly over-estimated. It is part of the history of the 20th July that even in this circle of men, in which church figures played an important role, opposition to an assassination was abandoned. Indeed, this was demanded in view of the fact that only in this way could the conscience of thousands of men be assuaged. Above all, the Kreisau circle makes clear the different conditions in which a German Resistance movement had to operate from liberation movements in other countries; what it was to love the Fatherland and to want its defeat! At all events, the subsequent preoccupation with Europe was long before ardently discussed and anticipated by Moltke and his friends. "For us," Moltke wrote to a friend in 1942, "post-war Europe is less a question of frontiers and soldiers, of top-heavy organizations and grandiose plans than the question as to how the image of man can be re-established in the hearts of our fellow-citizens."[50]

It may be said that post-war Europe was conceived and considered more far-sightedly and honourably by the Kreisau circle than by some politicians of the victorious nations, whose thoughts about the future did not go beyond Germany's unconditional surrender. If we look at the views of Trott zu Solz on politics between East and West, his objections to the "peace programme of the American churches" or Steltzer's memorandum of July 1944,[51] which was not considered by the allies; or if, recalling the long

121

series of dubious trials, we read the forward-looking directives of the Kreisau circle on the judgment of criminals, we are left with the impression of how powerless all the painfully acquired knowledge of the one side was to influence the policies of the other, and how in this matter nothing was granted either to the Germans or to their victors.

VII. INDIVIDUAL PERSONALITIES

WHEN, in the history of the 20th July, we speak of groups and circles, and even of parties, and try to place individual participants, we must remember that these classifications are of a later date. In those days it was the régime alone which held all the positions of power and ruled absolutely; one which, according to its daily pronouncements, wanted only good, did good and apparently had Providence on its side. There were no Socialists and no registered members of the "Kreisau circle". Everyone had, in some way or other, to play their part and prove day by day their useful participation in the total war. But amongst these were some who knew of each other that, behind their masks, they held quite different ideas about the state of affairs from those they had to express in public. All that was known was : one might have broken with Hitler, after at first supporting him; the other might have been seven or ten years ago, when there were still parties, a member of the *Stahlhelm* or in the Social Democrat Party in the Reichstag, a follower of Gregor Strasser, or a Catholic publisher. The present attitude of such a person could only be guessed. All who did not cling obstinately to the old had learned something over the years, perhaps re-learned something. Former allegiances meant nothing; new ones came into being as a result of contacts in daily life, or by chance encounter. The circles interlocked. Consequently later classifications have only very approximate validity and, in the case of some participants, it is impossible to place them in any category. We shall describe four such men in detail; but others could be mentioned who defy classification.

We know Count Fritz-Dietlof von der *Schulenburg* as a born "frondeur" of extraordinary pertinacity, who worked like a ferment in many circles simultaneously. He was born in 1902. His father subsequently became a General who made a name for himself as an Army Commander in the First World War. As Chief of Staff of the Army Group "Kronprinz", he was one of the few outspoken opponents of Ludendorff and his total warfare; and he tried to persuade the Army High Command to make a compromise peace in 1915–16. Fritz von der Schulenburg inherited much from his father. While his brothers were more the traditional type of officer which comes from old Prussian families, he had both the attributes of a nobleman and a restless desire to inquire into the fate of other men. After a lively student "corps" period in Göttingen and Marburg, this trait brought him increasingly into touch with social questions and occasionally gave him, during his years as a *Referendar* and *Assessor*, the reputation of being a "red Count". In the year 1932 he gave up his four years' work in Recklinghausen : during an impending crisis he had told his superior *Landrat* that he could not agree to shots being fired at German workers. He went to the office of the Oberpräsident in East Prussia. The situation there seemed to him intolerable to the point of explosion. He and his friends felt that basically a breath of fresh air and a shaft of light was needed in the whole antiquated and dessicated bureaucracy of the economic and administrative system. In 1932 he joined the Nazi Party. Although he had reservations about Hitler's person, he thought his movement, with its drive and revolutionary spirit, which widely caught the enthusiasm of the young, promised at last to get away from worn and hopeless paths. In Königsberg, Schulenburg met a circle of young people who thought on similar lines. They combined solid ability in their profession with ardent readiness to accept new ideas and they established contact with Gregor Strasser. In the stimulating atmosphere of this border city, the group had boldly anticipated developments and built up the administration and economy in the hope that there would soon be change and action throughout the Fatherland. The change came. Schulenburg became political adviser to the Oberpräsident and Head of the Personnel Office of the Gauleiter, Koch. In those days, Koch, as a thorough-going Prussian, loved simplicity or, at any rate, the appearance of simplicity and sought an agreement between the Protestant Church and the new régime.[1] But the high expectations of Schulenburg and his friends were quickly and thoroughly dashed. Corruption in the administration of the Gau became apparent. Schulenburg opposed it. He lost the battle and was posted as *Landrat* to the Samland coast by Koch who was involved in the affair; and a year and a half later, in the summer of 1937, he was forced to leave that post, too. As Landrat of Fischhausen, who governed rather than administered, he was, it is said, often draconian; but he began with himself and, after a year, achieved a situation, in which the Samland was free of debts and continued afterwards to remember him with respect and gratitude. In 1937 he was offered, and he accepted, the position of Berlin Deputy Police President. Of this he said : "I had to decide whether I should leave the service or become Hitler's Fouché : I chose the latter."[2] Schulenburg established good relations with the Police President, Count Helldorf, for many years SA leader in Berlin. This fact and Olbricht's influence later ensured that he and his police were available to co-operate on the 20th July. Because the Police President attached particular importance to representation and liaison and led an active private life, Schulenburg got the work. But this, as he had hoped, provided him with insights which he would not otherwise have had, and enabled him to find and bring together people who thought on similar lines. And, from now onwards, he worked at this with determination. He saw the Blomberg and Fritsch affairs at close quarters in the course of his duties and was active in support of Beck's plans for an uprising in the summer of 1938. In the winter 1938–39, perturbed by the persecution of the Jews and the imminence of war, he planned, with new urgency, a coup with his friend, Count Nikolaus Uexküll. They divulged their ideas to Claus Stauffenberg, who at that time was a cavalry captain in a garrison on the Rhine. With Counts Yorck and Berthold Stauffenberg and the official in the Ministry of the Interior, Otto Ehrensberger, Schulenburg worked out a draft for a new German constitution.[3]

From August 1939 until the summer of 1940 Schulenburg was Deputy, in fact acting, Oberpräsident of Upper and Lower Silesia, with a total population of 7 million. The Oberpräsident, Gauleiter Joseph Wagner, had so many other offices, that he left the government to his Deputy, to whose views he increasingly adhered. Schulenburg was devoted to the government of his province. "Silesia must be an example to others," was his motto among close friends. By this he meant that, in this instance, a German should so stand out for its legality and its law-abiding administration that it would attract all those forces in the Reich which wanted to see constructive work and were opposed to rule by force. Schulenburg faced even senior dignitaries without fear. For instance, he told a meeting of Gauleiters in Stuttgart that officials of his region who resisted the attacks of the Party with appropriate methods were certain of his special protection; and he acted in accordance with this principle.[4] When Himmler urged him personally to accept a senior rank in the SS, Schulenburg remarked that he could not reconcile this step with his Christian conscience. And when, after Poland's defeat, the number of encroachments increased in the territories which were added to Silesia, Wagner,[5] with Schulenburg's encouragement, did not hesitate to discipline those responsible. In the spring of 1940 Schulenburg was expelled from the Nazi Party as "politically unacceptable" and had to resign his office. He refused the offer of the State Secretary that he should remain with the new Oberpräsident on the grounds that he could not work under a man who had so little regard for probity, and left Silesia. He joined the Army, spent a short while in France and then from autumn 1940 was in Poland where he looked into an abyss which profoundly shocked him. As a platoon commander in an infantry company, often involved in heavy fighting, he took part in the Russian campaign. In the winter he was able to get posted for a while to the Ministry of Economics in Berlin. He had told his intimate friends that the real decision would be made at home. The next summer he was in the central sector of the Eastern front—still a Lieutenant, then guest of the staff of Army Group South, where he admired Manstein's strategy and saw the conquest of Sevastopol; and in the autumn he was in the Ministry of Food in Berlin. In the summer of 1943, he managed to get on the staff of General Unruh, whose task was to "comb through" the European theatre behind the fronts with the aim of finding personnel fit for front-line service. Schulenburg intended to use this post to serve the conspiracy. From the winter onwards he was in Berlin where at last the coup d'état was being prepared and required his presence. For him it was a time of climax which would bring either liberation or the inevitable end. Sometimes it seemed impossible to justify any longer his stay with the reserve battalion, and it must have appeared almost inexplicable, when he declined very important administrative posts—in Norway or in the Government-General of the Ukraine. In July 1944 he had to give in; and he was appointed Head of the Military Administration in Lyons. But he delayed his departure and feigned illness, in order to be in Berlin on the day of the uprising. On the evening of the 20th July he was arrested with his friends in the Bendlerstrasse and brought to trial on August 10. His proud remark before the Judge has been preserved: "We have taken this upon ourselves to save Germany from unspeakable misery. I am aware that I shall be hanged for it. But I do not regret my actions and hope that another will carry them out, at a more favourable time, to save us from chaos."[6] In a personal letter written on this day there is an echo of this: "What we did was insufficient, but, at the end, history will judge and acquit us. You know that I was inspired by patriotism." Schulenburg was executed on the same day as Berthold von Stauffenberg and his friend, Kranzfelder. He was forty-two and the two others thirty-nine and thirty-six years old.

Schulenburg was perhaps of all the men of the 20th July the one most born to be a conspirator. He was imbued with his cause and keen to act, a spectacular deceiver of all big-wigs in the Party and régime, who took refuge behind a reserved appearance and was bold in spite of a sluggish exterior. He had a fascination for the young and he himself was still full of effervescent youth. A State Secretary was once horrified that "this badly brushed and almost negligently dressed young man, totally devoid of military bearing, should be the famous Count".[7] But this Count was more of a "character" than numberless others who went about elegantly turned out and were concerned about their appearance. He was a Prussian; and had Prussian principles in his striving for just administration, spartan austerity and honest officials—above all, in the way he insisted on starting with himself. "The Fatherland was more important to him than anything else and its plight oppressed him, as if it were his own suffering."[8] He was not cut out to be a Prussian officer and attached no importance to this, although he belonged to the regiment with the Potsdam guards' tradition and had many great friends in it.[9] But he insisted on getting into the war and enjoyed the excitement and the facing of dangers with his men. This we can see in a moving tribute which he wrote for a young friend, his company commander, who was killed in action.[10] His own attitude to his men is exemplified by the farewell scene, when he was summoned home from the fighting. He rode over to the members of his platoon who were installed in a Russian house. While the men lay stretched out in the dark recesses of the room—with the Russians around the fire—he had each one come to the table in turn and talked, as is the way, jokingly and yet seriously with them, gave them brandy, and took leave of each. The soldiers were very devoted to him. When he lit a cigar at the beginning of an attack, everyone knew that he possessed the concentrated calm to lead them well. Schulenburg has finely described those moments in the experience of a soldier when he commends himself to God and accepts his fate. The way he speaks of "quiet confidence" in one of his letters is very characteristic of this inwardly brave man : "I wish to have quiet confidence in God and what He brings us, so that I accept His decision without turning a hair." He combined this "quiet confidence" with remarkable gifts for reconnaissance. It is reported that, in spite of near-sight and virtual night-blindness, he went on patrol through a forest thick with the enemy, to set an example as a platoon commander. He kept on asking the soldier with him : "I rely on you : tell me what you see !" and, from the answers of his trusty friend, was able to reconnoitre the situation safely.[11]

It was typical of him that, although he never wasted a minute, he never seemed to be outwardly in haste. Whatever he did, he did with zest—whether he was working with associates, talking, playing with children or going to bed. His friends were often surprised how little he depended on his surroundings. He could sleep, or immerse himself in books, in any situation. He commented on his Freiherr vom Stein from the running board of a vehicle and in the din of war he learned the second part of Faust by heart. Schulenburg did not have the lankiness of some of the Mecklenburgers. He was of medium height and rather slim; but he was physically adroit; a runner, rider and swimmer. Some sabre-wound scars and a flat-ended, hooked nose—the result of a sports injury and a sabre cut—gave his face an insolent and angular character, to which the monocle, usually fixed in his eye, also contributed. The very clear eyes only took on colour when he was angry or very happy. But all the more lively was the powerful and scornful tongue in conversation. Noticeable, too, were the large, delicate ears. It was not difficult for Schulenburg to act the haughty Junker and, with an almost mask-like face and outrageously tough look, to cope with insults, or annoying requests, or to quell smart opportunists. But behind this there was another Schulenburg: full of life, youthful, enthusiastic about great aims, a man who had Eichendorff's love of nature, and hated the all-devouring cities, was mindful of his neighbour's welfare and ready to share everything with him.

It is not surprising to find volumes of verse amongst this man's travelling possessions. We know, too, that he particularly loved Stefan George's poem "Der Gehenkte", and it is said that when he returned from the Crimea in August 1942 he read George's great war-poems to friends in Bucharest. Before he finished, he left the room and was later found to be in tears.

It is said that Schulenburg's way of speaking had something very distinctive about it. He expressed himself quietly and rather slowly, almost monotonously and without pathos. Sometimes his ideas seemed only to take shape in utterance; but his unadorned speech, accompanied only by a clenched, raised fist, must have had something inexplicably impressive, often spell-binding about it. Wherever Schulenburg operated he found friends, particularly amongst the younger people, who were stirred by him and who, from then onwards, stood by him and on whose co-operation he could later count. After a successful coup d'état, he hoped to give jobs to some of these, as well as to a great number of professionally able, personally reliable, non-party men, whose names he had noted on secret lists he left behind. In spite of the Judge's insulting attacks, he remained silent at his trial about names which would have shown how systematic and comprehensive his work had been. In consequence, many of these were never prosecuted.

Once his decision was taken, Schulenburg organized his official duties consistently and with expert dissimulation, in order to be of the greatest use for the uprising. Sometimes he undertook a difficult task only because he wanted to win over a certain man whom he had in mind. In such cases, it was frequently not arguments that were decisive, to which he was not sufficiently amenable,[12] but rather a kind of atmosphere, which directed him sometimes very strongly, almost like a divining rod, to certain men and groups. It is extraordinary how many men were brought together through him. There was hardly a bridge within the Resistance groups or a conspiracy formed in which "Fritzi" Schulenburg did not have a hand. He was there when Beck, Popitz, Jessen and Planck were drafting the Basic Law of the State; he made contacts with Goerdeler, who supplied him with information; he worked for Tresckow; he won over Stauffenberg; he became the latter's intermediary with Leber and the Socialists and the intermediary between Kreisau and the officers; and he maintained contact with Paris through his friend Hofacker. In doing so he did not seek any "seniority" in the conspirators' state and he was, as his relationship with Stauffenberg showed, always ready to serve the younger man, whose superior strength he was aware of, as helper and loyal supporter.

Schulenburg distrusted plans for a revolutionary reconstruction of the state. He once said that, to ensure that the state was irreproachably run, it would be sufficient that the bell of Potsdam rang in every man's heart. He judged empirically. The experiences he was able to acquire as a young man in senior administrative posts provided him with many ideas as to how certain measures could banish despotism, and a better balance could be established in relations between town and country, between local authorities and the state, and between the provinces and the Reich. The memorandum, which he worked out at the beginning of 1944 with precise details for simplifying and reconstructing the administration, has not reappeared. According to this, some fifty-eight Reich authorities were to be dissolved and their functions handed over to nine responsible ministries.[13]

He was very concerned about the flight from the land, a process which had been accelerated in Hitler's Reich, and which he saw as a symptom of man becoming absorbed in the masses. He was also concerned about the excessive growth of industry and the facelessness of the great cities and all over-centralized administrations. He considered how the rebuilding of cities should in future be controlled. He also gave thought to how, against the prevailing current of the time, it would be possible to achieve sound but limited and easily recognizable structures with clear responsibilities in the social, communal and political spheres without relapsing into an atomistic state. He cared for crafts and skills and inveighed against the anonymity of mass products. It was typical of Schulenburg that he translated his ideas into practical rules for himself: in the city, where he lived, he always frequented the same streets, bought from the same grocer and from the same paper-man, so as to get the feeling amid this urban vastness that the district had an intimate character and was not lacking in human contacts.

In one matter, Schulenburg's attitude emerges very clearly : in his ideas for a reorganization of the Reich.[14] The Basic Law of the State, which Beck and Popitz possessed, and in the preparation of which Schulenburg took part, contained a demand for the period after the coup. This read : "The inequality of the present provinces in respect of size, and economic and financial strength, as well as the lack of uniformity in the administrative structure of the various territories of the Reich, make a reorganization of the Reich essential. Prussia will complete her mission as architect of the Reich by renouncing the constitutional integration of her provinces." To provide a technical solution to the problem, Schulenburg thought it necessary to use the statistical aid and experience of the highest Reich authorities. The difficulty was that, after a great number of plans had been submitted, Hitler had forbidden further work on the problem of Reich administrative reform. But Schulenburg, who was then at the Food Ministry, got access to the Reich Office for Territorial Organization. Two of the officials employed in it, Oberregierungsräte Isenberg and Muthman, worked for some time under the eyes of their superiors, in the closest co-operation with Schulenburg and in contact with Dr Albrecht Haushofer, on principles of Reich administrative reform under the cover of "Reorganization of agricultural marketing associations". Twenty-seven kinds of administrative boundary were counted, all of which overlapped : political boundaries such as those of the Länder, the Prussian provinces, and government districts, etc.; the boundaries of the Military Districts, the railways and post office directorates, the Chambers of Commerce, the Land employment offices, the Land agricultural associations, the boundaries of the National Socialist Gaue, etc. To achieve a simpler and more manageable Reich and provincial government, it was decided, after detailed consideration, to bring together all territories into administrative units larger than the existing Gaue, subsequently to be called Reich Gaue. These would be balanced from the point of view of population distribution and density, and as regards boundaries determined by economics, by communications and as far as possible by natural factors, and the type of soil. On a "map of main centres" the Reich was divided into thirteen territories with thirteen city centres. From this map arose a new one with ten future Reich Gaue, which had the cities of Königsberg, Berlin, Breslau, Hamburg, Hanover, Leipzig, Cologne, Frankfurt, Stuttgart and Munich, as their centres (individual alternative solutions were left open). Where present, a navigable river was not regarded as a boundary but a main artery of the area. Schulenburg used the discreet assistance of the Reich Office for Territorial Organization for other tasks as well; for instance, to lay the foundations for the reconstruction of cities, for the movement of industry to bring about a sensible relationship between town and country; and for housing estates and for land reform, which was also very close to his heart.

The plans, in so far as they were not destroyed, fell into the hands of the Gestapo after the 20th July. Himmler is reported to have said that draft laws and proposals found amongst Schulenburg's possessions were such as could be put into force in a very short time and could have been substituted for the National Socialist pattern of government without difficulty. The State Secretary in the Ministry of the Interior at the time, Stuckardt, who was not one of the conspirators of the 20th July and whose place Schulenburg was to take after the coup, went further. He said repeatedly that administrative reform as planned by Schulenburg was the only possible one to restore order in the Reich in the shortest possible time.[15] This very dangerous and suspect work in Berlin ended for Schulenburg in a curious way. He was given a farewell party. And he did not know later how it had ended— usually he was never the worse for liquor. At all events, it seems, he found himself in the early morning lying across the lines of the S-Bahn (electric railway) in an outer district of Berlin which he otherwise never frequented. Railwaymen came to his aid : a train was only a few metres from him. The next morning he came back laughing, with some scratches on his face and a torn sleeve. This time matters had gone too far ! . . .

In the court's interrogation files at the end of July there is a statement of Schulenburg's that the movement, which led to the 20th July, started with the breach of February 4, 1938 (Fritsch's dismissal). He gave as his reason for participation the fact that power had become the criterion for all action in the state. The leaders, he said, had departed from the principles of simplicity and modesty which they had earlier preached. The Party's struggle against the state had broken the back of the civil service. The state had abandoned the principles of justice and had become a police state, invading every sphere of life; it paid homage to a disastrous centralism and reduced the people to masses who were ruled by force and propaganda. The state had departed from its religious basis and pursued a foreign policy which had brought the whole world against Germany. In the occupied countries a short-sighted policy of suppression and plunder had been carried out, instead of

131

winning over the subject peoples.[16] Schulenburg, as he once simply confessed, had offered to act to get rid of Hitler, but he had had no opportunity. He spent the Easter of 1944 with Stauffenberg on his country estate, Trebbow. In the weeks that followed he was at his side with advice and action. On July 15 we see him entering a friend's home "looking a little different, outwardly composed, but inwardly in great turmoil, as could be sensed from the fact that his smile disappeared more quickly than usual from his strained face, which then looked chiselled in bold ruggedness". He asked the friend to go to Frau Leber, who was lying under supervision in a hospital, with the news that they were on the track of her arrested husband. . . . The next day he came back happily with some good news. "While he spoke, he walked up and down my minute room with small, quick steps. It made me suddenly think of a cell. Then he pulled a crumpled 20 mark note from the pocket of his uniform jacket, which was never buttoned up according to regulations, and said : 'Buy roses for her with it. For you must go there again, to bring further news. Tell her I am going to France in four days and tell her also that we will do our duty. Nothing more. And be careful. You don't know what danger you could be in and I don't want to be responsible.' "[17] On the evening of July 18 Schulenburg went to the family in Trebbow. From Schwerin he called his wife to say he was coming on foot and wanted to celebrate her birthday, which was on the 20th, in advance, that evening. The children were to be got out of bed again. In this way he took his departure without divulging anything. When he drove away again in the early morning and sat on the driver's seat he, the Lieutenant, waved his cap like a civilian, bowed low and gravely and went off, to the laughter of the gesticulating children. In Berlin he received the news that his brother had been killed in Normandy. The next day, the uprising was to be attempted.

Friends had predicted early on that he would end up either as a minister or on the gallows.[18] The latter was to be the fate of this man who had always tried to be a "minister", or servant, of his people.

If a person wished to compose an Homeric catalogue of the heroes of these times, he would certainly depict a meeting in the Kingdom of the Dead with the lofty, blond, Friesian figure of Nikolaus von *Halem*. Even among the shades Halem would evince his individuality. He was variously connected with other men of the Resistance, but had gone his own ways and provided the inspiration for his own circle—and on this course he died. He had no direct connection with the 20th July. But for several of his friends, who were preparing the decisions of the 20th July, first concern over his uncertain fate, then the news of his death sentence in the last weeks, were an outward, and, much more, a personal reason for action. He cannot therefore be omitted here.

Amongst his fellow-pupils of the former Rossleben *Ritterakademie*, Halem had the reputation of having an independent, self-confident nature, talented in debate. He easily mastered his work, always looked much too young and yet had something of the imperturbability of a philosopher. When Hitler first appeared on the scene, he belonged to the circle of Karl von Jordans, the politician of Catholic background who, like Edgar Jung, tried to exercise a modifying influence on the new régime in Germany through Franz von Papen. The events of June 30, 1934, to which Jung fell a victim and from which Jordans only escaped by chance, helped Halem to recognize the failure of what was still virtually a "parliamentary" opposition and prompted him to act on his own. Hitler was for him the enemy of morality, who had risen from the underworld, the destroyer of all worthwhile spiritual and patriotic values. He once called him in conversation the "messenger of chaos". In February 1938 he tried, with Germans from the Reich, and Austrian friends, to persuade the military leaders in Vienna to use force against Hitler's threat to intervene and to prepare to assassinate him, should he really march in.[19] The attempt failed and the plans became known. Wilhelm von Ketteler, Halem's close associate, disappeared. Some days later his body was recovered from the Danube below Vienna; he had almost certainly been disposed of by drowning. Roman Hädelmayer, an Austrian, who was also involved, had to endure torture and terrible years of imprisonment in Dachau and Buchenwald, until he was unexpectedly released five years later. Thanks to the silence of both, Halem was not touched. It would not have required much to seal his fate, as he was already on the black list: two years earlier he had helped a Jewish acquaintance to flee to Czechoslovakia. Near the frontier the refugee, with whom Halem was driving, lost his nerve, drove like lightning through the German, and rammed the Czech, barrier. He was unhurt and was saved. Halem had to bear the consequences. He reported to the German frontier police, was arrested but got off, thanks to his firm defence at the trial.

In the first years of the war he worked in the Reich Office for Industry in Berlin and, thanks to his eloquence and powers of persuasion and his always astonishingly good information, became the centre and inspiration of a circle of like-minded people. In this circle hopes and plans for a coup were considered very realistically.

To the objections of wives that they were all risking the lives and happiness of their families, Halem, who was very attached to his own, gave soothing answers, which were really meant to avoid discussing dangerous matters. "Remember", he said to one of the friends, "there are only a few who have the courage to act for something beyond their private life.... There are reasons which oblige us not to think of self and family, but only to help the cause of justice, honesty and honour.... I advise you to tell your wife nothing of your activities, not even in hints. It is always easier for women when they know nothing."[20]

Like Schulenburg, Halem came into close contact with Joseph Wagner, the Gauleiter of Westphalia-South and Silesia, who was perhaps chiefly "converted" by him. And through Fabian von Schlabrendorff, he remained in touch with the opposition in the Army. Several times he went abroad on behalf of an Upper Silesian concern, a steel works—to Italy, France, and Sweden; and he sought to talk with influential people who would be ready to take up with the Germans the struggle against the dictatorship in Germany.

In January 1941, in a conversation in Berlin, Halem expressed the view that it would be wrong to expect senior officers in the Army and industrialists to exercise a moderating influence and so limit the war and finally change the régime. He thought that a man like Hitler would cast his spell over Germany until his last breath. There was only one solution for anyone who was clear-sighted and resolute : Hitler must be assassinated. After that, the régime could be changed, attempts could be made to negotiate with the Allies and the fronts could be withdrawn to the 1939 boundaries. Austria and Czechoslovakia would have to be restored as independent states.[21] Schlabrendorff, who had taken part in this conversation, was soon afterwards posted to Lieutenant-Colonel Henning von Tresckow at the Army Group Centre in Posen. He was a very energetic man who tried to force on developments in accordance with Halem's ideas, even when Halem himself was already under arrest.

Halem thought he had found the man, to whom could be entrusted the attempt on Hitler's life, in an active officer of the First World War and later leader of the Oberland Free Corps. This man was a controversial, somewhat turbulent, swash-buckling character. He had known Hitler since the first Bürgerbräu speeches, had been a Party member for a while, then emerged as an opponent and a member of the Communist Party. He was badly treated in concentration camps by the new men in power, then released again. He founded "action groups" with former Communists in various Gaue, and he himself, with many others, kept a watch on all Hitler's movements in Berlin. Halem was able to get this man,

134

Beppo Römer, a job in Berlin for a while and so help him financially during the complex preparations. But nothing came of it. The payments made under a false entry had to cease. Römer was betrayed and the police took him, and with him, a large group who were exposed, it seems, largely as a result of Römer being tortured. One hundred and twenty people were executed.[22] Halem was arrested on February 25, 1942, three weeks after Römer, and at the same time as Herbert *Mumm* von *Schwarzenstein*, who had to give up his diplomatic career in the Hitler period and who, with Halem, had devoted himself to the preparation of a coup. After more than two years' imprisonment Halem and Mumm were sentenced to death by the People's Court on June 16, 1944. "See what you have done : you have sunk yourself," Freisler called to Halem; and Halem answered finely and proudly : "A ship can sink, but it does not need to haul down its flag." Four months later Halem was executed with the men of the 20th July. He himself wrote that their end was ". . . sad and without lustre, but also without guilt and without disgrace".[23]

According to a report, Halem himself was seriously tortured at least twice. But evidently he was strong enough to preserve the secret of his friends and to speak only well of three particular names put to him—those of Schlabrendorff, Guttenberg and Dohnanyi. Like Mumm, he betrayed none of his friends. He was "a diplomat of the great school, a realist with a sarcastic sense of humour", and was perhaps akin to Trott zu Solz in his youthful ability and manner. Like him, Halem did much to initiate talks outside Germany. He had the special gift of being able to win people over easily by getting to the heart of things and by his quick and striking formulations. Tall, strong, blond and blue-eyed, Halem united in his person, as another of his friends says, cunning and courage, drive and deliberation, frankness and skill, great knowledge and real wisdom.[24] We see the whole man in the letters he wrote from prison, which have been preserved. They are among the most impressive testimonials to be found in the annals of those days. To his friend, Carl Ludwig Freiherr von Guttenberg, he wrote after the 20th July, when each day he had to reckon with death :[25]

"See that in the life and thought of my sons their father does not remain a blot and a wound about which the less said the better. Spare them, at least, this festering consequence of my misfortune, for which they were in no way responsible. Only your friendship can preserve H. and the children from the drab mediocrity that so often engulfs widows and orphans. It is an experience which penetrates to the very depths when this foreground, the 'I' begins to

135

become so shadow-like. How retrospect changes in character, when it suddenly seems advisable to resort to it as one's only perspective! How much there is, about which, all at once, I can now laugh, quite merrily and gently, for, thank heavens, I have not yet forgotten how to laugh! Rather, I have, in a number of situations in my life, found new strength and a new zest for laughter. But when I look back I see more shadows than light. I now see for the first time how much I have lived my life only as a reaction to forces, needs and impulses, and how little I have actually moved in the course of all this, how little progress I have made in the sense of a higher reality. Thus, the darkness always emanates from me, the brightness from other people, including you! And if I, conscious of the disgraceful injustice done to me and my own rights, look, with tense concentration and undiminished strength, at every possibility of tearing this loathsome strangling noose from my neck, then it is, above all, because of an ardent desire to do what remains to be done, to complete what is unfinished, to speak out what has been given to me for this purpose in the form of ideas and to grow upwards into a higher stratum of life. . . . Greet my friends and pass my request on to them. Make it your responsibility to keep them at it a little. I think of you all with the greatest affection. Every happy laugh still rings in my ear, every serious word passes through my mind, every piece of good advice, every look, every act of friendship, is still real and distinct for me. They clothe me like a suit of mail against a thousand little miseries. Who knows, my dear fellow, perhaps one day we shall sit together again over a good glass of wine and think of the old times with laughter and sadness. But if not, then I want to thank you today for the gift of your friendship and the many pleasant hours we have spent together : from them, according to their measure, grew, as from few other things, the richness of my life."

A few minutes before his execution on October 9, 1944, Nikolaus von Halem wrote with shackled hands :[26]

"Dear Mother, I have now overcome the last little tremor that seizes the top of the tree before it falls; and so I have attained the goal of humanity, for we can and ought to endure consciously what the plants undergo without consciousness.

Farewell, I am being fetched. A thousand kisses,

Your son."

*　　*　　*

Like Nikolaus von Halem, Dietrich *Bonhoeffer* had no direct part in the 20th July. He was arrested on April 5, 1943, and did not see freedom again. But, until his disappearance, he belonged to the circle of those who thought it wrong to look on tolerantly at something which was recognized to be disastrous, and who tried, on their own responsibility, to bring about a change. The part which Bonhoeffer played in the internal problems and deliberations which preceded the decision to stage an uprising can be seen today from a memorandum of his which he wrote for himself and his friends, in the form of a defence of their activities, at the turn of the year 1942–43. This memorandum, which avoids all specific reference to contemporary events, is a unique document of this time and is worth reading and pondering. Entitled "After ten years", it appears at the beginning of the volume of personal reminiscences of the prison period which Eberhard Bethge, a friend of Bonhoeffer, has published. Some passages from the memorandum may give an idea of Bonhoeffer's thoughts and attitudes and, at the same time, provide proof to the perceptive of how little these men thought in terms only of Germany :

"If we do not have the courage to evoke again a genuine feeling for human reserve and to fight for it in our personal lives, then we shall perish in an anarchy of human values. The insolent disregard of all human reserve is as much the mark of the rabble as the inner uncertainty, the haggling and currying for the favour of the insolent, as lowering oneself to the level of the rabble is the way to become part of the rabble. When we no longer know what we owe to ourselves and to others, where the feeling for human quality and the ability to maintain reserve is extinguished chaos is at hand. When, for the sake of material comfort, we tolerate impudence coming too near, then we have already given ourselves up, then we have allowed the flood of chaos to break through the dam we were pledged to defend and made ourselves guilty of a crime against humanity. In other times, it may have been the duty of Christianity to champion the equality of men; but today it is Christianity which must passionately defend respect for human reserve and human quality. . . . We are in the middle of a process in which all classes of society are being reduced to the state of the rabble and, at the same time, we are seeing the birth of a new sense of nobility which binds together a circle of men from all previous social classes. Nobility springs from, and thrives on, sacrifice, courage and a clear knowledge of what we owe to ourselves and to others, and the natural demand for respect which is due to a person, as well as an equally natural deference towards the humble and the mighty. . . .

"The great masquerade of evil has wrought havoc with all ethical ideas. The fact that evil appears in the form of light, or beneficence, of historical necessity, and of social justice, is utterly confusing for

137

someone nurtured in our traditional ethical system. . . . Obvious is the failure of the rationalists who, with the best intentions and naive misunderstanding of reality, think that they can with a little reason put the world to rights. . . . Worse still is the failure of all moral fanaticism. The fanatic thinks he can oppose the power of evil with pure principles. But, just as the bull thrusts at the red rag instead of its carrier, he grows weary and succumbs. . . . The man of conscience defends himself single-handed against the overwhelming odds in situations which demand decisions. But the extent of the conflicts in which he has to choose—with only his very own conscience to guide and support him—tears him to pieces. The many specious and deceptive guises in which evil approaches him make his conscience anxious and uncertain, until, at last, he is content to have a salved conscience instead of a good one, until, that is to say, he deceives his conscience in order to avoid despair. . . . The sure path of duty seems to lead out of the confusing variety of alternatives. Here an order is seized on as something most certain : the giver of an order carries responsibility for the order, not he who carries it out. But, by confining ourselves to the sphere of duty, we never run a risk of doing something on our own responsibility; and that is the only way of getting to grips with evil and defeating it.

"Who would deny that in obedience, duty and calling, the German has always achieved the limits of bravery and self-sacrifice? But the German preserved his freedom—and where in the world has there been more passionate talk of freedom than in Germany, from Luther to the philosophy of idealism?—by freeing himself from his own will in the service of the community. Calling and freedom were for him two sides of the same thing. But, in this, he misunderstood the world. He did not realize that his readiness to subordinate himself and to stake his life for the cause could be exploited for evil ends. . . . It transpired that the German still lacked an important basic perception : that of the need for free, responsible action to take precedence over calling and duty. . . .

"But it is a fact that historical success creates the only basis for the continuance of life and it is very questionable whether it is ethically more responsible to take the field like Don Quixote against a new age, or to admit one's defeat, accept the new age, and agree to serve it. . . . So long as the good is successful, we can afford the luxury of regarding success as ethically irrelevant; but, once evil means lead to success, then the problem arises. Faced with this situation, we find that neither theoretical criticism and dogmatism —that is to say, the refusal to face facts—nor opportunism, which is self-surrender and capitulation before success, are appropriate to our task. We must be neither outraged critics nor opportunists, but must bear our share of responsibility for historical developments, from case to case, and at every moment, whether as victors or vanquished. . . . Talk of going down like heroes, in the face of an inevitable defeat, is really very unheroic, because it does not dare look into the future. The ultimate question, a responsible man asks, is . . . how is the coming generation to continue to live?

"Folly is a more dangerous enemy of the good than evil. We can protest against evil, we can unmask it and, if necessary, we can prevent it by force. . . . But against folly we have no defence. . . . For this reason it is necessary to be more cautious with folly than with evil. . . . When we look closer, we see that every violent revolution, whether political or religious, strikes a large part of humanity with folly. . . . That the fool is often stubborn ought not to disguise the fact that he is not independent. . . . He is under a spell, he is blinded, he is misused and mishandled in his very nature. Having thus become an instrument without will, the fool will be capable of every evil, and, at the same time, incapable of recognizing evil. Here lies the danger of a diabolic exploitation. . . . However, it is just at this point clear that it is not education but only liberation which can overcome folly. In this we must accept that genuine, inner liberation is, in most cases, only possible when it has been preceded by external liberation. Until then, we shall have to renounce all attempts to convince the fool. This state of affairs will also explain why, in such circumstances, we try in vain to discover what 'the people' really think and why, for the man who thinks and acts responsibly, this question is, also, so superfluous.

"I believe that even our mistakes and errors are not in vain, and that it is not more difficult for God to cope with them than with what we imagine to be our good deeds. I believe God is not a timeless destiny but that He waits for, and answers, honest prayers and responsible action.

"Optimism is, in its nature, not an opinion about the present situation, but a vital strength, a strength of hope where others resign, a strength to hold one's head high, when everything seems to fail, a strength to bear defeats, a strength which never leaves the future to the enemy but claims it for oneself. There is certainly also a cowardly, foolish optimism, which must be condemned. But no one should despise optimism as a will for the future, even when it is mistaken a hundred times. It is the health of life which the sick should not impugn. . . . It may be that the Day of Judgement will break tomorrow; then we can readily stop working for a better future, but not before.

"For us there is only the narrow, and sometimes hardly discernible, way of regarding each day as though it might be the last, and yet to live in faith and with a sense of responsibility, as though there were still a great future. 'Houses and fields and vineyards shall yet again be bought in this land,' Jeremiah must proclaim—a striking contrast to his predictions of war just before the destruction of the Holy City—a divine sign and pledge of a great new future, when all seems at its blackest. To think and act for the sake of the coming generation, while being ready each day to go without fear or anxiety—that is the attitude which is practically forced upon us and which, to hold to bravely, is not easy, but necessary."

Bonhoeffer was born in 1906 in Breslau into an academic household. His father was the famous psychiatrist, Professor Karl Bonhoeffer. Dietrich grew up in Berlin during the period of the First World War. In later years he had happy memories of holidays spent in the Harz and Weser Mountains. The age differences of the eight brothers and sisters, the coming and going of many different people in the hospitable home and a deliberately severe form of education taught the young man how to be independent and to hold his own at an early age. But it also taught him to face the world openly and receptively, to be aware of his duty and to be of assistance to others. He was absorbed in music and found in Schütz, Bach and Handel the strains which appealed to his own kind of piety. This piety found expression in an inner and outward contentment. Even within the silent walls of his cell, the memory of this music remained with him. For him the pastor's calling was a tradition of his forebears. But a more powerful impulse for him was the unanswerable, tormenting accusation against the Church that it was no longer able to win over the whole, strong man, and that it was being restricted either to care of the under-privileged, and spiritually needy, or to anaemic intellectualism. He saw before him the task of recasting the message and office of this Church in such a way as to win over also the man of this world who, in his words, had "become of age". On completion of his studies, Bonhoeffer wanted to go abroad to get a wider view of the problems that interested him. After years spent in Spain, the USA and England, and, after a period as a student pastor in Berlin, he was appointed in 1935 director of the Preacher's Training College of the Confessional Church in Finkenwalde. This Church had recently been constituted to resist the interference of the new régime. Shortly afterwards, he was relieved of his private lectureship at Berlin University. During the war Bonhoeffer went on missions for his Church to Geneva and Stockholm, where he met church leaders of neutral and enemy countries, some of whom he had known from earlier days and were friends of his. He left them in no doubt where he and a whole circle of determined men in Germany stood, and asked them to persuade the politicians of their own countries not to let the struggle of the Opposition in Germany be extinguished, but to encourage it, and make it clear that their own actions were directed against Hitler and not against Germany.

At these meetings, as a British report also confirms, Bonhoeffer showed his inward solidarity with Germany and proved that "one could approach the non-German world with clean hands, without betraying the Fatherland".[27]

As a pastor, Bonhoeffer had, as someone says who saw him in many situations, a unique quality in that he spoke simply and assuredly with the ordinary man and without condescension; yet he moved easily in the sophisticated world and won unqualified respect. He shared neither the Church's prejudice for the weak and spiritually poor, nor the world's for position, honours and money; and an obvious strength emanated from his open and refreshing confidence.

During the first one and a half years of his imprisonment there was no serious evidence against Bonhoeffer which would have permitted a sentence. Only when, in October 1944, papers were found in Zossen, which revealed Oster's efforts over the years to bring about a coup, was Bonhoeffer's role proved; and from then on his fate was tied to that of Oster and Canaris. He was hanged with them on the same day, April 9, 1945, as the enemy approached. Schlabrendorff, who was for a long time a fellow-prisoner and cell-neighbour, describes[28] the amazing and constant cheerfulness of the man who became his friend. He tells how Bonhoeffer, after an air-raid, jumped, like a cat, through the open cell-door of the paralysed Dohnanyi, in order to have a short talk with him, and then got away unnoticed behind the backs of the guards. This he did with a strength, artfulness and agility, which one would not have expected from Bonhoeffer's almost corpulent build. But he himself once expressed the wish from his cell that a baptized infant, named after him, should have the strong calves of the god-father, his freedom from headaches, and his good palate. For other virtues, he said, he would have to look elsewhere. . . .

A few days after Dietrich Bonhoeffer was executed, the husband of his twin sister, Hans von Dohnanyi, suffered the same fate in Sachsenhausen. In Berlin, shortly afterwards, when the Russians were already over-running the city, his brother Klaus followed. He had been a lawyer and legal adviser with Lufthansa. Klaus Bonhoeffer, with other prison inmates, was shot in the back of the neck and killed by the guard acting on orders, as the group crossed the street. He had been preceded by Rüdiger Schleicher, a

Ministerialrat in Berlin, who had married the eldest Bonhoeffer daughter,[29] and Lieutenant-General Paul von Hase, the uncle of Dietrich and Klaus Bonhoeffer, who had been among the first of those accused in connection with the 20th July to be sentenced and executed. Only Justus Delbrück, who belonged to the family by marriage, saw the liberation at the beginning of May. But he was re-arrested by the Russians in the same month and died half a year later in their captivity.

Before all this misfortune, which came to the family, Dietrich Bonhoeffer wrote to his parents :[30]

"A life which can be fully developed, professionally and personally, and be so balanced and completely fulfilled, as was still possible for your generation, can no longer be expected by ours. Therein lies the great renunciation which is imposed on, and required from, us younger men, who still have your life in mind. The uncompleted, fragmentary nature of our life we find particularly hard. But even the fragments can point to a higher fulfilment beyond that of man. I must think particularly of this when I hear of the death of so many of my best pupils of the past.

"Even if the force of external circumstances breaks our life into fragments, as the bombs do to our houses, it should be seen, where possible, how the whole was planned and conceived; and people will, at least, be able to recognize, with what material we built, or were to build here. . . ." (February 20, 1944).

Dr Wilhelm *Ahlmann*, a friend of Jens Jessen, who was born in the same year (1895) and also came from Schleswig-Holstein, was fated to lose the sight of both eyes before he was twenty-one. The family tradition of several generations of sea captains, mayors and district officials in Northern Dittmarsch made him by disposition as much a man of action as a thinker. Forced to look inwards, the blind man, by systematic studying, mastered law, political and social science, history, including that of the Church, psychology and philosophy, and constantly pitted himself against men who provided him with contacts with the outside world. In this way, he did not suffer any deprivation and was able to develop in his fourth and fifth decade such a full life that, in his case, honour, friendship, and homage seemed more appropriate than compassion.

The prosperity of his home allowed him an independent existence. During the war he moved between Kiel and Berlin. Housemaid and servant catered for his surroundings which even in the bad years were notable for their atmosphere of calm, relaxation and courteous hospitality. These domestics arranged, in accordance with a perceptible routine, for guests to be received and entertained whom the host preferred to have alone or in groups of his own choice. This is another reason why there is no record of his talks with Stauffenberg. But others recount how this unusual figure knew of all the happenings of the time, and how powerfully he was able, merely by his presence or withdrawal, to act as mentor to those of his friends who were involved in the events of the day. What he imparted was not instruction, but encouragement and strength to do what was right and an almost physical faith that neither suffering nor death can inhibit exemplary conduct in the cause of freedom. To an ordinary, straightforward person, he could give the impression of wearing a mask, because he made no confessions and, it appeared, only approached matters with a part of himself, while the other part remained a mystery. He knew, as only few men can, how to listen appreciatively and positively and, with his sightless glance, to encourage the speaker and his ideas or, perhaps, to direct them. He liked to challenge and contradict, to lay and solve traps. He groaned and audibly expressed his pleasure. And when he spoke of conduct in the hour of danger, or of victory over death, distant forebodings seemed to pervade the quiet talk.

Men of the most varied intellectual callings sought his company and later regarded the hours they had spent at his side as memorable. The conversations with him, it seems, had this characteristic : that, however detailed, professional and intellectual they were, they always revealed and expressed the true, manly qualities which could form the basis of life for the individual and for the community. They always sought to get to the bottom of things, whether it was a question of a new legal system, of stoicism and Christianity, of British class problems, of Pascal, or of modern music. It was the same when once a conversation about the war situation was summarized in the words : "We are our own worst enemies." This signified that it was not enough to criticize National Socialism, which was only an outward form; it was also necessary to grasp and overcome the nature of the disaster implied in the loss of human standards and the eclipse of the individual.

Claus Stauffenberg, who was introduced by Jessen, spent several evenings with Wilhelm Ahlmann. His driver spoke of this without then knowing the name of the mysterious blind man. But he noticed Count Stauffenberg, whom he had to drive to so many visits and talks, had an obviously special relationship with this man; and he himself was involved to the extent that sometimes, as he waited in the car on the street at night, he was brought food, drink and cigarettes with the compliments of the owner of the house. It is certain from what has now become known that Stauffenberg, who in these months was taking advice from all sides about an interim political solution, profited from his contact with Wilhelm

Ahlmann and sought this man's practical understanding of what was possible. If it is literally true, as one report says, that Wilhelm Ahlmann opposed Stauffenberg's plans for "political and ethical reasons", so it is equally certain that Stauffenberg was strengthened in his resolve by contact with this extraordinary, very self-possessed and strong man, this "vita sibi concors" in Seneca's words. Stauffenberg's resolve was the product of a similarly strong and harmonious personality.

Wilhelm Ahlmann died as a result of the 20th July. On December 7, 1944, he felt compelled to shoot himself "in order, as a latter-day Stoic, to preserve his own freedom and to remain silent in the interests of his friends".

VIII. HENNING VON TRESCKOW
NEW ATTEMPTS AT A COUP IN THE ARMY

DURING the war years 1942–43 there were two main circles in the Army which were concerned with a coup. One was in the High Command of the Army in Berlin round General of the Infantry, Friedrich Olbricht, and the other was in the staff of the Army Group Centre in the East round the then Colonel i.G. Henning von Tresckow.

Friedrich *Olbricht* was born in 1888. He was the same age as Oster with whom he was in close contact. In the Polish campaign he served as Divisional Commander and was awarded the Knight's Cross. Thanks to his ability as an organizer and negotiator, he was made Chief of the General Army Office in the Army High Command in the Bendlerstrasse. This post brought him into touch with all elements of the Army on the fronts and at home, and he must have been one of the best known figures among his fellow officers. Outside office hours, many visitors, including men on leave from the front, came to his house to drink wine and to talk. He often met Beck and he knew Stülpnagel and Falkenhausen, the two Military Commanders in Belgium and France, as well as Witzleben. But, in addition, he had contacts with civilians in the Resistance movement, largely through his acquaintance with Goerdeler, whom he had known in his years as Chief of Staff of the IV Army Corps in Dresden and Leipzig in 1933–38. He met Popitz; and Hassell looked him up when he was in Berlin.

Olbricht was of medium height, well-built, without being corpulent. In spite of the glasses which he wore, he was regarded by the ordinary soldier as a fine-looking General, and he was admired because he was affable and approachable, for all his official strictness. Sometimes his Saxon intonation was noticeable in his way of speaking, and his irony—he came from Dresden; but, generally, the Berliner was uppermost in him with his quick wit and lively personality and his generous, polite and sociable nature. He supported an uprising without personal ambition and solely out of patriotism; and he gave it valuable service as "technical organizer in difficult and dangerous single-handed work".[1] He did not care about his rank and he was satisfied with a secondary role, when he found the younger members more able and stronger than himself, and his own burden almost unbearable. The war, which he thought

145

wrong and nonsensical, had deprived him of a son to whom he was very attached. In the book of interrogation reports his words, as an Adjutant remembered them on the night of the 20th July, are reproduced : "It is over with me and my plans. Stauffenberg, the leading horse, and I, will now be brought to account. I cannot avoid that. Tell my wife, that, just as a soldier falls in battle, so in this I have acted according to my conviction."[2]

From the beginning, Olbricht had spoken freely to this Adjutant, to whom he was also attached as a man : Lieutenant-Colonel Fritz von der *Lancken,* before the war the head of a country boarding school. In his home in Potsdam he kept the explosive which was used in July 1944. He was executed.

Until his dismissal at the end of 1942, General Georg *Thomas* acted in close co-operation with Olbricht and had opportunities to meet him in the course of his official duties. From 1934 he was Head of Military Production and Armaments Office of the OKW and obviously had wide knowledge of armaments and military economics. He was impressed by the potential strength of Russia, and after a study trip in 1933 he advocated a peaceful settlement with the Soviet Union. In 1935 he clashed with Hitler over his Japanese policy, shortly after he himself had concluded an economic treaty with Chiang Kai-shek on Hitler's behalf. In 1937 he supported Schacht in opposing the apparently limitless expansion of credits and armaments projects. In August 1939 he produced memoranda and statistics calling for the abandonment of the war plans, on the grounds that they could not be justified economically. But Keitel announced on August 28 that Hitler did not share these reservations, because he had Soviet power on his side. Thomas was arrested after the 20th July and was released after the war.

With Henning von *Tresckow* the younger generation of officers opposed to Hitler comes on the scene. These officers were at that time Lieutenant-Colonels and Colonels. Tresckow and his friends believed that, against a power such as Hitler's, no warnings and no reminders from an earlier and better tradition and no attitude of superiority and no wise speeches could be effective—only action itself, as a result of clear determination and readiness to accept the challenge. They knew the objections which were always encountered from above. With the clear reasoning of the General Staff they considered the necessary conditions and the consequences of such action. Their hearts told them to act. They resolved the dilemma of the soldier's oath, after much searching of heart, by asking : whether the oath did not bind the soldiers to overthrow the oath-breaker himself in his role of destroyer, in order to safeguard the life of the Fatherland?

Henning von Tresckow[3] was born in January 1901 into a Prussian officer's family which could trace its ancestry back to the fourteenth century. An ancestor had made a name for himself as defender of Neisse under Frederick the Great. The king had called him one of his good generals, of whom, he said, he did not have too many.... The young Tresckow grew up on his father's property, Wartenberg, in the Neumark, and acquired great physical prowess. Even when he went to the *Realgymnasium* in Goslar and the war made its impact, Wartenberg remained his home; here he felt he had ties with the land. In 1918 he was platoon commander on the Western front with his elder brother, Gerd, who was unselfishly devoted to him. Gerd von Tresckow surrendered himself after the 20th July. He was arrested and took his life in prison.

After taking part briefly in the revolutionary fighting, Tresckow went in for banking. He became a broker on the stock exchange with an astonishing talent for getting on in such a sphere. In 1924 he went on a world tour and spent six months in South America.

After his return he left what was for a young man a very favourable situation and managed, thanks to Hindenburg's recommendation, to get into the Reichswehr. He began as a Second-Lieutenant in the 9th Infantry Regiment in Potsdam which, in the meantime, had taken over the tradition of the 1st Prussian Foot Guards Regiment, his old unit. In 1932 he went to the Military Academy as Captain and was among the best of the year's intake. For three years before the Second World War he worked in the General Staff with (later) Lieutenant-General Heusinger in the Operations Branch, which came under Colonel-General Beck's influence. He went through the Polish campaign, now a Major, as GSO I of a division. Thereafter, he had the same function in Army Group Staffs, first under (later) Field-Marshal von Rundstedt in the West and then under Field Marshals von Bock and Kluge in the East. He was in Army Group Centre from 1941 until the summer of 1943. On October 1, 1943, he had command of a regiment for a short time and then became Chief of the General Staff of the Second Army under Colonel-General Weiss. On January 30, 1944, Hitler made him a General at forty-three.

There is much evidence to show that Henning von Tresckow developed an extraordinary ability in the art of leading troops. In the reports we constantly come across opinions such as "a soldier of quite considerable stature" or "a man far above the average". It is also known that Kluge valued his services highly as a GSO I. He became indispensable for him with his almost inexhaustible capacity for work, his quick and alert brain and his ready way of putting forward his views and offering practical help. In the Army

147

Group, Tresckow had, apart from the Marshal, whose operational gifts he greatly admired, the Chief of Staff above him. Towards them and to all senior in rank to himself, he showed tact and courtesy without any self-abasement. For the others, Tresckow was clearly, because of his humanity, the man who counted in this senior staff camp in the field. He often expected unusual things from those who worked under him, but he was always there to back them up and support them. Tresckow had also the confidence of the Army staffs, right down to the individual troop officers, and this confidence stood some severe tests. They knew that he did not just pass down orders from above which might demand senseless losses, but took the greatest trouble, where possible, to avoid them, to change them or water them down.

Sometimes Tresckow seemed to be the born *grand seigneur* who bestowed and received honours; but there was nothing overbearing about him. He himself seemed to live only to serve a cause and he won over others to it, thanks to a personality which combined professional competence and compassionate moderation. It is reported from his entourage that, while he was extremely cautious and silent about his secret affairs, he had an open manner, as few others had, and that everyone came away with the conviction of being his special friend. In this way, everyone automatically did his best for him—and even those who disagreed restrained themselves under his bridle. If he took on a difficult job for one of his close friends, his word was not so decisive as the absolute certainty that he was ready at all times to do what he asked from others.

Tresckow hated drill and, when he could, avoided uniforms. He regarded it as his task not to let the young officers under his care become too great specialists. He invited them to evenings, where the talk and conversation was about non-military matters, about historical figures, ethnology or other intellectual subjects. Tresckow himself was remarkably eloquent. Here his uncompromising nature and deep feeling for the Fatherland often came to the fore with passionate intensity, when he had to decide between what was honourable and base. His attitude to Hitler was also like this: rational considerations made him an opponent, but even more so, as one person said, "antipathy to everything which was rooted in baseness". What happened in 1938 and 1939 outraged him. And he went into the war with the intention of helping to bring about Hitler's fall at the first opportunity that offered, and so to extirpate those characteristics which he had introduced amongst the Germans. He felt himself affected by every misdeed perpetrated in the name of the Germans. "You and I, also, will be counted amongst the guilty," he said on such an occasion to one of his officers. It struck him as a personal misfortune when another city at home fell in ruins, when another division was senselessly destroyed, and no one raised a hand. . . .

The invasion of France turned out differently from what Tresckow, like Beck and many others, had expected. He recognized Hitler's achievement; but, as a direct participant, he was dismayed by Hitler's orders to halt the tanks before Dunkirk, which had allowed the British to escape. A war with Russia, in the preparations of which he had taken part at the Army Group Command in Posen, he regarded as the presumptuousness of a great dilettante—so long as Britain remained completely undefeated; and he considered how it might be possible to bring about Hitler's fall after the first reverses. But events proved stronger and carried Tresckow with them : victories, enormous numbers of prisoners, the penetration of his Army Group 800 kilometres deep into unknown territory, right up to Moscow. Then, because it was too late in the year, there was paralysis due to the *rasputitsa*, the period of mud; and, after it, the freezing cold and the turning point on December 6, when the exhausted soldiers were faced with an army of one hundred divisions which seemed to come from nowhere and laughingly made nothing of the winter. Now the one preoccupation was the battle and the lives of the soldiers. Field-Marshal von Bock went and in his place came Field-Marshal von Kluge. Tresckow, who was relentlessly opposed to Hitler and thought his delusions and obstinacy were responsible, had, as GSO I of the Army Group, to endure with Kluge the winter struggle to save the armies which were defending themselves so fiercely and bravely. Tresckow remained with Kluge for more than a year and a half, first only as military assistant to the Marshal, then later as a warning voice who tried, with increasing frankness, to persuade him to undertake independent action against Hitler.

In the course of 1942 a circle of sympathizers was won over. Here Tresckow's direct yet discreet nature and his faculty for establishing human contacts achieved wonders. Many who worked with him in those years were not aware of the ideas he held. Others, when some misfortune broke, encountered his "beaming, wise and kindly eyes"[4] or heard a gently ironical word addressed to themselves from his wry lips and suddenly knew where he stood, and where they stood with him. He was often content with the certainty of inward agreement and he hesitated to burden even willing officers, who were very devoted to him, with more information than seemed necessary to him. But he had complete faith in those who were won over, and was never disillusioned. A young cavalry Captain tells how, when newly appointed as Kluge's personal Adjutant, he reported to Colonel Tresckow. Tresckow in his first talk with the Captain stressed, nonchalantly and without any inhibitions, that his main duty would always be to influence the Marshal in the right direction politically and to use every opportunity "to keep him up to the mark". Tresckow knew, of course, that the cavalry Captain was the friend of one of his friends.[5]

Tresckow was repeatedly able to bring about transfers and appointments, which he could use for his purposes. Often the Army Personnel Office under Schmundt was able to help him without, however, suspecting his motives. His contacts extended to Führer Headquarters, to the Army Group South and to Colonel-General Beck's centre in Berlin. His ardent wish to get one of the Marshals to lead a revolt against Hitler and to be that Marshal's first assistant, was never fulfilled. Field-Marshal von Bock ignored his pleas, without betraying him : but one of Tresckow's associates, Hardenberg, remained with Bock as Adjutant, even when the Field-Marshal was in retirement. Kluge, with whom we might say Tresckow argued almost daily, he repeatedly won over for his plans; but Kluge thought he could only act once Hitler was dead. Field-Marshal von Manstein expressed himself in the same sense : in opposing plans for a coup, he always stressed his responsibility for the fighting troops. As a result, he failed to take advantage of an opportunity to make Tresckow Chief of Staff of his Army Group. Later, Tresckow also dared to approach Colonel-General Guderian, who after his disciplinary dismissal, lived privately in Berlin. Tresckow hoped to bring about a reconciliation between him and Kluge and to persuade them to act in common.[6] He himself called it going "into the lion's den". In spite of his dismissal in front of Moscow, Guderian was not considered an opponent of Hitler. His energy and military ability were highly regarded. Guderian wanted time to think it over—these were anxious days for Tresckow—and then declined.[7]

There was a remarkable group of men which, like a circle of peers, formed round Henning von Tresckow in the Eastern field camp in the years 1941–43, without others having the slightest knowledge of what really bound these men together. They differed in manner and years; but they were all devoted to the GSO I, who, in periods of difficult decisions, showed great discrimination in his judgement and who was the epitome of bravery. Many of them were traced after the 20th July and had to die. Two fell later in action. Several remained untouched and to them we owe much of the picture of Tresckow.

In the first rank among these friends was Colonel Bernd von *Kleist*. Like Tresckow, he had come from the Guards' Regiment and had lost a leg in the First World War. In spite of his lameness and difficulty in walking, he was again in active service and played the part of an unchallengeable censor in their circle—disciplined, sober, and serious. He was never known to exaggerate, even in inveighing against the enemy. "An excellent military insight", Schlabrendorff says, "enabled him to foresee events of which others hardly had an inkling. His untiring industry helped to make him indispensable in his post. In our circle he exercised the greatest influence and was a knight without fear and without reproach. When I once asked him, how he judged the prospects of the Russian campaign, he answered: 'The German Army will fight against Russia like an elephant which attacks an ant-hill. The elephant will kill thousands and thousands, even millions, of ants; but it will eventually be defeated by the number of ants and eaten to the bone.' "[8]

Colonel Georg *Schultze-Buettger* had been Adjutant for several years with Colonel-General Beck and had, it seems, acquired there the calm of a man of intellectual judgement. He was not impressed by what in the turmoil of events struck others as sensational and he always looked for the essential. In company he was remarkable for his ability to recount anecdotes and to recall experiences; and he always knew how to go to the heart of things. Tresckow was able to get him posted as GSO I in the Army Group South, so as to have one of his men near Field-Marshal von Manstein.

Colonel, later General, Freiherr von *Gersdorff* had a lucid and lively mind. He was gripping in conversation, witty and eloquent; courageous and carefree, when he was doing something for friends. He had been in the cavalry and was an elegant figure, lightly built. As the Abwehr representative in the Army Group, he was particularly valuable to Tresckow.

Lieutenant-Colonel Alexander von *Voss*, Schultze-Buettger's successor and, before that, a General Staff officer with Witzleben in Paris,[9] was a profound and passionate nature. He was an officer with whom Tresckow had had close contact for a long time. We read that he could "as little tolerate a mean spirit, as he could remain silent over a great joy". He had close connections with Karl Heinrich von Stülpnagel, to whom his wife was related. After the 20th July he shot himself.

Fabian von *Schlabrendorff* was born in 1907 into the Brandenburg branch of the family and was by profession a lawyer. At the beginning of 1941 he was brought by Tresckow to the Army Group as ADC. Tresckow had met him for the first time just before the war, when he returned from a trip to England. He got to know him as a very lively, unusually determined political opponent of

Hitler, who knew many people. Schlabrendorff gave him information about what was going on in the Government, which otherwise he would not have known. Originally he belonged to the patriotic "Young Conservative Group". But Schlabrendorff also had contacts with Hitler's opponents on the Left, for instance, with Ernst Niekisch. He was a friend of Halem and joined Oster's circle in 1938. In August 1939 he was in England and informed both the Foreign Secretary, Lord Halifax, through Lord Lloyd, and Churchill, in a personal conversation, that the conclusion of a treaty between Hitler and Stalin was to be expected and that war was imminent and would start with an attack on Poland, whatever proposals for mediation were made. He told them the German Opposition would try, with all its strength, to prevent such a disastrous development. On September 3, 1939, Schlabrendorff had the job, as he says, of informing the British, through an official he knew in the British Embassy in Berlin, of Hammerstein's plan. It was hoped after the first promises that Britain, in spite of the declaration of war, would not fail to support a coup in Germany. Tresckow jokingly called Schlabrendorff his "Kornak", or Indian elephant guide, who must direct him in political affairs. The close co-operation between the two lasted until Tresckow's death.

Other officers who were close associates of Tresckow and who often took messages for him to the Reich were Counts Carl Hans von *Hardenberg* and Heinrich von *Lehndorff*. Hardenberg, who came from the Mittelmark, was a physically strong man, calm by nature with ready advice in all situations. This came from his practical experience as a landowner who administered his own estates. Lehndorff was an even younger landowner, who had a very old family estate in East Prussia going back to the time of the German Orders. He loved hunting in marsh, field and wood; he had an open character, and was always ready to help his friends and was keenly sought after by them. Near Borisov, where he worked on the staff of Field-Marshal von Bock, during the advance into Russia, he learned of an act of devilish inhumanity, on the part of the SS, and was not able to stop it. From that day on, he burned with shame and saw no alternative but to work with all his strength for the liberation. Since parts of the headquarters were on his property and he could visit many staffs inconspicuously, his role was often of great value. Important talks took place at Lehndorff's castle; and for this he was later executed. In a last letter, which he wrote to his family, he said: "You can always be sure that I did not light-heartedly destroy your future, but that I worked for an idea which I believed did not justify my taking family and private matters into account. . . . My confirmation verse: 'Watch ye, stand fast in the faith, quit you like men, be strong' must guide me to the end."

Others of Tresckow's entourage can be mentioned here only by name : Major Ulrich von *Oertzen*, of whom something will be said later : Captain *Eggert*; Lieutenant Hans Albrecht von Boddien; Captain of the Cavalry Eberhard von *Breitenbuch*; the two brothers Freiherren von *Boeselager*, with one of whom, Georg von Boeselager, Tresckow enjoyed a particularly fine and intimate friendship.

A service report on the twenty-six-year-old Cavalry Captain and Troop leader Boeselager, called him "a spirited cavalry officer, who thinks boldly and surely in taking decisions, but who is modest and unassuming, the idol of his men. . . ." At twenty-nine, as a Colonel, decorated with the Knight's Cross, oak leaf and swords, he was killed on the invasion front in France during at attack by the cavalry brigade which he led. His body was brought back to his home on the Rhine. When he was about to be buried, the order came to withhold military honours from him, because it transpired that he was the "Lieutenant Freiherr von Boeselager" of the Army Group Centre, who had, until then, been sought in vain for his role in the attempted coup of the 20th July. His comrades, when asked about him, had always replied : "We have no Lieutenant Freiherr von B."

Boeselager came from an old Westphalian family which had settled near Bonn, on the Rhine, in the time of Napoleon. The grandparents' generation had been connected with the Counts of Stolberg, with the Swiss baronial family of Salis-Soglio and with the Hungarian nobility. The father, a Münster cuirassier in the First World War, was a popular and modest country aristocrat with a passion for hunting; and the mother a cultured, church-going woman, who had ten children. She brought them all up herself and was strict with them to the point of imposing corporal punishment. The young man was tireless in his enjoyment of the open fields and woods, riding, hunting and indulging in other adventures. He was always the leader of a band, although the smallest and most highly strung of the brothers. At the Jesuit Gymnasium, Aloysius College, in Bad Godesberg, which he went to in accordance with family tradition, he learnt more about character than about academic subjects. All this formed the background to the choice he had to make in 1934 : whether to be an officer or a priest. He chose to be an officer, but, it seems, inwardly kept the way open to the other vocation. A report from his division indicates that he was a "born officer", under whose command no one showed fear, even in overwhelming danger, and that his clear, sanguine

153

judgements constantly earned the confidence of other men of much higher rank. They said he had a "feel" for terrain : he only needed to cast one look at it, to know how to proceed in it for reconnaissance, flank attack or a feint against the enemy. Boeselager met Tresckow at the beginning of the war in Russia. In talks, which often lasted all night, and as a result of tormenting questions as to what he owed both to God and to himself, he gradually came to agree with Tresckow on the need for them to co-operate. It would have been much easier for him to live for glory and to be just the brave front-line soldier, cherished and praised by so many whom he himself loved. Instead, he would have to face the disappointment and regrets, even the contempt of his men who, until then, had been devoted to him, and had no idea of what was going on. Friends would use the word "traitor" and demand excuses and explanations. But Tresckow's manly friendship gave him the strength to take the stand he had to, and Boeselager did everything he could to bring about the liberation of the Fatherland.

Tresckow was the first of them to meet his death by suicide. When, at midnight on the 20th July, the failure of the attempted coup became apparent, he decided to kill himself before he was seized. To avoid disadvantages for his family and, perhaps for his accomplices among the officers, he chose a special way. One of those close to him describes the morning. Tresckow asked this person whether he would accompany him : he agreed, but shortly afterwards received orders from the Field-Marshal, who wanted him. "In front of the barracks in Ostrov, where the Army High Command was, stood the great open car of the GSO I in the morning sun of a wonderful summer's day. His driver waited with me as I sought, as was usual, to report that I was off to carry out Model's orders. Then came Tresckow, calm and composed as always. When I told him that I had received orders, Tresckow expressed his great regret. He took me a few steps aside and said : 'I should so much have liked you to be a witness of my death.' I was startled and asked Tresckow what he planned. He replied he did not want to give our opponents the satisfaction of getting hold of him. He wanted to go to the 28th Rifle Division and to walk alone into the forward area there. With a rifle, hand-grenades, and a pistol he wished to feign an engagement there and take his life. He intended it to seem as though he had encountered partisans. Tresckow bade me farewell with complete calm and ended 'Au revoir in a better world.' It is remarkable how someone can be so calm and confident two hours before his death."[10] At the Division Tresckow took Major Kuhn with him, who had for long taken part in the secret plans, and drove forward. The driver reported that the two officers got out to reconnoitre further on foot. Major Kuhn, when they had gone on a few hundred metres, turned back to the car and called for the General's map. The driver ran with it to him. At this moment firing and the bursting of hand-grenades could be heard from the wood, where the General was. They hurried to help him, but he was already dead. It was assumed that he had been attacked by partisans. A few days later Major Kuhn went over to the Russian lines.

Schlabrendorff, who in a long talk during the last night had tried in vain to persuade Tresckow not to kill himself, remembers some of Tresckow's last words : "Now the whole world will attack us and abuse us. But I am still absolutely convinced that we have acted rightly. I believe Hitler to be not only the arch-enemy of Germany, but also the arch-enemy of the world. When in a few hours' time I appear before the judgement seat of God to give an account of my deeds and omissions, I believe I shall be able to answer with a good conscience for what I have done in the struggle against Hitler. Just as God once promised Abraham that He would spare Sodom, if only ten just men could be found in it, so I hope that God will not destroy Germany because of us. None of us can complain about his death. Whoever joined us, put on the shirt of Nessus. A man's moral worth begins only when he is ready to give his life for his convictions."[11]

In addition to the reasons which officers like Olbricht, Tresckow, and Beck had as early as 1938–39 for acting against Hitler, the war brought new experiences which made it imperative for them not to let matters continue. It was not, at first, so much a question of criticism of Hitler by the military experts, who thought his basic decisions to fight in Russia and the Mediterranean were wrong and his faulty estimate of Germany's strength disastrous. In fact, General Halder was dismissed in September 1942 for such opposition and his successor, Zeitzler, broke down in the early summer of 1944 for the same reason.

But of deeper significance for the revolt was the argument that had been going on for some years, particularly since Stalingrad, about a new "war-time top level organization"[12] an attempt to change the command system set up by Hitler, which was based on a division of responsibility between the Army High Command (Russia) and the High Command of the Wehrmacht (other war theatres) and which also gave Hitler direct authority down to divisional, even company, level. It was thought essential to form a Great General Staff and an Eastern High Command out of the General Staff of the Army, so as to restore the unity of command,

155

to simplify the leadership and to give scope to ability and responsible authority. Professional suggestions and conversations on these lines, which were the consequence of too many unfortunate experiences, were followed by Hitler like the plague in his Headquarters; for they seemed dangerously close to ideas of a coup. They certainly implied a demand that the decision of February 4, 1938 (Hitler's assumption of the Supreme Command of the Wehrmacht) and the decision of December 1941 (when Hitler had made himself Commander-in-Chief of the Army) should be revoked. The People's Judge, after the 20th July, repeatedly encountered these complaints against Hitler and amongst the first papers of the conspirators, which were laid before him, was a draft order for a temporary war-time top level organization.

Of most significance of all for the decision in favour of a revolt were the experiences which these soldiers had undergone, not as officers but as human beings, when they became witnesses and even tools, of the massacres of thousands of human beings not involved in the fighting. When the war made it necessary to kill and to conquer, they accepted this law as soldiers, like the other side. But butchery and fury, as a result of racial madness, invaded the earth on which they stood, called forth Nemesis and would, if allowed to continue, poison the lives of their children and grandchildren. This is the way Tresckow saw it, whose words we know, and the way many others saw it, whose horror is attested. Officers, who were no more than aware of these outrages perpetrated in the name of Germany, had no peace of mind and put themselves at the disposal of those who were proposing to take action. "Whoever joined us, put on the shirt of Nessus," Tresckow said.

After the Polish campaign, the measures taken by the SS and the SD in Poland, which were completely contrary to all the laws of war, became known in the Army High Command thanks, in particular, to Canaris and Wagner, but also thanks to officers in command of troops. Indignation and disgust at these measures had prompted men like Halder to decide in favour of a coup d'état. Colonel-General Blaskowitz, as even the troops learned, had been removed from his command because of his protest to Hitler. He had, as Oster's circle knew, demanded the punishment by court martial of the SS leaders and SD leaders under his command.[13] In the spring of 1940, following this experience, and with the agreement of the Army, the SS police formations were removed from the jurisdiction of the Army, and executive authority in the occupied Eastern territories was handed over by the Army to the SS police leaders. The Army was not to be associated with measures which the police and administration regarded as politically necessary.

156

At the beginning of April 1941 Oster and Beck knew of orders which showed that in the war then being planned for June against Russia the principles of humanity and the laws of war would be disregarded.[14] In May, some weeks before the expected date of attack, Tresckow heard in Posen of two orders which profoundly disturbed him. The "Commissars' order" made it mandatory for the Army to execute all civilian and military Commissars who came into its hands. And the order on martial law deprived the local inhabitants of any legal rights in cases of offences and crimes against the Army during the advance into Russia—even the right of summary courts. It also made offences and crimes against local inhabitants by German soldiers virtually immune to punishment. Gersdorff recorded the immediate reaction of Tresckow: "Remember this hour. If we do not succeed in persuading the Field-Marshal to do everything, even to exert his own influence, to get these orders countermanded, Germany will have finally lost her honour, and that will be felt for hundreds of years to come. Not only Hitler will be blamed, but you and I, your wife and my wife, your children and my children."[15]

In spite of many incensed protests from various sides, Brauchitsch was not able to get Hitler's orders withdrawn. He merely tried, by issuing an additional order on the maintenance of discipline, to give the Commanders means to get round the other orders. Inquiries at all three Army Groups make it probable that the majority of Commanders did not carry out the orders and some did not even pass them on. But, in spite of his energetic efforts, Tresckow was not able to achieve what he hoped would be a more important move : that the three Army Group Commanders, Marshals Bock, Rundstedt, and Leeb, should together demand from Hitler that the orders be withdrawn and that, in the case of refusal, they should give up their posts. It is clear from Hassell's diary, how disastrous it was thought in the circle of Beck, Goerdeler, Oster and Popitz that the orders were accepted by the Army : "Brauchitsch and Halder have already gone along with Hitler's manoeuvre to extend to the Army the odium for the murders, which until now, rested only on the SS. They have assumed responsibility and by certain . . . additions . . . deceived themselves and others. Hopeless sergeants !"[16] Beck wanted to goad Brauchitsch with a letter; but the attack, which began on June 22, prevented it.

Early on during the advance into Russia, Tresckow heard of the new massacres against the Russian population, particularly the Jews, called for by an extermination plan of the SS. This he learned from his intelligence officer, Gersdorff, and from Oster's contacts with the leader of the *Einsatzgruppe,* SS Gruppenführer

157

Nebe. His own Army Group staff also came into contact with it, when, just in the vicinity of the staff camp at Borisov, some thousands of Jews were shot in Nebe's absence. Nebe, according to Gersdorff, usually coped with his murderous assignments by reporting that the victims had been executed when, in fact, they had not. In addition to the experience of the SS's extermination policy behind the backs of the fighting troops, they learned later of a cruel and huge round-up of men fit for work and their compulsory transportation to the Reich on the railway line used by the Army.

During the advance into Russia the troops, as Tresckow learned from all the Army Group reports, found the population very friendly. They regarded the advancing Germans as their liberators from the Soviet yoke. Tresckow thought that, if they could be persuaded to co-operate by correct behaviour and human moderation, it would not only reinforce the struggle against Bolshevism but spare German lives. But to what depths were they now sinking with this incomprehensible megalomania? Must the soldier now see all that he fought for disappear in hate and revenge? Was the Russian not being driven on to fight a patriotic war against Germany?[17] But Germany and all Europe was, as an officer of the same Army Group, the GSO I of the Fourth Army, had written in his diary on November 5, 1941, "handed over to the criminal will and diseased ambition of a madman".[18] Not a few, who encountered on the staffs the same cruel, mad actions, were only saved from the hopeless despair by absorption in their heavy duties or by volunteering for the front.

In his unremitting search for a successful form of intervention, Tresckow became convinced that, only if Hitler died, would the soldiers feel freed from their oath of allegiance and the way be cleared for action. From 1942 onwards his conscience prompted him to advocate passionately to those who thought the responsibility too great the terrible but inescapable duty they had to assassinate the tyrant. He dismissed all objections about so-called Prussian or German officers' honour and so-called Christian morality. The higher and more sacred morality, which this genuine Prussian officer and pious soldier of God felt in his breast, left only one way.... An oath was a reciprocal undertaking. Hitler had broken his a thousand times and so often lied to, and deceived, his people that an oath made to him had no further validity. To overcome the problem of the oath, Tresckow told his officers, they should disregard their own persons and think of their obligations to the whole people. This was when the Army at Stalingrad was fighting its last battle. Hitler, "the author of all evil", he said, must die. Once, pausing suddenly on a walk, Tresckow said to one of his close friends : "Is it not monstrous that here are two Colonels of the General Staff of the German Army talking about the best way of killing the Head of State? And yet it is the only way to save the Reich and the German people from the greatest catastrophe in their history."[19] But he saw this salvation, essentially, as a matter of conscience. However much he hoped for a "renewal", as a result of a successful coup, it seemed to him more important, even if defeat was now almost inevitable, that Germans themselves should revolt, in spite of the prospect of failure.

After the first great frontier battles in Russia, Tresckow, following a journey to the front by State Secretary Planck and General Thomas, resumed contact with the group in Berlin and sent Schlabrendorff to Berlin at the end of September 1941. He was to look round for "useful resistance nuclei" at home and to inform himself of the international situation. In a conversation Hassell pointed out "the old dilemma : if we wait until the whole world sees there can be no victory, then we have lost the chance of a tolerable peace. But we cannot wait. Whatever happens, the inheritance will be evil."[20] Hopes in Brauchitsch, which were revived in the late autumn of 1941, were again extinguished, when he was relieved of his post on December 19. It was the same with an attempt, undertaken by Beck and Goerdeler after their disappointment, to get Witzleben, who was Commander-in-Chief in the West in Paris, and Falkenhausen in Brussels, to support a move. Both Generals rejected a special move by the Army in the West as utopian.[21] From the spring of 1942 onwards, when the worst of the winter crisis in Russia was over, the contacts between the Berlin group round Beck, Oster, Hassell, Canaris and Dohnanyi and the Tresckow circle were again reinforced, particularly when it seemed likely that Kluge could be persuaded to make a move. In the autumn of 1942 Goerdeler visited Smolensk, and according to a report, his arguments "broke the ice with Kluge". Goerdeler had also, as he said later in Berlin, found the "full understanding" of the Commander-in-Chief of the Army Group North, Field-Marshal von Küchler.[22] In December, Goerdeler, Olbricht, and Tresckow met in Berlin. Before separating, they agreed that Tresckow would prepare, and be in charge of, the first move from the Army Group and that, within about eight weeks, Olbricht would have organized matters in Berlin, Cologne, Munich and Vienna to enable the Army to take over power after the assassination had been carried out.[23]

No details are known of the preparations Olbricht made and which went on in January and February. H. B. Gisevius, who was now working secretly with Olbricht, as he had done with Witzleben

In 1938, has described how difficult, even impossible, it was, even for Nebe, to get access to the necessary documents, such as those relating to the SS strongpoints in the Reich and the forced labour camps which were also the strong-points for the *Totenkopf* (Death's Head) units. "We had therefore to make our preparations quite independently and to co-ordinate these with the military measures to cope with 'internal unrest' prepared by Olbricht under the code-name Valkyrie."[24]

At this time, January 1943, a meeting took place in Berlin in the house of Count Peter Yorck. It had been particularly asked for by Schulenburg and had been the subject of preparation for weeks. It was meant to serve as a political forum and to bring about agreement. Beck, Goerdeler, Popitz, Jessen, Hassell, Yorck, Schulenburg, Trott, Gerstenmaier and perhaps one or two others, were present. Mierendorff and Haubach were absent for "police reasons". At this discussion, it seems, it was a question of the Kreisau circle meeting Goerdeler, particularly in economic and social matters, on which they had so very different views. Trott spoke on foreign affairs, with emphasis on the aim of European unity, Yorck on administration and Reich reform, Moltke on co-operation between the Churches and the unions, Gerstenmaier on relations between Church and state and on social questions. In the social sphere the "younger" members were not ready to accept Goerdeler's efforts to create a bridge, because they felt he wanted to restore the old and was opposed to the new start and the new constructive policy they wanted. Hassell acted as mediator. "There was agreement," Gerstenmaier's report ends, "on the need to bring about the coup d'état as soon as possible. Beck briefly wound up the meeting with the remark that he must first see how strong were the forces which were actually available."[25]

Tresckow went straight to work, once the decision had been taken. It was clear to him, and sometimes he even said it, that he would have to undertake himself the heaviest and "dirtiest" work; this meant constant self-control and strain in a distasteful exercise. It would have been more to his liking had he thought he was destined to take the extreme step of meeting Hitler in the open with arms. But every sober appraisal told him that this old and "highly respectable way" had very little chance of success. A secretly activated bomb seemed to offer better prospects. But if it were to be this, it was essential to act with complete technical mastery of the means, so as not to be guilty of half-measures. So, Tresckow, who was GSO I of an Army Group engaged in a severe winter battle—it was the winter of 1942–43—himself undertook the difficult tests and preparations. The mid-day walks over the

Dnieper meadows near Smolensk, which he took alone, or in company, even in times of heavy work, provided the opportunity. Gersdorff was always getting him new equipment from a sabotage section under his command in every conceivable disguise. He provided a British plastic bomb known to have a high explosive capacity which could be kneaded into any form desired; in addition, British chemical time fuses, which were noiseless, could be handled easily and inconspicuously and were very reliable. Most of them had been obtained when they were dropped by British aircraft. Tests had shown that it was particularly necessary to know exactly how long the fuses took to burn, so as to be able to work with them to the precise minute. The time the fuses took to burn, according to the maker, were, it turned out, based on average room temperatures; in the cold they were found to act more slowly. Tresckow made the first bomb single-handed and himself set its fuse. There were failures. New attempts became necessary. Tresckow persevered and only few people could calculate what it must have cost a man like him to learn to be an assassin. The last tests confirmed the reliability and the explosive power of what he had managed to put together and the duration of its fuse could now be accurately predicted.

The winter struggle for Stalingrad was nearing its end. Those officers who knew what had happened were very bitter. This was not just a fate brought about by a change in the fortune of the war. This was a judgement on the frivolity, superficiality, and megalomania of a leader, who had lost all sense of moderation and reality.[26] There had been hopes in connection with Stalingrad that the troops encircled there and, above all, Colonel-General Paulus, would openly defy Hitler's orders and try, as was originally thought possible, to make the break-out and so start a revolt. Hitler had forbidden this break-out with false promises. Beck and Olbricht were clearly involved in such plans.[27] But Paulus, promoted by Hitler to the rank of Field-Marshal, went into Russian captivity on February 3, 1943, with what was left of his former 300 000 men.[28]

At the end of February Olbricht reported to Tresckow that the preparations were concluded. Canaris came to Smolensk at the beginning of March with Dohnanyi and General Lahousen. Details were discussed. After various delays, Tresckow, through General Schmundt, the Chief Adjutant, was able to get Hitler to announce he would visit the Army Group Centre on March 13, 1943.[29] Some time before, at Tresckow's instigation, an "Army Group Centre Cavalry Regiment" had been formed from the reconnaissance units of the divisions, under Lieutenant-Colonel Georg von Boeselager.

He soon had it firmly under his control; his officers were so devoted to him that they would follow him however unusual the undertaking. Boeselager was ready with his regiment to remove Hitler on his next visit. Kluge, to whom Tresckow made the proposal, rejected an undertaking which required his orders and which would force him from then onwards to come out into the open. Kluge did not think success was possible, if he were attacked by troop commanders who were loyal to Hitler, especially Model who was in the vicinity. He thought they would have to try at once to liberate Hitler at all costs.

Tresckow's plans were also affected in another way. Hitler came and the visit went according to plan. The conference, in which Tresckow participated with the other Army leaders, took place in Kluge's office. A bomb explosion here would have been quite possible; but this would also have killed the leaders of the whole Army Group, whose services would be needed at the critical time of the coup. The same applied to the joint lunch. Hitler ate what his cook had prepared and his physician sampled. During the lunch Tresckow spoke to one of Hitler's staff, Colonel Brandt, and casually asked him whether he would take a small parcel of two cognac bottles for Colonel Stieff in the High Command. Brandt agreed. In the meantime, a code-word announcing the imminent start of the operation was sent to a colleague of Oster's, Captain Gehre, in Berlin. Gehre was to warn Oster through Dohnanyi, who in turn would warn Olbricht. After the lunch Hitler, accompanied by Kluge and Tresckow, drove back to the air-field. Schlabrendorff waited there with the parcel in a brief-case. When Hitler had taken his leave of the officers of the Army Group and turned to the plane, he set the fuse and, on a sign from Tresckow, gave the parcel to Colonel Brandt, who took it and entered the plane behind Hitler. Brandt was to be killed on the 20th July by Stauffenberg's bomb. Shortly afterwards, Hitler's plane and, behind it, another with other members of his staff, followed by some fighters, set off for East Prussia. Tresckow talked with Kluge as they drove back. Kluge knew nothing of the incident. Schlabrendorff sent a new code-word to Gehre in Berlin. . . . From his description it is possible to picture the tremendous tension of those moments. They knew that the inconspicuous parcel was in the plane and that its acid was silently eating away the wire which must soon break and release the firing-pin. In thirty minutes from take-off the armoured plane must explode in the air and perhaps nothing more would be found of the Führer. There would be talk of an accident; Kluge would have a free hand; and in the confusion the planned revolution would be completed. The half-hour passed and there was no special news of the flight. Finally, after two hours, Headquarters reported that the Führer had landed and had resumed his work.

Schlabrendorff called Berlin to cancel arrangements. It seemed bad enough that the attempt had been a failure. But its discovery would mean death not only for Tresckow and Schlabrendorff but also for their leading accomplices. The recipient of the parcel, Colonel Stieff, was not then one of the initiated. After considerable thought, Tresckow decided to phone Colonel Brandt and ask him not to hand over the parcel, because it was the wrong one. The right one would come on the following day. From his answer, it was clear that nothing had yet happened to it. Schlabrendorff decided to fly in the courier plane the next day to Headquarters on some military pretext. He went to Colonel Brandt and exchanged the parcel for one which now really contained two bottles of cognac.... "Today I can still feel the anxiety I experienced when Hitler's aide, unaware of what he was holding, handed me the bomb with a laugh and so violently jogged the parcel that I was afraid the bomb would explode belatedly, for the fuse was still set." In the sleeper-train to Berlin he locked himself in the compartment and opened the parcel with a razor blade. The acid had been released, the wire had been eaten through, the firing-pin had been pushed forward, but for some inexplicable reason the small detonator had not ignited and the two charges remained intact.

A few days later an exhibition of captured weapons and other captured equipment of the Army Group Centre was opened in the Berlin Armoury (Zeughaus). General Schmundt told Tresckow that on March 21, Heroes' Memorial Day, Hitler would visit the exhibition for half-an-hour after the ceremony. Göring, Himmler and Keitel, were expected to be with him. Tresckow spoke to Rudolf von Gersdorff. He, as intelligence officer of the Army Group, was to accompany Hitler through the exhibition. Gersdorff was determined to do more and to sacrifice his life in the task. He drove to Berlin. He received the explosive from Schlabrendorff who woke him as he still lay fast asleep in his hotel in the early morning, and went to the Armoury with a bomb in each coat-pocket. Before the visit began, and before Gersdorff set off the fuses in his pockets, Schmundt came up to see him : there were not thirty minutes available, as had been foreseen, but only eight to ten. Tresckow followed the ceremony on the radio in Smolensk with a watch in his hand. When the commentator, ten minutes after he had reported the Führer entering the exhibition, announced that he had reappeared at the War Memorial, it was clear to Tresckow that Gersdorff could not have acted : the shortest fuse available, and the one which Gersdorff had been given, required fifteen minutes to burn in the cold rooms of the Armoury.[30]

An assassination in Führer Headquarters was considered as another possibility. Tresckow himself, or one of his colleagues, was from time to time taken by Field-Marshal Kluge with him to Hitler's conferences. But what excuse could be found to keep the Marshal away? For it was essential to have him for the coup; he would be needed as a leading figure during the first days of the new régime. When it was impossible to proceed further, a plan took shape to make a joint assassination attempt with pistols, when Hitler next visited the Army Group. Experience had shown that there was no prospect of an individual being able to fire, and to fire accurately, under the eyes of a vigilant staff. Seven officers were ready to take part in a joint attack. But Hitler did not make another visit to the Army Group and, after 1943, he only rarely left the highly-guarded inner area of his Headquarters. It became ever more difficult to plan an assassination.

Tresckow was bitterly disappointed by this continued failure. In the summer of 1943 he decided to ask for two months' sick leave, which he hoped to spend in Elmau. Before he got away, the Army Group was involved in very heavy fighting, first in its own offensive ("Citadel", near Kursk from July 5), then in the enemy's big attack (Orel, from July 15). Mussolini was arrested on July 25, and Italy threatened to defect. When Tresckow arrived in Potsdam on July 30 or 31, he was determined to remain in Berlin and to devote himself solely to the aim of an early coup. There had been great doubts whether, in the event of an assassination, the plans would have ensured a seizure of power. Tresckow regarded it as vital to prepare the day 'X' on General Staff lines, right down to detailed orders and ordinances, and to check and elaborate, in the light of recent experience, the "Valkyrie" operation—that is to say, the measures planned with the knowledge of the Army Command to cope with internal unrest. Only in this way could any of the major front-line Commanders be expected to go ahead.

Before leaving Smolensk, Tresckow had been able to achieve something with Kluge, who gave him some hope, in spite of previous bitter experience. During a walk—Gersdorff was on Kluge's other side—he told him of the attempts they had made and of which Kluge had, until then, no idea. "We think, Field-Marshal, that is the only way the German Reich and the German people can be saved from complete catastrophe," declared Gersdorff, whom the Field-Marshal had taken by the arm. Kluge was speechless for a moment and then said : "Boys, you have me on your side !"[31] Goerdeler reported that Tresckow had visited him in

164

August and assured him Kluge, Manstein and Küchler, the three Army Group Commanders in the East, realized that there must now be "action" and that even the SS Generals Hausser and Sepp Dietrich, who were under the command of the Central Group, "would co-operate".[32]

Tresckow set up his secret "staff quarters" in a relative's house in Neubabelsberg, which he was able to take for himself. Here during the weeks of August he worked out the military plans for that day 'X', painstakingly, on his own, and with few helpers, and in touch with Olbricht and the initiated.[33] At the same time, he sought contact with the political elements of the Opposition movement to Hitler. Great difficulties had arisen. Oster, under heavy suspicion, had had to withdraw to private life and was closely watched. Dohnanyi, Dietrich Bonhoeffer, and Josef Müller, who, like Oster, belonged to the Abwehr, were arrested; and Canaris was hardly in a position any longer to do anything. Beck was absent, owing to a grave illness, which made it seem unlikely that he would ever return. Weizsäcker, who until then had provided important support in the Foreign Office, was removed from the scene and became Ambassador to the Vatican.[34] Only Goerdeler was active in all directions and tried with renewed fervour to combat both the thesis of the "psychologically unfavourable moment" and general depression engendered by the set-backs. In a long memorandum of March 26, 1943, he appealed to a new group amongst the officers and, when everything seemed paralysed, he urged Olbricht to act, in a passionate letter written after the surrender of Tunis on March 12, 1943. "Stalingrad and Tunis are the greatest defeats in German history since Jena and Auerstädt." He thought he could serve the cause by offering to Olbricht to appear in person before Hitler. "I would tell him what needs to be said. Surprises are possible, if not probable. But the risk must be taken. But it is not too much if I ask for an assurance that there will then be immediate action."[35] At the same time Goerdeler handed over to the Swede, Wallenberg, in Stockholm, a memorandum to be forwarded to Churchill. This contained the promises of a new government and proposals that the bombing attacks should be limited, particularly during the period of the coup.[36]

The series of defeats and retreats, which signalized the year 1943, aroused doubts in several who, until then, had had an unthinking faith in Hitler. But the Allies themselves, by their demand for unconditional surrender, had again made it more difficult for Germans to break with Hitler. By giving them no option but the harsh terms of surrender, they forced even the opponents of Hitler to see him and the Fatherland as one, and to support him.[37] How greatly minds were ensnared was shown, some weeks after Casablanca, by the memorable occurrence in Munich: the passionate appeal to their fellow-students made by the *Scholl* brother and sister[38] and their friends. This was drowned in the tumult of events, and the impact of their deaths was undermined by abuse or icy silence. In the same way, the death of an entire army on the Volga, which had prompted these young people to speak up, was realized in all its horror by only a few people at home. But if the fire did not really catch on, as these young Germans gathered round the "Weisse Rose" (White Rose) had hoped, the group of persons who lived only for a change of régime consolidated itself. Individuals and groups intensified their exchanges, and thought was given to finding a way out of the hopeless and desperate situation. There was agreement about the aim of overthrowing Hitler and trying to end the war as soon as possible. But opinion was divided about how this should be done and what kind of régime should be put in place of the existing one. So far there had been no unifying will. Sometimes, it looked as if the Resistance movement was quarrelling in the shadows in a desperate struggle for places in the future government. There were also different opinions about the question of an assassination. There were weighty elements, including Goerdeler, who took the view that the struggle against violators of the laws should not begin with a formal violation of those laws. In addition, there were differences about the moment to choose. Some of the Socialists were opposed to risking a coup before the Allies had landed in Central or Western Europe and were ready to march straight to Berlin and the Eastern frontier of the Reich. But after some members of the conspiracy had been arrested by the Gestapo and others were increasingly threatened, it hardly seemed possible to delay any longer. Their problem was: they had to act, but were powerless; and they had to wait, but had no time to lose.

By the autumn of 1943 the situation on the fronts was constantly deteriorating for Germany. The war on two fronts was being felt in all its weight, thanks to the participation of the USA. In Russia, the summer offensive, which began on July 5 on the Kursk front salient, collapsed after little more than two weeks. It was not able to prevent the carrying out of a big Russian offensive, which in August deprived the Germans of Orel and Kharkov, and in September of Smolensk, and which threw them back to the Southern Dnieper and cut their communications with the Crimea. In September 1943 the whole front was approximately 2 200 kilometres long and ran from Leningrad via Lake Ilmen to the area of Nevel, from there between Vyazma and Smolensk via Bryansk to the

Dnieper (Cherkassy-Nikopol) and reached the Black Sea at Odessa. There was strong Russian pressure in the central sector, particularly near Nevel, and in the south in the direction of Kiev. Southern Italy was in the hands of the Allies. In the occupied countries from Scandinavia to the Balkans no new front had arisen, apart from the growing Resistance movement; but there were increasing expectations of an enemy invasion in France. The once successful U-boat war had failed after heavy losses as a result of the hitherto superior radar invention of the enemy. The air attacks, made generally by American forces by day, and by British forces by night, reduced more and more towns and industries to ashes during this summer and could no longer be adequately countered by the defence. More than seven million German troops (including ten Rumanian and six Hungarian divisions) were under arms on the fronts and in the occupied territories; and about four millions of them were in Russia. The new weapons, of which there was mysterious talk, had so far played no decisive role. They had not been able to stop the retreat. But it was not the retreat itself which caused the greatest concern, but the stubbornness and lack of imagination of the Supreme Command which, day by day, became increasingly apparent. The forces were not equal to their over-extended task. But Hitler was not open to advice to cut his losses and he could not achieve a political solution in the West with Churchill and Roosevelt, or in the East with Stalin. There was no knowing how much longer Germany could hold out, thanks to the bravery of her soldiers and the discipline of her war economy. But it looked as if the greatest sacrifices in men and material were yet to come.

Yet Hitler still spoke this summer, as he had in his speech of November 5, 1938, of *Lebensraum* and of the German mission to be the leading power in Europe. We have part of a speech he made to the Army Group Commanders shortly before the summer offensive: "Without Lebensraum the German Reich and the German nation cannot exist. It must be the leading power in Europe. . . . In the last resort man lives from the earth and the earth is the prize-cup which Providence gives to people who fight for it. I do not want to make war for five years and in the last five minutes let this cup out of my hands for the sake of some vague hope. . . ."[39] In this address Hitler emphatically declared that he was not interested in any policy for the populations of the conquered Eastern territories : no policy should alter the slaves' fate of inferior peoples.

Hitler's supporters who, now more than ever, ought to have acted as his sober advisers in these weeks, were gravely shaken by the

167

deteriorating situation but still prepared to take refuge in a mad faith that their wishes would somehow be realized.

* * *

On October 14, 1943, at a meeting of Commanders in Bad Schachen, Heinrich Himmler reviewed the internal situation in Germany, as seen by the Security Police, and also drew a picture of the hard struggle and of the aims for which, in his opinion, it was being fought.[40] These sentences are to be found in a record of this speech, which he made before a select audience :

"Another question is that of defeatism, particularly amongst the educated and prosperous classes. I remind you here of a time, when, without doubt, a great wave of defeatism was going through Germany. It was the time when the news came that the Duce had been deposed. Fascism was finished and Italy was out of the war. You will have read in the paper that Herr Regierungsrat[41] so-and-so, waiter X or factory-owner Y, who spoke in defeatist terms, were condemned to death by the People's Court and that the sentences have already been carried out. . . . What sort of impact does it have when a Regierungsrat says : We must make peace; we cannot win the war. Besides, the Führer has done this and that wrong. . . . What sort of impact does it have when precisely a man who is supposed to be educated and from whom the small man expects leadership, speaks like that? When someone like that begins to destroy faith, confidence, loyalty and obedience in the peaceful, decent German, the damage could be very great. . . . When a man of position, in an office and with honours and of mature age, acts in this way, then he becomes the pitiless victim of the laws of war and is executed. And we publish such information because, only in this way, can a life of failure be of use to the German nation, so that thousands of other stupid gossipers can be taught a lesson. For that reason I am always in favour of hard and merciless punishment where necessary. . . .

"One thing we must know. It is only if we remain true to the oath that we have sworn to our supreme war lord, if we are loyal, faithful and united, that we can, and will, achieve the victory that is one day destined to be ours. There may be grave crises : we will certainly experience some new ones. We must never lose faith : we must always strike back; and then one day the war will be at an end. 'Old Fritz' (Frederick the Great) needed ten years to establish Prussia as a European power. For us the end of the war means that the way will be open to the East, the creation of the Germanic Reich and, in this or that way, the incorporation of 30 million of our kinsmen, so that, in our lifetime, we shall be a people of 120 million Germans. . . . That means that we can then turn to peace, in the first twenty years of which we are determined to rebuild, and ease the strain on, our villages and towns, and push the frontiers of the German-speaking people 500 kilometres to the East. And that means, gentlemen, that we shall then want to have an Eastern defence frontier that will always be fluid and will keep us virile and from which we can gradually move into a military safety area for our grandchildren and great-grandchildren. This we must have in a future war in order not to collapse under the bombs of the enemy.

"That, gentlemen, is the meaning of peace : this wonderful future which we want to think of. When we look thus into the future, the sufferings and dangers that have to be endured now grow less, because they are small in comparison with the greatness of our time in which—and this cannot be grasped often enough in our hearts—we have the fortune, as Germanic people, to have found after two thousand years a leader, our Führer, Adolf Hitler. Let us show ourselves to be worthy of him and let us have the stature to be his loyal and obedient supporters."

On November 7, 1943, the Chief of the Wehrmacht Operations Staff, Hitler's most immediate adviser, General Jodl, spoke in Munich to Reich leaders and Gauleiters about the strategic situation at the beginning of the fifth year of war.[42] Jodl told the meeting in a speech which, even to the use of particular expressions, bore the stamp of Hitler's way of speaking, that, after the winter fighting of 1942–43 and the loss of four allied armies, Germany had gone over to the defensive, while the enemy, with their mastery of the air, had also won the initiative on the ground, as was shown in their joint summer attack in Sicily and in the East (both began in July 1943. "Italy's betrayal" had had in this crisis a worse effect than had been publicly announced. The overall situation was now "difficult" and further serious crises could be expected. But particular hopes were to be placed on new technical war equipment which could counter the enemy's superiority in the air and make it possible to resume U-boat warfare successfully. Above all, hopes were to be based on the ethical and moral basis of the struggle, which gave its stamp to the entire attitude of the German people and made the Wehrmacht an absolutely reliable instrument in the hands of its leader.

"The strength of the revolutionary idea," Jodl said, "has not only made possible a series of incomparable successes, but it enables our brave troops to achieve—even in defence and planned withdrawals—feats which perhaps only the Russians, but no other people, could perform and which render utopian all our enemy's hopes of a military collapse. . . .

"My profound confidence is based on the fact that, at the head of Germany, stands a man, whose whole experience, will and aims, make him predetermined by fate to lead our people to a brighter future. Despite all contrary opinions, I want to say here that he is the spirit behind, not only the political, but also the military, conduct of the war, and that the strength of his will and the creative wealth of his ideas in the field of strategy, organization and arms technology, pulsate through the whole German Wehrmacht and hold it together.

"It is now up to us all to suppress faint-heartedness and to create in ourselves the basis of that confidence from which alone victory can grow. . . . A war is only lost when one regards it as lost.

"At this hour I would like to acknowledge, not in words, but from the depths of my heart, that our confidence and faith in the Führer is unlimited; that for us there is no higher law and no holier duty than to fight to the last breath for the freedom of our people; that we are determined to reject all weakness and neglect of duty; that all the threats of our enemies will only make us harder and more resolved; that we do not indulge in any cowardly hope, as though others could save us from Bolshevism, which will sweep away everything, if Germany falls; that we would defend even the ruins of our country to the last shot, because it is better to live among them than in slavery; that we will be victorious, because we must be victorious, since otherwise the history of the world would have lost its meaning."

THE TWENTIETH OF JULY

IX. CLAUS AND BERTHOLD STAUFFENBERG

AFTER Stalingrad and Tunis, September 1943 brought the third capitulation of the year : the surrender of Italy announced on September 8 and followed on the 9th by the Allied landing on the south Italian mainland. As was realized later, this could have rapidly led to total disaster for Germany if her opponents' Supreme Command had been bolder.

Mussolini had been arrested on July 25. On September 10 Hitler warned the German people in a broadcast that anyone hoping for a revolt in Germany was making a "fundamental mistake", both about his, Hitler's, personal position in the nation and the attitude of his political comrades-in-arms, his Field-Marshals, Admirals and Generals.[1]

On the same day the "exceptionally gifted General Staff officer" whose name remains linked with the 20th July began his task in Berlin. He was Lieutenant-Colonel Count von Stauffenberg, the "seriously war-disabled" officer whom Goerdeler had a few weeks earlier mentioned for the first time to confidants as a possible hope for the Resistance movement. Until then his name had not been put forward in this connection.

Claus, Count Schenk von Stauffenberg was born on November 15, 1907. The ancestral seat of the Stauffenbergs was in a Swabian valley near where their castle had once stood. They were the lords of the manor in a small parish there and patrons of the church, with their own family pew in the gallery. It was said that, in a fit of high spirits, one of his titled ancestors offended a Hohenzollern neighbour by telling him he was not good enough to look after the Stauffenbergs' swine, and was consequently banned from tournaments for three years. Another ancestor had been Prince Bishop of Constance and a third one Prince Bishop of Bamberg. Through his mother, Countess Uexküll by birth, Stauffenberg was descended from Gneisenau and related to the Yorck family.[2]

His father, Lord-Marshal Count Stauffenberg, who was in the service of the Royal house of Württemberg, was given accommodation in the ancient Renaissance castle in the capital, and from there the three boys attended the Eberhard-Ludwig Gymnasium. Bonds of intimate friendship, rare between brothers linked Claus and Berthold, two years his senior. Their association with Stefan George, the poet, and his circle had a decisive influence on their character.[2a]

As boys, they lived in a world of their own; on a rock in the Jura mountains near Lautlingen they kept a castle to which even their own family were barred access. At school the brothers and their friends formed a group which devoted itself to poetry and the appreciation of art and music.[3] Even strangers noticed them as they met each morning at certain points and made their way to school together.

The brothers played leading roles in several school festivals and theatricals. Some fellow-students particularly remember Claus Stauffenberg as William Tell. Once, scenes from Julius Caesar were staged at the Stauffenberg home while the parents were away. The boy Lucius—portrayed by the fifteen-year-old Claus Stauffenberg —made a deep impression as, on the eve of battle overcome by sleep, he played his song to Brutus—brother Berthold. At that time Claus loved playing his cello, and some of his fellow-students thought he would later devote himself to music. But in his adolescence he chose a different career.

Putting aside his equally strong leaning towards architecture the eighteen-year-old Stauffenberg joined the Reichswehr. He was trained in the Bamberg Cavalry Regiment, to which other members of his family had belonged before him,[4] and coming top at the cavalry tests he was commissioned at the age of twenty-two. He had a real passion and an inborn skill for riding and handling horses. When he was billeted on a farmer he one day came across a young mare among the draught-horses—"an enchanting personality" as he put it. He bought the mare, trained her to perform the passage and levade and won a prize with her in the difficult dressage test. At the Hanover Cavalry School he rode with future Olympic champions who were then preparing for a tournament.

The years 1936 to 1938 were spent at the Military Academy in Berlin. A whim prompted Stauffenberg to write a paper on "The defence of the homeland against enemy paratroops". To his astonishment it won him a first prize, and even during the war the paper was regarded by Ministerial experts as the "basic work" on the subject.

But the critics were less kind about another of his papers which had deeply absorbed him : after a survey of earlier methods of fighting, Stauffenberg tried to show the "unaltered character" of the cavalry "especially in times of surprising changes of method", and to re-define the task of the cavalry in a modern war of movement and armour. After passing his interpreter's examination he was able to make a trip to England. It was a great experience and broadened his outlook. His travel notes, passed from hand to hand, have been lost. On the journeys which he and his friends undertook from the Military Academy Stauffenberg often acted as spokesman. Once, as they were standing on top of the Hohentwiel Rock he drew an outline of the great Staufen Empire and said they were to "consider themselves at its centre".

After he had finished his course at the Military Academy, they made a final trip to study the Rhine crossings and he used the occasion to persuade the group to pay a joint visit to the Imperial cathedrals on the river. He acted as leader. At the end of the trip he made a speech on the Rhine in which he evoked the region's centuries-old history. Then, turning to the time when national states would have passed away he forecast a new role for the Rhine as the main artery of Europe. Of the past he spoke not like an intellectual observer but seemed more of a co-actor, one who had been there himself and now was called upon once again to make decisions. Thus his portrayal of the past became a living example for the present.

He combined a broad and passionate view of things with a charming ease of delivery; there was clarity without dryness, depth without gloom in his speeches. It is not known whether Ludwig Beck was present on any of these journeys or on what occasion he joined the young circle. Stauffenberg spoke of him with great respect and he knew of Beck's moves from close observation, even in 1938.

At the Academy Stauffenberg was regarded as very industrious but nobody actually saw him doing much work. According to the interrogation reports one of his comrades described Stauffenberg as "top-boy". He outshone the rest by his intellectual ability. This, combined with his temperament and skill as an orator, enabled him to carry the whole course before him.[5] Stauffenberg, they thought, had the strength to overcome the narrow military way of thinking. Jokingly they also referred to him as the new Schlieffen, and a General of the old school said he was "the only German Staff officer of genius, likely to become a worthy successor to Field-Marshals Moltke and Schlieffen". Another comment by someone who had seen the thirty-year-old officer for the first time : "Impossible to tell in what way he will take a hand one day, but I can see there is action hidden in this man." At about that time the sculptor Frank Mehnert created a statue of a young sapper.[6] It was put up on a bridge across the Elbe in Magdeburg. Mehnert gave it Stauffenberg's features : a vigorous, relaxed and clearly defined body, and a head which reflected a unity of the sensual and spiritual, uncommon in those days. Ludwig Thormaehlen who made a model of Stauffenberg's head[7] and who met him many times gives this account : "At this time, the end of 1924, Claus von

175

Stauffenberg was seventeen, two-and-a-half-years younger than his brother, and of quite a different nature. Even at this early age his cheerful and enthusiastic approach to everything around him gave the impression of absolute reliability. His spirit showed itself in the way he acted—loyal in attack, serene in reproach, energetic in the support and defence of the just claims of others. He was modest and reserved, yet alert and ready for vigorous action, and of charming disposition—all of which made him instantly attractive. He was a born soldier and marked out for a position of authority. From the outset he aroused great hopes as a gallant defender or even creator of sense and order and as protector and patron of any righteous cause.

"Stauffenberg's most striking feature were his eyes, which at once revealed his serenity and magnanimity, his commonsense and goodwill. They were a metallic, dark blue. His face, without appearing round, was broad and well-proportioned. He had powerful high cheekbones, a vigorous, faintly cleft chin, and a firm resolute forehead with slight bulges above the eyebrows—evidence of alertness, acute observation, will-power and tenacity. Another notable feature was his aquiline nose and his well-shaped, curved mouth. His slightly wavy hair was dark, shiny and brushed to lie flat on his head. As a youngster he was a lively, roguish lad, but— as his face showed—he rapidly grew to early manhood. He was tall and lithe and had strong, well-trained limbs. Later, his slight stoop and the way he walked indicated the horseman—and he was a superb equestrian. All three brothers possessed that rare quality— a warm heart. As Claus grew older his features resembled more and more those of his ancestor Neithardt von Gneisenau as was clear from family portraits.

"Perhaps his brothers inherited more unusual qualities, but his was a wonderfully balanced personality, the perfection of courageous, alert, vivacious manhood, an abundance of talent which was no unmanageable burden to him. Not only was he liked—he evoked immediate enthusiasm and delight, wherever he appeared. His vivacity and his positive attitude to himself and anything of worth was infectious; it swept everyone else along and made present and future seem easy and full of hope. Worry, scepticism and scruples dissolved into nothing in his presence.

"Like his brother Berthold he was the 'master', in the most self-evident way: he was a free, exalted person who knew nothing superior to himself, nothing to induce in him an attitude of submission or devotion, except where he freely recognised superiority in intellect and rank."

As a boy Stauffenberg was delicate and often ailing. Even when

176

he was about to enlist in the Reichswehr he was afraid of being rejected because of his weak constitution. Later he toughened himself to withstand any strain and physical effort. He did not go short of anything, enjoyed life whenever possible and always appeared to be on the go, lively and agile. The story goes that once, after military manoeuvres, he rode in three days from the Swabian Alb to his beloved Bamberg.

Even when things were at their tensest at Headquarters he only reluctantly gave up his early morning ride, although he might have had a sixteen- or eighteen-hour working day behind him and was facing another one as long. Someone who saw him quite often during that time remarked on the speed with which he worked, his powers of concentration, his brightness night and day and said, "his nerves and health, which he certainly did not spare, were enviable".[8]

Not only descent and identity of profession linked him with Gneisenau, his character and physical appearance too made him a genuine "Gneisenau-grandson". He had great self-confidence and was aware of his power over others. But no one found him conceited. He was not envious and was surprisingly unconcerned about his own position and authority. To him applies the phrase "of a people free and proud that overcomes the low instincts of envy and jealousy" and the sentence which he later incorporated in his oath of allegiance : "We bow to rank ordained by nature."[9]

Despite his specialized abilities he did not give the impression of being an expert. What impressed observers most strongly was that he always saw a problem in its entirety and based his judgement of details on this secure foundation. People from quite different walks of life were his close friends. They were all actively involved in intellectual and artistic pursuits which he did not give up even during the last few months before the 20th July when one objective required his entire attention. He was a frequent contributor to a number of historical and poetical works produced by his friends. While he was fighting in Africa he learnt of the death of Frank Mehnert the sculptor, who had been very close to him. Mehnert was killed in battle on Lake Ilmen. Another younger friend of his, a gifted poet who had been writing about Prince Eugen, had lost his life six months earlier at Sevastopol.[10]

Even in the daily company of his fellow-officers Stauffenberg often discussed historical, political, social and artistic matters. His mind was occupied with the pressing question of how to save life from becoming submerged by the overgrowth of a technological civilisation. Mere exposition of the evil made him impatient and he had no time for the almost inevitable lamentations of intellec-

177

tuals confronted by a world which they basically detest. What attracted him were, above all, ideas for doing things differently. At the same time he kept his eye soberly on an attainable objective and on the people with whom it could be achieved. There is a significant story about a delegation of senior students asking the young Stauffenberg—he was about sixteen then—to become their leader and to advocate "the idea of a Youth Ring at school". Stauffenberg is said to have replied that he knew of no idea, he only knew human beings. . . . His attitude was neither determined by the conflict of generations which was so marked in the years after the First World War nor by the clash of ideologies which ten years later became a topic of controversy dividing the world.

His charm and ease made one forgive his forceful and uncompromising manner; and his ruthless will was made bearable by his cheerful calm which allowed no pathos. They said his "magnificent" laughter was unique; once on a night express a man who had not seen Stauffenberg for many years recognized him by his laughter through the closed door of a sleeping compartment. Many who later recalled meeting Stauffenberg agreed with what a lieutenant told the People's Court : he always smiled when he spoke. He was never without supporters. Wherever he went he soon had "his band of conspirators". Later, many friends and comrades from the Cavalry and the Academy days again appeared at his side.

In the summer of 1938 Captain Stauffenberg was posted to the 1st Light Division at Wuppertal which was under General Hoepner's command until November—it became the Sixth Armoured Division after the outbreak of the war. In the months of the Sudetenland crisis Stauffenberg was this division's GSO II and moved with it to the assembly area in the Thuringian Forest. After the German invasion of the Sudetenland he took part in a Quartermasters' tour of inspection at the end of which he and two comrades staged a witty and sarcastic burlesque for the senior officers. With remarkable boldness and supreme disregard for the position on their flanks they expertly drove a fictitious armoured column as far as the Urals. As supply officer Stauffenberg performed unbelievable miracles of improvisation, imaginatively pursuing a strategy which recommended that "if you get into a mess you must pull yourself out by your own boot laces". And when for example the armoured column ran out of petrol in the Ukraine, you simply conquered Baku, quickly laid an overland pipe-line and brought up the missing fuel. The whole scheme was run under the recurrent magic formula : "Under the master's guidance all goes well." In the late autumn came the burning of German synagogues. During that autumn and winter Stauffenberg's thoughts were focused on Gneisenau's plans for an uprising. In January 1939 he invited a group of officers to hear a lecture on Gneisenau. He introduced it himself in terms which discreetly, yet unmistakably referred to the contemporary situation. At the end of the lecture, which lasted nearly two hours and was warmly acclaimed, he remarked, with his characteristic laugh : "So you see, we have learnt how *he* did it."[11]

In the early days of the war Stauffenberg was with the Sixth Armoured Division belonging to Kleist's Armoured Group in Poland and France. A fellow-officer said he was as well-known in the division as the General. He was in it, heart and soul, worked hard and still had time for everybody. Another report described him presiding over a conference :[12]

"Stauffenberg, tall, slim and agile, a man of decided personal charm, received us with radiant and genuine kindness. He saw to it that each of us had a drink, a cigar or a pipe. He gave news, asked questions, enquired into seemingly unimportant matters and told the latest anecdotes that were going the rounds from the divisional reconnaissance unit to the field bakery. He jumped from one subject to another and interrupted conversations because he first wanted to hear what the last entrant had to report. Thus the best part of an hour passed without any of our questions having been decided, until—quite informally and casually—he said : "Right, I think, this is how we're going to do it. . . . Then, left hand in his trouser pocket and holding a glass of wine in his right, pacing up and down the room, deep in thought, stopping now and then, or reaching for the map—Stauffenberg announced the details of the Quartermaster's orders. . . ."

The same reporter from the Armoured Division used these almost panegyric phrases :

"Those evening talks among three or four of us in the billets near St Omer are unforgettable. Time and again we admired the vast intelligence, mature judgement and tremendous knowledge of this highly gifted man—and he was only thirty-two then. Never before or since have I taken part in discussions on such a high level. He was revered and admired by his comrades, collaborators and subordinates, esteemed by his superiors whom he faced with pleasing frankness and without a trace of subservience, fully aware of his own value and dignity, always and in any situation able to choose the right tone and suitable manner : thus he was, radiant and handsome as Alcibiades 'pleasing to man' and truly 'a darling of the Gods' as one of his comrades once put it."

Another acquaintance from the Armoured Division recalls Stauffenberg's remark : "There's nothing more wonderful than a

179

victorious campaign alongside a friend." Yet this man, who was so pre-occupied with the technology of modern battles, saw war as something out of its temporal context and without romance. In the company of friends he could enjoy the charm of the country-side, take pleasure in an attractive bivouac and rejoice in a victory. But in this elation at success in battle there was none of that intoxi-cation to which some of his fellow-officers initially succumbed, none of that delirious desire to use Germany's might to reduce the world to shambles. When, unexpectedly, France seemed about to be defeated, Stauffenberg remarked that it was all senseless, unless France and Germany could be brought closer together. Now (he said) we must be magnanimous, we must at last create something new out of the ancient enmity and, with bravado, he added : if they gave him a free hand he would do it. At the time when Hitler halted the tank advance on Dunkirk and the British succeeded in embarking, Stauffenberg was posted to the General Staff of the Army. At the Organisation Branch he was put in charge of the "Peace-time Army" Department where he had the job of making sure that the Army's organisation and equipment always matched the continuing modifications of weapons and the needs of war. He had to work closely with field commanders, evaluate their experience, and examine and test their suggestions. Occasionally, Stauffenberg also had to guide and instruct delegations of foreign officers who were intended to see something, but not too much, of the German Army.

Stauffenberg saw more than two-and-a-half years of war from Headquarters. They were years packed with crucial events; 1940—the cease-fire with France; the attempt to grind England into sub-mission by air attacks; 1941—the German thrust into the Balkans; the landing on Crete; the broad advance into Russia; the German declaration of war on the United States; 1942—the disastrous winter in Russia; the assault in North Africa which took the Ger-mans as far as Egypt; the push to the Caucasus and the Volga; the enemy landing in Tunisia and Morocco; the sacrifice of the Sixth Army at Stalingrad. . . . In those years Stauffenberg and his Branch took part in every Headquarters move : from Godesberg to Belgium, to Fontainebleau, to the Brandenburg Heath near Zossen; to East Prussia; to Vinnitsa in the Ukraine and back to East Prussia. He made frequent journeys to senior staff officers at the front and in the occupied countries, and to top-level military authorities in Berlin. He paid visits to various commanders : at Borisov on the Beresina river, in the Crimea, in Finland, Belgrade, Paris and Athens.

We have a personal account by Rudolf Fahrner of a meeting

with Stauffenberg in those days.[13] It refers to a journey through the Ukraine where Stauffenberg inspected volunteer forces from Azerbaidjan and other parts of the Soviet Union. He set great store by getting the right leaders for these units under his care. He did not want them turned into hired and misused auxiliaries but to form them into freedom-loving battle groups retaining their own customs and traditions. Stauffenberg's escort said they often encountered a splendid type of man—male dancers and singers who gave performances in the guest's honour, and he thought it remarkable that these people from an entirely different part of the world took to this visitor and accepted him like one of their own indigenous masters.[14]

Although Headquarters consisted of hundreds of sections and sub-sections and even its lay-out was impossible to survey, Stauffenberg had ample opportunity of keeping well informed through friends and acquaintances in Operations Branch; in the "Foreign Armies, West and East" Department; in the Abwehr, in Signals and with Generals in the Ordnance branch. Determined to get an over-all view of the situation, Stauffenberg supplemented the information obtainable at Headquarters by knowledge he gained on his journeys, by verbal and written reports he received and any information his brother let him have from the Naval War Command. However hard pressed, he always managed to find time to listen and ask questions particularly of men just back from battle. He enjoyed offering them hospitality, let them talk of their tough time at the front, and asked about everyone he knew. The soldiers' successes and failures interested him and he analysed them quietly in his mind. Anyone coming to Headquarters with a request would receive advice and help from Stauffenberg, whenever possible. At least he would try to see that an unbiased report on the situation— and this was often difficult—reached the competent authority. There was the case of a repeatedly unsuccessful petition, concerning Russian civilian workers, which despite all kinds of obstruction Stauffenberg is said to have brought to the attention of those responsible. He even added a sharp rider describing the treatment of Russian civilian labour as "an irresponsible provocation of the East".

An elderly comrade in Stauffenberg's regiment, who served at Headquarters as a Reserve Officer, said that at the end of a long working day at one or two a.m. he quite often went over to Stauffenberg's office for a chat or a drink. "I never opened the door without finding Claus on the telephone (he writes), piles of paper in front of him. The receiver in his left hand, a pencil in his right he would be tidying the files at the same time. He was always talking animatedly, and depending on the person at the other end of the phone he would be laughing—and this was the most usual—or scolding, he rarely managed without either; or else he would be giving orders and explanations, writing at the same time either his signature in large, expansive letters or short, remarkably precise comments on the files. Next to him there was usually a clerk who in the intervals rapidly took down comments, letters and memoranda. Claus always meticulously observed the routine trappings of senior staff letters. He could tackle several matters simultaneously with complete concentration and had an amazing ability to sift the essential from the unimportant at a glance. He expressed himself with clarity. His remarks, interposed at lightning speed, were invariably to the point and quite often perplexed the person to whom he was talking. An innate graciousness, tact and charm towards his military seniors, freedom and ease when dealing with men of equal rank—these were the outward reflections of Claus' great personality which readily commanded respect and confidence. Sartorial appearance which others consider an equally important mark of distinction meant little to him amidst the momentous happenings which completely absorbed him.[15]

At the beginning of 1943 Stauffenberg was given an active service post. He arrived in Africa in mid-February and became the GSO I with the Tenth Armoured Division which was then covering the Afrika Corps' retreat to the Tunis bridgehead from a hard-pressing enemy superior in numbers and armament. For many months the division had to fight their tough English opponents in what has been described as an exemplary withdrawal.

Stauffenberg had ignored a slight knee wound from an artillery shot. It had now healed, but after only seven weeks' service with the division he was hit by a burst of fire from a low-flying enemy plane and brought back on April 7, seriously wounded. His face, hands and knee were shot to pieces and he could no longer see. Not until a few days later when the bandages were taken off his head at the military hospital in Carthage, did he know that one eye had been saved after all. He was taken home and put in a military hospital at Munich. For weeks he lay there with a high fever from his wounds. No one seemed certain whether he would pull through. His head, arms and legs were bandaged. The Kaltenbrunner Reports (p. 305) say that "despite his serious condition, he declined any pain-killing and sleeping drugs and with great willpower rapidly recovered from his wounds".[16] It was not so much the wounds that seemed to depress him as the feeling that he had been wrenched from his career without having achieved any of his plans.

But soon an inexplicable change was noticed. Friends who only two weeks before had seen the Count hovering near death were amazed at his entirely new self-confidence and vibrant energy. There was no longer any point in discussing his recovery with him. At the end of April he dictated a letter to General Olbricht saying he hoped to be available again in three months. Evidently, Stauffenberg was referring to some understanding which already existed between the two men.

Once, when he was alone with a friend, he told him confidentially that he had meanwhile been offered the post of Chief of Staff to General Olbricht at OKH, which might provide opportunities for decisive action. Soon afterwards, the same friend received a type-written letter to which Stauffenberg had for the first time added his signature with his crippled left hand. An old General who visited Stauffenberg at the beginning of May was impressed by his lively and assured conduct of the conversation, though he was still suffering from fever. The General noted how Stauffenberg freed several fingers of his left hand from the bandages in order to write. The large number of high-ranking visitors calling on the Lieutenant-Colonel caused astonishment at the military hospital. Gifts arrived from Germany, the Ukraine, France, Italy and Greece. It was like a wave of friendship, affection and hope enveloping him. How many of his visitors sensed what was going on in his mind? "You know, I have a feeling I've got to do something now to save the Reich", he once remarked in passing and in an almost frivolous tone to Countess Nina, the mother of their four children, "as General Staff officers we all share the responsibility".

*　　*　　*

"You ask me about Stauffenberg's political views : I don't think one should try to classify them. He had a remarkable capacity for grasping any situation that arose, and other people's views of it. Yet he was not influenced by opinions, intentions or 'programmes'; he was driven by an urge to action, by inner forces transcending the confines of current political theses and anti-theses. You cannot label people of such temperaments 'right' or 'left', you cannot classify them as opponents or supporters of some trends. This is what makes them 'pregnant with the future' and stamps them as the potential initiators of something new."[17]

Rudolf Fahrner wrote this in 1950. Since then he has enlarged upon it in an extensive account of his collaboration with Claus and Berthold Stauffenberg. And so he becomes the most important surviving witness to the intentions and conduct of the Stauffenberg brothers. His observations may help to clarify Claus Stauffenberg's relationship to Hitler and the events of his time.[18]

They show two things : Stauffenberg cannot be fully understood simply by labelling him as a "brilliant and talented" officer who, in addition to his profession pursued intellectual and political interests; but it is equally wrong to say that he began as an enthusiastic National Socialist, then, after a presumable conversion, turned away from Hitler and found his way to the Resistance; nor would it be correct to call him pro-Communist, citing as alleged evidence his interest in contacts with the East and in plans for social reform.[19] All Claus Stauffenberg's original impulses seemed to be directed towards political action; this is borne out by the afore-mentioned description of him as a youth : "From the start he aroused great hopes as a gallant defender of sense and order." It was this urge towards future action that prompted his decision to become an officer. Many of the discussions in Stefan George's circle in which the young officer and his friends took part turned upon the question of what could be done to promote the growth of a new state structure in Germany. Fahrner's account of these conversations gives a clue to what was on Stauffenberg's mind. It is true that Fahrner scrupulously refrains from attributing this or that remark to any particular speaker, but he says there was agreement on all important points. Fahrner's account, therefore, is of great value as a source about Stauffenberg, unequalled by any other testimony, especially as hitherto scattered reports can now be fitted in to a wider context.

"From about the autumn of 1936"—Fahrner writes—"no matter how absorbed we were with intellectual work nor how great Claus' interest in it, all our meetings with him centred on the same theme : when, how and where could there be a change?"

According to Fahrner, Stauffenberg—himself a man of action— watched and judged Hitler's ascendancy and impact with deep, objective interest. He saw in him the type of a modern leader of the masses with an astonishing capacity for "beating the drum". To him, Hitler was a man who often merely adopted contemporary ideas, he used them just as it suited him but was able to simplify and make them politically effective, thus inspiring large numbers of people to devotion and sacrifice even against their own interests. Stauffenberg was stirred by the magnetism this man was able to generate, by his vehemence which made what seemed impossible in a stagnant world suddenly appear feasible; one could imagine that the crust of bourgeois traditions which had grown from the nineteenth into the twentieth century, had successfully been cracked and that—even in opposition to Hitler—a new order might

184

emerge. After all, it was unmistakable that Hitler, despite the obvious baseness of his character, was also appealing to deep-rooted and genuine desires for a "renewal" and that even men of high ambition and idealism were thus indirectly drawn to him.

From the record of their conversations it seems that these were the points which Stauffenberg regarded as important as he watched Hitler's rise to power : evidently Hitler's aim from the start had been the abolition of democracy by seemingly democratic means. This procedure had defeated the entire Party system and state administration in Germany. Hitler's rise had partly been due to the action of Germany's adversaries, indeed it had only been made possible by it. The Versailles idea of establishing "peace" had provided Hitler with the strongest arguments, and for years he had appeared as the champion of the just causes of all nations. He had a remarkable way both of urging revision and renouncing claims : he seemed to show that there were other possibilities of reaching an understanding among European nations than outworn conventional methods of diplomacy.

Hitler's great impact was in part due to his social welfare measures. In this field of government he did more than many other leaders of the masses and "mere" military men who "once in power invariably fail to solve social problems, which in turn causes their downfall. They often do not realize that they are merely living off and misusing the remnants of an outdated social order." And so Hitler founded an internally effective opposition to communism.

It had to be remembered that "leadership of men and masses has always been an inescapable and important political affair which cannot be left to just anybody, without potential harm, and that it need not automatically imply the use of fraud".

Fraud : It seemed that Hitler often used his ability to "turn ideas into primitive but genuine simple propaganda slogans", not consciously, just following a primitive instinct—"which is why he was a relatively well-meaning swindler with a comparatively unperturbed belief in what he did". Hitler, of course, had a political reason for this use of both crude and subtle fraud; but even so this did not apparently exclude the possibility of the deceiver himself becoming convinced by and accepting his own oft repeated fraudulent arguments as true.

This is how Fahrner concludes the account of his conversations with Stauffenberg : "I was particularly struck by the fact that, although Stauffenberg set great store by an 'objective' assessment of Hitler, he was very reserved and sceptical when anyone made a purely derogatory remark about the man. Claus suspected such

185

observations of being just emotional and politically biased. He warned against precipitate hope; he was indifferent towards any kind of over-emphasis; I noticed that he discussed some aspects of these matters which he did not mention to me thoroughly with his friend of longer standing, Frank Mehnert. All this merely reinforced my impression of his political talent and competence."

According to Fahrner, Stauffenberg's determination to act revealed itself undisguisedly for the first time in the winter of 1938–39. Fahrner said that when he went to hear the lecture on Gneisenau at Wuppertal he felt embittered by what had been happening. Walking through the wintry forest he asked Stauffenberg whether the whole Wehrmacht was putting up with what had been committed in the name of Germany on the "Kristallnacht" (the night of anti-Jewish excesses, organised by Goebbels, November 9, 1938). It was then that for the first time, Stauffenberg had openly spoken of plans and the possibility of a revolution. He said they could count on Hoepner; and mentioned Beck—with great reserve, as on all previous occasions, but all the more impressive for that—as the central figure of the anti-Hitler opposition within the Wehrmacht. Fahrner said that Stauffenberg urgently warned against putting faith in wider circles of senior officers, let alone in the by then enormously inflated Army. And he had used the words : you cannot expect people who have broken their spine once or twice to stand up straight when a new decision has to be made.

Several months later, in the spring of 1939 Fahrner had another meeting with Stauffenberg. "Half-joking—half serious", Claus told him of a tank exercise he had just attended : he had been travelling all day in a small tank to find out how the armoured troops were doing and under what conditions they were fighting. Almost in passing, but very seriously and emphatically, Stauffenberg remarked : "The idiot is making war." According to Fahrner, what was constantly on Claus' mind was that Germany, having already lost some of her best blood in the First World War, was now threatened with the same fate for the second time within a generation.

After his return from the campaign against Poland, Stauffenberg was visited by his uncle, Count Nikolaus von Uexküll,[20] whom he greatly admired. With him came Count Fritz von der Schulenburg whom Stauffenberg knew well from earlier days. Stauffenberg's entourage noted how deeply moved, indeed disconcerted, he was by these talks. Only later did it become known that the two visitors had told him new details regarding the dangerous trend in the Reich, and tried to induce him to intervene or to seek as quickly as possible a post from which he could take action—they are said to have suggested that he become Adjutant to the Commander-in-Chief of the Army. Stauffenberg is reported to have declined saying he was not ready for that.

Once war had broken out, he did not at first look upon it as Hitler's enterprise but a matter involving the Fatherland; and it never occurred to him that one might, if only inwardly, withdraw from it. To the last day he devotedly carried out the duties his position and job demanded of him.

In the early days of Hitler's victories, which went beyond all expectation, Stauffenberg objectively acknowledged the "Führer's" part in them, as he saw it, and he emphasized this vis-à-vis many a critic. But he was never heard to join in any apotheosis of "the greatest war-lord of all times". To him it was essential for the glory of victory that the victor should succeed in "making something" of the new situation : he felt that Hitler's failure ever to come to the right terms with France was one of the main reasons for Germany's eventual collapse. A significant scene related by Colonel-General Halder—and one of which similar personal accounts by others exist—occurred at the end of June 1940 when Hitler had ordered preparations for a great victory parade in Paris at the Arc de Triomphe and in the Tuileries. (The parade, incidentally, was later cancelled.) Halder recalls a conversation with some of "his" younger General Staff officers; Stauffenberg and Merz von Quirnheim, his friend from the Military Academy, were the main speakers. They conjured up a frightening image of a heartless victor without any sense of proportion who would become the country's disaster and they argued that soon it would be necessary to oppose and, if need be, bring him down.[21]

During another conversation, which again turned on the possibilities of a revolt and which took place in the spring of 1941— between the Balkans campaign and the beginning of the war against Russia Stauffenberg is on record as saying : "He is still winning too many victories." As to later events, Stauffenberg thought Hitler made strategic blunders by abandoning plans to invade England (which he regarded as promising) and by refusing (out of jealousy of Rommel's popularity?) to provide the means for a potentially successful invasion of Egypt and the conquest of the Suez Canal. Of the campaign against Russia, Stauffenberg said Hitler made that fatal move because he was at a loss and had simply run out of any ideas.

A conversation reported by a former officer at Headquarters[22] and said to have taken place in the winter of 1941–42—the time of the first winter disaster in Russia—shows that the internal situation in Germany was even tenser. The officer saw a portrait of

Hitler above the writing desk in Stauffenberg's study. Stauffenberg noticing his surprise, said : "I chose this picture. And I put it up so that whoever comes here shall see the man's expression of madness and the lack of any sense of proportion." They talked about the precarious war situation, the disastrous failure of the supreme leadership, the threat from the East and Hitler's excesses. At the end of the conversation the officer asked Stauffenberg what way out there was. Came the terse reply : "Kill him." They both agreed that the difficulties were enormous; especially in the midst of war. Such action was permissible only to a man who, once Hitler was gone, had the necessary self-confidence to assume power and to lead state and Army during the emergency.

As Head of a Department in the Headquarters Organisation Branch—Stauffenberg was constantly arguing against the chain of command Hitler had set up in the Army and the Wehrmacht. It was based on a separation of powers, copied from political life, which gave Hitler personally complete and unchallengeable authority but created constant tension among his senior subordinate commanders by putting them on an equal footing with many others. It crucially weakened their effective exercise of power.[23] More and more the three services drifted apart; there were the rival theatres of operations of the OKW (Wehrmacht Operations Staff, Jodl) and OKH (Chief of General Staff, Zeitzler);[24] the SS was acquiring more and more privileges, and other organizations and offices directly responsible to the Führer daily threw the supreme leadership into ever worsening anarchy. This kind of "top level command structure" established and secured Hitler's military omnipotence. No protest against him was effective since, at best, it could only come from a representative of a divided authority. Together with other men at HQ Stauffenberg struggled stubbornly to get things changed : at least he wanted to see a Commander-in-Chief on the Eastern front with his own responsibility and freedom of action. Even after Hitler had expressly forbidden any further discussions on this subject, Stauffenberg emphatically continued to work towards the same objective. He is known to have made representations to several commanders and to have tried to persuade them to make at least a demonstrative gesture. Several of the men thus approached seemed fully to agree with him, and thought it was indeed high time to restore the independence of military command in order to prevent disaster. But they lacked self-confidence as they felt tied by their difficult and demanding daily tasks at the front. They thought he, Stauffenberg, ought to get things going! They were willing, "to place themselves fully at his disposal in the event of a successful coup d'état (to quote Freiherr von Gersdorff, who was ordered by Kluge to visit Manstein in the summer of 1943).[25]

In the light of such experience, Stauffenberg was heard to speak angrily of Army Group Commanders who, at most, could bring themselves to the decision that after a successful coup d'état they would pledge obedience to the new leadership of the state.[26] According to Goerlitz, the Field-Marshals whom Stauffenberg received in those days appeared helpless and reluctant to make up their minds. And it was this which partly decided Stauffenberg to act on his own. But he did not hold it against any man of lower rank who simply wanted to mind his own business, loyally do his duty and just act like an ordinary human being completely absorbed by his own joys and sufferings. Stauffenberg often talked about the need for order and hated any kind of excessive "revolutionizing" based on thoughtlessness or folly. Such "revolutionaries", he felt, were pretending to rouse their followers to free decision and action whereas in truth they merely wrenched them from the place where they belonged and where alone they could prosper. This was what Stauffenberg had in mind when he was taking part in Fahrner's study of Gneisenau and suggested that the portrayal of the radical and extremist organisation of the popular rising against Napoleon should be deleted. "He reasoned that such ideas and practices might potentially be taken up by some future opponents of Germany and by exponents of anarchism at home and abroad. In his view, such forces must be unleashed only if (as happened in Gneisenau's days) enough strong moral curbs were available within the state and community—which was no longer the case. (He looked upon any form of guerrilla war as undermining the last humane and chivalrous rules of battle and he later predicted that the organisation of and support for the partisans in the Balkans, and especially in Greece, would rebound on its originator, Churchill—which is what happened.)"[27]

Two reports of October 1942 mention Claus Stauffenberg at Headquarters in Vinnitsa. One[28] tells of a couple of lectures, on German agricultural policy in the occupied Eastern territories and on the European food economy, being given to some forty General Staff officers under the chairmanship of Colonel von Altenstett. At the end of one of them Major Stauffenberg asked for the floor and spoke for about half an hour. One of the lecturers later reported that in a brilliant speech Stauffenberg expressed what was to him at the time a most surprising view on German policy in the East. According to this report, Stauffenberg argued as follows : "Feeling responsible for the replacement of troops in the East, as he did, he was watching the disastrous course of Germany's Eastern policy with horror. We were sowing hatred which would one day be avenged on our children. Any examination of the replacement issue made it absolutely clear that victory in the East was possible only if Germany succeeded in winning over the local population. Stauffenberg said he was therefore particularly interested in my lecture from which he deduced that something on these lines was at least being done in matters of agricultural policy. For the rest, the only thing our policy in the East was likely to achieve was to turn the masses there into Germany's enemies. It was scandalous that at a time when millions of soldiers were staking their lives not one of the leaders had the courage to speak to the Führer openly about such matters, though it might be at the risk of his own life." The lecturer added : "I remember the incident so well because at that time no one dared to mention this in public. I was deeply impressed by Stauffenberg's arguments, especially as they were put forward with such conviction that you felt certain he himself had the courage he demanded of the leaders. I was greatly surprised that it was possible to speak so openly in a circle of General Staff officers, and even more so at the fact that the chairman of the meeting far from refuting Stauffenberg's criticism declared that they all felt the same."

The second account[29] describes a personal visit to Stauffenberg at about that time. A room at the hut where he lived; a table, bed, chest of drawers, with a picture of his wife and children, a book and a few torn out pages. Cordial welcome. The conversation quickly became topical. Stauffenberg gave a clear and sober outline of the situation (Halder had just been dismissed from his post as Chief of the General Staff). He felt that any decisions that were or were not taken in those weeks were crucial to the whole war. He thought the prospects were poor because Hitler had become a prisoner of his own doctrines and the military leaders were obeying any of his orders. In the evening the visitor joined a fairly large circle of younger officers. Count Stauffenberg was leaning lightly against the edge of the table; various topics were discussed. Quite spontaneously one of those Stauffenberg monologues developed which, born on the spur of the moment and without plan, often galloped away yet always had the effect of a powerful appeal, all the more gripping since he gave himself up completely to the cause and spoke without personal ambition. Some officers said they were sick and tired of their jobs at Headquarters and wished they were at the front to forget about it all. Stauffenberg did not admit to such an attitude. What sort of ideas were these for officers destined to lead? What kind of false heroism to have themselves killed by the enemy, like hundreds of thousands of others "in faithful discharge of duty". It was nothing but cowardly

evasion and no better than Field-Marshals using the excuse:
"We're merely acting on orders"; and "We're only soldiers". An
entirely different outlook was needed. A man whom office and
honour had raised to a position of leadership reached a point where
he and his task became one and other considerations no longer
applied: he was responsible for everything. How few there were
who in fact behaved like that or at least felt they ought to! The
majority were just petty bourgeois people with a nice little income
or trade and holding the rank of General. They were drawing
their pay, doing their "duty", trusting in the Führer and looking
forward to their leave—on whom was the Fatherland then to rely?
Stauffenberg—so the report recalls—cited a verse from the "Return
of the Dead", starting with the words:

"One day when this generation has purged itself of shame and
thrown off the fetters of the tyrant . . ."

As two different reports show, 1942 ended in deep despair for
Stauffenberg. All his attempts during the summer and autumn to
persuade responsible Army leaders to make common cause against
Hitler had failed. Even his last hope had foundered: to use the
desperate position of the Sixth Army at Stalingrad, wantonly caused
by Hitler, to get the Generals jointly to refuse any further orders
from the Führer. As one report puts it, "Stauffenberg was now
fully convinced that the catastrophe had become inevitable, and
he was dejected".

In January 1943, when his service at Headquarters had ended
and his turn came to be posted to the front he was heard to say:
"It is time I disappeared from here." In the preceding few months
he had been so daringly outspoken that it seemed necessary to get
out of the line of fire for a while. He forecast what in fact later
happened in Africa.[30] From Tunis he sent a frank and, as he
remarked to friends, "devastating" report to Zeitzler, the Chief of
the German General Staff whom he held in high regard because
of his courageous stand against Hitler during the Stalingrad crisis.
To his colleagues Stauffenberg made it clear beyond doubt that not
the military position or the strength of the opponent but Hitler
alone heralded disaster. Soon Stauffenberg was to be wounded and
nearly die. But the task for which he felt responsible made him
unexpectedly recover and brought him in close touch with his
brother Berthold.

* * *

Berthold Count Schenk von Stauffenberg served as a senior
judge (Marineoberstabsrichter) in the Naval Command in Berlin.

After their boyhood together in Lautlingen and Stuttgart, Berthold had begun to read law and political science—apart from many other subjects that interested him—with a view to joining the diplomatic service at a later date. Two fellow students later said that he never seemed to find work very hard as he had an innate gift for languages and for remembering legal clauses. It was almost with envy—something which Berthold himself did not know—that his colleagues would see him return from riding, at his leisurely, slightly rolling gait, looking slim and refreshed while others had been hard at work with their tutors.

The afore-mentioned account by Ludwig Thormaelen speaks of the great impression the nineteen-year-old Berthold made at a first meeting.

"I had never before seen such a close and clear combination of nobility of mind and heart, of intelligence and spirit, of a relaxed yet challenging disposition." About Berthold's relationship to Stefan George he said : "Berthold Stauffenberg can scarcely be described as a disciple of George's. From the moment he entered his circle there was nothing more to shape, to educate. If there had been room for that, it had already been accomplished by the impact of poetry and George's works. The poet felt a firmness and complete lack of affectation in Berthold von Stauffenberg's behaviour and character which he accepted as 'sui generis' and as of equal rank. It was Berthold who was to give his younger brother support and encouragement."[31]

Having passed his Referendar examination and completed the required training in court and in the administration, Berthold von Stauffenberg went to the Institute of International Law in Berlin (Kaiser-Wilhelm Institut) to hear Viktor Bruns. A little later he wrote a dissertation on the legal position of the Russian trade delegations—a work which also aroused interest abroad. In 1931, the twenty-six-year-old Berthold was offered an editorial post at the International Court at the Hague by the Clerk of the Court, Dag Hammarskjoeld's brother. There he wrote a comprehensive commentary on the Court's statutes : "A work of fundamental significance (according to Makarov) which retained its importance even after the foundation of the International Court of the United Nations because the Statute of this Court mirrors, with only very few deviations, the statutes of the old Cour Permanente". In 1934 he returned to the Institute in Berlin. He remained a member to the end of his life and made important contributions to its publications, the "Fontes iuris gentium". He often travelled outside Germany. He published works in French and English, both of which he spoke fluently, and knew enough Italian and Russian

192

to be able to study legal sources in each of these tongues. He specialized in military law and was kept extremely busy with the laws of naval warfare, with German prize law and theories on the strategy of aerial warfare. At the beginning of the war he was called up and posted to the Naval Command as adviser on international law. His duties brought him into regular contact with the German Foreign Office and he quite often negotiated with representatives of neutral powers.

His position, which linked him with both naval strategy and politics, enabled him to get an overall picture not easily obtainable in a purely military post. The legal opinions he gave were those of a sober judge who knew that there were reasonable and unreasonable men among Germany's enemies, too, trying to do the best for their countries. At his post in the Naval Command he acted, whether deferred to or by-passed, as an incorruptible and moderating influence. He spoke rarely during the daily situation conference; but when he did, he briefly and clearly defended his own firm views and, without getting heated, put an end to any indecision by judging in accordance with the law. It was not an easy task in the midst of a tough war to check the spread of brutality in naval warfare. In few cases can those who benefited from his intervention have known that Stauffenberg was behind a decision : the starving Greeks, for example, received Red Cross grain shipments from the United States thanks to his care and untiring effort. His comrades noted that he never indulged in vilification and no one ever heard him say anything spiteful against Hitler.[32]

Berthold von Stauffenberg did not seek to influence or persuade others. But, as one observer who was frequently in touch with him put it, there would have been no need for him to give orders : people did what he wanted in anticipation. He never made a show of his great specialized knowledge as many others might have done —he had no need of that either. Listening to him was enough for many a man to decide on the merits of an issue. To those around him it was obvious that he was still living in another world, and that knowing his job was not his most important concern. He scarcely spoke of the spiritual world in which he moved[33] but it was absorbed and mirrored in his whole behaviour and his manner of speaking.

Something of this emerges from a report by one of his fellow officers[34] : "I knew Berthold von Stauffenberg only briefly, outside his and my own sphere. We met in a strange world of war. One became lonely and silent being thrown together with so many comrades on the large operations staffs. And so one doubly welcomed a genuine encounter, and was glad to strike up a friendship."

He describes how they spent their off-duty hours tearing about the countryside often keeping silent for long stretches and stalking deer : he tells of their swims in the forest lake, their conversations and of Stauffenberg's appearance. Stauffenberg (he says) was aware of the prestige and obligations attaching to his ancestral name but he was completely free from feudal romanticism. He was an exclusive person by nature, but not in the social sense. His manner, too, was aloof : he knew the rules of the game, but he did not really give the impression of being good at it. There was still something of the boy in him, modest, awkward, good-humoured, reserved. . . . Quite a few people had given up trying to get closer to him because he made no attempt to keep a conversation going. What he did say was direct and simple and always reflected his own views. He felt that only if he could make a contribution of his own was it worth saying anything. His sense of originality was eccentric rather than conventional. Serenity was the most essential thing to him; this was the source of great and creative thoughts, as well as comfort and enjoyment." His fellow officer found it significant that Berthold "did not take sides as a South German, as a lawyer, as a noble-man or as a Catholic", and he went on : "He was not only intellec-tually but also artistically free. To him the arts were reality. He had an eye for sculpture and loved great classical music. But his strength he drew from poetry. This was where his soul had its roots; it was here that he found his great ideals and norms. To some he may have seemed undecided, inactive, unsociable, un-approachable, disinterested and inflexible. But poetry and the arts were the source and condition for his calm and composure, his modesty and reserve, his straightforwardness and stubbornness."

Another observer who met Berthold Stauffenberg in those late days gave this account[35] when questioned : "I hesitated for a long time before answering your question about my encounters with Berthold Stauffenberg. I tried to tell you what he was like, but I soon realized how little even the most accurate portrayal of his appearance and manner brings out his character—which is so vivid in my mind. One gets nowhere near the real man by speaking of his fine, lithe, tall body, of his bearing which had nothing affected, rather something prim—at times a little awkward—about it. I know of no one who, despite being such a remarkable person and unusual type, is so difficult to describe. While his brother Claus was full of thrusting, extrovert strength, Berthold's nature seemed to be entirely turned inward. This reflected the riches of his life—riches that were not amassed but innate and had grown to abundance perhaps because he had had the good fortune to meet many great men. It seemed that this character allowed him to answer questions almost without deliberation and he appeared to be able to provide the reply by his very being—and with the incorruptible certainty of a touchstone."

During the summer Claus Stauffenberg received several visits from his brother in Munich. In August he was able to leave hospital. He had lost his left eye, his whole right hand, and only the thumb and first two fingers remained on his left. His leg injuries had healed without leaving any stiffness. Meanwhile he had learnt to write quite tolerably with his remaining fingers and was able to dress himself, by using his teeth to help him. He would good-humouredly reject any offer of assistance. The expansive and thrusting movements whereby he overcame his impediments, as if it were a matter of course, seemed to come quite naturally to him. Despite the severe damage to his limbs he was fit, and nothing was broken in his body. His physique and facial expression had acquired a new and deeper substance which could appear heavy and almost menacing. But as soon as Stauffenberg began to speak, his former self-possession and infectious, sparkling liveliness broke through— he was free from the bitterness of a fanatic invalid.[36]

On about August 10, Stauffenberg secretly stayed in Berlin, where he met Olbricht and Tresckow. It was agreed that after his recovery he would start work at Olbricht's department on October 1. During the second half of August and the beginning of September the two brothers were together in Lautlingen. They are known to have gone for daily walks in their native countryside, often for hours at a time, so as to be able to talk privately. Rudolf Fahrner, who was invited to join them for the last week of their stay, said their discussions in twos and threes centred on basic issues of a new political, religious, economic and social order. He has given some examples:

"Even in political life man cannot prosper without allegiance to God and there must be no interference with or prejudice against those who are still so committed to the Christian churches;

"Customs and traditions that have grown naturally cannot be replaced by self-seeking artificial concepts because some things need time to grow;

"There are ways of inducing the citizens of a nation freely to accept the necessary differences of position, wealth and prestige which occur in any society.

"To what extent are agreements among peoples pre-destined in the nations themselves and are they not perhaps nearer fruition than ever, provided they are furthered rather than hampered by the powers that be? Differences between European nations, for example, could be resolved in the way tribal differences were settled; indeed, the differences could even prove fruitful.

"How can people fit to govern be recruited from all sections of the population? Is it possible, and if so how, to establish popular representation in Germany, perhaps on an entirely different basis than that of conventional political parties—perhaps building on the political reality of a system of local communities, vocational groups or associations of common interests which might be given a public voice of their own in Parliament instead of deviously pursuing their objectives through self-interested parties or by parleying with such parties?

"Relations between entrepreneurs and workers must be based on their common tasks, and their joint responsibility towards the community as a whole and towards the individual human being.

"Technology, industry and economy in relation to the State: notwithstanding their importance, they must serve the community and must not deliberately and systematically create needs which become man's masters.

"The strength that flows from voluntary renunciation: a voluntary distribution of large estates initiated by their owners (and beginnings of such a trend were already apparent) could set an effective example and could lead to new forms of a social welfare economy.

"Those in positions of leadership need, in their deliberations and actions, the assistance of people not tied to office, with independent minds—the type of men with whom wise rulers in the past used to surround themselves.

"Rigid rules and dogmas should be applied only with the greatest caution, because the most important consideration in any given situation must always be to provide and keep open opportunities for people to develop."

The report ends: "We thought that after Hitler's overthrow and Germany's foreseeable defeat in the war there would be opportunities—missed for such a long time—for great and unselfish decisions by many people, for the realization of new ideas and numerous changes. What mattered was to make use of them."[37]

On September 10 Stauffenberg was to undergo an operation by Professor Sauerbruch which the doctors had already postponed for four weeks. The operation would have made it possible to fit an artificial hand to the stump of his right arm. On September 8 it was learnt that Italy had capitulated. On September 9—the day on which the Allies secured a beachhead at Salerno—Stauffenberg, to the astonishment of even his closest relations, suddenly cancelled the appointment for the operation, and, pushing aside all plans for convalescence and recovery, went to Berlin without giving any explanation. He had the rumour put about that because of the renewed festering of a splinter wound the operation had once again been postponed and he had lost his patience.

Political events were moving ahead, but the real reason for his hasty departure seems to have been the news that Tresckow would, unexpectedly, once again manage to be in Berlin for several weeks. Stauffenberg moved to his brother Berthold's house in the Tristanstrasse in Wannsee. Officially, he spent the three September weeks on convalescence leave. But this leave camouflaged a time of maximum tension : it was a time of plans and preparations for the uprising.

X. THE CIRCLE OF CONSPIRATORS

AT the beginning of October 1943, Lieutenant-Colonel Count Stauffenberg took up his post as Chief of Staff in the General Army Office in Berlin. It was agreed that his predecessor would stay on for a month to allow Stauffenberg to get acquainted with the work and that he would take over the office from November 1. This arrangement was possibly influenced by the fact that further developments were expected in October which required Stauffenberg's full attention.

As the largest of three departments, the General Army Office came under the Commander-in-Chief of the Reserve Army and Chief of Armaments, Colonel-General Fromm. It was also housed in the same building, in the Bendlerstrasse, at the former War Ministry. Olbricht's department had to provide the reserves in men and material needed at the front, either by drawing on existing resources or procuring new ones.[1] Year by year the task had become more difficult; not only was there a steady decline in the number of potential recruits and inadequate armament production, but with the growing separation of power more and more authorities, Ministers and plenipotentiaries of the Führer were trying to prevent the Army Office from laying hands on men and materials and were forcing it into bitter and often fruitless competition.[2]

In the past Stauffenberg's work brought him into contact with a large number of people and authorities. Every day he was faced with almost insuperable difficulties of reinforcing the troops in the field now that the fifth year of war had begun. His independent judgement, expert knowledge, quick grasp of essentials and the ability to remain pleasant even when issuing strict orders—all these were obviously great assets. His colleagues soon felt that despite his physical impediments Stauffenberg was marked out for high office. Some of them, therefore, tried to get into his good books at that stage. Even when the going was tough and people were showing the effects of the constant strain they were living under—air raid alerts and the destruction in the city—visitors never found Stauffenberg agitated. In an air raid, he would reluctantly go to the shelter and set a bad example to others by being the last to descend, with the bombs already crashing down. Stauffenberg had about him a kind of aura which even strangers visiting him sensed very quickly. He was always the same, whether he received a

198

Lieutenant or a General, or addressed a gathering of his collaborators. Frequently he appeared to be occupied with official business until far into the night. Many people who had dealings with him later found it almost impossible to believe that the same Stauffenberg, besides this, bore a much greater and far more dangerous responsibility.

Someone who knew him in those days wrote : "No one who has met Claus von Stauffenberg is likely to forget him. A Colonel who looked like a poet with a pale face beneath curly hair, young but intensely serious, badly disabled, yet in full control of himself, more than that, the moment he began to speak in his soft, clipped manner everyone else fell silent. He did his many-sided and difficult job, at the same time carrying on with the tremendous task he had set himself : everywhere he put out feelers towards the other groups, prepared military plans, and went through the tensions and dangers of this double-life. Again and again he had to fight the whole battle emotionally, intellectually and in practical terms. Despite this superhuman strain, he would briefly discuss any caller's affairs with him, in complete composure—and in a few minutes everything was clear and settled. . . ."[3]

Only very few even of Stauffenberg's immediate collaborators in the General Army Office knew what action was being taken and planned. To the others it must have been obvious that he was not a staunch supporter of Hitler—in fact one of his woman secretaries remembered a remark he made at the time of the disaster in the Crimea : "It must be unique in the history of a nation for its leader always to issue orders which bring the people nearer and nearer to ruin."[4] But it was still a long way from a sober statement of misgivings or momentary bitterness to action. Ever since his arrival in Berlin Stauffenberg had been determined to act—this resolve was as typical of the man as the extreme care with which he chose his allies and the strict secrecy which he demanded of them and of himself. Under ingenuous cover their joint preparations were fitted into the daily duties at his office. Service reasons were advanced as an excuse for essential meetings and discussions in Berlin, and, where this was not possible, they met at night.

Since the autumn of 1943 air raids on the blacked-out city had become an almost nightly affair. There were fires; no public transport; it was difficult to get home and detours had to be made through rubble-strewn, burning streets. And often the few hours of rest were disturbed by the terror of new air raid alarms. Yet even when things were at their worst Stauffenberg managed to sleep soundly and showed admirable physical stamina. On one occasion there was a heavy night raid in the immediate vicinity of his staff

HQ where an anti-aircraft battery was situated, and there were some casualties. But Stauffenberg, with the sirens wailing overhead had slept through it all. Some people even thought he deliberately refrained from seeking shelter underground so as not to cause panic among his men. It is said that when the quiet click of the telephone at his home in Wannsee woke him, giving advance warning of an air raid before the sirens sounded, he would rouse the other people in the house but go back to sleep again himself until the alarm was given; then, having been wakened by the others, he would go down to the shelter and continue sleeping. When bombs dropped somewhere nearby he would make his way to the slit trench, his boots squeezed under his arms, and then, standing up or squatting down go to sleep again in the trench.

Schulenburg disclosed during later interrogations how Olbricht's Chief of Staff prepared the secret plot and how individual conspirators were assigned different tasks. The interrogators described it as a "crafty system" :[5] only very few men were let into some of the secrets, such as the proposed use of explosives; more, but still only a very small number, were told of the assassination plot. A somewhat larger circle were informed about the plan to use force —and stage a coup d'état—though nothing was said about getting rid of Hitler. But with the majority of the conspirators (still according to this interrogation report) only the seriousness of the situation, the danger of its getting worse and the possible need for declaring a military emergency were discussed. Only those directly concerned with a specific matter were told, and even they only as much as they had to know to do their job. Beck acted in the same way. To him, as the report put it, secrecy even vis-à-vis his closest confidants had become second nature. Those who asked for more information were told that Beck had given personal orders to disclose only what was vital for a fellow-conspirator to know; and unless absolutely necessary no names were to be mentioned. Officers were familiar with this type of instruction through Hitler's order of December 11, 1941. This laid down that no officer must be told more of any secret plan or told of it sooner than necessary for its execution. Some who were associated with the revolt but had not been let into any secrets, successfully invoked this order in court to defend themselves. Beck's and Stauffenberg's attitude sometimes aroused mistrust, even opposition, among the rank and file, especially as Stauffenberg insisted that he himself must be "kept fully informed also about all political and personnel matters" (according to a statement reported by Goerdeler). Apparently, Stauffenberg used many nocturnal meetings and discussions to counter such opposition in person and to restore authority and unity in the whole enterprise.

Stauffenberg tolerated no carelessness that was liable to imperil the scheme. If he got wind that there was danger from the Gestapo he would warn the likely victim and other conspirators and cut their contact with the threatened person. He himself used a varying pre-arranged system of go-betweens to organize meetings which might incriminate the participants. He demanded the same discipline as he imposed upon himself from his junior assistants—but he did his best to see that they got their leave and had some fun. At home, even when ladies were present, he personally opened the glass door to new arrivals. He did not allow introductions and "private" conversations. He was always a good host even when there was but little refreshment to offer, and set the tone of lively and invariably frank discussion. He provided blankets and beds when it had become too late for the others to return to town or so that everybody could snatch just two or three hours' rest before getting back to the maps and plans on the floor—as happened quite often. What he would have liked best he said on his arrival in Berlin would have been to set up a special home—a sort of "home for bombed-out officers"—presumably to organize the nucleus of his little state.

He did not waste time on himself, made the best use he could of his remaining fingers and otherwise left things in the care of his orderly, who was also his driver. The man, who came from the Swabian Alb, helped him to dress and undress—not much time was allowed for that—looked after food and drink and was available at the office or when they travelled. Though the orderly was his confidant there was no familiarity; their partnership was regarded as so exceptional that even Stauffenberg's successor tried very hard to secure the services of this orderly. But he was quickly disappointed.

Until the end of 1943, Berthold Stauffenberg worked in the Naval High Command building on the Tirpitzufer, next to Fromm's and Olbricht's office. Because of the heavy air raids the senior naval officers moved to a remote hutted camp outside Berlin known as "Koralle", but Berthold frequently went to the city to meet his brother and other associates either there or at their evening rendezvous in Wannsee.

Claus Stauffenberg's discussions with the other conspirators mainly centred on questions of tactics, but he talked absolutely freely to his brother. During these talks the day's events fell into perspective. The two men looked at the planned revolt from every angle, weighing the potential chances of success or failure with an intimacy shared by no-one else. Outsiders could glean little from their conversation : they always avoided mentioning names or else circumscribed them with 'Homeric epithets' to such an extent that their own wives, who occasionally were present in the room, were scarcely able to make out what they were talking about. Those who later conducted the investigation against Stauffenberg found that he had not disclosed any secret information even to his orderly, who was with him every day and attended all these meetings, in order not to involve him. One of the investigators of Stauffenberg's part in the plot is known to have exclaimed spontaneously : "Typical Stauffenberg !"

From Claus Stauffenberg or his brother or Tresckow we have nothing in writing about the motives, aims, scope and organization of the attempted coup d'état.[6] Claus Stauffenberg and Tresckow were spared all interrogation by their early death. The same applies to the small circle of people who must be assumed to have had full knowledge of the military plan. By July 21 all of them were dead without having been questioned : Beck, Olbricht, Merz von Quirnheim, Oertzen. The Quartermaster-General committed suicide on July 23 before he was arrested. Berthold Stauffenberg was presumably subjected to a thorough interrogation. What is on record as his testimony explains motives and objectives but contains nothing about the scope and organization of the plot. So as not to have to mention names, he probably declared that he had nothing to do with his brother's military planning. All the others with military responsibility in Berlin and at Headquarters, who had been assigned major or minor spheres of the conspiracy, died violent deaths.

As historical source material the record of their interrogation is not very useful, except for data and facts which are supported by several other authorities. This is because in their evidence the conspirators, who were fighting for their lives, tried wherever possible not to incriminate anyone but only those already dead. Indirectly some of their statements allow a glimpse of Stauffenberg, particularly when they answered questions on how he persuaded various people to join him.

The same applies to the civilian associates whose links with Stauffenberg's inner circle had been discovered and who were executed. On the whole, their evidence is of limited value, but it does contain some unqualified statements which, like Berthold Stauffenberg's testimony, give important clues as to the purpose and motives of their actions, though not about the military overall plan. Yorck and Schulenburg are two examples.

No more than ten of the conspirators of the Bendlerstrasse are still alive and none among them was fully initiated into the military plan. Each had been assigned a special job (i.e. Gerstenmaier, Gisevius and Otto John) or carried out military orders (Kleist, Hammerstein, Cords, Fritzche, Oppen and Georgi); the three or four survivors from the Naval Command were alloted similar tasks by Berthold Stauffenberg (as for example Traber, Jessen, Bauch and perhaps also Kupfer).

There was no reason why Tresckow should have passed on details of the plan, which had been drafted in Berlin, to his confederates in Army Group Centre from which he had been transferred. These men played no direct part in the action that was to be launched from Berlin. Until his death Tresckow maintained close relations with Schlabrendorff. Although Schlabrendorff was in extreme danger, he escaped death, and he has disclosed details of the military plan which Tresckow revealed to him. But he has first-hand knowledge mainly of the earlier conspiratorial activities in which he took part himself.

Rudolf Fahrner—as far as is known the Stauffenberg brothers' closest collaborator—occupies a special position. He was not an officer and escaped persecution. He had associated with them frequently from about 1936 onwards and since autumn 1943 had been one of their advisers on constitutional planning. He had helped to draft their appeals, among their guests at Wannsee and "Koralle" in July 1944 and took part in military or political discussions. But even he had no inside knowledge of the military preparations as a whole.

*   *   *

The full plan for military action (the staff plan) has not been found, nor has it been possible to interrogate any of the conspirators who knew all the details. Consequently we can only make deductions about the plan from the actual events on the 20th July. Only tentative conclusions are possible because certain things went unforeseeably wrong and they determined the course of events on that day. But an assessment can be made on the basis of the written orders issued on the 20th by the Berlin centre. Some of these orders—the text of which is available—became known through their recipients, who kept and published them after the war. They were then reprinted, together with the reports of interrogations by the Kaltenbrunner Office; what was published were presumably the full texts as they were found. It is worth noting that in every case these were orders which had already become operative, i.e. which had been taken to the Signals Branch to be transmitted. No orders that were still pigeon-holed and might have been intended for some later "X-day" have been printed. The time of issue was stated on the orders, which helps to establish whether the operation went according to plan or was unexpectedly delayed.

Other valuable sources are some of the memoranda and drafts which were discovered in connection with the conspiracy and published together with the interrogation reports. But closer examination shows that most of the writings reproduced or quoted are papers by Goerdeler, such as his memorandum "Das Ziel". This memorandum is repeatedly cited as being of fundamental significance. Herman Kaiser is erroneously quoted as its author (KB 130, 138, 170). The plans for simplifying the administration and for dividing the country into Gaue (KB 207) are based on Goerdeler's and Schulenburg's ideas. "Thoughts on reforming the educational system" (KB 342) may, as stated in the KB reports, have come from the pen of Hermann Kaiser. In his comments on the conduct of the war and the structure of the top level command (KB 291) Meichssner, undoubtedly in agreement with Stauffenberg, expressed demands which had often been discussed by responsible officers. Unfortunately only extracts of the memorandum by Trott zu Solz are published; there is no other record of it. This memorandum ("Europe between East and West") (KB 34, 173) is an important document on the Stauffenberg circle's views of foreign policy. There is also a brief account, with no indication of the author (KB 33), of a six-page paper which must be assumed to be a memorandum by one of Stauffenberg's closest collaborators and to which he, in fact, made reference.

Another fairly important clue to the intentions behind the revolt are the appeals to the German nation and the Wehrmacht which were to have been issued at the moment of the actual revolt. The appeals, which fell into the hands of the Gestapo have been published together with the interrogation reports. Unfortunately the version of the appeals which Stauffenberg regarded as the final one has not become known. What has been published are previous versions drafted by various authors and found together with Goerdeler's papers in the Askanischer Hof (not at the Bendlerstrasse!)[7] The President of the Court attributed the authorship of some of the appeals to Stauffenberg, who had nothing to do with them. Of the version which Stauffenberg considered final, only two copies were made at his express wish, in the first days of July 1944. One was deposited in "Koralle" outside Berlin and the other handed to him for his own safekeeping. The woman secretary who had typed and kept the "Koralle" copy has said that she destroyed it after the 20th July. No light has been shed on the fate of the other copy by later writings on the subject; the second copy must have been among the papers destroyed at the Bendlerstrasse during the night of the 20th. Rudolf Fahrner, the co-author of these appeals, has rendered their content from memory.

From the entire source material on the attempted uprising the story is easy to comprehend where it is based on the activities of the Resistance movement and especially on Goerdeler's abundant writings; as to the active nucleus of the conspiracy, especially Stauffenberg's personal role, written sources give at least a clear outline.

*　　*　　*

The above-mentioned, unsigned manuscript speaks of the "imminent disaster" and the need to avert it by forcible intervention. According to the interrogation reports, Stauffenberg dropped the paper from his pocket "during his attempted escape" on the night of 20th July at the Bendlerstrasse. Here is a summary of the six-page plan, outlining some of Stauffenberg's arguments of which there is also other evidence :

"If the present course continues, defeat and destruction of the country's manpower and material strength is inevitable. Imminent disaster can be averted only by removing the present leadership. The original ideas of National Socialism were largely correct but were perverted after the Party's advent to power. The new leaders, by giving priority to selfish interest and allowing the growth of corruption and political favouritism represent government by men of inferior moral calibre.

"The treatment by Germany of the occupied countries is a major cause of the bad situation as a whole. And the Russian campaign is the beginning of the end. It started with orders to kill all commissars and went on with letting prisoners of war starve to death and organising man-hunts for civilian labour.

"The leadership has failed to prevent a war on two fronts. The present régime has no right to drag the whole nation down with it to its doom. The most important aim after a change of government is to ensure that Germany continues as a factor in the power game and that the Wehrmacht, in particular, remains a usable instrument in the hands of its leaders.

"There have been various political opportunities to exploit differences in the enemy camp. But they will diminish with each new military setback, especially if the invasion is launched. Therefore, quick action is necessary."

This manuscript—of which there is no other known record—could have been written by one of Stauffenberg's associates. This assumption is supported by the content of the paper and its style, which is matter-of-fact, devoid of complaints or accusations, and could well reflect Stauffenberg's manner of speech; only the monotonous repetition of some German verbs suggests that Stauffenberg's views were merely reported by someone else. The notes may have emanated from Stauffenberg or someone close to him in the autumn of 1943, or even as late as May 1944. The initial situation is described as in a military project : Germany is doomed to perish with her irresponsible and corrupt rulers who have forced her to sacrifice irreplaceable manpower.... The objective is summed up in a double challenge : Hitler and his régime must be eliminated, but Germany must remain capable of action as a political and military power.

For Beck, Tresckow and Stauffenberg the two demands were inseparable. If Hitler's overthrow or death alone were aimed at, without establishing a new government, the war could possibly be brought to a swift end; but eight million soldiers would be abandoned, the homeland exposed to chaos in a clash with invading enemies and hatred unleashed in a civil war. But if both objectives were to be pursued—what a colossal undertaking ! Was it possible in the middle of a war to attack, overthrow and replace a "totalitarian" government in the final display of its power? What if the disaster they were trying to avert were only to be made worse by the undertaking they had launched with the purest of motives? There were major considerations for and against action. What arguments were there to dissuade them? Hitler's continuing power to spell-bind the German people as a whole and the front-line troops in particular; the undeniable fact that he personified, and seemed inseparable from Germany's might in war; the danger—and one not to be minimized—of a new "stab-in-the-back" legend and, finally, the attitude of Germany's opponents, as proclaimed at Casablanca; their one-track minds had become as rigid as Hitler's and they refused to recognize that there was "another" Germany.

But there were compelling reasons for action if the German people were to be spared the incalculable sacrifices which the road to defeat under such leadership was bound to exact. Something had to be done to establish a responsible government which could not be ignored by the Allies. And action had to be taken if the German people were to be given the chance of changing their ways and showing repentance, through their own efforts and not under foreign compulsion.

Only by such self-imposed atonement could the peace be fruitful and a new political life begin. By this means only would the Germans restore their moral freedom and true image and, to quote the ancient Romans, harmony with their gods and spirits whom they had desecrated by their actions.

The drafting of appeals and guidance of the thinking majority were a genuine duty to Stauffenberg, and he put his mind to it with great persistence. And having decided what to do, he paid little heed to the argument that he and his movement stood alone among a people still entirely devoted to Hitler.

Dietrich Bonhoeffer, without then knowing anything about Stauffenberg, once remarked : "A man who thinks and acts responsibly need not worry about approval. His only concern must be the imperative need of the hour."

Not education but only liberation could overcome "folly". "In this we must accept that genuine inner liberation is in most cases only possible when it has been preceded by external liberation." Bonhoeffer added that in such circumstances we try in vain to discover what the people really think and why "for the man who thinks and acts responsibly this question is superfluous."[8]

There were, of course, convinced opponents of Hitler, and people who even hated him and his régime and badly wanted a change but with whom arguments against forcible intervention weighed so heavily that they did not want to hear of it. But Claus and Berthold Stauffenberg were destined for action.

Rudolf Fahrner's notes confirm that from the start Claus Stauffenberg did not assess the German situation purely as a military expert; even years before the war he had been ceaselessly engaged in political planning with the aim of a revolutionary change in Germany. Significantly, his vocabulary does not include the words "Resistance" or "Resistance movement" but there is the term "a German uprising" which he may have adopted from his study of Gneisenau, Napoleon and the Freiherr vom Stein. Stauffenberg does not seem to suggest that history could repeat itself, but the initial situation is comparable : for Gneisenau or vom Stein one important aim was to defeat Napoleon, but their most important goal was the rise of a stronger and socially renewed Germany. Similarly, to Stauffenberg the term "uprising" meant the overthrow of Hitler, for which military preparations were needed. But Hitler's fall was intended only as the starting point for Germany's political rebirth.

A long way back—even before the National Socialists' "accession to power"—Stauffenberg had drawn attention to Hitler's potential impact. Stauffenberg rejected any too facile criticism of Hitler's influence and never underrated it as so many of the "Führer's" enemies seem to have done. But Stauffenberg did not succumb to the man's spell unlike many others on whom it had the effect of turning them into his enemies. Judging by various accounts, especially Fahrner's, Stauffenberg was a political force sui generis, capable of observing a phenomenon such as Hitler objectively and making his own decision to act against him.[9] Meeting Hitler face to face merely reaffirmed Stauffenberg in his own strength. Such confrontations are known to have made much good will, anger and ideological conviction melt away in many a resolute enemy of Hitler's even in would-be assassins who were ready to kill him. But Stauffenberg's "imperviousness" was a quality completely independent of his time. Thormaehlen called him an "impassioned guardian" of his people. The KB reports suggest that this may explain how Stauffenberg with just a few words, won over so many to make common cause with him.

*   *   *

The people who were actively engaged with Stauffenberg in preparing the revolt were identified by the Gestapo investigators, with the exception of very few who knew about the plot but did not play a major part in it. The active conspirators either committed suicide or were handed over to the court and the executioner. They are not identical with "the" Resistance movement from which they shut themselves off by their special role and a secrecy which the others often felt to be excessive. The Kaltenbrunner Office's interrogation reports list their names and draw a few correct conclusions about the pattern of the rebellion but the characterization of the conspirators is distorted and hardly usable for a historical portrayal.

Claus Stauffenberg's first and closest collaborator at all levels—human, political and military—was his brother Berthold. From the day Claus started work with Olbricht until the 20th July Berthold was at his side all the time, thanks to his employment at the Naval High Command in Berlin. Fahrner declared that without his brother Claus Stauffenberg would not have taken it upon himself to launch a revolt in 1943–44.

Rudolf *Fahrner* was associated with both brothers. He was closely acquainted with Friedrich Wolters and knew Stefan George personally. The sculptor, Frank Mehnert, who many years before had been Stefan George's companion, remained the link between the friends until his death on Lake Ilmen in February 1943. He provided a powerful impetus for political action based on moral responsibility. Apart from intellectual matters, in which they were all interested, they had been discussing this topic at their meetings ever since 1936. In 1935, because of growing political difficulties with the régime, Fahrner left Heidelberg University where as a young professor—he was born in Austria in 1903—he had been lecturing on German language and literature. In later years he taught at universities in Spain, Greece and Turkey. When Stauffenberg made his acquaintance Fahrner had just completed a critical study of E. M. Arndt which, in examing a historical subject, at the same time dealt with a contemporary issue : the then newly raised question of the relationship between the human spirit and the state. Claus Stauffenberg showed particular interest in a new work of Fahrner's on Gneisenau which had been suggested by Frank Mehnert. Their association continued after Mehnert's death. Claus Stauffenberg often discussed political questions with Fahrner. And although he hesitated to expose Fahrner to danger, in October 1943 and June–July 1944 he brought him in among the planners of the revolt because he wanted his help with drafting the appeals and the proposed oath of allegiance.

Among the officers with whom Stauffenberg worked for the revolt Henning von Tresckow should be mentioned in the first place. Stauffenberg is said (KB 368) to have "occasionally described him as his mentor". During his visit to Berlin in August, Stauffenberg had vital discussions with Tresckow on what would have to be done. The two men no longer felt it necessary in their consciences to justify their plans. When, four weeks later, Stauffenberg returned to Berlin, Tresckow had already done good groundwork by collecting information and drafting orders and making preliminary arrangements for an attempt on Hitler's life.

We know nothing about the relationship between Tresckow and Stauffenberg in earlier years or about the date when Stauffenberg learnt of Tresckow's assassination attempts in March 1943; at that time Stauffenberg was involved in the fighting during the retreat in Tunisia. Colonel-General Halder mentioned in a more recent statement that Tresckow attended the discussions in Paris at the end of June 1940, when Stauffenberg reportedly said that the only possible way out might have to be the use of force against Hitler.[10] If that was so, we can assume that the two were also in agreement in the intervening years during which Stauffenberg repeatedly visited Army Group Centre. The two men were together for some weeks in September 1943; and—as witnesses testified—they discussed their plan right down to the minutest detail that General Staff officers might require. They were totally absorbed by their undertaking and in a high state of tension, when they discussed these matters with their confederates and they took a considerable risk in travelling across Berlin with incriminating documents in their brief-cases.[11]

At the end of June 1944, Stauffenberg was for the last time confronted with a situation which made it imperative to decide whether action could or ought to be taken. He quickly sent a messenger to Tresckow, who was in Poland. Tresckow's emphatic "Yes" probably made it easier for Stauffenberg to prevail in Berlin and to "cross the Rubicon".

Shortly before the blow was to have been struck for the first time, in the first week of October 1943, Tresckow had had to return to the Eastern front. But he sent Ulrich von *Oertzen*, a close friend of his, to Stauffenberg. The young major—born in 1915 in the Neumark—was a true paladin to both, who touched many a heart. He brought devotion and expert knowledge to the perilous enterprise, sacrificing the chance of personal happiness during his short leave. The day after the 20th July the officer who was guarding him let the young major take his own life.[12]

In General *Olbricht*[13] Stauffenberg found a receptive superior ready for the risky enterprise and who provided the necessary cover for the Colonel's activities. Olbricht knew a vast number of people and had contacts in Berlin, at Headquarters and in the Army's Operations Branches. All these connections were now open to Stauffenberg. Far from standing on the dignity of his rank, Olbricht was at all times ready to give his younger colleague all the help he could, either through personal intervention in his capacity as departmental head or as a General in handling affairs involving other Generals and Field-Marshals. By agreement they quite often set out to recruit new associates and their collaboration is said to have been at its best when they decided to concentrate on one or two officers at the end of a major service conference. A report by someone who was invited to one of these meetings illustrates how well they understood each other : Olbricht pretended to be Stauffenberg and, imitating his courteous phraseology, asked for orders.

During the battle for Stalingrad and shortly afterwards Olbricht had been trying, with increasing impetuosity, to get support for the planned coup d'état from his superior, Colonel-General *Fromm*; and he had introduced numerous visitors to him who spoke in a similar vein. Olbricht felt that without orders issued by the Commander-in-Chief of the Reserve Army these troops could not be expected to back the uprising.

Fritz Fromm, born in 1888 in Pomerania, one time budget officer of the Reichswehr Ministry, and later for several years head of a department at OKH, had been appointed by Hitler in 1939 to the posts of Chief of Armaments and Commander-in-Chief of the Reserve Army. In many ways he was a strong man, such as Hitler would require to head a department, and he had been outstandingly successful in the recruitment of new troops and in many organizational matters. In 1943, Hitler must have become increasingly distrustful of him : this is indicated by Keitel's insulting demand that Fromm give a written justification of his actions. The incident is confirmed by Kaiser.[14] After this Fromm never said anything that might be held against him, although it was well known from private conversations what he thought. The general opinion is that Fromm was driven by ambition and desire for personal prestige. His grand manner owed nothing to ancestry but was born of his physical appearance—he was very corpulent and 2·04 metres tall. According to Kaiser, however, he gladly left the work at the office to others. He enjoyed his food and drink and went hunting. Other powers in the state pushed him more and more into the background and there was nothing he could do to prevent it. He continued to reject Olbricht's repeated overtures but let it be known that after a successful "change-over" he would side with the new men. In summer 1943 the pressure on Olbricht, especially by Goerdeler and other civilian confederates, became almost unbearable. At the same time his relations with Fromm grew increasingly tense. After Stauffenberg had joined Olbricht's office there began a rivalry for his services. In 1944, Fromm insisted on having "the toy" himself—as Stauffenberg put it, and to make him his own Chief of Staff. Before taking up his post, Stauffenberg had had a straight talk with Fromm and let him know what was in his mind. Fromm raised no objections and merely sought an assurance that his special friend Wilhelm Keitel would not be forgotten in the "clean-out". Even Stauffenberg was unable to persuade him to more active co-operation.

Olbricht arranged Stauffenberg's contact with Colonel-General Beck, whose serious illness had kept him away throughout the year and who had returned to the active circle only in September. Physically he still showed traces of what he had been through. He had aged beyond his sixty-three years and seemed more spirit than flesh. But his dynamic will-power was unbroken; and without demanding it he resumed his role as co-ordinator and at the hub of the circle.

It is not known whether Stauffenberg had met Beck in the preceding years. But his new encounter reinforced their relationship and showed how they complemented each other. As far as Stauffenberg was concerned, Beck's uncompromising, noble personality and his strong sense of responsibility dispelled any misgivings which some other younger conspirators felt about the "old man's" resolve. On several occasions, Stauffenberg had to arrange opportunities for Beck and Olbricht to meet. At first, he himself met Beck while accompanying Olbricht; later they were often alone or with other groups. Beck, who stuck to men of his own generation, held different views on quite a few things. But, as he told others, Stauffenberg gained his complete confidence. And Stauffenberg, who owed a great deal to Beck, acted in accordance with the pledge he had given him.[15]

In Olbricht's and Fromm's departments Stauffenberg met a number of people initiated and ready to take part in the plot. Lieutenant-Colonel i.G. Robert *Bernardis* (an Austrian born in Innsbruck in 1908) had fought in the Polish and French campaigns and during the first year of the war against the Soviet Union. In 1942, because of illness, he had been transferred to the General Army Office where he had an important and absorbing job, first as Head of Department and later as "Gruppenleiter" responsible for "personnel and field army replacements". He worked for the uprising very persuasively in his own departmental position, as the interrogation reports bear out. His relationship with Stauffenberg was one of comradeship and trust. On the 20th July he was among those who acted openly, without reservation. He was one of the first to be sentenced to death and died on August 8. One of Bernardis' collaborators, Major i.G. Egbert *Hayessen* (born 1913) had the important job of passing on orders to the Berlin Command and was to be the City Commandant's aide on the 20th July. It was found that another member of the department, Lieutenant-Colonel i.G. Joachim *Sadrozinski* (born in Tilsit in 1907) was also in league with Stauffenberg.

Another active supporter of the revolt was Captain of the Reserve, Hermann *Kaiser*. Born in 1885 in Remscheid, he came from a family of teachers, was repeatedly decorated as a Second Lieutenant in the First World War, and during the inter-war years taught history, mathematics, physics and art appreciation at the Oranien Gymnasium in Wiesbaden. Kaiser's history lessons, the study groups on the history of art which he arranged at his home, and the excursions to Worms, Speyer and the Einhart basilica in Michelstadt remained unforgettable to one of his former pupils who later lived for many years in Tokyo. He said that his memory of Hermann Kaiser enabled him to understand the "deep, one might almost say mystical link between teacher and pupil in the Far East. There has always been veneration of the 'master'. Hermann Kaiser was a German idealist, a soldier but not a militarist, an educator of the young, a teacher, a human being whom his pupils will not forget to the end of their days." Once Hitler was making a speech in Darmstadt which offeneded Kaiser. In full view of his Commander and fellow officers, he ostentatiously left the hall. And if one of his comrades was about to give him the Hitler salute, he would say: "Drop it! You look like somebody who wants to give a blessing where there is nothing to bless."[16] At the insistence of Beck, Olbricht, Stauffenberg and Goerdeler he left Olbricht's office and became Fromm's war diarist. In this post he played an important liaison role. For Stauffenberg, who worked with him a great deal and had particular faith in him, Kaiser made the required notes and drafts, some of which can be found among the depositions of the interrogations; he also took messages for him, including communications with Goerdeler, and organized rendez-vous. Published fragments from his private diary provide impressive evidence of the events at the Bendlerstrasse in 1943 and of the feeling of hopelessness among the anti-Hitler confederates which Stauffenberg encountered on arrival at the Bendlerstrasse. An entry on 27.6.1944, reproduced in the KB reports (p. 356) gives an idea of the style of his often cryptic diary jottings: "18.00 at Beck Praise of Diocletian and relaxation in one's own garden, when it is suggested he take over the government." The reports on the investigation describe Kaiser as "one of the moving spirits behind an attempted assassination". Kaiser had been earmarked for the post of liaison officer with Military District Command XII (Wiesbaden), in the case of a successful coup d'état.

Major Hans-Juergen Count von *Blumenthal* was born in 1907, the same year as Stauffenberg. He was seriously wounded and worked from 1941 onwards in the General Army Office, eventually as Head of the Replacements and General Army Affairs Branch (KB 333). In the weeks before the 20th July Stauffenberg is known to have sent for him frequently. His driver—wearing a track suit —would wait for him at a given point near the Dueppel camp to which his (General Weidemann's) office had had to move from the Bendlerstrasse. Blumenthal had behind him the Potsdam tradition —his father was tutor to Princes of the House of Hohenzollern, his mother born a von Schulenburg. But his own thinking was influenced by F. W. Heinz, the former editor of the "Stahlhelm", and from the outset he had regarded the peace between the German Nationalist Party (Deutschnationale) and Hitler as a misfortune. As time went on he became even more convinced of this and he defended his views with rebellious independence. He was close to Dohnanyi and Oster, and was a childhood friend of Merz von Quirnheim. Witnesses said that when he was interrogated he refused to give the names of others who knew of the conspiracy. Blumenthal was earmarked for the post of liaison officer for Military District II (Stettin).

We have already mentioned Lieutenant-Colonel Fritz von der

213

Lancken, born in 1890, Olbricht's aide-de-camp, in whose country house at Potsdam various meetings were held and where from time to time explosives were stored.

Colonel Siegfried *Wagner*, an officer of the older generation and former *Stahlhelm* leader, who was working at Fromm's office, sympathized with Goerdeler's ideas. He regarded it as one of the tasks of the military to pave the way for an uprising in spite of the war. Count Blumenthal shared his views. Wagner's name was later mentioned less frequently than many others, but some people who knew him described him as one of the most clear-sighted planners. He is said to have prepared a precise escape route for Goerdeler. It is not known why Goerdeler made no use of it. After the 20th July, Colonel Wagner forestalled his own arrest and sentence by committing suicide.

Karl *Sack*, a senior Ministerial official and Judge Advocate-General, was born in 1896, and like Oster was the son of a parson. Five times seriously wounded in the First World War, he had been working in the military law branch since 1934 and was its head from 1942 onwards. Ever since he and Count von der Goltz had succeeded in throwing light on to the background of the "Fritsch Crisis" he had been waging a constant secret war on the Gestapo. He often shielded the Resistance movement and audaciously supported it even in dangerous situations. He was a friend of Oster's and worked closely with Dohnanyi. But he tried in vain to save him from trial and certain death. He collaborated with Olbricht and his circle till the 20th July. He also formed the link with Canaris and the men of the Confessional Church. In the last month of the war he was murdered by the SS, together with Dietrich Bonhoeffer and Canaris.[16a]

The Quartermaster-General at OKH, General (Artillery) Eduard *Wagner* (born 1894) was in daily touch with Fromm's and Olbricht's departments—although his own office was in Zossen. Their contacts were both about service matters and the planned coup d'état.

Until Ludwig Beck's departure, Wagner had been one of his Quartermasters, had taken part in Beck's attempts to organize a coup in 1938 and 1939 and remained loyal to him. In 1941–42 he started new attempts to prepare a revolt. His main aim was to force Hitler, through joint action by the Army Group and Army Commanders, to hand over the supreme command. In his capacity as Quartermaster-General he had on several occasions and at decisive junctures emphatically warned Hitler against over-ambitious and impracticable plans for an offensive. His warnings were as futile as were his reminders of the danger facing the Sixth Army in

Stalingrad. His official position, his freedom of movement between the staff departments at home and at the front, and his frequent attendance at Führer HQ, all this enabled him to be a great help to the Resistance and get reliable men promoted or appointed to commanding positions. Through his previous activities Stauffenberg was well known to Wagner, and once when he visited Claus in hospital he suggested (although Stauffenberg was not overjoyed at the idea) that after his recovery he would like to have Claus transferred to the Quartermaster-General's department. Stauffenberg and Wagner discussed, in particular, what steps would have to be taken at HQ and how to co-ordinate action at the various focal points.

Staunch support for the planned uprising came also from Professor Jens *Jessen*, a Reserve officer employed at the Quartermaster-General's department, a man full of ideas and energy, who took personal risks by offering asylum to members of the Resistance. Being in charge of the permit issuing office (Qu 6) he was able to open important avenues. Also active at the Quartermaster-General's office, and later sentenced to death like Jessen, was Lieutenant-Colonel i.G. Günther *Smend* (born in 1912) temporarily aide de camp to the Chief of the General Staff, Zeitzler. An official report stresses his courageous bearing in court. Another important collaborator of Stauffenberg's was the later Artillery Ordnance General at OKH, Fritz *Lindemann,* whose main task was to put out feelers to Corps Headquarters whose Commanding Generals or Chiefs of Staff were mostly his former comrades from the Reichswehr. He had two confidants in particular at the Military District Headquarters in Berlin who held themselves ready for a revolt and were supporters of Stauffenberg : the local Chief of Staff, Major-General von *Rost*,[17] and the war production officer Colonel of the Air Force, Hans *Gronau.* Like the Quartermaster-General, General Lindemann was able to do a great deal for the co-ordination of the Resistance thanks to his freedom of movement between Berlin, the Führer HQ and the General Staffs of the different Army Groups. After the 20th July he went into hiding. A warrant with a prize on his head of half a million Reichsmark was issued. Even so he found people to hide him. But in September he was betrayed, and the house in Berlin where he was staying was surrounded. Attempting to jump from a third-floor window, he was seriously wounded by three shots. He underwent an operation in a prison hospital. According to one report he tried to end his life by tearing off his bandages. But he failed to forestall the executioner. The three people who had harboured him in their Berlin flat—the architect Gloeden, his wife and mother-in-law—were all executed.

Colonel Helmuth *Stieff*, a friend of Lindemann's, was born in East Prussia in 1901, the same year as Tresckow, and was also the son of an officer. Stieff was promoted to Major-General after January 30, 1944. He took part in preparing the revolt and was one of the inner circle of conspirators. From September 21, 1941 he had been the GSO I of the German Fourth Army then advancing towards Moscow. The General and the Chief of Staff being no longer available he was thrown upon his own resources throughout the disastrous winter of that year. In October 1942, he became Chief of the Organisation Branch at OKH. He owed this promotion to his outstanding expertise, his keenness and his gift for organization and improvisation.

When he was promoted on January 30, 1944, he was the youngest officer to have risen to the rank of General and, as people liked to note, the Army's smallest General—light, agile, full of vitality and a passionate horseman. They worked hard in his department, but Stieff let them have a good time, too, and always managed to be obliging, amiable and in a good mood. But he was not a frivolous man. More than others an officer of his calibre was always expected to prove himself and "push himself forward"; yet at the same time Stieff had a deep and lively sense of responsibility as a German and as an officer.

The published letters of the years 1932–34[18] show that his attitude towards Hitler's "national revolution" was akin to Beck's. The things he saw and heard on a trip through Poland in November 1939 and which were corroborated by Colonel-General von Blaskowitz outraged him : "I am ashamed of being a German", he wrote. "This minority which sullies the name of Germany by murder, plunder and arson will prove the misfortune of the whole German nation unless we put a stop to these people soon. What has been described and proved to me by the most responsible authorities on the spot is bound to rouse the avenging Nemesis. Otherwise this rabble will one day do the same things to us decent people and terrorise their own nation with their pathological passions."[19] A letter dated 23.8.1941 marks Stieff's break with Hitler : "Every day that passes here (at Führer HQ) strengthens one's dislike of this proletarian megalomaniac. Only yesterday we had another taste of his attitude, in writing. It was *so* outrageous in tone that I can only say : anyone who puts up with that does not deserve any better. And the other side *must* gradually become convinced that they can go to any length if people swallow everything without a word of protest. At any rate my respect for certain people has sunk very low ... the whole thing is simply disgusting and disgraceful !" His experience with the front-line troops in the East—

216

presumably also in his contacts with Tresckow—roused him even more against Hitler, the "bloody dilettante" who was senselessly demanding unjustifiable sacrifices, the man who had introduced and permitted a régime that was defiling everything with its horrors and crimes. In a letter dated November 19 Stieff described the deportation of Jews from Germany to Minsk, which he had witnessed, as "unworthy of a nation that calls itself civilized. One day all this is *bound* to be avenged on us—and rightly so! What impudence that a few scoundrels should plunge a good people into misfortune. Everything has become even worse than it was two years ago in Poland." And on January 10, 1942, with his Army in a dreadful plight, Stieff wrote: "All of us have brought so much guilt upon ourselves—for we are after all *co-responsible*; I see in the judgement falling upon us no more than a just atonement for all the crimes we Germans have committed or permitted in the last few years. Actually, it satisfies me to see that there is, after all, retaliating justice in this world! Even if I myself should be its victim. I am tired of this horror without end." A letter written in Berlin on August 6, 1943, indicated that he had met Olbricht and probably also Tresckow there and decided to take an active part in the overthrow of Hitler. He said he did "not want to shirk a responsibility decreed by fate". He undertook to deliver a letter from Olbricht to Kluge. His next assignment was to bring up and store the necessary explosives and to prepare the attempt on Hitler. The lady who received these letters said that on September 8 Tresckow, who was then again staying in Berlin, told Stieff the details of the assassination attempts he had planned.

In his department Stieff was able to count on three officers: Lieutenant-Colonel i.G. Bernhard *Klamroth* (born 1910 in Berlin),[20] Major i.G. Joachim *Kuhn* and First Lieutenant of the Reserve, Albrecht von *Hagen* (born 1904), in civil life legal adviser to a bank. Stauffenberg was Stieff's Chief of Staff for four months; then Klamroth, his former colleague, succeeded him. Kuhn was a friend of Stauffenberg's, and Hagen had served with him in the 10th Armoured Division in Africa.

There was no doubt that Bavarian-born Lieutenant-General Adolf *Heusinger*, Chief of HQ Operations Branch, shared their ideas and took an identical view of the situation. It was known that together with his assistant, Colonel i.G. Heinz *Brandt*, he was waging an exhausting struggle with Hitler during the daily situation conference. He considered that the command structure must urgently be changed if a catastrophe was to be avoided. He, therefore, took an important part in the "conspiracy" to set up a new top level command and found that many senior Army

217

Commanders with whom he discussed the matter agreed with him. In spring 1944 he had to absent himself for several weeks owing to illness. Tresckow unsuccessfully tried to persuade him to let him come as his deputy to HQ and thus close to Hitler. Schlabrendorff's view is that this was not because Tresckow lacked the right qualifications but that it had something to do with Tresckow being so extraordinarily active. Heusinger probably saw through this attitude, and in any case it did not conform with his own great outward reserve.[21]

General Erich *Fellgiebel*, another high officer at HQ who worked for the revolt, was born in 1886 in Silesia. He grew up on his father's estate in the province of Posen, but it was the years he spent at the Johannis Gymnasium in Breslau which decisively shaped his character. He had a great gift for exact natural sciences and had received a classical education which was broadly based on his wide reading, including such authors as Kant and the ancient Greek philosophers. Physically he was tough and agile, at home in field or forest, a superb horseman—in fact he managed to keep a riding horse as a "cart horse" for a long time in Hitler's immediate entourage despite the Führer's express prohibition. He had been working in Signals, holding General Staff positions during the First World War, and after 1934 was assigned to reorganize the Signals service. He was on good terms with Beck, Freiherr von Fritsch and Karl-Heinrich von Stülpnagel, but had been openly opposed to Keitel even before February 1938. He was outspoken in his criticism and knew that his telephone conversations had been tapped since long before the war. He opposed attempts to minimize Hitler's early victories which he regarded as an achievement, but from the late summer of 1940 he stubbornly argued at conferences against Hitler's plan to make war on Russia. Although with his bespectacled face, his shrewd, watchful and independent manner,[22] and his passion for horses he represented the type of General which Hitler loathed, he was retained in his post as Chief of Signals of the Wehrmacht, because he was virtually irreplaceable. This was one of the ten most important war offices and through it Fellgiebel was always in Hitler's immediate entourage. Stauffenberg had established close contact with the General during his term at HQ. They were frank and close friends and there was no doubt that Fellgiebel had the courage to act and give all necessary assistance. Only Fellgiebel's often violent outbursts and the fact that he was too trusting and not cunning enough was liable to cause misgivings during the preparation of the revolt.

Other collaborators of Fellgiebel's in Signals who came to know about and took part in the revolt were Colonel Kurt *Hahn* (born

218

1901), next in seniority to Fellgiebel at HQ; Captain Max Ulrich Count von *Drechsel* (born 1911), ultimately envisaged as liaison officer for Military District VII, who had transferred from the Stahlhelm to the SA and volunteered for the Wermacht in 1934. Like his friend, Major Leonrod, he had belonged to Stauffenberg's cavalry regiment in Bamberg (KB 296). Lieutenant-General Fritz *Thiele*, born in Berlin, in 1894, who was the most senior Signals officer at OKH in the Bendlerstrasse,[23] had been initiated into the plan by Fellgiebel. His collaborator as Chief of Signals Inspectorate VII was Colonel *Hassell*.

Among the men in the Abwehr who worked for the coup was Colonel i.G. Georg *Hansen* (born 1904), first as Head of a department, then as successor to Canaris. In June–July 1944 he attended various meetings at Stauffenberg's place in Wannsee. Other confederates in different sections of the Abwehr were : Captain of the Reserve Theodor *Strünck*, an insurance manager whose house in Berlin was a frequent meeting place; Captain of the Reserve Bernhard *Letterhaus* (born 1894), in charge of a publishing department, and a former Deputy of the Centre Party in the Prussian Diet. Later he did liaison work between the military conspirators and the Catholic Resistance circle, centred around the Ketteler house in Cologne. Others included : Regierungsrat Hans Bernd *Gisevius*; Dr Otto *John*, legal adviser to the Lufthansa, who worked together with his brother Dr Hans *John*; Captain Dr Ludwig *Gehre*, who according to the interrogation reports had been working hand in hand with Stauffenberg from autumn 1943 onwards and disappeared a few months before the 20th July because the Gestapo was trying to arrest him; Colonel Wessel *Freytag* von *Loringhoven* (born 1899) and Lieutenant-Colonel Werner *Schrader*.

Lieutenant-Colonel i.G. Joachim *Meichssner* was serving as the Army's representative at OKW. He was born in Deutsch-Eylau in 1906, attended the same class as Stauffenberg at the Military Academy and was devoted to him. Meichssner himself was committed to the planned revolt from deep personal conviction. According to the interrogation reports his father, "a fanatical pastor of the Confessional Church", wrote to him : "What is being done against the Church is a stab-in-the-back." They mention Meichssner's criticism of the military leadership under the heading of top level war command structure (KB 437, 291). The reports also assume that he was the officer intended to carry out the assassination but had "abandoned his plan because his nerves could not stand the long period of waiting" (KB 178). As the top-ranking officer in the Wehrmacht Operations Command in Berlin his job after the 20th July was to pass on all information to the equivalent

Command at Führer HQ, until the net closed around him and he was caught.

Another of Stauffenberg's close contemporaries, who was later actively implicated in the secret plot, was the Head of the "Foreign Armies, West" Department at OKH, Colonel i.G. Alexis Freiherr von *Roenne*. Of Baltic origin, he was deeply rooted in the Protestant faith of his native region. The memorandum he later wrote in prison under the title "The Aim was the Salvation of Germany" was a remarkable assessment of the situation and a clear explanation of the motives of the by then outlawed conspirators (October 1, 1944).[24] Another potential accomplice ready to play his part (KB 259) was Regierungsdirektor Count Michael von *Matuschka* (born 1888), who was Roenne's collaborator in the months before the 20th July.

Two junior officers, very close to Roenne and friends of Schulenburg's, worked directly under Stauffenberg on 20th July: Captain Friedrich-Karl *Klausing*, decorated and seriously wounded during the campaign in the East, who was promoted to Captain in 1943 at the age of twenty-three and served at the General Army Office from April 1944 onwards; and Captain Hans *Fritzsche*, a little older than Klausing who was transferred from front-line service as unfit to the reserve of the 9th Infantry Regiment in Potsdam. He had joined that regiment in 1935 to get a commission after being forced to flee from Heidelberg University because he had rebelled against some SD measure. Major Ludwig Freiherr v. *Leonrod*, who had regimental ties with Stauffenberg, was to be liaison officer for Military District VII (Munich). On the 20th July he was assigned the duty of making arrests and guarding prisoners in the Bendlerstrasse after Count Drechsel had been allotted his post in Munich. Major Leonrod's confessor, Chaplain Wehrle, discussed the question of tyrannicide with him and, as he said under interrogation, the priest encouraged him. Later the two were confronted in court. Both were executed (KB 262, 288, 304, 311, 435).

Two other friends of Stauffenberg's from his Academy days began to take active parts in the planned coup at the end of June 1944: Colonel i.G. Eberhard *Finckh*, born 1899, who had a distinguished record as a Quartermaster with Army Group South at Stalingrad. In June 1944 his superior, the Quartermaster-General, entrusted Colonel Finckh with the formidable job of organizing the supply for the German troops in France, who were being attacked by the invasion army, and transferred him to the staff of the Commander-in-Chief, West.[25] The most marked feature of this burly figure who inspired confidence was the contrast between his white hair and the fresh, almost youthful colouring of his face.

Finckh gave the interrogators an impressive account of a meeting with Stauffenberg when passing through Berlin on June 23, 1944. Stauffenberg, he said, came straight to the point: the situation in the East was untenable and a breakthrough in the West was only a matter of time. "Of course, we no longer have any proper Field-Marshals. They're all in a blue funk and don't contradict the Führer when he gives orders. They know the situation is serious, but they don't assert their views strongly enough." Finckh added that Stauffenberg's outbursts were so fascinating, "that you had hardly time to think, let alone produce a considered reply (KB 305, 306, 313). The other of the two men who attended the talks with Finckh on June 13 was Colonel i.G. Albrecht Ritter *Merz* von *Quirnheim* (born 1905), the son of the former Head of the German War-Archives. He had been brought to Olbricht to succeed Stauffenberg as Chief of Staff so as to have a reliable man for the day of the revolt. This was Stauffenberg's own suggestion. Merz was lively, cheerful and unsentimental, and, although basically refined and amiable, he had the strength to get his way. Originally a convinced adherent of the Hitler movement, he later felt increasingly outraged at what was going on in Germany. As far back as 1940, in France, he would have liked Stauffenberg to agree to the future plot and coup d'état.

First Lieutenant of the Reserve Werner von *Haeften*, born 1909, was Hans Bernd von Haeften's aforementioned brother. Until the outbreak of war he was a legal consultant in Berlin; he served as infantry platoon commander on the Eastern Front and was decorated. After being seriously wounded in the pelvis he joined Olbricht's office in November 1943. Claus Stauffenberg, who made him his ADC, found in him a devoted helper in planning the revolt. Haeften, then thirty-five, looked much younger. He had very fair curly hair, and with his infectious cheerfulness and good humour he quickly established friendly relations. More than anyone else he assimilated Stauffenberg's way of living and helped create an atmosphere around Claus into which the younger men joining the office felt themselves quickly absorbed. In conversation Haeften revealed how the developments in Germany gripped and stirred him to action; but he had his own bracing sense of humour and reassuring calm which were especially welcome to anyone who met him in those days of misery and destruction. This is how one of the younger men who spent the last weeks with Haeften described him: "At first, you would not have believed that a head like his could think out such ideas and become so deeply involved in such responsible and dangerous affairs. Inwardly he was full of a joy which illuminated everything else. As he was on that first evening, so he continued. I never found him depressed or downhearted, although he could be serious. . . . Not once did he speak about his links with the men who later became involved in the 20th July nor did he say whether he himself was one of them. . . . He loved his friends and did everything in his power for them. . . . Werner rarely mentioned that he was having a lot of other work in addition to his office duties. Occasionally he would remark that he had had a late night, not going to bed before midnight, two or three o'clock, though he did not for a moment sound annoyed about it, nor did he ever complain that it was all too much for him. He arrived punctually at the office every morning—usually driving his little Mercedes with Colonel Count Stauffenberg at his side. And when he overtook me on the way from the underground station to the Bendlerstrasse he stopped, if there was room in the car, or at least he gave me a cheerful wave." The same report pictures Haeften on the late evening of the 20th: "The last time I saw him was after the officers' conference. He was not in despair but seemed still hoping for success, although the likely outcome of the enterprise was becoming all too clear. Perhaps I ought to say I did see an expression of sadness in him; it was a sadness not about himself, his own fate and that of his friends but rather about the inescapable misery Germany would continue to suffer and about the coming destruction. I never saw Werner again."

The man who wrote this, Captain Helmuth *Cords,* himself took an active part in the events of the 20th July. He was detailed to check security measures in the Bendlerstrasse. Other young confederates in Stauffenberg's and Haeften's circle worthy of mention are: 2nd Lieutenant Ludwig Freiherr von *Hammerstein,* the son of Colonel-General von Hammerstein; 2nd Lieutenant von *Oppen,* whose family estate in Altfriedland Stauffenberg had visited as late as July 1944; 1st Lieutenant Ewald Heinrich von *Kleist-Schmenzin,* Captain Axel Freiherr von dem *Bussche* and 1st Lieutenant Urban *Thiersch.*

Major Roland von *Hösslin* of Munich, born 1915, had been a close associate of Stauffenberg's for many years. In whatever capacity he served in the war he always proudly wore the Seventeen of the Bamberg Cavalry Regiment on his shoulder. In the war in Africa he was awarded the Knight's Cross for his service as leader of a reconnaissance detachment at El Alamein. He was heart and soul a front-line officer but was so severely wounded that he could later only serve as an instructor at home. He was recalled to the Armoured Troops School II at Krampnitz near Potsdam and it was from there that he frequently went to see Stauffenberg in the winter of 1943–44. Somebody later recognized him from a picture[27]

222

remembered meeting him during a visit to Stauffenberg's place in Wannsee although Hösslin's name had not been mentioned. He was particularly struck by the fact that the two men were of similar type and by their robust yet sensitive relations in Berlin in those days. Stauffenberg went to see Hösslin in February 1943 when the Major lay seriously wounded in the Charité hospital. That was before Stauffenberg himself left for Africa. According to the interrogation reports Hösslin, whose part in the conspiracy evidently made a great impression, was closely questioned. He repeated Stauffenberg's arguments which had convinced him of the need to dare a last attempt to save Germany. His own views are on record : "As to the present situation, I should merely like to add that I thought it madness, after exhausting the Army's fighting strength in Germany, to wage a partisan war on two fronts against fully equipped modern armies. There can be no 'Battle of the last Goths' on Mount Vesuvius for a nation of eighty millions." Hösslin confirmed in court that Stauffenberg was regarded as the "coming man in the General Staff" (KB 373, 478). It may be assumed that arrangements were made with Hösslin as to which task the Armoured Troops School would undertake on the day of the revolt. But in spring 1944 Hösslin was put in command of the Armoured Reconnaissance School at Insterburg. He was then charged with carrying out the emergency measures decreed for Königsberg in co-operation with Lieutenant-Colonel Hans Otto *Erdmann* (born 1896)—another confederate who was the GSO I at Military District HQ. Erdmann was to pass on to him the code word "Moewe II". ("Moewe I" was intended to call up stand-by units for the Commandant of OKH Headquarters) (KB 372).

Two weeks before the 20th July the Armoured Reconnaissance School was transferred to Meiningen in the interior of Germany as Insterburg was in danger from the advancing enemy. It was there that Hösslin was arrested on August 23, 1944. In October, Hössling, then twenty-nine, and Blumenthal were put to death.

First Lieutenant Heinrich Count von *Lehndorf-Steinort*, born 1909, has already been mentioned as one of the members of Tresckow's circle. His estate, Steinort, was in the area of the East Prussia HQ ("Mauerwald"). Foreign Minister Ribbentrop set up his headquarters at the Count's castle. Lehndorff became an important link between Stauffenberg and HQ on the one hand and Stauffenberg and Tresckow on the other. Stauffenberg assigned to him the job of liaison officer for East Prussia where his uncle, Count Dohna-Tolksdorf, was intended to become Political Representative. Arrested in Koenigsberg, Lehndorf managed to escape, but was seized again. At the interrogation he explained his complicity with clear arguments against the National Socialist régime and Hitler and said it was better, even at considerable risk, to do something than let things drift towards the chaos of Bolshevism (KB 257, 258).

Colonel Fritz *Jäger,* born in Württemberg in 1895, had known Stauffenberg since 1942 and Olbricht since March 1943, through Gehre and Kaiser. He was Commandant of an Armoured Troops School and tank commander decorated with the Knight's Cross. Stauffenberg had him at his side for any task that required determination and authority. On the 20th July he arrested SS-leaders and Generals and was charged with leading the assault on the Prinz-Albrecht-Strasse (Gestapo, SS-Security Head Office) and on the Propaganda Ministry.

Stauffenberg personally maintained contact with the President of the Berlin Police, Count Wolf-Heinrich von *Helldorf* (born 1896). Meetings were held in the Bendlerstrasse at Stauffenberg's office and at the house of Count Gottfried von *Bismarck-Schönhausen,* the Regierungspräsident of Potsdam, who was also involved in the plan. SA-Gruppenführer Helldorf, well known as a fighter in the early days of the Nazi movement, had favoured the idea of an uprising since 1938; in 1941 he turned against Hitler—out of concern for Germany, as he himself declared (according to KB 104)—and was ready to use the police of Berlin in support of Stauffenberg's planned coup. Certain features of his personal life, Schulenburg said, such as his SA record, made it advisable to appoint, after a transitional period, Tresckow rather than Helldorf as Chief of the German police. Another man who collaborated with Helldorf and Gisevius was the Chief of the Criminal Police, SS-Gruppenführer Arthur *Nebe* (born 1894), who had been ready for a conspiracy ever since 1938.

The co-operation of Lieutenant-General Paul von *Hase,* Commandant of Berlin, a post of special importance for the day of the coup, had been secured by Olbricht and Stauffenberg, who initiated him into the plot. Two of his officers, Lieutenant-Colonel in the General Staff, Hermann *Schöne* and Major Adolf Friedrich Count von *Schack* were also "in the know".

At the Military District III HQ, in Berlin, Major-General Rost, who had been willing to take part in a revolt was succeeded as Chief of Staff by Major-General Otto *Herfurth* (born 1893, in Stuttgart). His participation could be relied upon whereas it was impossible to approach the Commanding General. With a view to replacing him, Stauffenberg approached and won over Lieutenant-General Karl Freiherr von *Thüngen* with whose Franconian family he had been in touch since his Bamberg days. Thüngen was told of the conspiracy.

Because of frequent personnel changes it was difficult for Stauffenberg to infiltrate reliable allies into the most important service units likely to be required for the coup. But there were Colonels Harald *Momm* and Martin *Stein* at the school in Krampnitz, whom he knew well from his cavalry days; General *Hitzfeld* of the Doeberitz School, who was all for the revolt, and Colonel Wolfgang *Müller*, who had for a long time been in touch with the anti-Hitler Opposition.

Stauffenberg had also personally summoned, persuaded and instructed the following officers in their duties as prospective liaison officers of the Military Districts : Captain (Cavalry) in the Reserve Friedrich *Scholz-Babisch*, a Silesian farmer; Lieutenant-Colonel von *Sell* from Berlin, ADC to the venerable Field-Marshal von Mackensen; Colonel Count Rudolf *Marogna-Redwitz*, chief of the Abwehr office in Vienna; Lieutenant-Colonel i.G. Hasso von *Böhmer* (born 1904) a friend of Tresckow's; and Major Georg-Konrad *Kissling* (born 1892), a Silesian farmer who was to serve as agricultural expert.

The man Stauffenberg placed in the Naval High Command was a resolute ally and friend of his brother, Lieutenant-Commander Alfred *Kranzfelder*, who served as liaison officer between the Naval High Command and the Foreign Office in Berlin. The same age as Claus Stauffenberg (born 1907), he came from a family of lawyers in Bavaria. As a boy, his mountains and forests meant everything to him; he knew the stars and wondered about their movements. Later he decided to become a naval officer to see something of the world. On his voyages he was particularly impressed by the East. The great serenity of the Hindu priests, their power to master life from within and rise above good luck and misfortune was something the sensitive Kranzfelder, who was later steeled in the struggle against illness, always regarded as a goal worth pursuing. He had been top of his class at the Naval College in 1927. One of his fellow-officers described him as an "imaginative, complete officer whose interests ranged beyond his profession, a man sure of himself, independent, full of clear, bold plans and with a natural flair for politics".[28] Another officer, who was taken into their confidence by Stauffenberg and Kranzfelder and who remained unidentified by the Gestapo, said the two were "among the very few members of the Naval High Command who retained their soul and human dignity when all hell broke loose". As soon as Claus Stauffenberg came to Berlin, Kranzfelder joined forces with him. The report by the same officer showed that Kranzfelder must have felt himself in constant danger. He described a long walk at night which the three of them took through the forest of Eberswalde in November 1943. Kranzfelder kept on hearing steps behind them and believed that they were being followed and spied upon, until it was found that he had been worried by the flapping of his own leather coat. But in that month he also once joined a family of friends in the shelter during a heavy air raid on Berlin where, forgetting the present, he told the gathering of a Bach and Mozart organ concert which he and some others had attended a few days earlier in Paris.

Kranzfelder was consumed by one thought alone : how to bring off the planned coup. Even his engagement, soon to be followed by the wedding, did not deflect him from his dangerous path. His fiancée said the plan might fail with unforeseeable consequences. In that event she would commit suicide, to die with the other victims. Kranzfelder rejected the thought : even if he died, she must live, marry another and have children so that she might "implant in them the good qualities of our nation".

Kranzfelder's complicity seems to have been betrayed by an irrelevant long-distance call which, as a matter of routine, had been taken down by Göring's "Search Office" and which was not understood in its proper context until after the 20th July. According to the interrogation reports Kranzfelder, when charged with not having reported these treasonable activities replied : "It was mainly the fact that the two Stauffenbergs were involved which prevented me from doing so" (KB 297). The reports also indicate that Kranzfelder was instructed by the conspirators to observe, after the assassination, at the Naval Command in "Koralle" how Rear-Admiral Dönitz and Admiral Meisel were reacting to incoming orders and especially whether Dönitz would obey the summons to report to Field-Marshal Witzleben. To show that the attempt had been successful it was arranged that Berthold Stauffenberg should telephone and say that he was sick (KB 55, 116).

Reports say that Kranzfelder was taken to be executed together with Berthold Stauffenberg and Schulenburg. At the Naval High Command some officers later spoke scathingly of the scoundrels who had raised their hands against the Führer; but on one occasion an officer ventured to suggest to a young Admiral that the day might come when he might be glad if his own son were allowed to serve in the training ship "Alfred Kranzfelder".

Among Berthold Stauffenberg's and Kranzfelder's associates in the Navy who were ready to take personal action were Commanders Sydney *Jessen* and Werner *Traber*; also in close touch with Berthold Stauffenberg was Lieutenant-Commander Kurt *Bauch*, who in civil life was professor of the history of art.[29]

At the High Command of the Air Force, Major i.G. Friedrich *Georgi* (born 1917), General Olbricht's son-in-law, knew about the plot. According to his evidence a plan was drafted under the code word "Pericles" to include the Luftwaffe in joint action. Georgi was arrested together with Olbricht on the 20th July.[30]

An important link in the planned revolt outside Berlin—at the second focal point of events—was General Heinrich von *Stülpnagel,* the Military Commander of Paris, previously mentioned in connection with the plan of September 1938.

Two other senior officers also involved at that time but later, in autumn 1943, suspended from active service either as a punishment or a sign of disgrace, had agreed to being brought in on the day of the coup and to assuming important tasks: they were Field-Marshal Erwin von *Witzleben* and Colonel-General Erich *Hoepner.* After Stalingrad, Witzleben had renewed his contacts with Beck, and in the autumn of 1943 was initiated into the new plans by Beck and Olbricht. He kept his links with the Bendlerstrasse alive through his former ADC, Major Count Wilhelm-Friedrich zu *Lynar,* in whose house many meetings took place, and through Captain Count *Schwerin* (KB 43). According to the interrogation reports, Witzleben only came to know Stauffenberg in May and June at General Olbricht's office. Stauffenberg's acquaintance with Hoepner dated back to his service days in Wuppertal (1938–39) and the subsequent campaigns in Poland and France (1939–40), Major-General Hans *Oster* was willing to act as liaison officer with the Dresden Military District.

*　　*　　*

While these officers were in charge of the military side of the revolt there was another circle of men responsible for its political aspect. Stauffenberg—and this has been held against him—took the same intense interest in the political as in the military planning and obviously laid more stress on the character and efficiency of the men involved than on their political programmes. It was found that not only did he frequently call for reports on political conversations and preparations (KB 523) but that he himself often proposed and attended meetings and discussions. In addition, he tried "to obtain access to the most comprehensive sources of information possible about events abroad and the enemy's attitude" (KB 173).

First, we must mention Count Fritz von der *Schulenburg* who from the beginning of his Berlin days stood by Stauffenberg and was himself dedicated to the idea of preparing the revolt. His most distinctive characteristic was his genuine devotion to this patriotic task. His strength in adversity made him irreplaceable; and the conspirators profited from his friendship with Stauffenberg. His chief role was to put Stauffenberg in touch with the political Opposition to Hitler. He had many contacts with those men irrespective of his personal views. Through him Stauffenberg quickly obtained an idea of the people he could rely on and with whom he could continue to plan. In Schulenburg he possessed an indefatigable spokesman and pioneer wherever preparatory and direct action was needed. Schulenburg applied himself thoroughly to the problem of a new state administration and the selection of reliable officials likely to be needed for it.[31]

Stauffenberg seems to have had his first meeting with *Goerdeler* in September 1943. He continued to collaborate with him nearly until the 20th July. He owed much to Goerdeler's expert knowledge, his courage, his great activity and contacts with people, and was able to rely on the Political Representatives whom Goerdeler suggested. In their political discussions and assessment of the situation and the methods to be chosen there were moments of crisis and tough argument. But they did not stem from any personal feud. The two met for the last time on July 18, 1944.

Joseph *Wirmer* (born 1901), a Berlin lawyer, was closely associated with Goerdeler; but he was also in touch with men of the Roman Catholic and Socialist Resistance. Wirmer—an ex-member of the Centre Party—had been expelled from the National Socialist Lawyers' League because of his hostility to the régime and his legal work on behalf of persecuted Jews. He was a very active man and his house became an important meeting place for discussions among representatives of various movements. Stauffenberg was among the visitors.

Hassell's diaries reveal that Stauffenberg met *Hassell* for the first time in November 1943, together with Popitz in Jessen's house. The interrogation reports show that during the months preceding the 20th July he was in frequent touch with trade union circles and with the Socialists, as for instance Leuschner, Maass, Jakob Kaiser and members of the "Kreisau circle" such as Haubach, Gerstenmaier, Delp and Reichwein. The meeting places were the house of Maass in Potsdam, the house of Yorck and the Princesses' Palace, Unter den Linden in Berlin.

Advisers and political allies among Stauffenberg's own entourage who were ready for action included : his nephew Count Peter *Yorck* von *Wartenburg*, at the time Oberregierungsrat to the Reich Price Commissioner in Berlin; and Adam *Trott* zu *Solz*, Legationsrat in the Foreign Office, both of whom have already been mentioned in connection with the Kreisau circle. (Moltke was arrested

228

in January 1944.) Yorck was engaged chiefly with matters of domestic and social policy and ecclesiastical affairs, while Trott dealt with foreign policy planning and kept in close touch with Hans Bernd von *Haeften*; then there was Count Carl Hans von *Hardenberg* (already mentioned in connection with Tresckow) descendant of a former Chancellor, consultant on the future state administration and a popular friend on whose country estate of Neuhardenberg near Küstrin important week-end conferences were held; Freiherr Kurt von *Plettenberg*, a member of the Prussian Crown Prince's household ("Kammerpräsident"), who openly favoured a new concept of the state and was as much esteemed for his unassuming nobility as his reliability.

Special mention must be made of Count Ulrich Wilhelm von *Schwerin-Schwanenfeld*, who was completely devoted to the task and whose unobtrusive contribution to political planning was most effective. He was born in 1902 in Stockholm, at about the same time as Schulenburg in London. From October 1943 onwards he seems to have maintained close and frequent contact with Stauffenberg. Although they had not known each other before, in company they immediately pretended to be old, intimate friends so that the stranger's frequent visits to the General Army Office should not arouse suspicion. In the ensuing months the two did, of course, become good friends, and Schwerin, who from 1938 had frequently acted as a go-between for Beck, Goerdeler, Hassell, Oster, Popitz, Wagner, Jessen and Yorck, from then on devoted himself entirely to Stauffenberg and the exciting conspiratorial plans.

The son of a diplomat who had grown up in foreign capitals, Schwerin was in constant touch with political life thanks to a circle of relations and friends and his innate, passionate patriotism. Now he turned to a new and unexpected task : the care of large hereditary agricultural estates near Danzig in Western Prussia and in Mecklenburg. His background and involvement with so much bigger issues did not really equip him for the role of a self-interested landowner. Nor did he seem to have the right physique for the part—he was excessively lean and agile. Time and again he and Stauffenberg discussed plans for agricultural reform and approved schemes which, for Schwerin, involved far-reaching and voluntary personal sacrifices in favour of a new political order. His view was that the wealthier people must set a voluntary example to put into effect a "revolution from above" such as Freiherr vom Stein had urged.

Having seen varied service at the front and at home Captain Schwerin worked at the Quartermaster-General's Office from the autumn 1943 onwards, in collaboration with Jens Jessen. What his friends particularly cherished was his clear-minded and prudent firmness, his independent way of life which was free from envy and the respect which he showed for his friends. At Beck's request he "offered his services as collaborator in civilian matters" in November 1943. Schwerin was arrested in the Bendlerstrasse together with Schulenburg, Yorck and Berthold Stauffenberg and was the last of them to be executed in September. In a farewell letter Schwerin wrote : "I am going to my death with the firm conviction that I have wanted nothing for myself and everything for our Fatherland; of this you must be sure, always, and you must tell our sons again and again."[32]

Two other men of Stauffenberg's own family—apart from his brother Berthold—took a major personal part in his planning and activities : his mother's brother, Count Nikolaus von *Uexküll*, and his nephew, Cæsar von *Hofacker*.

During the interrogation Uexküll, a retired Colonel, born in 1877 in Hungary, an extremely popular aristocrat of the old Austrian school, cultured and pro-German, took the line that the principles of National Socialism were betrayed by its leaders and representatives. In his view they still needed to be introduced as a clean and just "German Socialism" (KB 448 ff). Assigned as liaison officer for Bohemia and Moravia, he was arrested a few days after the 20th July. He turned down an offer to save himself. And he thought it was right to tell the Court that he had been heart and soul in the plot and had acted from the deepest conviction. He was executed on September 14 together with Count zu Dohna-Tolksdorf, Count Matuschka and Chaplain Wehrle.

Cæsar von *Hofacker*, whose father was a General from Württemberg who had made a name for himself in the First World War, served with distinction at the front from 1914 to 1918. Later he worked in the United German Steelworks and joined the National Socialist Party in 1937. He was a generous manly figure who demanded decisive action and who could see things in their wider context. He was rooted in tradition, self-confident, yet sincerely affectionate towards his numerous friends and had a unique way with his children. His impetuous and noble appearance commanded authority and he had an unusual gift of persuasiveness.

Commanding a Group in the Air Force he had been in action against the enemy until 1940, but later as a Lieutenant-Colonel in the Reserve he was posted to the economic department of the Military Governor in Paris. He had gained some knowledge of France between the wars and established quite a number of personal contacts. Hofacker made no secret of his views among friends and office colleagues : he considered the political attitude of the German leadership towards France shortsighted, imprudent and in every moral respect disastrous and reprehensible. He sent a closely reasoned memorandum to State Secretary Freiherr von Weizsäcker who very much regretted that Hitler paid no attention even to him as Secretary of State.

A friend who visited Hofacker in the summer of 1943 in Paris recalled his remark that relations between France and Germany were bad because of a hopeless misunderstanding. Then, with passionate oratory Hofacker had evoked a stirring vision : they must meet and shake hands on the Douaumont, the colours of the Reich and the Tricolor must fly side by side above the old and the new graves, and over a road the two nations with a common destiny would thenceforth follow together. . . . Through his friend Schulenburg he learnt that strenuous efforts were being made to force a change. Hofacker met Stauffenberg after his recovery and they had a vital discussion in Berlin during the second half of October. At about that time he managed to get transferred to a post—although no one knew what his specific task was—in the immediate entourage of Karl Heinrich von Stülpnagel, the German Military Commander in France. Together the two men prepared the ground in Paris for the day of revolt. Hofacker was intended to become liaison officer with the French Government.

After the 20th July he refused to take advantage of chances to escape which German and French friends offered; it seems he still had the idea of joining a revolt from the West. His behaviour under interrogation was fearless and aggressive. He startled the others by asserting that he had acted with the same justification on the 20th July as Hitler had done on November 9, 1923. He said he assumed sole responsibility for what had happened in Paris and was only sorry that he had not himself been chosen to carry out the attempt on Hitler—in which case it would surely not have failed. He said he had several times offered himself to Stauffenberg for that purpose. When the interrogator asked how a man with wife and four or five children could do such a thing, Hofacker is reported to have cut him short with the remark : "What do I care about wife or children where Germany is at stake !" Judging by the reluctant statement of an observer, Hofacker's speech must have been so pungent and devastating in its condemnation of Hitler that the interrogators, who had never heard anything like it, found it difficult to tear themselves away. Afterwards they described Hofacker as the most dangerous internal enemy they had come across in Paris. "A dangerous enemy of the state, but what a man !" was the verdict of Oberg, one of Hofacker's opponents from the SS.[33]

The accounts by fellow conspirators and interrogation reports suggest that in his nine months in Berlin Stauffenberg found the strongest backing for his political plans and actions in Julius *Leber*. Their first meeting was arranged by Schulenburg. At once Stauffenberg was attracted by Leber's personality, power of judgement and energy. Similarly, Leber found the young Lieutenant-Colonel quite different from what he had expected; for he distrusted the military although—as an "ex-officer and Graudenz artillery man" (KB 199) —he himself had a soldierly mentality. Two uncompromising characters met and became allies. From their conversations it is known that they were not intending to stage a "revolution of old men", and were less concerned with fixed programmes and the preliminary lists of Ministers than with having the very best men on the spot "at the moment of freedom", after Hitler's death. "To bring about the coup," Leber said on several occasions, "I'd be willing to make a pact with the devil. What happens afterwards will sort itself out as long as we consider the will to shoulder responsibility and to build a new society as the decisive factor."

Leber and Stauffenberg nevertheless discussed the "afterwards" in great detail. They always started from the assumption that democracy could not be established among the Germans by government proclamation but had to be put into effect gradually by thoroughly planned and active guidance. Hence Leber was constantly preoccupied with the thought that despite all their revolutionary drive, they would have to proceed cautiously in abolishing and replacing the safeguards and institutions of the "totalitarian" state.

Annedore Leber has described one of the evening meetings with Leber and Stauffenberg. Air raids were a regularity at that time, and when the alert was given, it was customary for visitors to leave Leber's place quickly : this was in order to avoid the risk of it being found out who had gathered there in case the house was hit by a bomb. Stauffenberg had already left when Frau Leber, her mind still on the earlier discussion, asked Julius : "Do you two believe your plan can succeed?" "I don't know," he replied, "I have only one head, and I can't use it for anything better than this cause."[34]

It only remains to mention Wilhelm *Ahlmann* after Leber. Authority and freedom, the future structure of the state, economic and social problems—these were the topics Stauffenberg and Leber frequently discussed and analysed from every conceivable angle. According to Fahrner these talks took place in August–September 1943. Stauffenberg had similar discussions with Ahlmann, as can be inferred from the sparse data about meetings which Stauffenberg sought to arrange as often as possible. Clearly, the two did not discuss the "eternal Kingdom" nor engage in some brilliant intellectual speculation; they debated what responsible men could achieve in practice, questions which the blind Ahlmann approached realistically but with an awareness of the need to preserve spiritual values. It is not reported whether Leber and Ahlmann ever met. Ahlmann in his isolation fell under suspicion four and a half months after the 20th July and was brought to the point where he asked his loyal friends for a weapon to kill himself, which he did. The fact that he chose to die by his own hand and so joined Stauffenberg is testimony to his place in the history of the rising. Jens Jessen, who had introduced Stauffenberg to Ahlmann, was executed a week before, on November 30. Julius Leber was put to death on January 5.

*　　*　　*

We have mentioned one hundred or more men, who according to the interrogation reports and survivors' testimonies worked with Stauffenberg for a coup d'état. Not even twenty of them lived to tell the story. But we could list an almost equal number of additional participants : Staff officers or officers serving outside Berlin who undertook individual jobs; officers who dropped out of the active circle because of their transfer or recall before July 1944; civilians brought in to help reshape Germany politically who might have been linked through Goerdeler or Leuschner and many of whom were identified and sentenced. Besides, there were ramifications the courts failed to discover and which by decision of the conspirators were not disclosed even later.

In view of the differing degrees of inside knowledge and the variety of the functions of the people involved in the uprising it is impossible to define each one's exact role and their mutual relations. But it is clear that Stauffenberg maintained personal, direct contact with each of them; moreover the people working for an uprising were not brought together through large-scale, though covert, recruitment as if for the formation of an illegal Party; on the contrary—and this was repeatedly noted by the investigators—it was conscious and restricted selection determined by close comradeship in regimental or war service, friendship and blood ties by which they came together and united. For reasons of secrecy alone, there was never any question of trying to recruit as many people as possible. From time to time Stauffenberg needed a reliable and efficient man for a specific task or a key position; he had to look for him either among the people whom he personally knew to have proved themselves or he had to go by recommendation as far as he had access to them in the home territory or the

Reserve Army. Judging by the interrogation reports, he hardly ever (except in cases like that of Captain von dem Bussche) resorted to recalling men from the front. In any case, even a man in his high position found it difficult to arrange a recall—something that could only be done by devious means. But one frequently comes across a report that "an officer was summoned" from his post in the Reserve Army to Berlin by a telegram from the Bendlerstrasse, without anyone else knowing anything about it; the officer, either already known to Stauffenberg or secretly "tested", was courteously received by him, almost like a friend. And (still according to the report) Stauffenberg won him over and told him what part he was to play. There is mention of the "atmosphere of the house" having helped to elicit a spontaneous, even enthusiastic "Yes". On several occasions Haeften's name is added (cf. KB 306). Not once did any of the men thus approached betray Stauffenberg or Goerdeler, who went about things a different way. In the only case of refusal which the interrogation brought to light the would-be recruit, who felt himself unable to carry out the task, tried, although unsuccessfully, to find a replacement. Neither of them, though aware of their dangerous position, ever considered betraying Stauffenberg (KB 313). Fahrner, too, confirms Stauffenberg's procedure in selecting his confederates : as so many were already in danger, Claus and Berthold Stauffenberg avoided involving people unless absolutely necessary by making them privy to their plans. That was the Stauffenbergs' way even when they were certain of the newcomers' allegiance and knew that if let into the secret they would "have taken part with joy and would have risked any danger".

Within the conspiratorial circle itself difficult decisions had to be made. Not only were there inevitable arguments about seniority, ambition or vanity and personal differences among the widely differing types of people concerned. The leaders of the enterprise were left with the often tricky problem of deciding just how much responsibility to give any individual. For this depended not only on whether he was willing to play his full part, whether he was dependable, honourable, talented and knew his job. It was clear that at the decisive hour steadfastness, strong nerves, physical courage and imperturbable calmness would be required, and many a willing man worn down by months of nerve-racking preparations and the restlessness of the bomb-shattered city might in the end not stand up to it all. There had already been cause for such concern over the participation of Colonel-General Beck, whose utter devotion was beyond all doubt. And Field-Marshal Witzleben was no longer in full vigour since his illness eighteen months earlier. Similar decisions had to be faced in many other cases, for example,

234

that of Lieutenant-General von Hase, a steadfast, very able and dedicated officer of Beck's generation, Commandant of the city of Berlin, who was expected to perform duties which would have been easier for a youthful, rough dare-devil. Occasionally a young energetic officer was attached to an older man in the hope of adding the qualities of youth to circumspection and experience; in other instances it had to be left to Beck to use his authority and persuade senior men to give up their part in favour of a junior and more forceful colleague or to accept a subordinate position.

In dealing with the men engaged on the political side of the plan, the leaders had to try to give scope to those ready to put new ideas into action even where they seemed to be conflicting. At the same time it was necessary to counter some "fixed ideas and dogmatic views" strongly held by individuals when they took no account of realities and would have proved fruitless. The tasks the revolt would bring had to be solved by the men available, with such qualifications or limitations as they possessed. Sometimes wilfulness and notions of prestige had to be indulged, but care had to be taken to ensure that, irrespective of a political party's previous demands, the will to create a new Germany should prevail.

XI. PLANS AND PREPARATIONS

THE plan for the coup d'état envisaged three phases : the assassination, action to be taken within the first few hours after it (the state of military emergency), and the political and military repercussions.

According to Schulenburg's evidence (KB 89) Beck, Olbricht and Tresckow had expressly affirmed at their meetings that there must be an attempt on Hitler because without his forcible removal the plan "would involve too great a risk". Tresckow, who had discussed the need for a change in the preceding months with Stieff, told him openly at the beginning of August 1943, possibly on the 6th, that he now felt it necessary to get rid of the Führer by assassination. He thought the "enemy's war potential was overwhelming" and said it was a matter of military commonsense to consider the war as lost. It was, in fact, the historic duty of General Staff officers, in the interests of the nation, to prevent defeat in the Second World War, which was a certainty under the present leadership" (Stieff's evidence, KB 88). According to Stieff, Tresckow had added that "at the conferences which he had been told to attend as GSO I of Army Group Centre, together with his Commander-in-Chief, he had become convinced that an attempt on the Führer was perfectly feasible during Hitler's situation conference". We must assume that at that meeting with Tresckow or during later discussions with Beck and Olbricht, Stieff declared himself ready to plan the assassination with his group, and to carry it out at one of Hitler's daily situation conferences which he had to attend. According to another report (Schulenburg, KB 89) Colonel Meichssner, too, was approached in September, and told of the preparations. He is said to have promised to get ready to make the attempt. Being a member of the OKW's Army staff, he and his Commander, Keitel, were expected as occasion demanded to put in an appearance at the "noon situation" conference.

Tresckow used the same means as before to get his explosives : via the Abwehr through Colonel von Freytag-Loringhoven. And in September he once again obtained the necessary British-made explosives and handed them over to Stauffenberg in October, when he had to return to the front. From Stauffenberg they found their way to Stieff.

From the start, no military force worth speaking of was available and the idea of stirring up an open mass rising had to be discounted. This was why Olbricht had based his plans for a coup on a camouflaged usurpation of power. He would make use of the established chain of command to issue the orders envisaged in the "Valkyrie" Plan he had drafted. In the late winter of 1941–42 he had, with support from Canaris, laid plans for proclaiming a state of emergency in which at a moment's notice the mobilization of adequate forces in the homeland could be decreed in the event of internal unrest. Hitler had agreed to this plan after the number of prisoners-of-war and foreign workers employed in Germany exceeded four million in 1942.[1] More than double that number was expected for 1944. It was arranged that orders to launch operation "Valkyrie" were to be issued by the Commander of the Reserve Army, i.e. Colonel-General Fromm, to the Military District Commanders and to the Army Group Commanders. Only in a special emergency was the Military District Commander authorized to put "Valkyrie" into effect in his territory, but his duty was immediately to inform the Commander of the Reserve Army.

The first comprehensive emergency plan for Operation "Valkyrie" was dated May 26, 1942. Modifications adapting the orders to changed circumstances and intended to make them more effective were issued in secret to the Military District Commanders on October 13, 1942, and July 31, 1943. The modifications of July 31, 1943, which, it may safely be assumed, were pushed through by Olbricht with a view to the planned revolt, ordered the preparation of "operational fighting groups" whose units were to be ready for action within six hours (Stage 1) and on receipt of a further order (Stage II) to be formed into battle groups at top speed (cf. KB 160).

A later "Secret Command Matter" of February 11, 1944, which bore Stauffenberg's signature (KB 165) referred to the need of "organizing, at short notice, 'Valkyrie fighting groups' into effective fighting formations for service at the front". It also ordered each Military District to concentrate the existing "Valkyrie fighting groups" into a reinforced Grenadier regiment, with this significant rider : "Personnel designated as replacement of troops in the field must not be kept back by Military District HQ." This modification was presumably also connected with the intended coup.

Tresckow and Stauffenberg incorporated "Valkyrie" as an emergency scheme into their plan but prefaced it by two General Orders which were intended to clarify the spheres of competence and to ensure the proper execution of the "Valkyrie" orders.

The first General Order prepared for issue began with the usual brief reference to the situation : I. "The Führer Adolf Hitler is dead. An unscrupulous clique of Party leaders, remote from the fighting front, have tried to exploit the situation, stab the struggling army in the back and usurp power for their own selfish ends." Under heading II it was stated that the government of the Reich had proclaimed a state of military emergency and at the same time transferred both the supreme command of the Wehrmacht and the executive power in the Reich to the undersigned Field-Marshal. In this capacity the new Commander-in-Chief declared (under heading III) that he was delegating the executive power in the military territory at home to the Commander of the Reserve Army, and the executive power in occupied territories to the Commanders-in-Chief West, South-West, South-East, Army Group South-Ukraine, North-Ukraine, Centre and North, to the Wehrmacht Commander Ostland and the Wehrmacht Commander in Denmark and Norway. The following units and authorities would be subordinated to these holders of executive power within their orbits : all units and branches of the Wehrmacht, the Waffen-SS, the Reich Labour Service, the Todt Organization; all public authorities, the entire police force—regular, security and administrative police; the entire NSDAP; and the traffic and transport authorities and public utilities. The Waffen-SS was to be immediately incorporated in the Army. The holders of executive power were given the task of maintaining law and order and public security; of safeguarding the system of communications and of eliminating the SD. Any resistance was to be ruthlessly suppressed by force of arms. The final paragraph read : "In this hour of supreme danger to our country, unity within the Wehrmacht and the maintenance of discipline are of paramount importance. I therefore proclaim it the duty of all commanders of the Army, the Navy and the Air Force to give full support to the holders of executive power in the fulfilment of their difficult task, and to secure compliance with their orders from all subordinates. To the German soldier a historic task is entrusted. Whether Germany is to be saved will depend on his energy and bearing."

According to one interrogation report (KB 41), when Beck approached Field-Marshal von Witzleben as early as February 1943, shortly after Stalingrad, the Field-Marshal placed himself at his disposal as Commander-in-Chief of the Army, "when things are ready". In September 1943, he was prepared to put his signature to General Order I when it was submitted to him.

In the second General Order, instructions were issued by the Commander of the Reserve Army in his capacity as Commander-in-Chief of the home territory (which authority had been delegated to him by the new Commander-in-Chief of the Wehrmacht). He transferred executive power in the Military Districts to the Commanding Generals and District Commanders. These, thereby, also took over the powers of the Reich Defence Commissioners, who were members of the Party and appointed by Hitler. The following immediate measures were to be taken :

(a) Systematic military occupation of the postal and Wehrmacht communication centres, including broadcasting installations.

(b) The following were to be relieved of office and arrested forthwith : all Gauleiters, Reichsstatthalters, Ministers, Oberpräsidents, Police Presidents, senior SS and Police Chiefs; all Heads of the Gestapo, the SS Administration centres and Propaganda Bureaux, as well as the District Leaders.

(c) The concentration camps were to be occupied, the commandants arrested and their guards disarmed and confined to barracks.

(d) If any Waffen-SS leaders were unsuitable or offered resistance they were to be arrested; any units putting up resistance were to be disarmed. "Incisive action by superior forces to avoid worse bloodshed" was ordered.

(e) Security Service (SD) and Gestapo centres were to be occupied and the regular police called in to assist.

(f) Liaison with the Navy and Air Force was to be maintained : "Joint action is to be ensured."

It was further announced that to deal with political questions arising from the state of emergency a political officer would be appointed to each Military District, who would also be the temporary Head of Administration and Adviser to the Military Commander. In addition, the Commander-in-Chief of the home territory would despatch liaison officers to each Military District Commander to ensure a mutual flow of information. The second General Order concluded with the words : "No arbitrary or revengeful action must be tolerated in the exercise of executive power. The population must be made aware of the difference between the behaviour of the new authorities and the wanton methods of the former rulers."

The Order had to be signed by Fromm. As he had shown reluctance until the autumn of 1943, it was decided not to submit the Order to him. In case Fromm continued to refuse co-operation even after Hitler's death (which was hardly likely in view of his remarks), Witzleben was to appoint another Commander of the Reserve Army. Hoepner also a Colonel-General—and two years older than Fromm—was ready to take his place. The second General Order could be immediately followed by the Valkyrie-II Order, unless it were decided to issue it a few hours or a day ahead under the specific heading of Valkyrie-"Exercise".

The focal point of Operation "Valkyrie" was Berlin. Here a detailed master plan had to be prepared : individual orders had to be ready for the commanding officers and the troops carrying out the occupation; for the Wehrmacht garrison Commander, to whom not only the Guard Battalion but also the units of the Berlin garrison, the troops stationed in Spandau and the Army Weapons Schools were subordinated; for the Armoured Troops Schools in Krampnitz and Gross-Glienicke; for the Infantry School in Döberitz; the Officer Cadet and the NCO schools in Potsdam. If necessary, the troops in Wünsdorf (Armoured Troops School) and Jüterborg (Artillery School), which were between thirty and eighty kilometres away, would have to be brought up as second reinforcements. Most of the orders had to be issued in two versions : as preliminary orders, to be given at the appropriate moment by telephone with the brief introductory explanation : "Internal unrest; state of emergency; Army has executive power"; and as written orders to be handed to and discussed with the Commander concerned upon his reporting at the Bendlerstrasse. Both orders to the garrison Commander and to the Commandant of the Armoured Troops School in Krampnitz have been preserved (KB 38–40).

The Commandant of Berlin was given the task of sealing off the Government quarter, for which he was to use the Guard Battalion. The streets constituting the limits of this area were exactly defined. Any infringement, even by Ministers, was, if necessary, to be prevented by force of arms; Goebbels was to be arrested and special surveillance kept on the Propaganda Ministry and the SS-Head Office. The Guard Battalion was to be reinforced by two battalions of the Armoured Troops School and by "Valkyrie" emergency units. Another of the Commandant's assignments was to occupy specified objectives, important Reich offices, communication centres, press and newspaper offices.

In addition, he was to use shock troops to occupy the headquarters of the Reich authorities and arrest the most important officials; to despatch a shock detachment under the command of a General to the SS-garrison commander; and to keep the Hermann Göring Regiment in constant readiness but confined to its quarters until further orders.

The orders to the Guard Battalion were based on a list of the most important SS, State and Party authorities which were divided into two groups.

Twenty-nine objectives were to be occupied in order of priority (the first ten mostly SS-centres, ten Government offices and nine Party offices);

Thirty-two other objectives, to be occupied later, were numbered on an attached map; deviations from this order by evacuation or other changes were permissible (KB 28).

The Commandant of the Armoured Troops School was to be ordered by telephone to march with five battalions—his own three "Valkyrie" battalions and one from the Officer Cadet School and the NCO School at Potsdam—into the Tiergarten-Bendlerstrasse area; in addition an operational motorized unit was immediately to occupy the Königswusterhausen and Zeesen transmitters. In Zeesen, force might have to be used against a Waffen-SS company. On arrival in the Bendlerstrasse, the Commandant was to receive precise instructions to reinforce the Guard Battalion by five battalions, to use the bulk of his units for the protection of the Bendler-block and to hold himself ready for action elsewhere; besides, he was to organize reconnaissance to the south in the direction of the Waffen-SS garrisons at Lichterfelde and Lankwitz, and to have available a shock detachment with heavy arms for possible despatch to the SS garrison commander.

A special directive concerning procedure against the Waffen-SS was drafted. It was regarded as very important. The method of attack on SS-barracks was specified. Access roads were to be sealed off; heavy arms and shock troops to be used for surprise action; two officers with despatch riders, who would keep in visual contact, were to issue the call to surrender to the most senior SS officer— its exact wording was prescribed, ending with : "I must ask you to issue any necessary orders from here in my presence." The directive added : "In case of refusal or resistance the SS-leader is to be shot, the sentries disarmed and the disarming of the entire SS unit to be enforced." Ruthless use of arms was also made obligatory "at the slightest sign of resistance" from SS formations.

A state of military emergency for the whole Reich was proclaimed by "Martial Law Decrees", five of which have been preserved (KB 70). These were some of the regulations :

The following are recognized as entitled to bear arms : the Wehrmacht, police and specially authorized guard units. All other persons must immediately report the possession of arms.

All marches, demonstrations, assemblies in closed premises and the preparation of leaflets are prohibited.

Trade, industry, and transport must continue; the Reich Food Organization and trade associations, the Todt Organization, the Reich Labour Service and the National Socialist Motor Transport Corps will continue under new supervision; so will the National Socialist People's Welfare which will be placed under the control of municipalities, districts and provinces to whom its tasks revert.

The Labour Front will be kept on under the new leadership of a Commissioner.

Civil servants, workers and employees will stay at their posts; all leave is suspended and everyone must be available to his superior even during off-duty hours.

Party officials and others are forbidden to carry out any activities ordered by the Party. They are to obey exclusively the orders given under the State of Emergency Decree.

The assets of the Party and its formations, excluding the Labour Service and the Todt Organization, are temporarily confiscated. Martial law will be applied to anyone removing or altering any asset, disposing of or forging documents, registers and files etc.

Imprisonment for not less than three years, penitentiary up to fifteen years or life, confiscation of property or death will be imposed for any contravention of these orders, for any incitement to commit violence or cause damage to property and for looting.

Drumhead Courts Martial of three members each were set up. "The Courts Martial decide their own procedure with reference to the principles of the Reich Code of Criminal Law Procedure. Courts Martial summon the accused or have him brought into Court, give him a legal hearing, if need be, take evidence from witnesses and immediately pass judgment.... Courts Martial verdicts are final and must be carried out forthwith."

A separate Martial Law Decree ordered the confiscation of direct and indirect assets, including shares, rights, etc., of the leaders of the NSDAP down to district leaders. It also extended the competence of Courts Martial to try crimes of murder, deprivation of liberty, blackmail and bribery "which were committed by abuse of power and authority against defenceless people or out of avarice". The Decree said these offences "call for swift punishment because they arouse particularly strong and righteous popular indignation".

A special order demanded the immediate closure and custody of such offices and premises of the Party and its organizations as were not to continue under a Commissioner. Experts from the Labour Exchanges were to be brought into the German Labour Front.

Members of the Party and its organizations not immediately required for continued service were to be called up or directed to other work within the shortest possible time and their jobs no longer to be considered "reserved occupations".

Another Decree (KB 75) prohibited all private travel for three days. All telephone conversations, with the exception of local calls and calls which had to be specially booked, between civil and Wehrmacht authorities were temporarily suspended; and the same applied to private telegrams. The most extensive versions of the General Orders, Supplementary and Martial Law Decrees which have been preserved as a result of the events of the 20th July are found in the Kaltenbrunner Reports. But in addition to those documents there must have existed a very detailed plan, a "calendar", presumably in Lieutenant Haeften's handwriting. This plan distinguished between preparation, anticipatory measures and action on "X-Day". It demanded that every move be camouflaged and that during the coup itself the transmission of commands must be rapid, but clear (KB 35).

Thorough discussions and preparations were necessary to arrange for the control of communications. The aim was to seize the network on the day of the insurrection so that the conspirators' own orders and messages would go through whereas the opponents' signals could be stopped. Successful action in Berlin depended on its suddenness. But knowledge of it had to be kept from Führer HQ and the SS and Party Leaders who were in communication with it. The revolt required time to unfold and the conspirators had to try to keep their opponents as long as possible in the dark about their plans after the assassination so as to retard their counter-moves. Telephone, teleprinter, telegraph and broadcasting played a vital role in this, but the difficulty of interfering with these means of communication was obvious.

There was no focal point that could be seized by a coup de main and blown up. The Army, Air Force, SS, Police and the Foreign Office were able to use not only the public postal network but also their own intricate systems of communication which included a whole series of repeater stations and switching centres. At HQ in East Prussia these installations were housed in several bunker-type buildings, some distance away from one another. The individual communication centres were, though to a limited degree, able to take over from one another. To cut off the "Wolf's Lair", the Führer HQ proper, was relatively easy but to isolate the nearby spacious HQ with which Himmler, Göring and the Foreign Office were connected was more difficult. Here not only the major switching centre "Anna" but at least three other repeater stations— Lötzen, Insterburg and Rastenburg—had to be cut off as well. A variety of similar operations had to be considered when Hitler made Berchtesgaden his HQ. In that case the repeater stations at Salzburg and Munich had to be disconnected.

In Berlin the conspirators had to reckon with an even more complicated communications network. The Kaltenbrunner Reports contain a statement based on Colonel Hassell's evidence, according to which Olbricht had asked him "as early as 1943, after Stalingrad" to make a survey of the "telephone exchanges of the *Reichspost* and the telephone network of the Foreign Office, the Ministry of Propaganda, the RSH, the Police HQ etc." That survey was brought up to date in April–May 1944. Twenty Signals officers were detailed to occupy the individual centres in an emergency. Wehrmacht communications in Berlin were routed through two distinct centres, the big switching centre "Zeppelin" in Zossen (40 km south of Berlin) and the multi-storeyed communications bunker in the Bendlerstrasse—the centre of Germany's war Signals service with its wide ramifications, where two hundred civilians were employed in addition to the men from the Signals Corps.

Even if it had been technically possible to blow up all central communication channels, it can be inferred from the evidence that such action was never contemplated. It would have meant a grave danger to the Army in the field and would have deprived the new leadership of the vital close contact with the fighting front. All that could be envisaged was to put the communication system temporarily out of action.

Some passages in the Kaltenbrunner Reports indicate that the conspirators had carefully considered the possibility of preparatory action even before the coup. But it was agreed that the complete isolation of Führer HQ from contact with the outside world could be undertaken only after a successful assassination attempt (KB 330). This meant, of course, that men with authority to give orders would have to be ready at the few key points. Resolute, decisive and swift action would have to be taken.

Stauffenberg and Olbricht were able to count on the most senior Signals officer as their ally : General Fellgiebel, who was Chief of Signals at OKH (with Colonel Hahn as his Chief of Staff), and Chief of Wehrmacht Communications at OKW (with General Thiele as Chief of Staff). He was, therefore, in charge of all means of communication of the three arms of the Wehrmacht and also had authority to give instructions to the network of the German Reichspost.

Fellgiebel had pledged his unreserved collaboration. He had been in agreement with Beck since 1938 and, according to the interrogators (KB 258, 296), in 1943 and 1944 he "was one of the most eager advocates of an assassination attempt, one of the most active members of the conspiracy". Fellgiebel told his two Chiefs of Staff as much of the secret plans as they needed to know. They were ready to do what was necessary, after a successful attempt, Hahn acting from HQ and Thiele in Berlin. There is no record of their plans for joint action and it is hardly possible to reconstruct them after the death of the three confederates. We depend on deductions from the events on the 20th July and individual observations by other associates. Apparently, it was planned that Fellgiebel who always had local access and was able to observe from close quarters what was happening should inform Hahn, presumably in code, that the attempt had taken place. Hahn's job was then to inform Stieff and to order that communication between his area and the outside world be cut and "all communications be placed under the control of 'Anna' " (as is stated in KB 330 with reference to July 1944). Either Stieff or Hahn were to put Thiele and the Quartermaster-General Wagner into the picture, and Thiele was to let Olbricht know. In addition, Thiele was to organize the blocking arrangements for "Zeppelin"; and together with Colonel Hassell, who knew all about the plot, he was to ensure that the various communication centres of Berlin were occupied and that signals operations at the Bendlerstrasse were not interrupted. The assumption was that even if "Zeppelin" was blocked, communications at the Bendlerstrasse could be kept open for the new leaders. They had taken care that Fellgiebel's signal to Olbricht of the attempt on Hitler would pass through as quickly as possible without attracting the attention of any surveillance clerk, and that once the message had been received communications should be blocked.

Apart from the twenty officers to be sent to occupy communications centres in Berlin, e.g. the Foreign Office, Propaganda Ministry, Reich Security Office and Broadcasting House (KB 376), fifteen Signals officers who are mentioned elsewhere were to stand by for the occupation of repeater stations (KB 330).

The take-over of the radio transmitters was regarded as a special task and was discussed with individual Commanders. The transmitters concerned were the Deutschlandsender in Koenigswusterhausen, the nearby Sender Zeesen—both in the south of the city— the Sender Tegel, in the north; and the Broadcasting Tower and Broadcasting House in the Masurenallee. According to an earlier version of one order (KB 40) which was found, the surprise attack on the transmitters in the south was entrusted to a fully operational motorized unit of the Armoured Troops School in Krampnitz consisting of a tank company and a company of grenadiers. On the 20th July the same order seems however to have been given to the Infantry School in Döberitz.[2] It is not known why the change was made. The intention was to take over all broadcasting installations intact—sabotage was to be avoided. The radio was to broadcast the first appeals and proclamations within a few hours after Hitler's death.

On the territory of the Reich, responsibility for putting the military emergency into effect lay with the Commanders of the Military Districts. Based on the "Valkyrie" orders, they were to assert their authority against the Reichstatthalters (the Reich Defence Commissioners), the Gauleiters and their staffs, the SS and its formations and Cadet Schools, military Commanders "loyal to the Führer", especially in the Luftwaffe, and they were to suppress any rebellion from any other quarter whatsoever. Only where their own forces were inadequate, where more serious fighting developed or a Commander resisted was Berlin to take action. It was impossible to make sure in advance that the Commanders would co-operate. All that could be arranged at the planning stage was, wherever possible, to attach to the commanding officers men cognizant of the plot who would be able to take a hand in the situation and report any trouble immediately. Independent of this precaution the Centre was to send a liaison officer to each Military District Commander. Preliminary arrangements were made by Stauffenberg, who initiated suitable officers into the plan and gave them instructions. As these officers had to be summoned at the very beginning of the coup their names became known to the Gestapo on the 20th July from telegrams that had already been despatched. Only two of thirteen men named survived, thanks to special circumstances. These are the names given in the Kaltenbrunner Reports:

Military District I (Berlin): Lieutenant Count Heinrich von Lehndorff
Military District II (Stettin): Major i.G. Count G. H. J. von Blumenthal
Military District III (Berlin): not named
Military District IV (Leipzig): Major-General Hans Oster
Military District V (Stuttgart): not named
Military District VI (Münster): not named
Military District VII (Munich): Major Freiherr L. v. Leonrod
Military District VIII (Breslau): Captain (Cavalry) of the Reserve, Fr. Scholz-Babisch
Military District IX (Cassel): Lieutenant-Colonel von Sell
Military District X (Hamburg): not named
Military District XI (Hanover): Colonel Sigfried Wagner
Military District XII (Wiesbaden): Captain of the Reserve, Hermann Kaiser
Military District XIII (Nuremberg): not named
Military District XVII (Vienna): Colonel Count Rud. v. Marogna-Redwitz
Military District XVIII (Salzburg): Colonel Armster

Military District XX (Danzig) : Lieutenant-Colonel i.G. Hasso v. Boehmer
Military District XXI (Posen) : Major of the Reserve, George Conrad Kissling
Bohemia-Moravia : Lt.-Col. Count Nikolaus v. Uexküll

The plan was that after the attempt, the first moves to put the emergency into force should be taken suddenly, avoiding all publicity. The surprise element—with radio silence and maximum possible shut-down on news—was to facilitate action against the leaders of the State and Party. But within a matter of hours a most important task would arise : the nation would have to be told, the conspirators would have to explain what had happened, seek support and establish a Provisional Government.

The events of the 20th July and later investigations have thrown light on Stauffenberg's, Tresckow's and Olbricht's military plans. But the evidence and statements in the Kaltenbrunner Reports are equivocal and strangely vague about the planned political moves. The happenings on the day itself give no clue because no political statements were made or actions taken, and because those involved on the political side had time to destroy incriminating papers. No document is known—perhaps none ever existed—that could be regarded as the insurgents' representative Government programme, for which so many people have been looking. The documents before the Court were individual writings by Carl Friedrich Goerdeler which—in more or less accidental sequence—had fallen into the hands of the Gestapo as for example : his 1941 memorandum, "Das Ziel", which was quoted most frequently to illustrate the political aims of the conspirators (e.g. KB 130, 138, 170, 206). His "Government Proclamation" No. 2 (3rd version) (KB 147), the draft of a broadcast address (KB 213), two manuscrips for unspecified use "We assume that . . ." (KB 249) and "Material for . . ." (KB 265). Two other MSS, which belong to the same category but were not placed before the People's Court, were published at a later date : an appeal by Goerdeler, presumably dating from the end of 1943, the text of a programme from spring 1944 which Ritter has magnified into "The Government Programme of the 20th July, 1944".[3]

Goerdeler had to contend with the demands of the Socialists and trade union representatives who, like himself, wanted to see law, decency, political liberty and respect for human rights restored to the country. But in social and economic policy they distrusted his liberal attitude, his advocacy of a competitive society with a corporate system and his appeal to reason in economic matters. They had drawn up a programme of their own ideas which were still

247

being discussed in May 1944. In the aforementioned programme of early summer 1944, which was evolved after violent disputes, Goerdeler apparently tried to come to a compromise agreement by making concessions which earlier he had not felt in a position to offer. He appears to have been successful in as much as it was agreed that after the uprising he, as Chancellor, should make the first political decisions.

Among the political proposals for the transition period were the suggestions by the Kreisau circle—a "Basic Law on Economic Prerogatives of the Reich" formulated by Paul Lejeune-Jung. This laid down the claims of the state to mineral deposits, water rights, etc., which in a largely socialized system would have involved far-reaching political intervention by the state.[4]

Other proposals for the transition period included a detailed plan for the structure of the state and the administration and a plan for the reorganization of the military leadership, about which Schulenburg, Goerdeler, Schwerin, and Meichssner gave evidence and parts of which were contained in the Martial Law Decrees and in a Draft Decree on the provisional organization of the top level war command.[5]

There was also a "Provisional Constitution" for the transition period "until all sections of the population can take part in working out a final constitution for the German Reich". This Provisional Constitution had been drafted by Popitz together with Jessen, Hassel, Planck and Beck. In addition, there was a draft law on the state of emergency by Langbehn and Jessen, which has been lost, but with directives for its application by Popitz, which have been preserved. These directives defined the position of "political representatives" who were to be assigned to each Military District Commander as advisers. Since Jessen closely collaborated with Beck, Olbricht and Stauffenberg until the 20th July, it must be assumed that the draft laws in his keeping would have been applied, suitably adapted to given circumstances, especially as the "political representatives" were in fact appointed.

Stauffenberg had been pressing for suitable men to be chosen for these jobs since the autumn of 1943 (KB 357). The selection turned out to be a difficult task for Goerdeler, Jakob Kaiser and Leuschner. They had to meet and talk with each prospective candidate individually. It is not known to what extent the recruits were let into the secret plans. At any rate, later most of the people involved in the coup were able to defend themselves in such a way that they escaped death though not imprisonment. Eight of the twenty-seven men listed were hanged. The names are not all identical on different lists. The one which was available at the teleprinter centre

248

in the Bendierstrasse on the evening of the 20th July and which fell into the hands of the Gestapo contained the following names :

Military District I (Königsberg) : Count Heinrich zu Dohna-Tolksdorf
Military District II (Stettin) : Oberlandforstmeister v. Willisen Ewald Heinrich v. Kleist-Schmenzin
Military District III (Berlin) : not named
Military District IV (Leipzig) : Kaufm. Direktor Walter Cramer
Military District V (Stuttgart) : Baurat (ret.) Albrecht Fischer
Military District VI (Münster) : Captain of the Reserve, Bernhard Letterhaus; Landrat Sümmermann (his successor)
Military District VII (Munich) : Otto Gessler, former Reichswehr Minister
Military District VIII (Breslau) : Police President (ret.) Fritz Voigt for Lower Silesia; Kaschny, lawyer (for Upper Silesia); possibly Lukaschek, lawyer
Military District IX (Cassel) : Oberpräs. (ret.) Gustav Noske; Minister of State (ret.) August Fröhlich (Thuringia)
Military District X (Hamburg) : Gustav Dahrendorf; Premier (ret.) Tantzen
Military District XI (Hanover) : Mayor Dr. Arthur Menge; Hermann Lüdemann
Military District XII (Wiesbaden) : Staatsrat (ret.) Ludwig Schwamb, lawyer; Bartholomäus Kossmann, lawyer, Minister of State (ret.) in the Saarland Government)
Military District XIII (Nuremberg) : Gerhard Böhme
Military District XVII (Vienna) : Karl Seitz, ex-Mayor of Vienna; Josef Reither, Austrian farmers' leader
Military District XVIII (Salzburg) : Franz Rehrl, former Landeshauptmann of Salzburg; Anton Mörl-Pfalzen, former Security-Director of the Tyrol
Military District XX (Danzig) : Freiherr Hermann v. Lüninck, Oberpraesident of Westphalia (ret.)
Military District XXI (Posen) : Min.-Direktor in Prague, Colonel Vollert

At about the same time as the political officers were recruited, the list of members of a Provisional Government was discussed at Beck's request. The choice of the prospective holders of office was not reached without great difficulty. This was more than just a contest for the allocation of posts in accordance with the proportionate strength of the parties. And there was more to be weighed up than the political ambitions of old-style Parliamentarians : every man who was willing to be considered for office had to take a most unusual decision requiring plenty of courage and genuine conviction. "In such a situation," Rothenfels wrote, without denying that differences existed among the conspirators, "other principles of selection operate than in the conditions of normal political life, and we may therefore assume that a group of genuine leaders emerged."[6]

Even before that Goerdeler had sought to produce a group of people who would be capable of forming a new government.[7] And Beck now entrusted him with this task (cf. KB 532). The allocation of posts which had presumably been made in December 1943 was scarcely changed before July 1944, although alternative appointments—to depend on ensuing events—were left open until the last moment. Only five of the thirty-five people named in the list survived. This was the Provisional Government:

Provisional Head of State: Ludwig Beck as "Generalstatthalter" or "Reichsverweser". In certain circumstances Leuschner was later to stand as candidate for the office of Reich President, if the country remained a Republic. Secretary of State: Count Ulrich von Schwerin-Schanenfeld.

Reich Chancellor: Carl Friedrich Goerdeler. The Chancellor's press officer was to be Carlo Mierendorff; after his death (December 1943) Otto Kiep was mentioned and later, if Kiep could not be saved from execution, Theo Haubach. Leber was designated as Goerdeler's successor in the post of Chancellor. But for the period of transition and the representation of Germany vis-à-vis the Allies during that time Goerdeler was the first choice.

Vice-Chancellor: Wilhelm Leuschner. Second on the list (in case Leuschner became Reich President?) was Jakob Kaiser. Secretary of State: Count Peter Yorck.

Minister of the Interior (with control of the police): Julius Leber. Secretary of State: Count Fritz Schulenburg.

Foreign Minister: Ulrich von Hassell or Count Werner Schulenberg.

Finance Minister: Ewald Loeser, a director of Krupp's and former high City official (Stadtkämmerer) of Leipzig.

Minister of Economics: Paul Lejeune-Jung.

Minister of Public Worship and Education: Staatspräsident (ret.) Eugen Bolz. Also named were Kurt von Schuschnigg, former Austrian Federal Chancellor, and Adolf Reichwein. Secretary of State: Hermann Kaiser.

Minister of Justice: Joseph Wirmer, lawyer.

Minister of Agriculture: Minister (ret.) Andreas Hermes; another list contains the names of Freiherr von Lüninck and Hans Schlange-Schöningen, who had been Reich Commissioner for Eastern Relief under Brüening in 1931–32.

Minister of War: Colonel-General Erich Hoepner or General Friedrich Olbricht. Under Secretary of State : Count Claus Stauffenberg or Friedrich Olbricht.
Minister for Reconstruction (if such an office were established) : Bernhard Letterhaus.
Minister of Transport: Stadtbaurat (ret.) Wilhelm zur Nieden, a collaborator of Goerdeler's in Leipzig, or Matthäus Herrmann, trade unionist.
Minister of Posts (if a separate office established) : General Fellgiebel; Under-Secretary of State : Lieutenant-General Thiele.
The Police was provisionally to be placed under Count von Helldorf and later Major-General Tresckow.
In addition, an Austrian was to be appointed Government Spokesman ("Sprechminister").

This is not the place to speculate whether a Provisional Government of this complexion would have achieved anything but its joint negative aim—to settle accounts with Hitler; whether it would have produced anything of its own, anything new, and won the support of the people, the majority of whom still clung to Hitler. Socialist reports in particular say that many more people all over Germany were ready for a revolt and far more organizations were working for it than could become apparent.

For the transition period two problems loomed large : what relations could be established with the powers at war with Germany, and how could peace be brought about? Suggestions for Germany's prospective internal organization had been formulated over several years, but foreign policy decisions were still open. These began to play an important part in the consultations from August to October 1943 when preparations had to be made for the coup the conspirators soon hoped to launch. Those taking part included Ulrich von Hassell, Goerdeler, Adam von Trott zu Solz and Count Werner von der Schulenburg who had been Ambassador to Moscow until June 1941.

So far none of the Allies had given any assurance on which the Resistance could have counted. Feelers put out towards Britain in February 1940—before the German attack on Norway and France —had shown the British Government still willing to meet a new German Government half way. But all later attempts were rejected —as for example a "Peace plan" of Goerdeler's in the summer of 1941, which was sent to Churchill and Eden,[8] via the social educationist Siegmund-Schultze and Archbishop Temple of Canterbury. Equally unsuccessful were efforts to obtain Allied assurances by two clergymen, Hans Schönfeld and Dietrich Bonhoeffer, who passed on details about an insurrectionist movement in Germany to Bishop Bell of Chichester in May 1942, in Stockholm, which were then passed on by him to Eden.[9]

Similarly, the President of the United States rejected two approaches: the first had been made by Trott in November–December 1939, the second was a mission with which the American journalist Louis Lochner had been entrusted in Berlin at Wirmer's house in November 1941 before the United States came into the war. But Lochner was interned, and not until the United States had been in the war for six months and he was released in June 1942 was he able at least to try to bring his information to Roosevelt's notice. (He was not received by the President and was told to abandon his mission because of its "most embarrassing nature".)[10]

After the victory at Stalingrad in 1943 the Soviet Union increasingly asserted its power. Stalin had had a Treaty of Alliance with Britain since May 22, 1942, but at the insistence of the Americans (Cordell Hull) the Soviet Union had not been promised any territory in case of victory although she had been bearing the brunt of the war. Now Stalin used the toughness he had shown in politics against his Allies in the war against Germany—and he was successful. Roosevelt's and Churchill's Declaration (January 24, 1943)—to continue to wage the war together until Germany's unconditional surrender—had been issued without Stalin but presumably for his benefit. Apparently it was not enough for him. With the help of the "Union of Polish Patriots" founded in Moscow, he "took the wind out of the sails" of the Polish Government in exile in London, and the British promised him Eastern Poland (as far as the Curzon Line) for which Poland was to be indemnified with German territory. In May the Comintern, whose alien character was an impediment to Stalin's European policy, was abolished; and in June secret negotiations for a separate peace with Germany were resumed: they had been started at Russian initiative in Stockholm six months earlier. In July, the "National Committee of Free Germany" was founded among the prisoners of Stalingrad, and its appeals publicized the possibility of a separate peace with a Germany that would rise against Hitler. An offer by Japan to act as mediator for a separate peace between Russia and Germany was turned down, and the offer reported to Washington in September. Meanwhile, there had been a meeting between Roosevelt and Churchill (Quebec, August 1943), and—apparently as a result of an assessment by a "high military authority"—the mood among the Americans had completely changed in favour of Russia as the coming power which would be needed to defeat Japan. It was feared that the Japanese might make their own arrangements with Germany. Even in Octo-

ber the American Secretary of State Cordell Hull—the same man
who in 1942 had urged a tough attitude towards Russia—made
unexpectedly generous concessions at the Foreign Ministers' Conference with Eden and Molotov in Moscow. And at the beginning
of December Roosevelt and Churchill met Stalin in Teheran. It
was here that the advance dismemberment and sacrifice of Germany
was carried out. But this became known only much later. Soon
after Teheran, Peter Kleist, who had been negotiating in Stockholm on Ribbentrop's behalf with the Russian diplomatic go-
between, was able to report the final words of his partner who was
now withdrawing : the American offer had been so generous that
Germany could no longer take part in the bidding. The Trojan
horse which Stalin used to storm the American fortress was his
threat with the "National Committee of a Free Germany".[11] Later
it was suspected that Stalin wanted to get results from the Stockholm negotiations only in order to blackmail his allies.

In view of these political developments in 1943, the attempts of
the German Resistance to deflect the Anglo-Saxon powers from a
clearly disastrous path proved abortive. In January, Trott zu Solz
had handed a memorandum to the American, Allen Welsh Dulles,
who had just taken up his post as Roosevelt's special delegate and
European observer at the Embassy in Berne. Parts of the text of
this memorandum were later published.[12] The constant answer
that Germany must suffer military defeat, he said, drove the men
of the German Resistance to the conclusion that it was useless to
continue the conversations. The Allies failed to understand that the
Germans were themselves an oppressed people, who lived in an
occupied country, and that tremendous risks were taken by the
Opposition in continuing its activity. But the Opposition believed
the Anglo-Saxon countries were filled with bourgeois prejudice and
hypocritical theories. There was a strong temptation to turn East.
The reason for the eastward orientation was the belief in the possibility of close relations between the Russian and German peoples,
although not between the present governments. The memorandum
continued : "Both nations have broken with bourgeois ideology,
both have suffered deeply, both desire a radical solution of social
problems which transcends national limits, both are in the process
of returning to the spiritual (but not the ecclesiastical) traditions of
Christianity. The German soldier has respect, not hatred, for the
Russian. The Opposition believes that the decisive development in
Europe will take place in the social, not in the military, realm.
When the campaign in Russia stalls, after the German Army has
been thrown back, a revolutionary situation may arise on both sides.
Fraternization between Germans and imported foreign workers is

also an important element. Hitler has been forced to play up to the labouring classes and has given them an increasingly strong position; the bourgeoisie and intellectuals and generals are of less and less importance. Hitler will fall and the brotherhood of the oppressed is the basis upon which a completely new Europe will be built."

It must be assumed that the memorandum contained not only admonitions or even rebukes, but also practical proposals which have not been preserved. What is available shows no trace of friendliness towards the Soviets : Hitler and Stalin and their régimes are equal sources of oppression. Europe, after its bitter ordeal, is about to lay the foundations of a new worth-while life and is calling on the United States to recognize the true situation and give help.

While in Stockholm (from May 19 to 21) Goerdeler drafted a new memorandum on the composition, proposals and demands of a new German Government. The contents of this memorandum were communicated to London by the Wallenberg brothers. Goerdeler developed the idea of future European economic unification, of a joint European reconstruction effort, of a Europe disarmed vis-à-vis its own members and armed, depending on the circumstances, only against the Soviet Union and the Far East. He emphasized that the future of Europe and of the white races could be founded only on their free alliance and not on new degradation. And he concluded with the afore-mentioned words : "We ourselves will bring Hitler and his fellow criminals to justice because they have stained our good name. But we will also defend our independence."[13]

In August, Churchill's reply, which had been obtained by devious routes, was handed over in Berlin by Wallenberg : it was to the effect that Goerdeler's communications continued to be desirable as information material. Goerdeler sent back a message announcing that a coup was expected in September or at the beginning of October, and requesting that Berlin, Leipzig and Stuttgart—the cities which were most important for the revolt—should be exempted from bombing raids until October 15. Once again he specifically emphasized the dangers threatening Europe if Russia were helped to victory. He also stated that immediately after the coup a new government would despatch Fabian von Schlabrendorff (who was not unknown to Churchill) to Stockholm for armistice negotiations.[14]

The men of the Resistance asked themselves in vain whether they should assume any willingness on Britain's part to come to terms. Goerdeler was inclined to think so, especially as the bombing seemed to decrease as he had requested. Trott, after another reconnaissance trip to Stockholm, thought the opposite (KB 505). In view of apparent feelers from the East, it was possible to wonder whether the desired goal could not be reached by negotiations with the Russians.

The term "Eastern solution", which was used in the interrogation report of November 21, 1944 (KB 493), has led to serious errors in descriptions of the attempted German uprising. If it is held that the supporters of an "Eastern solution" were Communists and wanted to see Germany become a member of the Soviet Union or its satellite, then there *never was a single* advocate of such a solution. Not even Reichwein, although he was quoted as having said in evidence that Russia was the great and powerful country of the future which had important raw material and manpower resources at its disposal. No European policy, he was quoted as stating, was possible without or against Russia (KB 492). If the men of this Resistance circle spoke of an "Eastern solution" they used the term in the sense that the political climate offered understanding and joint steps with Russia, without and, if necessary, against the West. It is possible that some men—as perhaps Reichwein, Langbehn and Trott—had ideas of their own about the intrinsic qualities of the Russian people, about a similarity of Russia's and Germany's social conditions and potentialities, about Russia's importance in contrast to an over-civilized West and so on —but none of these concepts induced the Opposition to consider an "Eastern solution" as a tactical move.

During the consultations in the autumn of 1943 an "Eastern solution" seems to have been seriously considered alongside a "Western solution" to which the Opposition had adhered until then. But the decisive voices seemed to have advocated a "compromise solution" as suggested by Hassell and Trott. Hassell was in favour of using every opportunity in the given situation. On August 15, 1943, he wrote in his diary : "There really is only this one expedient left—to make either Russia or the Anglo-Americans understand their interest in a sound Germany. Actually, a healthy European heart is to the interest of the East as well as the West. In this game of staying on good terms with both sides I prefer the Western orientation, but if necessary I would put up with an agreement with Russia. Salzmann (he means Trott) agrees with me entirely; the others are doubtful for theoretical and moral reasons, which I understand. But they are gradually coming round." On December 5 he added : "(Werner Schulenburg) swears that it is possible to come to terms with Stalin; in my view he is unduly optimistic. Of course, I, too, see in this game of playing with both sides the only opportunity for a new régime, but not in the sense of double-dealing. It is vital to show fairness towards England. This must be supplemented by keeping open the possibility of an understanding with the East."

He found that Schacht agreed "that a loyal policy of reaching an understanding with the Anglo-Saxons must be tried and any double-dealing must be avoided. The threat of an understanding with the other party in the game, Stalin, remains in the background. Unfortunately, the whole thing is probably a *fata morgana*."[15] The conversation took place at the time of the Teheran Conference.

Through confidants at the German Foreign Office, Schulenburg had learnt about the Russian peace-feelers in Stockholm. The aim was apparently to bring the Ambassador himself into the conversations, which Hitler, however, refused. Schulenburg, who had parted with Stalin on good terms, perhaps thought it might be possible in this way to come to an "agreement" about a revolt. He also offered to make a direct approach. Tresckow arranged for a reconnaissance to be carried out at Army Group Centre for a spot on the front where a crossing might be feasible. This probably happened in November. A diary entry at the end of December 1943 shows that Hassell no longer thought the idea of a separate peace with Russia practicable. Schulenburg's efforts probably also came to an end at about that time, and the West again began to figure more prominently in the deliberations. There may be a connection between this and the unsupported report that round about Christmas Moltke had intended to use a duty trip to Ankara to fly to Cairo wearing the uniform of an American officer, in order to contact an Allied General. This was the time when the coup was expected to be staged.[16]

The "generous offers" whereby the Allies delivered themselves into Stalin's hands, remained secret at the time. The nature of these offers became manifest later only through their terrible fulfilment. Hassell, Goerdeler or Trott knew nothing about them. Some of the reasons which prevented the British Government from making any promises were known : the British were determined to avoid a repetition of "Wilson's 14 Points" which might afterwards be used by the vanquished as a permanent means of pressure; they were cautious not to create mistrust among the Russians by making any separate pledge to the Germans. They were disappointed because for years they had heard talk about a counter-move and a new Government, but they never saw any action. But the German Opposition also clung to its conviction that Britain's vital interests and Churchill's proven statesmanship could not in the end permit the Soviet Union to become too powerful in Europe. And so, the Germans argued, Britain would not obstruct determined action by the German Resistance, especially in view of the danger that, if repulsed, the Opposition might turn to the East.

Thus in the end, after many futile attempts, the only thing left open to the planners of foreign policy was to have the right men for the job and the necessary channels of communication ready to establish contact with the West and the East immediately after the assassination. These were the men selected (according to KB 503):

for *Madrid:* Otto John, who had access to British circles;
for *Stockholm:* Count Werner Schulenburg, to negotiate with Russia, and possibly Schlabrendorff for negotiation with Britain with Wallenberg as intermediary;
for *Berne:* Gisevius who had access to Dulles and thus to Washington;
for *Rome:* an unnamed person to negotiate with the Pope.

As soon as possible—according to Trott's evidence—negotiations were to start in London and Moscow. Those in Moscow were to be conducted by Schulenburg and possibly also by General Köstring whom he knew well as the former military attaché; the negotiations in London were to be handled by Trott, accompanied by General von Falkenhausen.

"Not knowing what attitude the world will adopt towards us"— to quote a phrase from Goerdeler's intended broadcast speech—the leaders of the revolt had to make an all-out effort to secure the backing of the German people. The first appeals had to be ready to be broadcast and the first proclamations to be printed. Addresses to the German nation, the troops and Government declarations had to be prepared. The Opposition leaders had given a great deal of thought to all these matters. They had discussed and approved, made changes and re-drafted much of the material. Obviously, it was difficult to arrive at generally accepted versions, for this is where freedom had its first say. But they realized that they were addressing a misguided, not only an oppressed nation. There had to be explanations and clarifications but they had to be concise and stirring. The people would have to be told that the situation was extremely grave, and they would have to be disabused of the falsely inflated faith in victory which had no base in reality. Yet it was essential to make them realize that healing forces were at hand. They had to be given new courage to turn their backs on the past and continue as a nation. The Resistance leaders knew what they had to say, but it was difficult to find honest, sober, clear words which had not yet been perverted and flogged to death by Goebbels.

Goerdeler, who had a natural gift for drafting such appeals and proclamations, was their first and most prolific author. Hassell and Wirmer also took part in the drafting while Beck, with Tresckow's help, prepared the announcements to be made to the troops. Most of the texts which have been preserved are presumably drafts revised by several people, and not the final versions. They contain repetitions and contradictions. Nevertheless, even where they are couched in fairly conventional terms, they still impress as evidence of an ambitiously planned uprising.[17] According to the Kaltenbrunner Reports (KB 501) Leber, Reichwein and Mierendorff also contributed draft appeals, but there is no other record of this. All that has been reproduced from these drafts are some catchphrases, which makes an assessment impossible.

Stauffenberg himself tried to bring out his own versions of the appeals. In the last week of October 1943 he asked his brother to summon Rudolf Fahrner by telegram to come and see him in Berlin. He received him in the early morning after an all-night journey, and at once disclosed to him his short-term plans—the attempt was expected to be staged within about ten to fourteen days. He asked Fahrner to formulate the proclamations which would have to go out at the start of the revolt. He told him to differentiate between essential statements to be put out immediately and others that might be held over for a later announcement. What mattered most, he impressed upon Fahrner, was to find the right human touch and words manifesting a new patriotism.

Fahrner says the drafts were first discussed with Stauffenberg; then came consultations with both brothers, and finally their effect was tried on other occupants in the house and certain visitors. Later, Stauffenberg took the drafts to several "important allies". When he returned with some objections, further alterations were made. These proclamations seem to have been lost but Fahrner made some notes from memory at the prison camp in August 1945 and this is what he recalled :[48]

"It was announced, without further explanation, that Hitler was dead. There followed a few sentences about settling accounts with the other Party chiefs and a short outline of their past activities and plans for the future. From these the Resistance leaders deduced that it was necessary to take action and their duty to do so. The Head of the Provisional Government, who had signed the document but whose name was not disclosed to me, gave an assurance that he and his associates wanted nothing for themselves. As soon as possible (or, according to another version, after the return home of the troops) the people would be asked to vote freely on the future constitution of the state for which a new system would have to be found. He pledged that he himself and his collaborators would observe strict legality in everything and they would not do or permit anything that contravened divine or human justice. In return, he demanded unconditional obedience during the period of provisional rule. Crimes and other breaches of law committed under the Party régime would be suitably punished, but there would be no persecution for political convictions. The Provisional Government would do everything in its power to restore external peace as quickly as possible. It was made clear that after what had happened, peace was bound to mean the greatest sacrifices and losses to Germany. But it remained true that each individual and the nation as a whole could endure anything, no matter how hard and bitter, with courage and unshakable faith in the future, if punished, purified and reconciled with God they were willing to bear their fate.

"The proclamation to the Army was similar in content. Here it was more a matter of putting an end to the senseless crimes of war and renouncing all lust of conquest and threats to other nations. The new Government solemnly vowed not to stake the life of a single German unless it was absolutely necessary for the direct defence of women, children and the homeland. Sensible leaders would bring the armies home as soon as possible. Until then the soldiers were urged to hold out.

"The proclamation to the women appealed to them to help and nurse their menfolk who had had to endure and would still suffer so many physical and spiritual injuries. The women were urged to use their power of sympathy and love with which they were so richly endowed by nature to bring about the necessary reconciliation, overcome the past and build a new life.

"In my view this third appeal was as important as the others because women seem to possess a special insight not based on reason alone and a sense of higher values, which cannot be suppressed as easily as men's by fixed ideas, accepted dogma and blindly pursued objectives. Claus and Berthold agreed with me.

"Nothing was to be said about Hitler until everything could be explained and all facts disclosed. It had to be clear that this was a matter of settling accounts with him, of restoring law and order and therefore of creating a new German state. This was why conventional phrases and well-worn excuses had to be avoided, however much consideration had to be given to the people involved and to the desired impact at home and abroad, in particular."

XII. ABORTIVE ATTEMPTS
THE STRUGGLE FOR A DECISION

FIELD-MARSHAL KLUGE, who had told Beck, Olbricht and
Goerdeler in September 1943 that he was ready to act, was
seriously injured in a car accident on October 12. He was out of
action for nearly nine months. At the end of October preparations
in Berlin were concluded and the group at HQ declared itself
ready. The coup could be expected to take place any time after
the beginning of November.[1] News might come any day. There
were postponements. After several reconnaissances of the locality
Stieff said it was impossible to get the explosives into the conference room and set them off there. The attempt was not made.

Stauffenberg drove to Headquarters to see for himself and find
a possible solution. The plotters were facing two formidable
obstacles : Hitler had used all his ingenuity to make himself
inaccessible and he continued to exert a personal spell to which
even officers who opposed him succumbed.

Security arrangements scarcely equalled in their thoroughness
kept Hitler and his daily entourage in the Mauerwald in East
Prussia and on the Obersalzberg cut off from the outside world.
No outsider had a chance of penetrating into the close circle of
servants, cook, physician and guards—on the Obersalzberg, there
were also some women in this community. For years past the
"instincts of an animal of prey for his own safety" had been
ascribed to Hitler. With his well-nigh infallible instinct he sensed
whether the people he met were susceptible to his personality and
arguments. If they were in any way antagonistic his caution or
defence was alerted. Presumably, he regarded the intimate circle
within which he moved as safe. Moreover, he avoided setting foot
in any surroundings which he did not dominate completely. For
many months he had not visited the battlefront. If special occasions made his presence in the Reich unavoidable, he had arrangements for his journey by train or air made under the seal of
strictest official secrecy, and reserved his choice of travel until the
last minute. In addition, the time set for departure, arrival, a
public appearance or audience was usually changed just before the
event. He is also said to have had himself represented by a
"double"—although there does not seem to be any proof of this
story. It was impossible to get him on the short walks at Head-

260

quarters which rarely took him beyond the innermost "security ring". Access to this area was possible only with a special pass, reserved to very few people, and in addition the Secret Police watched over his every step. Only a few officers—and none of his opponents—were allowed to attend the nightly private meetings with Hitler which could last from midnight till the early hours of the morning and at which the participants were usually treated to one of the Führer's interminable monologues. The forces for an attack from the air or on land on this innermost sector were neither at hand nor could they be assembled inconspicuously. Count Lehndorff, who was in favour of the Opposition's plans and who certainly knew his way about the area as it was his property, emphatically counselled against any use of force: the whole territory was secured against a potential enemy paratroop attack by several rings of concrete dugouts, pillboxes and barbed wire entanglements. Strong SS forces were stationed there and, in addition, Himmler's and Göring's nearby field HQ could at a moment's notice call on their not inconsiderable escort troops in case of an attack. In the absence of any other propitious event, the conspirators had to depend on striking during the so-called "mid-day situation" conference which was held daily from about 1-3 p.m. and to which even Hitler's opponents had access as they were called in as military experts. At the entrance to the security ring, reserved to Hitler, a pass bearing the holder's name had to be shown. All weapons had to be discarded outside the conference room. SS-Oberführer Rattenhuber, a man of awe-inspiring height, and his "Rattenhubers", who were unimpressed even by a General's stripes, guarded the inner compound.

But what Stauffenberg must have found even more discouraging than Hitler's inaccessibility was the fact that the Führer's personal spell had scarcely diminished. Even brave men who cursed Hitler and were ready to act against him simply did not find it in themselves to stand up to him and to preserve their inner freedom against the man. Stauffenberg had encountered this on several occasions during his previous work at Headquarters but now, in the changed circumstances, it was somewhat disquieting. Obviously, this spell was inseparably tied up with the whole public boosting of the "Führer" and the painstaking measures for his safety; it was reinforced by the German soldier's unshakable oath of allegiance which bound him to the supreme warlord. But undoubtedly it was also nourished by Hitler's great successes and—like a fakir's spell—it continued to emanate from the Führer's person. Incidents, such as the one related by Plettenberg,[2] which became known later, were probably no secret to the Resistance even at the

261

time : an Air Force officer was deer-stalking near Führer Head-quarters—something for which permission was hardly ever given. Hearing a noise, he took cover and released the safety catch of his gun. Hitler, unaccompanied, appeared on the path. Seeing him, the thought flashed through the officer's mind : this is the decisive moment. He must die, now. He tried to take aim—but could not raise his gun. His arms would not move. Back went the safety catch. He shouldered his rifle—this he managed to do—and walked on. Hitler paled on seeing him. The officer saluted. Hitler, looking perturbed, acknowledged the greeting and passed by. Date of the incident : summer 1942.

The Resistance leaders also knew that Georg von Boeselager, who had an outstanding record of bravery on the Eastern front, had refused to kill Hitler. He confessed to his friend Tresckow that he was not sure whether on his own he would be cold-blooded enough to dare to make a revolver attempt on Hitler—at the head of his cavalry he would have ventured even against vast odds to break into the Wolf's Lair to seize the Führer.

But the most important factor was that to a German officer assassination of the Head of State had always been something entirely alien, a monstrous and detestable act. It was indeed a major step from this conviction to affirm that assassination was necessary. But the most passionate affirmation did not yet mean ability to do the killing. Persuasion or even the resolute will to action was not enough : as was found, a man of very special character was needed, one who would dare in his conscience to make the decision and bear the consequences of his deed. It was hardly possible to expect one man alone to do it. A way had to be found for simultaneous action by two or more people. But how?

An earlier suggestion of Tresckow's came to mind and this was now regarded as the most promising idea. The fighting on the Eastern front had shown it to be advisable to modify the German uniforms; work on new models had advanced far enough and it would shortly be possible to submit them to Hitler for approval. Himmler and Göring, too, were expected to be present on the occasion. Since Stalingrad they had attended very few functions together. The usual practice was for a young front-line officer to conduct the demonstration of the models, and the Chief of the Organization Branch had to be present. If they were both prepared to carry a bomb on them and to throw it, or themselves, on Hitler there might be a chance of success. But they would have to be ready to sacrifice their lives.

Looking round for a front-line officer who might take on this task at Headquarters, Schulenburg mentioned his friend Captain

Axel von dem *Bussche* to Stauffenberg. Von dem Bussche was at the time a Company commander on the central front in Russia. Stauffenberg arranged for him to be recalled. Von dem Bussche has described how in October he and Schulenburg went to see Stauffenberg at his auxiliary headquarters at Düppel near Berlin. The young officer said Stauffenberg radiated "relaxed self-assurance". He remained alone with Stauffenberg for some time. Despite his black eye-patch, he said, Stauffenberg appeared indestructibly strong and aristocratic. Youth was talking to youth. Von Bussche himself was only twenty-four and Stauffenberg thirty-six—and this automatically appealed to the best qualities of this gallant officer. Stauffenberg did not try to persuade or plead with him : without anything being said it was agreed that in such an emergency the best sons of the nation must act for all. Their deeds alone would determine the future. Stauffenberg seemed to be the destined leader of Germany's youth—and von dem Bussche prepared himself for his task.

Later, when some other young officers openly or privately condemned the severely wounded von dem Bussche, he told them what he had gone through and what had made him decide. He had joined up in 1937 to become an Army officer and served the first few years of the war, confident in Hitler, unquestioning and ready for any test. In Count Schulenburg, who was also stationed with the Ninth Infantry Regiment at Potsdam, he found a friend and mentor. Both had witnessed the mass murders in Polish and Russian towns evidently carried out on orders from high authority. As Army officers they had been unable to take action. But, said Bussche, having become aware of what was really going on he began to feel more and more ashamed. Until then he had taken the oath of loyalty to the German warlord seriously and never questioned it; but now he was facing another situation : the Führer himself had broken the oath to God a thousand times. And a true liegeman had not only the right but, by old Germanic usage, the duty of rebellion against a renegade. For any of his comrades who had ever looked upon events in this way—he declared—there was only this choice; to seek death at the enemy's hand in "violent, desperate battle", as some of the better men had done; desert to the enemy, escape abroad, or else risk his life at home against Hitler. And that was how he had responded to Stauffenberg's approach.

Before the expected date of the coup von dem Bussche paid several visits to Headquarters to discuss details with Stieff. They were agreed : "Each one can and must be prepared to give his life." That was the only way. Each would take a bomb with him

263

when the uniforms were to be demonstrated. Bussche wanted to have a German explosive charge which he could ignite instantaneously and which would go off with an audible hiss within a fraction of a second. The men who knew about this plot were told, and the plans for action in Berlin and the rest of the Reich were once more gone over and memorized. Bussche remained at Headquarters from November 23 to 25. Describing this period of waiting, Bussche said : "In those sunny days of late autumn in the woods and lakeland I had that feeling of premonition which a soldier has before the attack."

There was a delay in the arrival of the uniforms to be modelled. Enquiries were made while everyone waited. Then news came from Berlin that the items had been destroyed in the heavy air raids of the previous few days and that it would be impossible to replace them quickly, especially the leather equipment. Bussche suggested they should immediately show Hitler some other uniforms and equipment, no matter what. But the modelling session was cancelled. Shortly afterwards an incident occurred which might have exposed the whole plan. According to a report (KB 128), Stieff, who on November 20 had asked for leave—probably for a few days only—instructed Major Kuhn to take the British explosives, which were still stored with him, back to Stauffenberg. Kuhn decided to store them in a hide-out. But on November 28 he and Lieutenant Hagen were observed by the military police busying themselves under a wooden watchtower in the forest at the Headquarters. The police started digging and found the explosives, wrapped in roofing felt, but they were unable to establish the identity of the two officers who had put them there. The officer of the Abwehr who was entrusted with the investigation, Lieutenant-Colonel Werner Schrader, knew about the plot, and at the gravest personal risk managed to prevent intervention by the Gestapo. His complicity was established after the 20th July, but he had meanwhile taken his own life. The explosives were returned to Freytag-Loringhoven.

Before anything was discovered about the storage place of the bombs, Kuhn and Hagen tried to obtain new explosives. Kuhn met a friend, Major Gerhard *Knaak*, when passing through "Mauerwald" in November. He told Knaak, who commanded a Pioneer battalion near Orsha, about the plot. Hagen obtained access through Oertzen, who was on the Army HQ staff. And this meant that in the same month, November, Stieff was able to procure new explosives, this time German-made, from the Pioneers. Klamroth and Hagen looked after them until they were later taken to Stauffenberg. But this type of explosive proved unsuitable for the

264

planned assassination—the fuse made a noise and it took about four seconds to set off the bomb. Freytag-Loringhoven, in charge of Abwehr II at Canaris' office, had, therefore, once again to be asked for explosives. He managed to obtain a different, allegedly more effective type.

A few weeks after the first failure new uniforms were ready for exhibition. Hitler's agreement to view them seemed to have been obtained for the week before Christmas and preliminary warnings went out to the conspirators concerned. For some reason or other the display was, however, put off indefinitely and they felt they could no longer rely on it ever taking place. On December 26 Stauffenberg is said[4] to have been asked to take the place of Olbricht, who was ill, at a manpower reserve conference at Führer HQ in East Prussia. He decided to take the explosives along with him. Having got them through the various check-points he found that the conference had been cancelled and Hitler had already left for Berchtesgaden. Confronted with that situation, Stauffenberg is said to have proposed to do the job personally and blow up both Hitler and himself. But Beck and Olbricht are reported to have emphatically rejected this idea. Stauffenberg was considered irreplaceable for the planned coup d'état. Besides, there were doubts whether a man with his physical handicaps would be able to carry out the attempt. Bussche was urgently recalled by his Division, which was engaged in very heavy fighting near Nevel. When Stauffenberg subsequently wanted to summon him back the Divisional Command refused to let him go because of the catastrophic situation at the front. Two days later the daring young Captain was seriously wounded and maimed. This meant a stay of nearly twelve months in hospital, doubly agonizing because of the overhanging threat of revenge by Hitler's men after the 20th July.

Towards the end of January there was a new opportunity for exhibiting the uniforms. Schulenburg suggested that another young officer take von dem Bussche's place—Ewald Heinrich von *Kleist*, a friend of Schulenburg's, the same age as von dem Bussche. Schulenburg thought he would be able to take on the job and on January 28 summoned him by telegram. Kleist, who was on leave at home, was told what was involved and accompanied Schulenburg to see Stauffenberg. His father, von Kleist-Schmenzin, a Conservative from Pomerania, was a deeply religious man and a determined enemy of Hitler's. He had always uncompromisingly opposed him with his upright character and conduct.[5]

One Saturday afternoon Stauffenberg had a six-hour talk with the young Kleist. From time to time Schulenburg joined them.

Stauffenberg made the position clear to Kleist: before long the consequences of the recent Teheran Conference would make any revolt in Germany senseless and impossible. Stauffenberg and the men who had to regard themselves as the leaders of the German Army and the nation had one supremely important task in this emergency: they must act without delay. Everything was prepared for the attempt, he said, but for one reason or another they had not been able to bring it off, so far. However, there would shortly be an opportunity which would have to be seized without fail. He was not pressing Kleist, he said, he was merely asking him whether he thought he could do it and whether he felt something in him that compelled him to make a decision that might require sacrificing his life. Kleist spent the following Sunday at his native estate in Pomerania, where he had grown up, and asked his father's advice. After serious consideration, his father concluded that if the moment of such challenge came it was his son's duty to meet it. . . .

Stauffenberg hurried to make the final arrangements and informed his associates that the date for modelling the uniforms, and thus the attempt, was to be February 11. Himmler was expected to be present. February 11 came—and neither the exhibition nor the attempt took place. According to Kleist, the reason was that Major-General Stieff had been told at the last minute that Himmler would not be attending.

Meanwhile, Tresckow was trying hard, on his own, to find an opportunity to kill Hitler. He sought in vain to have himself appointed as Adolf Heusinger's deputy so as to have access to Hitler. To revive the earlier idea of a revolver attack on him at Orsha or Minsk proved impossible because Hitler no longer paid any visits to the Army Group. Kluge had been succeeded by Field-Marshal Busch, with whom rebellion against Hitler could not even be discussed. But Tresckow managed even now to devise a new opportunity for an attempt. Almost by accident—he was Chief of Staff to the Second Army—he learnt that one of his associates, who was Busch's ADC, would have to accompany his Field-Marshal on a flight to one of Hitler's situation conferences at Berchtesgaden on the following day. Tresckow, with Oertzen at his side, unexpectedly interrupted the ADC's preparations by asking him whether he was aware of his responsibility at the forthcoming visit to Hitler; as far as the future conduct of the war was concerned, Tresckow said, the ADC had it in his hands to spare Germany endless suffering at home and senseless, incalculable sacrifice at the front. Oertzen pulled a small bomb from his brief-case. He explained its mechanism and suggested that the bearer of the bomb should hide

266

it under his uniform, set it off, throw his arms around Hitler from behind and hold him till the bomb exploded. The Captain said he was prepared to make the attempt, but thought he would make a better job of it if he shot Hitler with a pistol. Tresckow told the conspirators to hold themselves ready for the following day, March 9, 1944, when Field-Marshal Busch, Keitel, Jodl, Schmundt and others were to attend the conference on the Obersalzberg. When they entered, Busch's ADC started to follow him—having left his holster and pistol outside, but carrying a loaded Browning with the safety catch released in his pocket. But the SS-Sturmbann-führer who had just announced Hitler's arrival stopped him with the words : "Today, please, no ADCs !" Protests were of no avail. The officer had to wait alone in the ante-room without setting eyes on Hitler, but convinced that he had been "recognized". From time to time one of the SS-men on orderly duty entered the room to see what he was doing. Tresckow later thought that some of his tele-phone conversations might have been tapped and that instructions might, therefore, have been sent to Berchtesgaden that only officers who were known there should be admitted to the situation con-ference that day.[6]

These tense weeks were filled with plans, action, hope and dis-appointment. But many details of what went on have been lost to posterity because the men involved are dead. Between March and May 1944, as Schulenburg's (KB 90) and Kranzfelder's (KB 116) evidence seems to confirm, the plans for a military revolt were in abeyance because "it was no longer possible to put them into effect". But political moves, both inside and outside Germany, continued.

In April 1944 Trott sent yet another message to Mr Dulles in Berne and through him to the Western Powers. The text, which is preserved in Dulles' book and which he received through the go-between Gero von Schulze-Gaevernitz, shows Trott as the spokesman of the "German labour leaders"—mainly Julius Leber. Trott spoke of the growing Communist underground movement which was being supported by the "Free Germany Committee" in Moscow and the Russian Government, and which was proving more and more tempting through its "constructive ideas and plans" for Germany's post-war reconstruction. But by comparison the West was offering nothing with regard to the future of the centre of Europe. The labour leaders in Germany were emphasizing the need to fill this vacuum as quickly as possible. "If it is permitted to continue, German labour leaders fear that in spite of military victory the democracies may lose the peace and the present dic-tatorship in Central Europe be exchanged for a new one."[7] There followed detailed proposals to show how the vacuum could be filled, how the German workers could be won over to the Western democracies and what steps should be taken in war to prepare for peace.

At about the same time (the end of March and the beginning of April 1944) Dulles received through Gisevius a memorandum from Beck and Goerdeler. It described the situation in terms similar to Trott's, but then referred to the coup d'état as something that would definitely take place. Beck and Goerdeler no longer sought assurances *before* a coup but only asked whether London and Washington would be willing *after* Hitler's overthrow to enter into direct negotiations with the plenipotentiaries of the new Government, without insisting on the Resistance group simultaneously dealing with Moscow. This procedure would have been at variance with the Casablanca Declaration. Beck and Goerdeler had in mind the example of Finland, which had recently begun one-sided peace negotiations with Russia, and apparently would have liked to use the same procedure, but leaving Russia out. They stressed that their principal motive and that of their collaborators was a desire to prevent Central Europe from coming ideologically and politically under the control of Bolshevism : in such an event Christian culture and genuine democracy would disappear in Europe and the present totalitarian tyranny would be exchanged for another. The dangers of such a development should by no means be underrated, especially in view of the completely proletarianized millions now populating Central Europe. If negotiations had first to be carried out with Russia, a different set of men, not the Resistance group, would be ready to do so.

But here a further step was taken which signified a clear decision in favour of a "Western solution". The Opposition group offered to enable a swift occupation of Germany by the Anglo-Americans by ordering the German Generals in command on the Western front (Rundstedt and Falkenhausen) to give up resistance and to facilitate the landing of Allied troops. Likewise, arrangements could be made for receiving Allied parachute troops in key points in Germany.[8]

When these urgent approaches were received in London and Washington the British and Americans were busy with the preparations for the greatest invasion project of all time, involving millions of men. This Allied landing was to bring down the bulwark of the European heartland over which the Western powers already had almost unchallenged air supremacy. All other reasons apart, this was not the moment to have victory presented on a platter. The way it was done was so uncertain that it was perhaps merely an attempt at delay. And so Beck and Goerdeler were left without reply. Nor could they read an answer to their approaches in Churchill's speeches which they followed most carefully. Not until May 24—twelve days before the great landing—did the British Prime Minister declare in the House of Commons that the Empire would fight on together until the unconditional surrender of the Germans and would not entertain agreements on the lines of Wilson's Fourteen Points. That would merely give the Germans a new pretext for complaints about a future dictated peace.[9]

A brief note, dated May 25, 1944, a record of which has been preserved, mentions Stauffenberg's name for the first time in connection with negotiations with the Allies. This note, which according to Captain Kaiser's own evidence (KB 126) was written by him for Stauffenberg, contained eleven main points. These were not intended as demands, but subjects for negotiation with the enemy :

immediate cessation of the war in the air;
abandonment of the invasion plans;
avoidance of further bloodshed;
continuance of Germany's defence capacity in the East; evacuation of all occupied territories in the North, West and South; avoidance of any occupation;
a free government; independent constitution determined by Germany;
full co-operation in application of armistice conditions and in preparation of peace;
1914 Reich frontiers in the East; Austria and Sudetenland to continue as parts of the Reich; autonomy for Alsace-Lorraine; the Tyrol as far as Bozen and Meran to become German;
energetic reconstruction and German participation in rebuilding of Europe;
Germany herself to settle accounts with those who committed crimes against the nation;
recovery of honour, self-respect and respect from others.

The same report, obviously based on Kaiser's evidence, stated that Stauffenberg had "had two contacts with the English, through go-betweens". The one was believed to have been through Count Gottfried Bismarck-Schönhausen, the Regierungspräsident of Potsdam. Like Goerdeler, the Count was a friend of the Wallenberg brothers in Stockholm. His acquaintance went back ten years further than Goerdeler's. There was no clue as to the identity of the other middleman. In June Stauffenberg told Goerdeler that he had had an opportunity of getting a direct message through to Churchill which the British leader would find on his desk in about a week. He mentioned Bismarck's name in this context. Apart from this link with the British Government, Stauffenberg had been trying from about May or June to establish direct contact with the American High Command—General Eisenhower and the American Chief of Staff, General Marshall. It is not known how such a contact was to come about, but there are reports which indicate that it was established, possibly via Madrid, in July. On this subject Trott was reported to have said under interrogation (KB 507) : "He (Stauffenberg) has time and again expressed the opinion that in view of the catastrophic strategic position of the Anglo-Saxon forces vis-à-vis Russia, no Allied Army leader was likely to become more reasonable towards Germany. This leads me to suppose that he did receive certain feelers, if not offers, from military quarters on the enemy's side." Trott afterwards mentioned that Stauffenberg might possibly have been taken in by one of Eisenhower's special agents. But immediately afterwards he continued : "From my last conversation with Stauffenberg I came away with the definite impression that a positive opportunity to establish contact with the Americans, probably with the US military High Command, must have recently offered itself to Beck. What made me think so was that Stauffenberg emphasized : 'The old boy has reasons for holding different views from mine.' "

According to another report (KB 175) Trott stated that Stauffenberg, apparently on the strength of "other contacts in the military sphere" had said in July 1944 that "because of the rapid advance of the Soviet Union the West would negotiate, but not with the present Government". The statements made by Strünck under interrogation may point in the same direction; he is reported to have said that in mid-July Gisevius, on returning from Berne, reported that negotiations with England were possible; in any case, the Americans were for ending the war in Europe quickly, so as to have a free hand in the Far East. Eisenhower, he went on, was instructed by the State Department not to demand unconditional surrender in case a Beck–Goerdeler Government was formed.[10]

Whatever the truth or legend about Stauffenberg's personal relations with the Western Allies, it must be remembered that in the hopelessly entangled and deadlocked political situation of July 1944 his most promising hope was for a move on the military plane— "between opposing commanders". The entry into the heart of Europe of Soviet forces posed—even if for no more than two or three days—primarily a military and not a political problem. If in such a tense situation an acceptable German leadership offered its Army to help the Allied High Command stem the Russian thrust instead of worsening the chaos, then no Army leader who was guided by military necessity would reject such an offer. This is how Stauffenberg may have argued : a new German Government which had got rid of Hitler must assume that the Western powers would prefer their own advance and Germany's withdrawals to be orderly rather than chaotic. And it would be up to the German leaders to give convincing proof of their control of the country and to make their co-operation acceptable both to the military and political Command in the enemy camp. There was nothing else left than to trust that in some form or other the new German leaders would win approval. Berthold Stauffenberg and Trott quoted various utterances by Churchill to show that he was just as able suddenly to change direction in victory as he was willing to limit Russia's advance. It was from Churchill that Claus Stauffenberg and his collaborators expected support for their plans, even in July 1944— not out of any pro-German sentiment, but from sober consideration of the need to maintain a balance of power.

The constant failures and the repeated postponements of the attempt in an increasingly dangerous war situation imposed an almost unbearable burden on the wide circle of conspirators. For a long time they had been doing two jobs, often in most difficult external conditions, which imposed an excessive physical strain. Besides, there were ominous signs which made them fear that it might not be possible to keep the secret any longer and that bloody vengeance might break loose any day. There was a terrifying rise in the number of arrests and executions on political grounds.[11] Moltke and Gehre had been arrested; so had Kiep and others who had been meeting at Frau Solf's house. Canaris had been relieved of his post. Himmler had told him threateningly that he knew about plans for a revolt in the Army and that he would put a stop to the activities of men like Goerdeler and Beck. Hassell realized that he had been put under surveillance. Popitz was in grave danger. Many of the conspirators were deeply distressed when they heard on June 16 that Halem had been sentenced to death. In addition, a report from enemy sources put out by Reuter's spoke about plots being hatched by a German Resistance movement, and the agency claimed that the General Staff officer who was to kill Hitler had already been chosen.

All this could easily have led the conspirators to decide that the whole thing was futile and that it was better to split up and simply make sure that the abandoned plot was not discovered. Some felt that—from an objective point of view too—the moment for useful action had been missed long ago and they withdrew.

Among the civilian associates who were not yet abandoning the idea of a coup, there was growing distrust of the military who, they felt, did not really want to do anything at all and had betrayed them. This mistrust was nourished by the experience they had had over many years with "the" Generals. Those who knew of Stauffenberg's role in the conspiracy had looked upon him with confidence and hope; but now it was he, above all, who had to endure the reproaches, voiced and silent. And these became more frequent because he would not tell the civilian conspirators exactly why things had gone wrong so far. Stauffenberg seems to have maintained great reserve even towards Goerdeler, after once having given him his word of honour. Of course, in those months Goerdeler was in increasing danger, and great caution had to be exercised in letting him into the secrets of the preparations for the assassination. But, as is implied by a report (KB 177) Stauffenberg was angry at "being constantly pressed by Goerdeler to make the attempt. There was an insinuation that Stauffenberg had been making big promises and was not keeping them. Finally, Goerdeler was told that Stauffenberg knew he had pledged his word of honour and there was no need for Goerdeler to nag all the time."

Several reports indicate that some things had changed since the autumn. In the beginning, Beck, leaning heavily on Goerdeler,[12] had still represented the political centre-group; but during the winter and spring, Stauffenberg, relying on the younger members and Leber, had enhanced his own political influence and had dispensed with Goerdeler's role as intermediary in relations with the Socialists (Leuschner, Maass, Haubach and Reichwein) or in putting out foreign political feelers. To the younger members of the Resistance this meant that they had to become politically more active and had to examine and discuss the "constructive" elements of Goerdeler's schemes. Understandably, this offended Goerdeler and was bound to incriminate him, which is why a great deal of these alleged disputes and squabbles within the Resistance was recorded in the Kaltenbrunner Reports. They referred to several missions to Stauffenberg with which Wirmer, Schwerin and Jakob Kaiser were entrusted, and to joint visits by Stauffenberg and Leber to Wirmer, who acted chiefly as Goerdeler's but also Leuschner's intermediary. Repeatedly mentioned are also two major meetings at Wirmer's house in mid-May and mid-June (KB 179, 211), and a conference at the Esplanade Hotel on June 16 which Beck, Goerdeler, Leber, Leuschner, Stauffenberg and others attended. The point at issue, according to these reports, was to resolve differences between Goerdeler and Stauffenberg, who was said to have remarked that there was too much talk of "restoration" : he did not wish to see former conditions revived. Leber is reported to have reproached Goerdeler with having illusions in foreign policy, holding out-moded economic views and being altogether tied to the big industrialists. The reports also note differences between Leber and Leuschner, apparently caused by the radical programme which Leber had drawn up for the contingency of Germany's disastrous military collapse (KB 212). But it seems largely to have been a question of different assessments of the foreign political situation. In Leber's view total occupation of Germany was inevitable, even if the conspirators acted at once. And he demanded that clear preparations be made for that eventuality. He also warned Trott when he set out on his reconnaissance trip to Sweden in the second half of June that in no circumstances must he try to pursue a policy aimed at dividing the Allies. Their only chance was Hitler's overthrow, the proclamation of a Government of the Resistance and an open armistice offer by its members.[13]

At many of these meetings Jakob Kaiser exercised great conciliatory influence. After months in hiding he was probably the only man to come through unscathed, and he has emphasized that the picture of disunity, argument and personal offence which the official reports present is grossly exaggerated and that, notwithstanding the seriousness of the discussions, the Resistance never lost the strong bonds and the feeling of collective commitment towards Germany.

To depict the attempted uprising as no more than a manifestation of ambition, personal animosities, stubbornness of old "reactionaries" and the intolerance of confused youth is a falsification of events—even though it may be explained by the plight of the men under interrogation and by the situation of those who reported the story.

Stauffenberg spoke to Goerdeler, who was already being hunted by the Gestapo, only two days before the attempt. According to Goerdeler's report, they parted close allies without Stauffenberg having told him of the imminent moves. He impressed upon Goerdeler that he must keep in strict hiding, but be accessible at all times—there is hardly any doubt that Stauffenberg looked upon him as the first Chancellor.

After about May 20, Stauffenberg seems to have gained a new impetus. He asked for the explosives which were in Stieff's care to be sent to him. They were the explosives obtained from the pioneers in Orsha. Klamroth and Hagen arrived with them on the courier train on May 25 (KB 55, 94). On the same day Stauffenberg drafted the points to be discussed with the Allies, as the aforementioned note of Kaiser's shows. He asked Leber "whether it was not in Germany's interest to make it easier for the Western Allies to cross the German minefields. In that way the dreaded collapse of the Eastern front could be averted."[14] At the same time, while still Olbricht's Chief of Staff, he was working on a memorandum for Fromm. An unconfirmed eyewitness report said that Hitler, on seeing the memorandum, exclaimed: "At last a General Staff officer with imagination and sense!" As a result, Fromm—who, according to this report, had not been in personal contact with Hitler for two years—was again invited to conferences. Stauffenberg, too, was being kept in mind for these meetings. On June 7 both he and Fromm were summoned to the Obersalzberg and Stauffenberg was introduced to Hitler during the situation conference.

A conversation which became known to Schwerin-Krosigk probably took place at about the same time. Colonel-General Guderian and Himmler had been discussing the need for some personnel changes in the General Staff on the grounds that some of the Staff officers had been away from the front for too long and were slow to make up their minds. The Chief of the General Staff, too, would have to be replaced. Guderian suggested that Himmler should put this to Hitler at a convenient occasion. The report continued: "Himmler was ready to do so if Guderian could name a suitable successor. Guderian proposed Stauffenberg as the 'best horse' in the General Staff." Himmler is said to have agreed at once.[15]

The memorandum may well have provided the final impetus to Stauffenberg's appointment. At any rate, the appointment had been under discussion for some time and was probably decided soon after May 20. It must have given him new hope for his plans. The post of Chief of Staff to the C.-in-C. of the Reserve Army offered Stauffenberg two things he needed: the chance to activate the entire command system of the Reserve Army, either jointly with the Colonel-General or as his "deputy" without him—at least for a brief period; and the opportunity of attending conferences at Führer HQ. He was to take up this post temporarily as from June 15 and officially on July 1 at the same time being promoted to Colonel in the General Staff.

In May it was generally felt that important new developments were in the offing on the front. In the West, an Anglo-American invasion attempt to open up a second front had to be expected. After weighing up all the arguments against it, Beck was convinced that a landing attempt was imminent. If it succeeded it might pave the way for a situation which the Resistance itself had thought of creating. If it was defeated a German offer would be doubly effective. The situation in the East was regarded as even more threatening, although there was scarcely any alarm to be noted in public discussion. The disproportion between Germany's and the enemy's forces moving up in growing strength against Army Group Centre and in the South was known. At the beginning of June Tresckow said he was convinced that the Russians would soon launch a major offensive on the central sector. At great cost, half of the encircled German divisions had managed to escape from the Cherkassy cauldron, and Germany had suffered grievous losses when the Crimea, cut off since the autumn, had to be evacuated.[16] These divisions had not been relieved for three years and, with hopeless loyalty, were continuing to defend the front which had been pushed back in severe winter battles. Little did they know that they were being ruled by a "war-lord" who had become desperate, unbending, passive and unimpressed by any sacrifice, however great.

On June 6, General Eisenhower's invasion armies, with the support of superior air forces and the fire-power of a mighty "Armada", established themselves on the Normandy beaches; and they held out for forty-eight hours—the period which Rommel and the other military leaders on the German General Staff regarded as crucial for further operations.

Two weeks after the start of the landing, on June 17, the two Field-Marshals von Rundstedt and Rommel, who were responsible for anti-invasion defence, met Hitler in France and warned him that bravery alone could not avert the imminent disaster. In their view the enemy was superior in "all three dimensions", especially in the air. This meant that all German movement was paralysed, but for insignificant military traffic at night; and so the Allies would gain their immediate objectives—seize a large port (Cherbourg) and break out of the encirclement—as soon as Germany's fighting power, in the absence of reserves, was exhausted. The time when this would happen was foreseeable. But once the enemy broke through, improvisation against superior forces would be impossible and no effective line of defence in France could be established. Only immediate, strong reinforcements could avert collapse.

Hitler, more than ever convinced of the incompetence of his Generals, promised new forces. But he emphatically drew the Field-Marshals' attention to the bombardment of London with the new secret weapon which had begun the previous day. In Rommel's and Rundstedt's presence he dictated a violent explanatory report on the new "weapon of retaliation" (V2), predicting panic and the collapse of England. The Field-Marshals' suggestion that it might be better to aim the new weapon against the enemy bridgehead and the embarkation ports in Britain was rejected by an Ordnance General whom Hitler had called in to advise: the V2, he said, to date only had an accuracy of fire within a 15 to 18 km zone. Rommel's suggestions for different treatment of the French, his criticism of the excesses of the SD, his comments on the military and political situation in Germany which called for a rapid end to the war—Hitler rejected them all with the abrupt retort that Rommel should worry about his own invasion front. Without waiting for the meeting with front-line commanders which had been arranged for the following day, Hitler returned to the Berghof the same night.[17]

None of the help promised to the troops on the invasion front materialized. Several days after Hitler's visit to France a heavy Soviet attack was launched against the central sector of the Eastern front. In the very first assault the Russians broke through the German lines at several points. Strong enemy forces swept across the sparsely held hinterland towards the frontiers of the Reich. The Army High Command had to throw all available reserves into battle, and in the greatest haste the Commander-in-Chief of the Reserve Army had to offer the Eastern front reserve units, some of which were incomplete and not fully operational.

On June 29 Rommel and Rundstdet again went to see Hitler to report on the impending collapse in the West and to urge him to take a major decision : to abandon secondary theatres of war, withdraw untenable front lines, and concentrate on defending the threatened heart of Germany. They were given trifling promises and, for the rest, were told to mind their own business. A few days earlier, the Chief of the General Staff, Zeitzler, had violently clashed with Göring at the Berghof. Göring "insulted the Army and accused it of cowardice, in the presence of the ADCs" (KB 91). At the end of March Zeitzler had unsuccessfully asked to be relieved of his post, on the occasion of the dismissal of Field-Marshals Manstein and Kleist; now, after a bitter encounter with Hitler which had followed a conference of Army leaders in the East, he reported sick on June 30—his robust health had given out.[18] Lieutenant-General Heusinger, Chief of the Operations Branch, deputized for him.

In the West and the East the enemy was breaching the German lines, but nowhere did Hitler meet the changed situation with radical decisions.[19] He turned down every proposal to establish a new defence line to which German forces, abandoning some territory, might retreat : even for the Supreme Command it became rigid dogma, "Cling to every inch of soil !" "Victory or death !" and "Hold at all cost !" On duty, people felt they had to show a certain elation at the fantastic prospect of the new weapons. But obviously Hitler himself was in the grip of the terrible situation.

He raged against his Generals, and tried to pin the blame for every reverse on someone who could be court martialled. He heaped abuse on the "plutocratic-capitalist" enemy in the West. It was reliably reported that during a discussion of the situation in France he "foamed with rage" and declared he would give up the Eastern front before allowing a Western victory to restore the rule of democracy and the lie of Christianity. He would rather have chaos. He had made remarks like this after Stalingrad : "If the German nation does not want to understand me and refuses to fight, it will simply have to perish." His illusions of an heroic end were old-Germanic and Wagnerian or reminiscent of Felix Dahn's "last Goths on Vesuvius"; and he tried to make them come true by issuing the most reckless commands, going as far as ordering the self-destruction of the nation.[20] As Goebbels put it : "If the enemy invades Germany he shall find a 'silent land'."

*   *   *

For Stauffenberg his first meeting with Hitler had been an important experience. It took place at a "situation conference" the day after the invasion had started. For the first time the new military situation was discussed. Himmler was present at the meeting. Stauffenberg later told some friends that he strongly felt the paralysing effect of the "stale atmosphere" of the place, which was cut off from the outside world. There was no trace of frankness and sincerity. He saw for himself how Hitler managed to get a complete hold over officers whose views before entering had been entirely different, sober and objective. But Stauffenberg was almost surprised to note that he himself was not affected by any of this. He said that only two of the men who had attended this situation conference—and among them were staunch opponents of Hitler—Colonel Brandt and he himself remained firm, sober and did not waver. He also made another observation : at one moment during the situation report when everybody was studying the maps spread out on the table Hitler, his right hand trembling, looking worried, suddenly cast a searching glance at Stauffenberg across the long table; then after quickly reassuring himself that there was no danger he again turned his attention to the reporting officer. Stauffenberg is said to have remarked, with his own plans in mind, he found "it was quite easy to move about in the immediate vicinity of the Führer" (KB 91). This experience is important because it was said Hitler did not show any surprise when he heard the aforementioned Reuter report. But, so the story goes, he remarked with his old bitterness that some members of the General Staff had long been harbouring the idea of getting rid of him. From that day onwards he forbade any transfers within Headquarters of which he was not told before; he is also said to have tightened security precautions even further and to have given express orders that an eye must be kept on the brief-cases conference members were carrying.[21]

On June 15 Stauffenberg took up his new post under Fromm; from then on he seems to have gone all out to prepare the coup as fast as he could. Previous plans were re-examined and brought up to date, new associates were enlisted where necessary and "initiated" officers in positions of command were asked to renew their pledges.

There was one difficulty over the Guard Battalion in Berlin, which had been given an important job in the planned revolt. At the end of May a new Battalion Commander, Major Ernst Otto *Remer* had been appointed. The conspirators had tried various ways of getting some information about him. Of humble origin, he had taken his matriculation at a classical Gymnasium and joined the Army at the age of twenty in 1932. He was commissioned in 1935. Although at one time a Hitler Youth leader, he did not make a name for himself later as a Hitler and Party zealot. From his remarks against the SS one might have expected that he could be won over for the plot. Remer was undeniably a good soldier and had plenty of courage. Until then he had been fighting at the front and Hitler had only recently decorated him with the Oak Leaves to the Knight's Cross. He was described as a somewhat unsure, minor personality, without firm convictions. He was therefore not the right type of man to bring into the conspiracy; yet to replace him might have attracted the attention of the Gestapo. It was highly probable that he would join the Opposition once Hitler was dead, but in any case they had to be vigilant so as to be able to replace him, if necessary, on the day of the attempt. General von Hase and Major Hayessen were prepared for that contingency.

The Resistance in the Bendlerstrasse received an important reinforcement in Stauffenberg's successor, Merz von Quirnheim, whom Stauffenberg had personally accommodated at his home in Wannsee.

Now to Paris, where the German Resistance had begun to receive strong support in the last few months. This was of great significance in the new situation. It was now a question of reaching agreement on joint action.

General Karl-Heinrich von Stülpnagel had managed to form his own group of resolute conspirators. For a long time there had been an understanding between Beck and Stülpnagel; and it will be recalled that this was further strengthened by Schulenburg's activities in the West in the summer and autumn of 1943. Caesar von Hofacker had been transferred to a post close to Stülpnagel in the same autumn, after having served three years as Head of the Iron and Steel Department. The two men immediately agreed to start organizing their own group. At the time time Hofacker was acting as go-between with Berlin. He was free to go and see Stülpnagel any time he liked, and they often met in private after work. Hofacker secured another collaborator, his friend Dr Gotthard von *Falkenhausen*, who had read law and was working as a banking expert at the German Embassy in Paris. He was a nephew of General Falkenhausen, the Wehrmacht Commander for Belgium and Northern France, whose HQ was in Brussels. The young Falkenhausen had contacts with the conspirators in the Reich. We know from him about his conversations, as Stauffenberg's guest, with Count Nikolaus Uexküll and Freiherr von Plettenberg, and about a talk with Helmuth von Moltke, who came to see him in Paris. Falkenhausen gave advice on economic and particularly on foreign policy matters. Schulenburg himself had won support for the planned revolt from Freiherr Friedrich von *Teuchert*, a senior administrative official on the staff of the Military Governor of Paris. Teuchert, a native Franconian, was in close touch with Hofacker and had in turn secured the agreement and co-operation of another high official in the war administration, Walter *Bargatzky*. In addition, Regierungsrat Dr *Horst*, a brother-in-law of Lieutenant-General Speidel, and Verwaltungsrat Dr *Thierfelder* also placed themselves at the conspirators' disposal. Thanks both to Stülpnagel's sure instinct for the right kind of man and Hofacker's recruiting efforts, the chief of the military administration of the Governor's staff, Ministerialdirektor Dr Elmar *Michel* also promised to take part in the revolt.

In addition to securing the support of these officials, whose knowledge of administration was bound to acquire special significance in the event of a successful coup, Stülpnagel and Hofacker had also formed a network of military helpers. There was Lieutenant-General Hans von *Boineburg-Lengsfeld*, who had served with the German forces at Stalingrad and was now the Army Commander of Greater Paris under Stülpnagel. He himself has reported that he told Stülpnagel in the summer of 1943 that he was willing to play his part in a revolt. He had been given the task of manning his staff HQ and the most important posts in the garrison regiments under his command with people who, though not privy to the plot, could be relied upon. Stülpnagel knew that his attitude was shared by Dr Hans *Speidel,* for several weeks in 1942 his Chief of Staff with the rank of Colonel, later Chief of an Army Staff on the Eastern front and now back in the West as Lieutenant-General. Colonel i.G. *Kossmann*, since 1942 Speidel's successor under Stülpnagel, also knew and shared his superior's thoughts. The link with the Army Staff was Dr Reinhard *Brinck*, a Frankfurt lawyer who served as Captain, then Major, of the Reserve in the Abwehr Branch of the Commander-in-Chief, West, in St Germain.

In July 1944, Stülpnagel took his Chief of Staff, Colonel i.G. Otfried von *Linstow*, into his confidence; Boineburg's Chief of Staff, Colonel i.G. *Unger*, was also let into the secret. It took Unger some heart-searching before he came to the conclusion that force which strangled justice and conscience could be broken only by force. And he was satisfied that the oath of allegiance to Hitler must not stand in the way.[22]

Stülpnagel deliberately kept the circle of the "initiated" small, but in addition to them he had gathered around him men on whom he could, as far as was humanly foreseeable, rely at the time of action, although he had not incriminated them in advance. The Military Governor of Paris maintained close service relations with the Wehrmacht Commander in Belgium and Northern France as a matter of course, and so no suspicion was aroused by the despatch of a liaison officer from the Brussels staff to Stülpnagel. All this was of great use in the preparation of the coup. Both Generals were at one in their assessment of the situation, kept nothing secret from each other and were prepared to lend a hand in a revolt.[23]

Speidel took up his post as Chief of Staff of Army Group B under Rommel in La Roche Guyon on April 15, 1944. Thereby the hitherto limited circle of men who knew about the plot was significantly widened. For it was seen that the relations of *Rommel*, who for years had been regarded as Hitler's own Field-Marshal, with his Supreme Commander were very strained. Rommel evidently thought the war must urgently be brought to an end, if necessary against Hitler's decision. He no longer believed it could be won and he was furious that Hitler showed no appreciation of the serious warnings he had been given on two occasions when they confronted each other. Rommel was also deeply moved by the urgent pleadings of men from his native Swabia : they begged him to agree to save the Reich at this late hour; his was the only name which had the almost legendary power to win the nation's allegiance.[24] In Berlin, the circle around Beck was still treating the news of Rommel's readiness to co-operate with reserve, and Stülpnagel's staff, too, placed their hopes primarily on Speidel. Meanwhile Rommel and Speidel were discreetly but resolutely going ahead with their plans. As early as April 20, 1944, Stülpnagel and Speidel met in Paris. On this occasion the Military Governor heard from the Chief of Staff that Rommel had fundamentally changed his attitude towards Hitler. On May 15 Rommel and Stülpnagel had a meeting at Kossmann's remote cottage near St Germain. Rommel, who had undergone some of his training at the Dresden War College together with Stülpnagel, now submitted to his senior colleague the plan which he and Speidel had evolved : it envisaged the arrest and trial of Hitler by a German court; armistice negotiations with the West on the basis of the immediate evacuation of occupied Western territories and immediate cessation of bombing raids by the Western Allies; retention of a shortened defence front in the East; and, finally, the formation of a new Provisional German Government led by Beck, Goerdeler and Leuschner. Stülpnagel agreed with the main provisions of the plan and left no doubt about his readiness to place himself under the command of the junior Field-Marshal.

Five days later, on May 20, 1944, Rommel spoke with equal frankness to Field-Marshal von Rundstedt, who as Commander-in-Chief, West, was his immediate superior. Rundstedt's Chief of Staff, General (Infantry) Günther von *Blumentritt*, and Colonel i.G. Rudolf *Zimmermann*, the GSO I, were present at the interview, but Rommel failed to persuade Rundstedt to adopt a more definite attitude. In June, General von Falkenhausen was in La Roche-Guyon and told Rommel that he was ready for any plan. Through Hofacker Berlin was being kept up to date on the way things were going. General Eduard Wagner, the Army's Quartermaster-General, brought Rommel details about the day-by-day preparations which had been made at the High Command, but he found the Field-Marshal resolutely opposed to an attempt on Hitler's life.

The enemy landings on June 6, 1944, and the alarming course of the battles in Normandy made heavy demands on all conspirators in the West. They, like the leaders of the Resistance in Berlin, were vitally interested in maintaining a strong and coherent defence. They felt that only this would enable them to face the Allies as a negotiating party after a successful coup. Hitler himself endangered this defence by constantly interfering in the war. The military leaders were thereby stripped of freedom of decision and tied down to the rigid fulfilment of Hitler's increasingly senseless demands. His visit to the Western front on June 17 and 18—into which he had almost to be forced—was virtually useless, except for the fact that his hasty and unexpected departure from the bomb-proof bunker at Margival was bound to convince Rommel how hopeless was his original plan to capture Hitler. The Field-Marshal thus seemed to get closer to the Resistance group in the Bendlerstrasse, but the main thing was that he became more determined to "get on with the job". Two of his subordinate Army leaders, Colonel-General *Dollmann* and Colonel-General von *Salmuth,* as well as the C.-in-C. of Armoured Group West, General Freiherr Leo *Geyr von Schweppenburg,* were willing, according to Speidel's testimony, to follow Rommel even if it meant disobeying the Führer's orders. Lieutenant-General Count Gerd von *Schwerin,* Commander of an Armoured Division, outlined his views on the political situation in a memorandum to his Commander-in-Chief and explicitly offered himself and his troops for the struggle against "internal enemies"; General Freiherr von *Lüttwitz,* who also commanded an Armoured Division, did likewise.

On June 25, Colonel i.G. Eberhard Finckh, who had come from Berlin, reported to Rommel and told him that Stauffenberg was preparing an attempt on Hitler. Even now, Rommel declared, he could not approve that kind of action. The German people who had elected Hitler should also try him. It nevertheless seemed clear that the Field-Marshal had come closer to the views of Beck and his confederates, and there was reason to hope that he would not fail them at the decisive hour. Finckh was cordially received by Hofacker and Stülpnagel and told them what Stauffenberg had to say.

At about the same time Trott zu Solz had once again travelled to Sweden as Stauffenberg's emissary to find out something about the situation abroad. "I must know what England and the United States would do if Germany were to be compelled to start negotiations at short notice." That was Stauffenberg's instruction, as Trott stated under interrogation (KB 175). At the same time, Trott was to bring back news about the "Free Germany Committee". The Resistance leaders had heard that some "good" men were members of the Committee—including Merz's brother-in-law, Major-General Korfes—but the whole set-up was considered to be too much under Russian direction for the Opposition to be interested in joint action. Stauffenberg remarked that he did not think much of proclamations from behind barbed wire (KB 174). If no co-operation could be established with that Committee the Resistance leaders at least wanted to be sure that no undesirable interference in the coup would come from that quarter, especially when approaches were being made to the West. Julius Leber thought that a similar reassurance was also necessary in Berlin, and, against the advice of Leuschner and others, he arranged a meeting with leaders of the Communist underground who were known to Reichwein. The first such meeting between Leber and Reichwein on the one side and three men on the other took place on June 23 at a doctor's flat in East Berlin. A second was to be held on July 4, but Leber decided not to attend it because he had been recognized by one of the people at the meeting, and contrary to previous agreement had been spontaneously addressed by name.

In addition to the invasion of France, the last ten days of June had brought an attack on the central sector in Russia which Beck and Tresckow had forecast. It was not yet possible to assess the scope of the assault, but its severity could well indicate that it was meant to lead to a quick decision in the war.

The leading planners of the revolt now faced their most difficult decision. Their Yes or No would be final and irrevocable in the judgement of future generations. Germany's defeat was approaching. They would not have an opportunity for independent action much longer. Soon foreign armies would rule. Perhaps it was already too late to launch a revolt that would achieve its purpose.

Emphatic opposition and serious misgivings were voiced in the inner circle of conspirators even by brave men who, until the Allied invasion, had advocated a coup. They pointed out that after the invasion of France and Russia's successes, the inevitable military sequel would be Germany's unconditional surrender. Even if a different régime could be established in Germany before it was all over, they argued, it would be foolish to expect anything else than a "Diktat" of the stronger from enemies who felt sure of victory. This downward trend could no longer be arrested. Whoever intervened at this moment—whether successful or not—would always be damned for having been guilty of Germany's defeat. No salutary lesson would be learned; instead a new, venomous "stab-in-the back" lie would be born and the people would curse the men who had striven for the nation's good. Hitler would always be regarded as the betrayed hero, who with his unerring certainty, unknown preparations and his secret weapons would have achieved victory in the end. From the military point of view, too, serious doubts were raised. It was argued that a coup d'état now could lead to nothing but chaos, which would be much worse than bringing the war to an end under Hitler. With such prospects in view was it still defensible to risk the lives of so many important men on an uncertain venture? Did not a sense of higher responsibility demand that in the hour of defeat there should still be men at hand whom both the Germans and the Allies would regard as representing Germany?

Colonel-General Beck, who also felt serious misgivings, took this view of the probable future : Germany vanquished and occupied, and deprived by the occupying-powers of her own political freedom of action—that situation could not be changed by the coup d'état. But the revolt could prevent incalculable sacrifices and destruction which had to be expected in the final phase; moreover, it could demonstrate to the rest of the world—and for that purpose Beck was ready to use his prestige with the German Army and abroad—that there were still people in Germany determined to stop the crimes committed in the usurped name of the nation. To revolt would at least make it possible for the inescapable defeat to be borne with dignity and decency. It could have the effect of preventing Germany from being overrun by the Eastern powers. But, as his conversation with Hassell on June 28 showed, Beck by then had little hope of the coup taking place.

After the start of the invasion Goerdeler once more asked for Jakob Wallenberg's opinion of the situation. Wallenberg's reply, brought back from Stockholm on June 20 by Gotthold Müller, finally dashed all hopes that the Western powers might be willing to negotiate. But Wallenberg had expressed his personal conviction that after a successful coup Germany would be in a quite different and stronger negotiating position, which would be seen from the result of such negotiations. Goerdeler, usually of titanic courage, was beginning to lose heart. He now hardly believed that action was any longer possible, however much he still thought it was needed. Goerdeler had sought a few days' quiet at Rauschen Spa near Königsberg, in his native region; but he was tormenting himself, fighting for a last glimmer of hope. Yet he felt so cut off from the "younger ones" that his word no longer carried any weight.[25]

But irrespective of any foreign-political prospects, hopes and disappointments, the "younger ones" had come to a clear-cut decision, even though they knew defeat was near, to accept the plan Stauffenberg advocated and for which he was working. Tresckow, asked to give his advice, agreed that this decision was inescapable.

Stauffenberg tried urgently to get in touch with Tresckow. Stauffenberg had learnt that the Chief of the General Staff had summoned the Army Commanders to East Prussia, for a conference at HQ, to which he would go from Berchtesgaden. Tresckow, who was on the central sector where his troops were engaged in a bitter defensive battle, was also invited to attend. Count Lehndorff was sent to meet him. The talks took place at Lehndorff's estate, at Steinort am Mauersee, where Hitler's Foreign Minister had set up his elegant "Field Headquarters". Schlabrendorff, who accompanied the General, later gave this version of Tresckow's view which, he said, had been put forward with deep conviction : "The assassination must be attempted at all costs. Even should that fail, the attempt to seize power must be made. What matters is no longer the practical purpose of the coup, but to prove to the world and to future generations that the men of the Resistance movement dared to take the decisive step and to hazard their lives on it. Compared with this objective nothing else matters."[26] Tresckow urged Stauffenberg to see that the war in the West was brought to an end immediately. By issuing false orders a gap could be opened in the Western front—while the Eastern front should be defended as strongly as possible until the Anglo-Saxons had seized control of Germany. He suggested that Stauffenberg should at once see Rommel.

The final decision lay with Stauffenberg. He knew the arguments against this course of action. He came up against them every day in discussion. There was a terrible logic in many of them, which he did not deny, but he was convinced that the reasons demanding action were stronger, for the sake of the future, not his own prestige. He agreed with Tresckow, it no longer mattered that the coup might fail.

*   *   *

Lieutenant Urban Thiersch, a young artillery officer who, at Stauffenberg's instigation, had been transferred to Berlin from July 1, has given an account of his first visit to the Bendlerstrasse. The report, which is here reproduced in full[27] vividly describes the atmosphere the young officer found in Berlin :

"After my arrival on July 1, I drove through different parts of the capital to report at various offices. Most streets showed signs of the destructive bombing raids—some of them very recent—such as I had never seen in any city before. Churches, administrative buildings, factories, schools and dwelling houses had been reduced to ruin and rubble. Most shops had rough boards instead of window panes and were unattractive. By day the streets seemed deserted, only in the late afternoon and evening hours hurried crowds thronged the railway stations and streets leading to the suburbs seeking a quiet night's rest away from the dangerous city centre. I felt anguished seeing or talking to these people. Many of them were probably going about their daily jobs and tasks. Some grumbled, others were still unshaken in their faith in the salvation of the Fatherland and the future, anxiously shunning any thought of impending disaster; yet others saw it coming, but doing their duty unfailingly seemed to give them a certain steadiness. Yet over it all there hung the paralysing, leaden nightmare : they were being hunted and driven and there was no way out.

"When I got to OKH in the Bendlerstrasse, I found an entirely different atmosphere. I asked my way to the Chief of Staff's office on the second floor, facing the road, and reported at the spacious and elegant ante-room. There was a lot of activity. Officers—most of them wore the red stripes of General Staff members or Generals' badges of rank—were pacing up and down or sitting on the narrow upholstered benches. Some were engaged in cheerful, others in heated, conversation. I had been waiting for a few minutes when a young officer entered from Stauffenberg's room, greeted me like a friend and ushered me in. The officer was von Haeften. Stauffenberg held out his left hand. He was radiantly alive and so self-assured that it made one think his serious mutilations did not handicap him in the least. He politely asked about my journey and accommodation in Berlin, and had cigarettes offered to me. Stauffenberg and his ADC talked to each other very frankly. Except among soldiers on the front I had rarely come across such a relationship.

"We were interrupted by the ringing of the telephone and Stauffenberg got involved in another conversation. It was a pleasure to watch him conduct the telephone conversations—giving brief and definite orders, behaving with natural courtesy towards important people, and always in command of the situation. Of course, I was unable to pay much attention to what was being said because I was too fascinated by his appearance : the fine proportion between his powerful head and body; he was wearing riding breeches with the red stripe and a lightweight white tunic. His complexion was fresh and healthy, his sound eye flashed unimpaired, as if kindled by some fire from within, and independent, it seemed, of whatever cheerful or serious emotions his face registered. The other half of the face, with the black patch covering the eye, appeared less active, yet it had peculiar power because of the bold features, the shape of the head and the imprint of his experience. And looking at him from that angle only this part of the face gave Stauffenberg something remote, something monumental.

"The telephone conversation completed, he turned to me again : 'Let's get straight to the point,' he said, 'I am committing high treason with every means at my command.' We then talked about the utterly hopeless military situation. A coup could not change it but could save a great deal of bloodshed and terrible chaos. The present ignominious régime, however, would have to be removed. Gravely he added that it was doubtful whether the revolt would succeed. But worse than failure would be to succumb inactively to disgrace and paralysing tyranny. Only action could bring inner and external freedom.

"Although what he said was just what I felt, it was something else that drove me to support this plan wholeheartedly and at the risk of my life. There was nothing hypnotic or mystical about Stauf-

286

fenberg, but one could sense that he had some unassailable power of genius which made one want him to be the leader, and which made one feel sure it would be wonderful to work for him and with him. Looking at him one realized that this man had broken the spell which had made people submit to mean brute force as the only way of getting things done. His personality was proof that great strength can combine with supreme natural dignity. I recalled a passage of Jean Paul's about the difference between genius and talent. It said something to the effect that genius is an indivisible simple force which cannot be split into individual elements and therefore cannot be suppressed.

"We then talked about my task and he asked me to remain in the ante-room until my future chief, Colonel H., arrived. Waiting in the narrow corridor, from which three open glass doors led into the large ante-room, was a most interesting experience. I thought the people waiting here or talking to one another were under some subconscious tension which mounted whenever Stauffenberg came out of his office to greet somebody or call him in. But whether he was speaking to subordinates or superiors his candid and cordial manner always seemed to sway the others. At one time he stood fairly near to me talking to a tall, slim man—a northern type whose eyes seemed to be thoughtfully trained on something far away. I could sense a special mutual respect from the way they spoke to each other. I assumed they were old friends. He was Colonel H.—Stauffenberg quickly and lucidly explained my new duties. He made the necessary decisions easy.

"A little later—von Haeften was just arranging a luncheon appointment with me—a smart senior officer in SS uniform entered the ante-room. With an upward glance von Haeften sighed : 'How do we get rid of that man Helldorf?', and then went to Stauffenberg to announce the arrival of the police chief. Stauffenberg soon emerged. To Helldorf's verbose congratulations on his appointment as Chief of Staff, Stauffenberg replied with a cheerful and friendly, 'Too kind, Herr Präsident', and managed to dismiss him quickly.

"Towards noon quite a number of officers, NCOs and officials gathered. I understood that the old Chief of Staff, a General, who was leaving the office, intended to say goodbye, and Stauffenberg was to welcome his new colleagues. The glass doors were shut and all I could see was Stauffenberg stepping forward after his predecessor's speech. You could sense the interest roused among the gathering. All attention was focused on Stauffenberg who spoke freely and with assurance, now and then bending his head back slightly. Soon the doors opened again and everybody went back to their own offices, most of them in a good mood after his final, presumably jovial, remarks."

Towards the end of June Rudolf Fahrner, summoned from Athens by Stauffenberg, arrived in Berlin. Stauffenberg explained why nothing had happened yet. The men who in the previous October had taken over the preparations at HQ, he said, had been inactive, and all assassination attempts so far had failed. But now there was a chance that something would be done in the very near future. Fahrner, who was asked to revise the October proclamations writes : [28] "The proclamations had to be adapted to the new political situation both at home and abroad. Secret foreign political negotiations had shown that the Western powers rejected any help or support from the German Resistance against Hitler and that they preferred Germany's total subjugation to any contact with an anti-Hitler movement. The military fronts had advanced much closer to Germany. The liberation movement at home now comprised so many sections and groups that it was possible to speak about it in different terms from those of October 1943. Fewer and sharper words could be said about the settling of accounts— political and military—with the Nazi régime. Many things that still required justification in October 1943 no longer needed any. What had to be said about the future that lay in store for the nation would have to be expressed even more soberly, simply and briefly. The appeal to the women would be dropped because some of the people consulted about its terms thought they were too novel and would not be well received. But some of the ideas were taken over from this appeal into the general proclamation."

The revised appeals were once more discussed with all concerned and finally approved by Claus Stauffenberg. Then at the Naval War Command, Fahrner dictated them to Stauffenberg's secretary, straight on to the typewriter. Earlier versions were destroyed. One of the two newly typed copies was kept at the Bendlerstrasse, the second was locked in Berthold Stauffenberg's safe in case it was needed as a replacement.

Fahrner, who had been staying for about a week as Claus Stauffenberg's guest in Wannsee and with Berthold Stauffenberg in "Koralle" near Bernau, gave a very personal account in his memoirs which underlines the historic importance of this period. With his permission we quote from his manuscript.

"In those days Claus, though basically serious, was cheerful; and in spite of all the demands made upon him, his intellect was unburdened, fertile and full of sparkle. A few illuminating words of his, and a whole complex of problems seemed solved. Never a consultation without laughter; devastating, but indirect, references by the score; paraphrases that hit the bull's-eye every time; and always there was that dry, smiling and salutary candour with which he described the situation. It was characteristic of his way of speaking. Amidst all the claims on him in his capacity as Chief of Staff and as the leader of the Resistance movement, throughout all the consultations, visits, telephone conversations, instructions and planning—he always seemed at ease, with a ready answer to spiritual problems, willing to hear about intellectual activities and offering his valuable advice. I had recently brought the two brothers Alexander Stauffenberg's poems. Claus read all of them—I can't imagine when—and in between the pressing tasks of the day he discussed them in detail with me and even with Berthold before the joint poetry reading on the last evening.

"I can still see Claus having breakfast with Merz von Quirnheim on the balcony in the morning sun. Some wasps were after their honey and ready to sting. They sent Claus running. The one good thing about his injuries, he joked, was that, without worrying about being misrepresented, he could now openly show his fear of wasps. Before that he had always had to conceal it.

"Late in the afternoon of July 4—I was to leave for the Alps on the 5th—Claus and I went for a walk through the garden suburb of Wannsee. Once again we discussed something a lot of people talked about in those days : whether, in view of the war situation which made the complete occupation of Germany inevitable before long, there was still any point in staging a revolt, or whether it would be better for us to keep our strength intact and be ready for action after Hitler's defeat by external powers. If we acted now we could still save a lot of property and much more human life and happiness—and not only of Germans. But even heavier weighed the knowledge that the whole affair was not a matter of outward success. It was a command of moral purification and of honour that had to be obeyed. I asked what the chances and possible consequences were. I suggested that if the revolt succeeded we should simply stop all fighting against the enemy in the West and throw everything we could into the defence of the Eastern front, but then realized that such plans had already been given thorough consideration. But what engaged us most on this walk was the question whether, everything else failing, Claus himself ought to try to assassinate Hitler. Claus, of course, as Fromm's Chief of Staff, had access to Headquarters and Hitler himself. But it seemed vital that Claus should be available for what needed to be done after Hitler's overthrow. Here is a situation for analytically-minded historians : ability to reshape the state, in a cruel, almost hopeless, clash, driven by the urge and duty to purify Germany. When Claus

289

put this question straight to me I faced a most difficult decision. When I said yes, 'Yes', he responded with an indescribable expression in his eye and a word that sealed our commitment. I remember seeing him wear the FINIS-INITIUM signet ring on the remaining second finger of his left hand.[29]

"A hectic evening followed that afternoon. Immediately after we got back Stauffenberg had to deal with an almost non-stop series of long-distance calls. The telephone kept buzzing and he himself was putting through calls which Berthold, who had meanwhile arrived from 'Koralle', and I both overheard. Very little was said in between the telephone conversations—but in those hours a whole abyss of problems and events seemed to open up : the urgent needs of the front, especially in the East, whose defenders called for reinforcements and replacements in their untenable situation; the misery of thousands of German men, women and children fleeing from the East to Germany to avoid falling into the hands of an incensed enemy. Yet the German troops had to try to stem the flood of refugees to prevent the disintegration of their own front. At the same time, there was much friction between the Party's defence experts and the Army authorities, crass selfishness among Party and armament departments waging a private war within a war; air raids caused suffering and shortages of vital materials. There were difficulties in the Home Army, delays in the execution of orders, personal news, good and bad, about friends and acquaintances. There were recriminations, people had to be comforted, some were in despair. Bold new advice had to be given, perseverance counselled and rescue operations organized. Stauffenberg's replies on the telephone were a reflection of these grim realities. Claus' whole body was involved : alternately, he would sit down, lean or, occasionally, lie across a table, stand still or walk up and down, the receiver in his hand. His remarks showed that he shared the thoughts and feelings of the people on the other end of the line. He planned, anticipated, sorted out what needed immediate action and what could be postponed, and separated justifiable from unjustified and inflated claims. Some matters were followed up through several conversations until they were clarified —with Stauffenberg rapidly switching from one subject to another, settling issues, giving encouragement, making promises, rejecting ideas and terminating further discussion about them.

"It was 11 o'clock at night when we sat down to dine. Thanks to some good friends there was even some wine. A memorable, quiet night followed. Now all three of us were united in the contemplation and discussion of Alexander Stauffenberg's poetic work, 'Der Tod des Meisters'. The brothers exchanged impressions and ideas with which I was already familiar from my conversations with each individually. New agreements, considerations, points of view and trends of thought emerged. One work and comment on it led us to several major issues of poetry. We were all deeply involved. Then we went back to the beginning once more and read aloud the work we had been discussing. It was nearly dawn when we parted for a brief rest."

* * *

The same night something else happened that had the effect of a fuse being ignited. Individual accounts convey the daily increasing tension that hung over the next two weeks until the 20th July.

When Stauffenberg arrived at the office on July 5, news reached him through Haubach and Trott that Reichwein and his companion had failed to return home after a meeting the previous evening with some members of the underground, and that the Gestapo had also arrested Dr Leber early that morning. The blow had struck very near home. Was it about to be followed by others? Undoubtedly the Nazis had managed to seize the two men because one of the members of the Resistance had betrayed them. Stauffenberg was shaken at the thought of Leber being under arrest, the very man whose strength would have been a vital asset in the revolt. Stauffenberg did not doubt his steadfastness, but every day's delay meant danger to his friend's life and to the prospects of the uprising.

And from Paris came news of a change in the High Command. Two days earlier Rundstedt had been forced to make way for the returning Kluge.[30] In view of what had gone before this gave rise to some hope. Tresckow acted quickly: he dispatched Georg von Boeselager to Kluge to explain the situation in the East, and to ask him to give orders which would lead to a swift surrender in the West while the Eastern front could still be held. Kluge replied that an Army Commander in the West could not do such a thing; in any case it would soon be unnecessary as the enemy was strong enough to achieve a break-through.

On July 6, Stauffenberg flew to HQ at Berchtesgaden with the explosives in his brief-case. According to KB 130, he told Stieff: "I've got the lot on me." He had no commission which would take him near Hitler on that day, but he apparently intended to try, for the last time, to persuade the group at HQ who had the opportunity to make an attempt to kill Hitler, to do so. The following day was the date set for the showing of uniforms at the nearby Klessheim Castle not far from Salzburg. Hitler and Himmler had at last promised to attend the session. Stieff was to be in charge. It is not known whether another conspirator was to take part in addition to Stieff, nor what had been arranged between him and Stauffenberg. Stieff maintained silence about this episode at the interrogation. As it was, Stauffenberg had little hope of the attempt being made. On his return in the evening he talked with noticeable emotion and fiery impatience about the situation at Berchtesgaden and declared that now he would have to take charge of that as well.[31] None the less, he would be available for Berlin. His enquiries at HQ had made him think it feasible to combine the two actions. Fellgiebel would transmit the news and then block all communications. Within two or three hours after the start of the coup Stauffenberg hoped to be at the Bendlerstrasse. Objections were raised : the Chief of the General Staff could not at the same time lead an assault party; he, Stauffenberg, who would be indispensable after the deed and who personified the entire enterprise, could not be the assassin. Would not his physical disabilities make the success of the attempt doubtful? Besides, it was too great a risk to take on such a dual role. Stauffenberg brushed the objections aside, arguing like this : in the past such reasons might have been valid, but not any longer. Now was the last chance for settling accounts, for decisive action which affected all of them. His resolve prevailed. Even on earlier occasions, when other plans misfired, people had been looking to him because he had access to Hitler; but then, upon sober reflection, they had thought it impossible to expect him to kill Hitler. Now that he offered to do it, at such a time, they felt that despite weighty arguments against it, this was the only conceivable solution. Perhaps it would bring salvation. The young officers in particular who had learnt of Stauffenberg's decision stood devotedly by him, irrespective of what might happen to them.

On July 7, despite Stauffenberg's doubts, they expected the alarm to be given from Berchtesgaden. But the only news they received indicated that the demonstration of uniforms had taken place without incident.

On July 8, disconcerting news came from the Eastern front. Army Group Centre had ceased to exist. Any initiative to resist now only came from smaller units which had managed to hold out here and there, in front of, and in between, the enemy's assault troops. Russian spearheads had got as far as the Vistula. The Soviet Command itself was presumably surprised at its success on the central sector. It was believed in Germany that the Russians had merely intended to pin down German forces in order to relieve pressure in the south.[32] Beck and Tresckow concluded that the

Russians would take advantage of their unexpected strategic position and, without worrying about their lagging right flank, press the attack across the Vistula towards German territory. This meant that Russian armoured troops could be expected outside Berlin within ten days. Near Kovel and Dünaburg (Dvinsk) a "second Stalingrad" was beginning to take shape for the 250 000 men of Army Group North, whose land communications with the Reich were certain to be cut before long.

Urban Thiersch's account says that everyone was extremely worried that day at the Bendlerstrasse. Something had to be done, the next day if possible. Stauffenberg himself would take action. It was suggested he should inform his superior, Colonel Hansen.

"I waited to see Stauffenberg. Eventually he came along the corridor, walking with firm, calm steps and talking seriously to two companions. Greetings were brief as he was busy with urgent matters. At that moment a heavy, sombre burden seemed to lie upon him."

On July 10, it was known for certain that twenty-seven divisions of the former Army Group Centre had been annihilated by the Russian assault. Enemy armoured forces were now barely 100 km from Rastenburg HQ. The southern sector was expecting the Russian offensive to begin any day. Reconnaissance had shown that the forces assembled there were even stronger than those on the central front.[33]

On the following day, Tuesday, July 11, Stauffenberg again flew to HQ Berchtesgaden. In his leather brief-case he carried official papers and the explosives. He was accompanied by Captain Klausing, who had offered to help him as Haeften had fallen ill. Klausing drove him to the situation conference on the Obersalzberg and was awaiting his return at any minute to take him to the airfield at Freilassing. But Himmler did not attend the conference. Stauffenberg came back only after it had ended—without having accomplished anything. He had telephoned Olbricht in the meantime. Stieff quoted Stauffenberg's remark : "Shouldn't we do it, anyhow?" (KB 130). On the way to the airfield Stauffenberg briefly discussed communication problems with Fellgiebel and Stieff (KB 146).

Back in Berlin, Stauffenberg met Caesar von Hofacker, who had arrived the previous evening from Paris. On July 9, Hofacker had talked to Rommel. The Field-Marshal and his immediate superior, Kluge, had clashed bitterly during their first meeting. Rommel was furious that Kluge was "blindly copying the Berchtesgaden style" although he knew nothing about the real situation. In Rommel's view, an enemy break-through in the West, and therefore collapse in France, was to be expected within two or three weeks. According to Hofacker, Rommel seemed determined to take action on his own responsibility. He wanted to bring the war in the West to an end as quickly as possible before the defences on the invasion front collapsed. In Paris, Bargatzky had already drafted a letter in Rommel's name to the British C.-in-C., Field-Marshal Montgomery. But Rommel, Hofacker reported, thought independent action in France was impossible and he was urging a first move in the Reich, while still rejecting the idea of an attempt on Hitler; in his view it must be possible to have him arrested by reliable tank troops. Hofacker said he himself had been unable to get near Kluge, but it was known that Kluge, too, regarded a pure "Western solution", such as Tresckow demanded, as impracticable and thought an initiative from Berlin and from Headquarters was indispensable. He was in favour of a joint demarche of all C.s-in-C. with Hitler. It was felt that once Hitler was removed, Kluge would unhesitatingly support the revolt and immediately take steps to bring about an armistice in the West.

On the same day Lindenberg had arrived as Otto John's emissary from Madrid. John was pressing for the quickest possible action, as only very little time was left. John said he could very quickly establish contact with General Eisenhower through the American military attaché. He sent word that the Western Allies would insist on unconditional surrender, vis-à-vis the Russians as well.[34] John was urgently summoned to Berlin.

That same evening Hofacker and Stauffenberg went to see Beck (KB 136). One report suggests that in view of the extreme urgency they concluded that next time they would have to act even if Himmler and Göring were absent.

On July 12, a code signal was received from Paris, from which it could be inferred that Rommel and Kluge had come to a new, more propitious understanding. They had met in La Roche-Guyon. Kluge, who now shared Rommel's opinion about the situation, had agreed to take immediate soundings among the Commanding Generals and Army leaders as to how long they thought the front could be held. The outcome of this enquiry would be reported to Hitler, together with certain demands with a time limit. Rommel had made some additional proposals for action in case Hitler, as was to be expected, refused. Kluge did not disclose what he had decided to do.

Goerdeler urged Stauffenberg to act without delay, remarking that now "a frontal break-through must be made".

On July 14, orders came from HQ summoning the Commander in Chief of the Reserve Army and his Chief of Staff to make a report on the following day. The innermost circle of the Resistance decided to order "Operation Valkyrie" two hours before the expected attempt, to make sure the Army units and especially the tanks from Krampnitz would arrive more quickly in Berlin. Prearranged advance warnings in code were issued to the conspirators. Hitler's situation conferences had hitherto been held at the Berghof near Berchtesgaden. Now they were again to be held in East Prussia. Hitler had moved his HQ to Rastenburg after rebuilding operations there had been completed. Because of the war situation it had become imperative to have the Supreme Command nearer the Eastern front. This meant that the Resistance in Berlin was forced to adapt itself hurriedly to a new situation as far as communications were concerned. General Wagner made the necessary arrangements with Fellgiebel, Stieff, Hahn and Thiele.

On the same day, July 14, Rommel drafted a letter that was to be flashed by teleprinter to Hitler via the Commander-in-Chief, West. It announced that the Allied break-through was imminent, which in the circumstances, set out in great detail, was bound to decide the war. Hitler was asked to "draw the proper conclusions" without delay, i.e. to end the war in the West. According to Rommel, the letter was intended as the ultimatum to Hitler which he and Kluge had agreed. ("If he does not draw any conclusions, we will act.") On the following day the letter was shown to Kluge. As was later established, he did not pass it on until July 23.[35]

On Saturday, July 15, Stauffenberg and Colonel-General Fromm, who knew nothing about any of this, flew to East Prussia. Once again Klausing accompanied Stauffenberg. According to another—unconfirmed—report there was also a Colonel whose job would have been to set off a second explosive charge; it is not stated whether this was to reinforce the first, intended as a safeguard in case the attempt failed, or for use against a second person possibly Himmler. The officer is said to have been recalled from his division to the High Command to carry out a special assignment. At 11 a.m. in Berlin, General Olbricht issued the "Internal Unrest" code signal (Valkyrie I) and the situation conference began at the "Wolf's Lair" at 13.10.

Shortly after the start of the conference Stauffenberg left the room, apparently to make a telephone call. He returned very soon only to find that the conference, barely started, had already finished. Hitler had left the room and Stauffenberg was sent to a special conference with Himmler. This was to discuss the organization of fifteen new divisions to come under Himmler's command. According to Klausing's evidence, Stauffenberg learnt on the way to the meeting that Himmler would not be there. Afterwards,

Stauffenberg and Colonel-General Fromm had to attend yet another conference.[36] Soon after 1.30 p.m. Stauffenberg reported failure to Berlin. The "Valkyrie" alarm was cancelled and the units which had already set out in full marching order returned to their barracks.

One interrogation report said that on the morning of July 15 Fellgiebel and Stieff (and through them Stauffenberg) received an explicit request from General Wagner that action should be taken only if the Reichsführer SS Himmler was present (KB 330). The request is said to have been brought by a liaison officer who had been in Berlin only the previous day. When Stauffenberg returned in the evening he must have been furious about the order that divisions were to be put under SS command (KB 94).

Meanwhile, in Belgium the Military Governor, General von Falkenhausen, on whose co-operation the Resistance relied, had been unexpectedly relieved of his post and replaced by a Gauleiter. Although no longer holding office, Falkenhausen remained in the vicinity of Brussels.

On Sunday, July 16, Stauffenberg went to see Beck. The military arrangements of the previous day had revealed important shortcomings. The necessary changes were made to prevent a recurrence. The Colonel-General offered to discuss the matter in detail with General Olbricht. They had managed to explain the movement of troops on July 15 as an exercise to test arrangements in case of internal unrest. So as not to give himself away, Olbricht had quickly gone to inspect the units involved. This time he got away with a dressing down from Keitel, but it was unthinkable to set the troops prematurely in motion a second time.

Two attempts having failed, the possibility of a separate peace with the West was re-examined. Goerdeler, who was pressing for such a solution, through Gisevius, had suggested that he and Beck should immediately fly to Kluge and Rommel to bring about a surrender (according to Gisevius) or an armistice (according to Goerdeler's later account).[37] Beck refused. He was of the opinion that to achieve this the attempt on Hitler was vital. But he did not conceal his serious doubts as to whether it could still be made. Stauffenberg swore that whatever happened, next time he would act.

That Sunday evening, Schulenburg, Trott zu Solz, Schwerin, Yorck, Merz von Quirnheim, Hansen and Hofacker all gathered with the Stauffenberg brothers at Claus' home at Wannsee. Hofacker was to return to Paris on the next day (KB 57, 91, 101). He reported on how things were going in France, and Trott spoke on the foreign political situation. Nothing definite is known about that gathering, as all nine men present were executed. According to the reports of Trott's interrogation (KB 175), the three possible choices were once again discussed : a "Western solution" breaking off the struggle in the West, withdrawal of troops as far as the West Wall, defence in the East with a view to an early end to the war; the "Berlin solution" temporary seizure of command and communications system, orders to Army Groups that they must fall back, which instruction Führer HQ would be unable to rescind; and the "Central solution"—attempt on Hitler as the preliminary to a "Western solution". According to the interrogation report, Stauffenberg thought even a wholly "Western solution" still possible; but they agreed on the "Central solution". According to Hansen's evidence, Trott assumed the enemy would be willing to negotiate once the Hitler régime had been overthrown. It was suggested that negotiations should take place both with the Western and the Eastern military leaders (KB 101). They parted. The only course now was to do the decisive deed and to accept whatever Fate had in store.

In the morning Goerdeler had travelled to Leipzig to say goodbye to his family. He was expected to return on Tuesday morning. Hansen had also arranged for an aircraft to be held ready should Beck decide to fly to the West.[38]

July 17 saw the launching of the expected major offensive on the southern sector of the Russian front. Germany had nowhere near adequate forces to face it. Within the first three days the Russians made penetrations on a very broad front. The threat to the eastern frontier of the Reich was growing more serious. The Gauleiters or Statthalters of the regions concerned were appointed Reich Defence Commissioners.[39]

More bad news came from the West on July 17. Caen and St. Lô had fallen. This marked another step forward by the enemy before their break-through to the Greater Paris area. Even worse news : the night before, Rommel had been seriously wounded on his return home from the battlefield. He was unconscious. There were doubts whether he would recover. It was learned that shortly before this Stülpnagel had reached a definite agreement with Rommel; Rommel had declared himself willing, at the moment an attempt was made on Hitler, to do his part for the revolt, openly and unconditionally even if Kluge were to show himself hesitant or evasive.

Stauffenberg was informed by Kranzfelder that there were rumours in town that Führer HQ was to be blown up that very week. When misgivings were voiced Stauffenberg replied : "There

is no longer any alternative. The Rubicon has been crossed"
(KB 117).

Nebe reported through Gisevius that at lunch on the previous
day the Chief of the Gestapo had decided to issue a warrant for
Dr Goerdeler's arrest. Kaiser undertook to warn Goerdeler. Stauffenberg, too, had a brief meeting with him. According to Goerdeler's later notes, Stauffenberg told him that he "was in direct
touch with Churchill and that the British leader had received
the demand that in case of the coup all German territory must
remain within the Reich or be united with it".[40]

A few days earlier, Dr Leber's whereabouts had been traced : he
was in the prison of the SS Head Office in the Prinz Albrecht-
Strasse. During an excited conversation with Trott zu Solz, Stauffenberg, on hearing of Leber's position, is said to have exclaimed, time
and again, with utmost agitation : "We need Leber, I'll get him
out, I'll get him out!" Through Schulenburg he sent this brief
message to Frau Leber, who was in a Berlin hospital : "We are
conscious of our duty."[41]

During the afternoon of July 18 a summons from Headquarters
arrived for Stauffenberg to report to Hitler on the 20th (KB 21).
In the evening of the 18th and on the 19th, Bernardis prepared the
material which Stauffenberg needed for his report. He was to
inform Hitler on the progress being made with the new "Volksgrenadier" divisions.[42]

Dr John arrived from Madrid, ready to take any communication or proposal to the Allies. He confirmed that nothing but Germany's unconditional surrender to Russia as well would be acceptable (KB 441).

Outwardly, July 19 was no different from other days at the
Bendlerstrasse office. Only a handful of people among the hundreds working there knew what one of them was facing. An officer
who had arrived that day in Berlin and had some business with
Stauffenberg, has described his impressions of the visit.[43] He wrote :

"Early on July 19 I went by train from our office in the East
to Berlin. My job was to go to OKH in the Bendlerstrasse and
clarify with the appropriate department some questions regarding
the Gauleiters' and the Military District Commanders' duties in
matters of supply and administration, in the event of Soviet forces
invading military districts on the eastern frontier of the Reich. As
Allied bombers were over Berlin even in the morning, our train
was held up for hours en route and I only arrived at the Bendlerstrasse at about 2 p.m. At that moment a new air raid alarm was
sounded and as I mounted the stairs in the main block everybody
was hurrying down to the air raid shelters. The officer on duty

left it to me whether to go upstairs, despite the alert. He said I would find the GSO I there and could talk to him. The GSO I was Count Stauffenberg.

"I found him on one of the top floors : a friendly, relatively young General Staff Officer—I supposed he was about thirty-eight —with a black patch over one eye, wearing breeches with the crimson stripe and the white tunic which was generally being worn on hot days at offices in the homeland. 'Do stay until the conference at 15.00,' he suggested, 'then we can deal with your business at the same time.' I agreed. Meanwhile I went to see a comrade from the First World War who was working on the same floor. And at the time arranged I went to a little hall where about thirty officers had gathered for the conference. Count Stauffenberg took the chair and asked me to sit down by his side. I liked him. If he had not been wearing the uniform of a General Staff Officer he might have been taken for an artist or scientist with that narrow, intellectual head of his. His dark hair and the black eye-patch made his face seem a little pale. He was resting the artificial arm with the leather glove on the table as he began to speak.

"Count Stauffenberg nodded and smiled as he accepted a cigarette and a light from me, and started quietly and soberly to deal with the various points on the agenda. Now and then he good-humouredly called out to some fidgety young officers, and I was struck by the way he occasionally addressed his more intimate colleagues on the General Staff with 'You chaps, back there'. Otherwise he conducted the conference calmly and objectively so that the fairly extensive agenda, including my own business, was dealt with in a matter of two hours.

"I tried to remember what impression Count Stauffenberg had made on me as I stood facing him and later sat by his side. There was not the slightest indication of what must have been going on in his mind. He showed no sign of nervousness, but appeared to be absolutely calm and relaxed. The man must have made a super-human effort to give an impression of calm to the world around him. Looking back upon those hours I spent with him I realise he must have been weighed down by a tremendous burden of thoughts, doubts, anxieties, fears and disappointments which made him decide to stake everything the following day."

At the afternoon conference on July 19, over which Stauffenberg presided, the necessary signals for the next day had to be prepared in a hurry. Most of the messages were to be passed orally in a pre-arranged sequence. Telephone and teleprinter—where agreed code words were to be used—were reserved for very few matters because it was known that the entire system of communications was tapped by the Gestapo. There was little time left, and in view of the difficulties of communication it was impossible to check once more whether everyone involved in the plot was receiving messages. Both Hoepner and Witzleben were under surveillance and had to be brought to Berlin without attracting any attention. As if a major surprise raid had been planned, the men needed on the following noon would suddenly have to be there, ready for action.

For Stauffenberg's close friends, whom he had met during the previous days and evenings, this was not the time to speak of failure and certain death. But we know that in those hours some of the confederates, discreetly, and with loving care, made provisions for their families. And they bade farewell to their wives and children without letting them sense the imminent danger. Who can guess what the scattered groups of conspirators discussed during that July night to while away the hours of waiting? Berlin again had its almost nightly air raid warning which drove people to the shelters.

That evening Stauffenberg had set off for home shortly after eight o'clock. On the way through Dahlem he ordered the driver to stop by a church. Some of the people of this bustling city, which was anxiously awaiting the night, had paused to attend a service. Stauffenberg entered through the open door. He stayed for a while at the back of the nave, and then returned to the car to be driven home. He spent the rest of the evening alone with his brother.

XIII. THE TWENTIETH OF JULY

SHORTLY after six o'clock in the morning of the 20th July Claus Stauffenberg, accompanied by his brother and his driver, left his home at Wannsee. In the city they were joined in the car by Lieutenant von Haeften. Berthold Stauffenberg drove with them to the Rangsdorf airfield where they found the Quartermaster-General's aircraft waiting. Major-General Stieff was there ready to join them. After a flight of several hours they landed at Rastenburg in East Prussia at 10.15. The pilot was instructed to stand by from noon onwards to take them back to Berlin. The camp Commandant had sent a car to meet them. After half an hour's drive through the woodlands, they reached the Führer Headquarters. The first gate, which gave access to an extensive minefield and ring of fortifications, was about three kilometres from the centre. A second gate had to be passed to get into a large compound surrounded by electrified barbed wire. From this gate it was another 800 metres to the officers' check-point and from there a further 200 metres or so to the entrance to the innermost compound, Security Ring A, where Hitler lived and worked.[1]

Even after its reconstruction, the "Wolf's Lair" Headquarters was a gloomy camp of huts dispersed in a forest. The number of bunkers—cube-like, windowless concrete blockhouses with camouflage paint—had been increased; the previous bunkers had been reinforced—they were said to have walls and ceilings six metres thick. To protect them againt incendiary and small splinter bombs, most of the original huts had been given a half-metre thick outside coating of concrete, leaving room for normal-sized doors and windows ("Speer-Baracken"). The "Lagebaracke"—the conference hut—was of similar construction. This hut, together with the bunker where Hitler lived (Führerbunker I", later Gästebunker"—the visitors' bunker) and the dogs' enclosure for Hitler's bitch, were contained within the innermost Security Ring, which was surrounded by barbed wire fences $2\frac{1}{2}$ metres high and constantly patrolled by SS guards and Secret Service officials. Here even the highest officers were admitted only with a pass issued by SS-Oberführer Rattenhuber in his own handwriting.[2]

After reporting to the camp Commandant, Stauffenberg went to have breakfast at the so-called tea-house with the Commandant's ADC, Captain von Möllendorf. Stauffenberg was wearing his cap and belt and, under his left arm, he was clutching a bright leather brief-case. He stayed with General Buhle, the Army's representative at OKW on whom he had to call on business, until noon. Both men arrived at Field-Marshal Keitel's office at about 12 o'clock. Stauffenberg made a brief report and continued in conversation with Keitel. As Mussolini's visit was expected at 14.30, the "midday situation" conference had been advanced to start at 12.30. Only the most urgent matters were to be brought up and the number of persons attending was to be restricted as far as possible. After Keitel had repeatedly cast impatient glances at the clock, they got ready shortly before 12.30 to walk over to the conference together. Keitel, Buhle and Keitel's Adjutant, Lieutenant-Colonel von John, were waiting outside the hut for Stauffenberg who had entered the ante-room to fetch his belt and cap. He was delayed a bit—it had meanwhile gone 12.30—so that the General called out into the corridor asking him to hurry up. Shortly afterwards Stauffenberg appeared. He had used the few moments of privacy to break the capsule in his brief-case with the help of little tongs which he could operate with the only three fingers he had. There was no going back; the bomb would explode within about fifteen minutes.

As they walked to the conference hut—which would take them about three minutes—Keitel's Adjutant offered to carry Stauffenberg's brief-case, which he thought must be cumbersome for the one-armed officer. Stauffenberg thanked him kindly, but declined. He was engaged in casual conversation as they passed through the checkpoint to the Security Ring and proceeded towards the conference hut.

The officers attending the meeting stood chatting at the entrance until Hitler's military Adjutant, Colonel von Below, asked them to go in. Shortly afterwards Hitler appeared, and the conference began. The Army was represented by Lieutenant-General Heusinger and his chief colleague, Colonel Brandt; the Air Force by General Korten, Air Force Chief of Staff; the Navy by Admirals Voss and von Puttkamer and Commodore Assmann. Himmler was represented by SS-General Fegelein; Göring by General Bodenschatz. Hitler's Chief Adjutant was General Schmundt, his Adjutant Lieutenant-Colonel Borgmann; and Major-General Scherff was there as Head of the War History Section at OKW. Hitler was followed by his personal Adjutant, Sturmbannführer Günsche. Below, previously Hitler's Air Force Adjutant, also stayed for the conference. The Wehrmacht Operations Staff was represented by

General Warlimont and Colonel Weizenegger, in addition to Major Büchs, who was Colonel-General Jodl's Adjutant. Jodl himself, the most senior officer next to Keitel, arrived only after the meeting had begun. Legationsrat von Sonnleithner attended as representative of the Ministry of Foreign Affairs. The shorthand writer was Dr Berger. As was later established, the list of participants contained a total of twenty-five names.

The conference room was at one end of the hut.[4] To get to it from the entrance in the long wall, one had to walk along the central corridor past the telephone room and a cloakroom, taking about eight paces to the right and then entering through a double-winged door. There were altogether ten windows, in the opposite long wall, and in the narrow wall on the right, all of which were open as it was a hot, sultry day. The room measured about 5 by 12 metres. Walls and ceilings were covered with white pasteboard. In the middle of the room there stood an oak table, about 6 metres long and 1·2 metres wide. Its top, a good 10 centimetres thick, rested on two massive oak supports. Hitler's place at the table was recognizable by a chair positioned at the centre of one of the long sides nearest the door. On the table the required maps were spread in pre-arranged order, one on top of the other. Hitler's polished spectacles were ready for him even before the conference began.

When they entered, Keitel heard Stauffenberg tell the telephone operator, a sergeant, that he was expecting an urgent call from Berlin. He said he would like to be fetched immediately as he required the information for his report. Lieutenant-General Heusinger had already begun to outline the situation on the Eastern front when Stauffenberg and Keitel entered the conference room.[5] Hitler turned briefly towards the two officers and acknowledged their salute. Keitel introduced Stauffenberg who, he explained, had come to report on the use of the *Sperr-Divisionen*, which were intended to block the enemy's advance. Hitler shook hands with Stauffenberg and said that first he wanted to hear the end of the report on the general situation. Heusinger continued. Keitel, only half listening to the words, looked nervously around and briefly left the conference room. As was later established, he had suddenly noticed Stauffenberg's absence and had gone out to look for him. (Another report said that General Buhle had gone to find Stauffenberg.) When Keitel returned and took his place behind Hitler, Heusinger, according to his later account, was just ending his report with words to this effect: "West of the Dvina, strong Russian forces are driving northwards. Their spearheads are already south-west of Dvinsk. Unless at long last, the Army Group is withdrawn from Lake Peipus, a catastrophe..." A deafening roar

cut his sentence, dazzling flames shot up and smoke filled the room
—the time was 12.42.

Shortly afterwards Stauffenberg's car stopped at the checkpoint
about 200 metres away, demanding to be let through. The guard,
alerted by the roar of the explosion, refused to open the barrier.
According to one report,[6] Stauffenberg, without wasting words, got
out of the car, went to the guard room to see the duty officer who
knew him and demanded to use his telephone. He dialled, spoke
a few words, put back the receiver and said : "Lieutenant, I am
allowed to pass." The barrier was opened. The logbook entry said :
"12.44, Colonel Stauffenberg passed through." Ninety seconds later
the alarm was sounded. At the outer checkpoint South, Stauffenberg was faced with portable wire entanglements, double sentries
and the duty NCO, Sergeant-Major Kolbe of the Guard Battalion,
who flatly refused to let him pass. Stauffenberg asked to be put
through to the Camp Commandant's ADC and telephoned :
"Colonel Count Stauffenberg speaking, from outer checkpoint
South. Captain, you'll remember we had breakfast together this
morning. Because of the explosion the guard refuses to let me pass.
I'm in a hurry. Colonel-General Fromm is waiting for me at the
airfield." Replacing the receiver he said : "You heard, Sergeant-
Major, I'm allowed through." Kolbe insisted on receiving direct
permission and telephoned again. Captain von Möllendorf's reply
"May pass" cleared the way. Stauffenberg told the driver to hurry.
En route Haeften tossed an unused parcel of explosives out of the
car. Shortly after 1 p.m. the two officers reached the airfield,
boarded the waiting plane, and were airborne at 1.15 p.m.

The distance to be covered was about the same as from Lake
Constance or from Budapest to Berlin, and the flight took two and
a half hours. To Stauffenberg, burning with impatience, the time
must have seemed endless, perhaps agonizing because of the
enforced inactivity and uncertainty after his first decisive action.
Had they carried Hitler's dead body from the wreckage at the
camp? Was the news black-out effective? What about Berlin? Had
they sounded the alarm in time? Had things worked better than
five days ago? Were they already on his tracks? When the air crew
were interrogated, they were unable to give any information about
the two officers' conversation during the flight. There are two
accounts of the landing : one says that the aircraft flew over the
outer suburbs of Berlin at about 15.45 and landed shortly afterwards at Rangsdorf. The two officers could see nothing unusual.
Haeften first went to telephone the Bendlerstrasse. When Olbricht
answered, Haeften gave the code word which signified that the
attempt on Hitler had succeeded. Olbricht's first words made it

clear that he had not yet issued the signal for action and three hours had passed since the explosion! Agitated, Stauffenberg demanded that they act without waiting for his arrival and rushed to the car. As his own driver was not yet there, he asked for an Air Force vehicle to be put at his disposal. The second report, based on later information, said that Stauffenberg landed at 16.05 and that the conspirators at the Bendlerstrasse had taken action, despite his absence, ten minutes earlier.[7]

On his drive through Berlin, Stauffenberg saw nothing conspicuous either in the suburbs or in the inner city: it was a calm, bright summer afternoon and the people had no idea what was afoot. He arrived with Haeften at the Bendlerstrasse between 16.30 and 16.45.

Meanwhile, three-quarters of an hour had passed since Olbricht and Merz von Quirnheim had set the revolt going. It is known that at 15.50 they brought out the long-secreted file of orders. The liaison officer, Oertzen, was given the vital order to be handed over to General Kortzfleisch, the Wehrmacht Commandant of Berlin, which would command him to alert all units of the Guard Battalion, the Spandau garrison, and two Army Weapons Training Schools. The General, who was not privy to the plot, was summoned to the Bendlerstrasse. To speed things up, Lieutenant-General von Hase, the Berlin garrison Commander, who came under the Wehrmacht Command, was informed directly by General Olbricht. Major Hayessen, acting as liaison officer, was on his way to Hase, who was awaiting instructions. By 16.10 the troops under Hase's command had been alerted, and the Commander told to report for orders at the garrison HQ, No. 1 Unter den Linden. At 16.00, Lieutenant-Colonel Bernardis had begun to alert the troops outside Berlin, i.e. the Armoured Troops School in Krampnitz; the Armoured Training Classes in Gross-Glienicke, which were ordered forthwith to occupy the broadcasting stations of Königswusterhausen and Zeesen; the Infantry School in Döberitz; the Grossdeutschland Reserve Brigade; the Cadet School and the NCO School in Potsdam. At 16.15 Merz gave the alarm to the guards in the Bendler block, who were part of the Guard Battalion. Klausing took orders to the duty officer, Second Lieutenant Arnds, to block all exits and to stop all transit traffic. Olbricht gave verbal instructions to the officer to use force if any SS units moved up.

The first signals and orders having been issued, Olbricht went to see Colonel-General Fromm, who was at the time listening to a reporting officer. Olbricht begged him to interrupt the audience, and when he was alone with Fromm[8] he informed him that Hitler had been killed. General Fellgiebel, he said, had given the news. Olbricht proposed that Fromm, as Commander-in-Chief of the Reserve Army, should act at once and issue the "Valkyrie" alert to the Military District Commanders. Fromm hesitated : he said he could take such a step only after having satisfied himself personally that Hitler was dead. He proposed to telephone Keitel. After Haeften's report, Olbricht was certain that Hitler was dead. He was bound to expect Fromm's co-operation when confirmation was obtained. He picked up the telephone and demanded an urgent call to Führer HQ. To his surprise he was put through immediately. The time was 16.10. Keitel answered. He confirmed that an attempt had taken place, but the Führer was alive and only slightly injured. He said he would tell Fromm more about it later; at the moment he was in conference with Marshal Graziani, while the Führer was conferring with Mussolini. Keitel then asked : "By the way, where is your Chief of Staff, Colonel Stauffenberg?"

Fromm replied that Stauffenberg had not yet reported to him. Olbricht thereupon left the room without revealing the slightest sign of agitation.

Meanwhile, Merz had continued to put out "Valkyrie" orders. At 16.20 the President of the Berlin Police, Count Helldorf, was summoned to the Bendlerstrasse. At about the same time, Beck came, wearing a dark civilian suit. He had been fetched by Schwerin. With him, or shortly after him, arrived all the confederates. They had been holding themselves ready nearby. Other people in the building, who were not involved in the plot, did not notice their arrival.

Tension was high when the conspirators learned that Stauffenberg had just driven into the courtyard. He and Haeften bounded up the stairs and entered Olbricht's big office : Stauffenberg, tall and slim, walking even more lightly than usual, flushed and out of breath, reported briefly what had happened and what he himself had seen : a tremendous explosion, flames and smoke, and the hut being wrecked. "As far as one can judge, Hitler is dead."[9] In reply, Stauffenberg was told that inadequate and contradictory information had been received through General Thiele.[10] The impression, he was told, was that the attempt had failed and that was the reason why the signal to launch the revolt had not been given. Keitel, they said, had just been on the phone to Fromm and confirmed that there had been an attempt, but that Hitler had got away unscathed. Stauffenberg declared that, after what he himself had seen, Keitel was trying to deceive them and playing for time. It was unlikely that anyone could still be alive, and at the very least Hitler must have been severely wounded. There was only one thing they could do now: use every minute and act. He demanded to be put through to Hofacker in Paris and told him that decisive steps must now be taken in the French capital. For the time being, it was decided to delay the despatch of Hansen and Dr John to Madrid. John was present at this meeting.

Count Helldorf reported that the police were standing by. Olbricht informed him of the attempt on Hitler and of the imminent proclamation of a state of siege; the police would be under the orders of the Army and Helldorf was to issue the appropriate orders. The President of the Police was about to leave when Beck insisted[11] that Helldorf be told that the situation was not at all clear. They must all agree on how to face any statements their adversaries might put out. Beck declared his own attitude and begged all present to make it theirs, too: no matter what was being put about, irrespective even of what was true—ar far as he, Beck, was concerned, Hitler was dead. That would determine his action from now on. And to avoid confusion among their own ranks, they must not deviate from that line. It would take hours to secure incontrovertible evidence from HQ that Hitler—and not his double—was alive. By then the coup in Berlin would have to be concluded. Everyone felt that Beck's clear and determined statement made it impossible any longer to shirk the crucial issue. Beck thus proclaimed his wholehearted support for Stauffenberg, who, of course, had already made his decision.

Olbricht urged that Fromm be told what had happened before news from outside could reach him. As Beck thought it advisable not to act as spokesman at this stage, Olbricht and Stauffenberg went to see Fromm. Olbricht told the Colonel-General that Stauffenberg had just confirmed Hitler's death. Fromm said Keitel had assured him Hitler was alive. He added that in these circumstances he could not give the all clear for Operation "Valkyrie". Stauffenberg retorted: "Field-Marshal Keitel is lying, as usual. I myself saw Hitler being carried out dead." "In view of this," Olbricht interposed, "we have sent out the code signal for internal unrest to the Military District Commanders." Fromm leapt to his feet—and according to the account he himself later gave in the camp—banged the table and shouted: "This is rank insubordination What do you mean by 'we'? Who gave the order?" Olbricht: "My Chief of Staff, Colonel Merz von Quirnheim." Fromm: "Fetch Colonel Merz at once!" Merz entered and admitted to having sent out the code signal without Fromm's approval. Whereupon Fromm declared: "You are under arrest. That's all for the moment." Another report quoted this additional exchange: "Go to the teleprinter, at once, and stop the issue of orders." Merz replied drily:

307

"Colonel-General, you've just put me under arrest; my freedom of movement is therefore restricted." And he sat down in a chair.[12]

At that moment Stauffenberg, completely composed and calm, said : "Colonel-General, I myself set off the bomb at Hitler's conference. It was as if a fifteen-centimetre shell had hit the place. No one in that room can still be alive." Fromm : "Count Stauffenberg, the attempt has failed. You must shoot yourself at once." Stauffenberg : "I shall do nothing of the sort." Olbricht intervened and, turning to Fromm, said : "Colonel-General, now is the time for action. If we fail to strike now, our Fatherland will be ruined for ever." Fromm : "Olbricht, does this mean that you, too, are taking part in this coup d'état?" Olbricht : "Yes, sir. But I am only on the fringe of the circle that will take over power in Germany." Fromm : "Then I formally put all three of you under arrest." Olbricht, speaking with determination : "You can't arrest us. You don't realize who's in power. It's we who are arresting you."

There was an argument and a scuffle between Olbricht and Fromm. The incident ended with the entry of two young officers—Haeften was one of them—from the map room. They pointed their pistols at Fromm. He gave in and was taken to his Adjutant's room next door where he was put under Major von Leonrod's guard. The telephone cables were cut. Olbricht made it clear to Fromm that they would shoot if he tried to escape. At the door, Fromm walked into Hoepner, an old acquaintance of his, who regretted meeting the Colonel-General in such a situation and told him that he was to take over his office. Fromm said something to the effect : "Yes, Hoepner, I'm sorry too, but there's nothing else I can do. I believe the Führer is not dead and that you are wrong. I can't sign the 'Valkyrie' order for you." The officers of the branch were then summoned to the map room adjoining Fromm's office. Hoepner, attired in the uniform of a Colonel-General and accompanied by a Captain with his pistol drawn, briefly told them of Hitler's sudden death and of the steps taken to protect the Reich.[13]

Men of the Guard Battalion unit on duty at the Bendlerstrasse were posted at all entrances to the building and the bomb craters at the back of it by Lieutenant Cords, who had been put in charge of the sentries at the gates. Anyone entering the building had to produce an orange pass signed by Stauffenberg. And no one was allowed to leave the building without a pass or signed orders. Captain Fritzsche was assigned by Stauffenberg to guard the corridor and the map room on the second floor. Stauffenberg's ADCs were Captain Klausing and Second Lieutenants von Kleist, von Oppen and von Hammerstein.

It was shortly before 17.00 when an SS-officer,[14] accompanied by another man, arrived at Olbricht's ante-room. He demanded to see Count Stauffenberg, "on orders from the Chief of the Central Reich Security Office". After a while Stauffenberg entered, greeted Kaltenbrunner's emissary in as civil a manner as he would a guest, and asked him to come into his room. According to Gisevius, he soon returned, laughing : Herr Piffrader, he said, had been instructed to interrogate him about his astonishingly hasty return from Hitler's HQ. By way of reply he had put Piffrader under arrest. In fact, the SS-Oberführer, who had come accompanied by his Adjutant and two detectives in civilian clothes, had been ordered to arrest Colonel Stauffenberg unostentatiously. It had been assumed that Stauffenberg would be at the Bendlerstrasse. At that time they still knew nothing of what had happened there. Piffrader and his Adjutant were arrested by Colonel Jäger and Lieutenant von Kleist and put under guard in a separate room. The guard at the gate arrested the men waiting in the car as well so as to prevent any news from leaking out. An Obersturmführer of the SS who was seen near the building was also taken into custody.

Meanwhile, the General in command of Berlin, Kortzfleisch, had arrived and asked to see Colonel-General Fromm. When he was taken to Colonel-General Hoepner instead, he refused to recognize his authority, loudly protested that Hitler was not dead and said he would not declare a state of siege in Berlin. Olbricht was fetched, who in turn sent for Beck. But Kortzfleisch continued to protest and invoked his oath of allegiance. With unusual ferocity, Beck snapped at him : Was he talking of an oath? Hitler had broken his oath on the constitution and his word of honour to the German people a hundred times over. How dare Kortzfleisch invoke his oath to a perjurer! But the General remained adamant. He was arrested and put in Olbricht's room. General von Thüngen, who was waiting, was sent to the Hohenzollerndamm to take over the command of the Military District. Kortzfleisch managed to escape for a moment from Olbricht's office. The sentry raised his gun to shoot, Captain Fritzsche intervened, the General was seized near the staircase and again put under arrest in the room of Olbricht's Adjutant. During the argument about his release, Kortzfleisch is reported to have said : "Let me go home and leave me in peace."

By 17.00 the leaders of the units under the garrison Commander had been given their marching orders and directives. At 17.30 all detachments involved in Operation "Valkyrie", including those outside Berlin, had been alerted.

The second phase of the alert which had to be put into action via the teleprinter branch had begun between 16.30 and 17.00. Captain Klausing arrived at the signals bunker with the Order No. 1, signed by Witzleben and Stauffenberg, to be sent to the Commanders-in-Chief in the field and the Military District Commanders. From 17.35 onwards, the signals went out to twenty recipients. The second of the prepared General Orders, signed by Fromm and by Stauffenberg, and calling on the new Executive to take immediate action was written down by a woman secretary under Merz's supervision and handed over by Klausing. It was sent out from 18.30 onwards. Another teleprinter signal over Witzleben's signature announced the appointment of Colonel-General Hoepner as Commander-in-Chief of the Reserve Army and in the home territory.

At 18.30 confirmation was received that the Government quarter had been sealed off by three companies of the Guard Battalion. No General or Minister was allowed to cross the barrier line.

So far the broadcasts on the German radio had contained nothing specially noteworthy. But at 18.45 the Deutschlandsender broadcast the communiqué from Führer HQ which had been trailed for many hours : it said that an attempt with explosives had been made on the Führer. A number of his entourage had been seriously wounded, several others only slightly. He himself had escaped with minor injuries. There was surprise and consternation. Was the purpose of the communiqué merely to mislead? Beck thought this was quite probable. He therefore felt it doubly urgent for himself to make a broadcast. But the orders to seize the two transmitters, which had been sent out two hours earlier, had not yet been carried out. Urgent enquiries by Stauffenberg, Merz and Olbricht followed. Soon incoming telephone calls began to show the impact of the communiqué. From the commanding officers in the Reich who had meanwhile received the alert orders and were in disagreement with one another, came incessant requests to speak to Fromm or, as he was said not to be available, to Stauffenberg. In reply, Stauffenberg declared with utmost certainty that Hitler was dead, Keitel was lying and the broadcast communiqué was intended to deceive. The Army, he said, had taken over, the action would be continued and had not met with any obstacle so far....[15] He arranged for an urgent teleprinter message of similar content to be sent to all Commanders-in-Chief at 19.15. Meanwhile Merz in his steadfast, matter-of-fact, but audacious manner saw to it that orders were transmitted and carried out; General Olbricht explained the as yet not entirely clear happenings to the thirty-five or forty officers of his branch whom he had summoned.[16] There was a striking contrast between the conspirators, who were up to their eyes in work and under extreme strain, and the growing number of others waiting in idleness or agony; some of these, who had been assigned specific tasks were waiting for the signal to get going (like John, Gisevius, Gerstenmaier, Sack, Counts Schulenburg, Yorck, Hardenberg and others); then there were quite a number who were only accidentally involved and whose subdued, impatient or completely uninformed talk increased the tension in the offices and corridors.

By 19.00 the Artificers' School had at last begun to set up their base at the Armoury and the Army Weapons Training School had done so at the Royal Palace : but the bulk of the troops had not yet arrived. The first tanks were expected at about 19.30. Only then would the conspirators be sure that they had gained their first start over the SS. The Commander of the Armoured Troops School II in Krampnitz, Colonel Gläsemer, reported for duty. But as he hesitated to undertake the task he was given, Merz had him arrested on the fourth floor and put under a Captain's guard. The main body of Gläsemer's troops were again ordered to stand by at the Victory Column while some detachments were to secure the General Army Office. No news had yet been received of an attack on the Reich Chancellery and Goebbels' Ministry or of the seizure of the Broadcasting Station. Colonel Jäger was despatched to Town HQ Unter den Linden to instruct the Commandant quickly to assemble a reinforced assault party, march on the Propaganda Ministry and arrest Goebbels.[17] New moves were made with a view to speeding up the occupation of the radio transmitters. Beck was urging them to hurry : it was vital to get the appeals to the German people broadcast before Hitler could speak.

Shortly after 19.00, telephone connections were established with Army Group North in the Baltic area, for which Colonel-General Beck had asked. General Kinzl, Chief of the Group's General Staff, answered and was told by Stauffenberg that from now on all orders would be issued from Berlin by Beck and Witzleben. Beck then took over the telephone and formally ordered immediate steps to withdraw the Army Group from its hopelessly exposed position to the Dvina and East Prussia. This action by Beck might still have saved the Army Group. This was the order the Chief of Operations Branch (as there was no longer a Chief of General Staff) had tried to get issued at noon. Both that and later efforts proved abortive.[18]

At about that time Colonel Merz received a telephone call from the Organization Branch of the Army High Command in East Prussia reliably informing him that the attempt on Hitler had failed.

Then came the report that the first tanks had arrived in the centre of the city. Scouts reported that extensive formations of armoured troops and infantry were moving up along the major approach roads. From now on even the man in the street realized that something out of the ordinary was happening. People assumed it to be connected with the attempt on the Führer which had been reported on the radio an hour earlier.

At 19.30, Field Marshal von Witzleben arrived at the Bendler-strasse. He had come from OKW at Zossen.. In uniform, with his cap and Marshal's baton, he entered Fromm's office, briefly saluted Stauffenberg, respectfully reported to Beck and went with him to Fromm's study. A few minutes later Beck called in Stauffenberg and then Schwerin. As far as could be observed from the ante-room, the Marshal was mercilessly critical. Now and then he banged his fist on the table and Beck replied heatedly. Counts Stauffenberg and Schwerin stood like "marble columns".[19]

After 20.00, with the Beck–Witzleben dialogue still going on, tension and uneasiness in the other rooms began to mount. And it was fanned by conflicting rumours coming in from outside. Tele-phone messages were pouring in, confirming that the orders from the Bendlerstrasse had been received. But for many recipients they created a conflict of loyalties because Keitel had issued instructions from HQ forbidding the acceptance of any orders emanating from the Bendlerstrasse. In some cities, for example in Paris, they were ready to carry out the "Valkyrie" order. At 20.00 Merz had tele-phoned Colonel Finckh in the French capital : "Tanks on the move. Carry on." But in Berlin things were moving very slowly indeed. Even the vital first objectives, such as the occupation of the Broadcasting Station and Goebbels' Ministry, and the arrest of the top leaders of the SS, had not yet been attained, despite repeated enquiries and the despatch of forces for these purposes.

Witzleben, the most senior officer in authority, whom many had expected to clarify the position, left the Bendlerstrasse again at 20.15. Very little became known of what had been discussed but the impression was that the Marshal thought the whole enterprise had failed and was not going to have anything more to do with it.[20]

At about 20.15 news came via Major Hayessen from Town HQ Unter den Linden that Major Remer was with Goebbels, had in fact been there for some time, and was not getting on with his job. Hase drove to the Military District HQ. For about one and a half hours the Guard Battalion had apparently taken no action and a go-ahead Staff officer was sent to take Remer's place. But the take-over failed. Nor had Colonel Jäger managed to launch the attack on Goebbels' Ministry because, he said, he had not suc-ceeded in obtaining the necessary troops.

Olbricht and Stauffenberg tried everything to marshal more troops, even calling on any police forces that might be drawn in. Stauffenberg particularly urged Potsdam to despatch at once the reserve unit of the 9th Infantry Regiment. Meanwhile telephone contact was maintained with the Military Districts throughout the Reich. Nuremberg had received the state of siege order at 19.45. Vienna came up at 20.30 (General Freiherr von Esebeck), and Stettin shortly afterwards. Hoepner took both calls. Both Vienna and Stettin had already received an order from Keitel. In the end Hoepner, as he later told the People's Court, gave up contesting Keitel's instructions. But the telephone calls from Field-Marshal von Kluge were even more disturbing. Beck tried to pin him down by reminding him of their earlier discussions and of the fact that he, too, was privy to the plot. Beck was agitated, and sought to persuade Kluge; yet as the only witness to the conversation, a young officer, recalled, his language was remarkably "operational", considering the fever pitch of the situation. To him, Beck appeared like a vision of the "Old Fritz" at that moment . . . Kluge's replies seemed to be unsatisfactory. He was obviously speaking in the presence of Stülpnagel and Hofacker. The Resistance leaders in Paris reported that so far everything was going according to plan.

Colonel-General Fromm, who had hitherto been under guard in his Adjutant's room, was granted his request to go to his private chambers. He had given his word of honour to Hoepner that he would not attempt to interfere and would not in any way try to seek contact with the outside.

After 21.00 the Deutschlandsender announced that the Führer would shortly make a broadcast and that Reichsführer SS, Himmler, had been appointed Commander-in-Chief of the Reserve Army.

A few minutes later Colonel Köllner came from the signals bunker with the text of HQ orders which had been received by teleprinter for re-issue by the Bendlerstrasse. These orders announced Himmler's appointment and forbade all Military District Commanders to accept any orders from Witzleben, Fromm or Hoepner. Olbricht decided that the HQ orders were not to be put out.

At about that time the Guard Battalion units which had undertaken to guard the Bendler block began to withdraw. All efforts to prevail on them to stay proved futile. These were their Commander's orders, they said : to assemble in the garden near Goebbels' official residence. The only guard left was a detachment of about thirty-five men at the main gate of OKH. More and more reports were coming in from outside of other troops withdrawing from parts of the inner city or of those still on the approach roads turning back. By 21.30 there was not a single tank to be seen in the Government quarter and in the vicinity of the Bendlerstrasse. Incoming telephone calls indicated for the first time that a counter-movement was being organized : General Reinecke, Chief of the General Wehrmacht Office, it was understood, had been ordered to storm the Bendlerstrasse with all available troops and SS units. Counter-orders had also apparently been issued by the Armoured Troops Inspectorate, and these units were said to have been instructed to assemble in Fehrbelliner Platz.

The telephone kept buzzing, and most of the callers wanted to speak to Stauffenberg. He was also taking over conversations with people who were expressing doubts. One eyewitness described how Stauffenberg grabbed the receiver from another speaker, sank into a chair and listened. "I could feel his tension," Otto John's report stated. "Seconds went by, then he spoke loudly and rapidly : 'This is Stauffenberg . . . yes, all orders from the C.-in-C. of the Reserve Army . . . yes, of course . . . that's right . . . all orders are to be carried out immediately. You must occupy all transmitters and signals centres. . . . All resistance must be crushed. . . . It's very likely that counter-orders will be given by Führer HQ. . . . Don't believe them . . . no . . . the Wehrmacht has taken control, nobody except the C.-in-C. of the Reserve Army is entitled to give orders . . . do you understand . . . yes, the Reich is in danger, and as always in times of danger the soldiers take charge. . . . Yes, Witzleben has been appointed Supreme Commander. . . . It's only a formality, you are to occupy all signals centres. . . . Understood? Heil !' " On another occasion Stauffenberg was heard to shout into the receiver : "The time has come for officers, and officers alone, to assert their authority" (KB 298).

Various reports suggest that at about 22.30 Olbricht gathered his officers together in his department. He had already addressed them once or twice earlier that evening. After hearing a brief report from the Second-Lieutenant of the guard at the gate, Olbricht said that, as the Guard Battalion detachment had been withdrawn and no replacements were available, the officers would have to take over the protection of the building themselves. He allocated the various duties. There were no objections. Each of the six exits was to be manned by a General Staff officer. Lieutenant-Colonel von der Lancken was put in charge. Then the officers were dismissed. After this conference individual officers,[21] with Lieutenant-Colonel Herber as their spokesman, returned to Olbricht. "What's the real game?" they wanted to know. Olbricht told them something to this effect : "Gentlemen, for a long time we have been anxiously watching the way things were going. There is no doubt, we're heading for disaster. We have had to take precautions. These are now being put into effect. I beg you to support me."[22] Olbricht was in full control of himself, only the slight redness of his face betrayed his emotion. The atmosphere in the office was grave and heavy: no one dared rebel. So far "nothing had been said or done against the planned coup, although everyone knew that the military leader of the attempted assassination was with us, at the Bendlerstrasse. Of course, the onlookers were separated from the conspirators, but there had been no arguments throughout the afternoon and evening."[23] But now a dangerous mood of rebellion was noticeable in the faces of some of the speakers. The most determined group gathered in the office of Lieutenant-Colonel i.G. Pridun, Olbricht's GSO I, an Austrian, where they pledged themselves to stand by their oath to the Führer and to crush the dangerous revolt. The chief spokesmen, in addition to Pridun, were Lieutenant-Colonel i.G. Herber, Olbricht's GSO II; von der Heyde, who as the real GSO I was Pridun's superior, and Kuban. Ordnance Major Fliessbach had, presumably at Herber's instigation, requested arms from the Spandau arsenal. These had first been refused but were now being delivered by lorry and taken up to the second floor. The officers divided up their tasks and got their tommy-guns ready for action.

While these officers were preparing for armed action, without Olbricht's knowledge, Colonel Müller of the Infantry School in Döberitz reported to him. It was about 22.40. Müller had come to ask for written authority to take over command at the School. He said he was prepared to launch an immediate attack on the transmitter and to put an end to the delay that had arisen through the Commander's absence. He proposed to send the demonstration battalion, which was just returning from a night exercise, to take over guard duty at the Bendlerstrasse. The orders, dictated by Merz and signed by Olbricht, were the last to be issued.

It is still not known exactly what happened in the next few minutes: the conspirators and others involved in the enterprise were in a state of excitement and agitation; it was difficult to know what was going on at different places. All this explains why the reports by survivors—inasmuch as they gave any account of the events at all—differ so greatly. The time was about 22.50 and the commotion and noise in the corridors indicated that there was another incident afoot. A group of about six or eight officers and NCOs, armed with pistols, tommy-guns and hand-grenades and led by Herber broke into General Olbricht's room. At the threshold, Herber demanded an explanation from Olbricht. His enquiries from HQ, he said, had shown that Olbricht's information was apparently wrong. Until everything was cleared up, neither Olbricht nor Major Georgi would be allowed to leave the room. If they tried, Herber and his men would shoot. Olbricht, seeking to calm Herber, said he himself knew no more than what he had told the officers, and he suggested that they should ask Colonel-General Fromm.[24] His son-in-law, Georgi, had nothing to do with the matter. Stauffenberg looked in, but turned immediately to leave again. Herber's men tried to hold him back, but a moment later he managed to push his way into the ante-room, and from there through Merz's adjoining office into the corridor. Both he and Haeften ran along it. Shots were fired after Stauffenberg, possibly by Fliessbach or Herber, and he was heard to shout: "What's up? Who is that shooting?" Some ten shots were fired. According to Herber's later evidence, he himself was shot at when he appeared in the corridor. From inside, apparently from Merz's room, two shots rang out, aimed at the armed men in Olbricht's ante-room where Schwerin, Yorck, Klausing, Gerstenmaier and Berthold Stauffenberg were waiting at that moment. A woman secretary whom Claus Stauffenberg overtook in the corridor noticed how he suddenly jerked, having apparently been hit in the left arm or in the back. Bleeding, he moved on. Meanwhile, Georgi had also managed to force his way out of Olbricht's room and into the ante-room. In a brief-case he was carrying papers Olbricht had just handed to him with orders not to let them fall into the hands of the Gestapo. It was virtually impossible to pass along the corridor because of the shooting, but thanks to some lucky chance Georgi managed to get out of the Bendler block at 23.05. Klausing, too, was able to escape, but Gerstenmaier was driven back. After about five minutes the shooting in the corridor was over. The intruders challenged everyone at gun point: "For or against the Führer?" General Olbricht was put under arrest in his own office. Later, at about 23.15, Merz von Quirnheim and Captain Ramin, who had only that day taken up his duty as Merz's ADC, and Olbricht were disarmed and taken by a strong armed escort (including Heyde, Herber and Fliessbach) along the corridor. The others remained under guard in Merz's room.

In the front rooms the intruders met Hoepner and Beck, Stauffenberg and Haeften.[25] They demanded to see Colonel-General Fromm. Where was he? Hoepner pointed to the floor below, to the General's official quarters.

Seconds later Fromm, flanked by armed men, appeared in the door of his office. He told those present that he would now deal with them in the same way as they had treated him in the afternoon. Brandishing a pistol he shouted: "Put down your weapons!"

316

One report says that Haeften raised his pistol and aimed at Fromm. Stauffenberg waved him off, apparently determined to let the inevitable take its course. Fromm declared "those in the room" under arrest. When asked to lay down his weapons, Colonel-General Beck replied : "You wouldn't demand that of me, your former Commanding officer. I will draw the consequences from this unhappy situation myself." As Beck reached for the revolver lying behind him on his suitcase, Fromm warned him to keep the gun pointed at himself. Beck said a few more words : "At a time like this I think of the old days . . ." Fromm cut him short : "We don't want to hear about that now. I ask you to stop talking and do something." Beck said something else and fired, but the bullet only grazed his head and he reeled back. "Help the old man," Fromm said, whereupon two of the escorting officers approached Beck who had slumped into a chair. Fromm told them to prise the pistol from him, but Beck resisted. Meanwhile, turning to the others in the office, Fromm said : "Now you, gentlemen, if you have letters you want to write you'll have a few moments to do so." Olbricht said he would like to. Fromm invited him to sit down. "Come over to the round table where you used to face me." Hoepner was writing at Fromm's desk, the others stood in silence. Fromm left the room for a while.

Meanwhile a platoon from the Army Weapons School had arrived. The men were about to be detailed to various defence duties in the building when, between 23.00 and 23.15 a Company Commander of the Guard Battalion, Lieutenant Schlee, moved up with fairly strong forces, threw a ring of sentries round the building, occupied the entrance and the signals bunker and proceeded to make arrests. When Fromm re-entered his office he was accompanied by officers of Schlee's assault party and the former Commander of the Guard Battalion, Lieutenant-Colonel Gehrke. He said : "Right, gentlemen. Are you ready? Please hurry up, so as not to make it too hard for the others." Hoepner put the page he had written on the table, Olbricht asked for an envelope and sealed his letter. Fromm then made this announcement : a summary court martial,[26] which he had set up, had just passed the death sentence on four officers—"Colonel in the General Staff, Merz; Infantry General Olbricht; this Colonel—I cannot bring myself to name him—and this Lieutenant." With these words he ordered a previously assigned young officer standing next to him to carry out the sentences in the courtyard. In view of the large number of people present, he once more pointed out the four condemned men : "This gentleman here, the Colonel; this General with the Knight's Cross; this Colonel in the General Staff and this

Lieutenant." The four were taken away, Beck, still dazed, asked for another pistol. One of the five officers standing behind his chair handed it to him. Fromm asked Hoepner to follow him, and the two crossed the empty little map-room into Stauffenberg's study. They returned shortly afterwards, and Fromm gave orders to take the Colonel-General to the Wehrmacht's remand prison. According to Hoepner's later evidence, Fromm gave him, as a former friend, the choice between shooting himself and arrest. Hoepner chose the latter. After the two men had left the room a shot rang out behind them. Even after aiming a second bullet at himself, Beck was still alive. Fromm asked an officer of the Guard Battalion to give him the *coup de grâce*. The officer could not bring himself to do it, and passed on the order to one of his subordinates. The sergeant shot Beck in a small side room.

To date, no one who saw the four sentenced officers on their way down the stairs or witnessed their execution, has given an account of the event. All we have are descriptions by casual eye-witnesses, which vary in detail. In the turmoil and with the, by then, usual black-out against air raids, evidently few people saw the shooting, which took place a few minutes after midnight. The firing squad consisted of ten NCO's under the command of Second Lieutenant Schady. The scene was lit by the headlights of an army truck parked in the yard. It was the courtyard of Nos. 11–13 Bendlerstrasse, which was surrounded by buildings and to which entrance was gained by a large iron gate below the front building. The four officers were led out through the door by which they normally entered to face the tommy-guns of the execution squad, in front of a sand pile placed there for use in air-raids.

The best-supported account says that all four stood in line when they were being shot—the observer remembered particularly the difference in the height of the officers standing side by side with the light shining on them.[27] The sight of the youthful Haeften clinging to life in the face of certain death must have been heart-rending. Olbricht went to his death calmly, without saying a word. Merz is reported to have stepped in front of Stauffenberg when the order to fire was given. Stauffenberg died with the cry on his lips : "Long live our sacred Germany."

Shortly after the shooting, with the bodies still lying on the blood-stained spot where they had fallen, Colonel-General Fromm emerged from the doorway. With a conqueror's bearing, which considering his corpulence was quite impressive, he strode across the yard to review the detachment lined up along one side. He made a brief speech which he ended with "Heil Hitler". Then, while there was still silence all round, he turned in a somewhat forced, pompous manner towards the exit, called for his car and disappeared.

At the same time—it was 00.21—Fromm had this teleprinter signal flashed to all authorities which had previously received orders from Witzleben, Hoepner and Olbricht: "Attempted putsch by irresponsible Generals bloodily crushed. All ring-leaders shot . . ." (KB 76). After Fromm's departure, Major Remer, and shortly after him General Reinecke, appeared at the Army Office. The men suspected of complicity and the secretaries were waiting in their offices to which they had been confined. There was Bernardis, who having been found convulsed with pain, had been brought to the Army Office; von der Lancken, whom Remer himself had arrested; and others, not on the Staff, such as Count Berthold Stauffenberg —wearing naval uniform—Schulenburg, Yorck, Schwerin and Gerstenmaier. Ramin, although he was not involved, was there too. "Gentlemen," General Reinecke addressed them, "you are under arrest. You will hear your sentences from the Führer himself." A search was then made of the more remote premises and further suspects were arrested. Armed men had sealed off each end of the corridor; there was no chance of escaping by the windows, but there were no guards in the rooms. According to Gerstenmaier, even before that the conspirators had begun to burn in the ashtrays any incriminating documents they could lay their hands on. According to another account—which is not borne out by the Kaltenbrunner Reports—the Gestapo seized the iron box and its contents in Olbricht's room. It presumably contained some of the plans. Important documents had previously been removed by Georgi. Gerstenmaier tried to make a get-away. He stepped through the door unhindered and got as far as the back stairs along the corridor, when he was stopped by a major. At Lieutenant-Colonel von der Heyde's orders he was taken into custody in an NCO's office with a single guard watching him. Gerstenmaier was able to form some idea of what was happening from the conversations he overheard. Shortly after his entry the execution squad's salvo could be heard. His friends had as yet no idea of the scene in Fromm's office, the "court martial verdict" or of the execution of the four officers.[28] Towards 1 a.m. strong SS forces broke into the building and occupied every room and entrance. They were led by SS-Hauptsturmführer Skorzeny, the man who had abducted Mussolini from the Gran Sasso nine months before. Skorzeny had been taken from the night express on its way to Vienna when it was realized that he would be needed. He was soon followed by the Head of the Central Security Office (RSH), Kaltenbrunner. Without as yet knowing who was friend or foe, Skorzeny introduced himself to each individually and, after various misunderstandings, sought to bring some order into the confused situation. He had the eight men suspected of complicity taken to Merz's room, where he personally searched them for arms and ripped off their orders and decorations, which he flung into an upturned steel helmet behind him. With Skorzeny's SS men standing guard over them, the prisoners were then forced to listen to Hitler's broadcast over the "Grossdeutscher Rundfunk" in silence. With the exception of Ramin, they all felt that they were already on the way to their own execution. They were only waiting to be fetched. At last, hand-cuffed in pairs, they were taken two at a time, first to Fromm's rooms and from there downstairs to the courtyard. They were told to get into cars and were driven away to the RSH prison in the Prinz-Albrecht-Strasse.[29] Upstairs in the various offices the troops were camping down, apparently without really knowing why they were still there. The women secretaries and anyone else that might have been involved in the events were told to write reports on what had happened. No one was allowed to leave the building. Some of the younger officers who had taken part, like Fritzsche, Klausing, Oppen, Kleist, Hammerstein and Cords, had, however, managed to get away. The attempt to shed some light on events was hampered by the fact that the chief participants were dead. During the night the SS officer, Piffrader, was bitterly reproached for not having prevented the executions. And Colonel-General Fromm, who had gone from the Bendlerstrasse to see Goebbels, was that same night taken into "honorary custody".

Beck's body was now taken downstairs from the little room next to Fromm's office, where it had been left. Even on the following day traces of blood could still be seen. The other four bodies were still lying at the place of execution. Now all five were put on a truck and taken away by a sergeant to be buried during the night. No one was to mention the names of the dead or discuss what had happened, and the place of burial was to remain secret. The same night the sergeant gained entrance to the old churchyard of the Matthäus Church in Schöneberg along the Grossgörschenstrasse, where he and his companion dug a grave for the five bodies. Two police sergeants, whom the verger had summoned, were given no answers to their questions. They shone their torches on the bodies : three officers "with Generals' stripes", one Lieutenant, and an elderly man in a dark suit. . . . The area superintendent was wakened and asked to come to the cemetery. After a hint by the sergeant from the Bendlerstrasse, he agreed not to make any further enquiries and to lend a hand with the job. The five men set to work and covered the dead with soil. As dawn broke on

July 21, the burial site was deserted, with nothing to indicate its location.[31]

In Berlin all the troops that had been alerted were again returning to their barracks. But in some other cities[32]—for example, in Prague, Vienna, Frankfurt and Paris—the state of emergency ordered by Fromm and Witzleben still continued.

In Paris, where the ground had been most carefully prepared, the revolt proceeded according to plan.[33] The first of the prearranged signals indicating that the attempt was to take place on that day—the code word "Exercise"—was passed in the morning from the Quartermaster-General's office in Zossen to Colonel Finckh, the Deputy Chief of Staff to the C.-in-C., West, whose office was in the Rue du Surène. At about the same time, the code word from Berlin was received by Lieutenant-Colonel von Hofacker at the Military Governor's office. The two men quickly telephoned each other to confirm. They knew that Stauffenberg, carrying the explosives in his brief-case, was now on the way to East Prussia. The fate of the Reich hung in the balance while they themselves, with an outward air of casualness, still had to carry out their routine duties on that sultry summer day. Their special task would only start when the second code word was issued. Hofacker informed Stülpnagel and the confederates.

At about 14.30, Finckh received from Zossen the second of the prearranged signals "Finished", denoting that the attempt on Hitler had been carried out. His job now was to inform General Blumentritt, who was acting for the C.-in-C. West at St. Germain, that there had been a putsch by left-wing SS circles in Berlin, that Hitler was dead, that a new Government had been formed under Beck and Goerdeler, and that Witzleben had assumed the Supreme Command of the Wehrmacht. Finckh set out at once for St. Germain-en-Laye, about twenty kilometres away.

The only thing Stülpnagel and his men could do during the oppressive hours that followed was to sit and wait. His luncheon guest at the Hôtel Raphael had been Professor Weniger, the author of a work on "Goethe and the Generals". They soon parted and Stülpnagel went for a little stroll on the roof-garden of the Raphael, as usual supporting his back with the left hand. According to Teuchert, Hofacker told him he did not rate the chance of a successful attempt very high, but he was convinced that, once launched, the enterprise must be carried through no matter what risk : "We can't worry now whether everybody will keep his oath. But if this thing goes wrong, it'll certainly be the hangman for us."

The unbearable tension was relieved only after 16.30, when Stauffenberg, back at the Bendlerstrasse, spoke on the telephone to Hofacker. In a few hurried words he told him that he himself had seen a big flame leaping from the hut, and that he was convinced that Hitler could no longer be alive. "The way to action is open," he said.

Hofacker rushed over to Stülpnagel to report what he had heard. Together with the General and Colonel von Linstow, his Chief of Staff who was initiated into the plot, they began to set their plans in motion. They first summoned General Oberhäuser, the most senior German signals officer in France. He was instructed to cut all radio and telephone communications between France and Germany which were under his command, except the lines needed for traffic with Berlin. After these precautions the Resistance leaders in Paris considered it impossible for their adversaries in the Reich to interfere by countermanding signals and orders, especially as there was bound to be confusion in Germany in the next few hours. Furthermore, Oberhäuser was ordered to occupy the Paris transmitter with the help of a number of men who had been told part of the plan.[34]

Having seen Oberhäuser, Stülpnagel spoke to the Chief of his military administration, Dr Michel, who was not given any assignment for the time being. The next to report was the City Commandant of Greater Paris, Lieutenant-General von Boineburg-Lengsfeld, and his Chief of Staff, Colonel von Unger. Both had been summoned by telephone. They, too, were told by Stülpnagel that according to news just received a rebellion by the SS in Berlin had removed Hitler, and it was feared a dictatorial régime might be formed which would negotiate with Russia. This must be prevented, he said, by quickly arresting the senior SS leaders and SD men in Paris and other French cities. The two officers agreed without reservations to undertake this task. They were given a specially prepared map showing the SD and SS quarters. While still at Stülpnagel's office, Boineburg alerted Lieutenant-Colonel von Kräwel, Commander of No. 1 Garrison Regiment. The time was nearly 18.00.

Meanwhile, at St Germain, Finckh had announced Hitler's death and the formation of the Beck–Goerdeler Government. It was about 15.30. General Blumentritt—tall, hefty, dark-haired and wearing pince-nez—was on the side of the anti-Hitler movement. But the jovial and agile General, who was of Bavarian extraction, had not been told anything of the day's preparations. Without any sign of dismay at Finckh's disclosures, he tried to contact Field-Marshal Kluge at La Roche-Guyon. But he only succeeded in

322

getting hold of General Speidel. With the Normandy battle reaching its climax, the Field-Marshal had gone to the front as usual. As Blumentritt was afraid that the telephone might be tapped, he merely hinted at what had happened and said that he would go over to see Speidel personally. Meanwhile, neither Blumentritt nor Speidel were in a position to take any action without Kluge's knowledge and orders and, therefore, had to await the Field-Marshal's return.

Only the previous evening Kluge had moved to La Roche-Guyon battle headquarters and personally taken charge of Rommel's Army Group which had been without a Commander since July 17. So far Speidel had not found a suitable opportunity for tackling the difficult job of telling Kluge of Rommel's plans and preparations, which were now far advanced. Besides, Speidel himself had apparently been given no hint of the imminence of the revolt by Hofacker after the latter's return from Berlin on July 18. From 9 a.m. until the afternoon of the 20th July, Kluge had been in conference at a concealed spot in a wood, with operational commanders of the gravely threatened eastern Normandy front. No one present at the meeting, not even the senior leaders of the front-line SS units, made any secret of their view that the position was hopeless. Now these men's main concern were the immediate exigencies of battle. And they found it hard to accept that Hitler was responsible for everything that was happening in those days to themselves and their troops. But, as the war diary drily records, they all agreed that "with what troops we have left a change of battle tactics offers no solution to our difficulties and large-scale measures, as for example the complete evacuation of the Mediterranean and Biscay sectors, must be considered". It is not certain whether the advocates of this idea realized its implications—but Kluge certainly knew that until then the entire strategy had been dictated by Hitler. Kluge, a master tactician and skilful field commander, must have admitted to himself that these commanding officers were right to rebel, that their criticism, even if they did not know it, was directed at Hitler alone and that nothing was less likely than their demands being fulfilled.

Kluge returned between 17.00 and 18.00 to La Roche-Guyon, where Speidel was waiting to report to him. Still preoccupied with what he had just heard at the military conference, Kluge listened to Speidel's brief account of the latest developments on other sectors of the front, followed by Blumentritt's news that Hitler was dead and a new Government, headed by Beck, had been formed. Speidel added that available reports seemed to leave room for doubt and that it had not yet been possible to obtain confirmation or additional news. But Blumentritt had said he might call personally and he would surely be able to explain the position in more detail. Kluge said nothing and showed no emotion. As was the practice on important occasions, he asked for Field-Marshal Sperrle, the Air Commodore of the Third Air Fleet, to come over. He also gave instructions for the Military Governor and his Chief of Staff to be summoned to La Roche-Guyon at 20.00.

The summons reached Stülpnagel at 18.15, just as he and his collaborators were discussing the next steps to be taken in Paris and the major provincial cities. About a quarter of an hour later, the officers at the Majestic also heard the surprise announcement from the Deutschlandsender, that Hitler had escaped unscathed from the attempt and that he had received Mussolini as planned. Rumours to this effect had already been going around for about half an hour. Immediately after the announcement, Beck telephoned Stülpnagel. The Colonel-General outlined the position to his old friend; it was just possible that the radio announcement was a trick by the SS; but even if the attempt had really failed—and Beck admitted that there were some clear indications of that—it could make no difference to the operation already launched. The die was cast. The only thing left was to carry on with the fight. Stülpnagel placed himself unreservedly at Beck's disposal and gave an assurance that before long the entire SD and the senior leaders of the SS in Paris and the rest of France would be under lock and key. He could not say what attitude Kluge would adopt and asked Beck to have a word with the Field-Marshal himself. The call was transferred to La Roche-Guyon.

So far, Kluge had only heard the first, still unconfirmed, report of Hitler's death, which had been passed on by Finckh, via Blumentritt and Speidel. When he picked up the receiver he was not surprised to hear Beck say that events had taken a favourable course; but he immediately gave him to understand that he would first have to be absolutely sure of Hitler's death and of the situation at the Führer HQ before agreeing to Beck's request that he, Kluge, should give the signal for a general revolt. While he was talking to Beck he apparently received a written text of the broadcast announcement that the attempt had failed. He now asked more insistently whether Hitler was really dead and what the true situation at HQ was. Beck was neither able to vouch for Hitler's death, nor to give definite news from the "Wolf's Lair", but he countered with the question : was it not irrelevant whether the man was dead or merely severely wounded, if they acted with determination to create a *fait accompli*? Finally, Beck asked Kluge firmly whether he approved of the action in Berlin, and whether or not he put himself under his orders. Kluge evaded a direct "yes" or "no", and said that until he knew definitely what had happened he could make no decision. Beck reminded him of their previous conversations and of what had been agreed between them. But Kluge considered himself absolved from any commitment if the attempt had misfired. He said he would consult with his collaborators and call back in half an hour.

A little later, after 19.00, Kluge was again called to the telephone to speak to Falkenhausen in Brussels. Falkenhausen had already spoken to Beck and was now having to decide what to do about orders from Berlin. There was, after all, the possibility that the attempt had failed. Not long before, on July 9, Kluge had personally told him that it was absolutely necessary to act if a catastrophe was to be averted—and Falkenhausen had begged the Field-Marshal to intervene as quickly as possible. Now Kluge said he would first try to find out what the true situation was and would get in touch with Falkenhausen later.

The first General Order from the new Supreme Commander of the Wehrmacht, von Witzleben, arrived in La Roche-Guyon at 19.28. After many conflicting and confusing signals this was the first service message to reach Kluge. Irrespective of its special content it was couched in the usual terms of a military command. Blumentritt testified that the order made a very strong impression on Kluge, especially as it was accompanied by a supplementary instruction which described the broadcast announcement as false and read: "The Führer is dead. All measures ordered are to be carried out with maximum speed." Kluge now appeared ready to act and discussed the necessary moves with his Chief of Staff. The most important thing was to secure an armistice in the West as quickly as possible. This depended on a cessation of the rocket attacks on England. Immediate orders to this effect would have to be given. The Germans having renounced this form of assault, the enemy would have to be asked to stop the bombing, in return for which the evacuation without resistance of the German-occupied territories in the West would be offered.

Less than half an hour had gone by and Kluge was still talking to Blumentritt, when an order arrived from Field-Marshal Keitel forbidding all commanding officers and authorities to accept and carry out orders from the Fromm–Witzleben–Hoepner group. This created even more confusion. Blumentritt was told to find out from Führer HQ what was really going on. Although contact was established with the "Wolf's Lair", neither Keitel nor Jodl, not even the latter's deputy, Warlimont, could be reached—which was unusual and again made Kluge inclined to believe Witzleben and

325

Beck. A call to the SS commander in Paris, Oberg, who could presumably have been informed by Himmler, also failed to clarify the situation. Even the SS knew no more than what the radio had said. Such was the irony of the situation, that what made Kluge decide in the end was the view of one of the "initiated" at HQ who said he thought the attempt had failed. Blumentritt had managed to get hold of General Stieff in East Prussia, whom he knew well and who told him that the Führer was alive and well. That news determined Kluge's attitude. The attempt having failed, he regarded it as senseless to co-operate with Beck and Witzleben; and he told neither Berlin nor Brussels of his decision, although he had promised to do so.

Round about that time—it was nearly 20.00—the First Garrison Regiment had been alerted and assembled in Paris. Major-General Brehmer, the Deputy-Commandant of the city, explained the position to the battalion Commanders. At the request of the regimental Commander, he gave express instructions that the arrests were not to be made "in the name of the Führer". Lieutenant-Colonel Kräwel discussed the details with the leaders of the assault groups, and Boineburg-Lengsfeld gave orders to storm the SD and SS barracks at 22.30. The focal points of attack were in the Avenue Foch and the Boulevard Lannes.[35] These were the orders : any resistance was to be crushed immediately by force of arms. The arrested leaders were to be taken to the Hotel Continental and the troops to allotted Wehrmacht prisons. Transport was arranged by regimental trucks which were standing by near the barracks to be attacked. Similar alerts had been issued to the major provincial towns.

Meanwhile, Field-Marshal Sperrle had arrived at Kluge's HQ. The two men had talked privately for about a quarter of an hour. Evidently Sperle knew no more than what had been announced. He looked sullen, declined an invitation to dinner and soon left. Immediately after that Karl-Heinrich von Stülpnagel, followed by Caesar von Hofacker and Dr Horst, entered the ancient Norman castle of the Dukes of La Rochefoucauld, nestling under the rocks. The officers were at once taken to Kluge who greeted them with his usual reserve. He then invited them to join him, Blumentritt and Speidel at the table. Without further introduction, he asked Stülpnagel to report what he knew. This was the start of the impassioned argument which went on for several hours and became more and more heated after long distance calls to Berlin and Führer HQ. The outcome was decisive : the 20th of July brought no change in the theatres of war and no change in the fateful course of events between East and West.

Stülpnagel was brief and asked that Lieutenant-Colonel von

Hofacker be allowed to speak. Hofacker gave a powerful account of the start of the revolt, named Stauffenberg as the driving force and author of the plan to kill Hitler, confessed his close ties with him and urged the Marshal to support the revolt now under way by decisive action. Kluge listened in silence and when Hofacker had concluded he gave Blumentritt a nod, indicating that he should read the teleprinter signal which had just come from Keitel. This said that the Führer was alive, the attempted coup by a handful of officers in Berlin had failed, and only orders from Führer HQ were valid. Thereafter Kluge declared the whole enterprise a failure and said it would be irresponsible to take action. Stülpnagel protested violently and demanded to be put through to Berlin again. The connection was quickly established but Merz's voice could be heard only for a few moments before some interference on the line made any further conversation impossible. Stülpnagel left the room for a while and paced up and down on the terrace.

Then they all sat down to dinner with Kluge who, according to Blumentritt, in vain tried to pretend he was light-hearted and at ease and spoke of what he had seen on his tour of the front—with no one paying any attention. They dined in silence "as if they were sitting in a house of the dead." Speidel, one of the three survivors of that dinner in the ducal chambers, said the "sinister atmosphere of that Dantesque hour" was unforgettable. Even before the end of the meal, Stülpnagel requested another interview with the Marshal. Blumentritt and Hofacker were present. Stülpnagel once again tried his hardest to win the Marshal over. He revealed what measures he had taken before leaving Paris. Kluge was outraged; he said he ought to have been consulted in advance, and now Stülpnagel must shoulder the whole responsibility. Stülpnagel retorted that he had been trying in vain to get hold of the Marshal during the afternoon. Blumentritt telephoned Paris. Stülpnagel's deputy, Linstow, informed him that the troops were out, that the arrests were in progress and could no longer be stopped. So far, everything had gone without a hitch. . . .

Stülpnagel pleaded with the Marshal: this was the hour for action, whether Hitler was dead or alive. Hitler did not matter any more, only Germany. He urged Kluge to come out into the open— for the sake of the German people—to seize the opportunity, put an end to the hopeless sacrifice, which he himself had condemned as criminal, and start immediate armistice negotiations with the enemy. There would be no treacherous attack from the rear by SS and SD troops—they had all been arrested. Steps had been taken which would make it possible to negotiate with Eisenhower and Montgomery that very night. The only way of bringing the revolt to a successful conclusion was to create a fait accompli by ending resistance, if necessary by capitulation in the West. Otherwise the revolt would fail.[36] General Blumentritt objected : such action was clear treason and in later days it would be described and despised as nothing but a stab in the back. The dispute, which was carried on in the presence of the other officers, was punctuated by telephone calls to East Prussia : Kluge spoke to Keitel and Warlimont at Rastenburg. The discussion became increasingly heated. And the internal struggle was still further aggravated by urgent telephone calls in rapid succession from the three Army Commanders-in-Chief, whose reports showed how desperate the situation in the field was : the defensive front of Caen was in grave danger, as a powerful, concentrated enemy assault had been launched against it during the evening. If at all possible, reserves would have to be brought up to prevent the German defensive ring from being broken. Hofacker was the chief spokesman. His chivalrous and courageous bearing, his deeply felt love of the Fatherland and his persuasive eloquence made him a counsellor to be heeded. Hofacker reminded Kluge that for many years he had approved of the idea of a revolt and had himself on several occasions shown readiness to co-operate. Yes, but only on condition that Hitler were first removed, Kluge interposed. Even now, he said, he would be willing to co-operate "if Hitler (he used the word 'the swine') were dead".[37] Hofacker kept on pressing him : it was up to the Generals to try to prevent the predictable catastrophe. There were situations in which a war-lord's greatest contribution was capitulation. They could not allow pitiable attrition to the last man and last round of ammunition to continue, and if Hitler was to have his way this would be inevitable. Only the future would show what could be saved by ending resistance in the West. It was quite probable that an invasion from the East could still be prevented. But, Hofacker argued, what the Germans at home would gain by asserting a will and responsibility of their own before the collapse on the front could not be over-rated. Disregarding the question of rank, Hofacker made a final attempt to persuade Kluge : "Herr Feldmarschall, your word and your honour are at stake. The fate of millions of Germans, the honour of the Army lies in your hands. . . ." Gloomy silence followed his words; and then came an irrevocable "No" from Kluge.

Stülpnagel obviously expected that Kluge would now have him arrested. But the Marshal merely said : "Consider yourself suspended from duty." He accompanied Stülpnagel down the flight of stone steps to his car in the courtyard of the castle and said : "I think, the only thing you can do now is to change into civilian clothes and go into hiding." The two men bowed slightly and parted in silence. Kluge did not shake hands with the General. It was nearly 23.00 as the Military Governor's two cars pulled out from under the towering chalk cliffs into the dark night.

Meanwhile, as Linstow had already told Blumentritt on the telephone, everything in Paris had gone according to plan. At 22.30, with deepening darkness, the assault began on the SS quarters. General Boineburg himself had been there half an hour earlier when his regiment assembled near the Avenue Foch. The raid was successful. There was no need to resort to the heavy arms which had been held in readiness. Not a single shot was fired. All SS barracks were attacked simultaneously. The shock troop commanders burst in, guns at the ready, rattled out the sharp order "Hands up!" and declared the inmates under arrest. Major-General Brehmer, to whom Hitler had awarded the "Blutorden" for his part in the march on the Feldherrnhalle in Munich in 1923, led the assault on the senior SS and police Commander's office on the Boulevard Lannes. The sentries offered no resistance. Brehmer, brandishing his weapons, burst into Gruppenführer Oberg's office and told him he was under arrest. Oberg, who was on the phone talking to Ambassador Abetz leapt to his feet and shouted something about an outrage, but surrendered when Brehmer sharply told him there had been a putsch by the SS in Berlin. Oberg even ordered his men to hand over their weapons. He was sure it was all a misunderstanding.

Lieutenant-Colonel von Kräwel broke into the headquarters of the SD in Avenue Foch. His example inspired officers and men— and all of them set to with real enthusiasm. On several occasions the officers had to intervene to prevent acts of violence. Kräwel ordered the officer on duty to issue a routine alert summoning to the office the leaders of the SS and the SD. One by one, as they arrived, they were arrested and disarmed. None of them attempted to resist. The only man missing was the Chief of the Security Service, Dr Knochen. He was discovered in a nightclub, called to his office, and arrested on arrival. After handing over his weapons to Lieutenant-Colonel Kräwel, he was taken to join the other officers already in custody at the Hotel Continental. The prisons of Fresnes, Cherche-Midi and St Denis were bulging with disarmed troops. After an hour—by which time the supporters of the Nazi régime had already won the upper hand in the Bendlerstrasse in Berlin— the set objective had been attained in Paris : the entire forces of the SD and SS had been put out of action and some 1,200 men were in the custody of the Army. Only a few had managed to escape through backyards and gardens.

But the shadow of failure was already creeping over the enterprise. It was still going well and with the exception of very few conspirators in Paris, no one was aware of the impending collapse. Linstow, who as Stülpnagel's deputy at the Hotel Majestic, was keeping watch and issuing directives, had to withstand a deluge of questions and threats, against which he was armed with nothing but his loyalty to the General and his comrades struggling in Berlin. He realized the implications of what was being done and what could no longer be undone. He had heard on the radio that the attempt on Hitler had failed; he also knew that Stülpnagel was nevertheless determined that the men arrested in Paris should face a court martial at dawn. From suspicious and threatening enquiries by Navy Group HQ West, he sensed that counter-forces were getting restive in Paris and that there was a growing danger of the marines being called in against the soldiers. A telephone conversation with Stülpnagel in La Roche-Guyon round about 21.00 indicated that Kluge had not yet made up his mind. But when Linstow rang the Bendlerstrasse once more at 21.30, he was again told that the official announcement on the Deutschlandsender was untrue.

It was nearly 22.45 when Linstow, hardly capable of speaking any longer, told his fellow conspirators at the Hôtel Raphael that all was lost in Berlin. Teuchert and Bargatzky quoted him as saying : "The struggle in Berlin is nearing its end. All is lost. Stauffenberg has just telephoned. He gave the terrible news himself. His murderers were already raging around the corridors outside his room." The two men gave the suffering Linstow what comfort they could, and helped him to abide by his decision not to rescind any of his orders before Stülpnagel's return. He stuck to his decision even when Blumentritt signalled Kluge's order to set the prisoners free. Linstow ignored the order.

The revolt had been crushed in Berlin and Kluge had decided to come out against Stülpnagel. In Paris the telephones were buzzing at midnight. The one thing that became increasingly clear from the numerous, confusing conversations was that the resurgent will of the man who had escaped assassination was marshalling new forces for battle.

There was Admiral Krancke, Commander-in-Chief of Naval Group HQ West, in Paris and in charge of some 5,000 men. At 21.35 Naval HQ received an Order of the Day from Rear-Admiral Dönitz intended to rouse the Navy's "holy wrath against our criminal opponents and their hirelings". Later, Dönitz himself asked Krancke for a pledge to obey only his and Hitler's orders. With growing suspicion, Krancke was following all incoming reports about events in blacked-out Paris. He was determined to take action, but uncertainty and rumours seem to have caused him to hesitate : everywhere there was talk of French Maquis who, in German Army

330

uniform, were said to have captured an Army barracks in a surprise raid after 22.00.

Field-Marshal Sperrle, Commander-in-Chief of the Luftwaffe in the West, whose residence was at the Palais Luxembourg, had laid down that in his zone no orders must be accepted or carried out without previous reference to his office and confirmation of their authenticity. It is not clear whether Sperrle's instructions were given before or immediately after his conversation with Kluge.

Not only Linstow, but also Colonel von Unger and Lieutenant-Colonel von Kräwel, noticed that the situation was beginning to change : they were receiving astonished, indignant and later openly threatening enquiries from the Navy and the Air Force. And while their own troops, having done their job, settled down for the night, the units of the other services in Paris were being alerted. Linstow, Unger and Kräwel always referred to the Military Governor as the source of their orders, adding that he was, at the moment, with Kluge. Subsequent enquiries addressed to Kluge were handled by Colonel Zimmermann, the only officer remaining in St Germain, who said he was unable to give any information and promised news later. The conspirators had the greatest difficulty in averting an attack by Naval and Luftwaffe detachments.

Stülpnagel hardly said a word during the return journey from La Roche-Guyon. He reached Paris after midnight and stopped at the Hôtel Raphael. Hofacker was still seething with anger at Kluge for "not having kept his word", as he put it. Boineburg and Linstow were waiting for them at the club in the Raphael. Stülpnagel and Hofacker told them what had happened and of the vain effort to win over Kluge. They discussed whether it was perhaps still possible to force the Field-Marshal's hand by convening an immediate court martial to try the senior SS leaders under arrest. The sentences would have to be carried out at once. Or was it feasible to arrest Kluge himself and issue orders on his behalf?

It was 01.00. Military music blared from the loudspeaker which had been set up by an orderly officer. And then came Hitler's speech, followed by addresses by Göring and Dönitz and the announcement of Himmler's appointment as Commander-in-Chief of the Reserve Army. To get a better hearing of what was being said the officers left their tables and gathered round the radio. Together they stood motionless : Stülpnagel, Hofacker, Boineburg, Linstow and Finckh. Shortly afterwards, Boineburg received a message from Kräwel that naval units had been alerted to free the SS : Admiral Krancke, he said, had given orders to disarm the Garrison Regiment and to arrest its officers. According to another report, an ultimatum from SS-General Sepp Dietrich was received at about the same time. He threatened to attack Paris with his Armoured Corps unless those under arrest were set free immediately. A telephone call from St Germain announced the imminent arrival of General Blumentritt : he would temporarily take over the Military Governor's duties. Stülpnagel and the other chief confederates expected him to come with warrants for their arrest, possibly even with court martial verdicts.

Stülpnagel gave himself half an hour to think things over. In a last gesture of rebellion, he and Hofacker once more explored every possibility—apparently even the immediate execution of anyone found guilty, an action which might create its own momentum. But they saw no way out. Finckh, too, now regarded their cause as lost. Hofacker was the last to give up. Towards 2 a.m. Stülpnagel ordered Boineburg to release the prisoners, return the files and bring the Gruppenführer to the Hôtel Raphael. Meanwhile, according to one report, Lieutenant-Colonel von Kräwel had decided with a heavy heart to forestall the imminent attack by the marines : he threw open the prison gates and restored their weapons and freedom to the SS.

Boineburg-Lengsfeld now rendered Stülpnagel a most difficult service. He went to the Hotel Continental, where the SS leaders were being held. He had all the proud and courteous self-assurance of a man of the world and was smiling when, monocle fixed, he walked up to the SS men and informed them, with a few explanatory words, that they were released. He requested Oberg, who was still livid with rage, to come to the Hôtel Raphael.

Stülpnagel went to the door to meet the SS leader. Politely, and with complete self-control, he apologized that it had all been a misunderstanding. Oberg, without entirely mastering his anger, replied coldly : "Herr General, you backed the wrong horse." But Stülpnagel showed him the teleprinter signals from Berlin and, supported by Ambassador Abetz—who was still prepared to believe him—he played his part so superbly that even the SS-General seemed to be momentarily satisfied. And despite Stülpnagel's own misgivings, it was agreed to tell the public that the whole affair had been an "exercise". Only Francke, who had arrived at the Raphael simultaneously with Blumentritt and the SD leader Knochen, inveighed against Stülpnagel. The time—it was well after midnight—and the setting—the officers seated in a circle in the hotel foyer—gave the whole scene a "worldly" yet sinister, ghost-like character.

By about 3 a.m. all SS and SD barracks had been evacuated by the Army. Disillusioned officers and men withdrew to their quarters. In other parts of France, too, the arrests that had been made without incident were countermanded. As General Blumentritt's war diary shows, he tried to cover up for Stülpnagel and to help the other confederates to a fairly painless retreat. He did this by allowing himself to be accused of hypocrisy by those who knew the truth about the Paris operation. But ostensibly he acted the part of an investigator and loyal follower of Hitler.

Soon after midnight, even before Hitler's speech was broadcast, Blumentritt suggested in St Germain that Kluge should send a telegram of loyalty[38] ("by the grace of Providence, the infamous, criminal attempt on your life, my Führer, has failed . . .") and he drafted one on his own behalf, as the most senior General Staff officer of the Army in the West. These telegrams appear to be cynical contrivances to suit his purpose, but his notes offer the explanation that he chose silence and deliberate hypocrisy in order to save his comrades. Before his arrival at the Hôtel Raphael at about 3 a.m., he drove to Naval HQ and the SD office to calm tempers and act as "appeaser". At the Raphael he and Oberg devised a "formula" which was intended to cover both sides against the Reich Security Chiefs and perhaps to benefit Stülpnagel, who was in the greatest danger of all. Blumentritt did not decree any arrests, although his presence at the talks in La Roche-Guyon made this incumbent upon him. He did not submit any reports on what had happened, and during the interrogation in the following days, when Hofacker had taken all the blame upon himself, Blumentritt was able to ensure that the investigations were restricted to a small circle of conspirators.[39]

But his attempt to shield Stülpnagel failed. On his return to St Germain at 4 a.m. he found an order from Keitel demanding that Stülpnagel should at once leave for Berlin "to report". Kluge himself had informed OKH of Stülpnagel's unauthorized action and Himmler had apparently also received news about what had happened through one SS signals centre which had been overlooked when the others were shut down. Stülpnagel received the order on the morning of July 21 "and took cognizance of it" without batting an eyelid, and without a single word of comment even joking as usual with Countess Podewils, his secretary.[40]

"Fate has decided against us," he said. Stülpnagel made an unsuccessful attempt to shoot himself that same day. Death did not come until five weeks later at the hands of the executioner. By then Kluge was already dead.

HEADQUARTERS

Events at Headquarters, the attempted assassination and subsequent happenings have been adequately documented by eye-witness

333

accounts. Hitler had requested that only the most urgent matters should be raised at the conference, and that the number of people present should be limited as much as possible. Accordingly, Göring and Himmler were not at the mid-day conference, which they had hardly ever failed to attend in those eventful weeks. It had been agreed that Stauffenberg should report because, in view of the daily setbacks on the front, it had become a matter of utmost urgency to get the new "Volksgrenadier" divisions operational as quickly as possible. When General Heusinger, who was reporting on the war situation in the East, began to go into details, Hitler rose from his chair to follow the information on the map. He bent across the table, leaning on his right elbow. Shortly after entering the room Stauffenberg left again, having whispered to Admiral Voss, who stood next to him (another account said it was Colonel Brandt, who sat in front of Stauffenberg) that he was going to enquire about a telephone call. He said he had been waiting for it but it had not come through yet; and would the Admiral keep an eye on his brief-case as it contained secret documents.[41] One account makes it seem likely that Stauffenberg left the closed brief-case near Hitler's place, propped against Colonel Brandt's chair. It was in Brandt's way when he wanted to study the maps and after Stauffenberg had gone he reached down and placed it on the outside of the right table support. It was from there that the flames shot up. There followed a deafening bang; some witnesses heard two. A hail of splinters of glass, timber, plaster and metal crashed down. The maps were ablaze. Part of the ceiling was suspended in flames, thick smoke momentarily obscured all vision, and only the cries of the injured could be heard. From the other part of the hut people rushed towards the exit, where they ran into the first of the conference members who, still half stunned, emerged gesticulating from the dense smoke. Their uniforms in tatters, blackened with smoke, some of them bleeding, they staggered out into the open. Two of the participants were found outside lying on the ground just as they were regaining consciousness. (Fegelein and Günsche, according to some witnesses, Scherff and Günsche according to others.) They must have been blown out of the window by the blast. The first seriously wounded were being carried along and laid down on the forest soil. Hitler appeared in the doorway supported by Keitel[42] and an ADC. He was barely recognizable, his face blackened with soot, his hair dishevelled and covered in dust and wood fibres. His jacket was almost undamaged, but his trousers of black cloth were hanging from his legs in shreds. He still seemed stunned and only took in the things that were shouted at him. He was taken to his

334

bunker nearby, where his personal physician examined him and began treatment.

Doctors and rescue workers were on the spot within minutes after the explosion and attended to the injured. Ambulances took the seriously wounded to hospital at Rastenburg, while those only slightly injured were treated on the spot or in their rooms. In great agitation, Keitel shook hands with anybody he met—even several times with the same person—and kept repeating: "The Führer lives, and now you'll see!" Jodl, who had been struck by the falling chandelier and whose head was bleeding, was pacing up and down outside the hut, cursing the eternal rebuilding work which he had always regarded as unnecessary and bothersome. He was convinced that a building worker (of the Todt Organization) had planted the bomb under the floor at the spot where there was now a huge hole.

The medical examination showed that Hitler had not been seriously injured. He had sprained his right elbow rather badly, had several bruises, a few abrasions and his eardrums had been punctured. The physician gave him his favourite injections to restore his vigour and insisted on Hitler having a complete rest, which annoyed the Führer. The special train that was to bring Mussolini was halted at Rastenburg station.

Bormann[43] was the first Party leader to arrive—he always made a point of being nearer to Hitler than anyone else and his quarters were closest to the inner compound. Himmler and Ribbentrop followed soon after—at about 1 p.m.—and congratulated Hitler. Göring came later "noisy and jovial". From now on, he said, all would be well. It had been discovered that some members of the General Staff had been engaging in the blackest sabotage;[44] they had deliberately kept the troops away from the front, and so on. Göring exaggerated more than the others by invoking Providence and interpreting Hitler's escape as a lucky omen, which promised victory under his leadership. Himmler made a brief report on what he had seen at the ruined hut, advanced the suggestion that some infernal device had been concealed there by a building worker and asked for authority to make further investigations into the crime. Hitler refused to believe that any of the building workers was responsible. He was inclined to think that the young officer[45] whom he had transferred to the front on the previous day was the culprit. An Adjutant reported that when he entered, Hitler "had the lively, almost cheerful expression of a man who had been expecting something terrible to happen and had now luckily survived it". The Adjutant quoted Hitler as saying that they had all been immensely lucky.

335

Reports about the injured were grave : eleven victims had been brought to the hospital; Generals Schmundt and Korten were so seriously injured that they were not expected to live. Colonel Brandt and General Bodenschatz were also very badly wounded; the stenographer, who had had his legs smashed was dying. All the others present at the conference, with the single exception of Keitel who had escaped unharmed, were injured. Hitler had been standing a few paces in front of Keitel, and the air pressure which escaped into the long corridor had flung him into the Field-Marshal's arms. Like that of all the others, Keitel's hearing was affected. Korten, Schmundt, Brandt and Berger died.

The list of conference participants was studied. It did not escape note that no one knew what had happened to Colonel Stauffenberg. Presumably he, too, had been taken to hospital. Hitler gave orders to search for him and turned to other matters. Shortly before 2 p.m. Himmler had contacted the Criminal Police in Berlin and demanded the immediate despatch of experts to investigate the crime. The conference hut personnel were questioned : the Signals Sergeant on duty said that the one-eyed Colonel, who had booked a long-distance call, came out again immediately after the start of the conference and, wearing cap and holster, left hurriedly without waiting for his call. Further enquiries established that Stauffenberg had left his brief-case behind and that he and the officer escorting him had passed through the checkpoint and the outer gate soon after the explosion. Suspicion hardened when confirmation came from Rastenburg airfield that the Colonel had taken off shortly after 1 p.m. He had given his destination as Rangsdorf (Berlin). But it was assumed that this had been a false trail and that he had since sought safety behind the Russian lines—which were scarcely 100 kilometres away. Even so, one account shows that Himmler made arrangements for Stauffenberg to be arrested should he land at Rangsdorf. Why this order was not received and carried out has not been established.

Towards 16.00 Mussolini's special train drew up at the little station of the "Wolf's Lair",[46] known as Görlitz, just as a light, thundery shower was coming down. Hitler was awaiting his guest, wearing a black cape, his right arm in a sling. He seemed to move a little more heavily than usual. On the short walk—a few hundred metres only—from the station to the forest camp he told Mussolini what had just happened, speaking in "a remarkably calm, almost monotonous voice", and immediately led him to the wrecked hut. The interpreter who accompanied them said : "The door was shattered and its broken parts were leaning against the opposite wall of the hut. The room itself presented a picture of

336

destruction ... tables and chairs lying in splinters all over the place. The beams from the ceiling had crashed down and the windows, complete with frames, had been blown out. The big map table was just a heap of cracked boards and broken legs. ..." Mussolini seemed genuinely horrified, and seeing this scene of destruction found it incredible that Hitler should have survived it. Hitler took up the thought and described his most unexpected salvation as proof that Providence still had a task for him.

On the way to the "tea-house", where their talks were to be held, Hitler walked over to a wire fence and addressed a few friendly words to some building workers : he said they had been wrongly suspected, but now the investigators had found a better clue. In the ensuing talks, which for some time were held among a fairly large group, but later between the two leaders alone, Hitler's attention was constantly diverted by interruptions : Göring came in, Himmler sent new reports, Keitel had exciting news, the press Adjutant submitted extracts from the first foreign broadcasts. As the quarter hours went by, it appeared that the assassination attempt involved wider circles than they had originally assumed.

At 16.20 Keitel reported a telephone call from the C.-in-C. of the Reserve Army in Berlin. He had enquired whether the news of Hitler's death was true. When asked who had put out that report, Fromm had named Olbricht who, in turn, was said to have received it from Führer HQ. Fromm had been unable to give any information on Stauffenberg's whereabouts. Upon receiving this news, Himmler ordered the Gestapo in Berlin to send a group of officers to find out what was going on at the Bendlerstrasse, and if Stauffenberg was there to arrest him inconspicuously. Until then it was still thought that the whole affair had been an abortive individual attempt by this General Staff officer.

Soon after Fromm's call, an unexpected number of Army Commanders telephoned, who wanted confirmation from Keitel or Jodl that Hitler was really dead. Suddenly it became clear from these enquiries that the C.-in-C. of the Reserve Army had activated emergency measures, which had been prepared, with Hitler's knowledge, for the contingency of internal unrest or his death. Keitel asked for an urgent call to the Bendlerstrasse; he wanted an explanation of this outrageous unauthorized action and he was going to have the order rescinded at top speed—but he failed to get hold of either Fromm or Olbricht.

Meanwhile the conversation had become even louder and more heated. No one bothered any longer about their Italian guests, and the assembled leaders showed their mutual hostility by shouting recriminations at each other. Admiral Dönitz, who upon hearing of

337

the attempt had flown to HQ, raged against the Army, whom he accused of treason. Göring joined in. But Dönitz quickly turned on the Air Force which, he said, had failed miserably. Göring defended himself. But soon he was involved in an even fiercer argument with Foreign Minister Ribbentrop, of whom he had always had a low opinion. Now he blamed him for the bankruptcy of Germany's foreign policy and threatened to hit him with his Marshal's baton. Eyewitnesses unanimously reported the following exchange: "Shut up, you champagne salesman." "I am still Foreign Minister, and my name is von Ribbentrop." Hitler had listened to all this for quite a while in brooding silence. When someone mentioned the 30th June, 1934, he flared up, uttering furious threats that from now on he was going to be ruthless. He would wipe out the lot of them and throw women and children into concentration camps— no mercy was to be shown to anyone! This inhumanity opened the eyes of some witnesses in favour of the victims of this day.

At 17.30 Hitler got through to Goebbels. He instructed him immediately to broadcast an announcement that there had been an attempt on his life but that he had emerged unscathed and that he was, at that moment, receiving the Duce as planned. So far Goebbels could give him no other information than that a group of officers at the Bendlerstrasse were apparently spreading the news that Hitler was dead. After prolonged reflection, Hitler came to the conclusion that as Zeitzler had gone, the post of Chief of General Staff of the Army would have to be manned by someone else. General Buhle having been wounded, Hitler decided to appoint Colonel-General Guderian, then Inspector-General of the armoured troops. The necessary order was issued.

Towards 18.00 Hitler accompanied his Italian visitors to the station. Mussolini had earlier made some request concerning Italian internees and had unexpectedly and effortlessly obtained Hitler's agreement.[47] This was the last time the two dictators met.

On his return from the station, Hitler had a phone call put through to the Foreign Ministry in Berlin. Apparently nothing was known there of any unusual happenings. All the State Secretary, Steengracht, had to report was that the Wilhelmstrasse was sealed off by troops who allowed no one to pass. He added that they were men of the Waffen-SS—"that is to say, our men," Hitler commented, somewhat relieved, when told of the telephone message. In fact, they were men of the Guard Battalion who, at that moment, were obeying the orders of the conspirators.

Hitler again asked to speak to Goebbels and criticized him vehemently for not yet having made the announcement over the radio. They were in such an agitated state that some even wondered whether Goebbels had not also defected to the rebel officers. Frightening visions of what was going on in Berlin and, at the instigation of the people there, in the rest of the Reich assumed enormous proportions in the remote forest camp. Anything seemed possible, and Hitler gave unrestrained vent to his old bitterness : he had never trusted the Army; the Generals had always been plotting against him. . . . After a while, the radio at last broadcast the statement for which he had asked. It was hoped that this would cut the ground from under the plotters' feet.

But it was soon clear that the announcement was not enough. Incoming telephone calls seemed to show that instead of fizzling out, the revolt was gaining ground. Hitler was fuming. From the Reich Chancellery it was reported that the Guard Battalion was demanding that the building be handed over. Meanwhile, Goebbels had let it be known that he was trying to get hold of the Commander of the Guard Battalion to convince him that the Führer was alive.

Exploiting Hitler's excitement, Himmler came up with a draft order expressing the Führer's decision to appoint the Reichsführer SS as Commander-in-Chief of the Reserve Army. Hitler signed, without even sitting down,[48] and implored Himmler to fly to Berlin and crush the criminal revolt at the Bendlerstrasse. He is reported as saying : "Shoot anyone who resists, no matter who it is. . . . The fate of the nation is at stake. . . . Be ruthless !" Witnesses never forgot the terror which these words—reminiscent of the 30th June, 1934—struck among the people in the "tea-house", and the chilling silence before Himmler, now all-powerful, said : "My Führer, you can rely on me." With a smile, half-hidden by his glasses, he raised his hand to salute and left. There is a picture of Hitler, taken presumably without his consent, which shows him at the door of the "tea-house" at that moment : shattered, deep in thought, sensing that his supremacy was being undermined, outraged and brooding revenge.[49]

While Himmler was getting ready to leave, the SS troops in Saarow and the SS Cadet School were alerted to march on Berlin. Meanwhile, Keitel was waging a ceaseless battle by telephone and teleprinter for control of all important authorities in the Reserve Army and the fighting forces. He gave warning that no note must be taken of the lies from the Bendlerstrasse and no one was to accept any orders from there.

Between 19.00 and 20.00 Goebbels telephoned again : he said Major Remer was at his side and would the Führer talk to him. "Do you know me, Major Remer, do you recognize my voice?" Remer said he did and briefly reported on the situation. "Major

339

Remer, I am speaking to you as Supreme Commander of the German Wehrmacht and I am giving you the following orders . . ." Hitler spoke with emphasis, and felt convinced that he had achieved the desired response. He ordered Remer to crush any resistance, adding: "You are directly responsible to me until Himmler arrives in Berlin." He now thought it imperative to address the German people without delay. On being told that there were no facilities for him to broadcast directly from HQ, he let fly again and complained bitterly. A recording van had to be fetched from Königsberg. When at last it arrived, the inmates at the "Wolf's Lair" were summoned to the "tea-house" to hear Hitler read his hastily drafted speech. According to a member of the audience, Hitler spoke in a toneless voice that was hardly in keeping with the self-assured words and showed that "his pride and confidence were shattered". The impatient Hitler had to wait for hours before the speech could be broadcast.

Between 21.00 and 22.00 General Herfurth, Chief of Staff to General Kortzfleisch, reported that there had been a military putsch but that he was firmly in control and had already re-asserted his authority. (None the less Herfurth was later executed because he had knowledge of the events of the 20th.)

After midnight Himmler reported on the situation from Berlin : the revolt, he said, had collapsed; the Bendlerstrasse had been occupied without a struggle by loyal troops; Stauffenberg, the would-be assassin, Olbricht and the other plotters most directly involved had been shot on Fromm's orders; Colonel-General Beck, allegedly also implicated, had been allowed by Fromm to shoot himself. All was quiet in the city. Investigations were proceeding to establish the circle of people involved and quite a number of arrests had already been made. At Headquarters, Generals Stieff and Fellgiebel were under strong suspicion and their arrest had been ordered.

Hitler wanted to be told the names of all who had played a prominent part in putting down the revolt. The first promotions and awards were made immediately, even before the situation as a whole could be surveyed. The only disquieting news came from Paris, but no clear picture about events there could yet be formed. Several telephone conversations had been held with Kluge, but he was highly suspect.

A little later—towards 1 a.m.—the German wireless broadcast Hitler's speech, which had been trailed for hours and had actually been recorded several hours earlier. How many Germans must have been waiting to hear this voice, in their homes or in the open, in still intact or hopelessly wrecked dwellings, or in dug-outs on the

340

battlefields. Perhaps at this hour after midnight there was, for the last time, something of that fever with which each of these speeches had been awaited in the first years of Hitler's rule. How much harm had been done since! But as yet the ring he had thrown around his people held firm and, not knowing any better, they continued even now to echo his condemnation of the "criminals", and his gratitude to Providence which had protected and preserved the Führer for Germany. How different was the impact of the speech on those who now knew that their hopes were shattered and they themselves faced certain death : the men under arrest at the Bendlerstrasse who were forced to listen to Hitler with their guards; Stülpnagel and Hofacker at the Hôtel Raphael in Paris; and Tresckow at his Staff HQ in Poland.

The man they had declared to be dead began :

"Men and women of Germany, I don't know how many times plans and attempts have been made to assassinate me. If I speak to you today it is, first of all, so that you should hear my voice and know that I am unhurt and well, and, secondly, that you should know of a crime unparalleled in German history.

"A very small clique of ambitious, unscrupulous, and at the same time criminal and stupid officers concocted a plot to remove me, and with me the staff of the High Command of the Wehrmacht. The bomb planted by Colonel Count Stauffenberg exploded two metres to my right. It seriously wounded a number of my faithful collaborators, one of whom has died. I myself am entirely unhurt, apart from some very minor scratches, bruises and burns. I regard this as confirmation of the task imposed upon me by Providence, that I should continue to pursue the aims of my life as I have done up till now. For I may confess to the nation that since the day I moved into the Wilhelmstrasse I have had but one thought—to do my duty to the best of my knowledge and conscience—and that ever since I realized that war could no longer be averted or postponed, I have known nothing but worry and work through days unnumbered and sleepless nights, and have lived only for my people.

"While the German armies have been engaged in a bitter struggle, a small group emerged in Germany, just as in Italy, which believed that it could repeat the stab-in-the-back of 1918. The allegation of these usurpers that I am dead is being refuted this very moment as I am speaking to you, my dear German comrades. The circle of these usurpers is very small and has nothing in common with the German Wehrmacht and, above all, nothing with the German Army. It is a tiny gang of criminal elements which will be ruthlessly exterminated.

"I therefore now order :

"1. that no civil authority is to obey any order from any office usurped by these people;

"2. that no military authority, no leader of any unit, no soldier is to obey any orders emanating from these usurpers; that, on the contrary, it is everyone's duty to arrest, or if they resist, to kill at sight anyone issuing or handing on such orders. To introduce order, once and for all, I have appointed Reich Minister Himmler, Commander of the Reserve Army. I have brought Colonel-General Guderian into the General Staff to replace the Chief of the General Staff who has been taken ill, and I have assigned a second proven Commander from the Eastern Front as his assistant.

"There will be no changes at other Reich offices. I am convinced that with the elimination of this very small clique of traitors and conspirators we shall at last create in the homeland the atmosphere which the fighters at the front need. For it is unthinkable that at the front hundreds of thousands, nay millions, of good men should be giving their all, while a small gang of ambitious and miserable creatures here at home perpetually tries to sabotage them.

"This time we are going to settle accounts with them in the manner to which we National Socialists are accustomed. I am convinced that every decent officer and every gallant soldier will understand that at this hour.

"I am particularly glad to be able once again to greet you, my old comrades in arms, and to tell you that once more I was spared a fate which held no horror for me, but would have had terrible consequences for the whole German people. I see in it a sign from Providence that I must, and therefore shall, continue my work."

After Hitler, Goering spoke :

"Comrades in the Luftwaffe, today an unbelievably squalid attempt to kill our Führer was made by one Colonel Count Stauffenberg, on orders from a miserable clique of ex-Generals who had to be thrown out because of their poor and cowardly leadership. As if by miracle, the Führer was saved by omnipotent Providence. Now these criminal usurpers are trying to cause confusion among the troops by putting out false orders. Any officers or other ranks, and civilians too, who act on behalf of these criminals and approach you to win you over for their abominable schemes must be immediately apprehended and shot.

"Wherever you yourselves are given the task of wiping out those traitors you must act ruthlessly. They are the same wretches as have been trying to betray and sabotage the front.

"Any officers involved in this crime have forfeited their place among the people, and the Wehrmacht, their honour as soldiers,

342

and have broken their oath of allegiance. Their destruction will give us new strength. The Luftwaffe will set its pledged loyalty and deep affection for the Führer against this treachery and will go all out for victory. Long live our Führer, on whom Almighty God has today bestowed his patent blessing!"

The last to speak was Dönitz, the Commander-in-Chief of the Navy:

"Men of the Navy, we are consumed with holy wrath and boundless fury at the criminal attempt on our Führer's life. But Providence has willed otherwise. It has protected and preserved the Führer for the German Fatherland in its fateful struggle.

"A small clique of mad generals, having nothing in common with our brave Army, instigated this murder in cowardly disloyalty, committing the most dastardly treachery against the Führer and the German people. For these criminals are nothing but the stooges of our enemies whom they serve with unprincipled, cowardly and false cleverness.

"In fact, they are utterly stupid. They think that by removing the Führer they can relieve us of the hard but inescapable struggle fate has imposed on us—and in their blind and fearful stupidity they do not realize that their crime would plunge us into terrible chaos and deliver us, defenceless, to the enemy. We shall put a stop to the work of these criminals. The Navy, loyal to its oath, stands faithfully by the Führer, and remains unconditionally ready for battle. It will ruthlessly exterminate anyone that turns out to be a traitor. Long live our Führer, Adolf Hitler!"

These speeches, which had been made in an as yet uncertain situation, were followed by this broadcast announcement:

"The plot of the criminal officer clique has collapsed. The ringleaders have either committed suicide or been shot by the Army. They include the would-be assassin Colonel Count Stauffenberg. There have been no incidents, anywhere. Others who are implicated in the crime will be brought to account."

LATER CLARIFICATIONS

Young Captain Klausing, when asked in the evening of the 20th whether everything was going all right, said: "It's always like that; it's the same in battle, too. You fire and you never know whether you've scored a hit. You only hear about that afterwards." It was impossible that day to get an over-all view of events from one place alone. Only later did a more coherent picture emerge from individual incidents.

Some of the happenings on 20th July were completely clarified

343

on the next day, others only at the subsequent trials and investigations. Then there were events on which no light was thrown
until after the war, when the reports of some of the people
involved became available. But a number of quite important points
still await clarification.

We have now had an account of the events and are left with
three main questions :

Why did the attempt fail?

Why was action not taken in Berlin until three hours after the
attempt?

What counter-forces in Berlin were responsible for the crushing
of the revolt?

I. As a result of information from the driver of the car which
had taken Stauffenberg to Rastenburg airfield, a little parcel
packed in wrapping paper was found by the roadside on the
morning of July 21. It was the one Lieutenant von Haeften had
thrown out of the car during the drive. It contained a charge of
1 kg. of a special explosive (Hexonit) modelled on a British explosive, two detonators, but only one of the two prescribed chemical-
mechanical thirty-minute time-fuses, with a British detonator.
Splinters were found which led to the assumption that a similar
explosive had been used in the conference hut—but there must have
been two time-fuses. It has never been established why Stauffenberg carried that second bomb and when or why he disposed of it
before igniting it. Did it make his brief-case bulge too much? Was
it to have been set off simultaneously with the other—and by
whom? Why was this not done? The investigating explosives expert
said that if the second bomb had also been used no one could have
got away alive.[50]

They had chosen a pure powder charge without metal casing (i.e.
non-splinter type) and a silent, apparently fifteen-minute time-fuse.
Stauffenberg relied on the experience gained with these bombs in
British Commando raids, on the numerous tests Tresckow had
made and on the advice of Sapper Major i.G. Kuhn. The explosives had been obtained by the Abwehr through Freytag-Loringhoven; they were then stored with von der Lancken in Potsdam,
and when required—e.g. on 6th, 11th, 15th and 20th July—were
supplied from there.

If 1 kg. of this charge had been exploded—even in the open air,
thus diminishing the effect of pressure—it was considered unthinkable that anyone standing within two or three metres of the
explosion could have survived. In enclosed premises the impact
was bound to be many times greater.

But the explosion at the conference hut showed that, although the bomb caused heavy destruction in the room, the solid oak table, even where it splintered into minute particles, greatly softened the effect, and that the pressure wave was able to escape into other parts of the hut and through the open windows. The thin walls separating the conference room from the two adjacent ones (the pantry and Hitler's rest-room) were shattered. The rooms in the centre of the hut were not badly damaged, while the worst destruction was wrought at the far end—a sign that the pressure wave propagated itself through the whole hut, travelling along the central corridor, and mainly through the layer of air beneath the floor boards and above the hardboard panels of the ceiling. At any rate, such was the force of the blast that two conference members were blown several metres through the window. The only ones killed were those who had been sitting or standing close to the bomb, unprotected by the oak table support. What saved Hitler's life was the fact that after Stauffenberg had left, his leather briefcase was shifted to the far side of the socle. Hitler himself did not pay much attention to the explanations of the explosives experts. For him, it remained a miracle and the will of "Providence" that he had escaped alive.

II. Obviously, the three-hour delay is closely linked with the way communications were handled after the assassination attempt. These questions have still not been fully clarified. The interrogation reports quote evidence by Fellgiebel, Thiele, Hahn and Hassell (especially KB 63, 329 and 376). Other sources are the official report of the RSH's Special Commission dated July 26, 1944, with references to communications procedures (KB 83); the report by Lieutenant of the Reserve, Hellmut Arntz (Fellgiebel's last ADC), which was written immediately after the end of the war; the report (first printed in 1961) by Lieutenant-Colonel Ludolf Gerhard Sander, the Wehrmacht Signals officer at Führer HQ; and finally —of relevance to the time sequence of events—the evidence of the driver who took Stauffenberg to the airfield. (This evidence is contained in a second-hand account.)

As regards communications at the Bendlerstrasse, the sources are the duty officer's report of July 22, 1944, signed by Thiele (KB 63); a comprehensive account by Wolfgang Müller, based on questionings, and finally information supplied by Thorwald Risler,[51] the Signals sergeant who was then serving at the Bendlerstrasse.

Eyewitness accounts differ even as to Stauffenberg's whereabouts at the time the bomb went off. According to Sander's evidence, which obviously formed part of the Special Commission's report, Stauffenberg was standing with Fellgiebel in front of the Signals bunker. Sander joined them at the very moment of a deafening explosion. Stauffenberg, he said, left barely thirty seconds later in a car which had been parked nearby, passing the wrecked hut—about 150 metres away—"while thick smoke was still belching from it and the maps, some of them torn to shreds, were still being whirled out of the window". He said Stauffenberg and Haeften were well able to see the conference hut from the road and were bound to get the impression that "the intended success had been achieved". At 12.43 Stauffenberg could have reached the officers' checkpoint by the direct route which Sander mentioned.

The other report, which is based on interrogations conducted by Kriminalrat Wehner, says nothing about Stauffenberg's brief stop near the Signals bunker. According to the driver, Stauffenberg, coming from the security ring, walked hurriedly towards the "teahouse" where Haeften was waiting. Together they came quickly over to the parking place where the driver called out "Herr Oberst" to signal where he was parked. The two officers got into the car and told him to hurry: "To the airport, as fast as you can!" Shortly before reaching the officers' checkpoint they heard the explosion. The driver said they were between 150 and 200 metres away from it. It may be assumed that, even taking this somewhat longer route, the car could have reached the checkpoint at 12.43. The events near the conference hut could at least be "partially" observed from the checkpoint (KB 86). It is possible that what he saw from there prompted Stauffenberg to remark later that it looked as if a 150 mm. shell had hit the place.

The interrogation reports contain this testimony by Berthold Stauffenberg: his brother had told him that the chemical fuse had to be activated by applying pressure. He did what was necessary, placed the brief-case containing the explosives in the conference room and then left. Even before his departure from the "Wolf's Lair", he heard a fairly violent detonation (KB 21). If this evidence can be accepted, it would make the version of the second report appear more probable.

Here is Sander's account of what happened after the explosion: soon after Stauffenberg's departure he was summoned to Lieutenant-Colonel von Below, Hitler's second Adjutant, who had himself been wounded in the head in the explosion at the hut. Below said to him: "Attempt on the Führer; the Führer is alive. Summon at once the Reichsmarshal (Göring) and the Reichsführer (Himmler). No news of the attempt must get out!" After that, Sander said, he arranged for "all telephone and teleprinter communications to be cut" and informed Fellgiebel "who agreed with this step". Shortly afterwards Sander was summoned to Hitler, who wanted to know when he would be able to make his broadcast. Fellgiebel, who had been pacing up and down outside the Führer's Security Ring (*Führersperrkreis*) was later told what had been discussed. The broadcast was planned for 21.00. Sander then telephoned General Thiele at OKW in Berlin, but he was temporarily absent. He therefore instructed the General's secretary to give him this message : "Attempt on the Führer—Führer alive—Führer to broadcast later today." Sander added in his report : "General Fellgiebel agreed and again stressed how important the message was." Sander then undertook to "request that the SD should tap all telephone conversations, under standing orders for all such situations" and said he would give the necessary instructions to the staff assigned this job. Fellgiebel meanwhile returned to OKH at "Mauerwald". Then followed this important sentence : "I don't know whether a communications shut-down was also ordered there" [i.e. in Mauerwald : Anna]. At about 15.00, he said, the communications clampdown for "Wolf's Lair" was lifted again "because of incoming calls from the various fronts".

Sander's conversation with General Thiele's secretary could have taken place between 13.15 and 13.30. He himself did not specify any time. According to Friedrich Georgi, Sander's report led to the questioning of Thiele's two secretaries who were on duty on the 20th July, but neither of the ladies could recall this telephone conversation, and both thought it unlikely that they would have forgotten such a disconcerting message, if it ever did arrive.

Sander's report implies that Fellgiebel merely "agreed" and that he took no action himself. But there is corroboration in other testimonies that Fellgiebel, realizing the failure of the attempt, decided to act as if Hitler had been killed. Without Sander noticing it (so these testimonies aver) he managed to set things in motion in the prearranged manner. Fellgiebel, as Chief of Signals at OKH Headquarters in "Mauerwald" had a confederate in his Chief of Staff, Colonel Kurt Hahn. The Colonel confirmed under interrogation that at 13.00 Fellgiebel—as advanced observer at the "Wolf's Lair"—issued orders to cut communications (KB 330). Arntz, the ADC, independently of this testimony of which he knew nothing, recalls Fellgiebel's unequivocal phrase, which had not however aroused the telephone tappers' attention : "Something frightful has happened. The Führer is alive. Block everything !"

Hahn's testimony—which is independently borne out by Arntz— further shows that the cut in communications was ordered in agreement with Stieff for both major switch-centres, i.e. "Anna" (HQ East Prussia) and "Zeppelin" (Zossen). Hahn specifically added that Wagner, the Quartermaster-General in Zossen, was put in the picture. The assumed hour of that action was about 13.15.

347

According to Arntz, the repeater stations at Insterburg and Rastenburg were blocked by the SS officers on duty, and the OKH
switchboard "Anna" and the repeater station Lötzen by Fellgiebel's men. The Kaltenbrunner Reports say that "after some
time"—probably 15.00 or 15.30—restrictions were eased to the
extent that only private conversations continued to be forbidden
while service calls under surveillance were permitted (KB 330).

Summing up, it will be seen that Sander secured the requested
communications shut-down for the "Wolf's Lair" area. In addition, Fellgiebel, without Sander's knowledge but covered by the
latter's arrangements, ordered the much more extensive isolation of
Headquarters. He did not resort to any fictitious announcement of
Hitler's death, which in any case would soon have been exposed,
but on his own initiative and credibly, as if on Hitler's orders, gave
instructions for communications to be cut. By this unauthorized
procedure, he assumed full personal responsibility for one important
particular action in the revolt. Since Hitler was alive, its sole purpose could have been to gain a few hours if meanwhile action was
being taken in Berlin, Paris and the rest of the Reich. When Hitler's order came to re-open all communications Fellgiebel was
unable to oppose it. According to the ADC's evidence, Fellgiebel
tried even then to have the signals network "operated exclusively
by reliable staff of his own" (is this how the orders given to Rangsdorf were held up?) and to "arrange by telephone that matters
concerning the Reserve Army in Berlin should be kept secret",
possibly by-passing Thiele. At about the same time, and with the
same deep disappointment as Stauffenberg in Rangsdorf, Fellgiebel
must have heard from Berlin that no use had been made of those
hours.

We do not know when Fellgiebel ceased to intervene and began
to concentrate on trying to save the men involved in the assassination attempt. According to Hassell's evidence (KB p. 377) Fellgiebel telephoned him in Berlin at 18.20. "What's going on there?
Are they all mad? The Führer is sitting in the 'tea-house' with the
Duce. Besides, there'll soon be news on the radio." At about that
time Stieff was talking in similar terms—from which it may be
surmised that the two acted in agreement. Quickly convicted on
this incriminating evidence, Stieff and Fellgiebel were the first
conspirators to be arrested at midnight, the time when Olbricht
and Stauffenberg were shot. Arntz, who had spent most of the day
with Fellgiebel, said that even in the afternoon the Chief of Signals
no longer had any illusions about his own fate and fully expected
to be shot. Arntz wrote: "He did not try to take his own life
because he wanted to give evidence and not to leave them, as he

put it, even with the semblance of right! Imperturbably calm, he spent the evening amongst his officers and the last few hours alone with me, talking about life after death, in which he did not believe. The call for which he had been waiting came towards midnight. Lieutenant-Colonel von John, Keitel's Adjutant, passed on the message: 'Herr General, the Field-Marshal requests you, in view of the unusual situation, to come and see him.' 'I'm coming', was the brief reply, and having put on his holster, his hand already on the door-handle of the car, General Fellgiebel turned once more to me: 'If we did believe in a Beyond, we could say: Auf Wiedersehen!'"

It has not yet been established beyond doubt when and how the first news of the attempt on Hitler reached Olbricht. There is no account by Lieutenant-General Thiele, who had been assigned to act as liaison between Fellgiebel and Olbricht. All the indications are that the lines between East Prussia and Berlin were out of action from about 13.30 to 15.30 for everyone, including Fellgiebel, Hahn and Thiele. This left only the period between 12.45 and 13.15 (at best 13.30) or a later hour after 15.30 for a code signal to be put through.

Friedrich Georgi, who was with Olbricht on the evening of the 20th July said that no news was received from Headquarters. One quarter of an hour after another went by as they waited and tried to make their own enquiries. It was after 15.00 (were the lines cut?) that Thiele managed to establish contact with HQ for the first time. But he did not hear that "an important item of news from Führer HQ is expected shortly". At Olbricht's insistence Thiele went on trying and managed to get a second call through at 15.45 from which it was learnt that "there were rumours at HQ about an attempt on Hitler, but nothing could be gathered about its success or failure". Georgi said that Olbricht found it impossible to decide, on the strength of the first vague information, to give the signal to launch the revolt because they could not possibly risk a repetition of the false alarm of July 15. But on the basis of the second message, which at least confirmed the rumours of an attempt, he had decided that the time for action had come and immediately gave the starting signal, at 15.50.

This account of Georgi's which he based on more recent research (his own eyewitness account written in 1947 did not contain anything about this aspect) would provide a convincing explanation as to why three hours were lost before the signal for action was given. But Georgi's testimony is not borne out by any other available evidence.

The People's Court questioned Colonel-General Hoepner about

the events which took place round about mid-day on the 20th
July. In his evidence he again spoke of the uncertainty which
hampered Olbricht during the hours between 13.00 and up to
nearly 16.00, and also about the forthcoming communiqué of
unknown content from Führer HQ which Thiele repeatedly mentioned. But Hoepner also referred to a telephone call from HQ
which, he said, Thiele received. Just after Hoepner and Olbricht
had returned from their lunch together, Thiele brought news of it
to Olbricht. From the context of this evidence this must have
happened at about 13.15. The exact words of the telephone
message were not disclosed but Hoepner's testimony implied that
it was a brief report about an apparently abortive assassination
attempt. Thiele obviously doubted the news and considered it
inadequate to warrant the go-ahead signal for a revolt of such
far-reaching consequence. Thiele, according to the evidence, left,
saying he would try to get more accurate information. Even at
15.15 he was vainly waiting for the communiqué, according to
Hoepner, and later he spoke to Fellgiebel. This may be a reference
to the conversation which, Georgi suggested, led to the orders to
launch the uprising.[52]

Sander's telephone call to Thiele (at about 13.15 or a little later)
would coincide in time with the call Hoepner mentioned. But if
we have to assume that this call never reached Thiele, we are left
with Hahn's evidence. This is, that shortly after the attempt on
Hitler's life, Hahn, on Fellgiebel's instructions, gave orders to shut
down the major switch-centre "Zeppelin" (Zossen). Consequently
Thiele would have been involved, and Wagner was put in the
picture. Any relevant message would have had to reach Thiele
direct or via the Quartermaster-General between 13.15 and 13.30,
and again it could have been the telephone conversation to which
Hoepner referred.

On the whole, these testimonies suggest that before the communications shut-down became effective, news was passed according to plan between "Wolf's Lair" (Fellgiebel), "Mauerwald"
(Hahn, Stieff) and Zossen (Wagner, Thiele). But nothing is known
about the form and content of these signals. The only thing on
record is Fellgiebel's clever brief phrase, which could not arouse
the suspicion of anyone tapping the lines and which made the three
essential facts quite clear: that the attempt had been made; that
it had failed; but that the action must still go on. Evidently Hahn
himself did not say whether he used the same short formula or a
more general phrase, or whether he confined himself to the word
"block!", which could also have been interpreted as a code-signal.
His phrase that Wagner was "put in the picture" suggests that he

used more rather than fewer words. In any case, no definite code word was used that would have signified the success of the attempt.

Wagner passed the message "Finished" without qualification to Finckh in Paris and, like Fellgiebel, obviously wanted to see the whole job completed. His complicity was discovered very quickly. But Thiele, a more careful, methodical man must have suffered a great deal from the uncertainty of the whole situation. Even those people of his entourage who were not involved noted that he was exceptionally worried and uneasy during those hours, and was continually in and out of his office. It may be that he did not want to break his oath to the General to whom he owed so much; and yet he found it impossible, even senseless, to impose the consequences of his decision on all the others, if Hitler was not dead. He was torn by this conflict, waited and hoped for clarification and therefore a solution, as the minutes went by. But he took no action. Only ten days later, when he had already become Fellgiebel's successor, was he identified as an accomplice in the conspiracy. The verdict was inexorable and he was executed, together with Fellgiebel, on September 4.

As for General Olbricht, he realized the risk of another false alarm : it would not only have meant certain death for himself but would have entailed disaster for the entire circle of conspirators. The reports which he received through Thiele—regardless of how and when they came—must have made him acutely aware of the uncertainty and risks in the situation, and caused him to hesitate to assume the tremendous responsibility for all the others involved. It is hardly likely that he yielded to weakness and dishonoured his reputation as a man of action.

One report, which refers to a conversation with Colonel Hahn, says that the 20th July was an exceptionally unfavourable date for the coup d'état because of the plans for re-organizing communications. In view of the war situation, preparations were in hand to transfer HQ from East Prussia to Zossen near Berlin. The 20th July had been chosen as the date for the switch : from that day on, all communications were routed via Berlin, they took longer and on the 20th it was more difficult than ever to control the network from East Prussia. Hahn is said to have exclaimed : "If only you had asked me. I'd have told you : any other day, but not today...."[53]

III. The prime reason for the failure of the coup in Berlin is that Hitler was not killed; but next in importance is the fact that the operation began only after the isolation of Headquarters had ended and when, therefore, the most vital premise for success had ceased to exist. It is amazing how far insurgent operations did

351

succeed under the circumstances, especially in cities like Paris. The coup in Berlin, begun under this double handicap, was hampered and finally halted by these five groups of officers or individual officers : the Chief of Signals at the Bendlerstrasse; the Commander of the Guard Battalion; the Commander of the Armoured Troops School in Krampnitz, in conjunction with the Inspectorate-General of the Armoured Troops and the Inspector in charge of the training of future officers; a group of officers at the Infantry School in Döberitz, and officers of Olbricht's department. None of the five organizations belonged to the SS. And in each of them counter-action started only once they were sure that Hitler was alive. None of them would have opposed action against the SS if Hitler's death had been confirmed.

(a) On the 20th July the Signals officer on duty at the Bendler-strasse was Second-Lieutenant Röhrig, who before his call-up to the Wehrmacht had been a music student, a pianist and an active member of the National Socialist Students' League. From about 16.30 till 21.00 various people such as Captain Klausing, Lieutenant von Haeften, Major i.G. Harnack and several women secretaries came in with teleprinter signals which he was instructed to transmit : the two General Orders; the launching of "Valkyrie"; phase II; Hoepner's appointment as Commander-in-Chief, Reserve Army; a statement repudiating the broadcast communiqué; the Martial Law and other Decrees. The officer's instructions were that he was not to ask about the content of the orders passing through his hands. He was not even authorized to disclose it to any of his superior Signals officers, even if he were a General. Röhrig's first misgivings were aroused by item IIc of the immediate measures ordered : the arrest of the concentration camp guards. That was at about 18.00. He became very uneasy : he was neither physically compelled to carry out his instructions nor was anyone of inspiring authority present to help him "sort himself out". None of the Signals officers privy to the conspiracy was there. To start with, he transmitted the signals as ordered. But when the radio announced that Hitler was alive, he could not stand it any longer. The Superintendent on duty agreed with him that something was wrong. His superior, a Lieutenant, was informed and then all other Second-Lieutenants off duty were brought in. They took over all outgoing lines and tapped every conversation, especially those of Stauffenberg and Merz. A double sentry was posted at the entrances to the switchboard centre, and at 19.45 Colonel Köllner, the departmental chief, was asked to come over.

Olbricht and Stauffenberg kept making enquiries and asking for confirmation that the individual Military District HQ's had received their instructions. Röhrig explained away the delays with "operational difficulties". A teleprinter signal handed in by Haeften at 18.00 "for top-speed despatch" did not begin to go out until 20.45. Only some of the addressees received teleprinter messages handed in after 19.00, whereas signals submitted after 20.00 were held back. But an intercepted teleprint from Keitel, which was handed to Röhrig by his subordinates at 21.00, was put through with utmost urgency to all previous recipients and issued simultaneously by radio. This was done although Olbricht, to whom Köllner had shown the teleprint, had forbidden it. It announced the appointment of Himmler as Commander-in-Chief of the Reserve Army and declared all orders issued by Fromm and Witzleben invalid. Röhrig informed some recipients by phone or special teleprinter signal that earlier teleprints they had been sent were invalid. When Lieutenant Schlee, a company commander of the Guard Battalion, was about to withdraw his men from the Bendler block, the counter-group took him into their confidence, and told him that they were on the track of a military revolt at the Bendlerstrasse and were sabotaging orders from there. "Immediate reinforcements" were promised and arrived at 23.15. Twenty men of the Guard Battalion occupied the Signals centre and set up machine-gun posts at all exits.

In the evening the senior Signals officers, Colonel Hassell (Chief of the Signals Inspectorate 7) and General Thiele arrived at the centre, both officers apparently trying to help clear up the situation. Their conduct aroused no suspicion of their being involved in the revolt. After a short while Hassell left again. Thiele then took over the frequent contacts with Führer HQ and received orders from there. Among the first was the award of an Order to the Signals officer and his Superintendent, who were later promoted.[54]

According to KB (p. 376), Hassell had been in league with Olbricht since 1943 and had undertaken to have twenty officers ready for the coup; their task was to operate the communications of the Foreign Office, Ministry of Propaganda, RSH, Broadcasting Station, etc. The officers were to report to Hayessen at the Town HQ. After Fellgiebel's phone call (18.20) and a further conversation with Thiele and Olbricht, Hayessen took no further part in the revolt, according to his own evidence. He got away with his life.

(b) Immediately after the event Major Otto Ernst Remer was hailed by Goebbels and his Ministry as the gallant and resolute officer who, loyal to the Führer, foiled the conspiracy of the 20th July. That very evening he received a personal long-distance call from Hitler, who promoted him to Colonel and, according to his own testimony, offered him an estate and the diamonds to the Knight's Cross—both of which, he said, he declined. But soon after the 20th even those who had gone out of their way to praise him as the saviour of the day, began to dispute his conduct and the service he had rendered. Goebbels himself is said to have remarked that Remer could easily have been shot as "a traitor to National Socialism"; and in October 1944, Martin Bormann, the Head of the Party Chancery, set in motion a review of Remer's "entire conduct" on the 20th July.[55]

From various post-war court investigations, there emerges the following sequence of events : Major Remer had just returned from a lecture on "National Socialist leadership questions" which Second-Lieutenant of the Reserve, Dr Hans Hagen, had given to his subordinates. It was then—shortly after 16.00—that he received news at his quarters in the Rathenowerstrasse in Döberitz that Operation "Valkyrie" had been ordered and that he was to report immediately to the General at Town HQ. While the troops were getting ready to march, Remer drove to Berlin. When he reported to Lieutenant-General von Hase, he found Lieutenant-Colonel Schöne, Majors Count von Schack and Hayessen and Lieutenant Erttel already there. Von Hase informed Remer that Hitler had had an accident, possibly a fatal one, that rioting was expected and that the Army had assumed executive power. He ordered Remer to have the Guard Battalion seal off the Government quarter and to ensure that no one, not even a General or Minister, crossed the barrier. In addition, he was to detail a company for duty at OKH in the Bendlerstrasse. On his return to Döberitz, Remer told his officers about the situation and the orders he had been given. The motorized advance detachments left, the Government quarter was sealed off as ordered and the SS and Leib-standarte sentries were disarmed. Remer reported personally to the General that his orders had been carried out. After a further conference he left Town HQ to arrange for reinforcements to seal off the area north of the Anhalter Station where the RSH was situated. Contrary to his later, entirely different, account, Remer had himself pointed out that it was necessary to use sufficient forces for this task.

Meanwhile, Second-Lieutenant of the Reserve Hagen had brought about a mobilization on his own. He had been present when Remer received the first news and when he issued his orders on returning from Berlin. He connected what he had heard with what he had seen the day before in the centre of Berlin : the dis-missed Field-Marshal von Brauchitsch driving past, wearing uniform. In a flash, everything seemed clear to him : a military putsch by Brauchitsch! In fact he wrongly put two and two together. But he told Remer of his suspicion and urged him to have a word with Goebbels to get things straight before acting.

In civilian life, Hagen was an adviser in the Propaganda Ministry and a regular contributor to Goebbels' weekly "Das Reich". Wounded in France, transferred to the Guard Battalion, then released, he was busy in Bayreuth on a commission by Bormann to write a "History of National Socialist Culture". He had gone to Berlin to organize an hour of commemoration in honour of the writer Haro Trüstedt who had been killed in action.

Meanwhile in Döberitz, Remer at first did not want to be talked into anything : his General's orders were all that mattered to him, and he was going to carry them out. But Hagen persisted, and expatiated on having seen Brauchitsch; then, Lieutenant-Colonel Wolters, whom Hase had assigned to Remer as liaison officer, suddenly disappeared without requesting dismissal. Remer said that Wolters seemed somewhat unreliable even before his disappearance. The two things together persuaded Remer to have a motor-cycle-combination issued to Hagen on which this official, blaring out "Military putsch by Brauchitsch!" whizzed through the city, to the Ministry of Propaganda, Goebbels' private residence, the Brandenburg Gate, Town HQ and back to the Ministry. In the end Remer was induced to join Goebbels, who arranged a long-distance call for him with Hitler.

While he was trying to find Remer, Hagen learnt from the first company of the Guard Battalion at the Brandenburg Gate that Battle HQ had been set up at Town HQ in Unter den Linden. When he asked for Remer there, he was told to go up to the General's office. He was still hesitating to do so when he came across two of Remer's officers on the staircase. He asked them secretly to tell their CO that he was at once to go and see Goebbels and that the situation had changed completely. That done, Hagen drove back to the Propaganda Ministry. Just before his departure, the officers in the General's room had been considering whether or not to arrest Goebbels. An officer called Remer out into the hall and gave him Hagen's message. Remer asked the officer to accompany him into the General's office where he made him repeat the message. He asked Hase whether in the circumstances he ought not to go and see Goebbels and get the matter cleared up, "otherwise we'll be in a hell of a mess". But Hase would have none of that and asked Remer to wait in the ante-room. Instead, Remer left the building and discussed the situation with his Adjutant, telling him that his, Remer's life was now at stake. Then

355

he took a long walk—he himself put it at half an hour—in the neighbourhood of HQ to sort things out in his own mind.

He finally decided to go and see Goebbels, in defiance of his General. He instructed Second-Lieutenant Buck to stand by with twenty men and rescue him, if necessary by force, if he failed to return within twenty minutes from the Ministry. His pistol at the ready, he burst into Goebbels' room. After some cautious reconnaissance, the Minister told him about the abortive attempt and the military putsch which was apparently in progress. Remer was then put through to the Führer on the telephone. The time was between 19.00 and 20.00, as various reports suggest.

It is impossible to be sure what other reasons prompted Remer's conduct. But two reports are of interest. One said that Remer had demanded the hand-over of the Reich Chancellery. This had been refused by Hitler's Adjutant, NSKK-Gruppenführer Albrecht, with the observation that Hitler was not dead. He told Remer that if he wanted confirmation he should go and see Goebbels who was just then on the phone to Hitler. The other report said that Remer received a telephone call from an officer who told him he was coming over from the Bendlerstrasse with instructions to relieve him. Shortly afterwards, Remer received yet another call, this time from a Sergeant he had known in the "Grossdeutschland" Regiment, who had overheard the first conversation. The Sergeant (so the report went) told him that the first caller, immediately after his conversation with Remer, rang up the Bendlerstrasse and said something to the effect that he was afraid Remer would make difficulties and see through the manoeuvre.[56]

Remer now gave orders to assemble the entire battalion in the garden near Goebbels' private residence in the Herman Göringstrasse, and to stop all troops moving up to the Brandenburg Gate and divert them to his HQ. The effect of this action was that the encirclement of the Government quarter was lifted and the guard withdrawn from the Bendlerstrasse. Remer retained his own Battle HQ at the guardroom at Town HQ, but did not go back there. At Remer's request, Goebbels addressed the assembled Guard Battalion on his behalf. All this must have happened round about 21.00. Two companies were then detailed to take over the local defence of the Reich Chancellery-Wilhelmstrasse and Hermann Göringstrasse block, while one was ordered to surround Town HQ. Several patrols were sent out to reconnoitre, to tell the Commanders of approaching units what was happening, ask them to halt and prevent them from any attack they might be planning on the "renegade" Guard Battalion. Agreement was reached—apparently before any shots were fired—with the Armoured Troops

356

Inspectorate in Fehrbelliner Platz. Remer said that he only realized during the evening that the centre of the conspiracy was at OKW in the Bendlerstrasse. Lieutenant Schlee's report—presumably at about 22.00—may have been the decisive factor. According to his own account, Schlee went to Olbricht's ante-room to report that he had to withdraw the guard. He was held by Merz. But at a moment when he was not guarded he managed to escape. Down in the street, the young Signals officer stopped him and informed him of the true position. Schlee suggested to Remer that the OKW be attacked with stronger forces. Goebbels asked Hitler, who agreed. Schlee was ordered to occupy OKW with a "battle group" made up of units of the Guard Battalion and Army Artificers and to "arrest all Generals".

Even before that, Hitler had asked Goebbels to put him in touch with one of his most loyal Generals whom he knew to be in Berlin—General Reinecke. He ordered Reinecke to take over command of the Berlin Commandant's forces, including the Guard Battalion, and to march with it on the Bendlerstrasse. This was at about 21.15. At 23.00 Schlee's "battle group" reached the Bendlerstrasse, occupied all entrances and exits, threw a ring of seventy sentries around the building and forced its way in. The advance of the armoured units and other troops gradually came to a halt after 21.00. Remer's move has been unduly dramatized; intervention from other quarters proved more significant.[57]

(c) Colonel Wolfgang Gläsemer,[58] the Commander of the Armoured Troops School II in Krampnitz—then the strongest force in the Berlin area—had received the order to launch Operation "Valkyrie" by long-distance telephone from Major Oertzen. He was instructed to march his men quickly into Berlin and make a reconnaissance of the SS barracks in Lichterfelde and Lankwitz. Gläsemer found the order odd and had his suspicions. Before issuing any instructions he, therefore, asked for a decision from the Armoured Troops Inspectorate. After some time, he received a reply which reflected the prevailing uncertainty: "General Olbricht's order is to be carried out, but in no circumstances must there be any exchange of fire with the SS." He thereupon dispatched a number of inconspicuous vehicles which might have been thought to be on a course of driving instruction, to the vicinity of the SS barracks; somewhat more laboriously than necessary, he got the School ready to march while he himself drove ahead to the Bendlerstrasse, accompanied by his Adjutant, Captain Schauss, who knew what was going on, but said nothing. Olbricht told him that the attempt on Hitler had succeeded, thus saying the opposite of what the radio had put out only a little

357

earlier. Gläsemer was ordered to stand by with the bulk of his troops at the Victory Column and to use the remainder to ensure the protection of the General Army Office. Merz von Quirnheim would give him more detailed orders in the ante-room. But Gläsemer argued violently with Merz, saying that they were putting the noose around their own necks, as had happened in 1918, and only the enemy would benefit. To isolate him from the others, he was taken to the upper floor. There he instructed his Adjutant to report to the Armoured Troops Inspectorate, and to take orders for the School from there, and nowhere else.

In the course of the evening—the time reported was 21.30—Gläsemer's ADC, Count Rothkirch, was able to gain access to him. He reported that the School's troops were drawn up at the Victory Column and that the Inspectorate had given instructions for them to be marched immediately to Fehrbelliner Platz. Colonel Gläsemer pretended to the Captain guarding him that on General Olbricht's instructions he intended to send these troops to guard the Bendler-strasse, and that he was going down into the courtyard to carry out the order. He made his way out and escaped.[59]

Colonel-General Fromm had summoned his Departmental Chiefs, Generals Specht, Kuntze and Strecker, to a conference at 18.00. They had already been waiting for some time and urgently demanded to be admitted. They were taken into Fromm's office and confronted with Hoepner, Beck and Olbricht. Hoepner explained to them that Hitler was dead and action was in progress to crush a putsch staged by the SS. There was no longer any chance of winning the war; the fronts would have to be held, but there must be an attempt to make peace as quickly as possible. What mattered most was unity in order to save Germany. He asked the three officers to mobilize their troops for the protection of the new Government. General Specht, who was the Inspector in charge of the training of future officers, objected, and there was a heated argument. General Kuntze, Chief of Training, also refused to co-operate in any way. They were taken to Fromm and all three were put under guard. But Fromm showed them a little-used side exit, asked them to make their get-away at a moment the guards were not watching, and to mobilize troops against the insurgents. These events must have taken place around about 20.30.[60]

Colonel-General Guderian, Inspector-General of Armoured Troops, was not in Berlin that day and could not be contacted. His deputy at Führer HQ was his Chief of Staff, General Thomale; and at the Inspectorate in Fehrbelliner Platz in Berlin, Colonel Bolbrincker was deputizing for him as Departmental Chief for Armoured Troops. In line with the information he had given to

Gläsemer, the Colonel kept "sitting on the fence" until round about 20.00, when he received an order from Thomale to crush the revolt, relieve the Government quarter and break the Guard Battalion's resistance at all costs. While attempts were being made to clarify the situation and prepare for action, Specht arrived with Fromm's request for help and with a more detailed account of what was going on at the Bendlerstrasse. The troops were therefore ordered to stay where they were until further instructions. Lieutenant-Colonel Gehrke, the former Commander of the Guard Battalion, tried to prevent any action against the battalion. He said the order was overtaken by events. Remer arrived and persuaded Bolbrincker and Gehrke to accompany him to Goebbels. Gläsemer came in and resumed command of the School. The troops stayed the night in Fehrbelliner Platz. There was no fighting, nor was any attack launched on the Bendlerstrasse. Instructions countermanding Fromm's and Witzleben's orders went out everywhere.

Evidently the Armoured Troops Inspectorate exercised the most effective control over the withdrawal of units during the evening. Guderian himself has said that he did not then know what was happening. At midnight he received a telephone call from his Chief of Staff, who informed him of Hitler's wish to appoint him Chief of the General Staff. At the next day's situation conference at the "Wolf's Lair" which marked the beginning of Guderian's new function, he was given decidedly preferential treatment by Hitler, according to an eyewitness account.[61]

(d) In the "Valkyrie" plan the Infantry School in Döberitz[62] was allotted the vital task of quickly occupying the Berlin region's radio transmitters, including the Deutschlandsender, with shock-troops. The School was also given the assignment of seizing the large concentration camp of Sachsenhausen (Oranienburg). The Commander of the School, General Hitzfeld, had offered his full co-operation to Olbricht and Stauffenberg, and during an inspection of his troops on July 15—the day of the first "Valkyrie" alert —Olbricht had expressed his particular satisfaction. But Hitzfeld, who had not been specially informed of the new date, was not there when the alarm was given in the afternoon; because of a bereavement he had gone to Baden for the day. Colonel Müller, who was on the staff of the School and who could be relied on to take resolute action in the event of an alarm, did not return from some outside duties until the evening; and only then, at a Berlin railway station, did he hear what had happened. When he got back to the School at 20.30 he realized that the troops had been under stand-by orders since about 17.00, and the officers were in a kind of "war council" mood and divided in their attitude. Some officers who were talking of a putsch—among them a young Major with the Knight's Cross—had prevailed upon the rest to hold back the troops until the situation was clarified. Müller managed to have a word on the phone with General Hitzfeld, who was shocked to hear of this situation and gave orders for "a ruthless attack on the SS". According to Müller, the majority of the rank and file were all for it. The demonstration battalion which had been intended for Oranienburg had to be recalled from a night exercise and could only get back in the course of the evening. Colonel Müller drove to the Bendlerstrasse. By 23.45, when he returned with written authority to Döberitz, the revolt had collapsed.

The inactivity of the Infantry School proved disastrous to the conspirators. If the School had gone into action immediately upon the alarm being given and if, as had been planned with Hitzfeld, its motorized detachment had set out without delay, the broadcast at 18.30 would in all probability never have been made. Instead, all Germany would have heard the insurgents' proclamations. And these would have had their impact, even though the revolt had failed.

(e) The fate of the revolt had already been sealed when the officers' counter-group in the Bendlerstrasse went into action. The importance of this move to these officers was that it was seen that they dissociated themselves from the mutineers to whom they had earlier succumbed. Herber and von der Heyde later explained their conduct by saying : "All of us would have been hanged."[63] One report said that some of the men who later so eagerly opposed the revolt behaved quite differently on that afternoon when news of Hitler's death came through : they ripped the insignia with the swastikas off their tunics and placed themselves fully at Olbricht's disposal. Pridun and Herber are said to have told Olbricht at 17.30 that they were prepared to co-operate against the Party clique which had no ties with the fighting front. Von der Heyde was sitting aloof, completely broken-hearted at the news of Hitler's reported death. At that time, too, Pridun and Herber are reported to have made their first request to the Ordnance Department for arms.

It was later stated in court that Herber had agitated more than the others for action, while von der Heyde subsequently managed to put himself forward as the leader of the counter-group. On the 20th July he only carried a dagger and did not use a firearm. According to Colonel W. Müller, on the morning of July 21 he said that it was his own and not Remer's intervention that had crushed the revolt. Three years later Heyde drew a different picture of what happened. Heyde, who had been at the Military Academy with Stauffenberg, is described as a somewhat colourless but very ambitious and verbose General Staff officer, who after the 20th July waged an exhausting struggle with Pridun for the position as GSO I.

Herber had previously been in the police force. He owed his position not to any special devotion to the Party or particularly ingratiating social manners—he had black hair, dark eyes and a somewhat shifty look—but to the zeal with which he made himself indispensable. Fellow-officers were amazed at the leading role to which he rose on the 20th: "No one would have thought such a thing of this wheedler. . . . If the attempt had succeeded he would have remained a loyal follower of General Olbricht."

Von der Heyde, Pridun, Herber and Fliessbach were promoted to the rank of Colonel; the Company Sergeant-Majors serving under von der Heyde became Second-Lieutenants, and Herber received an award he had not previously acquired, the Iron Cross, First Class—for his action against his own comrades.

Obviously, the armed assault by the counter-group made Fromm's swift court martial possible and spared the five chief conspirators more humiliating treatment by the SS. Shortly after 23.00 troops of the Army, and after midnight men of the SS, occupied the building. Someone who was not involved in the events described the scene on his arrival at OKW on the morning of July 21: a unit of company strength, tommy-guns and rifles slung over their shoulders, were marching out of the big gate, and broke into song.

XIV. VENGEANCE AND TRIALS

THE events of the 20th July came as a profound shock to the German people. The general reaction was one of indignation : for only few knew the background to the attempt, and those who did had to keep silent and bear the misfortune. One word on behalf of the unsuccessful conspirators meant being hauled before the People's Court and death for those who openly said what they thought. The public version of the event, and the announcements issued through official channels to the Wehrmacht, the Party and German missions abroad, made the action appear—as had the first speeches during the night—as the isolated deed of a "very small clique of ambitious, unscrupulous and criminally stupid officers". These morally corrupt men, it was insinuated, had no other aim than to remove Hitler and the leaders of the Wehrmacht to gain power for themselves. They were described as reactionaries, "in sympathy with the Jesuits" (Jodl) and "saboteurs of the German war effort" (Himmler); they were, above all, suspected of being in league with the foreign enemy, of seeking "a rapprochement with the Anglo-Saxons" (Jodl) or "peace with Moscow" (Bormann). In speeches up and down the country the confederates were reviled and slandered beyond measure. The normal reaction of the victors who had crushed a revolt would be genuine self-assurance and a sense of justification. There was none of that in their frenzied threats, their cursing and raving.[1] Instead, they proclaimed that as a salutory sequel to the plot there would be a merciless general reckoning : now, they said, it had become possible to get rid of what had long been sick and rotten, and there would be "a new and special reinforcement of Germany's strength in the current hard struggle for survival" (Ribbentrop).[2]

Three or four days after the attempt, thorough investigation established that much wider circles and plans were involved. The Gestapo felt compelled to set up its own "Special Commission for the 20th July" with a vast staff of 400 officials in eleven sections.[3] The investigation was conducted not only among the circle of people actively implicated in the conspiracy, but into the ramifications of an Opposition movement that was in no way connected with the events of the 20th July, but was brought to light in this connection, and dragged before the People's Court.

The Gestapo itself was surprised by the revelation of the wide network of the rebellion. Shortly before the 20th July, the official concerned with the Wehrmacht and seditious influences undermining the country's defensive strength had declared that nothing very interesting was happening in this sphere and that all material on any possible anti-Wehrmacht tendencies "had been pigeonholed". He mentioned, just in passing, that his department was looking into the question of whether "circles round Colonel-General Beck and Mayor Goerdeler are organizing a campaign of defeatism". Nothing more had been discovered, and not even the arrest of Leber had produced any repercussions—thanks, no doubt, to his unshakeable silence. The SS report on this situation pointed out, by way of explanation, that because of an incident some years previously, Heydrich had been expressly forbidden by Hitler to let the Gestapo meddle in Wehrmacht affairs. Heydrich, who had been cashiered from the Navy, had of his own accord intensified this ban to the point of prohibiting his men from associating with Wehrmacht members in any form whatever.

Himmler, too, was completely taken by surprise by the attempt on Hitler. Personally, of course, he may have considered anything possible, as had been shown by the frequently mentioned meeting with Minister Popitz and by various other feelers he had put out. And by then he may well have been prepared to give the SS motto "My Honour is Loyalty" any convenient interpretation. Stauffenberg himself said that he first met Himmler at the situation conference on the Obersalzberg on June 7 and that they talked about nothing of consequence. Himmler, he recalled, had helped him into his coat in his crippled state. This was probably soon after Himmler's conversation with Guderian, during which Stauffenberg's name had been mentioned. Later, on the way to the airfield, Himmler carried Stauffenberg's brief-case for him—hardly a gesture that pleased Stauffenberg as the case contained explosives which he had brought along "to test his nerves", and as Himmler then put it somewhat roughly on the ground. Stauffenberg described the SS leader as a man who combined bourgeois intelligence with dangerous and mad plans, and he found him either unsure of himself, evasive or grossly overbearing. But Stauffenberg meticulously returned his courtesies. And that was all there was to it, despite the sensation hunters who would have liked to make out that there was some secret link between the two men.

Himmler's "speech" on August 3 in Posen—where he had summoned the Gauleiters of the Reich to sound a deliberate fanfare of terror after the black 20th July—has been preserved, thanks to Reichleiter Bormann's collector's zeal.[4] It marked the peak of hatred and sinister threats. No punishment had yet been meted out since the 20th, but in this speech the entire process of vengeance was revealed—beginning on the next day with a "Court of Honour", and followed, five days later, with the first hangings. They continued till the end of the war, though they did not claim as many victims as Himmler had threatened. Then, envisaging punishment of others beyond the culprits, Himmler said he was going to introduce "a system of absolute liability on the grounds of kinship". "All you need do," he declared, "is to read up the Germanic sagas. When they proscribed a family and declared them outlaws or when they had a vendetta, they went all the way, without mercy. They outlawed the entire family and said: this man is a traitor, there is bad blood in that family—the blood of traitors—the whole lot must be exterminated. And in the case of a vendetta that was what they did, down to the last member of his kin. The Stauffenberg family will be exterminated, root and branch. (Applause.) That will be a warning example, once and for all."

In the same speech Himmler described the 20th July as "only the ultimate manifestation of a long trend" of the growing incompetence and sabotage in the Officer Corps, of the "intellectuals of the General Staff", indeed of the entire German Army—all of which had been going on since the First World War. He was convinced that the Officer Corps and the Army would never recover from this blow of the 20th July. He urged recruitment to the "National Socialist People's Army" whose first Grenadier divisions had just been placed under his command. On the day of this speech "Der Völkische Beobachter" wrote: "The marriage between Party and Wehrmacht has today become a living reality." The Wehrmacht had now also adopted the Party salute—the raised hand. In this speech to a Party audience Himmler violated the order Hitler had had to issue to stop the dangerously widespread public denunciation of the 20th July rebels: no one, Hitler decreed, must indulge in "attacks or insults of the Officer Corps, the Generals, the aristocracy or parts of the Wehrmacht as entities. It must always be stressed that the men involved in the putsch were a specific, relatively small clique of officers".[5]

The "absolute liability on grounds of kinship" which Himmler had threatened to enforce was not put into effect. But the next of kin and other relatives of the chief conspirators, from the oldest right down to the children, were put under arrest. At least twelve women over the age of seventy were among them, including the mother of the Stauffenberg brothers. Women even had to spend their confinement in prison. Children up to a certain age were sent to Party hostels, where they were destined to grow up under false names and where they were found, often after weeks of searching, at the end of the war. Kaltenbrunner's idea was to have all the arrested relatives taken to chalets in the Riesengebirge mountains for the duration of the war. This plan was being put into effect when the attack by the Red Army in January 1945 put an end to it. It is said that Göring's intervention was chiefly responsible for Himmler being prevented from carrying out his insane vendetta.

According to the SS, the discovery of two documents quickly gave the investigators a comprehensive picture of the ramifications of the revolt. One of them was found by sheer accident. Goerdeler's temporary lodgings in Berlin, the hostel in Askanischer Platz, had been destroyed in an air raid in the spring of 1944. By the time they began to search for Goerdeler, part of the house had been provisionally rebuilt and re-opened to boarders. The porter said that a fat envelope addressed to Dr Goerdeler had been found in a safe under the rubble. It had been left there before the raid but had never been collected. It was found to contain various drafts, appeals and a Government proclamation. The second find consisted of some of the diaries kept by Olbricht's and Goerdeler's go-between. The names entered were pseudonyms, but these were soon decoded. The identity of a fairly large number of people had also been established from the teleprinted messages confiscated at the Signals centre in the Bendlerstrasse. The cellar-prisons in the Prinz Albrechtstrasse were beginning to fill.[5]

Day and night the interrogations continued, with the inquisitors working on a shift basis. The available copies of reports sent to Hitler give the false impression of a calm atmosphere and of information volunteered. Maybe this did obtain—but how rare it must have been! It is much more likely to have been a terrible, cunning battle for information, with the men under interrogation nearing the end of their strength, then regaining courage, and the evidence frequently being extorted by force : some of the prisoners still showed the marks of this brutality when they appeared in court. There was a regulation permitting "rigorous interrogation", which had been practised ever since 1942 and which covered every, even the most callous kind of inhumanity during the investigations into the conspiracy. This regulation permitted harsher methods if the "prisoner is able to give information on important anti-state or illegal matters, connections or plans, but refuses to divulge his knowledge, and if this information cannot be obtained by ordinary investigation methods". "According to circumstances", it gave any resourceful interrogator a free choice among such penalties as : bread and water; a hard bed; a dark cell; deprivation of sleep; exercises to exhaust the prisoner and beatings. Where, by regulation, the rigorous methods were a means of obtaining evidence of other people's offences and not of a confession of the prisoner's own, there again a wide choice offered itself. And when the prisoner was near exhaustion, he could still be interrogated—without compulsion—about his own part in the affair. People already sentenced to death were kept alive as long as they could serve a useful purpose in the investigations. That was done with Trott, Hofacker, Goerdeler and Leber. Goerdeler was sentenced on September 8 and executed on February 2; Leber was sentenced on October 20 and executed on January 5. It has often been suspected that drugs were used on the prisoners, but in the case of Goerdeler this was denied by Ritter who was confronted with him during the investigations.

These investigations were carried out with great thoroughness. The bodies of the men killed in the first night were disinterred the following day. According to Himmler's speech at Posen, he had them identified, cremated and their ashes scattered into the fields. Tresckow suffered the same fate : his body had been recovered by the 28th Rifle Division on July 21 from a wood near the front line. Afterwards, an Order of the Day to the Second Army, whose Chief of General Staff he had been, paid tribute to him as an officer whose example should be followed, and he was specially mentioned in the Wehrmacht Communiqué. But when his complicity in the plot became known, some men were sent from the Gestapo HQ in the Prinz Albrechtstrasse to the place where he had been buried in his native soil. As they removed his body from the grave, they shouted insults at his relatives. The body was taken to Berlin, where one of Tresckow's closest assistants was under interrogation. He had so far resolutely denied everything. The interrogators now tried to break his resistance by presenting him with the unexpected, terrible sight of the dead officer.

Men who had been wounded by bullets received medical attention only to get them fit again for interrogation, and possibly for the agony of death. General Karl-Heinrich von Stülpnagel had been ordered to Berlin to report to Keitel after the unhappy night. On the way through the Meuse valley, he asked his driver to stop the car in a side road behind Verdun. He said he wanted to go for a little walk and told the driver to proceed to nearby Champs. The area was infested by Maquis, and his two companions who were anxious about his safety, stopped not far away behind a ridge. They heard a shot, then another, and rushed back to the spot where they had left the General. But he was gone. After some searching they found Stülpnagel floating in the green waters of the nearby canal. He was bleeding from a head wound, alive but unconscious. They took him back to Verdun and telephoned Paris : the General had been shot at by terrorists. The truth was soon discovered and served to prove Stülpnagel's guilt. The General, who went blind, was later executed. So was Jens Jessen, who could no longer walk, and Hans von Dohnanyi, whom they carried to his death on a stretcher.

The Special Commission was able to draw on the SS teleprinter and telephone network and search service, which covered the entire Reich and the occupied territories. In the sixth year of the war the coverage was extended rather than reduced. The SS was able to seize any new suspect, no matter how far away he was, within an hour perhaps, or they could immediately put him under observation. Without the victim knowing anything about it, as a rule, every aspect of his behaviour, what he said in his letters or who visited him at his home, was reported to Berlin.

Some tried to disappear, moving from place to place in Germany like the Wandering Jew—it was of little use. It was almost impossible to slip through the tight net of compulsory registration and controls which were difficult to by-pass, if for no other reason than that people had to buy food. Indeed, only a very small number succeeded, with help from people who risked their own lives, in remaining unrecognized until the end of the war or in fleeing into neutral neighbouring countries.[7] Only few of the conspirators at the front could bring themselves to desert to the enemy. Goerdeler, who knew of the warrant for his arrest even before the 20th, had sought refuge with some friends where he learnt that Hitler had set a prize of a million marks on his head. No one among the families that offered him shelter betrayed him, and, still free himself, he lived to see his friends taken away one after the other. He has left a simple, but shattering account of his flight to West Prussia where he wanted to see his birthplace and his parents' grave in Marienwerder once more before he was arrested. He probably no longer thought of fleeing abroad : he feared this might endanger the lives of the members of his family, and he had no passport under a false name. One morning, on August 12, he was resting at a remote inn near Konradswalde. He was exhausted and had temporarily dropped his guard. A girl from Königsberg, presumably quite guileless, recognized him; the million on his head later became too heavy a burden for her.[8]

Quite a number of the people involved in the revolt took their own lives. To them the prospect was unbearable : they would be dragged into an investigation where they were bound to succumb physically, and they were equally certain that they would never be allowed freely to state their motives. Others were driven to suicide more by the fear that they might not be able to withstand torture and might give away names. This was apparently the reason why the much-loved Freiherr Kurt von Plettenberg took his own life.

During the last weeks he had frequently met Stauffenberg. Contrary to expectations he had not been hounded by the Gestapo, but, being the man he was, he felt almost pained that he should be the only one to enjoy his freedom while all the others were lying in prison or had been put to death. In 1945 his turn came too. In earlier days he had taken boxing lessons to make up for his delicate constitution. Smilingly, he told a fellow-prisoner that they had given him twenty-four hours to think over whether he would voluntarily name the confederates he knew. When, on the following day, two guards took him away for interrogation—all this happened on the third floor of the court building—he suddenly broke loose, knocked the two men down with well-aimed blows and jumped out of the window.[9]

Ulrich von Hassell had reached Berlin via a difficult route from Upper Bavaria when the coup d'état was imminent. After the catastrophe of the 20th he did not want to run away from his fate. So he stayed. He knew when they would come for him; and when they did he received them "sitting at his writing desk".[10]

Count Hardenberg was dining when Gestapo officials broke in through the corridor and appeared in the adjoining room, the door to which stood open. He rose, calmly bowed to the Countess, and went to meet them. There was a shot—for a moment it looked as if there had been a struggle—Hardenberg sank to the floor; he had shot himself with a revolver through the left side of his chest. One of the intruders, too, had been wounded. A little later, when the attention of the guard was temporarily diverted, Hardenberg seized the paper-scissors from the writing desk and rammed them into his treacherous wound : but his heart survived the blow. He lost consciousness. Hardenberg made a third attempt—this time to cut his veins; the doctor, who alone was permitted access, agreed not to hinder him. But this attempt, too, was abortive. In the morning Hardenberg, having lost a vast amount of blood, was taken away. After custody in a cell for the injured, Hardenberg was transferred to prison. He was fated to survive it all and lived to see the collapse of Germany and the loss of his native region in the East.

The investigations produced a number of surprises. They explain the atmosphere of malevolent mistrust which had begun to affect everyone at civilian and military establishments. Men who only a short while earlier had been discussing officially what action to take against some of the conspirators, were suddenly found to be accomplices and arrested even while they were having lunch together. The Quartermaster-General, Wagner, had been talking to Kaltenbrunner about the most suitable investigation procedure to adopt when he was about to be arrested. He shot himself in order to be spared this humiliation. At times, arrests were being made on such a scale that the Minister of Armaments intervened to preserve the liberty of some men who were temporarily irreplaceable. Colonel Finckh, the Quartermaster-General in France, begged to be allowed to keep his job, at least until the crisis after the latest Allied breakthrough was overcome and a coherent front line restored. After that, he said, they could do what they liked with him. But no one listened.

The "Special Commission" continued its work throughout Hitler's life. As more and more people who had known about the revolt were identified, the prison population swelled. The investigators discharged their task with a meticulousness only possible under that type of régime. No more than a handful of people escaped detection and prosecution. There is proof that in many respects the character and scope of the revolutionary movement was correctly diagnosed by the investigators. Bormann and Hitler were told of the results of the investigation by the Gestapo at the Prinz Albrechtstrasse in reports summarized by Obersturmbannführer Kielpinski. At first they were made daily, later once every three days and in the end once a week. The reports, which have been preserved, vary greatly, depending on the prisoners under investigation and the interrogating officials, and are full of insults, bias and provocative remarks against the prisoners. All of them are based on an assessment of the situation which seems completely illusory to us today, just as the views of the conspirators appeared to the investigators at that time—although the rebel view soon proved to be the more realistic. None the less, it has to be stated that Kaltenbrunner's officials endeavoured to elucidate the motives which linked this unusual circle of men in rebellion against Hitler and that they did not suppress the conspirators' accusations against the Hitler régime. There are, for instance, explanations of the attitude of the officers, of the defection of formerly trusted Party members, and even of the motives of some who turned to the enemy.

Undoubtedly the investigators were influenced in their interpretation by the behaviour of the interrogated. It seems that to some of the prisoners, such as Goerdeler, Schulenburg and Berthold Stauffenberg, it was more important to demonstrate how deeply and genuinely they desired the overthrow of the régime than to defend themselves. Defence, they felt, would be of no avail in any case against death, which they believed to be their certain fate. It is conceivable that Kaltenbrunner personally gave instructions—as a controversial report by one of the Gestapo men, Kiesel, maintained —"that Hitler must be given an uncompromising account of the motives for the assassination attempt. So many men of distinguished character and office were involved in the conspiracy that Hitler would, it was hoped, receive the shock he needed to make the necessary changes."

Perhaps we shall never know the full truth of what was said during the interrogations. But even the expurgated versions in the Kaltenbrunner Reports contain condemnations of Hitler and his régime which were never allowed to become publicly known because the accusers would suddenly be seen to have become the accused. The interrogation at the Prinz Albrechtstrasse of Count Berthold Stauffenberg revealed that he was one of the very few who "remained utterly incorrigible and fanatic". "His short evidence," the Report continued, "was the clearest and most important document indicting Hitler that may ever have been written and shown to him. It manifested a type of German manhood with deep religious, political and artistic principles, utterly divorced from Hitler and National Socialism."[10a] The Kaltenbrunner Reports reproduced only a few extracts from Stauffenberg's testimony, including these passages :

"As regards domestic policies [reference is here made to the year 1933] we had fully endorsed most of the National Socialist tenets : the Führer principle, the idea of expert leadership responsible to itself and linked with the concepts of a healthy respect for rank and of a 'people's community'; the principle of common welfare before individual welfare; the struggle against corruption; emphasis on the role of the countryside and rejection of the 'big city' spirit; the racial principle and the will to build a new system of law on German foundations—all these seemed sound and full of promise to us.

"But nearly all the basic ideas of National Socialism were *completely reversed* by the régime.

"Instead of 'leaders with a calling', as a rule 'mediocrities', who exercised uncontrolled power, got to the top. The idea of a 'people's community' was violated by incitement against the upper classes and the intellectuals and by generally arousing resentment among the petit-bourgeois" (KB 447, 453).

Others besides Berthold Stauffenberg also turned the indictment of the conspirators into one of the régime, which they accused of having constantly betrayed itself. "The whole leadership has turned its back on the principles of simplicity and modesty which it preached in the early days of National Socialism. We want leaders who set an example by their conduct and actions.... We want a society again based on the sanctity and inviolability of law. . . . We want Germany to be purged of corruption and crime, and justice and decency restored for all without discrimination . . ." (Schulenburg, KB 454). "The first guiding principle ought to be : decency and justice. Another slogan was 'German Socialism'. That was supposed to mean that the ideas of National Socialism were to be largely adopted, indeed that some of them *were to be introduced for the first time*. I stressed that the future Government will have to be markedly different from the present régime, particularly in the administration of justice. . . . The leaders of the present National Socialist régime ought to be tried before a properly constituted court of law" (Count Nikolaus Uexküll, KB 449, 452).

First Hitler had asked for a big public show-trial with film, radio and maximum press coverage. But later he agreed with Himmler's misgivings and ordered a trial before the "People's Court", with limited seating capacity and a strictly selected audience. This meant he had decided against a court martial, which was the legally prescribed judicial authority for officers. He therefore arranged for an "Army Court of Honour" to be set up, the purpose of which was to expel from the Wehrmacht, and so hand over to civil courts, those officers who, judging by the results of the preliminary investigation, were likely to be found guilty. Field-Marshal von Rundstedt became President of the "Court of Honour". His assessors were Marshal Keitel, Colonel-General Guderian and Generals Schroth, Specht, Kriebel, Burgdorf and Maisel. The "Court of Honour" passed verdicts without personal testimony from the accused and merely on evidence from police files. Its first act on August 4, 1944, was the dismissal with ignominy from the Army of twenty-two officers, including a Field-Marshal and eight Generals.

Hitler demanded that the court proceedings be harsh and "swift as lightning".[11] The accused were not to be allowed to make long speeches and the standard punishment was to be death by hanging, which had to be carried out within two hours of the sentence. No visit from minister or priest was to be allowed. As President, Hitler appointed Roland Freisler,[12] who was already working at the People's Court. Freisler, an expert on Soviet law and methods of punishment, had played a leading part as a protagonist of the so-called "Gesinnungsstrafrecht"; according to this concept of criminal law the judge should base himself on his faith in Führer and nation and on "the sound sense of the people"; he should determine punishment not according to a law specifically prescribed for a specific deed. His sole guidance should be the offender's recognizedly hostile sentiments towards the régime from which the intent to commit the offence could therefore be deduced. The judge was not to be hindered by legalistic clauses. Freisler is on record as saying that the important thing was to "atomize" the accused.

The first eight defendants in the July conspiracy faced the People's Court in the Great Hall of the Kammergericht in Berlin on August 7 and 8. A bust of Hitler, swastika flags, the judges' robes—with Freisler in red—uniforms prevalent among the audience ... there were all the trappings of a show-trial. And the entire proceedings were recorded and filmed to let the German people, or at least Hitler, who wanted to see it all, take part in the trial.

This is what an eyewitness wrote later : [13]

"Never before in the history of German justice have defendants been treated with such brutality, such fanatic ruthlessness as at this trial. They were brought into the courtroom like common murderers, each held by the sleeves by two Gestapo officials. They wore no ties or braces. You could see from the defendants' outward appearance—and as the interrogation proceeded this impression grew even stronger—that after all they had suffered during their detention for preliminary investigation, they were longing for one thing only : a quick end to this physical and spiritual torture. One of them ... still showed the traces of torture. It was typical of the inhuman court procedure that not one of the accused was permitted to explain the motives for his action. All the defendants had to suffer this ex-lawyer to call them scoundrels, traitors and cowardly murderers. ... In this way the conduct of the proceedings ... turned into a travesty of a court trial, which was also shown by the fact that the President entered the courtroom at the head of his assessors like a second Robespierre—with a theatrical, brutal and merciless expression on his face which he seemed to have rehearsed before a mirror. There was nothing human in this repulsive, distorted face with its cunning, hypocritical, heavy-lidded eyes. ... In a voice that, contrary to all the rules about secrecy, must have blared like a trumpet call into the adjacent streets, he pronounced all eight defendants guilty of unqualified treason against the Führer, their liege, against everything the German people were and stood for, against German history, and all German men and women. In a pompous style, occasionally reminiscent of old Germanic sayings, he repeated the same phrases over and over again and finally sentenced all the defendants to be hanged for 'the most dastardly deed in the whole of our history'. He concluded his verdict with the boast : 'We are going back to life, to battle. We have nothing in common with them. The nation has got rid of them and has remained unsullied. We fight on. The Wehrmacht salutes you : Heil Hitler. We all salute : Heil Hitler. We fight with our Führer and follow him—for Germany. Now we have shaken off the danger, we march with total strength to total victory!' "

Only carefully vetted people were admitted to the trial and frequent checks were made to ensure that the audience included no unauthorized person and that only those entitled to do so were taking notes. Despite these precautions, people outside came to know how horrified those present at the trial were at the way it was being conducted. The Reich Minister of Justice, Thierack, himself complained to Bormann and Hitler on September 8, after the trial of Goerdeler, Wirmer, Leuschner and Hassell. But nothing was changed.[14] The accused were to be given no opportunity to make a statement. How many of them must have hoped to be able to tell their story and justify themselves before the German people at least once more before the hangman laid hands on them!

"It is not surprising," an account by one who saw it all says,[15] "that one witnessed so much courage and pride, yet can report only so few words of defiance. Only when the tiger in the presidential chair momentarily relaxed his vigilance to pounce, was a defendant able to make a bold retort. . . ." The remark by Hans von Haeften, the diplomatist, is well known : asked by Freisler why he had criminally broken faith with Hitler, Haeften replied : "Because I regard the Führer as the instrument of evil in history." In the short time he had left before his execution, Moltke was able to make some notes on his verbal duel with Freisler. What he had to state will always be read with horror and admiration. Leber is said to have behaved with his well-known courage before Freisler. Schulenburg, too, defied the insults hurled against him. According to one report, Freisler almost invariably addressed him as "Scoundrel Schulenburg" or "Criminal Schulenburg". On one occasion when the President slipped up and said "Count Schulenburg", the accused is said to have bowed and interrupted him : "Scoundrel Schulenburg, if you please!"

Photographs which have been preserved illustrate Ambassador von Hassell's defiant attitude and show the contemptuous silence of other defendants. They seemed to have passed all fear of torture and answered only the most essential points of the questions put to them. Fellgiebel is reported to have urged the President after sentence was passed : "Better hurry up with the hanging, Herr Präsident, or else you'll hang before us." And Witzleben said : "You can hand us over to the hangman. In three months from now the outraged and tormented people will bring you to book and drag you alive through the mud in the streets." Wirmer, with heavy build and professional legal expertise and court experience, proved a particularly tough proposition for Freisler : "If I am hanged, it's not me

373

who's frightened, but you. . . ." Freisler: "You'll soon be in Hell. . . ." Wirmer: "It'll be a pleasure, if you follow soon, Herr Präsident."[16]

The day came five months later. During a heavy air raid the People's Court had moved to the shelter. Part of the ceiling collapsed, a heavy girder broke loose and killed Freisler, who was about to read out the indictment against Schlabrendorff.

Germany's situation was getting desperate. The front lines were drawing closer and closer, and this was bound to cause Hitler grave anxiety. None the less, he obviously insisted on being told every day what progress the elimination of his opponents at home was making. According to Kiesel's report, he "devoured" the special daily summaries of new accusations, arrests, interrogation results and executions. Often upsetting the work of the officials in charge, he intervened with his own orders in current proceedings. If the only available report is correct, Hitler summoned both the President of the Court and the executioner and insisted that not even the slightest concessions must be granted to the condemned : they were to hang from meat-hooks like cattle; no one was to think of the executed as martyrs in the cause of freedom. He demanded—at least in the case of the first executions—that they be filmed, and he wanted to see those films.[17]

Perhaps the most desolate experience of the men whose lives ended on the gallows was not the vulgarity and the sneers of the executioners—they have probably been much the same throughout the ages ("they know not what they do"). What must have been even more shattering to the prisoners was the realization that he who was, or should have been, the leader of his people was no better than these petty stranglers. They knew that it was by his command that they were forced to appear in their final helplessness, in a scene filmed with pitiless efficiency by the whirring cameras, and so face once more this century's Anti-Christ.

Despite Hitler's orders to the contrary, the two prison chaplains at Plötzensee did have a few words with many of the condemned in the short time they had left between sentence of death and execution, before they departed from a life that had become agonizing for them. To some of the victims, the chaplains were at least able to wave a greeting and blessing from a distance as the men were led away to their death. These reports will always be read with deep emotion, not only because they deal with the final experience through which these men went uncomplaining and with praiseworthy self-control. Some of the Nazis executed at Nuremberg, too, are said to have borne their lot like men, but there is something else in the reports about the men of the 20th July; a

374

final reminder of how an exceptional and like-minded group of the best men of a nation combined in an attempt to turn the tide of evil and restore the rule of a higher law.

Only the first executions were announced : the many others which followed during the long final months of the war remained unknown to the German public, as did the inhuman cruelties inflicted on thousands of concentration camp inmates. Survivors later told what it was like to live in this separate, dismal world—a silent nod, a few stealthy words, help dearly paid for, or a gift—these were the only links with one's immediate camp neighbour afflicted by the same misfortune. In the midst of that filth and vulgarity were people of steadfast chivalry, and others who always had a word of encouragement or comfort. The long wait, the almost daily sight of death snatching another victim, and the unforeseen changes each hour brought—all this deprived death of its horror and made many a concentration camp prisoner walk unwavering along the path he would otherwise have trodden in desperate fear. Perhaps only he who has lived through a similar experience will understand the faith in destiny of those who have been hardened in the fire of such a furnace, who have become almost invulnerable and think otherwise of death than those who are free.

The unexpected discovery of some documents in September 1944 also gave Hitler an insight into the conspiracy during the 1938–40 period. In a safe in Zossen they found Beck's carefully collected documents, which he had failed to destroy when Dohnanyi was arrested, and parts of a diary by Canaris. Oster then gave evidence which suggested that the Resistance movement started as far back as the dismissal of Freiherr von Fritsch and which implicated the Army leadership. To Hitler, these were shattering revelations. But they were withheld from the public and even from the People's Court. Only when Canaris' complete diary was found during the last month of the war, did Hitler, in a fit of fury, have the whole group of men who had not yet been on trial, hauled before a drum-head SS court martial to be sentenced and executed on April 9. (Canaris, Oster, Dohnanyi, Bonhoeffer, Gehre, Strünck and Sack.)

In the last two weeks of the war a fairly large number of prisoners who, above the roar of battle, could already hear their liberators advancing, were treacherously shot without trial. It had been decided that under no circumstances must they fall into enemy hands. Some who survived that last peril and, marked by their bitter experience, regained freedom, were first dragged from camp to camp during a hazardous flight from the enemy who had already entered the country. The threat of death hung over them until the last moment of captivity.

The lives of the members of one of these refugee groups were also linked with the fate of the flyer, Countess Melitta Stauffenberg, née Schiller. As Claus Stauffenberg's sister-in-law—her husband, Alexander Stauffenberg, had been under arrest since July 24—she had herself first been taken into custody as a member of the Stauffenberg family. But later, as she had no knowledge of the planned revolt, she had been released for a special job : training night pilots at the Air War Training College at Gatow in the use of a device she had evolved, whereby night-fighter crash-landings could be avoided. Göring himself had conferred high decorations on the Countess. Making use of her freedom to travel around, she now saw it her duty to maintain contact among the separated members of various families, not only the Stauffenbergs. She found the escape route of the biggest refugee group, which included Alexander Stauffenberg, and once having located them, she was able to "drop in" on the same day and bring news and little gifts, accept messages to the outside world and help to look after the group's safety. Her aircraft was never armed. On one of her flights, on April 8, 1945, she was shot down by an Allied fighter over the Danube near Straubing.

*   *   *

The fate of two other men—Field-Marshals Kluge and Rommel —must also be recorded here : it is inseparably linked with the aftermath of the 20th July. What happened to them became known only after the war.[18]

Kluge, who had sealed the failure of the attempted revolt by his refusal to commit himself, survived the 20th July by a mere four weeks. General Blumentritt, next in seniority to him, later wrote in the prison camp : "Rather a Third World War than a repetition of the weeks after the 20th July. But an outsider *cannot* possibly understand that."

Kluge realized that the situation was hopeless in view of the material superiority of the Allies. He pitted his ambition as a great military expert against the enemy and shrank from no personal risk, however great, in an endeavour to hold the front. But there was also Hitler's growing distrust of the General. He blamed Kluge's "pessimism" for Germany's setbacks. Once proceedings before the People's Court had started, Hitler's suspicion was fanned not only by military reports. And his virulent distrust reached its climax when Kluge, on one of his usual visits to battle headquarters, had driven into the enemy-surrounded gap at Falaise, and during

376

twenty-four hours could not be contacted by Führer HQ. Hitler was convinced that Kluge had gone over to the enemy and ordered Field-Marshal Model, then commanding Army Group North Ukraine in Galicia, to take over his post immediately. On his return, Kluge had to hand over his command in France at an hour's notice. In a letter of August 18, in which he repudiated in great detail the criticism of his military leadership, he implored Hitler to end the war if the hoped-for new weapons failed to bring success. In a desperate final passage he wrote : "The German people have endured such unspeakable agonies that it is time to end this horror." And then this homage, amazing in a last letter, though it may have been meant as a challenge : "My Führer, I have always admired your greatness.... If destiny is stronger than your will and your genius, that is the will of Providence. You have fought a great and glorious battle, to which history will bear witness. Now show yourself great enough to end, if need be, a hopeless struggle. I part from you, my Führer, as one who in the knowledge of having done his duty to the end stood closer to you than perhaps you have ever realized."

It was August 19 and Kluge and his companions were driving eastward from Compiègne. When they reached the neighbourhood of Verdun they halted for lunch. A little later when the Field-Marshal's companions wanted to continue the journey, they found him dead near the spot where Stülpnagel had shot himself. The poison from a small phial had freed Kluge from his unbearable burden.[19]

When Hitler received Kluge's letter from Sepp Dietrich, his reaction was one of cynicism, even contempt, once he had been assured that the autopsy had shown that poison and not a heart attack had ended Kluge's life. What Hitler said on August 31 showed that Kluge would have also been hauled before a court. On the previous day Hofacker, Stülpnagel, Finckh, Linstow and Raht-gens—Kluge's nephew—had been sentenced to death and all, except Hofacker, had been executed. During the trial it emerged, for the first time, that Kluge himself had been heavily implicated, from 1943 onwards, and his staff since 1944. Blumentritt and Speidel were replaced, and Speidel was taken to the cellar prison at the Prinz Albrechtstrasse.

Until now Rommel had not come under suspicion. When the persecutions after the 20th July began he was desperately ill. The only remarkable thing was that the public was told in an almost casual way about a car accident in which the Marshal had been involved. Rommel, seriously injured, was taken to his native Alb valley near Ulm. No undue suspicion seems to have been aroused

377

by the fact that Party officials were asked to keep check of his convalescence, which was making good progress. As a result of a new report by Bormann, a conference with Hitler was arranged in early October, which was attended by Keitel, Himmler and General Burgdorf. On October 7, Rommel received a long-distance call from HQ inviting him to attend a conference in Berlin on the 10th. Keitel had apparently been told to discuss Rommel's next assignment with him and Rommel had found out about this from Burgdorf. On the advice of his doctors Rommel declined to go to Berlin and asked for a message to be sent to him through a reliable officer. General Burgdorf's visit was announced for October 14. Rommel had a hunch that evil was brewing. When a friend remarked to Rommel that Hitler would not dare to touch him, the Marshal declared calmly and with certainty : "Oh yes, he wants to get rid of me."

There are several accounts of what happened on October 14. At noon, Generals Burgdorf and Maisel appeared at Herrlingen Castle. Burgdorf was Head of the Personnel Department, having succeeded Schmundt who had been killed on 20th July; Maisel was the Army High Command's delegate dealing with the July conspiracy. Both were members of the "Court of Honour". After an hour's meeting, during which news came from the village that the castle was surrounded by SS troops, the Generals left again by the front entrance. A great change had come over Rommel's expression as he went to his wife and said : "In a quarter of an hour I shall be dead." He told her that he had been accused of complicity in the July plot. Hitler, he said, was offering him the choice between taking poison and facing the People's Court. He was not afraid of the Court, but he was convinced that he would never get to Berlin alive. And so he was choosing poison. He bid his wife and son goodbye, exchanged a few words with his ADC, and putting his hand on the man's shoulder, said : "Aldinger, this is it." Rommel repeated the essential points that had been put to him : on the way to Ulm they would hand him the poison; half an hour later news would be received that he had died in an accident. Everything had been pre-arranged, minute by minute. They had even described his own funeral to him in great detail. He had been given a promise that his family would not be persecuted. The Captain urged Rommel to resist, but the Marshal said the village was surrounded, it was impossible to get in touch with his troops as all telephone lines were being tapped. "I have, therefore, decided to do what, obviously, I must do." And so he left to join the two officers who were waiting for him in the garden. Without a word he stepped into their car. It was five past one. Shortly before half past one the two Generals

378

arrived at a hospital in Ulm, with the dead Marshal, and demanded that the doctor give him a "heart injection". They immediately telephoned Führer HQ and OKH and announced that the Führer had ordered a state funeral. When the chief physician of the hospital wanted to carry out an autopsy, Burgdorf snapped : "Don't touch the body! Everything has already been arranged in Berlin." An embolism due to Rommel's previous injuries was given as cause of death. When his relatives saw the dead Marshal they were struck by the "expression of colossal contempt" on his face which they had never seen in him when he was alive.

Later, news leaked out that the SS and SD troops which had accompanied the two Generals and surrounded the house and village had orders to shoot Rommel if there was the slightest incident. Under no circumstances was he to be allowed to get away alive. At the state funeral, Hitler had himself represented by Field-Marshal von Rundstedt, who seemed a broken and distracted man and, presumably ignorant of the true circumstances, read out an oration containing phrases like "his heart belonged to the Führer". The only Party leader present was Kaltenbrunner. An Order of the Day praised Rommel the Hero, and two steel-helmeted soldiers laid a huge wreath on his grave. . . . . At Nuremberg, Keitel declared that Hitler had personally instigated the attempt to kill Rommel, but that he kept up the pretence of an embolism even vis-à-vis Göring, Jodl and Dönitz. The Head of the German War Graves Board was ordered by Hitler to erect a memorial to Rommel and to invite designs from sculptors. . . . . But all attempts to adorn this grave with wreaths, memorials and speeches failed to silence rumours among the people that Rommel had not died a natural death, but had been killed by Hitler.

Speidel speaks of a "Socratic execution which the Field-Marshal must have regarded both as a sacrifice of his life and as a reveille to the nation" and he recalls a passage from Machiavelli : "The General whose achievement has brought victory and success to the Ruler is inevitably held in such high regard by the soldiers, the people and the enemy that these victories do not have the sole effect of making the Ruler favourably disposed. The Ruler must safeguard himself against his General. He must remove him or deprive him of his reputation."

Not only those directly or indirectly involved in the July conspiracy fell victim to the vengeance of Hitler and the régime they had assailed. A large number of people who had nothing whatever to do with the event, but who had caught the Gestapo's eye in another context were sentenced to death in this frenzied atmosphere, even for offences—real or presumptive—which normally would have been punished by imprisonment. It is known that in several instances Hitler himself ordered the executions after a sentence of imprisonment had been imposed by the Court—as in the case of General Heistermann von Ziehlberg, who had been sentenced by a court martial to nine months in gaol for "negligence in the execution of an order"; or in the case of General Count Sponeck, condemned to death for giving an unauthorized order to retreat in the Caucasus, but whose sentence had later been commuted to seven years' imprisonment.[20]

According to later research, about 5 000 Germans and other nationals were executed between the 20th July and the end of the war. This number does not include persons sentenced by courts martial. Of those directly involved in the revolt of the 20th July, between 180 and 200 lost their lives.[21]

The vanquished conspirators of the 20th acquired greater ascendancy over their executioners than was apparent to the outside world. The men who were going wild with staging more and more new trials and executions of the "traitors", themselves fell under the spell of those they punished. After the early outbursts in court, strict precautions were taken to prevent anything liable to cause unrest from reaching the public. But we now know that things were said in private in the guise of cautious "explanations", but which scarcely concealed the speakers' personal uneasiness. An investigating official was heard to say to one of the conspirators : "No doubt, you and your friends are good Germans. But you are enemies of the régime and therefore we must destroy you." Someone who was present at a Ministerial conference between Goebbels and Keitel, Bormann, Speer and others, quoted the Propaganda Minister as saying : "The men of the 20th July did not act frivolously. They were staunch patriots who took a desperate step in the last hour because they had doubts about final victory." And there is a letter dated August 30, from the SS Chief Kaltenbrunner (KB 323) to Reichsleiter Bormann, containing a selection of convincing accusations of corruption and political favouritism which had emerged during the interrogations. Undoubtedly, Kaltenbrunner welcomed the opportunity of being able to submit such a document but even he was deeply affected by the proceedings. Photographs of the trials show him looking gloomy as he sat in the row immediately behind the defendants. And when the widow of Hermann Maass, now knowing that her husband had just been executed, submitted a plea for mercy, an Under-Secretary in the Ministry of Justice exclaimed, genuinely shocked it seems, and secretly agreeing with the victims of the terror régime he represented : "The 20th July is getting beyond us. We can't control the thing any longer." No other demonstration against his leadership made such an impact on Hitler as the 20th July. Although he recklessly threw himself, and what was left of Germany's forces, into the inescapable final struggle, from now on his direction was anonymous and invisible. After the 20th July he never again spoke in public to the German people. One woman's simple remark—that he was living thirty metres below ground[22]—was soon on everybody's lips.

Hitler survived the 20th July by nine months and ten days. On April 30, 1945, he shot himself with a pistol in war-torn Berlin. In accordance with his instructions, his body was burned. It has never been found.

CONCLUSION

In the months after the 20th July the German leadership never, even for the briefest period, regained freedom of action, and it was unable to stop the progressive disintegration of the country's war potential. The enemy no longer needed to worry about Germany's air defences. In most cases it was now merely a question of calculating the quantity of explosives, steel and phosphorus that should be showered on her. The havoc wrought between the 20th July and the end of the war reflected this effort. Munich, Dresden, Bremen, Frankfurt on Main, Hamburg, Nuremberg, Würzburg, Stuttgart, Hildesheim, Braunschweig, and finally Berlin—to name but some of the cities—were virtually destroyed. It has been calculated that the air raid havoc, the destruction caused in the ground fighting and the demolition carried out by order accounted for much more than half the total war damage in Germany. The proportion of people killed in that period is even greater : more people lost their lives in the nine months of the war after the 20th July than in nearly fifty-nine months since September 1, 1939. Their number includes not only the German soldiers and their allies who died in battle, but also the civilians who were killed in air raids or while trying to escape, or during the invasion by the Russians, and men, women, and children who were taken prisoners-of-war or deported, and are listed as dead or missing.[1] After the 20th July Germany did not supply the fighting front with any new weapons or war materials of decisive significance. We know that various weapons were being developed and that some new ones were produced, such as jet fighters, or U-boats with Walther-engines. But production increasingly fell behind the required quantities. Much pioneer work in nuclear research had been done in Germany, but then it was decided not to develop a nuclear weapon and to go in for rockets instead, from which quicker and more reliable results were expected.[2] While Germany gained superiority in the construction of these long-range, remote-control missiles, they were not yet accurate enough for operational use. From June–July onwards the country's war effort was weakening, the fuel crisis in particular was threatening to get worse as a result of Allied attacks on the Rumanian oil fields of Ploesti and Giurgiu (the first took place on April 5, 1944) and on Germany's synthetic fuel industry (May 12, 1944). Albert Speer, who was the Minister in charge of armaments

382

at the time, gave it as his view at Nuremberg that technologically Germany lost the war in May 1944.

After the 20th July even Party and armament industry officials, until then exempted, were drafted to help the intensified "total manpower effort". But despite this no significant improvement was achieved. Himmler's representative who took over the job of C.-in-C. of the Reserve Army said, according to several testimonies, that he was unable to detect any sabotage in either Fromm's or Olbricht's office. Nor was there any subsequent proof provided of sabotage within the ranks of the Reserve Army, which might have been instigated by Olbricht and Stauffenberg or their supporters.[3] Available evidence suggests that the preparations for the revolt did not impair Germany's war potential. Even the sequel to the 20th July had no effect on the outcome of the war. The severe setbacks and the collapse of various fronts in June and July 1944 had nothing to do with the events in Berlin. They were neither cause nor consequence of the efforts to overthrow the régime, but they did provide a powerful stimulus to accelerate them.

In the light of a later analysis of the opposing forces' strength, the verdict of many German and enemy experts that Germany had lost the war even before the 20th July is unchallengeable.[4] All she could do was to try and prolong the final struggle until her still substantial resources were completely exhausted. Even men like Jodl and Keitel expressed similar views on the situation. As is now known from their confidential conversations, their military commonsense told them that after the successful Allied invasion of France there was no longer any chance of Germany's winning the war. Fundamentally, they then only relied on the illusory hope of a split among the enemies, which Hitler predicted.[5]

The main political event of the months before the end of the war was the invasion of Germany by the Americans and the Russians who represented two great powers of strongly divergent outlook. No advance preparations were made by Hitler to absorb the political shock of impending defeat and to soften the impact of collapse on the German people—if we disregard various abortive feelers put out by Himmler, which were concealed from Hitler. The Allies' insistence on unconditional surrender, of course, hindered any such move, but evidently the idea did not occur to Hitler. He was quoted as telling a meeting of Divisional Commanders a week before the 20th July : "No one concludes a separate peace with me." He never considered resigning or, if necessary, "sacrificing" himself for the sake of Germany, something which he ruthlessly demanded of others. Even within his inner circle, and right to the very end, he clung to the motto : Victory or downfall for the German people.

"The ones left after the war are inferior anyway, the good ones will have died in battle."[6]

But outside Hitler's immediate entourage, which he dominated, there were plenty of voices telling him the true position clearly and without reservation and demanding an end to irresponsible sacrifices. A number of reports agree on this. From the summer of 1944 onwards, the worse the situation grew the more stubborn and inaccessible did Hitler become. This, it is suggested, had something to do with his visibly increasing physical illness which has been described as Parkinson's disease (*paralysis agitans*) or as a nervous complaint due to degeneration which leads concurrently to a paralysing hardening of both physical features and psychological behaviour. His brain continued to function normally. His interpreter, who was last present at a discussion in December, confirmed that Hitler was in "full command of his mental faculties to argue". Observers believed that the mental edifice which he kept re-building for himself and in which he had believed, collapsed only just before the end "when, suddenly, he realized that he was giving orders to an Army which no longer existed. He then sat for two hours in front of his map in the Chancellor's bunker in complete silence and stared distractedly into the void. Like a bad captain he left the sinking ship and abandoned those he had led to their fate."[7]

On the 20th July no enemy soldier had as yet set foot on German soil. The Anglo-Americans were on the Rimini–Arezzo line in Italy, while in France they were still being contained within their Normandy landing areas. The Russians were only just fighting their way into Rumania and had not yet entered Yugoslavia, Hungary and Czechoslovakia (then the "Protectorate of Bohemia and Moravia" and Slovakia). In Poland, they still stood on the bend of the Vistula. Now available documents show that at that time no separate pacts existed among Germany's opponents about four-Power occupation. These agreements were not concluded until February 11, 1945, at the Yalta Conference (lines of demarcation, Oder-Neisse frontier, joint occupation of Berlin and Vienna), nor was there any agreement on the expulsion of Germans from Czechoslovakia, Poland, Hungary, Rumania and Yugoslavia. All that was decided later, in June 1945, at the Potsdam Conference. When the Allies gained control of Germany in April–May 1945 they took over a leaderless country which had been deserted by its Government at the very moment when it was invaded by the enemies it had roused.

If the revolt of the 20th July had succeeded, Germany's opponents would have been dealing with a legal, all-German Government both at the negotiating table and in case of an occupation of the country. They could not simply have ignored such a Government, just as they were unable to ignore Badoglio's Government in Italy, despite the demand for unconditional surrender. In July, Germany's ultimate fate—that of being torn asunder into opposing zones of influence and becoming a battleground between two parts of the world—was not yet inevitable. A later analysis suggests that if some form of a "Western solution", as contemplated by Stauffenberg, had been found, about a million German troops would have become available for the reinforcement of the Eastern front, provided the Western Powers would not have prevented such a move.[8]

The Allied break-out from the Normandy beach-head and the German defeat at Avranches—which, according to Eisenhower, decided the war—came five days after the attempted uprising. It marked the end of the period in which any action by Germany would still have had some purpose.

Asked in court what "he really wanted to achieve with a coup d'état", Count von der Schulenburg told the judge : "Wait three months ! The situation you will see then will be the one from which we started in our deliberations and decisions." Things took longer than three months—but what happened was just what the conspirators had predicted.

What happened on the 20th July did not prove that the plan for the revolt was unworkable, in fact, the success of the action in Paris showed conclusively that it was practicable. We cannot decide from the actual course of events whether the revolt came too late and whether it could have succeeded without causing the collapse of the fighting fronts and civil war. Anyone is entitled to his views on the matter—and they may well depend on his assessment of the relative strength of the contestants. Besides, the sequence of events on the 20th July showed that it was not the SS and the National Socialist Party but the Army which crushed the attempted revolt. It also showed that it was only Hitler's spell while he was still alive and not loyalty to National Socialism which prevented the majority of officers from actively joining the rebels. Had Hitler died, and a clear justification for the state of emergency been given, the picture would have been entirely different, even if the SS and the Party had meanwhile started a counter-movement. It is impossible to say what proportions a struggle between the two sides would have reached. In the Army the decision would have rested mainly with the Commanders-in-Chief of the Army Groups. From what was said afterwards, it may be assumed that after Hitler's death most of them would have agreed to the new arrangements and would have tried to influence their troops accordingly. According to Speidel, the leaders of the Waffen SS in France would also have given their support.

In the last resort, it also depended on the strength and authority of the Berlin conspirators and on the confidence they inspired, how Britain and the United States would have reacted to the Resistance movement in Germany and to the idea of Germany's breaking off the fight in the West without abandoning the defence on the Eastern front. There is reason to believe that the Western Allies would not have obstructed decisive military action, especially—as was seen later—since the soundness of the Casablanca formula was violently criticized and the British Prime Minister had said, although unofficially, he would be willing to drop it under certain circumstances.[9] The English historian, Wheeler-Bennett, in his book, defends Britain's policy of ignoring the revolutionary movement in Germany. He comes to the conclusion that it was fortunate that the revolt of the 20th July failed. And he offers this revealing explanation : otherwise the Allies would have had to agree to a negotiated peace, and that "would have been to abandon our declared aim of destroying German militarism". Equally, he is convinced that a successful coup would have led to a negotiated peace. His conclusions are, of course, at variance with other statements from the then enemy camp, with the Morgenthau Plan,[10] the Yalta and Potsdam Conferences, and the entire conduct of Germany's adversaries in the first post-war years. They show how hopelessly her enemies had meanwhile succumbed to their own propaganda, folly and hatred—concepts which they thought must be fought when held by the German nation. Years later various voices could be heard from the opponents' camp protesting that it had been impossible to realize what the 20th July had meant and what had been at stake at the time. If it was the Allies' intention to destroy German militarism, could not Stauffenberg, who himself was not in any way a German militarist, have helped to make clear to the Western leaders what was really at stake?

*　　*　　*

We may base our judgement of the events of the 20th July on these reliable assumptions : what was planned was to organize a responsibly directed revolt which would have used the existing chain of command of the Reserve Army, avoided chaos and civil war and led to a controlled change-over to a new, though provisional régime. It was impossible to carry out the plan without Stauffenberg being present. He was Fromm's Chief of Staff in Berlin. Although the events of the day took an entirely different

386

course, they showed how correct this assumption was. Stauffenberg, having decided that he would personally make the attempt on Hitler, also had to make sure that he would safely escape from Führer HQ and get back to his Berlin office as fast as possible.

To accomplish this task on the 20th July he acted in cold blood, logically and with great circumspection:[11] three and a half hours after the assassination attempt in East Prussia he took charge of operations at the Bendlerstrasse, 600 kilometres away, with a self-possession that allowed of no suspicion.

One may criticize Stauffenberg for having undertaken a double task in which he failed. But then one cannot escape the conclusion that without his decision there would have been no anti-Hitler move at all.

It may be objected that Stauffenberg ought to have had the courage to blow himself up with Hitler. But such arguments—however easy they may have appeared to the uninitiated observer at the time—are unfounded in view of the plan and the exigencies on the day of the attempt. Today this is no more than heroic posturing. There are authenticated reports that long before July Stauffenberg offered to risk his life and do the deed from which others had shrunk time and again. But the men who shared his responsibility prevented him.

Any serious analyst—except a narrow-minded critic—will understand that for a man of his type it cannot have been easy, indeed it must have been almost unbearably difficult, to know that his action at Headquarters would cost the lives of so many others—including some very close friends—while he had to make sure of his own escape. Only his comprehension of a necessity far transcending the fate of individuals could have given him the courage to take such a step.[12]

Stauffenberg knew just how near Hitler he had placed the deadly bomb a few minutes before it went off. And so, when he saw the explosion, which to him seemed like the impact of a 15 cm. shell, he felt sure the attempt had succeeded even when he was faced with Keitel's denial in Berlin. The fact that, contrary to all probability, his own eyes had deceived him determined the unexpected course of events on the 20th July.

As the incoming news was at first conflicting, then plainly unfavourable, the conspirators were quickly seen to divide into two categories: the ones who had joined the revolt only on certain conditions, the others who were ready to act in any circumstances. One began to hesitate, another made sure of a line of retreat, a third refused to do anything at all. Had the news been different they would all have wholeheartedly supported a change of régime.

But as the attempt had failed it became much more difficult, though not yet impossible, to attain the aims of the planned revolt, especially since three vital hours had been lost. And failure became certain once two or three of the men in key positions had decided not to join in.

From the point of view of historical research, it is futile to analyse the various individual setbacks of the day. As Hitler remained alive, we are left with a distorted picture of what could have been achieved with the plans and forces available.

* * *

"Anything that lies outside the ordinary course of action seems slightly mad to the cold rationalist : and you won't find a political dilettante who will not declare a General's enterprise that seems extraordinary to him as senseless, unless it turns out to be success-ful and so forces him to keep quiet. For only success induces ordinary people to admire extraordinary action. . . . In our case, the man who lacks spirit will think it much more prudent to eat his daily bread in peace and comfort with his family than to be shot dead for the sake of some imaginary honour, as they put it. The cautious man will seriously doubt whether the one who prefers to be shot is right in the head and he, for one, will go home and thank God that he is not like the other fellow."[13]

* * *

We do not have enough information to judge what action the prospective Provisional Government could have taken, what author-ity it would have wielded and what its chances of survival in such a difficult situation would have been. That government never came into being and all we have is a list of names.

The composition of the Provisional Government indicates that its first concern would have been to deal with immediate necessities, that no audacious innovations were intended and that it had made sure of the co-operation of experts. This did not exclude the possibility of giving an opportunity to the more go-ahead elements, once the transition was completed. Although the lists reveal that the prospective Ministers were drawn from particular political parties, the new grouping obviously was not really binding. In their combined strenuous efforts to establish a new régime the men of the Resistance had become so accustomed to working and being together that the necessary "compromises" were no longer looked on as a tug-of-war between parties, but as a genuine method—

388

and one that was indispensable in a living political organism—of working out a common policy. This unifying experience, which had made them all independent of party, class and denomination, and the uncompromising resolve to rise above the emergency, as Leber put it, would surely have become effective in the political actions of the new Government.

After the 20th July the men of the Resistance were criticized and attacked from many quarters and for many different reasons. This shows how little this unifying strength was understood and that during the war and in the immediate post-war period, the public in Germany and abroad was perplexed by the attempted revolt, or viewed it with irritation and hostility.

Here are some of the descriptions given to the men involved in the uprising:

... cowards; weak officers who had lost touch with the fighting front, who wanted defeat and undermined the fighting spirit—men of inordinate ambition; talented but unscrupulous officers who felt frustrated and neglected by Hitler, which was why they sought to usurp supreme power;

... traitors to the Fatherland; the enemy's tools in the destruction of Germany, who in self-chastisement and contrition at Germany's "outrages" saw salvation and moral right only in others... nationalists, worse even than Hitler—because they were disguised—who with all their talk about Europe and the community of the Western countries meant nothing but Germany's supremacy; men who wanted to get out of one war in time to play first fiddle again in the next one;

... left-wing revolutionary dreamers, who had knocked down Germany as far as the Rhine, nay all Europe, to the man in the Kremlin...

... right-wing reactionaries, who thought their time had come to cast off the fetters they had worn for years and to play politics again in good old German Nationalist fashion.

... Junkers, incorrigible aristocrats, who did not like the new people's state and whose sole ambition was that they and their like should once more get to the top—at Germany's expense.

. . . tools of the Church; an Opposition run by the clergy, who wanted to exploit the opportunity to launch a counter-blow against National Socialism, irrespective of the consequences to the Reich.[14]

It is unnecessary to defend the men of the Resistance against such reproaches. If they or the many opponents of Hitler in the post-war period included people to whom such criticism can be legitimately applied, it will be remembered that Stauffenberg joined an anti-

Hitler group which had existed for many years and had wide ramifications; he took them as he found them—some friendly, others
entirely alien to his own type—and it was he who led them to act
together in pursuit of their common aim. Undoubtedly, there were
men among them who were brought in only for the outward
appearance of the revolt although they stood aloof from its aims.
Such individual cases, therefore, should not make us draw conclusions about the inner ring of conspirators.

Historians will have to base their judgement on the entire community of people of different origins, ages and authority who united
for a common purpose : they included men like the former Chief of
the General Staff, who was acting from a high sense of responsibility and was rooted in the monarchical tradition; men brought up
in the days of the German Republic, whose attitude and ideas
exposed them to greater danger than did that of the old-established
class and who approached contemporary problems, especially social
and ecclesiastical questions, in a new, adventurous spirit; clergymen
who pressed forward beyond obsolete dogmas and who, though uncertain whether their superiors would approve, felt committed to
join in the dangerous enterprise; there were battle-scarred young
platoon and company commanders from the front who felt impelled
to action for the sake of their dead comrades and the men still
fighting; intellectuals who until then had thought of their spiritual
pursuits alone, but who now encouraged and helped the men of
action.

Among those involved in the revolt were large estate-owners and
humble wage earners; men from the middle class and many aristocrats; free-thinkers and believers; men of brain and men of brawn;
men who calculated cautiously, others who bravely professed what
they believed in. But those who elsewhere form the majority were
not found among the conspirators : the parasite, who wants to have
a good time; the busybody, who feathers his own nest; the luke-
warm and lazy, who lets things go as long as they do not hurt him.
There was, of course, some narrow-mindedness; they argued, as
Germans do, about ideas and dogmas; there was a tendency to
finish-everything-once-and-for-all; they made political mistakes;
and there was vanity—but as regards their commitment to a goal
that transcended the well-being of the individual and their willingness to make sacrifices in its pursuit, this community of men is
above reproach.

*   *   *

It is impossible to draw a contrast between the men of the 20th
July and those fighting at the front. The conspirators and their

390

associates thought like soldiers and did not run away from the harshness of modern war. They were passionately and directly involved in what was happening on the front, but they were utterly convinced that a leader had the right to demand such heavy daily sacrifices only if he was able to justify them by his own superior self-discipline and by the interests of the nation as a whole. By deciding to wrest command from this leader, the insurgents did not stab the fighting soldiers in the back. They did not dishonour the ultimate sacrifice which so many decent German soldiers—among them their sons and intimate friends—had made. They felt they were merely doing what the fighting and the dead were entitled to demand from them. Thousands died in the belief that under Hitler they were serving and fighting under responsible leadership. It may be argued that the revolt by Stauffenberg and his confederates ensured that these sacrifices were not wholly in vain.

* * *

"On the 20th July," a young officer said, "I told my comrades on the Eastern front that I was outraged by the mutineers in Berlin." But later he came to see things in a different light. And this is what he wrote about Stauffenberg and his confederates :

"The rebels realized that the execution of their duty, to which they were pledged by oath, was forcing them and countless others, for whom they felt responsible, to commit acts they knew in their consciences to be criminal. The unique, and to use a hackneyed phrase, tragic aspect of their situation was that there seemed to be a way out only if they themselves accepted the odium of breaking faith, allegiance and law by rebellion and violence. The only alternative was to let things take their course, in numb resignation, and at least to try not to become personally guilty of crime. For the sake of the community these men, as individuals, took upon themselves a deed which they clearly realized was questionable, but necessary and inevitable. How heavily this dual nature of the revolt weighed on their minds is evident from Major-General Tresckow's words about the 'mark of Cain' which all who had made common cause with him were bearing.

"These men did not make things easy for themselves. They hardly ever used the obvious excuse that it was Hitler who had broken his oath, that he himself never kept the faith which he enforced and demanded of everyone else. If anything in modern history can claim to be called a sacrifice, it is their deed. Fully aware of what they were doing, they undertook a crime to put an end to monstrous crimes which they witnessed.

"Anyone who honestly searches his conscience must realize that active rebellion was a hard decision; it was infinitely easier for a Christian to fall back on the catechism, for a soldier to invoke the sanctity of the oath or to say he was obeying an order. All of us who evaded the final decision in the great inner conflict of the past war at least owe silence to those who took a stand. They need no justification. And any attempt to oppose them and cast doubts on their deed condemns him who makes the judgement."[15]

* * *

At a time when the individual and whole nations are victims of "developments" which no one can approve yet no one can change —developments which seem to obey only the laws of gravity—the attempt of the 20th July carries its own shining message.

Stauffenberg and his confederates did not act as members of a profession, class, party or denomination. But they expressed their conviction that as true Germans they felt responsible for what was happening to the nation. Let others confine themselves to their day-to-day tasks, and with their limited horizon accept the small share of their own responsibility; Stauffenberg and his men were unable to ignore the command of humanity in their breasts. They felt the burden and misery, but they were proud, too, of being forced to take a stand and act for the sake of all. Of course they were tempted to ask themselves why they, of all people, should throw themselves against the tide when this was not their official duty; why should not they, like the rest, be satisfied, wihout being cowards, with doing what was asked of them? In any case, the outcome of the war was a foregone conclusion.

They decided otherwise. Today we know their reasons. They wanted to put an end to a war which was terrible in every respect and for all concerned. They wanted to end it in a reasonable manner so that the nations involved could once again find common ground and live together in peace, and so that all countries could be spared further, incalculable sacrifice and destruction. They wanted to take the initiative in getting Germany, by her own strong decision, to accept a new Government with which she could regain her freedom of action. The revolt was also meant to pave the way for new forms of political life and a coming-together of the nations —for which the peoples were ready after their great suffering. The exceptional situation had to be exploited before the wounds once again became scarred over. The revolt was positive proof that there still exists a sacred resolve to use human power to reshape the course of modern technology, which is sweeping the world to evil and bondage.

* * *

Moral Motives, a sense of responsibility for mankind as a whole —something most unusual in political life—played a great part in the uprising. It cannot be compared with other officers' revolts in which various groups struggled for power; nor can it be considered as an attempt by German non-political idealists to reform the world. The men of the 20th July were clear-headed and fully prepared to join and win the political battle. Their real enemy was Hitler. Their real task was to judge him and put a convincing leadership in his place. But their assault went beyond the person of Hitler; they were attacking the virulent and powerful evil of their day, of whose existence people scarcely knew, as all over the world they had come to accept a black and white version of life which presented no problems to them.

Dietrich Bonhoeffer once said it was symptomatic of the world in which he lived that "evil appears in the form of light or beneficence, of historical necessity or of social justice" and presents itself as progress. H. B. von Haeften described Hitler as "the executor of Evil in history". And in the Stauffenberg circle they spoke of the would-be-Christ, the Anti-Christ, who roused his opponents to action. There is an appropriate entry in Ulrich von Hassell's diary, in June 1940 : he tried to apply Goethe's interpretation of the "demonic" element in man to what was happening in his day. In Book 20 of "Dichtung und Wahrheit" Goethe wrote : ". . . they exert immense strength, they wield incredible power over all creatures and the elements themselves. . . . Not even a combination of all moral forces is of avail against them; in vain does the more intelligent section of mankind try to render them suspect as the cheated or cheaters, for the masses are drawn to them. . . . They cannot be overcome except by the Universe itself with which they have joined battle. . . ."

There is much evidence of this kind of thinking to be found among members of the Stauffenberg circle. It hardly suggests that they had themselves fallen too much under the spell of this man Hitler and had begun to glorify baseness. On the contrary, they saw beyond Hitler as a person : to them he was an important power, the "instrument of evil" in our time on earth. This reveals the true depth of their decision. It shows that their deed was not aimed just at the death of this one individual but was a *Revolt of the Spirit* that sought political power to meet the dangers from outside and within ("Hitler within ourselves") and strove to lead from misery to freedom.

Winston Churchill, who immediately after the July attempt had said some unkind things, is reported to have made this remark in the House of Commons in 1946 :

"In Germany, there was an Opposition which was quantitatively weakened by its sacrifices and by an unnerving international policy (Casablanca!) but which was among the greatest and most noble groups in the political history of all times. These men fought without help from inside or outside—driven solely by their uneasy conscience.... Their deeds and sacrifices are the foundations of a new edifice. We hope the day will come when this heroic chapter of the internal history of Germany is duly appreciated.[16]

Commemorating the men of the 20th July, Count Paul Yorck von Wartenburg said :

"They acted from a sense of responsibility which their conscience did not permit them to shirk : they acted on behalf of their nation in the knowledge of what Germany owed her illustrious men of spirit, her history, her culture, Europe and Christianity. They stood up against the nation's corrupters who had piled crime upon crime. And yet they had to break with traditional views and test themselves and their right to rebellion by the image of man they sought to create. They had to seek honour outside the laws of their class before they felt certain that they were called upon to act, before they could take the risk, indeed before they were allowed to sacrifice their own lives.

"Let us not deceive ourselves! Nothing of the mission our defeat entailed has as yet been accomplished spiritually. The German people has not gone through the searching of heart and soul and the suffering which the conspirators of the 20th July had to experience before they could act. We have not redeemed their legacy. For it is not enough to talk of freedom, yet think of a good life; it is not enough to fish out some dusty political ideals, re-varnish them and proclaim them to be truths. Our own political fate and the menacing vicinity of Bolshevism immediately confront us with this question about ourselves : what kind of people do we think we are? Force and utmost urgency demand an answer about man as such, about his very essence and nature.

"The 20th July 1944 has left the German people a name that ought to be burned into every heart—the name of *Stauffenberg*. His last words : 'Long live eternal Germany!' are his legacy to us. He imposes upon us a task and implores us.... The defence of liberty pre-supposes a class of leaders who know of the relationship between liberty, justice and love; a class of leaders who have been

394

trained to think on an historical scale; a class of leaders who feel called to serve and are not self-seeking. The men of the 20th July have won renewed recognition for all these views. And it is that which accounts for their unpopularity in a democracy that clings to fiction.

"But we—who have assembled here to honour their memory, praise them and contemplate their great suffering—we must know the worth of the gift the dead have bequeathed to us. We must want to learn from them and we must grasp that he who has no sense of the heroic in himself cannot understand heroes. Heroes are not just brave men. Solitude surrounds the hero. A flame burns in his heart. He accepts the challenge of his destiny and takes a stand against a whole world. His command is the one he gives to himself, and whether his ship lands safely or founders, he entrusts himself to God."[17]

*   *   *

An unpublished but authenticated report says that during his last weeks, even during the last few days, Stauffenberg was at pains to draft an oath which would bind the confederates together in the future as well. He assumed that the inevitable entry into Germany of occupation forces would bring new influences and a strong foreign element, and that some of the conspirators might waver or be forced to adopt an attitude that could be misinterpreted. He was certain of himself and his intimate friends; but he might not be with them, and so he wanted to provide something independent of himself for his confederates by which they would recognize one another.

The oath contained no reference to foreign occupation, no call to "Werewolf" resistance and violence. It simply stated in clear phrases, without foreign words, what binds the German to his Fatherland, what he must always preserve or achieve under a new régime for his own and other nations' sake.[18] The oath contained this passage : "We want a new order which makes all Germans responsible for the state and guarantees them law and justice; but we despise the lie that all are equal and we submit to rank ordained by nature. We want a people with roots in their native land, close to the powers of nature, finding happiness and contentment in the given environment, and overcoming, in freedom and pride, the base instincts of envy and jealousy. We want leaders who, coming from every section of the nation, are in harmony with the divine powers and set an example to others by their noble spirit, discipline and sacrifice."

Whether praised or criticized, regarded as strange or still effective

395

—these words by Claus and Berthold Stauffenberg clearly contribute more to the image of the two brothers and the revolt than many a direct statement they may have made in day to day affairs. The oath was intended as a pledge and guidance for the leaders. Rarely can spiritual planning and political effort have been more closely and courageously combined than in this call : and on the 20th July the men who were ready to carry it out proved that it was genuine. Berthold Stauffenberg, a man of independent political judgement and with a natural gift of deep reflection, carried on unbroken after the abortive coup as one of those who "wanted the best for his country and people".

Born to rise to a position of command and energetic leadership, Claus Stauffenberg, in order to save and keep faith with the others, took upon himself the stigma of would-be assassin (which, even today, he continues to be for many people who do not know the inside story). Only in his last words did he invoke what really filled his heart.

In these days of larger associations of states and nations it should be noted that Stauffenberg's oath strongly urges the Germans to cherish their native heritage, to be conscious of their nationhood and to shape their own destiny; and that it firmly denounces all "base instincts of envy and jealousy" against other nations.

*   *   *

In the memorial chapel of the cemetery at Lautlingen the names of Counts Claus and Berthold Stauffenberg are inscribed on reddish stone among those killed in the war. And to them as well as all the other men of the 20th July is dedicated a phrase, based on words from the Book of Maccabee which have acquired a new meaning : "They resisted the enemies of their nation and gave their lives for the maintenance of the law of God."

NOTES

In the case of non-German works, the references are to translations, where available.

IMT "The Trial of the Major War Criminals before the International Tribunal at Nuremberg". IMT in bibliography.

KB The so-called Kaltenbrunner Reports: "Spiegelbild einer Verschwörung". Under K. H. PETER in bibliography.

BZH 20. Juli 1944, "Sammelband der Bundeszentrale für Heimatdienst". Bonn 1960. Under BZH in bibliography.

I. LUDWIG BECK

1. FOERSTER, p. 121 ff.
2. WEIZSÄCKER on Beck: "This man with the fine, intelligent, responsible, almost melancholy expression, a Moltke redivivus" (p. 173). Manstein (FOERSTER p. 50): "If I have ever known an officer who, in my opinion, could have been the embodiment of Field-Marshal Moltke, it was Beck!"
3. HOSSBACH, p. 153.
4. FOERSTER, p. 42.
5. The very impressive letter of November 28, 1918, is reproduced in FOERSTER, p. 16 ff. Beck always took issue with the person of Ludendorff and his theory of "total war". Cf. Beck's studies "Der Anführer im Kriege" and "Die Lehre vom totalen Kriege" reproduced in BECK, Studien pp. 19 and 227. Cf. also WESTPHAL, p. 53 (discussion with Beck in the winter of 1937).
6. J. LEBER, Ein Mann geht seinen Weg, p. 157. Amongst the defending lawyers was Dr Karl Sack, later Judge Advocate General, who was executed for his participation in the 20th July. (*Translator's note:* SCHLABRENDORFF says it was Dr Alfons Sack, who defended at the trial, not Dr Karl Sack.) Hitler appeared as a witness in Leipzig. SHIRER p. 135 quotes from his statement reported in the Frankfurter Zeitung of September 26, 1930. Recently Thilo VOGELSANG, Reichswehr, Staat and NSDAP, p. 82 ff, p. 90 f. On the Reichswehr's relations with the Republic and NSDAP, FOERTSCH p. 13 ff, p. 19 (only in 1932 were registered members of the NSDAP accepted in the Army); KRAUSNICK, Die Vollmacht des Gewissens p. 179 ff; Hans von SEECKT, Gedanken eines Soldaten, p. 116: "What do I demand of the Army? Loyalty to the State! What do I demand of the State? Devotion to the Army!" For Reichswehr and von Seeckt cf. especially LEBER op. cit., also GÖRLITZ, Wallensteins Lager; and WHEELER-BENNETT and TAYLOR for British views. On the whole question especially VOGELSANG op. cit.
7. FOERTSCH p. 20 says it was a basic idea of the Wehrmacht leadership at the time (Schleicher) that the NSDAP should be given responsibility as soon as possible and so banish the danger of it becoming more radical. He quotes from Rosenberg's posthumous memoirs that General von Hammerstein told Hitler at this time: "If you come to power legally, that is all right with me. But, otherwise, I shall shoot." Cf. also in this connection the letter of the subsequent General STIEFF from this period reproduced in Vierteljahrsh. für Zeitgeschichte, Year 2, 1954, vol 3, pp. 295–98.
8. FOERTSCH p. 26 ff. describes the events based on the account given by General Freiherr von dem Bussche, who was involved as Head of the Army Personnel

Office. He refutes the legend, repeated by Göring in Nuremberg, that there was a threat from Schleicher and Hammerstein to stage a putsch with the Potsdam garrison. On Schleicher's attempt to act with the unions see LEBER op. cit. Cf. also DIEHLS p. 385.

9. Robert INGRIM, Hitlers glücklichster Tag, Stuttgart 1962, Seewald Verlag.
10. HOSSBACH p. 207; IMT XXV 402–13. Hossbach was present at the talks.
11. FOERSTER p. 70.
12. On the events in connection with Freiherr von Fritsch cf. the account based on his own observations by Hermann FOERTSCH, which treats the Fritsch crisis as a "turning point in the history of the National Socialist period". A source report also in Count KIELMANSEGG, Der Fritschprozess 1938, and in HOSSBACH, who (p. 156) writes in conclusion: "The reaction to the Fritsch case in the Officer Corps became for Hitler the test of the self-confidence and the independence of the Army." FOERSTER p. 92 for a memorandum on how Beck proposed to the C.-in-C. that the "insulting and humiliating attack on the Army" should be answered. HASSELL p. 39 writes after a talk with Fritsch on December 18, 1938: "The substance of his (Fritsch's) views: This man—Hitler—is Germany's destiny for good and evil. If he now goes into the abyss . . ., he will drag us all with him. Nothing can be done." KRAUSNICK, Die Vollmacht des Gewissens pp. 279–302 gives a survey of the "Fritsch crisis".
13. Beck had first received a confidential report of Hitler's remarks from Hossbach. HOSSBACH p. 218.
14. FOERTSCH p. 108 ff.
15. FRANÇOIS-PONCET, Als Botschafter in Berlin, p. 291.
16. WINNIG p. 83.
17. Summarized in DE MENDELSOHN p. 70; KORDT, Wahn und Wirklichkeit, p. 110 ff. FOERSTER p. 113 (Beck's memorandum).
18. FOERSTER p. 109, p. 114.
19. Statement made on oath about the meeting by ADAM, IMT XXI, 425, FOERSTER p. 142 writes: "Years later, when he (Beck) returned to these events and happenings, the usually so disciplined man was seized with passionate excitement. His figure then became tense, his eyes blazed with anger and contempt, and with finger raised dramatically, he exclaimed: 'Brauchitsch left me in the lurch!'"
20. FOERSTER p. 116 ff. and p. 121 ff. and KRAUSNICK op. cit., p. 314 ff.
21. Cf. M. BRAUBACH, Der Weg zum 20. Juli 1944, p. 16 and the report of his researches in "Hist. Jahrb., Year 76", 1957, p. 256. GISEVIUS p. 338.
22. FOERSTER p. 128 ff.
23. To break the resistance of the Generals and particularly to counter Beck effectively, Hitler, on August 10, 1938, did something very unusual. Short circuiting their superior officers, he summoned those Generals who, in the event of war, were earmarked as Chiefs of Staff of the Armies and Army Groups—"the younger generation"—to see him at the Berghof and spoke to them for nearly three hours to the effect that Britain and France would not dare to intervene in the armed conflict with Czechoslovakia, FOERTSCH, op. cit., p. 175 ff., MANSTEIN: IMT XX p. 659. On August 11 Colonel-General Fritsch was made "honorary" Colonel of the 12th Artillery Regiment in Gross-Born. On August 17 Hitler broke his pledged word and put the SS units alongside the Wehrmacht as special units at his exclusive disposal. IMT XXVI p. 190.
24. HOSSBACH p. 149.
25. The SS Report on the 20th July, whose value as a source is disputed, and which is based on the statement of SS-Standartenführer KIESEL (executed by

Tito) contains the sentences (p. 8): "In the coming events . . . he (Beck) was the great figure behind the scenes. He showed himself a master of the conspiracy. None of the participants could later remember a single occasion when Beck spoke to him about particular duties in this network of high treason, except entre deux têtes." BRAUBACH in his report on his research (note 21) stresses, contrary to Ritter, Beck's leading role even after his retirement. Stülpnagel, who was very close to Beck, was Halder's deputy. Cf. also details given by Frau Dohnanyi in SENDTNER in Die Vollmacht des Gewissens, p. 345 including "Beck was the sovereign. . . ."

26. Hitler to Reich Minister of Justice, Gürtner, as reported by SCHLABRENDORFF p. 44 (2nd edition).

II. BECK'S ALLIES

1. "Schwäbische Zeitung" of July 25, 1947: "Im Schatten des Zwanzigsten Juli" by I.W. On the disclosure of the dates of the attack and the question of Oster's "treason" see the chapter "The Oster problem" in SENDTNER op. cit. p. 499. The last section of this chapter is entitled: "A matter of conscience for Oster and his judges" and begins with the sentence: "Even after these investigations the final judgement on Oster must depend on individual conscience." At the same time Beck's knowledge and share of responsibility is discussed and weighed.

2. It is a remarkable symptom of the time that this General, who before had eagerly sought Olbricht's favour, immediately after the 20th July forbade the further tending of the grave of Olbricht's son in the Dresden garrison cemetery.

3. On Bonhoeffer cf. Chapter VII of this book. On Delbrück see SCHLABRENDORFF, also on Guttenberg (p. 35 ff. and p. 88 ff. of 2nd edition). Apart from those referred to here, the following men of the Abwehr, who worked as the allies and accomplices of Oster and Canaris, are named in PECHEL, p. 231: Colonel Wessel von Freytag-Loringhoven (cf. ABSHAGEN, p. 345); Colonel Rudolf Count von Marogna-Redwitz; Lieutenant-Colonel Friedrich Wilhelm Heinz; Lieutenant-Colonel Werner Schrader; Captain Ludwig Gehre; Lieutenant-Commander Liedig; Dr Theodor Strünck, salesman and insurance manager; Ulrich Count Schwerin-Schwanenfeld; Gesandter Otto Kiep; Klaus Bonhoeffer, Chief Legal Adviser of the Lufthansa; Pastor Hans Schönfeld; Dr Joseph Müller, lawyer; Dr Otto John, Legal Adviser; Regierungsrat Hans-Bernd Gisevius; Joseph Wirmer, lawyer; Otto Hübener, insurance manager; and Colonel Wilhelm Stähle. Ministerialdirektor and Judge-Advocate General Dr Karl Sack had close relations with Canaris. Only five of those named survived: Liedig, Otto John, Schönfeld, Gisevius and J. Müller (Dr Hans John, Otto's brother, was executed).

4. ABSHAGEN, p. 28. A characteristic anecdote of Canaris; when travelling by car through Spain, he liked to greet the sheep flocks with raised arm—one could not tell, he said, whether a senior official was amongst them (ibid., p., 166).

5. ABSHAGEN and LAHOUSEN, IMT II, 485 ff.; III, 7 ff. Ian COLVIN, Chief of Intelligence, London 1951. KRAUSNICK in "Neue Deutsche Biographie" Vol 3 (1957), p. 116 ff.

6. According to ABSHAGEN's (p. 265) assurance, Canaris, whenever there was even hypothetical talk of passing on military secrets to the enemy, in the sense of giving them a tip-off, expressly rejected this, saying "That would be treason (Landesverrat)."

7. WEIZSÄCKER p. 175.

8. During the night before, Canaris had tapped out to his cell-neighbour, a

Danish officer: "I die for my Fatherland. I have a clear conscience. As an officer you will understand that I was only doing my patriotic duty when I tried to oppose the senseless crimes with which Hitler is leading Germany to destruction. It was in vain, for I now know that Germany will go down to disaster. I have known it since 1942." ABSHAGEN p. 393.

9. SCHACHT p. 22.

10. RITTER (p. 532) fills out the picture of the General with some information from Hoepner's former Signals Officer. Hoepner gave his own order to withdraw on January 7, 1942, in deliberate defiance of the Führer's command. He reported the withdrawal to the prepared "Hoepner line" only once he had started. In taking leave of his officers, he said: "I would always act just as I did then. . . . I am going, knowing that I have done my duty to my Army and the people." To one of his divisional commanders, on the La Bassée Canal in France in May 1940, he said: "Don't the lives of men mean anything to you? You are a butcher, not an officer! A military success is only worthwhile when it is obtained with the minimum loss of men. Otherwise, one could put any fool in a military command."

11. In his work Stülpnagel thought it was important not to perpetuate the enmity of the two peoples, but to try to find again a basis of co-operation. His conduct was censured in official quarters for being too yielding. He received a telegram from Keitel telling him "not to promote French interests". See WESTPHAL p. 141, who was a colleague of Stülpnagel in the Armistice Commission. He was, incidentally, not a "complete" Prussian, but on his mother's side a grandson of the famous Bavarian General von der Thann of 1870–71. He had been to the Lessing Gymnasium in Frankfurt and had begun his military service with the 115th Hessian Life-Guards. SCHRAMM p. 42 writes that with Stülpnagel "the easy Hessian way of speaking always shone through the High German, and the well-born gentleman with his relaxed manners through the soldier's bearing". He was called in contrast to other Generals of his family the "blond Stülpnagel".

12. Stülpnagel's dismissal followed the famous scene in Poltava, Rundstedt's headquarters, in early December, 1941. Rostov, which had been taken on November 21, could only be held for a week. Rundstedt had insisted on the withdrawal of his Army Group behind the Mius. Hitler appeared with Halder and Brauchitsch at Rundstedt's and Kleist's headquarters. The argument was so vehement that Hitler looked as if he was going to fall on Rundstedt and tear off his Knight's Cross. Brauchitsch had a heart attack and shortly afterwards asked to be released from his post. Stülpnagel also occasioned a paroxysm of rage in Hitler. GÖRLITZ, Der Zweite Weltkrieg 1939 bis 1945, p. 573, ff.

13. Von TEUCHERT, former Colonel in the military administration in Paris, cf. XII of this book.

14. OKW trial at Nuremberg. Case XII pp. 1827–30.

15. HALDER, p. 52.

16. On Halder, cf. BOR, also KRAUSNICK in Vollmacht des Gewissens, p. 333 ff., SENDTNER, p. 393. In addition, KOSTHORST, RITTER; and WARLIMONT, Im Hauptquartier der deutschen Wehrmacht 1939–45.

17. FOERTSCH, p. 21 and p. 25 somewhat differently. Cf. K. D. BRACHER.

18. PECHEL, p. 153. Eight years after this meeting Brüning sent Pechel a letter which Pechel published in his "Deutsche Rundschau". In it Brüning gives his view of how Hitler rose in 1932–33. DIELS p. 146 provides a comment on this which, in many ways, is thought-provoking: "There is hardly a more impressive document of the impotence, the lack of imagination and blindness in face of the demonic forces of our time. . . . It is moving, and at the same time

profoundly disturbing, to see the cruel and terrible misunderstanding which guided this prototype of European, who combined Christian tradition and humanist ideals with the instinctively German military outlook. Hitler is rightly judged to be an 'impossible' negotiating partner; but there is no inkling of the demonic impact of this man—as though it were sufficient to decide proudly that one could 'naturally' never negotiate with a man like Hitler, without taking decisive action oneself!"

19. SCHLABRENDORFF, p. 33.
20. On Hammerstein's character cf. SCHWERIN-KROSIGK, 3rd ed., pp. 111–15, also WHEELER-BENNETT passim, especially p. 329 ff. (Hammerstein's attitude after June 30, 1934, and his efforts to secure the rehabilitation of Schleicher and Bredow). The former Reich War Minister, Groener, on Hammerstein in ROTHFELS, p. 192.

III. FIRST ATTEMPTS AT A COUP 1938–39

1. Erich KORDT, Nicht aus den Akten, p. 243.
2. KRAUSNICK in Vollmacht des Gewissens p. 341 ff. FOERSTER p. 109, PECHEL p. 151, SAUERBRUCH p. 533, KORDT Wahn und Wirklichkeit, pp. 122–28, GISEVIUS II, pp. 26–76, WEIZSÄCKER, p. 174. SCHACHT p. 22 ff. gives credit to two names for the proposed coup d'état: "It is clear from the subsequent course of history that this first attempt at a coup d'état, undertaken by Witzleben and me, was the only one which would have brought a change in Germany's destiny. . . ." Cf. also SCHLABRENDORFF p. 47 (2nd edition).
3. HASSELL p. 40,, entry for December 19, 1938: "The irresponsible attitude to war taken by our leaders angers and shocks him (Beck). He spoke particularly about the outrageous way people say it is 'certain to be only a short war'. Apparently he has drawn up another memorandum on the real conditions of a future war." See BECK, Studien, p. 47, for this memorandum "Germany in a future war". Hans SPEIDEL writes of this: "It is, in its exemplary terseness, documentary proof of the way the German General Staff correctly appraised the situation up to 1938. As far as principles are concerned in the study, it contains ideas for the present and the future. The prophetic observations of the time . . . were largely confirmed by the course of the Second World War." This exposition got through to the authorities it was intended for, but was looked on there as treason.
4. On both visits to England see KRAUSNICK op. cit., p. 327 (Kleist), p. 336 (Böhm-Tettelbach). Cf. also RITTER p. 489 (Böhm) and KRAUSNICK-GRAML supplement to "Das Parlament" of July 19, 1961, p. 416 (Kleist).
5. Erich KORDT, Nicht aus den Akten, p. 280 ff.
6. SCHLABRENDORFF p. 47 (2nd edition).
7. It was the night September 5–6. The diplomat got access to Downing Street inconspicuously through a back door. Horace Wilson and Winston Churchill were also acquainted with the message. Some days after Munich Lord Halifax said to the visitor who had talked to him on the night of September 5: "We were not able to be as frank with you as you were with us. At the time you gave us your message we were already considering sending Chamberlain to Germany." (ROTHFELS, p. 62 of American edition)
8. Kleist reminded Chamberlain "of the Jacobites at the court of France in King William III's time". (Brit. Doc. III, 2, p. 286 ff)
9. Military preparations: confidential talks with Brauchitsch on September 3, 1938, at the Berghof, IMT XXV, p. 462 ff.; talks on mobilization, etc., on September 9–10, 1938, in Nuremberg IMT XXV, p. 484.
10. KRAUSNICK in Die Vollmacht des Gewissens p. 345 reproduces the statement

made by Lieutenant-Colonel Heinz on August 11, 1952, to the study group of
"Europäische Publikation".

11. Erich KORDT p. 120. Similarly the interpreter, SCHMIDT, p. 440.
12. Hitler's speech in the Berlin Sportpalast on September 26, 1938, IMT
XXXIX, p. 23–30 (excerpts).
13. Goerdeler's letter of October 11 in RITTER p. 204, DULLES p. 47. In the epilogue
(PECHEL p. 221) is the first reference to the "demonic" Hitler.
14. ". . . they (the British people) should know that we have passed an awful
milestone in our history, when the whole equilibrium of Europe has been
deranged, and that the terrible words have for the time being been pronounced
against the Western democracies: 'Thou art weighed in the balance and
found wanting.' And do not suppose that this is the end. This is only the
beginning of the reckoning. . . ." Churchill on October 5, 1938, in the House
of Commons. In Winston CHURCHILL, Der zweite Weltkrieg, p. 399.
15. Details in KORDT and WEIZSÄCKER. See also CHURCHILL, HENDERSON, COULON-
DRE, GAFENCU, and SHIRER.
16. The next day, October 4, 1938, Churchill said in the House of Commons:
"Our leadership must have at least a fraction of the spirit of that German
corporal, who, when everything round him had fallen in ruins, when Germany
seemed to have sunk into chaos for all time did not hesitate to march against
the phalanx of victorious nations." IMT XXII, p. 102. Compare what Hitler
said at this time in his judgement of Britain in the "Elefant" in Weimar in a
conversation with Guderian: GUDERIAN p. 52. KIELMANSEGG op. cit., p. 136
recalls what Churchill wrote in 1935 in his Great Contemporaries (p. 261):
"It is not possible to form a just judgement of a public figure who has attained
the enormous dimensions of Adolf Hitler until his life work as a whole is before
us. . . . Such a final view is not vouchsafed to us today. We cannot tell whether
Hitler will be the man who will once again let loose upon the world another
war in which civilization will irretrievably succumb, or whether he will go
down in history as the man who restored honour and peace of mind to the
great Germanic nation, and brought it back serene, helpful and strong to the
forefront of the European family circle."
17. A judgement of the military and political situation can be found in Hitler's
conference on war aims on May 23, 1939, IMT XXXVII pp. 546–56.
18. Hitler's Reichstag speech of April 28, 1939, IMT XXXIX p. 32 (extracts).
Text of the speech which Hitler made to the Commanders-in-Chief on August
23, 1939, based on a secret memorandum in IMT XXVI p. 338. Hitler's
speech on September 1, 1939, IMT XXX p. 167.
19. Events treated in detail by KLEIST p. 25 ff., who was present in Moscow when
the Pact was concluded. Details also in sworn statement by GAUSS, who took
part in Moscow as legal adviser, IMT I p. 354. Cf. also KORDT, Wahn und
Wirklichkeit, p. 156 and p. 175, SCHMIDT p. 440, "Die Gegenwart" Year 1947,
Vols. 42–43, p. 11. Also GAFENCU, Préliminaires à la guerre à l'Est. On speech
of August 22, on basis of which WHEELER-BENNETT (p. 448) heavily criticizes
the Generals who took part cf. RITTER's reply p. 499: he casts doubt on the
authenticity of the document L3 used by Wheeler-Bennett. H. KRAUSNICK
(Supplement to "Das Parlament" of November 16, 1955, p. 706, No. 557)
tries to explain the document L3 as a forgery of Canaris's office intended by its
exaggerations (the planned extermination of the whole Polish nation) to
incite Britain.
20. On the events before the beginning of the war in August 1939 see especially
HASSELL, WEIZSÄCKER and THOMAS, Gedanken und Ereignisse and "Die
Opposition" (Notes of 1945). Also Erich KORDT, Walther HOFER, Die Ent-

fesselung des Zweiten Weltkriegs, A. J. P. TAYLOR, Die Ursprünge des Zweiten Weltkriegs.

21. KOSTHORST p. 156.

22. Erich KORDT, Nicht aus den Akten, p. 358 ff.

23. KORDT ibid. p. 271.

24. KORDT ibid. p. 357. On Halder's questions about an assassination see GISEVIUS II, p. 159. RITTER, p. 504 gives in this connection an assurance of Halder. Pressed by Grosscurth with proposals for assassination, he once said in a fit of annoyance that, if they wanted an assassination in the Abwehr, then the Admiral should arrange it himself. The following is reported from the Reich Chancellery on November 5: a General who was one of the participants in the planned coup—his name is not mentioned—had ended his statement and was about to go. Turning to him out of the blue, Hitler asked: "What else do you plan?" The General repeated part of what had been discussed. Hitler insisted that he did not mean that. He thought the General had something else on his mind. The latter became uncertain but denied everything and with difficulty kept his composure until Hitler dismissed him. He was convinced that the operation had been betrayed and he reported this to the conspirators. They proceeded to destroy papers and to obliterate all trace of the plan. On the evening of November 6, it became known that Hitler had no knowledge of the affair. On November 7 and 8 new moves were made and on the evening of November 8 the assassination attempt took place after a counter-move had been expected, as after the Röhm revolt (based on a report by Albrecht von KESSEL, cf. DULLES).

The reasons for which Brauchitsch later refused to take part in a coup were, according to Halder's statement, as THOMAS reproduces them: the German Army did not stage coups; there was also no personality to put in Hitler's place; the people needed an idea like National Socialism; Britain's struggle was aimed not only against the Hitler régime but also against the whole German people; and, finally, the younger Officer Corps was not reliable enough to execute such a political action. Halder, like Generals Stülpnagel and Wagner, had also doubts about opposing a man with a record of unbroken success, for whom hundreds of thousands of young Germans would enter the lists without question and be ready to sacrifice themselves. He said he could not allow the supreme military command to be split in two parts in war-time. (THOMAS's statement in a memorandum in Falkenstein of July 20, 1945).

25. Niemöller in KORDT, Wahn und Wirklichkeit, p. 229. Isa VERMEHREN, who like Niemöller was in the Dachau camp, supplements this information about Elser (p. 178) from what was being said in the camp. According to this, Elser had declared himself ready in 1939 (to whom, it is not said) to get a time-bomb into the Bürgerbräu hall for 40 000 RM. His special privileges during his imprisonment are then described as in GISEVIUS. According to another report which comes from the British Secret Service Officer Payne BEST (Venlo Incident, London, 1950, see WHEELER-BENNETT, p. 478 ff.), Elser was held in Dachau as early as October 1939 for "re-education" and was recruited there by senior authorities for the assassination attempt. Whether Hitler knew of this, is uncertain. Best was seized together with Major Stevens on November 9 at Venlo by agents of the German Secret Service and abducted to Germany from Dutch territory (story SENDTNER, Die Vollmacht des Gewissens, p. 450). He remained in German hands until the end of the war. Recently Best's account has been largely played down as invention or camp gossip.

As I learn from the Institut für Zeitgeschichte in Munich, new unpublished material makes it again probable that Elser carried out the attempt on his

own. On the usual explanation of the attempt until now ("a put-up propaganda trick on the part of Himmler's organizations") see RITTER pp. 250 and 505.
26. Erich KORDT, Nicht aus den Akten p. 370 ff.
27. KORDT ibid. p. 376. Hitler's speech of November 23, 1938, IMT XXVI p. 327 ff.
28. KORDT ibid. p. 377.
29. HASSELL p. 106.
30. SCHLABRENDORFF p. 61, 2nd edition, KOSTHORST p. 112, ff.
31. "Die römischen Friedensgespräche" clearly and critically set out in SENDTNER op. cit. pp. 436–85.
32. KOSTHORST p. 145, SENDTNER p. 485 ff. Here also confirmation on basis of statement by Frau Dohnanyi that the other side was informed at the wish of Beck: "We cannot be identified with this thing (violation of neutrality). We must be able to establish contact again. For this reason these people (The Vatican and Britain) must know with whom they have to deal and that there is a decent Germany which is capable of negotiating."
So far as one can see, the attack in the West was ordered and put off four times in November alone, and later some nine times. This period of the war has been entitled "the phoney war".
33. The "Wednesday Club" in Berlin was a private club which provided men of most varied branches of knowledge with the opportunity to meet and exchange ideas. It was founded on January 19, 1863, with rules drawn up by the former State and Education Minister M. A. von Bethmann-Hollweg, the grandfather of the Reich Chancellor. The historian I. G. Droysen was one of the founders. The rules limited the membership to sixteen. A new member could only join on the death or resignation of another. They met, with holiday breaks, on every second Wednesday evening in the house of the member whose turn it was to speak. Generally only members spoke; after that there was simple hospitality. The lecturer had to write down a record of his remarks and the discussion in a book of minutes. The first minute books have been kept in the Academy in East Berlin; the last three are in the Federal Archives in Coblenz. In 1943–44 the following gave lectures: Sauerbruch, von Hassell, Spranger, Stroux, Oncken, Pinder, Schadewaldt, Baethgen, Wilcken, Diels, Beck (May 31, 1944), Jessen, Popitz, Heisenberg and Fechter (July 26). This last meeting, in which only five members participated, including von Hassell, was the 1,056th and marked the end of the "Wednesday Club". Four of its sixteen members suffered a violent death as a result of the 20th July.
34. Ulrich WILCKEN, classical historian at Berlin University. His book on Alexander appeared in 1931.
35. FECHTER "Colonel-General Beck" in "Die Welt" August 21, 1948.
36. FECHTER op. cit. Cf. also the description of Beck in the same author's book "Menschen und Zeiten" p. 363 ff.
In the preface to the "Leadership of Troops", the manual of instructions for military commanders which he published in 1932 and whose influence extended far beyond Germany, Beck wrote: "War is an art, a free, creative activity, based on science." There have been those who thought that Beck's mastery of this art was only theoretical and that the element of Fabius Cunctator in him was an impediment to supreme leadership. That Beck was never able to prove his ability in the field carried much weight—even if the most experienced leader of troops in the Second World War, Field-Marshal von Manstein, expressed the conviction that Beck, if he had taken part in this war "would have stood in the very first rank as a Commander of armies". (FÖRSTER, Generaloberst Ludwig Beck, p. 50). Cf. GUDERIAN p. 26, WESTPHAL,

p. 151, HASSELL, p. 357, and the statement by Generals Fretter PICO and Hans SPEIDEL in various places.

IV. CARL FRIEDRICH GOERDELER
MAN OF THE RIGHT

1. HASSELL p. 158.
2. Walter HAMMER, Theodor Haubach zum Gedächtnis, p. 25.
3. Gerhard RITTER, Carl Goerdeler und die deutsche Widerstandsbewegung, Stuttgart, 1954. Quotations here from 3rd edition, 1956. RITTER tells of the great number of people with whom Goerdeler was in contact. PECHEL p. 209 and p. 221 gives the following names, some of which appeared in the Abwehr list: Fritz Goerdeler, his brother; Eugen Bolz (the former Staatspräsident of Württemberg); Joseph Wirmer; Paul Lejeune-Jung; Werner Count von Schulenburg; Erwin Planck; Franz Kempner; Eduard Hamm; Fritz Elsas; Carl Wentzel-Teutschenthal; Ewald von Kleist-Schmenzin; Friedrich-Karl von Zitzewitz-Muttrin; von Puttkamer-Nippoglense; Robert Lehr; Friedrich Justus Perels; Richard Kuenzer; Hermann Kaiser; Theodor Bäuerle; Paul Hahn; Theodor Strünck. Five of the named (Zitzewitz, Puttkamer, Lehr, Bäuerle and Hahn) survived the 20th July.
The following belonged to Goerdeler's wider entourage and died as a result of the 20th July: Walter Cramer; Reinhold Frank; Georg Conrad Kissling (committed suicide); Wilhelm zur Nieden; Friedrich Scholz-Babisch; Hans-Ludwig Sierks and Hans-Joachim Freiherr von Steinäcker. Others were released after shorter or longer periods of arrest: for instance, the Freiburg Professors Gerhard Ritter, Adolf Lampe and Constantin von Dietze; former Reich Minister, Andreas Hermes; Generaldirektor Dr Ewald Löser, Freiherr von Palombini, Professor von Erxleben and former Staatsminister F. W. Richter.
4. RITTER op. cit. p. 25.
5. RITTER p. 274.
6. Personal report of the publisher Gotthold MÜLLER, to whom these words were addressed. Müller confirms that Goerdeler, thanks to the death of his very dear soldier-son, Christian (May 1942), was more determined than ever on a coup. Christian G. had had a difficult time as a soldier because he had views similar to his father's (cf. RITTER p. 539).
7. Goerdeler's letter to Professor Kippenberg (Insel Verlag) from prison November 13, 1944, hitherto unpublished, in the possession of the Goerdeler family.
8. See Note 7. Among the special gifts to the Marshals that to Field-Marshal von Kluge was particularly in mind (SCHLABRENDORFF, p. 71; Diary of H. KAISER).
9. RITTER p. 279.
10. RITTER p. 287.
11. RITTER p. 335.
12. SCHWERIN-KROSIGK pp. 183–92. The following sentences are illuminating: "Schacht often showed a tendency to send others into the fire which he himself had made. He mercilessly let a 'poor fellow' get into trouble. If he came across an intellectual inferior, who allowed it, he exploited his weakness without compunction. He regarded intellectual limitation as moral guilt, for which restitution must be exacted. He himself did not suffer from it." Schwerin-Krosigk recounts a story characteristic of Schacht: Frank, the later Governor-General of Poland, greeted Schacht, who like other Ministers, had just been awarded the Golden Party Badge, in his loud way with the words: "Well, Herr Schacht, how do you feel, how are you?" Schacht looked down at him with unmoved face and said: "If we old fighters aren't all right, who should be all right in Germany?"

13. IMT XXXIII p. 531, there also Schacht's important letter to Hitler o November 12, 1932.
14. Nuremberg Documents 456 E.C. (quoted by SHIRER, p. 140).
15. SHIRER p. 252.
16. SHIRER p. 299. Cf. also Goerdeler's struggle with Göring in his memorandum on the foreign exchange question, August 1936. Goerdeler protested against Schacht's credit policy, based on the "Mefo-bills", which struck him as a fiscal swindle. Schacht remained unmoved. Goerdeler in his memoirs wrote of this: "When I showed him what nonsense this was, he pointed to the picture of Hitler and said: 'You are mistaken. He is a great man. He will lead the nation to happiness.'" On June 27 or 28, 1935, Hitler met Goerdeler as Price Commissioner and Schacht as Finance Minister, without others being present. After he was refused the plenary powers he asked for in order to reorganize the internal Reich administration, including finance, Goerdeler resigned. On Goerdeler's and Schacht's differing views on financial and economic policy and their relations with Göring, see the account in RITTER op. cit. pp. 76–87. The warning memorandum of the Reichsbank directorate (Schacht) to Hitler about the danger of a currency catastrophe as a result of unrestricted public expenditure in IMT XXXVI p. 366.
17. IMT XLI p. 267, other statements XXXIII p. 559.
18. Letter in SCHACHT, p. 26.
19. SCHACHT p. 48.
20. IMT XLI p. 279.
21. WEIZSÄCKER p. 176, p. 255 ff. Compare also the description in SCHMIDT, KORDT and KLEIST.
22. The so-called "Wilhelmstrasse proceedings" against von Weizsäcker and twenty other accused took place between January 6, 1948, and April 14, 1949. Another eight months were spent in written proceedings and revision of sentences. The efforts of the judges to weigh all the evidence of prosecution and defence responsibly and free from presumptuous infallibility and to decide justly is beyond all doubt. But it is also certain that in this case the court was dealing with matters which could not then, and never could, be decided within its own sphere of competence. Ernst von Weizsäcker was found guilty on two counts out of eight. But in its decision of November 12, 1949, the court changed its verdict on count I (Crimes of a war of aggression and crimes against peace) and amended the sentence. However, it upheld the verdict of guilty on count V, seeing a war crime or crime against humanity in that, for instance, Weizsäcker had "consented" to the abduction and presumed extermination of 6 000 French Jews. In this deportation, which was planned in the spring of 1942 by the RSH and carried out by it, the Foreign Office was only involved as an "interested department", without being its originator or entitled to make a decision. Weizsäcker's role in the Resistance movement was recognized by the court and regarded as an extenuating factor. On the other hand, it was said "One must not approve an act of murder or have a part in it, because one hopes in this way eventually to free society from the chief murderer. In this and similar cases, the accused Weizsäcker and Wörmann are pronounced guilty." One of the judges, Leon W. Powers, did not associate himself with this judgment because it was not within von Weizsäcker's competence to make a protest and it could not have achieved anything. He concluded: "To sentence them means inflicting on them punishment for the actions of another government office which they did not order and could not prevent."
23. SCHMIDT in his epilogue passes this judgement on the Foreign Office: "The clamp, which held together the old Office, was State Secretary Freiherr von

Weizsäcker, who enjoyed a high reputation with all officials and with all foreign diplomats, and who combined the greatest diplomatic skill with a high moral sense of honour. By a word, a gesture or a significant silence he knew how, at the appropriate moment, to inform us of his wishes in a way which could be understood neither by Ribbentrop's and Hitler's organs of control, nor by his later accusers in Nuremberg. This was because the former did not have the moral wave-lengths of a Weizsäcker on their primitive receiving sets and the latter knew nothing of such wave-lengths, as they had never lived under a dictatorship" (p. 559). The reservations about, and the attacks on, Weizsäcker which are contained in HASSELL's diary, have received more weight than they should have, thanks to post-war developments. They should be read as diary notes which mirror the drama of the moment and the various doings of the characters. It is understandable that Weizsäcker, who was in office, should have refused to have anything to do with the uninhibited and often imprudent conspiracies of Hassell and his friends outside; in addition there was a deep temperamental difference between the two men. From other sources it is known—and this can be seen again in Hassell's notes (p. 347)— that Stauffenberg also found it necessary to urge him explicitly to be careful. Weizsäcker wrote: "The existence of the diary notes shows that my warning was justified. Had they become known, the author, many of his colleagues, and I, too, and, above all, the cause of the Resistance would have perished. Diaries are safety-valves for moods of the moment. To publish them later without a commentary is usually an injustice to the author". (p. 343, cf. also SALIN p. 10). How far they agree with Hassell's observations about tribal characteristics, those referred to must themselves decide: "It is remarkable how often with Swabians, when one gets below the surface, one encounters lack of firm character and a peasant slyness concealed by bonhomie" (HASSELL p. 313).

24. Four other members of the Foreign Office were executed: Geheimrat Richard Kuenzer; former Botschaftsrat (and later banker) Albrecht Count von Bernsdorff; Gesandter Otto Kiep; and Legationsrat Herbert Mumm von Schwarzenstein.

25. "Programme" composed by HASSELL after discussions with Beck, Goerdeler and Popitz in January and February 1940. See his book, p. 381. On his participation in the preliminary discussions, see also ibid. p. 295 and the letter of the then Konsistorialrat Dr Gerstenmaier to W.U. von Hassell ibid. p. 379.

26. See HASSELL p. 385 ff.

27. Information from Frau Dr Cornelia Schulz-Popitz, see RITTER, p. 518 and p. 501. It is certainly not easy to define Popitz's political attitude. What RITTER has to say in various places does not at first sight make a coherent picture. It is clear that he opposed the "all too bourgeois" methods of Goerdeler's plans for a coup and, instead, put forward his own; and that he was at first named as the future Minister of Culture, then the Minister of Finance, but does not appear after the end of 1943 in the discussions about a future government. On the other hand, this should not imply a personal breach with the other men of the revolt. There is evidence that Stauffenberg met him several times, even in 1944, and that Goerdeler, despite information to the contrary at the trial, also visited Jessen at his house in 1944. Jessen was a close friend of Popitz. In the case of Popitz it is clear that expressions like "too bourgeois", "too conservative", "too reactionary", "old colleague of Göring's" indicate little about aims and ideas; and we must beware of regarding contradictions which emerge from reports and the court proceedings as important. Cf. HASSELL p. 121 and the account which Hans HERZFELD gives: "Johannes Popitz, Ein Beitrag zur

Geschichte des deutschen Beamtentums" in "Forschungen zu Staat und Verfassung", Berlin 1958, pp. 345–65.

28. HILDEBRANDT "Der Aufstand des Gewissens" in "Stuttgarter-Zeitung" March 1, 1947. Here also is the phrase often used by Popitz: "One cannot get out of an abnormal catastrophe with normal methods." Cf. also on Popitz, Rainer HILDEBRANDT, Wir sind die Letzten. Aus dem Leben des Widerstandskaempfers Albrecht Haushofer und seiner Freunde.

29. RITTER p. 362. Events concerning Popitz, Langbehn and Himmler in DULLES and HENK, p. 238.

30. Cf. Article "Nationalsozialismus" in the Wörterbuch der Volkswirtschaft, 4th edition, 1933. "In Memoriam Jens Jessen" in Schmollers Jahrbuch, Year 69, Vol 1, edited by Günther Schmölders.

31. Ohlendorf, chiefly known for his "work in the Einsatzgruppen" (extermination groups) IMT IV pp. 344–93, also XXXI pp. 39 ff. He was condemned to death in the Nuremberg trial of the Einsatzgruppen and was executed three years later in 1951.

32. FECHTER, Menschen und Zeiten, p. 407.

V. MEN OF THE LEFT

1. LEITHÄUSER, Wilhelm Leuschner, p. 184.

2. A. LEBER, Den toten, immer lebenden Freunden, p. 7. J. LEBER, in many places, for example pp. 253, 256 ("I could have wished that a fate had encompassed us which would have broken our programme but strengthened our hearts and our courage. Now the opposite has happened—we have broken hearts but an unbroken programme") p. 74: "What worries the party has at this time when everything is at stake! When the old Roman Empire finally collapsed in 1806, the Reichstag was busy checking and clarifying in all its aspects the question of the Eutin local elections. And later when the decisive hours of the German Republic come under the searchlight of history, it will only evoke a pitying smile that at this time the largest republican party quarrelled over the question whether a new cruiser should be built in 1931 or in 1932 ... I don't know how many new cruisers I would be ready to approve if, with that, I could save the Republic and democracy in Germany." This in 1929. Cf. in all this the essay in Leber's book "Thoughts on the Banning of German Social Democracy", June 1933, p. 185 ff.

3. On Leuschner see the book by LEITHÄUSER.

4. A. LEBER ibid. p. 7 cf. HENK p. 33.

5. Max Habermann went into hiding after the 20th July but was discovered on October 30 and arrested. He ended his life in the prison of Gifhorn because he "did not wish to betray the men who had given him refuge while in hiding". PECHEL p. 208: cf. W. MÜLLER, Gegen eine neue Dolchstosslegende, p. 60, 2nd edition.

There was contact with the Catholic workers' movement through Prälat Dr Otto Müller; the editor, Nikolaus Gross; and the publishing director, Bernhard Letterhaus. The first died in custody, the other two as a result of Freisler's sentence. On this PECHEL p. 205 and KB 380, 393.

Apart from Jakob Kaiser, Franz Leuninger and Heinrich Körner came from the Christian Trade Union movement. The first was executed: the latter was liberated from Plötzensee prison by enemy troops at the end of April 1945 but shot before the SS barricades. The day before the colleague and friend of Leuschner, Ernst Schneppenhorst, had died a violent death. Two of Leuschner's Silesian associates were together executed a few weeks earlier;

Fritz Voigt, former Police President of Breslau and Oswald Wirsich, former district secretary of the ADG (German General Trade Union Federation).
6. HENK p. 59 describes the organization in Hesse which extended to the smallest localities.
7. LEITHÄUSER p. 59. Leber and Stauffenberg had the same ideas.
8. LEITHÄUSER pp. 209, 210, 215, 223 and 224.
9. PECHEL p. 202.
10. A. LEBER ibid. p. 8: "With sadness one thinks also of the brave Maass, once the leader of the Social Democratic youth movement, standing in front of Freisler resolute and upright to the last minute of the trial. . . . When the President allowed him a final word it was noticed how Maass had waited for this moment, how his whole fiery and impetuous nature urged him to speak up so as to make his motives seem clear and pure to his listeners and posterity. . . . He began: 'I think I owe it to myself and the cause, when I state here before God and my conscience . . .' Here Roland Freisler's voice cut him short with 'You are making no statement here before God. You are only making a statement to the People's Court of the Greater German Reich!' Once again Maass tried to speak and once again Freisler interrupted him. Then the accused cast a glance of profound contempt at the man in the red robe and with proud resignation said 'I renounce my right to speak!' and sat down again. (Anonymous reporter in the "Schwäbische Zeitung" of May 10, 1946: "Märtyrer der Freiheit")
11. Even later, Haubach had something of the disciplined soldier in his bearing and liked talking of "militant socialism". Cf. PÖLCHAU, p. 123.
12. Walter HAMMER's impressive memorial essays for Theodor Haubach contain contributions from twenty people and Haubach's own views. Alma DE L'AIGLE published letters of Haubach.
13. The quotations from letters of Theo Haubach in DE L'AIGLE.
14. A. LEBER p. 10.
15. WEISENBORN p. 182.
16. "In memorian Carlo Mierendorff" p. XX.
17. ZUCKMAYER pp. 12 and 16.
18. ZUCKMAYER p. 31.
19. The story is told of one of his speeches in the 'twenties in Heidelberg at which a group of listeners left the hall and Mierendorff called to the leader of this group: "Stay in the restaurant, Herr Goebbels, if you have the courage to look a front-line soldier in the eye!" (In Memorian p. IX).
20. Op. cit. p. IX.
21. HENK p. 46. From this last period of Mierendorff's must come the words which STELTZER in his book, Von deutscher Politik (p. 75), says were spoken to Father Roesch: "I have lived without religion. But I have come to the conviction that only Christianity can give life meaning and content. And I now go this way to God. I think you will be glad, Father, to hear this from me."
22. A. LEBER p. 9. On February 22, 1944, Haubach spoke at the memorial service for Mierendorff at the Darmstadt cemetery and on March 12, without knowing of this, Zuckmayer spoke in New York in honour of the dead man before a select circle of Germans: "Not just his brave decision to stay in Germany and to defy the worst there, not just the hopes we placed on him for Germany's future, made his simple, plain, unpompous figure almost a symbol of a people in whose sound heart and rebirth we firmly believe. But in his whole personality, nature and work, in his character and actions, Carlo Mierendorff combined all that we may call German in the best and finest, and also in the simplest and most modest, sense . . ." (ZUCKMAYER p. 8).

23. HENK p. 34.
24. A. LEBER p. 6.
25. HENDERSON, Adolf Reichwein, p. 65 and p. 64.
26. Op. cit. p. 71.
27. Op. cit. p. 120.
28. Op. cit. p. 119.
29. Romai REICHWEIN "Der Vater", notes in archives of the Adolf-Reichwein-Hochschule in Osnabrück.
30. BOHNENKAMP, Hans. Gedanken an Adolf Reichwein, Brunswick, 1949, p. 15.
31. Guide to the Wood Exhibition, A description in Arthur von MACHUI in "Die Sammlung" Year 1, 1945, Vol 1.
32. HENDERSON op. cit. 159.
33. An English friend described Reichwein as combining "the contemplative wisdom of a Taoist monk with the ardour of an irreproachable crusader". BOHNENKAMP p. 9. Elsewhere we read: "His combination of bright vitality and sober scientific seriousness gave him a really magic attraction." (A LEBER p. 10). BOHNENKAMP adds: "His almost magic power of attraction came not only from the range of his mind, in which almost all his knowledge was based on practice, not only from the fullness of his experience and his toughness in bearing various vicissitudes, which is reminiscent of the similarly wiry and red-haired T. E. Lawrence, not only from his great and varied abilities but, above all, from the purity of his nature, which lay beneath it all and was always shining through. . . ."
34. On Ernst von Harnack cf. the life which his brother, Axel von HARNACK, published, also Otto JOHN's memories in the periodical "Blick in die Welt" (Vol 6, 1947), A. LEBER, Das Gewissen steht auf, p. 117. See also PECHEL for his own experiences with Harnack.
35. According to PECHEL's evidence, p. 204, Ernst von HARNACK established contacts between his friend Leber who had been released from arrest, and the Goerdeler circle, General von Falkenhausen and Hans John, legal adviser to the Lufthansa.
36. The Oberregierungsrat in the Reich Economics Ministry, Dr Arvid Harnack, and his American-born wife, Mildred, were arrested in the autumn of 1942, brought before the Supreme Military Court and sentenced to death for high treason. See Axel von HARNACK in "Die Gegenwart" on January 31, 1947.
37. A. von HARNACK, the life p. 64.
38. Theodor Baensch in HARNACK, op. cit. p. 65.
39. Cf. the description of Frau von Harnack in WEISENBORN, p. 184.
40. A. LEBER p. 13.
41. Otto Passarge in J. LEBER p. 271.
42. This and following quotation from J. LEBER, pp. 107, 254.
43. J. LEBER p. 120.
44. J. LEBER p. 258, letter of August 31, 1933.
45. A. LEBER p. 3.
46. A. LEBER p. 4.
47. This and following passage from letter J. LEBER pp. 255 and 256.
48. A. LEBER op. cit.
49. J. LEBER p. 265.
50. See note 2.
51. J. LEBER p. 289. The following ibid. pp. 156, 160, 173, 177.
52. Theodor Heuss in J. LEBER p. 294.
53. Gustav Dahrendorf in J. LEBER p. 293.
54. A witness of this moment wrote: "I shall never forget Leber's face when the death sentence was announced and he listened to it in silence without doing

his tormentors the favour of even turning a hair. I have never seen in my life
so much deep seriousness and calm moral sovereignty as I perceived in his
features" (Dr Paul SAETHE, Halver, in J. LEBER p. 293).
55. J. LEBER p. 295.
56. A. LEBER p. 14. Isa VERMEHREN op. cit. p. 44 describes a meeting with Leber in
Ravensbrück. "He said at once that there was no hope for him but thought that
the sacrifice of his own life was appropriate to the greatness of the undertaking
and asked me to give greetings to his wife in this sense."

VI. THE KREISAU CIRCLE

1. For information about Moltke and the Kreisau circle see the detailed report of
Marion Countess Yorck and Freya Countess Moltke; the letters of Moltke
published in the "Neue Auslese" and in GOLLWITZER-KUHN-SCHNEIDER; the
accounts of Pechel, Countess Dönhoff, Husen, Gertstenmaier and Hassell.
Also Dulles, Rothfels, and Pölchau. The texts of the Kreisau documents are to
be found in STELTZER who, in the same book, has made an authentic contribution to the political history of this period by giving his personal reminiscences
of the nature and work of the circle and by publishing his memorandum of
July 1944. On Moltke's attitude cf. ROTHFELS p. 116 who says it might have
recalled Gandhi's "non-resistance". GERSTENMAIER says no one ever heard
from Moltke anything like a moral rejection of an assassination attempt on
the tyrant. He only repeated: "*Our* concern is the day 'X': then we must be
ready." That the day "X" could mean a coup d'état or a catastrophe was
clear to all. Gerstenmaier warns against over-emphasizing the purely intellectual element in Moltke by taking too literally his description of events
before the court. In that letter ("We have merely thought . . ." etc.) he had
only adopted the agreed plans. Gerstenmaier spoke several times to Moltke in
the last days before his execution. He is convinced that, had he been free,
Moltke would have been with Yorck and himself in the Bendlerstrasse on the
20th July. SALIN reports a statement by a friend of Moltke, according to which
Moltke, after initial hesitations, declared himself in agreement with an
assassination as early as 1943. His later statements in letters were differently
worded with an eye to the prison censorship (p. 11, Note 12). PÖLCHAU (p.
112) alleges that Yorck tried to convince those of his friends who were still
hesitating of the need for an assassination.
2. "Hope is not my métier," Moltke once said calmly and good-humouredly to
another prisoner (VERMEHREN p. 28).
3. Cf. also the details in PÖLCHAU op. cit. of Moltke's interventions, in addition
"Neue Auslese" p. 5.
4. PÖLCHAU p. 112 cf. LILJE p. 62.
5. See "Neue Auslese".
6. The original of the famous "Convention of Tauroggen" of 1812 was kept in the
family (ROTHFELS p. 112).
7. VAN HUSEN ("In Memoriam Moltke and Yorck", unpublished memorandum)
stresses Yorck's sharp but fundamentally kindly wit and adds: "He was one of
those rare men who can convince without wounding his opponent."
8. To complete the three Kreisau talks there was one meeting at Yorck's in
Klein-Öls to discuss agricultural questions. No memorandum was drafted.
9. From one of these talks Yorck reported to the others that Stauffenberg had
told him with some indignation of a recent order of Kaltenbrunner providing
for "special treatment" in Auschwitz for 40 000 or 42 000 Hungarian Jews.
Those who adopt a cautious, academic attitude towards the oath of allegiance
ought to understand the impact of such experiences on the conspirators. Cf.

Moltke's letter of October 21, 1941, in which he speaks of the German atrocities he has learnt of in Silesia, France, Poland and Russia and of the action against the Jews and adds: "Am I to learn this and still sit at my table in a heated room and drink tea? Don't I thus make myself also guilty? What shall I say, when I am asked; 'And what did *you* do during this time?' " LEBER-MOLTKE op. cit. p. 201.

10. KB 110. Here also Yorck's statement that he was asked by Stauffenberg whether he would be ready to be State Secretary to the Reich Chancellor.

11. A. LEBER, Das Gewissen steht auf, p. 166.

12. HASSELL p. 379.

13. GERSTENMAIER in "Hilfe für Deutschland" Frankfurt/Main 1946 p. 8.

14. GERSTENMAIER "Der Zwanzigste Juli—Besinnung und Auftrag" in "Christ und Welt" of July 20, 1950. For the following quotation from GERSTENMAIER see "Der Zwanzigste Juli" Herder p. 38.

15. Alfred DELP "Tragische Existenz" 1935, "Der Mensch und die Geschichte" 1943.

16. DELP p. 112. From there, too, the following quotations which are taken from pp. 13, 102, 111, 163, and 178. On him see Alfred DELP, Kämpfer, Beter, Zeuge. Letzte Briefe und Beiträge von Freunden, Berlin 1955, Morus Verlag. In this the fine letter to the recently arrived god-child, Alfred Sebastian, written with shackled hands on January 23, 1945. In his appearance and movements Delp had something of the strength of a hard-working peasant.

17. DELP brought the "Bavarian group" into contact with Moltke through joint talks which often took place in his home in Munich-Bogenhausen and through individual encounters. And he sent the former Gesandter Sperr to talk with Stauffenberg in Bamberg in June 1944 (KB 331, 389 and 393).

18. Pastor BUCHHOLZ in "Die Neue Zeit" of October 1945; cf. LILJE p. 61.

19. Details according to STELTZER p. 74. On the participation of Church circles in the active conspiracy against Hitler and on the often noticeably timorous treatment these participants had at the hands of their own people after 1945 the statements of GERSTENMAIER in "Hilfe für Deutschland" ought to be heard for both confessions. There it says: "I do not believe that a single bishop of the two Churches had real knowledge of the military and technical plans for a coup d'état. None of them knew how Hitler was to be got rid of. But of those who certainly knew that he was to be got rid of, I have never heard one argue against it. I say that, first, because one must see the participation of the Church or, more properly speaking, the participation of its prominent members, in the policy of active resistance in the limits within which it actually operated. And, secondly, I say it because one should have the courage to admit this now before the world and the church, because this greatest and most costly attempt of the Germans to help themselves finally failed, and is concluded."

20. His reasons in STELTZER p. 10. Steltzer was also to show the British occupation authorities his courageous and almost puritanical attitude founded on personal integrity when, after 1945, he was Oberpräsident and then Ministerpräsident of Schleswig-Holstein.

21. His father, General von Haeften, later Head of the Reich War Achives and publisher of works on the science of war, became famous in the First World War thanks to his opposition to Ludendorff, cf. also ROTHFELS p. 15.

22. PECHEL p. 119.

23. From this letter of Trott's on August 14, 1944 (after the proceedings in the People's Court): "You will know that what hurts me most is that I may never again be able to place at the service of our country my special abilities and the experiences which I have been able to develop in what was an almost exces-

sively one-sided concentration on foreign affairs, and Germany's position among the powers. It was all an attempt arising from love of our country (for which I must thank my father) and knowledge of its strength, to protect its immutable rights among the changes and increasing difficulties of the modern world and to preserve its profound and indispensable contribution to civilization against the encroachment of foreign powers and beliefs. That is why I always hurried back in eager anxiety from foreign countries, with all their enticements and opportunities, to Germany where I felt I was called upon to serve." A. LEBER, Das Gewissen steht auf, p. 222.

24. "When he walked in the quadrangle of his Oxford college, in the moonlight, it was German poetry that came into his mind. This devotion to his own country and its destiny was obvious; he had no need to express it. He was well read in the literature of his own country, having a rather special attachment to the works of Jean Paul and being of the opinion that Hölderlin's was the best German poetry, better, even than Goethe's, although he revered Goethe's as the greatest German life." (Notes on Adam von Trott by G. E. COLLINS, unpublished, like the notes of ASTOR and OPPEN, in the possession of Frau Clarita von Trott.)

25. H. W. OPPEN, unpublished notes on Trott.

26. August FRANKE, Ein Leben für die Freiheit, Eine Besinnung auf die Männer des 20. Juli 1944 p. 18.

27. Albrecht von KESSEL see FRANKE p. 20.

28. "It was one of the chief charms of his nature that, in spite of this maturity, he had a youthful spontaneity and high spirits which made him perfectly natural company for much younger students." (COLLINS, op. cit.). "To me he was a teacher and elder brother as well as a well-loved friend. He was the greatest member of my generation in any country that I have met" (From a personal note by David Astor).

29. Trott worked for people who were persecuted by the new régime. In 1935 he published a volume of political and journalistic writings of Heinrich von Kleist, in which he clearly invoked Kleist as a warning to the present.

30. While still in China, Trott had written to English friends on July 20, 1938: "As long as you cannot regard all that has happened in Germany as a European phenomenon and a European responsibility, no progress can be made. . ." (FRANKE op. cit. p. 36). In October he returned to Germany. Opposing the efforts of foreign friends to help him, Trott said: "There are emigrés enough who in certain circumstances could help from outside. But there aren't Germans who are determined to stay in Germany to build a front against the others, as soon as circumstances allow it. If Germany is ever to be brought back to the community of nations, then it will only be by Germans who have stayed in the country and suffered there with the others all the humiliations and, finally, the defeat which Hitler will bring to the country." To the objection that he would fall a victim to the Gestapo, he replied that he could not avoid such risks (according to David ASTOR's notes). Here also the sentence on Trott: "He was the exact opposite of what Hitler represents. I believe he was more deeply and thoroughly anti-Nazi than any Englishman or American." Other English friends suddenly broke off their relations with Trott when they heard of his activities in Germany. The following sentences from his replies are worth recalling: "I have a growing suspicion that some of my friends equate the troubles of Europe with Germany as such and maintain their relations with me only to the extent that I happen to fit into your English life. I feel this judgement to be very untrue and unjust and I don't want to be accepted on this sort of compromise basis. . . . But I see the reason why his happens clearly enough and we are all under strong pressure, it seems to me, to think about it"

413

(FRANKE op. cit. p. 38). In another letter: "I do not feel that some sane solution is completely out of reach—but I don't think it can be reached by some new method or slogan, but through an act of faith which takes us right off the usual level of worry, complaint, and blame: in that sense, not in a resigned or desperate one, did I mean to say: one's happiness did not matter." (Unpublished private letter.)

31. Trott urged in the talks that Britain's readiness for war should be emphatically demonstrated, particularly by naval manoeuvres, and he gave a warning that something was going on with Russia—what, he could not say. At the same time he tried to arouse understanding for the situation in Germany and to persuade the British to make certain concessions which would take account of the legitimate elements in Hitler's demands. In this way the situation would be clarified for the Generals and further wild demands by Hitler could be rendered dubious even for the Germans. Whether Trott's report ever came to Hitler's eyes is uncertain, but it is improbable because Ribbentrop did not like it.

32. ROTHFELS's documentation in Viertelj. H.f. Zeitgeschichte, July 1959 "Adam von Trott und das State Department" with verbatim copy of the various documents. See also B. MALEY, "The drama of the German Resistance movement" in the weekly "Human Events" of April 5, 1946. Maley prints extracts from the diary of Felix MORLEY, who, like Trott, was a Rhodes Scholar and later became editor of the "Washington Post". Another peace-feeler addressed to Roosevelt (autumn 1941 by Hassell via Stallforth) arrived in New York on December 2, 1941, but reached Roosevelt only after December 8 (Pearl Harbour) according to Morley, see ROTHFELS, p. 142.

33. FRANKE p. 41.

34. FRANKE p. 42.

35. Cf. Ruheloses Leben by former Ambassador Rudolf RAHN p. 382.

36. The memorandum which Trott handed Visser t'Hooft in Geneva at the end of April 1942 is published in Viertelj. H.f. Zeitgeschichte in October, 1957, p. 388, together with Schönfeld's memorandum (Statement by a German pastor at Stockholm, May 31, 1942) with an introductory note by ROTHFELS.

37. FRANKE p. 56.

38. FRANKE p. 55. It is characteristic of Trott that for a time he read every morning in the old Prophets: "If we don't learn to speak like Jeremiah, so that our language is understood by a person who has a thousand sheep or only one, we cannot expect to be heard."

39. Reported by Frau Clarita von TROTT.

40. FRANKE p. 50.

41. PÖLCHAU p. 108. Details in STELTZER passim.

42. Cf. also the book by M. PICARD "Hitler in uns selbst", Zurich, 1946.

43. The letter is printed in "Neue Auslese", 2nd year, vol 1, p. 10. It ends: "We rely on you to carry the thing through without wavering and we are ready to do the little we are able. And then do not forget that there will be a very bitter end for us, when you are through with it all. We hope you realize that we are ready to help you win the war and the peace." For discussions and contents of the letter see also ROTHFELS p. 23.

44. See STELTZER p. 154 ff.

45. GERSTENMAIER in "Das Parlament" special number July 20, 1952, p. 4.

46. Cf. Note 17.

47. Cf. HASSELL p. 64.

48. KB 331, 388, 393. Unpublished note of Prince FUGGER-GLÖTT and Dr REISERT.

49. Exposition of the different views of Goerdeler and the Kreisau circle in ROTHFELS p. 123, RITTER, p. 303 ff. Cf. also HASSELL p. 379. "Chancy con-

spiratorial methods" amongst others "Neue Auslese" op. cit. p. 15. Cf. also
PÖLCHAU p. 113. ROTHFELS p. 130 gives the essential differences between
Goerdeler's views and those of the Kreisau circle. He does not share Margret
Boveri's opinion that there was a sharp antithesis between Goerdeler and the
Kreisau circle. But he rejects RITTER's judgement that the views of the
Kreisau circle were "half-baked dilettantism". "In contrast to the belief in the
infallibility of reason (Goerdeler), there was expressed here (the Kreisau
circle) the much less optimistic conviction of the need for a new basis of order
in a world devastated by demonic powers and repeatedly exposed to them. In
this dimension the contrast goes really very deep. Its political effects continue
into our own time and it is certainly not synonymous with the contrast
between people of rank and activists." Relevant also are the vivid words which
Helmut LINDEMANN in an epilogue ("Reichweins Schicksal als Frage an
unsere Zeit") writes about the impetus of the Kreisau circle in the book by
HENDERSON p. 187 ff.

50. Letter to Lionel Curtis, see note 43.

51. Printed in STELTZER pp. 81–96. Steltzer sent this memorandum to the other
side on his own responsibility as a warning to the Allies against a false post-war
policy (cf. p. 13, p. 80). The last sentence says: "The purpose of these remarks
is, from our knowledge of the situation, to draw the attention of the responsible
Allied authorities to the dangerous instability of the situation in Germany and
the occupied countries, and to justify our opinion that only by systematic and
agreed co-operation between the Allies and a competent and responsible
German government can very dangerous developments be avoided."

VII. INDIVIDUAL PERSONALITIES

1. The subsequent evil role of Koch in the "Reichskommissariat Ukraine" and
then in the "Reichskommissariat Ostland" is well known. There is a report on
that in KLEIST (p. 180) which says: "Neither Joseph Stalin nor his allies, nor
the opponents of National Socialism can today be the accusers or judges of
Erich Koch; for he did everything humanly possible to ensure that Germany
bled to death in the East. Koch, and the policy of blind and stubborn force
associated with his name, opened for the Red Army and its Generalissimo
Stalin the way to the heart of Europe." Cf. the statements made by the
emigré KAULBARS who worked for Canaris (KB 425 ff.) and the secret memorandum of the diplomat, Dr Otto Bräutigam (Nuremberg Documents 294–PS,
in excerpts in SHIRER p. 858), who courageously and clearly broached the
devastating and irresponsible effect of German behaviour towards the Russian
population, but obviously made no impact. He was Deputy Head of the
Political Department of Rosenberg's Ministry for the Occupied Eastern
Territories. Similar experiences were to become one of the main motives
among officers for the revolt against Hitler. Schulenburg visited Koch in his
new palatial governor's villa in Krasna (Makow) in 1941 shortly before the
beginning of the war in Russia. He was shaken by what he saw: "What a
contrast with the period 1932–33, when the same people appeared as revolutionary fighters for Prussian Socialism!" He was accompanied by Friedrich-
Karl Klausing (cf. Chapter X of this book). A hand-written report by Schulenburg on the visit has survived. There is an interesting record of a meeting
between Carl Burckhardt, at that time the League of Nations Commissioner
for Danzig, and Koch in SCHWERIN-KROSIGK p. 165.

2. WINNIG p. 79.

3. On this RITTER pp. 303, 520, basing his information on O. Ehrensberger.

4. Dr SEIFARTH, unpublished memorandum in possession of Countess Charlotte Schulenburg. In this, too, Schulenburg's words when leaving Silesia: "We have the misfortune to work in fragments."

5. A clearly well-drawn portrait of Wagner in VERMEHREN p. 142.

6. In spite of the strong attacks of the Court President, Schulenburg revealed nothing of the detailed plans for the administration and of the persons earmarked for the future tasks. "Even on the threshold of death, he renounced any claim to have been a good organizer, in addition to a good revolutionary —in order to be loyal to all of his colleagues. Many owe their lives to him" (unpublished personal account).

7. Unpublished personal memories of a friend in the possession of Countess Charlotte Schulenburg.

8. In a war-time letter of Schulenburg from Russia during the late summer of 1941 (printed in VON DEM BUSSCHE): "I believe that we are facing difficult times full of hardship and danger for the nation and the individual. Sometimes the prospect is so dark that one believes the abyss lurks just behind this darkness. . . . As surely as God did not allow this nation to sink after the great collapse of 1918, so now he causes it to be convulsed in great guilt, peril and suffering, so that under the cruel blows of fate, it may come to a deeper awareness of itself, and summon forth its real strength, be transformed, and arise purified. My heart tells me that, and my heart is right. . . ."

9. A particularly large number of officers, who turn up in connection with the 20th July, belonged to the 9th Infantry Regiment. An impressive figure, especially for the younger ones, was Major Wilhelm Dieckmann, lately Oberregierungsrat in the Reich War Archives in Potsdam and editor of many of the office's documents. He had a great knowledge of historical and political events, particularly in the period since the German Liberation Wars, and knew how to introduce this effectively into conversations with the younger officers, often in the form of Socratic questions. In this way he was able to prepare the ground among them. Even a person unfavourably disposed could not easily take exception to this sort of "Prussian". Dieckmann was hanged on September 13, 1944.

10. Detlef FRIEDRICHSEN, Ein Leutnant von der Infanterie, Leipzig, 1942, Reclam. In this also the following farewell scene.

11. Unpublished tribute by Hugo KÜKELHAUS, 1947.

12. Schulenburg once said of himself: "I am stupid in comparison with Moltke." In spite of their contacts he never had a personal relationship with Moltke and did not take part in any of the meetings in Kreisau. He was fond of Peter Yorck. At his house in November 1942 he met the Socialists for the first time.

13. Based on RITTER's account (p. 313 ff.) which is derived from "Plans to Simplify the Administration" in KB 206. Here it says the reorganization should go back to Stein's idea of reform. "The aim of administrative reform must be to create clear responsibilities and freedom to take independent decisions."

14. The information in the text comes from an unpublished note by Walter MUTHMANN, former Oberregierungsrat in the Reich Office for Territorial Planning in Berlin, and from his account in the Essen weekly: "Der Fortschritt" from October 7 to November 14, 1949. For other details see W. MÜNCHHEIMER, Die Verfassungs– und Verwaltungsreformpläne der deutschen Opposition gegen Hitler am 20.7.1944, Europa Archiv V 14, 20.7.50. RITTER (p. 314) reproduces a remark by Schwerin-Krosigk on Schulenburg: "He was as far from the extreme federalism of the Kreisau circle as he was from Popitz's centralism; the Reich Gaue planned by him were to remain genuine provinces (Länder)." Whose map it was that Moltke put forward in his talks, for example, in Munich (REISERT) is not clear. Those concerned with

416

these questions also considered the possible need of new frontiers or lines to which the German troops would, if necessary, withdraw. After the experience of the Sudeten conflict and that of later years, it was thought essential to examine objectively the true ethnic situation in the frontier zones of Germany and so to work out practical bases for future decisions, not only for the Germans themselves, but also for the enemy powers. It is known that Albrecht Haushofer, on the basis of his careful research into the language situation in Bohemia, made the authoritative proposals for the new frontier demarcation between Germany and Czechoslovakia in the Sudeten crisis. The precision of his cartographical work at that time was such that the British and French arbitrators decided on a number of roundings off in favour of German enclaves and language-islands. Now, too, he seemed to be the right man for this job and, in fact, he devoted all his expert knowledge and scientific responsibility to the task.

From the available memoranda and oral accounts, it is not clear whether the Kreisau circle reached agreement on Austria's future relations with the Reich. Conversations on this subject, as far as can be seen today, were conducted by Jakob Kaiser, Goerdeler, Leuschner and Habermann who visited the representatives of the Christian and Socialist Opposition in Vienna. There, of course, they must have discovered how the short period of National Socialist rule had, in some circles, put an end to the desire for integration with Germany which had been so strong after the First World War. But not everywhere will people have thought like Lois WEINBERGER, from whose memoirs, published in 1948, BRAUBACH quotes the remarks made in 1943 to the delegate of the Opposition in the Reich . . . "that we wanted Austria only to be a free and independent state—independent even of Germany" (p. 27).

15. MUTHMANN op. cit.
16. KB 145. Schulenburg's reasons are set beside the "government declaration" found amongst Goerdeler's possessions which echo the same claims "with fanatical hatred" (PECHEL p. 316, KB 147).
17. Ursula von KARDORFF, Der Zwanzigste Juli in Berlin, in "Stuttgarter Rundschau", Vol 7, July 1954.
18. SEIFARTH op. cit. Before the People's Judge Schulenburg called himself a "national Socialist". GISEVIUS II p. 219 thinks that at the end Schulenburg was closest to Claus Stauffenberg.
19. The action of Halem and his friends was the only one of this kind which was undertaken by Reich Germans to prevent the Anschluss with Austria. At that time even the opponents of Hitler thought that the aim of union was just and was strongly desired by the two peoples. Halem shared this view but rejected Hitler's method of disguised "rape".
20. Dr Karl MÜLLER, unpublished report in possession of Dr Fabian von Schlabrendorff.
21. Report on the talk in VERMEHREN op. cit. and SCHLABRENDORFF. Cf. the "statement" which Hassell drew up in February 1940 in Arosa for Halifax (HASSELL p. 127, ROTHFELS p. 140). This contains the condition "that the union of Austria (and the Sudetenland) with the Reich is not subject to discussion."
22. On Dr Beppo Römer and his insurgent group, RAS (Revolutionary Workers and Soldiers) there are reports by PÖLCHAU p. 95 (who saw Römer in prison) and PECHEL p. 81. Walter HAMMER, who got to know Römer and those arrested with him in Brandenburg prison, gives the number of executed as between thirty and forty (information in a letter).
23. Reinhold SCHNEIDER "Die Toten des Zwanzigsten Juli", tribute of June 22, 1949. Printed privately. Mumm von Schwarzenstein was executed only on April 20, 1945, together with twenty-seven others in Brandenburg.

417

24. See PÖLCHAU p. 87, SCHLABRENDORFF p. 19 (1st edition). K. MÜLLER op. cit.
25. The letter is published in R. SCHNEIDER op. cit.
26. Letter published by SCHLABRENDORFF p. 141 of 2nd edition repeated by PÖLCHAU p. 88 and by the special number of "Das Parlament" for July 20, 1952. In these passages is to be found the long letter written a few days before to his mother, which is the most impressive testimony that survives of Halem.
27. In a memorandum of Bonhoeffer's appear the sentences: "That it was possible for Hitler to carry out an act of relative historical justice is due, not least, to the willingness of Britain to make all those concessions to Hitler after 1933 which she denied the Weimar Republic. In this way Britain . . . stood on Hitler's side against the Opposition at home." Taken from a commemorative essay "Das Zeugnis eines Boten. Zum Gedächtnis von Dietrich Bonhoeffer" (Ökumenische Kommission für die Pastoration der Kriegsgefangenen, Geneva, 1945, p. 12 ff.).

On the other hand, Bonhoeffer always emphatically placed Germany's guilt in the foreground—even to the point of rejecting a deliberate political plan of action—and stressed the need of repentance and reparation towards other nations. In this, his attitude was close to that of Count Moltke. Cf. on this op. cit. p. 7 (a report of VISSER T'HOOFT) and the memorandum of George Bell, Bishop of Chichester, on his meeting with Bonhoeffer at Whitsun 1942 and its rejection by Eden on July 17, 1942, both in BZH p. 55.

At the meeting with the English bishop, Bonhoeffer spoke in particular about questions of a future peace and of the need for the Protestant Churches to co-operate. A year later, in the spring of 1943, these ideas had acquired greater urgency and a more concrete character because of the programme which the Freiburg professors, Ritter, von Dietze, Eucken and Lampe, had drafted and discussed with leading Protestants, including Goerdeler. They pinned their hopes on a coup initiated by the Army and thought it necessary to secure agreement amongst the Christian Churches on certain basic matters affecting a future peace. Bonhoeffer was chosen to conduct negotiations in Rome with the Pope and conversations in Geneva or Stockholm with the responsible leaders of the Protestant Churches of the world. A few days before he was due to leave for Rome he was arrested. The Gestapo learned of these happenings from a note which came into their hands when Dohnanyi was arrested (see WEISENBORN p. 89).
28. "Das Zeugnis eines Boten" p. 12 ff.
29. Rüdiger Schleicher, a doctor's son from Stuttgart, one of the many Swabians serving in the Berlin Ministries, was Ministerialrat in the Air Ministry and taught aviation law as a Professor at the University. He went to prison because he had not reported his brother-in-law. It was said that he must have known this his brother-in-law knew something about the 20th July. He never appeared before the People's Court and was treacherously murdered without a sentence on the night of April 23, 1945, with his brother-in-law, Klaus Bonhoeffer, Professor Albrecht Haushofer and others.

On Schleicher and Klaus Bonhoeffer see A. LEBER, Das Gewissen steht auf. Also Auf dem Wege zur Freiheit, Gedichte und Briefe aus der Haft, edited by Eberhard Bethge, 5th edition, Berlin 1954, Lettner Verlag.
30. BONHOEFFER, Widerstand und Ergebung, p. 80.

VIII. HENNING VON TRESCKOW
NEW ATTEMPTS AT A COUP IN THE ARMY

1. RITTER, op. cit. p. 344.
2. KB 368. Friedrich Georgi reports the words of Friedrich Olbricht on the

evening of the 20th July: "I do not know how posterity will judge our actions and myself. But I know with certainty that we have all acted without personal motive and only risked all in a desperate situation to save Germany from complete ruin. I am convinced that posterity will one day recognize and understand this." Repeated in LEBER-MOLTKE p. 14. Cf. also the description of Olbricht in Annedore LEBER, Das Gewissen entscheidet, p. 263 ff.

3. On Henning von Tresckow see SCHLABRENDORFF's book Offiziere gegen Hitler of which he is the centre. Also GERSDORFF, HEUSINGER, SPEIDEL, DULLES and others. My account is also based on details from oral descriptions, in particular from Frau Erika von Tresckow, Margarete Countess Hardenberg (née von Oven), Bernd von Kleist and others.

4. Unpublished remark in a letter by Count EULENBURG.

5. Captain Eberhard von BREITENBUCH, personal report.

6. Major-General von GERSDORFF, unpublished report and minute of his statement, Archiv der Europäischen Publikation. Manstein said later that he knew nothing of the possibility of having Tresckow as Chief of Staff. The version in the text is based on Tresckow and a remark made by him to Schmundt (according to SCHLABRENDORFF).

7. Based on Tresckow's oral report (SCHLABRENDORFF). GUDERIAN describes in his book his personal differences with Kluge which Tresckow sought to iron out (p. 284). Apart from Tresckow, General von Rabenau and Goerdeler tried to "recruit" Guderian. Guderian himself reports on his meeting with Goerdeler p. 272. He writes as though what Goerdeler urged had been wishful thinking without a real basis for action. After this and Tresckow's visit, it was feared Guderian would betray the men and plans of the Resistance. The main purpose of Rabenau's visit was, as SCHLABRENDORFF reports, to clarify Guderian's attitude and, if necessary, to dissuade him from reporting matters (p. 115, 1st edition). Tresckow's efforts to reconcile Guderian and Kluge also became known during the interrogation (KB 88).

8. SCHLABRENDORFF p. 142, 1st edition. In the 2nd edition more detailed.

9. In the winter 1941–42, Voss, on behalf of Witzleben, had seen Halder to ask him about his attitude to a military coup (SCHLABRENDORFF p. 82 of 2nd edition).

10. BREITENBUCH, see note 5.

11. SCHLABRENDORFF p. 153 (1st edition).

12. Cf. KB 291, 31, RITTER p. 536.

13. HASSELL p. 297, SENDTNER in Die Vollm. d. Gew. pp. 391, 405, SCHLABRENDORFF p. 59. Cf. Secret report of General Petzel to Commander of Reserve Army on November 23, 1939, IMT XXXV p. 88 ff. printed in LEBER-MOLTKE p. 172.

14. HASSELL p. 202; see "Der Verbrecherische Befehl" (supplement to "Parlament" on July 17, 1957).

15. GERSDORFF, see Note 6.

16. HASSELL p. 212.

17. HASSELL p. 214, BRÄUTIGAM (see Note 1, Chapter VII of this book), KAULBARS KB 426, also Vierteljahreshefte f. Zeitgesch. 1954, Vol 3, p. 309 (Hitler's address of July 1, 1942, in which he violently forbade all attempts to conduct politics with the Russians against the Soviet leaders). Similar, and for posterity hardly intelligible, refusals of the politician Hitler, who expected everything from his military dominance and avoided political ties, were constantly discussed in the circle of the Opposition movement. Several possibilities were discussed: the French were reported to have offered three Army Corps against Russia and participation in the war in return for a guarantee of the independence of France; the Greeks one Army Corps against Russia under the

same conditions. They were said to have been ready to hand over to Germany the officers' families as security.

On the attempts to persuade Hitler to make a generous peace and to offer the French an alliance for which they were ready to make military contributions, there is a vivid and detailed account in RAHN. Cf. especially pp. 271–78 —the words of Admiral Darlan: "Doesn't your Führer understand that the war cannot be won or ended with these methods? We French wouldn't mind if this were only to lead to a defeat of Germany. But sooner or later, it will lead to the collapse of the Europe we love. If France receives an assurance of an honourable peace and the maintenance of her Empire, we are ready to make a loyal contribution to the ending of the war. I would then close the Straits of Gibraltar with our fleet and have the 150 000 men we have under arms in North Africa march against the Suez Canal—if you like, under Rommel's command." On Russian attempts to get talks with Hitler, see Chapter XI.

18. Vierteljahreshefte f. Zeitgesch, 1954, Vol 3, p. 302, letters from Major-General Stieff. According to the SS Report (KIESEL), Stieff said at his interrogation: "I could not look on and see how this man with his obstinacy shatters his own work, like someone running amok. We are defending Kirkenes and Crete and we will lose Königsberg and Cracow."

19. GERSDORFF op. cit.

20. HASSELL p. 232.

21. HASSELL pp. 248 and 244. Cf. GISEVIUS p. 500.

22. HASSELL p. 281, SCHLABRENDORFF p. 66. According to information in RITTER op. cit. p. 535, Note 14, Goerdeler during his visit discussed with Kluge whether Hitler could be arrested during a visit to the Army Group. On his return he met Popitz at Königsberg railway station who was just on his way to Field-Marshal Küchler but who only "ran into open doors" there (ibid.).

23. SCHLABRENDORFF p. 67.

24. GISEVIUS p. 442.

25. HASSELL pp. 295, 380.

26. Goerdeler wrote in his notes that on November 24, 1942, a staff officer from one of the Corps of the Sixth Army appeared at Beck's and urgently asked him to help save the Army by a coup d'état at the right moment. Beck approached Manstein. RITTER p. 349.

27. GISEVIUS p. 440 and elsewhere.

28. Felix GILBERT, Hitler Directs his War, New York, Oxford, 1950, p. 17 ff. reproduces a stenographic report of the Führer's conference on February 1, in which he abuses Field-Marshal Paulus whom he has just promoted, for being so cowardly as to survive the surrender. "So many people have to die, and then one man like that besmirches the heroism of so many others at the last minute. He could have freed himself from all sorrow and ascended into eternity and national immortality—but he prefers to go to Moscow! . . . In this war, no more Field-Marshals will be made. I won't go on counting my chickens before they are hatched." Two days later, it was announced in the special Wehrmacht report: "The battle for Stalingrad is over. True to their oath, to their last breath, the Sixth Army under the exemplary leadership of Field-Marshal Paulus have been overcome by the superiority of the enemy and by the unfavourable circumstances confronting our forces." Cf. HEUSINGER p. 235, ABSHAGEN p. 225.

29. GERSDORFF (in PECHEL p. 160) speaks of another, earlier visit to Smolensk by Hitler. In fetching him from the air-field, Tresckow had wanted to hide a time-bomb in the side pocket of the car near to Hitler's seat, but was unable to carry out his plan because of the constant vigilance of the SS guards. SCHLABRENDORFF has no knowledge of the visit referred to here. In 1941,

before any assassination plans were ready, Hitler once visited the Army Group in Borisov. He himself came in a plane and a convoy of cars drove almost 1,000 kilometres from East Prussia, in order to collect him at the airfield and take him the two kilometres to the headquarters of the Army Group.

30. PECHEL p. 162. SCHLABRENDORFF p. 123 (2nd edition). Gersdorff's description, which forms the basis of Pechel's account, differs in some points from Schlabrendorff's.

31. Description according to GERSDORFF op. cit. Tresckow, who during leave in May, had had consultations with Olbricht, thought it essential that one of the major troop Commanders at the front should give the signal for starting the coup at home. (See RITTER p. 365.) Hence the new approach to Kluge.

32. RITTER p. 363.

33. Frau Erika von Tresckow, who was present during these exciting "convalescent" weeks that Henning von Tresckow spent in Berlin and helped write out his drafts, has given a report on this.

34. April 1943. An appreciation of the situation at this time after the Casablanca Declaration and the fall of Stalingrad in WEIZSÄCKER p. 340 ff.

35. Goerdeler's letter see "Die Wandlung" 1945–46, Vol 2, p. 173, GISEVIUS II, p. 261. RITTER p. 352 gives the facsimile of the whole letter (in possession of the family).

36. RITTER p. 334 ff.

37. "The Casablanca formula enabled Hitler to continue the war as leader of Germany for another two years. It mobilized the forces of despair in Germany, which now ranged themselves with the worshippers of success. It meant that the Allies had deliberately abandoned the idea of ending the war by political means. It created a vacuum in the heart of Europe and it is impossible to imagine what it cost both sides in blood and misery" (WEIZSÄCKER p. 342). Cf. the chapter "Unconditional Surrender" in ROTHFELS p. 156 ff. and in detail with information on sources KRAUSNICK-GRAML, "Der deutsche Widerstand und die Allierten", supplement to "Das Parlament" of 19.7.1961.

38. Inge SCHOLL, "Die Weisse Rose", Frankfurt 1952, Verlag der Frankfurter Hefte. Cf. also the tribute of Klara HUBER, Kurt Huber zum Gedächtnis, Bildnis eines Menschen, Forschers und Denkers. Contributed by his friends, Regensburg, 1949. Here also are the notes of Professor Huber for his famous closing speech in the People's Court on April 19, 1943, printed also in GOLLWITZER-KUHN-SCHNEIDER p. 256 and LEBER, Das Gewissen steht auf, p. 44. Huber was beheaded a week before the 20th July.

39. Vierteljahrsh. f. Zeitgesch., 2nd year, Vol 3, p. 311.

40. IMT XXXVII p. 498 ff.

41. WEISENBORN gives p. 265 the copy of the sentence on Regierungsrat Dr Korselt from Rostock who, because of a remark in a Rostock tram, was condemned to death by the People's Court on August 23, 1943. There also the copy of the death sentence on the pianist, Karlrobert Kreiten, who "tried to subvert the fighting resistance of his German compatriots and so helped our war-time enemy" (September 3, 1943).

42. IMT XXXVII p. 632 ff.

IX. CLAUS AND BERTHOLD STAUFFENBERG

1. Passages from Hitler's speech of September 10, 1943, reproduced by SHIRER, p. 916.

2. Countess Karoline Uexküll-Gyllenband's family was originally domiciled in the Baltic region but returned to the Reich at the time of the Swedish wars. The branch to which she belonged had been living in Swabia for many

generations. She herself suffered a great deal, but lived a free and daring life. For many years lady-in-waiting and friend of her queen, she presided over a large family of her own and took a very active part in the work of the parish. She lived to be over eighty, young in heart and adored by youth. Humiliation and arrest after the 20th July could not touch her. And greater even than her sorrow at the double loss she had suffered was her gratitude to her sons for having followed their chosen course.

2a. In his book "Mein Bild von Stefan George", Robert BOEHRINGER published photographs of the Stauffenberg brothers. George gave one of his poems in "Das Neue Reich" Berthold Stauffenberg's name as its title. Later, Berthold von Stauffenberg was named by George as his beneficiary in the event of the death of George's heir.

3. One of his fellow pupils in the inter-denominational class reports a significant incident. The Roman Catholic teacher had rudely belittled Luther and aroused lively opposition. Berthold Stauffenberg had remained silent throughout. But during the break, without any of his class-mates knowing about it, he went to see the teacher to protest, on behalf of the others, against this mean and unchivalrous behaviour. If anything like that happened again, he said, they would boycott his lessons.

4. Friends occasionally called Stauffenberg "Der Bamberger Reiter" (The Bamberg Rider), and in his book WHEELER-BENNETT reproduced side by side portraits of Stauffenberg and the "Bamberger Reiter"—the famous thirteenth century statue in his native city.

5. Colonel i.G. Eberhard Finckh, KB 305; on "one-sided military thinking" see GOERLITZ, p. 612; on "worthy successor to Moltke", personal remark to author by General KOESTRING.

6. The statue which the sculptor had personally helped to erect was destroyed by unknown vandals at the beginning of the war. The authorities showed no interest in prosecuting the culprits.

7. Ludwig THORMAEHLEN, Erinnerungen an Stefan George p. 220 ff.

8. Freiherr Dietz von THUNGEN, unpublished MS.

9. FAHRNER, see Note 13.

10. The "Erzaehlung" published during the war in a private edition and later by Suhrkamp Publishers was by Lt.-Col. Wolfgang HOFFMAN, who was killed at Sevastopol in August 1942. It has some bearing on the character of Stauffenberg, whom Hoffmann had met at HQ and in Berlin.

11. FAHRNER, see Note 13.

12. Erwin TOPF, article on Count Claus Stauffenberg in "Die Zeit", July 18, 1946.

13. At my request Rudolf FAHRNER wrote down his personal memories of 20th July in 1962–63. They have not yet been published. Fahrner gave me permission to read and use his MS. for my book.

14. On organization of Russian volunteer formations see MICHEL's paper—parts of which should be treated with reserve—and the more comprehensive work by KLEIST (p. 205 ff.), which also gives figures. He mentions Stauffenberg's part in the struggle against Bormann's and Koch's policy to subjugate the vanquished peoples.

15. Von THUNGEN, op. cit.

16. SAUERBRUCH, p. 550, confirms Stauffenberg's impatience: he says Stauffenberg refused to have the operation, just as he refused to have a "Sauerbruch-arm" fitted, because this would have meant more time in hospital.

17. Letter of 1950 from Rudolf FAHRNER to author.

18. FAHRNER, see Note 13.

19. FOERTSCH, p. 22, gives a description for which he quotes as source Peter Sauerbruch, a younger regimental colleague of Stauffenberg's: this says that 2nd Lt. Stauffenberg, then twenty-five years old, placed himself at the head of an enthusiastic crowd marching through the streets of Bamberg on January 30, 1933. He was wearing full uniform. Afterwards, he calmly accepted reproaches and criticism from his fellow-officers and superiors; and he told his comrades that the great soldiers of the Wars of Liberation seemed to have shown more understanding for such a genuine uprising of the people. Inquiries among Bamberg citizens who were in the town on January 30, produced no confirmation of any such event. P. SAUERBRUCH obliged the author with more detailed information. He confirmed Foertsch's recollection but added an explanation which is of importance for the understanding of the incident. According to Sauerbruch, Stauffenberg did not place himself as a young, active National Socialist leader of the people in officer's uniform at the head of civilians to lead the crowd on the march, thereby incurring criticism or punishment by his superiors. . . . What happened was obviously a much more personal matter. That day—or possible later (Sauerbruch, who as a cadet was not directly involved, does not exclude a potential error in the date because there were so many occasions in those days when it could have happened) there was some talk among officers about Stauffenberg in uniform having joined a marching crowd in the street. Criticized for that, he accepted the reproach and told his friends something to the effect that he happened to arrive on the scene as general enthusiasm was sweeping the people along, and he had found it impossible, as an officer in uniform, to turn into a side street. And after that he made his remark about the great soldiers of the Wars of Liberation.

The idea that an officer cannot remain aloof where the nation's great issues are involved, and the rejection of the caste spirit of the Officer Corps are quite familiar traits of Stauffenberg's. One is reminded of Hermann KAISER's diary (see "Die Wandlung" 1945–46, Vol. 5) where a similar view is expressed: "You only need to recall Scharnhorst, Clausewitz or Gneisenau to realize to what level today's officers have sunk." Stauffenberg's own ideas on this new movement can be gleaned from the text.

20. Count Nikolaus Uexküll, brother of Countess Karoline Stauffenberg, cf. pp. 294, 460.

21. Halder's evidence during the first hearing before Munich Court on September 20, 1948. As reproduced by GRAML in the supplement to "Das Parlament" of July 16, 1958, p. 359, Tresckow's name, too, is mentioned but I do not recall that from the hearing which I attended. In a similar way Caesar von Hofacker was motivated by his anxiety about Franco-German relations (cf. Chapter X).

22. Professor J. SPEER, Munich, formerly Freiburg, unpublished report. Speer was serving under the then Major i.G. Finckh at the Quartermaster-General's office and had been a school-mate of Stauffenberg's.

23. "Autoritäre Anarchie" in KLEIST p. 208: see also book of the same title by PETWAIDIC (Hoffmann & Campe, 1946): SPEIDEL p. 43 and also in extenso in the SS-Report (KIESEL). The officers' criticism of Hitler occupies a great deal of space in the interrogations, e.g. KB 291, 31, 406, 475, 525, 302 (The Moral Attitude of the Officer, Oster), 271 (on the "non-political" officer and the "soldier-only" cf. in this book: Stauffenberg's criticism of the Field-Marshals for making the excuse "we are only soldiers".

The nonsensical command structure is shown by Stauffenberg who cites the example of an African village, the evacuation of which had to be requested via Rome from Führer HQ; meanwhile, he says, totally unnecessary and avoidable losses had occurred merely because it took so long to put the order through (KB 294) (cf. Hagen's evidence before the People's Court on August 7, IMT XXXIII p. 325 ff. especially p. 337–38).

24. It had become customary for the representatives of one military branch to leave the conference room when those of another branch began their report.

25. GERSDORFF says that when he visited Manstein he was authorized "if necessary, to disclose the whole plot and to produce letters written by Goerdeler and Popitz which contained political and economic data". Manstein, who was in agreement in principle, refused to take part personally. Since Manstein declined to get involved in politics and had misgivings about a coup d'état because of the Army's attitude, Kluge's emissary did not disclose any further details of the plan to him. Gersdorff writes: "The most important thing was to ascertain that in case of a successful coup d'état, Field-Marshal von Manstein would be completely at our disposal: and that was guaranteed" (op. cit.).

   In summer 1942, Beck sent an urgent letter to Manstein (extracts in SCHLABRENDORFF's book p. 160, 2nd edition). Manstein's reply: "A war is not lost as long as you do not consider it lost" IMT XII p. 264. Goerdeler mentions another letter written by Beck to Manstein at the end of November 1942 (see RITTER p. 349). In his book 'Verlorene Siege' MANSTEIN says nothing about these matters.

   After Stalingrad, H. KAISER, in his diary on February 20, 1943, writes about the Generals who refused to join the plot: "One is ready to act when he is ordered to do so, another ready to give orders when action has been taken." (See Note 19.)

26. According to FAHRNER who had spoken to Stauffenberg soon after his visit to Manstein.

27. (See Note 13.) In conjunction with the remarks about the Generals in this book it will be seen that Stauffenberg, who allegedly undermined the new Army's oath of loyalty, in fact regarded a soldier's, and especially an officer's responsibility as a matter of supreme importance.

28. Prof. Otto SCHILLER, Agricultural College, Hohenheim. Personal report.

29. Erwin COLSMAN; personal report. Colsman was a Colonel in the Reserve and co-owner of his family's cloth factory in the Rhineland. He and Claus Stauffenburg were close friends and they often discussed matters which deeply interested Stauffenberg as an officer. He found in Colsman a man of sound judgement, a sense of honour and duty, and great patriotism. Colsman died in 1962. The author owes to him a great deal of information about his meetings with Stauffenberg. A visit to Hitler in Vinnitsa shortly before the end of August 1942 is described by SAUERBRUCH, p. 542: KOESTRING recalls a heated remark from a conversation with Stauffenberg during the same period in Vinnitsa: "I hate the Führer. I hate the whole rabble round him." COLSMAN emphasized, however, that Claus Stauffenberg did not take part in cheap sneers about Hitler. "Stauffenberg regarded Hitler as a worthy opponent."

30. KB 373, 395, cf. KB 293 and Hagen's evidence before the People's Court (Note 23).

31. Ludwig THORMAEHLEN, op. cit. p. 215 ff.

32. Accounts by: STREBEL: Obituary in "Zeitschrift fuer ausländisches offentliches und Völkerrecht" Volume XIII (1948) pp. 14–16: Prof. A. N. MAKAROV in "Friedenswarte", Zurich December 1947.

33. When the Gestapo searched Berthold Stauffenberg's office after 20th July for incriminating documents they found in the drawer of his writing desk a manuscript, apparently with his own corrections, of translations of Homer and the manuscript of a Life of the Kings Agis and Cleomenes from the latter days of Sparta.

424

The report by THIERSCH, mentioned in Note 35, refers to this translation of Homer. Speaking of Berthold Stauffenberg he recalls "The last time I saw him was in early July when, as I knew, he was preoccupied with the preparations for the coup d'état which was expected to take place very shortly. He and a friend of his had come to meet me at the railway station, and he appeared genuinely serene and relaxed."

34. K. BAUCH, Professor at Freiburg, unpublished MS.

35. Letter from Urban THIERSCH, sculptor, Munich, to author.

36. Anni LERCHE, General Olbricht's secretary at the Bendlerstrasse, wrote in an unpublished account of April 20, 1946: "One day he (Stauffenberg) told me that he was fit for military service. I didn't believe him and a few days later he showed me a certificate from the MO which said so. So he had done it! And at his insistence the doctor had issued him with this certificate. One really always got the impression of dealing with an entirely fit person. Once when I told him he ought to think of himself and have an artificial limb fitted, he laughed it off: 'Oh, I haven't got time for that now. I'll have it done some other time.' In his incredible modesty this man thought of nothing but his beloved Fatherland." The MO at the Bendlerstrasse (Carpentier) was 'in the know' and helped wherever he could.

37. FAHRNER, see Note 13.

X. THE CIRCLE OF CONSPIRATORS

1. The Chief of Armaments and C.-in-C. of the Reserve Army was in charge not only of the General War Office but also the Army Ordnance Branch with its many sub-sections, and the Army Administration Branch. Since 1943, General Olbricht had also taken over the affairs of the Army Replacements Branch (Wehrersatzamt) and thus was immediately subordinate to Field-Marshal Keitel. All personnel matters were therefore handled by him, and Lt.-Col. Bernardis was his personal assistant.

2. Only a few months earlier General von Unruh had unsuccessfully tried to "comb" the Reserve Army for fit men. The jobs of cooks and private barbers to this or that Minister were still regarded "reserved" (cf. KAISER's diary).

3. K. BAUCH, op. cit.

4. From a report by secretary Delia ZIEGLER.

4a. Countess Maria Stauffenberg, Berthold Stauffenberg's widow, gives this account: on a starlit night after a heavy air raid her brother-in-law, Claus, stepped out on to the balcony of their home at Wannsee, looked at the fires which lit the night skies, and recited some verses to himself. When they both went inside he opened the book containing the poem he had just spoken: Stefan George's "Antichrist" from his "Siebenter Ring". The Countess suggests that Claus Stauffenberg sometimes quoted it to win over men still hesitating to join the Resistance. And she says the poem circulated among Stauffenberg's associates as a sign of identity of those ready to take action (cf. E. ZELLER in "Bekenntnis und Verpflichtung", Stuttgart 1955, publ. Friedrich Vorwerk, p. 138, and also in Ludwig-Maximilians-Universitaet-Jahreschronik 1960–61, Munich, 1961, p. 77).

5. KB 521. According to Hofacker's evidence Stauffenberg's principle had been "that for the sake of the success of the plan each (confederate) should know only as much about it as was necessary for him to do his particular job". Hofacker added that he had argued about this with Claus Stauffenberg because he, Hofacker, had wanted to be an active accomplice in the deed and not only remain on the sidelines. Beck and Goerdeler had taken the same line as Stauffenberg.

425

6. An entry written on August 8, 1811, by Gneisenau reads: "Preparations for this popular rising are being made only in so far as they are necessary to bring it about. . . . Nothing is being laid down in writing among its participants, there has been no exchange of letters. But trusted men are carrying messages. They are being instructed by the leaders." (Letters, published by Botzenhart, Munich, 1937, Langen-Müller, p. 48.)

7. See Note 18 Chapter XI of this book; cf. RITTER 544. The People's Court was wrong in attributing this to Stauffenberg.

8. Dietrich BONHOEFFER cf. Chapter VII of this book—Friedrich MEINECKE wrote about the men of the 20th July: "He who put above everything else the task of saving Germany from the greatest catastrophe of her history also had the moral courage to suffer the insults which a second 'stab-in-the-back' legend was bound to heap upon his head. Beck and his men had this courage." (Die deutsche Katastrophe, p. 147.)

9. Erwin COLSMAN made a similar comment. Cf. Note 29 in Chapter IX.

10. See Note 21 in Chapter IX.

11. Margarete von Oven, later Countess Hardenberg, who for many years was secretary to Fritsch and Hammerstein, worked also for Tresckow and Stauffenberg with the same devotion, disregarding all danger, and helped to write the orders and drafts.

12. Hans-Ulrich von Oertzen, an ex-pupil of the school at Salem Castle, became a career officer in Signals. He had won several riding prizes in horse racing, occasionally also took part in motor racing, and joined the war as a young man full of ideals. His experiences in Russia changed him. . . . He took his place beside Tresckow and Stauffenberg and he, too, found fulfilment in a life of daring action.

13. Cf. Annedore LEBER Für und Wider p. 103 and in Das Gewissen entscheidet p. 263 ff. Cf. also Chapter VIII of this book.

14. Fromm was asked to state in writing why he had received Schulenburg and what they had talked about. He confirmed that they had spoken about the situation only "in a positive sense". Some time after Schulenburg's meeting, General von Rabenau made a similar approach to Fromm but the conversation offered no opening. (KAISER op. cit.) Rabenau was executed. As regards Fromm's knowledge and rejection of Halder's plans for a coup d'état of November 1939 see SENDTNER in Die Vollm. d. Gewissens., p. 420: about his certainty of victory in April 1940 see HASSELL p. 150.

15. Stauffenberg's driver reports that once, during an air raid, he had driven with Stauffenberg into the Goethestrasse when news came that Beck's house had been hit. He says that some streets were almost impassable because of torn-up pavements and debris. Stauffenberg had hurried him on—"nothing was ever fast enough for the Colonel"—and had not allowed him to stop even when he noticed that the drawn back hood of the open car had apparently caught fire, either from the heat or an incendiary bomb.

16. FRANKE p. 63.

16a. Examples of Sack's activity (KB 363): he intervened when danger threatened as a result of the arrest of Col. Stähle, who was a collaborator of Stauffenberg's and Goerdeler's. See also GROPPE Ein Kampf um Recht und Sitte 1959, 2nd edition, p. 38.

17. Von Rost always gave proof of his training in philosophy and was a great talker. He won quite a number of people over to the idea of an uprising but failed to persuade General Kortzfleisch, the Berlin commander and his immediate superior. Rost was put in command of a division in Italy where he was killed.

426

18. Published in the Vierteljahreshefte fuer Zeitgeschichte, 954, p. 300 ff.
19. Cf. Chapter VIII.
20. His uncle, Major Hans-Georg Klamroth, was also executed.
21. SCHLABRENDORFF p. 123. Heusinger published his memoirs of 1923–45 in 92 partly fictitious but largely historical incidents under the title Befehl im Widerstreit. Before the war Tresckow had worked under Heusinger and as CSO I of Army Group Centre he had been in frequent touch with him. Cf. HEUSINGER p. 213 ff. (Gespräche im November 1942) and p. 247 ff. (Gespräche im April 1943).
22. Description of Fellgiebel by Lt. d. R. Hellmut ARNTZ, his former ADC, not published.
23. He was Fellgiebel's Chief of Staff, in the latter's capacity as Chief of Wehrmacht Signals.
24. Notes by G. A. von ROENNE published in "Das Parlament", special issue on July 20, 1952. Roenne's last letters to his mother and wife were published several times, e.g. in "Das Evangelische Gemeindeblatt fuer Wuerttemberg" year 1947, No. 2. Regarding Stauffenberg's relations with Roenne see MICHEL ("Die Tat", Zurich, November 25, 1946).
25. In the SS-Report (KIESEL) Finckh is described as the "top ace" of all German Quartermasters-General. As Supply Chief of the Sixth (Stalingrad) Army he had urgently warned against Göring's airlift supply venture and had realized that the only possible solution was to retreat or break the encirclement (SCHRAMM p. 91).
26. Unpublished report by Helmut CORDS. Leonrod was quickly convicted and executed as his name was on the list of liaison officers. During the interrogation it emerged that a few months before the attempt he had sought the advice of Chaplain Wehrle of Munich, whom he knew well, as to whether knowing of a planned assassination was a sin. The chaplain was also sentenced to death because he had not reported this question. In evidence, Leonrod said he had felt he was bound by his oath as an officer, but Stauffenberg had impressed on him: "As a Catholic believer, you are bound in conscience by what you have been told about the military and political situation, to act contrary to that oath." (KB 262, also 288, 321.)
27. See BZH.
28. Kurt BAUCH, op. cit. The information from a fellow-officer is from an unpublished MS. by Commander Sydney JESSEN.
29. A recent very detailed account of the links between the Resistance and the Navy appeared in BAUM's contribution to the Vierteljahreshefte f. Zeitgeschichte, 1963, Vol. 1.
30. Georgi's statement, according to LEBER-MOLTKE Für und Wider, pp. 114, 115.
31. According to von dem BUSCCHE's verbal account, Schulenburg told a badly wounded friend, whom he visited in Insterburg in July 1944, that unless they managed to carry out the attempt they would have to pledge themselves on oath and combine in an "Order" so as to hold together a group of men who would know about one another and keep faith with the Fatherland in the days after Germany's collapse and foreign rule. The fact that Schulenburg knew of the oath, which had only just been drafted in Berlin, shows how close he was to Stauffenberg, who until then had told only very few friends about this highly confidential matter.
32. On Schwerin's account cf. HASSELL, SCHWERIN-KROSIGK, A. LEBER, Das Gewissen steht auf.
33. About Hofacker see SCHRAMM pp. 322, 400.
34. WEISENBORN p. 184, cf. also LEBER Ein Mann geht seinen Weg pp. 284, 291.

XI. PLANS AND PREPARATIONS

1. Cf. Chapter X.
2. "Deutsche Industrie im Kriege 1939–45", pub. by Deutsches Institut für Wirtschaftsforschung, Berlin 1954, pp. 46 and 139.
3. The Reserve Brigade "Grossdeutschland" in Kottbus had also been ordered on 20th July to occupy the Deutschlandsender in Königswusterhausen; cf. Note 63, on p. 537. I do not know how the two orders related to each other.
4. Goerdeler's appeal at the end of 1943: see SCHLABRENDORFF p. 149–57. Text of programme of early summer 1944: publ. by RITTER in "Gegenwart" of June 24, 1946.
5. "Skizze eines Reichsgrundgesetzes über wirtschaftliche Reichsgerechtsame." See BZH p. 31. According to KB 360, Lejeune-June was rejected as Minister of Economic Affairs by Strünck and Gisevius; but approved by Goerdeler on July 15, 1944.
6. The reports to Bormann and Hitler set great store by reproducing these drafts and the criticism on which they are based. On organization of state and administration: see especially KB 206, 59; on top-level war administration especially KB 291, 31.
7. ROTHFELS, Die deutsche Opposition gegen Hitler, p. 105.
8. RITTER in his book on Goerdeler, p. 617, enumerates the various lists of Ministers Goerdeler had suggested.
9. RITTER, op. cit. pp. 585, 324.
10. ROTHFELS op. cit. pp. 147–50; for the English "statement" by Schönfeld and a report by the Bishop of Chichester on his meeting with the two German theologians see Vierteljahrsh. f. Zeitgesch. October 1957; for the Bishop's memorandum of June 1942 and Eden's letter of reply of July 17, see BZH p. 50 ff.
11. ROTHFELS, op. cit. pp. 145–47.
12. Peter KLEIST 'Zwischen Hitler und Stalin' pp. 235, 243, 265. According to Kleist, the Russian negotiator stressed in particular Russia's disinterest in the war in Europe, and her future confrontation in the Far East: "There, in China, lies the fate of the next century; there, in China, the battle is going on for the control of the world; the master in the Kremlin will keep his powder dry and conserve his strength for China." On Hitler's reaction to this revealing disclosure see SCHMIDT p. 575. The former SD leader Walter HAGEN (pseudonym) reports a fairly important parallel undertaking in the Balkans. In his book H. says that in September 1943 Stalin evidently realized the danger— possible as a result of rumours from Quebec—of Churchill prevailing over the Americans with his plan for an Allied landing in the Balkans. He informed Tito that in that case he would approve of Tito's collaboration with the Germans for the purpose of a joint defence. Tito had earlier approached the German General Glaise-Horstenau in Zagreb regarding an alliance with Germany. Tito cleverly used the Yugoslav General Velebit for this approach. Hitler was informed via Himmler and Kaltenbrunner. His reply to Zagreb: "No negotiating with rebels. We shoot rebels." Does this feeler prove that the talks in Stockholm, too, were more than just a tactical move to bring pressure on the Allies?
13. A. W. DULLES, p. 165; ROTHFELS publishes the memorandum in his own translation, p. 164.
14. RITTER, op. cit. p. 335.
15. RITTER, ibid. p. 337.
16. HASSELL op. cit. pp. 327, 338 ff. End of chance of separate peace: p. 342.
17. According to Paulus van HUSEN see RITTER p. 523. In the course of the winter

428

Claus Stauffenberg had been gaining greater influence also on the formulation of political plans in collaboration with Leber, Trott and Schulenburg: but then those inclined more to the Right, particularly Gisevius and Goerdeler, began to stress Stauffenberg's Left-wing orientation and they even maintained he was pro-Soviet. East German (GDR) historians elaborated on this and managed to present Stauffenberg from their own viewpoint as the one and only praiseworthy leader among the whole "suspect bourgeois" movement of the 20th July. This misunderstanding, indeed deliberate misrepresentation, of Stauffenberg was encouraged by Sebastian HAFFNER's article published in "Contact" in London and reprinted in August 1947 in "Neue Auslese". Haffner writes: "This Government (with Leber as Chancellor and Trott as Foreign Minister) was intended to convert the military uprising into a genuine revolution, to bring together Germans and foreign workers under the old slogan 'Proletarians of all lands, unite!', to hand over power in the occupied countries to the Resistance movement and confront the advancing armies of the Big Three with a Europe which was forging its unity in a revolutionary sea of flames. To start with, this was no more than a conspiracy, but what a dream was behind it! . . . The man who dreamt it and inspired an elite of his contemporaries with it was Count Stauffenberg." The article had something compelling, something of the grand gesture, something of Stauffenberg's spiritual reach—something of a demonic genius, as Haffner called it. But although there may have been an element of truth in the interpretation, it was exaggerated and caused confusion by giving rise to false associations. The slogan "Unification of Europe through supra-national social revolution" may well have been used by Stauffenberg in some argument—although one would have looked for it rather among the Kreisau Circle—but if it is seriously linked with the obsolete slogan of "Workers of the World, unite!" the picture is abruptly reversed: nothing would have been further from these men's minds than to unleash an amorphous wave of revolution *from below*.

18. Appeal to Wehrmacht KB 199, RITTER 622, BZH 174; Appeal to Wehrmacht KB 202, PECHEL 304; Appeal to German people KB 139, PECHEL 305, BZH 159, WEISENBORN 142; Appeal to German people KB 140, PECHEL 309, BZH 162; Goerdeler's Government statement No. 2. 3rd version, PECHEL 314, BZH 167, KB 147; Goerdeler's appeal, possibly at end of 1943, SCHLABRENDORFF 149; Goerdeler's appeal (material) KB 165, cf. BRAUBACH "The Road to the 20th July", p. 47 ff.
19. R. FAHRNER, see Note 13.

XII. ABORTIVE ATTEMPTS: STRUGGLE FOR DECISION

1. Jakob Wallenberg and Gotthold Müller make it appear probable that an attempt on Hitler and thus the proclamation of a state of military emergency were expected for the end of September. No details are known; cf. RITTER p. 540 Note 44. My earlier statement that Stauffenberg's preparations in the General Staff were completed on October 10 turned out to be wrong. According to Fahrner, at the end of October Stauffenberg expected the start of the operation around November 10. Contrary to RITTER's information, p. 514 Note 48, Stauffenberg worked on the plans from September 10 and not from October 1 onwards.
2. August WINNIG, Aus 20 Jahren p. 178.
3. A. v. d. BUSSCHE 'Eid und Schuld' "Göttingen Universitätszeitung" of March 7, 1947. He gave evidence to the same effect at Nuremberg. Parts of this appeared in "Die Zeit" of July 22, 1948. He remarked: "I knew Hitler had to be destroyed when I witnessed the execution of 1 600 Jews in a little town in

the Ukraine. These men, women and children had to line up naked and then lie down in their own mass grave. There they were shot, one by one, irrespective of whether the person underneath was dead or still alive." (LEBER-MOLTKE "Für und Wider", p. 110.)

4. DULLES, p. 93. KB 90.
5. About Kleist-Schmenzin see SCHLABRENDORFF, pp. 12, 212; LILJE p. 55. "Proud and unbroken before man, but humble before God" (Schl.). "He was under sentence of death and knew that he was going to die. But no visible trace of disquiet disturbed the picture of perfect serenity in which natural and moral nobility were matched." (L) On pamphlet against Hitler 1932 see A. LEBER "Das Gewissen steht auf", p. 149.
6. Eberhard von BREITENBUCH, personal account.
7. DULLES, p. 171 ff. ROTHFELS, p. 160.
8. DULLES, p. 136 ff. RITTER, p. 393.
9. WHEELER-BENNETT, pp. 621, 619. Churchill's statements in the House of Commons of February 22 and May 24 and ATTLEE's (his deputy) of July 6, 1944.
10. KB 248, 364. GISEVIUS in his book gives an entirely different account: he says that after the Teheran agreements there was no longer any question of negotiations. The only thing that could have been attempted—as the future zones of occupation had not yet been fixed—would have been to let the Anglo-Americans get to the Königsberg-Prague-Vienna line before the Russians got there (cf. RITTER, p. 204, 552). The American historian Harold C. DEUTSCH, writing about the disappointing futility of all the reports Dulles sent to his Government (American Historical Review, January 1948, p. 338), says: "In which waste paper basket in Washington did these reports end up?"
11. Between April–June 1944, every day 200–250 Germans were put under arrest for "political reasons" (according to "confidential information from the Minister of Justice"). Even by October 1943 the number of people executed each month rose to ninety, according to the lists of three executioners which were found. The official so-called "Murder register" lists 3 400 executions in 1944. Between July 20 and August 8, 1944, alone 275 executions are mentioned—which had nothing to do with the 20th July. All these data are based on PECHEL, pp. 167 and 326. Walter HAMMER, who carried out a thorough research into the number of executions between 1933 and 1945, published his findings in WEISENBORN's "Der lautlose Aufstand" (pp. 258–59). According to this source the "Murder register", which does not include those sentenced by military tribunals, lists a total of 11 881 executions in the Reich between 1933 and 1944. Not counting executions ordered by military courts, the files of the Reich Ministry of Justice record 5 764 executions. In 1945, when apparently no more records were kept, about 800 executions are believed to have taken place. The total of those executed by order of military tribunals is estimated at about 20 000. HAMMER, in a report on the executions at Brandenburg penitentiary between 1940 and 1945 (more than 2 000), says that nine out of ten were put to death for their political or religious persuasion, and only one out of every ten could be said to have had a "criminal" record.
12. To illustrate the situation, HASSELL's diary entry for February 7, 1944 (p. 347) may be quoted (with the due reserve with which any diary needs to be treated): "In themselves the misgivings about Goerdeler's methods are justified. During the conference Stauffenberg was very adroit but was unable to dispel the objective doubts, at least some of which he shared in his own heart. But the crux of the matter is that Beck basically knows nothing about politics and has put himself entirely in Goerdeler's hands. The whole thing is of course a waste of paper, nothing is being done, in any case!" Cf. also pp.

228, 295 ibid. (Goerdeler: "a kind of reactionary"). According to Dr Gotthard
von FALKENHAUSEN's verbal account, Schulenburg stated on his visit to Paris
in the late summer of 1943 that the inner circle in Berlin did not consider
Goerdeler suitable for assuming the leadership in political matters: they were
urging that Stauffenberg should be given that role, too. Reinhard SCHWABE
("Tagesspiegel" March 9, 1947) says this remark was made among the closest
associates of Olbricht (von der Lancken): they were determined to "carry
out the revolt, if necessary, without Goerdeler". For Goerdeler's complaint
about Stauffenberg to Beck and the latter's reply ("this young hothead should
not be restrained too much"), see KB 248. Goerdeler says about Stauffenberg
in his memoirs written in prison in November 1944 (see RITTER, p. 540) that
he was a "high-minded General Staff officer, seriously wounded in Africa, who
later turned out to be a cranky, obstinate fellow who also wanted to play
politics". He continued: "I thought highly of him, but we did have several
rows. He was pursuing a dubious political course with Left-wing Socialists and
Communists and gave me a bad time with his arrogant stubbornness." To
treat these notes written in prison as an assessment of Goerdeler the politician
and revolutionary is bound to cause misgivings and seems unfair to Goerdeler.
What this man went through spiritually is certainly significant, but political
historians should have left it at that because it is irrelevant. Goerdeler is the
only member who played a central part in the revolt of 20th July who was
still able to write about it in detail *after* the event. It is therefore important to
keep in mind that, even allowing for his astonishing memory, what he said is
very much his own interpretation and cannot, therefore, be used as incontrovertible evidence about the 20th July.
13. Julius LEBER Ein Mann geht seinen Weg, p. 286.
14. Dahrendorf in LEBER op. cit. p. 286.
15. SCHWERIN-KROSIGK, p. 346.
16. Colonel-General Erwin Jaenecke, in command in the Crimea, had incurred
Hitler's disfavour because he had violently protested at HQ against the
senseless sacrifice of the Crimea Army. Through General von Rabenau,
Goerdeler had tried to contact him to "persuade him to take joint action with
the front line Commanders and the General Staff against Hitler". (RITTER, p.
390; cf. KB 490.)
17. SPEIDEL (p. 119) writes: "The reason for the hasty return journey is said to
have been that a V-missile hit Führer HQ shortly after our departure." No one
was hurt. The bunker "W II", which had been built for the planned invasion
of England in the autumn of 1940, was near Margival, not far from Soissons.
Hitler was accompanied by Generals Jodl, Schmundt, Buhle and Scherff;
Admiral Voss, Admiral von Puttkamer and Col. von Below—all officers who
were also present at the explosion on the 20th July. Report on what happened:
SPEIDEL, p. 112 ff.
18. Colonel-General Zeitzler, who had attracted Hitler's attention during the
planning and execution of the French campaign, had started his job with good
intentions—in one of his first orders he had urged General Staff officers—in
terms not usual in that milieu—to stop "seeing nothing but the holes in the
cheese". But later he changed his views considerably.
19. For example, Hitler's refusal to approve the General Staff's urgent recommendations to withdraw the Northern Army Group. His reasoning: this would
mean the loss of U-boat training facilities in the Baltic, and the shale of Narva,
and Germany's grip on Finland (HEUSINGER, p. 335). GUDERIAN reports him as
saying: "My Generals don't understand anything about the economics of
war" (p. 182). Similarly, as regards his refusal to evacuate the Crimea (cf.
Note 16). Reason: political considerations vis-à-vis Turkey.

20. The words "the last Goths" were soon used again by Freisler (IMT XXXIII 310, 316).
21. Statements by Hitler's Air Force Adjutant, von Below, in "Echo der Woche" of July 15, 1949.
22. SCHRAMM, p. 173.
23. SCHWERIN-KROSIGK writes about the General with whom he was in an American prison camp, p. 358 ff. Von Falkenhausen was arrested after the 20th July and narrowly escaped execution. Later he was gaoled and tried by the Allies, sentenced and finally discharged because of his failing health.
24. For example, by Freiherr von Neurath and the Mayor of Stuttgart, Strölin, who in turn was in touch with Goerdeler (see SPEIDEL p. 84 ff.; STRÖLIN, p. 32; KOCH p. 187 ff.; SCHRAMM, p. 32). YOUNG quotes a remark made by Rommel which Vice-Admiral Ruge, the Navy's liaison officer with Army Group B, remembered: "It is better to finish things quickly, even if it means our becoming a British Dominion. Better that than let the whole of Germany perish in this hopeless war. I know the man. He will neither abdicate nor commit suicide. He'll go on fighting without the slightest regard for the German people until there isn't a house left standing in Germany."
25. RITTER, p. 396, 551 and 412.
26. SCHLABRENDORFF, p. 129 (1st edition), p. 175 (2nd edition with minor alterations).
27. Urban THIERSCH, unpublished notes.
28. FAHRNER, Note 13, Chapter IX.
29. This was an unusual, broad gold ring which showed no ornamentation except the words *Finis Initium* in embossed letters. Stauffenberg wore it on the remaining third finger of his left hand. But in Court it was not the ring but a small golden cross on a simple chain which Stauffenberg wore round his neck that became important: it was used as proof of the theory that Stauffenberg was a "Catholic reactionary". In fact, the cross was an old heirloom of the Lerchenfeld family, which was the first present he ever had from his wife, a Baroness Lerchenfeld. Hermann Kaiser once saw the cross on Stauffenberg's chest when he was washing. He mentioned this in his diary and that was how the investigators learnt of it (KB 167). Neither ring nor cross were ever found after Stauffenberg's death.
30. Blumentritt reports a heated telephone conversation between the two Marshals towards the end of June. Keitel (exasperated): "What are we to do then?" Rundstedt (grimly): "What are you to do? You're to put an end to the war, you idiots!" Rundstedt had been with Rommel at the Obersalzberg and their talk with Hitler had been fruitless. On the day of his return he was replaced by Kluge (SCHRAMM 64).
31. HAFFNER (op. cit. p. 7) reports Stauffenberg's impatient exclamation: "I'll do it myself with my three fingers!" He adds: "He had the noble impatience of those who are destined to die young." Whether Stauffenberg did really say that and whether it was said on that day is impossible to determine.
32. HEUSINGER p. 329.
33. Major Oertzen, who had come from the Eastern front, exclaimed: "What is going on in the East is a disgrace. Isn't there anybody who'll bring the man who's responsible for it to book?" (Report by a woman secretary.) On military events: see HEUSINGER, p. 33 ff.; GUDERIAN, p. 303; GORLITZ, p. 637.
34. RITTER, pp. 404, 453: the following quotation ibid., p. 405.
35. SPEIDEL quotes the text of Rommel's teleprinter signal on p. 137 (also published in BZH p. 97). After setting out the strength of the forces—lost 97 000 men; replaced 6 000; lost 225 tanks; replaced 17—he writes: "In these circumstances we must expect the enemy to succeed in the near future—two to three

weeks—in breaking through the thin front, especially in the sector of the Seventh Army, and in pushing into the wide open spaces of France. The consequences will be incalculable. Everywhere the troops are fighting heroically but the unequal struggle is nearing its end. I must request you to draw the proper conclusions without delay. I feel it my duty as Commander-in-Chief of the Army Group to state this clearly. Field-Marshal Rommel." YOUNG (p. 12) quotes the rider which Kluge is said to have added to Rommel's letter to Hitler on July 23. SCHRAMM makes it appear probable that Kluge did not send on the letter until after July 26 (pp. 83, 303).

36. KB 21, 49; War Department files (see RITTER, p. 553). About this July 15, SCHRAMM (p. 117) writes—apparently based on what Hofacker had said—that Keitel "in his, at times, rather foolish zeal" stuffed some important papers into Stauffenberg's brief-case (which contained the explosives!).

37. RITTER, p. 407.

38. GISEVIUS, p. 498.

39. Army Group North Ukraine was being battered by two spearheads in the direction of Lvov-San. In the area of the Southern Army Group it was obvious that the enemy was trying to break into Wallachia and to push through to the Rumanian oilfields. On either front Germany's defence forces were utterly inadequate. One armoured division had even been switched to Army Group Centre. Instead, Operations Branch had asked for Army Group North to be brought back from Lake Peipus to reinforce the collapsing central front (cf. Note 19 of this chapter and HEUSINGER, p. 335).

40. RITTER, p. 550.

41. A. LEBER (p. 13) and Ursula von KARDORFF "Der 20 Juli in Berlin" in "Stuttgarter Rundschau" of July 1948.

42. On pp. 350 ff. HEUSINGER reports an incident during the situation conference on July 19: alarming news came in from Army Group North Ukraine which was having to withdraw the still intact XIII Army Corps that held the front between two major gaps created by the enemy. The Chief of Operations Branch called for an inquiry into what forces the Commander of the Reserve Army could still mobilize in the Government-General. Keitel suggested that Stauffenberg be summoned to report.

43. G.A. "Last meeting with Count Stauffenberg" in "Stuttgarter Zeitung" of July 20, 1950. On the following day, when the would-be assassin's name was revealed, the author of the article was most surprised to find that it was the same Stauffenberg whom he had met the day before. He concludes: "This act called for such unheard-of daring that it leaves one speechless even now; to think what this man, the leader of the German Resistance, must have gone through in the days before the 20th July!"

XIII. THE 20TH JULY

1. As regards the time sequence of events on the 20th July, the Kaltenbrunner Reports present an accurate picture on the whole. A comparison might be useful with the Opinion given by SERAPHIM before the Brunswick Court at the Remer trial in March 1952 (reproduced by KRAUS) and the tables in BZH. On topography and events at Führer HQ, see "Der Spiegel" IV/12 of March 23, 1950. This is a very mixed collection of reports, containing distortions and unfounded conclusions, and should, therefore, be treated with caution. But what is of importance is that, for the first time, the Opinions of explosives experts and results of interrogations by the Security Service and the Criminal Police are being evaluated: in this respect the collective report may claim to be treated as source material. For a somewhat more detailed description of the

"Wolf's Lair" see BZH. At the Nuremberg trial Jodl called the "Wolf's Lair" a "voluntary concentration camp".

2. "Der Spiegel", op. cit. says this about the conference hut: The "Lagebunker" ("Conference bunker") was a so-called "Speerbaracke"—a simple wooden hut about 45 m. long, surrounded by a 60 cm. thick layer of concrete and a 10 cm. thick layer of fibre-glass and pulped paper lining. The concrete ceiling was 40 cm. thick. In this massive outer casing openings had been left for the front door and for normal-sized windows. The concrete layer was intended to give protection against incendiary and small splinter bombs. So the hut was in fact anything but a mere wooden structure, an allegation which is often made in order to explain the failure of the attempt. Apart from the kennel for Blondy, the dog, there was not one wooden hut in the whole HQ—HEUSINGER (p. 352) gives this description of the "conference hut": "A brick-built annexe about 10 m. wide and 4 to 5 m. long attached to a concrete bunker. In one side wall, which formed the wall of the bunker, was the front door. Opposite on the right there were several windows, while there were none on the left side. Walls, ceilings, and floor were lightly constructed." The details of description about the windows agree with the "Spiegel".

3. For a list of people present and seating arrangement at the situation conference, see BZH, p. 115. This also names as 25th participant the stenographer Hagen who does not appear on the list.

4. This shows as untrue the frequent assertion that because of the summer heat the situation conference on 20th July was on this occasion held in the wooden hut, while its normal location was the bunker. The hut—"the conference hut" —was equipped for this particular purpose. Only in case of air raid danger would the situation conference be held in the "bunker-room".

5. HEUSINGER (p. 352 ff.) gives an eye-witness account in the form of a conversation said to have taken place. On German Wehrmacht communique of 20.7.44, see BZH, p. 109.

6. "Spiegel", op. cit.

7. Friedrich GEORGI in LEBER-MOLTKE "Für und Wider" (p. 114).

8. Accounts of this incident are based chiefly on these two sources: the description which Fromm, while under arrest, gave SCHLABRENDORFF (at that time Fromm hardly expected to be shot for cowardice); and on Hoepner's testimony before the People's Court (IMT XXXIII, 400 ff.). For plan of the rooms at the Bendlerstrasse—the scene of the events—see BZH p. 127.

9. Cf. pp. 403, 432, 433. HOEPNER told the People's Court that Stauffenberg had said: ". . . and all I saw was a large number of medical orderlies running across and cars being driven up." (IMT XXXIII, 402.)

10. On Signals, see also sub-section "Later Clarifications" in Chapter XIII of this book.

11. GISEVIUS II, p. 169.

12. SS-Report (KIESEL).

13. FRITZSCHE reports a strange mix-up: Stauffenberg had earlier given him the jacket of a General Staff officer and asked him to put it on Colonel-General Beck who was arriving attired in a civilian suit. Fritzsche, who did not know either of them, mistook Hoepner for Beck, offered him the jacket and even helped him into it. Fr. is convinced that in Court Hoepner deliberately lied so as not to betray him. (Personal account.)

14. SHIRER (p. 967) comments that Piffrader had "recently distinguished himself by superintending the exhuming and destroying of 221 000 bodies of Jews murdered by the Einsatzgruppen in the Baltic regions before the advancing Russians got to them".

15. There are several independent accounts of how Stauffenberg, alternately

using the two telephones, one on his own, the other on Fromm's desk, battled almost without respite—human, masterful, snapping orders, trying friendly persuasion, pleading in strong language, always speaking to the point, and in a frantic hurry. GISEVIUS II, p. 391, gives this sample: "Keitel is lying. . . . But don't believe Keitel. . . . Hitler is dead. . . . I can rely on you, can't I? Make sure your chief stands firm. . . . Hayessen, I rely on you. . . . Stieff has let us down. . . . Please don't you as well. . . . We must hold out . . . we must hold out."

16. "Olbricht had addressed his assembled officers. When he had finished he gave the salute with raised arm. Three or four of the 35–40 officers replied in the same manner, the others, including von der Heyde, who stood next to me, merely bowed. Some of them had already removed their Nazi insignia . . . in particular those officers who later fought us so bravely." (Letter by the then Lt. von KLEIST of 14.11.46. The final remark is also found in GERSTENMAIER.)

17. A report by Major of the Reserve H. KLAPPER, which I have seen, confirms that the two shock units of the Army provost patrol service, which with the support of troops from the local defence battalion and the Artificers' School, were detailed to occupy the Propaganda Ministry, were standing by at 19.00 at the corner of Unter den Linden and Wilhelmstrasse. They were led by Major Klapper and Captain Dangschat, both under the command of Colonel Jäger. Klapper then saw the defence battalion withdraw and learned that their leader had put himself under Remer's command. (Similar report in MÜLLER about the detachment of the Artificers' School which had been assigned the same task.) Originally it had been intended to order Remer's Guard Battalion to occupy the Propaganda Ministry and arrest Goebbels, but later it was decided to give the job to the patrol service. According to Klapper, no other Berlin unit was more suited for it in the circumstances, and the two assault groups had been formed from handpicked sergeants and NCOs. Jäger's move was foiled because the escort troops necessary for the attack withdrew in response to the broadcast announcement, and Major Remer intervened.

18. At 19.40 Kinzl telephoned Operations Branch at Führer HQ and passed on Beck's order to Count Kielmansegg, because Heusinger and Brandt were no longer available. "You know that this is the only sound solution. We have said this often enough. But we can't simply obey Beck without knowing what's going on. What are we to do?" As a result of Kielmansegg's negative attitude Beck's order was not carried out. (Report by KIELMANSEGG in "Die Zeit" of July 21, 1949.)

19. GISEVIUS II, 412. Individual aspects of this also elsewhere.

20. Witzleben drove to see the Quartermaster-General Wagner to report the failure of the attempt; then he returned home. He was arrested the following day, put on trial on August 7 and executed on the 8th. According to Witzleben, he had first met Stauffenberg through Olbricht in May 1944 and had hardly seen him since because he was taking the cure in Kissingen. He had for some time been suffering from stomach ulcers and gastric trouble (KB 366). He had been driven by Schwerin from Kissingen to Berlin on July 10 or 11.

21. These events were described in a note by W. MÜLLER about the trial involving Herber and von der Heyde at Neustadt camp on February 18, 1948.

22. According to what Bernardis, who had been present, stated in Court (IMT XXXIII 439).

23. Lt. Helmut CORDS, personal account.

24. This is how Dr Hans FRITZSCHE describes the events from memory: He had just entered General Olbricht's ante-room, when a Lt.-Col. with cap, eyeglass and tommy gun roared: "This is against the Führer. We stick to our Führer.

Where is Colonel-General Fromm? I want to speak to him, at once."
Olbricht came quietly out of his room to meet the Lt.-Col.: "You are armed;
I am not. We'll have to have a talk. You'll see Fromm. But first let's go and
see Colonel-General Hoepner." With these words, they went out into the corridor and walked along it. Fritzsche says that when he went out he saw his
friend Oppen and a group of about ten men standing there. They grabbed him,
one of them wrested his revolver from him and shouted: "What are you doing
here?" He says he answered: "I don't really know." Then a shot rang out.
As he was moving forward with the whole group, he saw—a few doors farther
on—Olbricht and the Lt.-Col. whom he took to be von der Heyde, and above
the landing he noticed Stauffenberg and Haeften. At that moment about five
shots were fired and Fritzsche says Olbricht cried out: "For God's sake, you
may have shot our friend, Stauffenberg!" There were cries from the secretaries
who hid under the tables. The armed group moved to the fore. A very old
Austrian Colonel of the Wehrmacht Propaganda Department, who had
obviously been called in and had nothing to do with the revolt, somewhat
helplessly came up to Fritzsche and asked him for information. Fritzsche says
he took the Colonel downstairs, and telling the sentry at the main entrance
that he was the Colonel's Adjutant, both were allowed to leave unhindered.

Fritzsche recalls that during a conversation later that evening Schulenburg
said: "We must empty the cup. We must sacrifice ourselves. Posterity will
understand us." (Personal account.) Dr GERSTENMAIER, who witnessed events
at the Bendlerstrasse from about 18.00 onwards, points out that everyone was
anxiously waiting for the radio to stop and the tanks to roll up. Three of them
were to drive with Gisevius to the Deutschlandsender. Between 20.00 and 21.00
orderlies in white tunics set the table at Olbricht's request, and all of those
waiting there, including the Judge-Advocate of the Army, Sack, who was "in
the know", sat down to eat. Only Olbricht and Stauffenberg, who were busy
all the time, did not join them. The only person who showed an appetite and
ate his meal calmly was Schulenburg.

Other eye-witnesses (apart from Fritzsche) who gave accounts of the sudden
entry of the counter-group: Friedrich GEORGI and the two secretaries, Anni
LERCHE and Delia ZIEGLER (for the latter's report see BZH p. 152).

25. According to the account in WHEELER-BENNETT (p. 661)—who does not
quote any source for it—Stauffenberg, wounded by a bullet in the back, was
half lying in a chair and found it difficult to keep upright. With him (says
Wheeler-Bennett) were his brother Berthold and Werner Haeften. When
they were taken down Haeften supported Stauffenberg. This account cannot
be correct as regards Berthold Stauffenberg, because he was being held in
Olbricht's rooms together with the group detained there, and was only
brought to the front room much later after the drumhead court martial verdict
had been carried out.

26. To my knowledge, no evidence was provided as to the composition of the
drumhead court martial. I assume that Lt.-Col. Gehrke was a member.

27. Personal account by a driver who watched the scene from a window in the
house opposite: he reports that Gerstenmaier was alone for a while, being
guarded in an NCO's room. This room, separated from the others by a corridor, had two windows facing out on the courtyard of Nos. 11–13 Bendlerstrasse, more or less above the spot where the executions took place. Two of the
people in the room apparently watched the scene that night from behind the
blackout curtain. G. thinks he heard Stauffenberg's voice, then a violent burst
of fire, followed later by separate revolver shots which he thought were the
coups de grace; finally he heard a triple "Sieg Heil".

28. The official who was assigned to conduct the investigation against Berthold

Stauffenberg later stated—and his evidence seems fairly reliable—that Berthold begged to be told whether his brother was dead.

29. All except Gerstenmaier, Ramin and Georgi were later executed. SKORZENY is convinced that Fromm had wanted the second group (Yorck, Schulenburg and others) also to be summarily executed during the same night, and that the shooting was suspended as a result of the intervention of Kaltenbrunner and Skorzeny who had brought an express countermanding order from Himmler.

30. From Himmler's speech mentioned in Note 4 Chapter XIV, it can be deduced that at his midnight visit Fromm failed to convince Goebbels that he was blameless. Himmler's speech contained this passage: He is so cunning and crafty that you cannot prove that he did not take part in this stupid revolution . . . the first impression of Herr Fromm, which both I and Dr Goebbels had when we met that night, as we had on other occasions in the history of our Party, was most peculiar. . . . I cannot help thinking that some uncomfortable conversation partners, not to say witnesses, were being quickly done away with, p. 381 ff. Meanwhile, Himmler and Kaltenbrunner were conducting interrogations at Goebbels' Ministry throughout the night. Fromm, Hase, Helldorf and Hoepner are reported to have been interrogated.

31. In his speech about two weeks after the 20th July (cf. Note 30) Himmler said of the men who had been shot on the night of the 20th: "They were disinterred the following day for proper identification. I then gave orders to burn the bodies and have the ashes scattered in the fields. We don't want the slightest reminder by a grave or any burial site of these people or of those who are now being executed." There is little doubt that Himmler's orders concerning the disposal of the five bodies were carried out. No other report about what actually happened is available. As to the bodies of those who were executed later, see Note 17, Chapter XIV.

32. In Vienna, the following were put under arrest: the senior SS and police leader; the Deputy-Gauleiter; the Inspector of the Security Police and the SD; the Gau Propaganda Chief and the President of the Police. (Gauleiter von Schirach was away from Vienna). Freiherr von Esebeck, General of Armoured Troops, and his Chief of Staff Colonel Kodré had begun to carry out their orders after confirming them with Stauffenberg. The liaison officer, Colonel Count Marogna-Redwitz, was at his post. On the following day, Gauleiter Schirach, in the presence of the Commanding Officer, stripped Lieutenant-General Sinzinger, who was in charge of the operation, of his Golden Party Badge and threw it at his feet. (SS-Report KIESEL IMT XXX-III, 413 ff.; KB 36, 104.) In Nuremberg, a Divisional Commander, Major-General Meyerhöfer, to whom the Commanding General had shown the orders from Berlin and who had been sworn to secrecy, informed the Gauleiter thus enabling him to mobilize his forces (unpublished report by K. WELLER). In Frankfurt on Main and Stettin, the City Commandants Major-General Rieger and Major-General Siegfried von Stülpnagel offered their co-operation; in Munich, things went off "without a hitch"; in Hamburg, the Chief of Staff (in the absence of the Commanding General) himself went to the Gauleiter and told him that he "had been instructed to arrest him, but that it all seemed to be such nonsense; whereupon Kaufmann suggested they first drink a bottle of wine and telephone Führer HQ to find out what was really going on" (according to Görlitz, p. 644). In Kassel, the Chief of Staff argued in favour of carrying out the Berlin orders (KB 36). In Prague, the orders had been received after 19.00 and General of Armoured Troops Schaal after talking to Stauffenberg had undertaken to see they were carried out. But after a long distance conversation with Hoepner he countermanded the arrests at 21.45. He had been unable to get hold of SS-Obergruppenführer Frank,

State Secretary in the Protectorate Government—according to KB 106. The situation is summed up in this remark; "The rapid collapse of the enterprise in the Reich was largely due to the undecided and irresolute leadership of Colonel-General Hoepner. As emerges from his interrogation, Hoepner was constantly being urged by Stauffenberg and others to 'put pressure on the Military District Commanders'."

The SS-Report (KIESEL) concludes that the arrests made in the Reich did not provide the basis for an indictment by the Chief Prosecutor. "The frequently mentioned teleprinter message had a rather comic effect in various places in as much as the District Commanders went to ask advice of precisely those men they were to have arrested first, i.e. the Gauleiters. There were no intuitive revolutionaries in the German Wehrmacht."

33. For events in Paris see SCHRAMM, further SPEIDEL, BLUMENTRITT, FALKEN-HAUSEN, BARGATZKY, TEUCHERT, Elmar MICHEL. For short official report by OBERG see KB 41.

34. One signals centre of the SS, unnoticed by Oberhäuser's men, had continued to keep in communication with the Reich. It is believed that even the Navy's and the Air Force's own networks were not completely cut off.

35. According to one report, the fortified buildings in Paris which had been intended for defence against outside attack were so devised, in agreement with Stülpnagel, that they would also be serviceable for an attack on the SS, with Avenue Foch forming the focal point. ("Wochenpost" 1948, No. 29. Report signed by Ernst HOFEN.)

36. SPEIDEL op. cit. TEUCHERT p. 20; MICHEL p. 9; FALKENHAUSEN p. 21; somewhat differently, SCHRAMM pp. 147–55.

37. FALKENHAUSEN p. 21.

38. SCHRAMM p. 208. SPEIDEL reports that in the morning of July 21, on instructions from Keitel and Goebbels, the NS-Operations officer of C.-in-C., West and representatives of the Propaganda Department in France, called on Kluge to submit a telegram of loyalty to Hitler for his signature; they also asked him to broadcast on the German network. The report has it that the telegram, somewhat toned down, was sent, but the broadcast speech was not made. When on the same day, July 21, Guderian, the newly-appointed Chief of the General Staff, reported to Hitler, the discussion also turned to Kluge, and Hitler said: ". . . in any case he knew of the attempt." As Jodl, Keitel, and Burgdorf (deputizing for the injured Schmundt) declared that Kluge could not be spared at the moment, Hitler took no action—and so he received his telegram of loyalty (GUDERIAN: Erinnerungen eines Soldaten).

39. SCHRAMM's account has also been confirmed to me by others: according to Schramm, Oberg tried to limit the trouble and to find a way which would not cause too much harm to Stülpnagel and his staff. At the time Stülpnagel's office looked upon Oberg as a crude blusterer rather than a dangerous SS-opponent (as for instance Knochen) and Stülpnagel is once said to have remarked: "If Oberg could do as he liked—I think he would be on our side."

40. SCHRAMM p. 225 "Fate has decided against us", ibid. p. 224, similarly Hofacker in conversation with Gesandter von Bargen ibid. p. 309.

41. Admiral Kurt Assmann in SHIRER, p. 1119. H. H. HAGEN in "Zwischen Eid und Befehl" gives a detailed account of what happened, but in many respects this differs from other reports and cannot be judged because no sources are cited. It says that in Keitel's hut, Stauffenberg released only the first safety catch of the mechanism and that he put the brief-case on the table in the conference room. Haeften appeared in the doorway to call him out to take the pre-arranged telephone call to Berlin; he apologized with a gesture to Hitler, and on getting up leaned on the brief-case, thereby setting off the

three-minute fuse. Stauffenberg had hardly left the room when a locality was mentioned which was obscured on the map by the brief-case. Schmundt (so it was said in 1958, but in 1950 it was Korten) picked it up and shifted it to the far side of the oaken support, next to Berger. Voss moved it again, "quite close to the oaken socle". When the explosion occurred Stauffenberg was still near enough to see Puttkamer being hurled through the window and landing in the grass outside the bunker.

Since Hagen appears to be amazingly well informed on some points but then makes quite a few deductions from demonstrably false data his account remains doubtful until confirmation becomes available.

42. Jodl said of Keitel at Nuremberg: "After the attempt on the 20th it was he alone who put his arms round Hitler and, with perfect calm, carefully led him into the open like a child. This is the first and quite unforgettable thing I saw when I regained consciousness." IMT XL, 472.

43. For characterization of Bormann see GUDERIAN p. 408: "A stocky, disgruntled, cheerless, taciturn, ill-mannered fellow."

44. An important moment in history: Göring could not know any facts as yet but promptly created the "stab-in-the-back lie", which Hitler used in his speech at 21.00.

45. Report by H.W. (presumably Lieutenant-Colonel Waizenegger) in "Stuttgarter Zeitung" of July 20, 1949. For the Adjutant's subsequent report see BELOW, "Echo der Woche" of July 15, 1949.

46. Regarding Mussolini's visit, see SCHMIDT (p. 580), who was there as interpreter; Eugen DOLLMANN (Roma Nazista, Milan, 1951, p. 393), who took part as SS liaison officer, and Rudolf RAHN (p. 386), who accompanied Mussolini as former German Ambassador in Rome.

47. "On that afternoon Hitler did not hold forth and Mussolini did not give any warnings. There was an air of farewell about the quiet and inconsequential conversation of the two; indeed this was the last time Mussolini and Hitler met." (SCHMIDT p. 582). (Schmidt's references to "holding forth" and "warning" are to accounts of earlier meetings between the two men.)

48. Teleprinter text KB 75. Time: 20.20. After announcing the appointment it said: "Orders to be accepted only from Reichsführer SS and myself (Keitel). Any orders from Fromm, Witzleben or Hoepner are invalid."

49. See "Frankfurter Illustrierte", Year 1949, No. 14.

50. Report in "Spiegel" (see Note 1) which also gives a schematic drawing of the explosive charge. See also report by the "Sonderkommission 20. Juli 1944" of July 26 in KB 83. In the afternoon of July 20 Claus Stauffenberg is reported to have said to his brother: "The only thing the English supplied did not work" (KB 55). The description of the bomb refutes Hagen's version (see Note 41).

51. Report by ARNTZ (unpublished). Report by SANDER in LEBER-MOLTKE's "Für und Wider" p. 205. Evidence by driver: "Spiegel" Report (op. cit.). Report by MÜLLER on what happened on 20th July, 1944, in "Das freie Wort" Duesseldorf July 19, 1952. Information by RISLER: personal observations made to author.

52. HOEPNER before People's Court (IMT XXXIII p 399 ff.); GEORGI, see Note 7 of this chapter.

53. KIELMANSEGG in "Die Zeit", July 21, 1949. Critics have often argued that Fellgiebel should have blown up the signals centre, etc. (He "failed miserably" said WHEELER-BENNETT, Nemesis p. 663.) But this hindsight wisdom on the events of the 20th July is not objective. To separate "truth and distortion" (SCHEIDT, "Neue Politik" Zurich, May 27, 1948) one must start from these facts: 1. The huge bunker in Führer HQ, which (according to SCHEIDT)

"would have been adequate to serve as a communications centre for a medium sized town", could only have been blown up "by several trunk-loads of explosives"—and that could not have been done if Hitler was still alive. 2. The signals installations were spread among several bunkers, distant one from another, partly built underground and all guarded by the SS. 3. There was no question of destroying the whole communications system of the Wehrmacht: if the coup d'état had succeeded the war command would have urgently needed an intact signals service. 4. The only objective could be— and this was constantly stressed (according to KB) by Fellgiebel and accepted by Stauffenberg—to cut off Führer HQ from outside telephone communications for a few hours after the attempt. This is what in fact happened for a limited period, although the attempt had failed.

54. A message dated July 22, 1944 (KB 63 ff.) by the Chief of the Wehrmacht Signals Administration contains a record of the incoming and outgoing teleprinter messages of 20th July:

	received	put out
1. Internal unrest (Witzleben)	16.40	17.35–21.03
2. Immediate measures by Military District Commanders (Fromm)	17.50	18.30–21.22
3. Valkyrie, second stage	18.00	20.45–23.00
4. As 1, but beginning "The Führer Adolf Hitler is dead"	18.30	only to Navy and Air Force
5. Hoepner (Witzleben) (Reserve Army Commander)	18.45	20.30–21.15
6. Radio communiqué refutation	19.15	19.45–21.12
7. Summoning of political "representatives"	19.15	19.45–21.12
8. Martial Law Decree 1	20.00	only to Mil. Dist. I and X
9–14. Martial Law Decrees 2–5 measures by Party, concerning travel, telecommunications	20.10–21.00	not put out
15. Telepr. Keitel: Himmler C.-in-C. Reserve Army	20.35	21.25–22.01
16. Fromm: Putsch crushed	0.10	0.15–1.15
17. Himmler replaces Fromm	4.08	4.15–5.15

55. Otto Ernst Remer, born 1912 in Neubrandenburg; classical Gymnasium; joins as cadet in Kolberg April 1, 1933. At the front since beginning of war, always commanding troops; nine times wounded; since May 15, 1944, commanding Guard Regiment Grossdeutschland (data according to HAGEN; see below).

Three official reports on Remer's intervention on 20th July are available: his own report of July 22, 1944 (see BZH p. 138); the report written by Lieutenant Schlee on July 23 (ibid. p. 145) and an account compiled by Captain of the Reserve Dr W. Hagen (October 16, 1944) which is an elaboration of a "short action report", made on July 21 but not now available. This was evidently provided at Bormann's insistence after doubts as to Remer's attitude had arisen (ibid. p. 148, KB 12). Later accounts by the participants: E. O. REMER Der 20. Juli (publishers: Deutsche Opposition, Hamburg, 1951); H. W. HAGEN Zwischen Eid und Befehl, Eyewitness account of events of the 20th July, 1944 (Türmer Publishers, Munich, 1958). There are also copious court files. In a private action which Remer brought against Senator Hermann Wolters in Bremen for slander, the Bremen Court on June 19 and 20, 1953, tried to obtain a true picture of Remer's conduct on 20th July. The Court had before it: Remer's evidence of October 28, 1949, before the Prosecutor in Oldenburg; the results of the Brunswick Trial of March 1952 (on which cf. Dr H. KRAUS who published the Opinions and sentence in that trial; Hamburg, Girardet 1953).

Remer has been repeatedly charged with having had pre-knowledge of the planned coup of the 20th July and having "defected"; this has been unequivocally repudiated by witnesses. Remer did not act primarily as Hitler's follower, but because he was a front-line officer who saw a dangerous situation in the making and felt called upon to deal with it. It is certain that at first he distrusted Goebbels and the voice which said it was "Hitler" speaking to him; it is equally sure that faced with the conflicting orders to go and see Hase and report to Goebbels, he hesitated, not knowing what to do, and quite aware of the danger he was in ("my head is at stake"). He had no particular ties with the Party, but he belonged to the generation of officers who had grown up in the days of Hitler and owed their rise to him. In November 1943 he received the Oak Leaves to the Knight's Cross from Hitler personally. In his position many officers would have taken the same decision if having to choose "between oath and orders".

Hagen was a writer on cultural history, trained by the National Socialists. Having been wounded, he was not even fit for garrison duty. He entered the scene of action of the 20th July accidentally, but he may be considered as Stauffenberg's most active opponent on that occasion. It was his impulse that started Remer's action, no matter how much he has tried to exalt "this great soldier Remer" in his October report. For his and Remer's action he claimed no more than that it put an end to a revolt which had already failed. Later he hit back against his critics by accusing those who had broken their oath on the 20th July; and he declared contemptuously, trying hard to substantiate his arguments with proofs from German history, that the ultimate reason for failure had been Stauffenberg's lack of strength to make a self-sacrifice. These are some of the high-sounding, feeble and spurious words he used about Stauffenberg's activity: "Death always hovers above the oath. And always death is the punishment for a breach of the oath. . . . The would-be assassin did not sacrifice himself—and the one moment when he left the bomb on its own sufficed to save his life. As if Providence could be expected to favour such inconsequential conduct! The self-sacrifice was missing!" (p. 82).

56. The National Socialist Motor Corps Gruppenführer Albrecht in Frankfurter Illustrierte 1949, No. 14 (July). On telephone conversations: verbal report by E. H. von KLEIST, an ADC of Stauffenberg's; on Olbricht's and Stauffenberg's orders Kleist had to make sure that the Guard Battalion did its job as ordered. The officer referred to in this context may have been Lieutenant-Colonel Wolters, who is mentioned as liaison officer by Remer.

57. General Reinecke, Chief of the General Wehrmacht Office, attended many of the trials of the 20th July conspirators. Seated on the right of the President of the People's Court, Freisler, he was also present at the trials of August 7 and 8. According to Reinecke, General von Hase, admitted "very courageously" that he had taken part in the conspiracy; and as one of his fellow-officers said, "he nobly and chivalrously described himself as its author and tried to save his comrades from the gallows". And he said nothing in Court to incriminate Remer. Bonhoeffer (p. 229) reports that on June 30, 1944, Hase visited him in prison, stayed there for five hours and brought him food and drink: an incident which testifies to this General's independent conduct.

HAGEN gives information about Remer's attempts to get the advancing troops to turn back and, above all, to prevent a clash between them and the

Guard Battalion. What made Remer the subject of criticism was not his behaviour on the 20th July but his later conduct. (Cf. Opinion given in Brunswick Trial by Lieutenant-General (ret.) FRIEBE, KRAUS, op. cit. p. 103.)

58. Gläsemer, who had previously either served with the troops or been ill in hospital, had only taken over the Armoured Troops School on July 15. Olbricht had used the "Valkyrie" alert that day to visit him in Krampnitz and to make sure, as far as possible, that he would support the revolt. But he found that the Colonel—white-haired, though not yet fifty, of medium height and rather thin—had such fixed views that it was impossible to talk to him about an uprising. He could only hope that some of Gläsemer's officers, who had been initiated in the plan, would carry him along. At an official function for officers at Potsdam, Stauffenberg arranged to be seated next to the Comdant of the Krampnitz School. He made a great personal impression on Gläsemer—who later spoke of him with the highest esteem—but evidently failed to achieve anything else.

59. According to MÜLLER op. cit. and GLÄSEMER.

60. MÜLLER, "Gegen eine neue Dolchstosslüge," 2nd ed., p. 87 ff.; KRAUS p. 149. Very different HAGEN, "Zwischen Eid und Befehl" who carries on a sharp polemic against Müller. The impression one gets is that Hagen bases himself on the individual stories of people involved in the conspiracy. But he takes great liberties with the chronology of events—to the point of distortion—and with the description of some of the accomplices' actions that evening so that even where he might deserve better he remains untrustworthy. According to Hagen, Kortzfleisch had himself set free by a guard and then arrested Olbricht and his fellow-officers "who had taken him into custody only a quarter of an hour(!) before". There is a description of how he threw a typewriter and telephone through the closed window of the room—next to Olbricht's—where he was locked up thereby alerting the guard in the courtyard. He then ordered the men to come up: a General was under arrest there (he said) and he was giving orders to release him. . . . "Schlee, who has served his way up from locksmith to one of the best company commanders of the elite Guard Regiment" arrived, freed the General and together with Kortzfleisch and General Specht took action against Olbricht (p. 42 ff.). The fact is that it was Olbricht's own group of officers which overwhelmed him. HAGEN also says that the arms brought from Spandau at Olbricht's instruction fell into the hands of Heber's counter-group on arrival.

61. KIELMANNSEGG, op. cit. (see Note 53). Cf. GUDERIAN, p. 308 ff.

62. For detailed account of events in Döberitz see MÜLLER, op. cit.

63. See MÜLLER for Court Note (Note 21 of this chapter). WHEELER-BENNETT (p. 654, Note 2) reports, without giving a source, that Major Jacob, an instructor at the Infantry School in Döberitz, succeeded in launching a surprise attack on the Funkhaus and expelled the SS Guard before they knew what was happening. (Translator's Note: Wheeler-Bennett in the English original does attribute the information, i.e. to the testimony of the officer charged with seizing the Rundfunk.) He occupied the building for some hours, and only evacuated it because he had no further orders from Olbricht, to whom he had reported his success, and because he received a personal telephone call from Goebbels, giving him the official and accurate account of the position. An explanation for this is given by HAGEN (op. cit. p. 39): the officer's report had been intercepted by a routine operation of the Propaganda Ministry and answered from there. According to the same source the Reserve Brigade "Grossdeutschland" (Kottbus) which had been told to occupy the Deutschlandsender was halted on the Autobahn outside Königswusterhausen on Remer's orders (ibid. p. 40).

XIV. Vengeance and Trials

1. Shakespeare, Henry IV, Part I Final lines:
   Rebellion in this land shall lose his sway,
   Meeting the check of such another day:
   And since this business so fair is done,
   Let us not leave till all our own be won.
2. The first regulations issued by Party and state authorities (see BZH p. 182 ff. Bormann, Jodl, Ribbentrop).
3. Regarding this and later matter see SS Report (KIESEL).
4. The speech was published in "Vierteljahrsh. f. Zeitgesch". Vol. 4, 1953, pp. 363–94. The editor, Theodor Eschenburg, comments: "To those in control a rebel is always evil; that is understandable. So is the fact that even two weeks after such an event feelings can still run high and lead to excesses. But even those who go out of their way to try to understand the situation and the resulting moral and emotional reaction find it impossible to grasp the narrow-minded primitiveness, the unbridled cynicism, the shameless degradation and absolute emptiness which cannot simply be explained as a consequence of the shocks of the 20th July."
5. See Note 2.
6. I have found no evidence for RITTER's statement (given as a certain fact on p. 412, as a rumour in Note on p. 558) that a list of Ministers was found in "Olbricht'e safe". According to KB 188, the wide political sweep of the Resistance movement was not realized until August 10 when the representatives of the trade unions and the former SPD were interrogated. The information about the planned allocation of posts, then appearing for the first time, was evidently culled from the interrogation and not from a list of Ministers said to have been found (KB 188, 210).
7. Several people were executed after the 20th for having given shelter to one or other of the accused, i.e. the architect Dr-Ing Erich Gloeden and his wife and mother-in-law, because they had hidden General Lindemann in their house for six weeks; Dr Fritz Elsas from Stuttgart, and until 1933 Mayor of Berlin, because he sheltered Goerdeler for a few days. By some strange coincidence two people escaped the same fate: Freiherr von Ploambini, who had also given shelter to Goerdeler, and Baroness von Palombini, who met Goerdeler, after her husband's arrest, on another two occasions.
8. The account which, according to KB 217, Goerdeler gave of his escape route after 20th July at his interrogation, mentions that he frequently spent the night in the open. By giving this information he obviously wanted to protect the people who had offered him shelter. In spite of this the Gestapo tracked them all down. For the individual stops Goerdeler made on his flight see RITTER p. 411 ff.—based on research by Reinhard Goerdeler. Regarding Helene Schwärzel (of Bad Rauschen) ibid. p. 415.
9. SCHLABRENDORFF p. 215, 2nd edition.
10. HASSELL p. 367.
10a. W. SCHEIDT "Gespraeche mit Hitler" in "Echo der Woche", Munich, October 1949. In 1944–45 Scheidt collaborated with General Scherff, the HQ historian.
    S. JESSEN wrote to me on May 21, 1954: "By a strange coincidence two SS guards outside my cell door in the Lehrterstrasse talked about Stauffenberg's execution (10.8.) and praised his manly bearing. That is how I learnt of his death. I can imagine what moral courage was called for and displayed in those days and months which were dominated by that paranoiac Freisler." Three years later, after many twists of fate, Berthold Stauffenberg's message, written on August 10 just before his death, reached his children: "My beloved children, My dear Alfred, My dear Elisabeth, Always think with pride of

your father, who wanted the best for his country and people. Be pure and strong, great and true, and remember always that you must live nobly, faithful to your birth. From now on life for your mother will be very, very hard, and I beg you to do all you can to make her life as beautiful as possible and to give her a little joy and happiness. You, too, should try to be cheerful and enjoy yourselves, despite the heavy burden. That will give you strength and make your mother happy. How I long to see you once more and hold you in my arms. I kiss you, my Alfred, and you, my Elisabeth most affectionately. Your father."

11. SCHEIDT quotes these remarks of Hitler's at one of the situation conferences very shortly after the 20th July (apparently Scheidt was present, deputizing for the injured Scherff) : "This time I'll make short shrift. These criminals are not going to be put before a court martial where their accomplices sit and where the trial is dragged on. They will be expelled from the Wehrmacht and put before the People's Court. They are not to get an honest bullet, they are to hang like common traitors! A Court of Honour is to expel them from the Wehrmacht; then they can be tried as civilians and they won't sully the reputation of the Wehrmacht. They've got to be tried at top speed; they must not be given a chance to say too much. And sentence must be carried out within two hours of its being passed! They must hang at once, without mercy. And most important, they must not be given time for long speeches. But Freisler will see to that. He is our Vyshinsky" (op. cit. October 7, 1949).

12. DIELS (p. 295) has this to say about Freisler: "This genuine revolutionary admitted to having started his career as a convinced Communist. While a prisoner in Russia, having mastered the Russian language, he got as far as becoming a Bolshevik commissar. But as early as 1924 he made a name for himself in his home town of Kassel as defence counsel in criminal cases against National Socialists. His knife-edged legal acumen found brilliant expression in theatrical eloquence. . . . In his mouth the law became a lever of power, fanaticism and revolutionary crimes. He could make one forget that extreme terror could follow from his philosophical dissertations on law and jurisdiction which he surrounded with the decorum of scholarly learning. It might have been a pleasure to tussle with such an agile mind. . . . Freisler was more brilliant, versatile and devilish than any of the prosecutors in the history of revolution. . . . I have learnt to hate Goebbels and Freisler like evil itself."
The People's Court had been established by an act of April 24, 1934, for the purpose of "trying cases of high treason", and there was no appeal against its verdicts. Regarding the "Gesinnungs-Strafecht" under which the "criminal sentiments" of the accused were punishable: once the law had decreed that the measures of June 30, 1934, had been taken in "legitimate self-defence of the state", Hitler made a speech to justify them before the Reichstag on July 13, 1934. He said: "A traitor to his country is to be punished, not according to the seriousness and extent of his actions but according to the views they manifest."
Gerd RUHLE, "Das Dritte Reich in Dokumenten", Volume 2; p. 245, Extract in LEBER-MOLTKE 153.

13. Peter VOSSEN, shorthand writer at the People's Court trials; see depositions of August 7 and 8, 1944 IMT XXXIII, 2999. His name, however, is not there.

14. See BZH p. 200.

15. "Der Dämon der Justiz", "Schwäbische Zeitung" of May 7, 1946.

16. On von Haeften, see Note 15; somewhat different account by MÜLLER p. 92 (2nd edition); on Moltke "Neue Auslese" p. 11 ff.; on Leber (cf. Chapter V); on Witzleben see MÜLLER op. cit. (not contained in depositions of court hearings); on: Wirmer see MÜLLER op. cit. I have been told by Ernst, who was

present, that Wirmer's secretary, having learned of his execution, appeared at the office in mourning; soon afterwards the Gestapo came for her. Nobody at her office knew anything about her fate. On "Scoundrel Schulenburg" see Ernst JÜNGER, "Strahlungen", p. 569.

17. Details in MÜLLER (op. cit.) and in notes by cameramen Stoll and Sasse "Das Schauspiel des Entsetzlichen" (BZH p. 209). Walter HAMMER in an article "Dienst an der Wahrheit" in the newspaper, "Das freie Wort", September 6, 1952, points out that, contrary to all other rumours, the hangings were carried out with the usual double-looped hemp noose. The bodies of the men executed in and near Berlin were handed over to the Anatomical Institute of Berlin University, with strict instructions that complete secrecy must be maintained vis-à-vis the families of the victims. Geheimrat Professor Dr H. Stieve, Head of the Institute, who knew that some of his own close friends were among the dead, explicitly put on record before his own death in 1952 that he had given orders for the bodies of all those executed for political reasons to be cremated untouched. He apparently arranged for most of the urns to be interred at the Marzahne cemetery. Later even this last service was undone when the place was bombed. Only very few of the dependants know where their relatives are buried. But Hammer also reports that on Hitler's orders the urns containing the ashes of the men executed for the 20th July revolt had to be taken to the Minister of Justice, Thierack "who saw to it that they disappeared and who is alleged to have clandestinely interred them in some forest glade or other whenever he drove to his estate in the Teltow district for the week-end".

18. On Kluge see SCHRAMM. His letter to Hitler also there in extract; it was first published in full by MILTON SHULMAN "Defeat in the West". Kluge's nephew, Lieutenant-Colonel i.G. Karl Ernst Rathgens, referred to the Marshal in court. For Rommel's fate see SPEIDEL, KOCH and YOUNG; for appraisal see YORCK, Note 18, p. 543. A portrait of the dead Rommel in "Parlament" special issue on July 20, 1952.

19. It is not known whether Kluge's letter ever arrived. Hitler's remarks of August 31, which are preserved in shorthand notes (see SCHRAMM p. 380) imply that Kluge would "in any case have been arrested", i.e. brought before the People's Court. Parted from the Führer whom he implored to end the war, separated from the men of the revolt to whom his intelligence told him he belonged; true to his oath but untrustworthy, a conscientious Prussian yet owing his material well-being to the Führer, seeking glory as a military leader and self-justification to his last hour—this is how Kluge departed . . . an important, memorable figure in the history of the uprising.

20. As Commander of the 28th Rifle Division, Ziehlberg had received a tele-printer signal to the effect that one of his Staff Officers, Major i.G. Kuhn, was to report to the central Army court in Berlin. The troops were just about to move into a new area. The General agreed to postpone his departure for Berlin until after the military operation. Meanwhile, however, Kuhn deserted to the Russians. When Hitler heard about it he ordered the General to be shot. Ziehlberg had been Halder's Chief of Personnel for General Staff Officers. (Cf. MÜLLER op. cit.)—In the early hours of the morning of July 23 telephone instructions by Himmler were received in Germersheim saying that Count Sponeck was to be shot at 7 a.m. In his speech ten days later, Himmler gave the date for this as the morning after the 20th July so as to give it more prominence as being a "first introduction" to the ruthless purge that was to follow. (Vierteljahresh. f. Zeitgesch. See Note 4 of this chapter.)

21. According to a British Admiralty press report, of July 20, 1947, based on captured German naval documents, 4 980 people were executed in the months following the attempt. According to Walter Hammer's research (see WEISEN-

BORN p. 258) this figure is possibly the total of the executions during that period and may be related to the figure of 5 764 executions which the Reich Ministry of Justice recorded for the whole of 1944. Hammer says that the immediate victims of the 20th July whose names are known numbered 180 to 200. See also his book "Hohes Haus in Henkershand" (2nd edition 1956, p. 118). In the SS Report (KIESEL), which Hammer rejects, approximately 700 officers are said to have been executed. ROTHFELS (p. 178) commenting on this difference between 200 and 700 says that the lists of the dead where between 180 and 200 names are given "presumably contain only the most prominent ones".

22. Commissar's statement (unpublished notes of Dr Gerhard WOLF quoted in RITTER p. 423). Declaration by Goebbels, reported by Otto JOHN in Hans-Jürgen BORENGRAVE's in "I remember Hitler". Borengrave says he was Signals officer in Führer HQ on the 20th July. Notification from Reich Ministry of Justice: verbal report by Frau Maass to publisher Gotthold Müller.

CONCLUSION

1. The tragedy of the German territories in the East is probably unique in the modern history of war, in that so little was done by the responsible leaders until the last hour, to meet the foreseeable invasion by the enemy. The population was left in the dark about the enemy's advance. In many places evacuation was forbidden on pain of death until the last moment; then the order to evacuate was given and thousands of lives were lost quite apart from the effect these circumstances had on the conduct of the war as a whole. The story of this immeasurable suffering and disaster, which had been threatening for a long time but to which the leadership shut its eyes, is more important for an understanding of the 20th July than many learned essays on treason and democracy under a tyranny. There is no need to remind the reader of the important part the defence of the German East played in the minds of Tresckow, Stauffenberg, Beck and Goerdeler.

2. On the military situation on the 20th July: see Opinion by Professor Percy Ernst SCHRAMM given in the Remer trial in Brunswick, published in KRAUS and BZH p. 98 (with colour map).

3. Remarks by SS Obergruppenführer Jüttner to several people in the office. As far as the people involved are concerned there is no proof whatever, although there have been many allegations, of actions which were attributed to individuals at the end of 1942 in the "Rote Kapelle" trials, such as the betrayal of production figures, of operational plans, of hindrance to Germany's war effort, etc. Considering their objective, Beck, Stauffenberg and Tresckow were bound to try to avoid any "decomposition" of the German Army. In his "Conversations with Hitler" SCHEIDT revealed that after the 20th July Hitler himself liked to put all the blame for failure at the front on the "conspirators", especially Quartermaster-General Wagner and General Fellgiebel, whom he hated. Strong resentment among the officers forced Bormann, in the autumn of 1944, to put out a counter-statement saying that no acts of sabotage by any member of the General Staff had been proved. The only case in which "Valkyrie" measures are shown to have interfered with reinforcements became known through Guderian: according to him, operational units which were to have been transferred on July 17 from Wünsdorf and Krampnitz to the fortified area of Lötzen, were held up for two or three days after Olbricht's request to Guderian or his deputy, Thomale. Olbricht's explanation was that he needed these units for a Valkyrie alert he had planned. There was no such character in the Wehrmacht as Carl ZUCKMAYER's Ingenieur Oderbruch in his

drama "Des Teufels General". On his return to Germany, Zückmayer realized that; and according to Karl STRÖLIN (p. 15), he said that he had been unable to assess the German situation accurately from abroad.

4. Cf. SPEIDEL (p. 127 ff.) on Rundstedt's and Rommel's visit to the Obersalzberg on June 29 and the subsequent telephone conversation between Rundstedt and Keitel. At the Nuremberg trial Jodl explained the continuation of German resistance by saying that it was the only way of saving millions of German women and children and the bulk of the Army in the East from the clutches of the Russians (cf. Note 1 of this chapter). At Rheims on May 6, 1945, Jodl gave Eisenhower this reason why Germany had continued to fight after the defeat at Avranches: "Hitler and I were of the opinion that our opponents would fall out over their German prey." (See BOLDT p. 66, cf. SHIRER p. 924.) For Jodl's and Keitel's relations with Hitler see WESTPHAL p. 85.

5. Müller: "Gegen eine neue Dolchstosslüge" 2nd ed., p. 36.

6. Cf. SPEER's memorandum of March 18, 1945, and Hitler's comment on it, IMT XVI 546–49. (Cf. Note 20 Chapter XII.) Hitler said after the fall of Stalingrad (according to WEIZSAECKER p. 344): "We'll win; if not, we'll go down with honour, fighting to the last man; that was also the motto of Frederick the Great." (Cf. Rommel in Note 24, Chapter XII.)

7. SCHMIDT p. 574; similarly WESTPHAL, RAHN and others.

8. "According to the war diary of the C.-in-C. West, the collapse in France cost nearly one million men and incalculable war resources. If a "Western solution" had been adopted, this million could have been preserved for the defence of the Reich which would have been tantamount to the defence of Europe." SCHRAMM on why the "Western solution" was not carried out; special issue of "Parlament" of July 20, 1952.

9. Karl von RUMOHR, personal account, unpublished.

10. Cf. SCHMIDT's survey (p. 566 ff.) and the chapter "Unconditional Surrender" of ROTHFELS (p. 156) and MOLTMANN. The "Morgenthau Plan" was signed in September 1944 at the second Quebec Conference by Roosevelt and Churchill: its intention was to deprive Germany of her entire industry and turn her into an agricultural country ("goat pasture plan" according to HULL). Both statesmen later dissociated themselves from this plan; Churchill called it an act of madness, and Roosevelt told his Secretary of War that he "did not know how he had initialled that particular language in the Quebec Agreement". It must have been done "without much thought" (J. F. BYRNES, Speaking Frankly, New York, 1947, p. 186).

11. Some people contrast Stauffenberg with the familiar image of the hero who does something extraordinary, indeed outrageous by ordinary standards, and sacrifices himself. These people think they have thereby done ample justice to their own and apparently the world's moral standards. But the 20th July and some other "ultimate" decisions have shown that a great and genuine act of sacrifice in an hour of decision in the twentieth century can look quite different. Indeed, one may say that not sacrificing oneself may be the greater self-sacrifice. (Cf. Note 55, Chapter XIII.)

12. Thomas ABT, born 1738 in Ulm; at the age of twenty-two professor in Frankfurt on Oder, then a Prince's tutor with Count Schaumburg-Lippe-Bückeburg as Herder's predecessor; died at the age of twenty-eight from a wound received at Kunersdorf; was an admirer of Frederick the Great. His book "Vom Tod fuer das Vaterland" inspired Scharnhorst.

13. Regarding the part played by the aristocracy: Count Fritz von der Schulenburg said in conversation with H. FRITZSCHE in winter 1943–44 (according to Fr.): "If I get out of this alive, I'll renounce my title. Then they'll see what sort of fellows we are." FAHRNER writes of Claus Stauffenberg that "through

447

him and around him, whatever his field of activity, there suddenly emerged people of another type than you would normally see in such settings; you only became aware of their existence through him. Every leader brings to light men appropriate to his type; it is wrong to assume that they don't exist, merely because they are not seen in the environment of people of different calibre.'' This observation probably explains why so many members of the aristocracy were active in Stauffenberg's circle. Count Alexander Stauffenberg, a professor in Munich, said in a speech. "As regards the preponderant share in this revolt of German aristocrats from every noble family: any German who does not suffer from class bias, will be proud to know that the most ancient and aristocratic families of the Reich, who are known to have lost their 'privileges' generations ago, once again claimed their original right: the right to give a lead to the German people by their way of life and to do so in death.''

14. There is no doubt that the Christian faith was a powerful driving force behind the men of the Resistance and gave them great strength, after the failure of the revolt, to endure sufferings which have been described as a new "persecution of the Christians''. (Cf. numerous writings by ecclesiastical authors of both Catholic and Protestant churches.) A significant report quotes Yorck's evidence (KB 167) "that in between political discussions ecclesiastical questions were frequently debated''. Concerning the attitude of the Stauffenberg brothers: during the weeks preceding the attempt, Claus Stauffenberg one day visited the Bishop of Berlin, Cardinal Count von Preysing, at Hermsdorf hospital. I was told by Monsignore SCHWERDTFEGER, who for many years was the Cardinal's private secretary and to whom the Bishop repeatedly spoke about Stauffenberg's visit, that Stauffenberg did not so much as mention an impending coup d'état or assassination, let alone did he seek to obtain the Cardinal's approval for such a deed. But, as the report shows, in their discussion of Germany's external and domestic affairs they reached a point which left no doubt that basically their attitudes were in harmony. Stauffenberg knew the Archbishop of Bamberg from his days in Bamberg. Asked about his own religious ties, Berthold Stauffenberg said, according to KB 455, that he was patron of the church in Lautlingen, that his family had ancient roots in the Catholic church and that they had valued a Catholic education for the children. Speaking also for his brother he added: "We are not really what are called Catholic believers in the proper sense. We did not go to church very often, nor to confession. My brother and I feel that Christianity is unlikely to produce anything creative.''

15. Personal letter (Dr K.E.H.) written at the time of argument about the reorganization of the German Army.

16. Efforts to trace this remark of Churchill's in Hansard have been unavailing. Nor does it occur in any of his writings. The only way of finding out was to ask him personally. According to SCHLABRENDORFF he acknowledged the sense of the passage and said it was not impossible that he might once have said something of the kind.

17. The speeches which Count Paul Yorck zu Wartenburg, German Consul General in Lyons—the brother of the executed Yorck—delivered at various commemorations, especially before youthful audiences, carry something of the challenge of the 20th July. The extracts are taken from a copy of his speech on the occasion of July 20, 1961, in the Bendlerstrasse in Berlin, a speech in Darmstadt and one addressed to officers of the Sigmaringen garrison on July 20, 1962.

On the subject of the responsibility of a senior commander and, in particular, with reference to Rommel's image, these passages from the 1962 speech are of interest: "The senior commander of troops alone has the over-all view and

448

expert training to judge the sense or senselessness of military operations. Quite simply he owes it to his men to lead them according to the best of his intelligence and to oppose impossible orders; equally, when a war is lost there comes a moment when the soldier must force the politician to start negotiations. The man in charge of military operations is responsible to his nation to ensure that this is done in good time and not, as happened in 1918, when it was already too late for negotiations. This responsibility is intrinsic, and no constitutional legalistic construction can diminish it. After Stalingrad, the Supreme Command of the Army and every Army Commander had the duty to confront the dictator with an ultimatum. This is what Rommel did as far as he was concerned and at his own risk in 1944, when the (Allied) landing was imminent and there was no longer the chance of an acceptable peace. But this late discharge of a duty which inexorably faces every senior commander transcends all his other military achievements. At the last minute, at the risk of his life he tried to defend his people's external freedom by a political decision, once he realized the futility of further fighting.''

18. Only the folly of the post-war years denied these men what every Frenchman, Swiss, Englishman, Dane and Greek was granted as a matter of course, and cast suspicion on their patriotism, denouncing it as nationalism hostile to others. Unquestionably, the 20th July demonstrated a breakthrough towards humanity, a revolt of conscience, an action far transcending any national frontier—and yet none of it conflicts with equally genuine tradition: every one of the confederates was deeply rooted in Germany, loved his people and country, and when the word Fatherland was spoken they blushed only because they knew that every day its false leaders inflicted bitter wounds on it, but no one stood up to act. Some of them described themselves in Court as national Socialists, using the specific term and yet playing upon words. Their bond with the Fatherland, of which they thought with gratitude, gave them the strength to sacrifice themselves and forbade them to pretend they were acting in the cause of mankind as a whole.

Here are two reports about Freiherr Ferdinand von Lüninck to illustrate this point: Lüninck, once Oberpräsident of the Province of Westphalia, was a Catholic. Asked during the interrogation whether he would have accepted the office of political representative for Danzig, even if he had been told that illegal methods were to be used, he is said to have replied: "I don't think I am obliged to answer such a question. But nevertheless I will answer it honestly: the highest and strongest bond I know on earth is that with my German Fatherland. In such a case I should, indeed, be facing a tremendous conflict of conscience; but I cannot unconditionally answer 'No' to your question if at the time I regarded the need of the Fatherland as so great that there would be no other way out'' (KB 137).

A fellow prisoner of Lüninck's reported a scene in the prison yard. They had been lined up three deep to receive the warder's instructions. A very old gentleman with a General's stripes seemed about to faint from weakness. The prisoner supported him saying something like "We've got to keep on our feet now, even if they're going to hang us''. At that moment he was nudged from behind and heard Herr von Lüninck say: "Fritzsche, what they do with us doesn't matter! But what is going to happen to Germany?'' (Personal account by Dr H. FRITZSCHE. See also BZH p. 191.)

BIBLIOGRAPHY
(For U.S. and British editions *see also* Appendix)

AHLMANN, W.: Tymbos für Wilhelm Ahlmann. Ein Gedenkbuch, herausgegeben von seinen Freunden. Berlin 1951.
ASSMANN, K.: Deutsche Schicksalsjahre. Wiesbaden 1950.
ANDREAS-FRIEDRICH, R.: Der Schattenmann. Tagebuchaufzeichnungen 1938–1945. Berlin 1947.
BARDECHE, M.: Die Politik der Zerstörung. Nürnberg oder Europa. Göttingen 1950.
BECK, L.: Studien. Published by Hans Speidel. Stuttgart 1955.
BOHNENKAMP, H.: Gedanken an Adolf Reichwein. Brunswick 1949.
BOLDT, G.: Die letzten Tage der Reichskanzlei. Hamburg 1947.
BONHOEFFER, D.: Widerstand und Ergebung. Munich 1951.
—— Gesammelte Werke, Munich 1958 ff.
BOR, P.: Gespräche mit Halder. Wiesbaden 1950.
BOVERI, M.: Der Verrat im 20. Jahrhundert. Hamburg 1957.
BRACHER, K. D.: Die Auflösung der Weimarer Republik. 3rd Edition. Villingen 1960.
BRAUBACH, M.: Memoiren zur neuesten Geschichte. "Historisches Jahrbuch" der Görresgesellschaft 70 (1950/51) pp. 388–401.
—— Quellen, Forschungen und Darstellungen zur neuesten Geschichte Europas. Ibid Volume 72 (1952/53) pp. 614–32.
—— Beiträge zur Zeitgeschichte. Ibid Volume 73 (1954) pp. 152–83.
—— Der Weg zum 20. Juli 1944. Ein Forschungsbericht. (Arbeitsgemeinschaft für Forschung des Landes Nordrhein-Westfalen 13). Cologne and Opladen 1953.
BUDDE, E. and LÜTSCHESS, P.: Die Wahrheit über den 20. Juli. Düsseldorf 1953.
BZH 20. Juli 1944. Sammelband der Bundeszentrale für Heimatdienst Bonn, based on special issue of weekly "Das Parlament" of 20th July, 1952. 3rd Edition (1960). Berto-Verlag Bonn.
CHURCHILL, W. S.: Second World War. 3 Volumes. London and Boston 1948 ff.
COOPER, R. W.: Der Nürnberger Prozess. Krefeld 1947.
COULONDRE, R.: Von Moskau nach Berlin. 1936–1939. Bonn 1950.
DEANE, J. R.: Ein seltsames Bündnis. Amerikas Bemühungen, während des Krieges mit Russland zusammenzuarbeiten. Vienna 1947.
DELP, A.: Im Angesicht des Todes. Frankfurt 1947.
DIELS, R.: Lucifer ante portas. Stuttgart 1950.
DÖNHOFF, Gräfin M.: Den Freunden zum Gedächtnis. Hamburg 1946.
DULLES, A. W.: Germany's Underground. New York 1947.
FECHTER, P.: Menschen und Zeiten: Begegnungen aus fünf Jahrzehnten.
—— An der Wende der Zeit. Menschen und Begegnungen. Both Gütersloh 1950.
FITZGIBBON, C.: 20th July. New York 1954.
FOERSTER, W.: Ein General kämpft gegen den Krieg. Munich 1949.
—— Generalstabschef Ludwig Beck. Sein Kampf gegen den Krieg. Munich 1953.
FOERTSCH, H.: Schuld und Verhängnis. Stuttgart 1951.
FRANÇOIS-PONCET, A.: Souvenirs d'une ambassade à Berlin, septembre 1931–octobre 1938. Paris 1946.
—— De Versailles à Potsdam. Paris 1946.
—— Politische Reden und Aufsätze (including: Achtzehn Monate bei Mussolini). Mainz 1949.

FREDE, G. and SCHÜDDEKOPF, O. E.: Wehrmacht und Politik 1933–1945. Documents with linking text. Brunswick 1952.
FURTWÄNGLER, F. J.: Männer, die ich sah und kannte. Hamburg 1951.
GAFENCU, G.: Préliminaires de la guerre a l'Est. Paris 1946.
—— Derniers jours de l'Europe. Un voyage diplomatique en 1939. Paris 1946.
GALEN, Kardinal Graf von: Rechtsbewusstsein und Rechtsunsicherheit. Rede in Rom, März 1946.
GISEVIUS, H. B.: Bis zum bitteren Ende. 2 Vols. Zurich 1946. 2nd enlarged edition. Hamburg 1948.
Special edition brought up-to-date by the author. Hamburg.
GOEBBELS, J.: Diaries 1942–43. Ed. by Louis P. Lochner. New York and London 1948.
GÖRLITZ, W.: Der deutsche Generalstab. Frankfurt 1950.
—— Der zweite Weltkrieg. 2 Volumes. Stuttgart 1951/52.
GOLLWITZER, H., KUHN, K. SCHNEIDER, R.: Du hast mich heimgesucht bei Nacht. Abschiedsbriefe und Aufzeichnungen des Widerstands 1933–1945. Munich 1954.
GRAML, H.: Die deutsche Militäropposition vom Sommer 1940 bis zum Frühjahr 1943. Supplement to weekly "Das Parlament", 16th July, 1958.
—— and KRAUSNICK, H.: Der deutsche Widerstand und die Alliierten. Supplement to weekly "Das Parlament", 19th July, 1961.
GREINER, H.: Die Oberste Wehrmachtsführung 1939–1945. Wiesbaden 1951.
GROPPE, Th.: Ein Kampf um Recht und Sitte. 2nd Edition Trier 1959.
GUDERIAN, H.: Erinnerungen eines Soldaten, Heidelberg 1951.
HAFFNER, S.: "Beinahe". Die Geschichte des 20. Juli 1944. "Neue Auslese" 2nd Year, No. 8.
HAGEN, H. W.: Zwischen Eid und Befehl. Tatzeugen-Bericht von den Ereignissen am 20. Juli 1944 in Berlin und "Wolfsschanze". Munich 1958.
HAGEN, W.: (Pseudonym für Walter Hoettl): Die geheime Front. Organisation, Personen und Aktionen des deutschen Geheimdienstes, Linz 1950.
HALDER, F.: Kriegstagebuch Vol. 1: Vom Polenfeldzug bis zum Ende der Westoffensive (14. August 1939 bis 30. Juni 1940) Stuttgart 1962.
—— Hitler als Feldherr. Munich 1950.
HAMMER, W.: Theodor Haubach zum Gedächtnis. Frankfurt 1955.
—— Hohes Haus in Henkers Hand. Deutscher Parlamentarier Leidenswege und Opfergang 1933–1945. Frankfurt 1955.
HARNACK, A. v.: Ernst von Harnack, ein Kämpfer für Deutschlands Zukunft. Schwenningen 1951.
HART, B. H. Liddell: Jetzt dürfen sie reden. Stuttgart 1950.
HASSEL, J. D. v.: Verräter? Patrioten! Der 20. Juli 1944. Cologne 1946.
HASSELL, U. v.: Vom anderen Deutschland. Aus den nachgelassenen Tage büchern 1938 bis 1944. Zurich 1946.
HENDERSON, J. L.: Adolf Reichwein. Eine politisch-pädagogische Biographie, published by H. Lindemann, Stuttgart 1958.
HENK, E.: Die Tragödie des 20. Juli 1944. Ein Beitrag zur politischen Vorge schichte. Heidelberg 1946. (2nd Edition.)
HERZFELD, H.: Johannes Popitz, in "Forschungen zu Staat und Verfassung" Berlin 1958.
HEUSINGER, A.: Befehl im Widerstreit. Schicksalsstunden der deutschen Armee 1923–1945. Tübingen 1950.
HILDEBRANDT, R.: Wir sind die letzten. Aus dem Leben des Widerstandskämpfers Albrecht Haushofer und seiner Freunde. Neuwied, Berlin 1949.
HOFER, W.: Der Nationalsozialismus, Dokumente 1933–1945. Frankfurt 1960.
—— Die Entfesselung des zweiten Weltkrieges. Stuttgart 1954.

451

HOGGAN, D. L.: Der erzwungene Krieg. Die Ursachen und Urheber des zweiten Weltkriegs. Tübingen 1961.
HOLLDACK, H.: Was wirklich geschah. Die diplomatischen Hintergründe der deutschen Kriegspolitik. Munich 1949.
HOSSBACH, F.: Zwischen Wehrmacht und Hitler 1934–1938. Wolfenbüttel 1949.
HUBER, C.: Kurt Huber zum Gedächtnis. Regensburg 1947.
HUCH, R.: Die Aktion der Münchener Studenten gegen Hitler. "Neue Auslese", 4th Year, Nos. 1 and 2. Munich 1949.
—— Grundlagen der Volkswirtschaftspolitik. Hamburg 1938.
ILLING, Gertrud: Der 20. Juli 1944. Burgscheidungen 1959. Published by Die Zentrale Schulungsstätte der CDU "Otto Nuschke".
IMT "The Trial of the Major War Criminals before the International Military Tribunal at Nuremberg, 14th November 1945–1st October 1946". 42 Volumes. 1949.
INGRIM, R.: Hitlers glücklichster Tag. Stuttgart 1962.
JESSEN, J. and others: Der Wettbewerb als Mittel der volkswirtschaftlichen Leistungssteigerung und Leistungsauslese. Berlin 1943.
JOHN, O.: Berichte über Harnack, Leuschner, Moltke, Mierendorff, Haubach, Reichwein, Dohnanyi in "Blick in die Welt" 6/1946–12/1947.
JÜNGER, E.: Der Friede. An die Jugend Europas. An die Jugend der Welt. Paris 1948, Tübingen 1949.
—— Strahlungen, Tübingen 1949.
KB see under PETER.
KIELMANSEGG, J. A. Graf v.: Der Fritschprozess 1938. Hamburg 1949.
KIESEL, G.: SS-Bericht über den 20. Juli. Aus den Papieren des SS-Obersturmbannführers Dr Georg Kiesel. "Nordwestdeutsche Hefte", 2nd Year, No. 2, February 1947, pp. 77–99.
KLEIST, P.: Zwischen Hitler und Stalin 1939–1945. Aufzeichnungen, Bonn 1950.
KLUKE, P.: Der deutsche Widerstand. Eine Literaturübersicht. "Historische Zeitschrift", 169 (1949), Oldenburg.
KOCH, L.: Erwin Rommel. Die Wandlung eines grossen Soldaten. Stuttgart 1950.
KOGON, E.: Der SS-Staat. Das System der Konzentrationslager. 3rd complete and enlarged edition. Frankfurt 1949.
KORDT, E.: Nicht aus den Akten. Die Wilhelmstrasse in Frieden und Krieg. Erlebnisse, Begegnungen und Eindrücke 1928–1945. Stuttgart 1950.
—— Wahn und Wirklichkeit. Die Aussenpolitik des Dritten Reiches. Versuch einer Darstellung. Unter Mitwirkung von K. H. Abshagen, Stuttgart 1947.
KOSTHORST, E.: Die deutsche Opposition gegen Hitler zwischen Polen-und Frankreichfeldzug, Bonn 1955.
KRAUS, H.: Die im Braunschweiger Prozess erstatteten moraltheologischen und historischen Gutachten nebst Urteil. Hamburg 1953.
KRAUSNICK, H.: Vorgeschichte und Beginn des militärischen Widerstandes gegen Hitler; in: "Die Vollmacht des Gewissens". Munich 1956.
—— see under GRAML.
L'AIGLE, A. de: Meine Briefe von Theo Haubach, Hamburg 1947.
LATERNSER, H. Verteidigung deutscher Soldaten. Plaidoyers vor alliierten Gerichten, Bonn 1950.
LAVAL, P. Pierre Laval parle. Paris 1948.
LEBER, A. Sozialdemokraten um den 20. Juli. Den toten, immer lebendigen Freunden. "Telegraf", 20.7.1946.
—— Das Gewissen steht auf. 64 Lebensbilder aus dem deutschen Widerstand 1933–45, Berlin–Frankfurt 1954.
—— Das Gewissen entscheidet. Frankfurt 1957.

—— Fr. Gräfin von Moltke Für und Wider. Entscheidungen in Deutschland 1918–1945. Berlin–Frankfurt 1961.

LEBER, J. Ein Mann geht seinen Weg. Schriften, Reden und Briefe. Berlin–Frankfurt 1952.

LEITHÄUSER, J. G. Wilhelm Leuschner, Ein Leben für die Republik. Cologne 1962.

LILJE, J.: Im finstern Tal. Nuremberg 1947.

LOTHAR, P.: Gespräche einer letzten Nacht. Hamburg 1953.

MAKAROV, Prof. A. N.: Berthold Stauffenberg. "Friedenswarte". Zurich 1947, pp.360–65.

MEINECKE, F.: Die deutsche Katastrophe, Betrachtungen und Erinnerungen. Wiesbaden 1947.

MENDELSOHN, P. de: Die Nuernberger Dokumente. Studien zur deutschen Kriegspolitik 1937–1945. Hamburg 1946.

MICHEL, K.: Ost und West. Der Ruf Stauffenbergs. Zurich 1947.

MIERENDORFF, C.: In Memorian Carlo Mierendorff. Darmstadt 1947.

MOLTKE, Graf H. J. v.: Einer vom deutschen Widerstand. Die letzten Briefe des Grafen Moltke. "Neue Auslese", 2nd Year, No. 1, Jan. 1947.

—— Letzte Briefe aus dem Gefängnis Tegel. Berlin 1951.

MOLTMANN, G.: Die frühe amerikanische Deutschlandplanung im zweiten Weltkrieg. In Vierteljahrsh. f. Zeitgesch., 7th Year, No. 3/1957.

—— Die Genesis der Unconditional-Surrender-Forderung in "Wehrwissenschaftliche Rundschau", VI, 1956.

MÜLLER, W.: Gegen eine neue Dolchstosslegende. Ein Erlebnis-Bericht zum 20. Juli 1944. Hanover 1947 (2nd Edition).

—— Was geschah am 20. Juli 1944? "Das Freie Wort" (Düsseldorf) 19th July, 1952.

MÜNCHHEIMER, W.: Die Verfassungs-und Verwaltungsreformpläne der deutschen Opposition gegen Hitler zum 20. Juli 1944. "Europa-Archiv" 5 (1950), 14th series.

NAMIER, Sir L. B.: In the Nazi Era. London 1952.

—— Diplomatic Prelude, 1938/1939. London 1948.

PARTSCH, K. J.: Stauffenberg. Das Bild des Täters. "Europa-Archiv" 5th Year, 20th July, 1950.

PECHEL, R.: Deutscher Widerstand. Erlenbach–Zurich 1947.

PETER, K. H. (Publisher): Spiegelbild einer Verschwörung. The so-called Kaltenbrunner Reports to Bormann and Hitler about the Assassination Attempt on 20th July, 1944. Secret Documents from the former R.S.H., published by Archiv Peter für historische und zeitgeschichtliche Dokumentation. Stuttgart 1961.

PETWAIDIC, W.: Die autoritäre Anarchie. Streiflichter des deutschen Zusammenbruchs. Hamburg 1946.

PICARD, M.: Hitler in uns selbst. Zurich 1946.

PÖLCHAU, H.: Die Letzten Stunden. Berlin 1949.

RAUSCHNING, H.: Die Revolution des Nihilismus. Kulisse und Wirklichkeit im Dritten Reich. Zurich 1938.

—— Gespräche mit Hitler. Ibid 1939.

—— Die Zeit des Deliriums. Ibid 1946.

RECK-MALLECZEWEN, F. P.: Tagebuch eines Verzweifelten. Lorch 1947.

REICHWEIN, A.: Abenteuer mit Mensch und Tier. Aus den Geschichten Adolf Reichweins. Munich 1949.

—— Schaffendes Schulvolk; re-published by his friends. Brunswick 1951.

REMER, O. E.: 20. Juli 1944. Hamburg 1951.

RITTER, G.: Das Regierungsprogramm vom 20. Juli 1944. Carl Goerdelers geplante Rundfunkrede nach Uebernahme der öffentlichen Gewalt. "Die Gegenwart", 1946 No. 12/13.

—— Carl Goerdeler und die deutsche Widerstandsbewegung. Stuttgart 1956. Cf. reference by Hans Herzfeld in "Histor. Zeitschr." Vol. 182 (1956) pp., 321–32; Max Braubach in "Histor. Jahrb." Vol. 76 (1957), pp. 254–58; Golo Mann in "Merkur" (1955) No. 7.

ROMMEL, E.: Krieg ohne Hass. Afrikanische Memoiren. Published by L.-M. Rommel and F. Bayerlein. Heidenheim (Brenz) 1950.

ROTHFELS, H.: The German Opposition to Hitler. An Appraisal. Hinsdale, Ill., 1948, Henry Regnery.

RUDEL, H. U.: Dolchstoss oder Legende? Rottach-Egern o.J.

—— Trotzdem. Vienna o.J.

RUDOLPH, L. von: Die Luege, die nicht stirbt. Nuremberg 1958.

SALIN, E.: Die Tragödie der deutschen Gegenrevolution. "Zeitschrift für Religions- und Zeitgeschichte", 1948, No. 3.

SAUERBRUCH, F.: Das war mein Leben. Bad Woerishofen 1951.

SCHACHT, H.: Abrechnung mit Hitler. Hamburg 1948.

SCHELLENBERG, Walter: Memoiren. Cologne 1959.

SCHLABRENDORFF, F. v.: Offiziere gegen Hitler. Nach einem Erlebnisbericht F. von Schlabrendorffs, published by G. von Schulze-Gävernitz, Zurich 1947. 2nd Edition 1950.

SCHMIDT, P.: Statist auf diplomatischer Bühne 1923–1945. Erlebnisse des Chef-dolmetschers im Auswärtigen Amt mit den Staatsmännern Europas. Bonn 1949.

SCHOLL, I.: Die weisse Rose. Frankfurt 1952.

SCHRAMM, P. E.: (Published jointly with Hans-Adolf Jacobsen, Andreas Hillgruber, Walther Hubatsch): Kriegstagebuch des Oberkommandos der Wehrmacht (Wehrmachtführungsstab) 1940–1945. Frankfurt 1961.

SCHRAMM, W. Ritter von: Der 20. Juli in Paris. Bad Woerishofen, 1953.

SCHUSCHNIGG, K. v.: Ein Requiem in Rot-Weiss-Rot. Zurich 1949.

SCHWERIN-KROSIGK, Graf L. v.: Es geschah in Deutschland. Tübingen 1952.

SENDTNER, K.: Die deutsche Militäropposition im ersten Kriegsjahr in "Die Vollmacht des Gewissens", Munich 1956.

SHIRER, W. L.: Aufstieg und Fall des Dritten Reiches. Köln-Berlin 1961.

SHULMAN, M.: Die Niederlage im Westen. Gütersloh 1949.

SKORZENY, O.: Geheimkommando Skorzeny. Hamburg 1950.

SPEIDEL, H.: Invasion 1944. Ein Beitrag zu Rommels und des Reiches Schicksal. Tübingen 1949.

STADTMÜLLER, G.: Schrifttum zur Geschichte der militärischen Widerstands-bewegung 1933 bis 1945 in "Die Vollmacht des Gewissens", op. cit.

STAUFFENBERG, A. Graf Schenk v.: Claus Graf Schenk von Stauffenberg, Lebens-bilder aus dem Bayerischen Schwaben, published by Götz Freiherr von Pölnitz. Munich 1954, pp. 449–67.

STELTZER, Th.: Von deutscher Politik. Frankfurt 1949.

STERN, W.: Zur Vorgeschichte der Verschwörung vom 20. Juli 1944. Von einem Autorenkollektiv des Instituts für Deutsche Militärgeschichte unter der Leitung Oberst W. Stern. East Berlin 1960.

STREBEL: In Memoriam Berthold Schenk von Stauffenberg. "Zeitschrift für ausländisches öffentliches Recht und Völkerrecht", Stuttgart 1950, No. 1.

STRÖLIN, K.: Verräter oder Patrioten? Der 20. Juli 1944 und das Recht auf Widerstand. Stuttgart 1952.

TAYLOR, A. J. P.: Die Ursprünge des zweiten Weltkriegs. Gütersloh 1962 (2nd Edition).

THOMAS, G.: Gedanken und Ereignisse. "Schweizerische Monatshefte". Decem-ber 1945.

454

TIPPELSKIRCH, K. v.: Geschichte des zweiten Weltkriegs. Bonn 1950.
VERMEHREN, I.: Reise durch den letzten Akt. Hamburg 1947.
WEINBERGER, L.: Tatsachen, Begegnungen und Gespräche. Ein Buch um Österreich. Vienna 1948.
WEINKAUFF, H.: Die Militäropposition und das Widerstandsrecht in "Die Vollmacht des Gewissens", op. cit.
WEISENBORN, G.: Der lautlose Aufstand. Bericht über die Widerstandsbewegung des deutschen Volkes. Hamburg 1953.
WEIZSÄCKER, E. v.: Erinnerungen. Munich 1950.
WENIGER, E.: Zur Vorgeschichte des 20. Juli. Heinrich von Stülpnagel. "Die Sammlung", 4th Year (1949), No. 8/9.
WESTPHAL, S.: Heer in Fesseln. Bonn 1950.
WHEELER-BENNETT, John: The Nemesis of Power. The German Army in Politics, 1918–1945. London 1954.
WINNIG, A.: Aus 20 Jahren. Hamburg 1948.
YOUNG, D.: Rommel. Wiesbaden 1950.
ZUCKMAYER, C.: Carlo Mierendorff, Porträt eines deutschen Sozialisten. Berlin 1949.

BIBLIOGRAPHY—APPENDIX

ANDREAS-FRIEDRICH, R.: Berlin Underground, 1938–1945; transl. from the German. New York 1945.
BOLDT, G.: In the shelter with Hitler; ed. E. A. Hepp, transl. E. Stern-Rubarth. New York 1948.
BONHOEFFER, D.: Prisoner for God: Letters and papers from prison. New York 1954.
BOVERI, M.: Treason in the twentieth century; transl. Steinberg. London 1961.
CHURCHILL, W. S.: Second World War. 3 Volumes. Boston 1948 ff.
COOPER, R. W.: The Nuremberg Trial. London 1947.
DEANE, J. R.: Strange alliance: The story of our efforts at wartime co-operation with Russia. New York 1947.
FRANÇOIS-PONCET, A.: Fateful Years: Memoirs of the French Ambassador in Berlin, 1931–1938. New York 1949.
GAFENCU, G.: Last days of Europe: A diplomatic journey in 1939. New Haven 1948.
GISEVIUS, H. B.: To the bitter end; transl. from the German. Boston 1947.
GÖRLITZ, W.: History of the German general staff, 1657–1945; transl. B. Battershaw. New York 1953.
GOLLWITZER, H.: Dying we live: The final messages and records of the Resistance. New York 1956.
GUDERIAN, H.: Panzer Leader; transl. C. Fitzgibbon. New York 1952.
HAGEN, W. (pseud. W. Hoettl): Secret front: The story of Nazi political espionage; transl. R. H. Stevens. New York 1954.
HALDER, F.: Diary, Vol. 1. Washington, D.C. 1950.
—— Hitler as war lord. London 1950.
HART, B. H. Liddell: German generals talk. New York 1948.
HASSELL, U. v.: The von Hassell Diaries, 1939–1944: The story of the forces against Hitler inside Germany, as recorded by Ambassador von Hassell, a leader of the movement. Intro. by A. W. Dulles. New York 1947.
HOFER, W.: War premeditated 1939. London 1955.
JÜNGER, E.: Peace. Chicago 1948.

KOGON, E.: The theory and practice of hell: The German concentration camps and the system behind them. New York 1950.
LEBER, A., ed.: Conscience in revolt: Sixty-four stories of resistance in Germany, 1933–45. Westport, Conn. 1957.
LILJE, J.: Valley of the shadow. Philadelphia 1950.
MEINECKE, E.: German catastrophe; transl. S. B. Fay. Cambridge, Mass. 1950.
MENDELSOHN, P. de: Design for aggression: The inside story of Hitler's war plans. New York 1946.
NAMIER, Sir L. B.: In the Nazi Era. New York 1952.
—— Diplomatic Prelude, 1938/1939. New York 1948.
MOLTKE, H. J. von: A German of the resistance: The last letters of Count Helmuth James von Moltke, 2nd ed. London 1947.
PICARD, M.: Hitler in ourselves. Chicago, n.d.
RAUSCHNING, H.: Revolution of Nihilism; transl. E. W. Dickes. New York 1939.
—— Voice of destruction. New York 1940.
—— Time of delirium. New York 1946.
RITTER, G.: The German resistance: Carl Goerdeler's struggle against tyranny; transl. from the German. New York 1959.
SAUERBRUCH, F.: Surgeon's life. New York 1954.
SCHACHT, H.: Account settled; transl. E. Fitzgerald. London 1949.
SCHELLENBERG, W.: Labyrinth: Memoirs of Hitler's secret service chief. New York 1957.
SCHLABRENDORFF, F. von: Revolt against Hitler: The personal account of Fabian von Schlabrendorff; prepared and ed. by Gero v. S. Gaevernitz. London 1948.
SCHMIDT, P.: Hitler's interpreter. New York 1951.
SCHOLL, I.: Six against tyranny; transl. from the German. London 1955.
SCHRAMM, W. von: Conspiracy among generals; transl. R. T. Clark. London 1956.
SCHUSCHNIGG, K. von: Austrian Requiem; transl. F. v. Hildebrand. New York 1946.
SHIRER, W. L.: The Rise and Fall of the Third Reich: A history of Nazi Germany. New York 1960.
SHULMAN, M.: Defeat in the West. New York 1950.
SKORZENY, O.: Secret missions: War memoirs of the most dangerous man in Europe; transl. J. Le Clerq. New York 1950.
SPEIDEL, H.: Invasion 1944: Rommel and the Normandy campaign; transl. T. R. Crevenna. New York 1950.
TAYLOR, A. J. P.: Origins of the second world war. New York 1962.
WEIZSÄCKER, E. von: Memoirs; transl. J. Andrews. New York 1951.
WESTPHAL, S.: German army in the West. London 1952.
WHEELER-BENNETT, J.: Nemesis of Power: The German army in politics, 1918–1945. New York 1954.
YOUNG, D.: Rommel, the desert fox. New York 1950.

GLOSSARY

Abwehr: Military Intelligence Service of the Wehrmacht.

Bendlerstrasse: When used in the text often a synonym for the OKH in Berlin The old War Ministry was located in a block bordered on one side by the Bendlerstrasse and on another by the Tirpitzufer. It contained offices of the OKH and OKW.

Berghof: Hitler's mountain retreat on the Obersalzberg above Berchtesgaden.

Einsatzgruppen: The special task forces of the SS/SD which, amongst other things, were made responsible for the work of human extermination in the East.

d.R. (der Reserve): of the Reserve.

Gau: Nazi administrative province.

i.G. (im Generalstab): of the General Staff.

NSDAP: National Socialist German Workers' Party—the official name for the Nazi Party.

OKH (Oberkommando des Heeres): High Command of the Army.

OKW (Oberkommando der Wehrmacht): High Command of the Armed Forces.

OKM (Oberkommando der Kriegsmarine): High Command of the Navy.

Prinz Albrechtstrasse: Gestapo Headquarters in Berlin. Also used as a prison.

Reichswehr: The name given to the Armed Forces 1919–35.

RSH (A) (Reichssicherheits-Hauptamt): Central Reich Security Office. Under Himmler, it controlled the Gestapo, the SD (Security Service) and the Criminal Police.

SA (Sturm Abteilungen): The Storm Troopers who constituted the Nazi private army.

SD: The Security Service.

SS (Schutz Staffel): The Nazi élite force, which also had military units (Waffen SS). The SS ranks with their Army equivalents are as follows:

Untersturmführer	2nd Lieutenant
Obersturmführer	Lieutenant
Hauptsturmführer	Captain
Sturmbannführer	Major
Obersturmbannführer	Lieutenant-Colonel
Standartenführer	Colonel
Oberführer	Brigadier-General
Gruppenführer	Lieutenant-General
Obergruppenführer	General
Oberstgruppenführer	Colonel-General

Stahlhelm: A right-wing ex-serviceman's para-military organization in the time of the Weimar Republic.

Unter den Linden: The main thoroughfare in central Berlin which ran westwards from the Armoury (Zeughaus) to the Brandenburg Gate. It contained many public buildings.

Wilhelmstrasse: Often used as a synonym for the German Foreign Office. The road ran south from Unter den Linden and on it were situated the Foreign Office, the Reich Chancellery and the Ministry of Propaganda.

INDEX

459

Pechel, Rudolf: editor of Deutsche Rundschau, 399, 400, 401, 402, 405, 408, 409, 410, 411, 412, 421, 429, 430
Perels, Friedrich Justus: of the Confessional Church, 405
Peters, Hans: former Professor of Constitutional Law, 107
Petzel, Gen. Walter, 419
Piffrader: SS-Oberführer, 309, 320, 434
Planck, Erwin: State Secretary in the Reich Chancellery, 37, 62, 129, 159, 248, 405
Plettenberg, Kurt Frhr von, 229, 261, 279, 368
Pölchau, Harald: Evangelical Chaplain in Tegel prison, 102, 409, 411, 414, 415, 417, 418
Popitz, Professor Johannes: Prussian Finance Minister, 37, 41, 61–3, 121, 129, 145, 157, 160, 228, 229, 248, 271, 363, 404, 407, 408, 416, 420, 424
Preysing-Lichtenegg-Moss, Count Konrad von: from 1946 Cardinal Bishop of Berlin, 448
Pridun, Lt.-Col. Karl, 315, 360, 361
Puttkamer, Admiral Karl Jesco von, 302, 431, 439
Puttkamer-Nippoglense, Jesco von, 405

R
Rabenau, Gen. Friedrich von, 419, 426, 431
Raeder, Grand Admiral Erich: 1935–43 C.-in-C. of the Navy, 58
Rahn, Dr Rudolf: Ambassador, 414, 420, 439, 447
Rath, Ernst vom: Gesandtschaftsrat in Paris, 35
Rathgens, Lt.-Col. Karl Ernst, 377, 445
Ramin, Capt. Barnim von, 316, 319, 320, 437
Rattenhuber: SS-Obersturmführer, 261, 301
Rehrl, Franz: former Landeshauptmann of Salzburg, 249
Reichenau, Field-Marshal Walter von, 18
Reichwein, Adolf: Professor of the Teachers' Academy in Halle; after 1933 village schoolteacher; later Deputy Director of the Museum of Folklore in Berlin, 77–82, 95, 113,

Reichwein—continued
228, 250, 255, 258, 272, 282, 291, 410, 415
Reinecke, Gen. Hermann, 314, 319, 357, 441
Reisert, Dr Franz: lawyer, 120, 414, 416
Reither, Josef: Austrian farmers' leader, 249
Remer, Major, Colonel, and Maj.-Gen. Otto Ernst, 278, 312, 319, 339, 340, 353, 355, 356, 357, 360, 433, 440, 441, 442, 446
Ribbentrop, Joachim von: 1938–45 Foreign Minister, 253, 335, 338, 362, 407, 414, 443
Richter, F. W.: Staatsminister in Saxony, 405
Risler, Thorwald: signals Sergeant, 345
Ritter, Professor Gerhard: historian, 52, 247, 366, 399, 400, 401, 402, 403, 405, 407, 408, 414, 415, 416, 418, 419, 420, 421, 425, 428, 429, 430, 432, 446
Roenne, Col. Alexis Frhr von, 220, 427
Röhm, Ernst: Chief of Staff of the SA, 12, 403
Röhrig: signals Lieutenant, 352, 353
Roesch, Augustinus: Jesuit provincial, 102, 409
Rommel, Field-Marshal Erwin, 36, 275–6, 280, 282, 293–4, 295, 297, 323, 376, 377, 378, 379, 420, 432, 445, 447, 448, 449
Römer, Dr Beppo, 135, 417
Roosevelt, Franklin D.: 1933–45 President of the USA, 36, 110, 167, 252, 253, 414, 447
Rosenberg, Alfred: 1934–45 responsible for ideological training in the NSDAP; Minister for the Occupied Eastern Territories, 397, 415
Rost, Maj.-Gen. von, 215, 224, 426
Rothkirch, Count, 358
Rundstedt, Field-Marshal Gerd von, 37, 147, 157, 268, 275–6, 281, 291, 371, 379, 400, 432, 447
Ruprecht, Crown Prince of Bavaria, 120

S
Sack, Dr Karl: Ministerialdirektor and Judge Advocate-General, 214, 311 375, 397, 398, 426, 436

467

469

Yorck von Wartenburg, Count Peter: Oberregierungsrat, 95, 97–9, 113, 116, 121, 125, 160, 202, 228–9, 250, 296, 311, 316, 319, 394, 411, 412, 416, 437, 445, 448

Z

Zeitzler, Col.-Gen. Kurt: 1942–44 Chief of the General Staff of the